Colette,
Merry Christmas 2013
Love you Mom

Missie,
Keep your Jesus Light as bright as it is now—as bright forever!! much Love DADDIE ♥
always.....M O R E (..)

Dancing in the Drought

Finding Joy in His Springs of Living Water

A Daily Devotional for Women

Brenda Gerland

To: Colette
Joyful Blessings!
Brenda Gerland
Psalm 42:1-2

xulon PRESS

Dancing in the Drought
Finding Joy in His Springs of Living Water
by Brenda Gerland

Printed in the United States of America

ISBN 9781628397635

Cover design:
Trevor Gerland
Cover photo:
Trevor Gerland Photography
www.TrevorGerlandPhotography.com

www.xulonpress.com

Foreword

There is a wall plaque in my home that reads, *Life isn't about waiting for the storms to pass. It's about learning to dance in the rain*. I thought those were profound words of wisdom—until I lived through a drought on Lake Travis near Austin, Texas.

After three years of watching the level of our lake—the source of water for Austin and surrounding towns—drop from the third to the second lowest in history, I decided that life is more about learning how to dance in the drought, not the rain. Dancing in the rain would be easy for me to do. It was waiting and living through the drought that was painful.

Watching the clouds roll in, listening to the thunder roar, I lashed out at God for repeatedly withholding His rain. Enduring days on end of gorgeous sunny, blue skies, while longing for thick, black ominous, rain-producing clouds to linger for weeks, I pleaded with God to share His water. Still nothing. That's what's been going on for the past three years.

Way back when, I grew up with my grandmother reading from the *Upper Room* daily devotional. As I progressed in age and in my spiritual maturity (unfortunately the aging came more quickly than the maturity), I still depended on my devotionals to get me going each day. Time after time, I read exactly what I needed to hear for that moment, for that specific situation in my life. It was in those daily readings that God opened my eyes to see His fingerprints all over the pages of my life, and the ones writing their God stories. I read how God worked in and through the lives of others, and realized He could do the same for me.

Somewhere along my spiritual journey, I got the idea to share my life—to write of my salvation and redemption. Surely, if the devotions written by others had been instrumental in my personal transformation, there just might be a woman out there who would find encouragement through the words of my stories. The Holy Spirit also urged me to share the life changing, God-incidences that occurred in my life.

Continuing with the idea of writing a devotional, I also thought it would be fun, and certainly much easier and faster, if other women participated in this project and contributed their God stories too. Emails were sent to over 250 special ladies God had placed in my path. If each one wrote one, maybe two devotions, there would be 366 in no time at all. This book was a done deal! I had it finished in six months—in my head. All I had to do was sit back and wait for the stories to flood my inbox, while I wrote a few of my own.

I actually prayed about and pondered this project for several years beforehand. I thought there was a clear green light from God to proceed. Oh, the green light was there. I just failed to read all the detour signs the Author (of my story) had for the book. After all, it was for His glory and purpose, so He certainly had the final say so in the finished product.

Very quickly it was evident not every woman shared my same passion for writing or documenting her encounters with the Father. I received an abundance of support through prayers and words of encouragement, which was a huge blessing and greatly appreciated, but where were the devos? Was God expecting me to fill in the gap and write more than the few I had anticipated? What was He up to?

Little did I know, but God was taking me on the journey of a lifetime! He was going to take me down roads I never dreamed of seeing. We were going to walk together, as He placed story after story on my heart to write. I tell you what—the three years spent compiling and writing these devotions have been the most rewarding, inspirational, transforming, humbling years of my life!

God could have led the Israelites to the Promised Land in a matter of months instead of 40 years, but that wasn't the plan. The journey was more important than the destination. If all the women had sent devotions, like I had envisioned, I would have missed out on the adventure. I would have missed the blessings of spending time with my Father. Just the two of us. The finished book isn't nearly as noteworthy as the lessons He taught me along the way. No, quick and easy wouldn't produce what God had in mind.

Dancing in the Drought wasn't even the original title, but about halfway through the project, after the Texas Hill Country and Highland Lakes were plagued with drastic drought conditions, I became consumed by the dry, parched land and the dwindling water supply. My focus changed from worshiping Jesus to being fixated on rain. Rain became my idol. God was out to teach me how to find joy in the drought—both the physical and spiritual. To want Jesus *more* than I longed for rain or anything else. To realize that Jesus is enough. He's all I need. Just as God is the only one who can bring the rain, He is also the only one who can fill the desires and longing of my heart.

I am not an author. I am a storyteller. God stories. Perhaps the greatest storyteller of all was Jesus, with His many parables. There must be something to this storytelling if Jesus Himself used that technique in His teachings. He shows up in my life, and I fill led to tell others what He has done. He rescued me from the pit of hell years ago. His amazing grace restored my soul. That loving act of redemption is nothing short of a miracle. Someone like me?

While begging and pleading for rain, Jesus was trying to tell me I had already received His gift of living waters. He had quenched my thirst and I needed nothing else. Through our time together, through seeking Him with all my heart, I found joy in His streams of living waters. A joy that made dancing in the drought—both the physical and spiritual ones—an actual reality.

Even after the 366th devotion was written, after the final editing was done, I discovered that God wasn't finished with this book yet. He had one very important lesson to teach me about how He answers prayer.

I mentioned that the desire of my heart was for hundreds of women to share their God stories, but that didn't actually happen as I envisioned. I was looking for the completed story to be sent to my inbox. What I realized after the fact, what God showed me the very day I was writing this page, was He had indeed used hundreds to complete this project. He had answered my prayers—His way.

What about all the online daily Bible verses that provided the exact Scripture needed for a story in the making? Or the devotions, written by others, that reinforced a thought the Holy Spirit placed on my heart? Those authors had a hand in this book and don't even know it.

All the people who lifted this project up in prayer. All the sweet friends who asked, during the course of the three years, how the book was coming. Even the husbands of my friends wanted to know. Yes, all who prayed and thought about this book were involved in the finished product.

You will note my many references to songs and how God spoke to me through music. Yes, He does know my love-language and how to touch my heart. All those song-writers and recording artists were instrumental through sharing their talents. (In case you want to hear a particular song or read all of the lyrics, you can Google the artist and title.)

All involved with Sunday morning worship at Austin Ridge Bible Church had a role in this book too. Whether it was a message from the pulpit or the incredibly talented praise and worship teams rocking the house, all contributed to the Sunday experience that inspired many stories.

You will note at the end of a few stories the name of someone who has gone home to be Jesus. Of those, I only knew one personally, but all had an impact on my journey. God will never waste a tear and even through death, He will use a life for His glory.

Then there were the people I encountered in the process of doing everyday life who touched my heart in such a way that I wrote about that specific God-incidence. They certainly had no idea they would be the main character in a God story for this book.

Yes, just as the heavens are higher than the earth, so are His ways higher than my ways and His thoughts than my thoughts (Isaiah 55:9). In His own way, my Father did indeed supply the hundreds for this book to be completed.

While I once longed for rain more than Jesus, I also longed for the "desires of my heart," devotions written by others, more than I yearned for my Father. After that final story was written, there were ultimately hundreds involved in this project. The desire of my heart had been met, and it took reaching the end to realize how God had answered my prayer. Yes, I had focused so much on God doing things my way that I missed the blessings He had already bestowed upon me.

Don't miss the treasures God has for you, scattered throughout your day. Take note of the people God places in your path. Maybe even start your own journal of God stories. Invite Him to reign on the throne of your life, being the One you desire over anything or anybody.

As my faith walk was influenced by the written words of others through devotions, I pray that you might also find hope and encouragement on these pages. The stories written by my friends are scattered throughout the book and noted with their name (or initials). There are a few contributors who are actually published authors, but for the rest of us, we are first-timers. Just a reminder, we are all ordinary women, sharing what God placed on our hearts.

May we all learn to dance in the drought that the trials of everyday life will bring, finding unending joy in His springs of living waters.

Acknowledgments

I am very grateful for the women who contributed their God stories. I don't have the words to express my sincere, heartfelt appreciation for your love and support. For some, it was difficult to put personal thoughts and experiences on paper for others to read. Thank you, girls, for stepping out of your comfort zone and sharing in this journey. (My friends are recognized after each of their stories.)

For those who covered me in prayer and encouragement, I am equally thankful. The power of your words sustained me! And there were the friends who were the inspiration for some of my devotions. Thank you for allowing me to write about you! While my heart's desire had been for hundreds of women to share their stories, in the end, there were hundreds who were used by God in His own specific way, for His purpose and ended up being part of this book. I remain in awe of His perfect orchestration of friendships, relationships and encounters resulting in the completion of *Dancing in the Drought*.

To my Java Dive Girls and LifeGroupers from Austin Ridge Bible Church: Thank you for walking with me on this journey, being such faithful prayer warriors and lifting me up when I became discouraged. Also, I am humbled that even after you knew my stories, you loved me just the same.

My husband, Austin, was instrumental in this project. He was not only a topic of discussion throughout this book, but also my most avid supporter. Austin prayed for this devotional every night, with his requests to God keeping my love tank full. Besides being the most patient, hard-working person I know, Austin is also a hopeless romantic and practical joker. A rather strange combination of personality traits, but the perfect mixture that helped me learn to laugh at myself, while feeling unconditionally loved. Thank you, dear, for keeping me supplied with lots of writing material!

My two sons, Zach and Trevor, were also the main characters in many stories, along with being huge supporters. It took being a mom for me to recognize the power of love—and how I do love both of you! Even though I sounded like a broken record, writing of my longing for you to come back to the Lord, thank you for allowing me to share my heart as I attempted to express my unending, unconditional love. Knowing the depth of my own feelings, it is still difficult to fathom our Heavenly Father loves you even more!

An added bonus in my life has been my daughter-in-love, Lauren. She loves my Zach so sweetly and the dynamics of her Cajun roots make life so fun. Lauren allowed me to pick on her in this book, yet still remained a source of encouragement.

I met my editor, Rick Weber, years ago at my previous church home in Katy, Texas, where we volunteered together in DivorceCare. During that time, he published *Pink Lips and Fingertips,* and his perseverance was my inspiration! He encouraged me to get started on this book and supported me the entire time. It was actually amusing to receive a male's comments about some of the stories, and he was an incredibly good sport about being immersed in a year-long devotional for women! He has quite a resume, especially in sports writing and editing projects of varying complexity, and his expertise was priceless. Please read more about him at www.rickweber.org.

Even though I lovingly give thanks to the many who had a role in *Dancing in the Drought*, Jesus Christ, my Lord and Savior, is the only reason this book was ultimately completed. Without His love, mercy and grace, I wouldn't be here today. He saved me from self-destruction years ago, and I give Him all the praise and glory for allowing me, along with some of my sweet friends, to share the stories God placed on our hearts.

O God, you are my God,
earnestly I seek you;
my soul thirsts for you,
my body longs for you,
in a dry and weary land
where there is no water.
Psalm 63:1

January 1

When I was woven together in the depths of the earth, your eyes saw my unformed body. All the days ordained for me were written in your book before one of them came to be.—**Psalm 139:15-16**

As I sat down to write the last devotion for this book, I realized there wasn't a story written specifically for New Year's Day. There I was, at the very end, but there was nothing for the beginning.

Hopefully you read the introduction and gained a little bit of background on how this book came about. If not, I will briefly tell you that my heart's desire was to have the fabulous women the Father had placed in my life write their God stories. My role would be to simply compile all of them. However, God had other ideas. While He led many women to share, His plans were for the two of us to work very closely together on the project. We embarked on this journey approximately three years ago and what an adventure it has been!

For those who have accepted Jesus Christ as Lord and Savior, we know how our story will ultimately end—we have the promise of eternity in heaven with our Father. Therefore, no matter what happens in "the meantime," we can live knowing the final entry of our last chapter. I don't know about you, but I think the words from today's Scripture reading are some of the most encouraging in the entire Bible. God knows every detail of what will fill those pages.

How did things go for you last year? Was it a year of trials or more joyful moments than you can even remember? Last January 1st, did you have expectations for the year to come, and if so, did it end up anything like you thought it would? Did you enjoy the journey with God, no matter what the circumstances, or were you anxious and fearful, trying to re-write the chapter?

As this book neared completion, there were some other events that were winding down as well. My Tuesday-morning Bible study had completed Priscilla Shirer's *One in a Million: Journey to Your Promised Land.* Just as God deliberately led the Israelites through the wilderness for 40 years, He led me on a three-year writing expedition. Like the Israelites, my dependence upon God grew stronger during my own wilderness excursion! God picked the perfect study to coincide with the completion of the book.

Also at the same time, our house remodel was finally finished after 14 months of living in the garage apartment. I can assure you that period of being under construction wasn't as bad as I expected—it was worse! But when we finally moved back into the house, those months seemed like a blur. The momentary trials were all in the past, and we were ecstatic with the finished product.

Life rarely goes smoothly or as planned. Most of us have more or less figured that out by now. In looking back on the past three years and this book journey, I am thankful beyond words that it went God's way, not mine. I spent three years spending more time in His presence than in my entire life. Now it's done—completed—and I can look back on how it all progressed with a huge smile and a heart full of thanksgiving. There was no way of knowing in the beginning what God had in store for my life, but honestly, it was a life-changer!

We don't have a crystal ball to view the future, to see how this year will unfold, but we do have a God who knows. Just as He knew exactly how long it would take me to complete this book—just as He knew every detail of the journey we would travel together in the process—He knows every detail of our days ahead.

The Holy Spirit encouraged me to begin each day of the book-writing process in hopeful expectation of an encounter with Jesus. Even though the project is done, I pray to never lose that desire "to fix my eyes on Jesus, the Author and Perfecter of my faith" (Hebrews 12:2).

Now I know why He wanted me to save writing this story for the first day of the year until the very last. God had another incredible lesson for me to learn—no matter how hard I tried to orchestrate the outcome of this devotional, no matter how I envisioned the whole process, it was going to happen His way. Such is life. Both mine and yours.

Our life stories have already been written in His book. While we know the ending, the chapters leading to that last line remain a mystery. But we do have the Father's assurance of that final entry.

I pray that as you allow Jesus to lead you through the days of this year, to His springs of living water, you find unending joy and peace. Peace that surpasses all understanding.

January 2

"Do not store up for yourselves treasures on earth, where moths and rust destroy, and where thieves break in and steal. But store up for yourselves treasures in heaven." — **Matthew 6:19-20**

When I was pregnant in 1984 with my oldest son, Zach, I craved ice cream. That's not very original, but it wasn't just any flavor of ice cream. I only wanted Blue Bell mint chocolate chip. Hopefully you have heard of that little creamery in Brenham, Texas. But some of you might be too young to know that way back in those days, mint chocolate chip was only one of the seasonal flavors and not available in the grocery stores except for certain months throughout the year.

Baskin & Robbins and other ice cream parlors carried that flavor and it had always been my favorite. When my cravings started, it wasn't time for mint chocolate chip to be in the stores, and the ice cream shops would only sell me a few scoops, not the whole five-gallon container. Oh, but I had an advantage. I just happened to be working in my dad's grocery store and I had connections!

I asked our Blue Bell salesman if he could sell me a five-gallon container of mint chocolate chip (that would normally be sold to the ice cream shops). The very next day, he had it delivered, saying it was an early baby gift. I was thrilled that I had so much ice cream and could satisfy my cravings. But I had a thought—what would I do when it was gone? I would be too embarrassed to ask the salesman to get me another five gallons. I would need to ration my servings and eat it sparingly. Perhaps I should just deny myself the pleasure of a big bowl of ice cream and only have a bite or two every so often, just to insure that I didn't run out. Before too long, I just stopped eating it altogether, for fear that I would consume it all and have none. I simply hoarded it!

A few weeks passed by and I couldn't stand it any longer. I just wanted a big bowl of the luscious, minty-green ice cream, so I broke down and went out to the freezer in the garage. Boy, was I in for a surprise when I opened the door! The freezer had broken and everything inside had thawed. That yummy green ice cream was now a sloppy, gooey mess all inside the freezer. My coveted five gallons of mint chocolate chip was lost, along with everything else in the freezer.

I still laugh about that little mishap. I didn't have the guts to tell the salesman what had happened. What was I supposed to say? *Yes, it's all gone, but I didn't actually eat it. Being afraid I would run out, I just saved it, then my freezer broke and it melted all over the place.* I only wish I had eaten the whole thing and enjoyed it, instead of hoarding it and missing out completely.

Fast-forward to January 2011. I developed a craving for Coffee-mate peppermint mocha creamer, offered only at Christmas. Knowing that it would be gone from the stores at the end of the year, I purchased the few remaining containers at the store. It had a very long shelf life and wouldn't expire until the following May, and I would certainly use it by then.

Shortly after stocking up on the creamer, I noticed that the refrigeration case was full of it again. I looked closer and saw written on the side of the container, "Now available year round." I laughed as I remembered the incident with the ice cream and what happened the last time I worried about running out of a coveted item.

You can imagine how overjoyed I was when, only a few weeks after the discovery of my melted ice cream, Blue Bell mint chocolate chip hit the stores again for a month. I did stock up with several gallons, but I can tell you I didn't hoard it. I enjoyed it as often as I wanted. That might be one of the reasons I gained so much weight, but it might also be the reason my son is so sweet!

Hoarding and craving ice cream or coffee creamer isn't a serious offense. However, hanging on to "stuff" instead of clinging to God's Word is. I want to crave the Father. That's not only the way to a healthier lifestyle, but also the way to eternal life.

January 3

Jesus replied: "Love the Lord your God with all your heart and with all your soul and with all your mind." This is the first and greatest commandment. And the second is like it: "Love your neighbor as yourself." —**Matthew 22:37-39**

As I was removing the decorations from my Christmas tree, I took off the ornament given to me by my friends, Susan and Steve. It held a special meaning because, tragically, Steve was killed the previous summer in a helicopter crash.

I sent Susan an email the beginning of December, just to say hello and let her know I was thinking of her. (Certainly not as personal as a telephone call or a face-to-face conversation, but it's what I did.) This first holiday without her husband must have been so painful for her. Wrapping up the University of Texas bling, I felt the urging to check on Susan since I never received a reply back to my December message.

As I reached for my laptop, I was diverted by a phone call from my husband. He asked me to look for something in his closet. After our lengthy conversation (he loves to talk), I saw the pile of dirty clothes patiently waiting for a trip to the washing machine, so I scooped them up. I walked by the unmade bed and threw the clothes on the floor to tidy up the room.

Twenty minutes later, I remembered that I had intended to send Susan another email. When I opened my mail, I saw that 10 minutes earlier, Susan had replied to my email sent at the first part of December. Sure, in my reply back I could tell her that I had just been thinking about her as I took the ornament off the tree, but I wish I hadn't delayed and had sent her a message 20 minutes earlier. It's not a matter of being first—it's about knowing I felt the nudge of the Holy Spirit and didn't make it a top priority.

I like to know that someone thought of me and sent an email or a Facebook message or phoned or better yet, sent a handwritten card. When I am feeling low, there is nothing like someone reaching out to me, to offer some words of encouragement or just to say hello. I feel that person is God with skin, showering His love on me.

I am certain Susan appreciated my speedy response back. Knowing her, she was pleased that I had been reminded of her sweet Steve when I took the ornament off the tree. But I also know that, personally, I would have been so very touched had someone reached out to me, without it being a reply to my email. Wouldn't she have felt more of God's love being lavished on her if only I had been prompt in my obedience to that small voice within me?

What a God-incidence, though. I felt God was teaching me a lesson in the importance of acting upon the calling of the Holy Spirit—not only a lesson in obedience but also one in timing. Who am I to tell God to wait? *Yes, God, I hear You, but I'm a little busy right now.*

Folks speak about their New Year's resolutions. I don't think it can be called a resolution when it is a commandment, but I am going to make Matthew 22:37-39 my daily goal. Jesus said it Himself: What could be more important than loving God and loving people as I love myself?

Is there someone on your heart you are being urged to contact? You know who it is. Don't wait any longer to shower her with God's love and yours. If the Holy Spirit puts that person on your heart, go for it—*now!*

God just put a very special someone on my heart whom I love dearly—my sister. Tomorrow you will read her story.

January 4

"Then all your people will be righteous; they will possess the land forever; they are the branches I planted, the work of My hands, so that I may be glorified." —**Isaiah 60:21 (HCSB)**

I was born and raised in Corpus Christi, Texas, which I considered to be a beautiful place—with the exception of the trees. Palm trees and mesquites were not my idea of trees. I envisioned something much more majestic. At mid-term during my senior year in high school, I realized I had enough credits to meet graduation requirements, so I moved on.

I am now blessed to spend my days on the family ranch—the dream of a lifetime. It's a beautiful place bordering the Colorado River, with rolling hills and massive live oak and post oak trees. Throughout the past decade, we have experienced some severe drought conditions that have taken a toll on some of these trees. This is natural and to be expected.

Recently, however, we had an event that was totally unexpected. At dusk one evening, the wind started blowing. It got stronger and stronger. We experienced severe straight-line winds for well over half an hour coming directly into the riverbank. Huge native pecan trees were uprooted, massive live oaks on the sides of the hills had their tops torn out or were split apart. The destruction was unbelievable. I was angry—how could something like this in such a short period of time destroy what had taken so long to grow?

After the anger subsided and the cleanup began, I remembered a very special man—Mel Brindley. My husband and I became acquainted with him when we were searching for a carpenter to help us restore an old house we lived in when we first got married. Mel had worked for the past 18 years at one of Camp Allen's three sites in the Houston area, which were owned by the Episcopal Diocese and named after Rosa Lum Allen. He painstakingly began working on our restoration. He did not waste the equivalent of a toothpick. We moved in as soon as the house was somewhat inhabitable. Mel continued to work quietly and always alone.

Unfortunately, Mel developed terminal cancer. After his death, we told his widow we wanted to do something special for him. She suggested a bench for the Mel Brindley Memorial Trail. The discovery instructor at Camp Allen dedicated hours to the creation of this trail, which begins at the conference center and continues along the rolling hills in the southeastern forests of Texas. There are markers along the way, each depicting a biological or historical teaching to foster in people the idea of stewardship of our natural world, while strengthening our understanding of God. The trail is such a fitting tribute to our special friend.

You see, Mel was not just a carpenter—he was a "woodsman." Throughout his life, he had developed the ability to perceive not only the natural beauty of the forest, but its spiritual beauty as well. He once said, "People think about God out here. It is evident that this is God's handiwork, something man can't duplicate." He helped people understand the unity of God and nature.

While I was viewing the collapse of these ancient trees as a tragedy, he would have seen it as part of the never-ending cycle of nature necessary to maintain a healthy and diverse forest.

Nancy Bonham Holt
Weimar, TX

January 5

Therefore confess your sins to one another and pray for one another, that you may be healed. The prayer of a righteous person has great power as it is working.—**James 5:16**

A friend once told me, "The Enemy lives in the darkness, in the secrets that we keep." The hope God gives us in response to that ugly truth is "even the darkness will not be dark to you; the night will shine like the day, for darkness is as light to you" (Psalm 139:12). There is nothing that God doesn't already know about us, and He loves us just the same.

God doesn't need us to confess our sins to others, but He wants us to. He designed His children to be in relationship with each other. A transparent relationship in which "love covers over a multitude of sins" (1 Peter 4:8 ESV) and in which we catch a glimpse of His unconditional love for us. We get to encourage one another and pray for each other. As James writes, "The prayer of a righteous person has great power as it is working" (James 5:16 ESV). God calls us righteous, and therefore we can be sure that our prayers are effective even as God is still working in our circumstance.

My marriage is a testimony that confession brings healing. My husband and I dealt with a sin in our marriage that only the two of us knew. We refused to share our struggle with others out of fear. For seven years, we prayed about the issue and truly sought the Lord's wisdom and strength, but we would go through cycles of victory and defeat. We were only obeying God in as much as we were comfortable. But the enemy continually spoke lies to us. *Your marriage is a sham. You are a failure. No one would love or respect you if they knew.* When you are deceived, you desperately need someone to love you, pray for you and speak truth to you.

It wasn't until we confessed our sin to other believers that we began to experience the miraculous healing of God. My husband shared with a pastor at our church. I shared with a trusted friend. The confession removed the bonds of shame and embarrassment. Sin had lost its power. We felt such freedom, walking in the light. God brought others into our life who had dealt with the same issue and He led us to resources that addressed our struggle. We never would have known that those resources were all around us if we had not humbled ourselves and confessed our sin.

He gave *everyone* over to sin so He could be merciful to *all* of us (Romans 11:32). There should be no fear in sharing our struggles with others. It is a testimony to God's power and faithfulness that while we were still sinners, Christ died for us. We are imperfect people in need of a perfect God. God did not wait to send Christ until we got our act together! Christ's death on the cross is sufficient! Live in the light and the freedom of God's forgiveness.

Anonymous

January 6

Let brotherly love continue. Do not neglect to show hospitality to strangers, for thereby some have entertained angels unaware.—**Hebrews 13:1-2**

Writing for this book has been a delightful adventure. By the end of many days, my mind is swarming with stories in the making. Too many ideas aren't always a good thing, though. One dilemma is allocating the time to write them all. (Believe it or not, even a retired Empty Nester is busy.) But most importantly, I must discern if the devotions swirling in my head are actually God-inspired.

On this particular morning, God made the decision-making process quite easy. I had a story already written in my head and I needed a verse to go with it. I pondered if it was actually worthy of writing, but the longer the words lingered in my heart, the more I felt it was something He wanted me to share. Then, when I read Hebrews 13:1-2 in one of my daily devotions, I knew God was in on this one.

I randomly gathered a few books from my bookshelf to begin my morning time with God. The first one I opened was the *Daily Guideposts* from the *previous* year. I turned to the current date and began to read. There they were, the God-breathed words I was searching for.

My precious golden retriever loves her daily stop-and-sniff walks along the neighborhood streets, taking in as many smells as possible. Since we walk slowly, I also have the opportunity to linger and dwell on the sights. However, on garbage day, there is one house that has intrigued me a bit. This is how the story unfolded:

Over the past few years, I have occasionally noticed a small box or sack placed on the garbage can at the curb of this house. I have wondered why the people just didn't take the time to place it inside. The garbage can wasn't overflowing, so certainly there was room. No, the bag or box just sat on the lid. Yes, I was quick to judge these people, thinking it would be so much easier for the garbage collectors if the homeowners just opened the lid and placed whatever it was in the can.

You are probably sharper than I am and have already figured out what was going on here. It wasn't until my walk on this particular garbage day that I understood.

Even though it was the first week of January, it was a sunny 70 degrees outside and I had on shorts and flip-flops. As I passed by, I noticed two unopened bottled waters on the garbage can lid at this same house. It took a second look for the light to turn on. I realized this family was thoughtful enough of the garbage collectors on this warm winter day to leave them something to drink.

Then I remembered the bags and boxes I had seen before. I am now positive they contained items for the men also, intentionally separated from the garbage. Here I had been so quick to judge this family, assuming they were making life tougher for the garbage collectors, all the while they were displaying random acts of love and kindness to total strangers.

God was certainly helping me write this devotion. He not only delivered the Scripture for me to use, He also took the opportunity for a teaching moment. First of all, I know I am way too quick to judge others and He wanted me to see my sin. But I also felt God nudging me towards the people I don't know who He places in my path each day—to offer a smile, a warm hello, a helpful hand, a bottled water on a warm day.

As I go out into His world today, may I go with eyes wide open, being mindful not to neglect the strangers—or possible angels—God has carefully placed in my life. Will you join me?

January 7

Finally, brethren, whatever things are true, whatever things are noble, whatever things are just, whatever things are pure, whatever things are lovely, whatever things are of good report, if there is any virtue and if there is anything praiseworthy, meditate on these things.—**Philippians 4:8 (NKJV)**

At the age of 25, a few months after rebounding from a difficult break-up, I married a family friend, five years my senior, who had pursued me from the time I was 16. Though we were Christians, neither of us prayed for the Lord's will for our upcoming marriage. And when Stephen began to get cold feet, being the "strong" woman that I was, I pressured him into our "shotgun" wedding by telling him it was "now or never."

The first months of marriage were neither blissful nor idyllic as I had dreamed. Instead, they were filled with shouting, harsh words, power struggles and regret—all occurring behind the scenes while we served in church.

Shortly after our 13th anniversary, I sought counsel from a divorce attorney about how to proceed with terminating the marriage. But in a "last-ditch effort" to stay true to my vows and my faith, I cried out to God and begged Him to speak His will into my life. In desperation, I made a commitment to fast, pray and read my Bible until I received His direction.

God's supernatural response came quick, clear and shocking, *I was to change.* I was to become more loving, forgiving and affirming, instead of fighting back, tearing Stephen apart with my words, and treating him with malice, bitterness and contempt. Though I was shocked at the revelation, deep in my spirit, I knew that I had heard from God and was humbled into obedience.

The Lord led me to meditate on all my husband's good qualities and all the reasons that I had been attracted to him before the marriage. The more I focused on the good, the more the bad faded away, and the more I grew to feel love for him again. In our first "altercation" after God had spoken, I prayed silently, begging God for His power to respond with love, and He did just that. My husband was so shocked at the change that he was speechless.

As the weeks and months passed, God helped me to become the loving and respectful wife that He had called me to be and I watched in sheer astonishment as my husband became the awesome, loving, spiritual head that God had called him to be. It was miraculous, and confirmed for me the truth of the Bible verse that reads, "Love covers a multitude of sins" (1 Peter 4:8 NKJV).

We have now been married for 19 years, and the last six have been happier than we could ever have imagined, reminding me that God can do amazing things when we seek Him with our whole hearts and when we meditate on the good.

Juliet West
Bee Cave, TX

January 8

With my lips I recount all the laws that come from your mouth. I rejoice in following your statutes as one rejoices in great riches. I meditate on your precepts and consider your ways. I delight in your decrees; I will not neglect your word.—**Psalm 119: 13-16**

During the many months and years of compiling this devotional, I spent countless hours in God's presence. I prayed before I ever sat down to write. Often in the middle of a paragraph, I stopped and asked for just the right words. I spent time, after I thought I was finished, reviewing and praying some more. Hours were spent reading commentaries on Scriptures.

All that said, one might think I would constantly have a joyful attitude with so much time spent in His presence. Unfortunately, that wasn't always the case. Many times I woke up with the Monday Morning Blues.

While this book was in the "production stage," my husband, Austin, was commuting between our house on Lake Travis in Austin and Houston because of his business. Come Monday morning, I knew he would be leaving and it would just be Holly, my golden retriever, and me until he returned on Friday. While I had plenty to keep me busy, with this book and other commitments, sometimes the thought of being all alone for the week just got me down before he ever left the house.

There were also some Monday mornings when I woke up expecting it to be a crazy, hectic week because I had too much on my plate. I found myself focusing on how I would get it all done by Friday instead of thinking about the day ahead of me. Instead of looking to find Jesus in my day, I was expecting to find stress and worry all week long.

On this particular day, my Monday Morning Blues was a combination of the two scenarios mentioned above. I am so thankful that others have poured out their hearts and their human frailties into the written word of daily devotionals. On this Monday morning, God was ready to lift my spirits and bring me back into His presence. All I had to do was delve into my stack of devotionals.

Sharon Young's *Jesus Calling* spoke directly to what was going on. (If you don't have that book, you must get it.) Through her unique style of writing, as if Jesus were talking, she wrote that the day was divided into 24-hour segments for a reason. As humans, we can't handle more than that.

Yes, "This is the day the Lord has made. Let us rejoice and be glad in it" (Psalm 118:24). "Therefore, do not worry about tomorrow, for tomorrow will worry about it itself. Each day has enough trouble of its own" (Matthew 6:34). These two verses were included in two other devotionals I pulled out that morning. Weren't they appropriate for the circumstances? I knew them by memory, but somehow they were like brand new words.

God is so good in the way He provides for me. Time after time, the devotions He leads me to read contain the exact words I need to hear. But I must do more than just read a story and learn the Scriptures He gives me. All Scripture contains verbs, and a verb describes an action, a state of being or an occurrence. For me to bring them off the pages of the Bible and to life, God commands me to put His words into action through obedience.

I could choose to disobey and sulk in my Monday Morning Blues or chose to obey and be back in His presence. I re-read Psalm 118:24 and Matthew 6:34 several times and my choice was clear. I would much rather rejoice, be glad and be without worry. It wasn't such a lonely Monday after all—God kept me company!

January 9

And we know that God causes all things to work together for good, for those who love God and are called according to His purposes.—**Romans 8:28 (NASB)**

When I first heard this verse, I was in a hospital, completely paralyzed. My neck had been broken in a bad car accident and doctors were saying that I would probably never walk again or be able to take care of myself. I was only 18 years old.

My sister was sharing her new faith in Jesus with me when she told me about Romans 8:28. She explained that she didn't know why our car accident had happened, but she did know that God could bring good from it.

We had both grown up going to church on Sundays and believing in Jesus. But she was telling me that the Bible says we need to receive Him as well (John 1:12). That is, we needed to accept His gift of dying on the cross for our sins and not just take it for granted. I also needed to ask Him to come into my life and to lead me according to His will. My sister said that if we want to have eternal life in heaven, as well as His promises (like the one in Romans 8:28), we need to be "called according to His purposes" (to want what He wants)..

I told her that I wanted this too, and she led me through a prayer that went like this: *Lord Jesus, I need You. Thank You for dying on the cross for my sins. Please come into my life and be my Savior and Lord. Thank You for forgiving me of my sins and for giving me eternal life. Please lead me to live according to Your will. Amen!*

I couldn't know then how much good would come from that simple prayer. It filled me with hope, right then, and over time the Lord has blessed me in so many ways. He used a terrible car accident to bring me to Him. To have Him in my life, to know Him, and to be able to walk through life with Him have made going through that awful wreck and the months of rehabilitation worth it.

I can walk and do most things again (though more slowly). He didn't give me complete healing, but there are many more blessings in my life now that I couldn't have had if I hadn't gone through that awful experience. My wonderful husband and children are examples of these blessings.

God really does cause all things to work together for good, for anyone who loves Him, and is called according to His purposes. He has proven it!

Jill Tanner
Austin, TX

January 10

How much more, then, will the blood of Christ, who through the eternal Spirit offered himself unblemished to God, cleanse our consciences from acts that lead to death so that we may serve the living God.— **Hebrews 9:14**

If you're a parent, you understand what it is like to try to get your kids to clean their rooms. You know, the room that you are almost afraid to enter for fear of what may be growing in it. There are dirty clothes, toys, books, papers, and, well, trash everywhere. And let's not talk about the smell. When you tell them to clean, what you get is everything stuffed in the closest, under the bed or in a dresser drawer you cannot open. That is their version of clean, right?

We do not like to tell our girls 15 times to clean their room, so when it seems they are rebelling against that dreaded chore, we have resorted to the infamous "trash bag." The sheer mention of the trash bag makes them cringe. We hear lots of, "Pleeeease, I promise to clean."

We will hang a trash bag on their bedroom door and give them one hour to clean their room. If it is not cleaned, then Dad and Mom get to clean the room with a trash bag. Anything left lying around is game for the trash, so if they want to keep it, they had better put it away. It is almost comical to listen to them rushing around upstairs before that hour ticks away.

Our oldest daughter has experienced the trash bag once; we actually placed her stuff in storage to see how long it would take her to miss anything we put in the bag. She must have been about 9 at that time. She is 15 now, and I do not think she has ever missed a single thing, but it did leave an impression on her. So much so that she gives grave warning to the youngest.

As I sat in a meeting the other day at church and mentioned this to the other ladies in the room, we all had a good laugh, but then wondered briefly how many times God hangs a trash bag on our spiritual door wanting us to become clean before Him.

And what is our own version of clean? What about all those sins we have asked forgiveness for that He so graciously threw away? How often do we dig that back out, then beat ourselves up time and time again? Or what about the trash we try to hide from our Father, hoping He will not see it? We joke to our kids that we know everything, forgetting that God really *does* know it all. I wonder how comical we must look to Him, thinking we can clean up our mess better than He can.

Truly, we are no joke. He loves us enough to want to forgive us. He tells us in His Word that we are forgiven, cleansed by the blood of Jesus Christ. That means when we ask for forgiveness, He throws our garbage away. As humans, we will always have trash that needs to be thrown out, but if we have placed our trust in Jesus, then the one perfect parent will always be waiting with a trash bag to toss out our mess.

Shanna Jacobson
Brownwood, TX

January 11

*And they will be called righteous tress, planted by the L*ORD*, to glorify Him.* —**Isaiah 61:3 (HCSB)**

The first time I read Isaiah 61:3 (from the HCSB) in a daily devotion, I wanted this book to be titled *Righteous Trees*. I had the title—that was a start. Me and the other "righteous trees" just needed to write 366 devotions to fill it up. Oh, but wait. There needed to be a front cover for the book. That would be easy. My younger son is an aspiring photographer, so he at least had one job on his agenda!

The next task was to decide what the cover would look like. The first thing I thought of was a picture of righteous, magnificent, stately looking trees. Besides living on a beautiful lake, I am surrounded by the most gorgeous trees here in the Texas Hill Country. Surely, I would have no problem finding the perfect grouping of trees. So the hunt began.

Soon I became overwhelmed with all of the trees that were potential candidates. I walk several times each week, so I always had my eyes open. The more I looked, the more "righteous" trees I found. Almost every one had possibilities, and I looked at them with a whole new set of eyes. They were all different, all unique and the exceptionally picturesque ones soon began to appear everywhere. How would I ever decide?

One morning in late spring, I was walking my dog, Holly, and I saw them! I knew I would know when I saw just the right ones. Here they were, literally right down the street from my house, and I had walked by them hundreds of times. Today the Spanish Oak, which was the largest, was majestic as her leaves were waving and calling out to me. *Hello! Look at me! I am the cover girl you have been looking for.* Had her leaves always been lime green? All of the other Spanish Oaks' leaves were a darker shade; these were distinct.

This yard had five different types of trees, and they all looked so healthy, so vibrant, so full of life and beauty. They seemed to be singing songs of praise and glory to God for the wonder of their creation as their leaves rustled in the wind. I had found my righteous trees. Different types of trees, of different ages, just like the women who would contribute stories to this book.

The first time Trevor came to shoot the pictures, it was actually drizzling. A very rare, but welcomed phenomenon in this drought-stricken area. The next time he was scheduled to come, there was an opportunity for a "paying" photo shoot, so it took precedence over mine. That morning, I walked Holly by the trees, just to tell them good morning and make sure they still looked gorgeous. As I stood and looked at them, the Holy Spirit told me to go home and read that verse again.

I didn't have to go home to read it; this one I knew by memory, and I stood there saying it over and over. It finally hit me and I just laughed at myself. I was so caught up with the name of "righteous trees" all I could focus on was just the words, not who was being referred to as righteous. "They" will be called righteous trees—they being the mourners in Zion who dwelt in Jerusalem. *We* are called to bear fruit, like trees, but it is spiritual fruit. *We*, as humans, are created in God's image, not the trees. *We* are called to glorify Him by our words, deeds and actions, by our love and reverence to God. Can a tree do that?

This book is going to be about real-life, righteous woman, giving God the glory for what He has done in our lives. There's nothing wrong with having some pretty trees in the picture, but we are here for His purpose, and it wouldn't be a book without us women sharing our stories, all for His glory. This book is about real lives, not real trees.

I'm glad circumstances didn't work out for my son to take pictures. Perhaps *Righteous Trees* wasn't supposed to be the title after all. I had only a handful of stories and I was already focusing on the title—and what the front cover would look like? I sensed the Holy Spirit telling me to wait on the title and see what God had in store for this journey.

January 12

They will be called oaks of righteousness, a planting of the LORD for the display of his splendor.—**Isaiah 61:3**

Remembering birthdays and other important dates isn't one of my better skills. Even when I make a note on my calendar, I slip up. The trick there is that I must look at my calendar, and sometimes I just forget. Facebook has been a huge help because I get an email at the first of every week alerting me to upcoming birthdays, but even that's not fail-proof. I have many friends who aren't on Facebook.

Last year, I started a new system to make sure I didn't let important dates go unnoticed. I started making a note of them in one of my devotionals I read every day, *Daily Guideposts*. There is a new one published every year, so the day of the week and the date correspond to the current year.

It has also been fun because many times the daily Scripture reading is very appropriate for the person whose special day it is. For instance, on my sister Nancy's wedding anniversary the verse was Isaiah 61:3, which I have cited above. I had originally wanted to title this book *Righteous Trees* after I read the translation of that same verse in the Holman Christian Standard Bible (HCSB) and just loved how "they," those grieving in Zion, were referenced: "And they will be called righteous trees, planted by the LORD, to glorify Him." Yes, we are all on this earth to bring glory to our Father in heaven.

I thought it was very special that the verse that influenced what I wanted to title this book happened to be the same one cited on their anniversary, just different translations. But there was also something else significant about the "oaks" of righteousness.

Nancy and her husband, E.M., live on an 800-acre ranch that is nestled on the banks of the Colorado River. They breed Angus cattle, and the Texas drought had been devastating to their livestock and their land. Along the road entering the property is a majestic, stately oak tree. It is at least 250 years old. Days before their anniversary, the huge oak had literally split in two, with one half still in the ground, but the other completely broken from the main branch.

Nancy called to tell me the sad news. She and E.M. had hauled water to that tree for months in hopes of keeping it alive. There were hundreds of oak trees on the property but none as beautiful and mighty. Now it had fallen victim to the lack of rain. It was located in the middle of a large pasture—it wasn't as if they could run a garden hose over to it. They had to haul water on the back of a truck. Nancy and E.M. had tried, but the old tree just didn't receive enough moisture.

Days later, my sister called again to let me know that the leaves on one half of the tree had already turned brown, but that the other half was still green. Perhaps the half that was still in the soil was going to make it after all. Did God save the big, old tree by allowing part of it to die since there wasn't enough water to supply the needs for the whole thing? Was God giving our righteous oak tree a second chance to display His splendor?

Hmm, that sounds a bit like my life. I go through periods of drought, but my Heavenly Father wants to restore my soul, renew my heart and give me another chance to grow in His love. Then the word drought became stuck in my head—the physical one that killed the big tree on the ranch and my own spiritual droughts that hinder my growth.

Apart from my Father, the one true vine, I can do nothing. I cannot survive the trials of life without His springs of living water to sustain me. Even in the middle of a drought, He will supply all I need. Hmm. That just might be a better idea for a title.

January 13

For those who are led by the Spirit of God are the children of God.—**Romans 8:14**

I am busy. Fortunately, Target is not. It's just a little after 8 a.m., and I can get what I need and go. Let's see, which aisle am I looking for?

My thoughts are interrupted by a loud woman on her cell phone. I can't see her but I can certainly hear her. Like too many other people using cell phones in public, her voice is loud, passionate, and insensitive to those around her. Blah, blah, blah, she goes on and on. Now she is saying something like, "Please don't do that. Please, no."

Can't she be a little quieter? I decide I am going to find her and see what she looks like. You know how you try to get a glimpse of what the bad driver on the road looks like, if they're too old to drive, or maybe talking on the phone? But her words are starting to haunt me. As I draw nearer, I see that she is quietly sobbing. Shame fills my heart as I witness her mysterious pain.

I start to turn away in respect for her privacy, but the Holy Spirit says, "Not so fast!" I stop and listen. God is speaking, and what He is telling me I would surely not come up with myself: *Go over to her and be with her.* Lately, I have been praying to be more obedient to God, so I walk slowly in her direction and wait for her to hang up. I don't know her, she doesn't know me. She probably wants to be alone. I might make a fool of myself. Suddenly she hangs up.

"May I help?" I hear myself say. She is thirty-something, blonde, chubby. Her face is wet with tears. Am I an unwelcome intruder? She looks at me. "He's so abusive, so mean. He always blames me, and now he's trying to take my home away! I don't know if I'm coming or going." More tears. And now some of them are mine.

I ask if I may pray with her. For a second, I wonder, *What if she doesn't want to pray in public, or at all? What if she doesn't believe in God, or even hates Him?* She answers, "OK." I take her hand and silently ask the Holy Spirit to pray through me. The words flow: "Lord, give this precious woman Your peace and guidance. Please make the man stop being mean to her; soften his heart and let him ask her for forgiveness. Let him also ask You for Your forgiveness." I pause a second to wonder if the name of Jesus would offend her. I finish the prayer, and she echoes: "In the name of Jesus." Whew!

It is a holy moment. In less than a minute, our hearts were bound to one another and to the Lord. I might never see her again or know the outcome. But I realize that God led me to Target this morning to be His ambassador. Such joy to be used by Him! I can trust Him. He has shown me how to hit the true target. I am flying high.

Ms. Hendle Rumbaut
Austin, TX

January 14

No eye has seen, no ear has heard, no mind has conceived what God has prepared for those who love him.
—**1 Corinthians 2:9**

Many of the women I asked to contribute a story for this book declined. I was totally naïve to assume everyone loved to write. However, even though they didn't send a story, many offered their prayers, which were just as important.

During the first six months or so after I began, hardly a Sunday went by that someone at church didn't ask me how the book was going. Just knowing that ladies were thinking about it encouraged me. My usual response was that it was going OK. However, that wasn't the actual truth.

The stories were coming in so slowly—how would I ever reach my milestone of 366? But yet I kept on telling that lie. I didn't want to admit that perhaps I had made a mistake with this little project. Maybe I just thought God was leading me to write/compile a book. If ladies weren't contributing, obviously I had approached it totally wrong. With God's truths in my heart, I made the decision not to quit, and I forged ahead. I refused to listen to that voice whispering the lies, telling me to give up. What I hadn't yet realized was that the journey between the start and the finished product would be the most important part of the whole process.

God opened my eyes to a whole new world—His world. Now when I am asked how the book is going, I respond truthfully: "It is going better than I ever expected." God is taking me on a personal journey of spiritual growth; we are walking hand in hand each day. Our relationship is flourishing beyond my wildest dreams. All because of this book.

Had every woman I asked shared a story, this book would be done. I can guarantee the stories would have been more interesting and certainly the variety would have made for a better read since I would have only written a few myself. My life would now be back to the way it was. But if God would have let things go my way, I would have completely missed His blessings.

Don't ever underestimate the significance in the little twists and turns of life. Every day I thank God for this book adventure we are on. Patience is not my best virtue, but I am learning how important it is to wait. If I had listened to Satan's lies or if all had gone according to my plan, I would have missed this joy God had planned for me.

His plan for my life—for your life—is beyond our wildest imagination. There will be bumps and some crazy, scary turns, but the journey is worth it. Hold on tight, enjoy the ride and keep your eyes wide open. You don't want to miss out on the lessons to be learned between the start and the finish.

January 15

Search me, O God, and know my heart; test me and know my anxious thoughts. See if there is any offensive way in me, and lead me in the way everlasting.—**Psalm 139:23-24**

Here in the Hill Country, we are plagued with Cedar Fever during the months of December through February. *Juniperus ashei*, known to most Texans as mountain cedar, is the culprit of this dreaded allergy. Cedar pollen from the male trees is released into the air in golden clouds and it travels for miles. Symptoms include itchy, watery eyes, runny nose, scratchy throat and sneezing.

I know many people suffer from allergies, but most regions of the country get a reprieve during the winter months. Not in Austin, where the cedars are found in great abundance. The past winter, I had been a victim of Cedar Fever and here it was again. I started off taking over-the-counter allergy relief medications. Nothing worked. The persistent runny nose caused a constant drip in the back of my throat, which resulted in a relentless cough, which led to sleepless nights.

Of course, this all started right at the first of December, just like the previous year, right when all the Christmas preparations were in high gear. I finally called the doctor about mid-December. Her office was swamped, but I could come and wait, and she might be able to see me sometime that day. I decided I was too busy to go sit in her office. However, after Christmas rolled around, I knew I could wait no longer. Averaging about three hours of sleep a night, I had to get some relief. Last year, I had some potent cough medicine that did the trick. With some much-needed rest and the proper medications, I knew the healing would begin this go-round.

I finally made it to the doctor and thankfully left the office with three prescriptions. I dropped them off at the pharmacy and had an hour to wait. I drove back home, got sidetracked writing and when I arrived back, it was after 5:30 pm. I just had this sneaky suspicion that something wasn't right.

Sure enough, they had nothing for me. It was too late to call the doctor. I would have one more sleepless night of coughing. I had to fight back the tears and tell myself to keep smiling and be kind and say nice words to the sympathetic pharmacist. After all, it was simply a human error. It wasn't his fault, and there would be a solution—tomorrow. I immediately heard the Holy Spirit sending me a message to remind me how blessed I was and give me a few things to think about.

At least I have insurance and money to cover my medicine. Think of all the millions of folks who don't! Think of those people who have lost their jobs and their insurance coverage; those who have no hope of relief because they simply can't afford the price of the wonderful drugs available.

At least I have the hope of tomorrow, when I know I can call the doctor and get the problem solved. Think of all those millions of children in such places as Africa and Haiti and India where all sorts of diseases kill every day. Those children who will never get the medicine to cure their disease. I have Cedar Fever, not malaria or AIDS. I have a very high likelihood of feeling better in a few days.

I did get my three prescriptions the very next morning and enjoyed the best night's sleep in almost a month. The next morning, I spent my quiet time with prayers of thanksgiving and seeking forgiveness.

The little talk with the Holy Spirit sure did make me more appreciative of the luxury of medicine and having the means to pay for it. However, I also realized how I had put all the focus on me and my circumstances. All I had thought about for days was poor little Brenda—I was tired and felt yucky. And I certainly hadn't spent any time thinking about or praying for God's other sick children.

Those prescriptions will do the trick by easing the discomforts of Cedar Fever in a few days, but I need Jehovah-Rapha for complete healing of my selfish spirit. He knows my heart and showed me my offensive ways. Through His mercy and forgiveness, I will experience some spiritual healing I desperately need.

January 16

For you knitted me together in my mother's womb. I praise you because you I am fearfully and wonderfully made, your works are wonderful, I know that full well.—**Psalm 139:13-14**

I was born missing my left arm below the elbow. It is all I've known my whole life, so I've had to learn how to do everything with just one arm. From tying my shoes to changing my baby's diapers, I just had to make it work. So for me, missing an arm was my normal. I did everything the other kids did growing up; I just happened to do it with one arm.

It wasn't until I was in high school that I realized how odd it was in a global context for me as a disabled person to live such a normal life. In 9th grade, I traveled with my church youth group to Latvia and Russia. At one point during the trip, we visited an orphanage. I soon discovered that the children there had not lost their parents, but instead had been shut away from the world because they were disabled in some way. From mental disabilities to missing limbs, these children were deemed too abnormal to mix with regular people and so were removed from where people would have to look at them.

I was shocked to hear that they were treated in such ways, but not nearly as shocked as they were to hear that I was able to exist as a normal person in my culture. I had opportunities and freedoms they would never have because their culture deemed them unworthy of participation. I've since learned that such treatment of the disabled is not limited to Russia, but is common in countries all over the world. Even here in America, 90% of babies diagnosed with Down syndrome are aborted as unwanted children.

But the scriptures tell us that God knit us together in our mother's womb and that we should praise Him because we are fearfully and wonderfully made (Psalm 139:13-14). It isn't just the people who fit some definition of normal or look the most beautiful on the outside who are wonderfully made—all of us are. God had a plan for each of us, and to reject a person because of a disability is to reject God's own creation.

It can be difficult at times to embrace people who are different than we are. They might look different, act different or even think different than us, but they are still God's precious creation, created in His image, fearfully and wonderfully made.

For me, I needed to see how people just like me are rejected from society to open my eyes to the ways I reject people as well. Since then, I have had to learn how to love and accept all others as beautiful creations of God despite how different they might be. I had the blessing of acceptance growing up, despite my missing limb. I now understand that extending the grace of that acceptance to others is simply part of what it means to be faithful to God.

Julie Goss Clawson
Austin, TX

January 17

He who trusts in himself is a fool, but he who walks in wisdom is kept safe.—**Proverbs 28:26**

Bible study had finally resumed for the spring semester at church, and we were well into Beth Moore's *Here and Now . . . There and Then, A Lecture Series on Revelation*. Thought-provoking, riveting and life-altering are words that come to my mind when I think of her ability to teach God's Word. But this isn't about her study—it's about what happened during it.

One of the weekly homework assignments was to journal about our personal "revelations" from God. How was God speaking to us? What was He showing us to change in our life? Was there any baggage we needed to leave at the foot of the cross?

During Lesson Three, I experienced an incredible *wow* week. God was going all out, placing the issue of trust, or more specifically the lack of trust, right in my face. These next few days, I am going to tell you about my encounters with God during this time.

I woke up in the wee hours one morning of this third week of Bible study, kind of half-asleep and half-awake. On such occasions, I try to pray or sing (silently) praise and worship songs. I just love music and receive great inspiration and pleasure from it. Third Day is one of my favorite Christian recording artists, and all of their songs touch my heart and speak to me. This time, it was their "Trust in Jesus." *I trust in Jesus, Blessed Redeemer. . .*

At some point I heard the soft, silent whisper of the Holy Spirit ask me, *Brenda, do you really trust Me?* It was like, *Whoa!* I sat up in bed, wide-awake now. My response to that question wasn't what God wanted to hear, but He already knew the answer.

Sure, I trust that God is God and He is who He says He is. I believe He is in control and that nothing that happens is a surprise to Him. I feel reassured that in all things God works for the good of those who love him, who have been called according to His purpose (Romans 8:28). I keep John 3:16 in my heart, holding tight to the promise of eternal life. So, what do I not trust about God? Why did the Holy Spirit ask that question?

For starters, God knows I have a tendency to place idols, like money and my children, and most recently rain, before Him. Plus, He is fully aware of all those details in my life that I attempt to control. Yes, I trust God, but there are times I trust myself more.

The very same morning I heard from the Holy Spirit with that thought-provoking question. *Jesus Calling* also spoke to me, giving instructions on how to trust God more. The daily devotion started off with words that were very clear and to the point: *"Strive to trust me in more and more areas of your life."* I was wowed with those explicit words. Everything written in that day's reading was exactly what I needed to work towards trusting God with all situations in my life.

I talk with other women and I know I am not alone. It seems we all wrestle with some trust issues here and there. I don't know about you, but I personally find great comfort in knowing that even the Apostle Paul had his own struggles with not always doing God's will. In his letter to the church at Rome, Paul describes his frustration: "For I have the desire to do what is good, but I cannot carry it out. For what I do is not the good I want to do; no, the evil I do not want to do—this I keep on doing" (Romans 7:18-19).

One of the countless attributes of Jesus I just love is that because He was fully human, He understands our struggles. *Jesus Calling* came to aid me with such caring words that morning. (I am thankful to author Sarah Young for such an incredible book.) Once again, God blessed me through the written word of someone else with His helpful hints on how to do life—life His way. The only way.

Dear Jesus, thank You for speaking to my need to trust You with it all. Oh, for grace to trust You more!

Little did I know that God had just begun working on this trust issue. Tomorrow, I will tell you what He did next.

January 18

He is like a tree planted by streams of water, which yields its fruit in season and whose leaf does not wither.—**Psalm 1:3**

Yesterday, I wrote about the first encounter I had with God during a week of wonderful revelations concerning my need to trust Him more. This second one came the very next day as I sat in church listening to a sermon titled "The Idol of Success."

Pastor Brad's sermons always leave me hungry to know more and to be more like Jesus. On this morning, he even said that "real" success is becoming more like Jesus in all that we do, which entails doing what is pleasing to the Lord, not what is pleasing to man. Of course, we must study the Word (to know what His commands are), and make time with Him a priority all week long, not just on Sunday morning.

Brad sited Scripture from Haggai 1:1-11. The Babylonians had destroyed the temple in Jerusalem, and the people had yet to rebuild it. Instead, they concentrated on their personal economic well-being and put their Father's work aside. God took away their gain because He wasn't being glorified or made the priority. "My house lies in ruins, while each of you busies himself with his own house. Therefore the heavens above you have withheld the dew, and the earth has withheld its produce. And I have called for a drought on the land . . ." (Vs. 9-11 ESV).

You may be wondering what in the world those verses have to do with trust. Please allow me to continue, showing you more Scripture that Brad referred to from Jeremiah 17: 5-8 (ESV):

"This is what the LORD says: 'Cursed is the one who trusts in man, who depends on flesh for his strength and whose heart turns away from the LORD. He will be like a bush in the wastelands; he will not see prosperity when it comes. He will dwell in the parched places of the desert, in a salt land where no one lives. But blessed is the man who trusts in the LORD, whose confidence is in him. He will be like a tree planted by the water that sends out its roots by the stream. It does not fear when heat comes; its leaves are always green. It has no worries in a year of drought and never fails to bear fruit.' "

The words from Jeremiah did compare the blessed man who "trusts" in the Lord against the one cursed because of depending on his own flesh. However, what actually grabbed my attention on that Sunday morning were the two references in both Haggai and Jeremiah to a drought.

You will read many stories in this book about the dry, parched land here in central Texas. I live on Lake Travis and during this time period, the water level was at its third-lowest in history. I had been praying for rain for so long, but I had never seen these verses.

Being overly consumed with the extreme dry conditions, I looked at weather.com every day to see if there was precipitation in the 10-day forecast. I relied on a weatherman more than I did the weather Maker. I even checked the lake level constantly to see how much farther it had gone down. Rain had become my idol!

As I sat in church, I felt the warmest hug from God. He knows me so well and how to get my attention. I can just hear Him. *Brenda is all-consumed with this no-rain thing. I'll just talk about a drought and she will listen for sure. But when it's over, she'll figure out the real lesson found in My Word.*

My Father so gently reminded me that morning, as I sat in His house of worship, of where my priorities must be. When I put all my trust in Him, when I place Him first in my life, my drought will end. I will be that tree planted by the stream of living water, strong and able to withstand the trials—death, unemployment, illness, wayward children, broken cars or computers, unanswered prayers, even no rain.

It does not fear. It has no worries in a year of drought and never fails to bear fruit. Doesn't that sound heavenly? I want to be the one who trusts so I can be like that tree!

January 19

Delight yourself in the LORD and he will give you the desires of your heart. Commit your way to the LORD, trust in him.—**Psalm 37: 4-5**

My homework assignment from Bible study (on the book of Revelation) was to journal ways that God was revealing Himself each week. I had no idea that in one week alone I would have so much to write about. After two encounters addressing the area of trust, He was still busy at work in me.

I have mentioned how, from time to time, I grew discouraged with the process of this book. I desired for other women to share their stories to be included in this publication, but it just wasn't working that way.

There were days when I questioned God about the project. I felt the Holy Spirit guiding me as I took this leap of faith in the first place—I had prayed and felt the doors open. I was excited about the adventure and loved every step of the journey. But why wasn't God helping me reach my goal of 366 stories?

Just when I needed a boost of encouragement the most, God provided His reassurance that He hadn't abandoned me or this book. Only hours before I received the devotion via email, my friend Judy told me she had finally finished it and to look for it in my inbox. When I opened the attachment, I was in awe of her first sentence.

Judy wrote, "Father, forgive me for my pride, my impatience and my self-sufficiency in attempting to live my life apart from total trust and dependence on You."

There it was again. The *trust* word. Judy's story was exactly what I needed to read that day, as I struggled with my own inability to live in total trust of my Father. He not only provided the written word of a fellow sister in Christ as a way of demonstrating His love and concern for me, He also proved His faithfulness to the project He led me to. In His perfect timing, He will provide the exact stories He wants for this book.

When I receive a God story from another dear sister, I am elated! When I open up that attachment in the email, I am opening a gift from God. He has sent a present not only to help me in the completion of this book, but He has also provided His sweet words of wisdom and truth to anyone who reads it. Yet, too often I lost sight that He is the publisher, writer and source of everything concerning this devotional.

This isn't my book. I do not determine who the writers will be or what the stories will reveal. God Almighty Himself is the final authority. On this day, He reiterated all that to me. On this day, He reinforced that I can truly trust Him and I cannot rely on myself or others.

Oh, just as a small bonus, He sent me another tidbit of encouragement. The day I gathered my thoughts and notes from my journal and actually wrote this story one of my sons who had been struggling with his faith walk, shared a link on my Facebook wall. *If God brings you to it, He will bring you through it.* Besides being thankful that my son liked these words and shared them with me, I could identify so well. God did indeed lead me to this book and He will be with me to the end.

January 20

I keep asking that the God of our Lord Jesus Christ, the glorious Father, may give you the Spirit of wisdom and revelation, so that you may know him better.—**Ephesians 1:17**

Studying Beth Moore's *Here and Now . . . There and Then, A Lecture Series on Revelation* completely rocked my world. Of course, everything the highly acclaimed author and speaker ever presented has been incredibly inspirational, but this one was exceptional.

Being involved in Bible studies has truly changed my life, and I am so thankful that God led me to enrolling in my first one back in 1997. I was such a baby Christian back in those days—I just didn't know it. I was simply playing the role and had never developed a relationship with Jesus. Just as all infants grow and develop at different stages, I was a late bloomer in my spiritual growth—a late bloomer according to my timetable.

After those years of stumbling in the darkness, I now know that all of life's events happen in God's perfect timing. Take for instance today's verse from Ephesians 1:17. I heard it during the second week of the study, but failed to write it down. I remembered that it was a verse that coincided perfectly with the study, since the weekly assignment was to record how God revealed Himself to us, but couldn't remember the Scripture reference.

As we finished the last lesson, God presented the Scripture to me again in one of my online daily devotions. Even though He had introduced it to me earlier, God knew it would have more of a profound impact on me at the conclusion of the study. And He was so right.

My journal was full of ways that God revealed Himself to me during the course of the Bible study. I *had* come to know Him better while in the Book of Revelation. I *had* grown in wisdom, gaining even more love and reverence for my God Almighty and the perfection of His Word.

Before delving into Revelation, I had preconceived thoughts that it would be scary. Afterwards, there was still a fear, but it felt different. I thought of the words from Proverbs 9:10: "The fear of the LORD is the beginning of wisdom, and knowledge of the Holy One is understanding." When the study was over, along with wisdom, I had indeed developed a more intense fear—a complete reverential awe of God's majesty.

I had to be honest with myself. After *Here and Now . . . There and Then*, I still didn't comprehend Revelation in its entirety, but I did understand that in the end, the full wrath of God will be known. Satan, and all of his followers will be defeated and sentenced to eternal hell, and the faithful followers of Jesus Christ will be rewarded with eternal life.

Revelation is full of harsh reality and incredible hope. God will fulfill His promises—both to unleash His anger toward sin, and to create a new heaven and a new earth. However, I needed to complete the study before the magnitude of that reality could be felt. For me to grow in wisdom, God knew I had to develop that reverential awe of Him first.

God knows exactly how to reach every one of us, and studying Revelation was His perfect teaching tool for me. Sharing the appropriate Scriptures with me, at just the right time, was part of His lesson plan too.

He gave me the insight to figure out that the wisdom to know Him better came from His hands alone. God's incredible gift (of wisdom) is received in His perfect timing, in His allotted increments. Just as I recorded my children's growth on a cute little chart, my Heavenly Father has mine at His fingertips. It is already completed, being made known to me as He sees fit, as I get to know the glorious Father better and better.

January 21

Naked I came from my mother's womb, and naked I shall return there. The LORD gave AND the LORD has taken away. Blessed be the name of the LORD.—*Job 1:21*

It has become somewhat of a treasure hunt, looking through the Bible and finding verses that are also lyrics of contemporary Christian songs. "Blessed Be Your Name" by Matt Redman is one of my favorites, and who better than

Job to write about the Lord giving and taking away? Then, after all that Job endured, he could still say, "Blessed be the name of the LORD."

We will all go through difficult situations. We will be called to endure trials that seem unbearable at the time. This is one of those verses I want to be able to have on the tip of my tongue during such circumstances. How comforting to be able to speak Job's words when all else is crumbling around me, and remember that he could still praise his Lord, despite losing everything he had.

I already know all of the lyrics to the song and you might also. Today, 1/21, let's ponder the treasure found in Job 1:21 and be blessed be the Word of the Lord.

January 22

Be still and know that I am God. —**Psalm 46:10**

I decided to load up the kids and take a quick trip to Waco to see some visiting family. I *always* underestimate the effort to pack myself and kids for these "quick" trips! As usual, I was running late and trying to pack the car with my then 3-year-old twins scurrying around at my feet.

"Don't forget to pack my bear-bear!" yelled one. "Where's my sparkly necklace and headband and bracelet?" yelled the other. "Mom, don't forget my light-up shoes and my elephant shirt and my alligator!" "If he takes his alligator, I get to take . . . " And the list goes on.

Meanwhile, I'm trying to block them out and remember more important things: kids' medicine, kids' bag, camera, snack bag, DVD player. My thoughts were broken by a piercing scream "MOOMMM, I *need* this!" I wanted to scream back, "Please just trust me! I am your mom, and I love you. I am perfectly capable of remembering everything you need. We may not take everything you want, but I will have everything you need." I knew that trying to articulate that sentiment to a whiny 3-year-old was futile, so I kept my thoughts to myself.

We finally made it to the car, started the DVD, and there was peace. It was then that the Holy Spirit brought to mind a verse from Psalms: *Be still and know that I am God.* I almost laughed out loud. How many times am I like a little toddler barraging God with requests? "God, can You please do this? Oh, and don't forget about that! And I really, really want this!"

I pictured God just smiling down at me like the loving Father He is and saying, "Please just trust in Me. I am God, and I love you. I am perfectly capable of taking care of everything you need. I may not give you everything you want, but I will give you everything you need."

As we were pulling out of the neighborhood, my son meekly asked, "Mom, where is my alligator?" It was then I started thinking of the things I forgot. This is where my analogy breaks down. Unlike me, God is all-knowing and never messes up. His plan for each one of us is perfect. He is completely sovereign and completely loving, and His plan for our lives will always fall within these parameters. This truth should not only give us peace regarding our trivial requests, but more serious requests as well.

Additionally, God is always eager for His children to come to Him with their requests. He loves when we pray—maybe even when we sound like whiny toddlers. But as He reminded me on this particular morning, He also loves it when we just come into His presence to sit quietly, to be still, to be at peace, to trust in Him, because we know that He is God.

Julie Zavodny
Austin, TX

January 23

"I am the true vine, and my Father is the gardener. He cuts off every branch in me that bears no fruit, while every branch that does bear fruit he prunes so that it will be even more fruitful. " —**John 15:1**

Have you ever asked yourself if you have bitten off more than you can chew? Have you ever reached the point where you must admit your plate is too full? Have you felt the "no" welling up inside, only to hear the "yes" come out of your mouth? If not, I would love to meet you and find out how you have kept yourself from falling into the trap of over-commitment.

Most of us know when we have gone too far in saying "yes," but it's all for good stuff, right? We know we will be stressed out, wondering how we will get it all done, but we jump on the new opportunity because it sounds fun and interesting, and certainly something God would want us to do.

All too often, even saying, "I will pray about it," never comes out of my mouth. "Yes" just blurts right out. Ninety percent of the time, when I agree to something without praying and giving it to God for clarity and direction, I realize, after the fact, I shouldn't have. Not because it was a negative thing to get involved with, but because I just didn't have time to do the other things God has called me to do. Unfortunately, one of the first areas that suffers is my prayer time. And what about my family? My children are grown and gone from home, but I have a husband to whom I am committed.

As this New Year is starting, I am beginning to feel the urgency related to this book. I have a deadline and so much left to do. Because of other obligations, I have discovered that the hours I need to devote to this book daily just aren't there. Must one or two of my other commitments go? Which one? Am I a quitter for giving in and admitting I can't do it all?

This book—not only writing my own devotions, but being involved with the women God has enlisted to contribute—has resulted in the most wonderful journey of my life! I spend my days in His most holy presence, writing, reading, researching, praying and pondering. I can't tell you how full and fulfilled my days are. I had no clue this was what God had in store for me when the idea for this book was placed in my heart years ago. However, I need to make room to complete what He has asked of me. It is time for God to do some trimming somewhere.

Just like when we cut back leggy shrubs and bushes so they will grow back healthier, thicker and fuller, this pruning will allow for a richer, more spiritual relationship with Christ. Every branch that God prunes that already bears fruit will be allowed to be even more fruitful. I should be excited about what God has in store for my life and not feel failure for what is discarded in the process.

Father God, You know what needs to be cut back. I pray to be able to discern what You want to prune. I ask for Your peace in knowing that if You ask me to take something off my schedule, it will be for Your glory and Your purpose. May I gain the wisdom to always look to You to help plan my calendar. I pray that You will take away this sense of urgency and allow me to cherish every day of this book journey that remains. Amen!

Sweet friend, I pray that you will also make room for what God has in store for you this year.

January 24

All scripture is God-breathed and is useful for teaching, rebuking, correcting and training in righteousness so that the man of God may be thoroughly equipped for every good work. —**2 Timothy 3:16-17**

OH, HOW YOU LOVE ME!

You are the Light of my life . . . Without You my days would be hopeless and full of strife.

You are the Strength of my life. . . Without You I would be weak and not a good wife.

You are my Way and my Truth . . . And now I have Faith and Hope and no longer need proof.

You are Patient and You are Kind . . . And before I knew You, my eyes were closed and I was blind.

From the moment I began to Delight in You . . . You have given me the Desires of my Heart and I know this is the beginning, only the start.

You make everything Beautiful in its Time and You have stilled and quieted my soul . . . Without You I was never completely whole.

You make me Lie down in green pastures and Lead me beside quiet waters . . . And I know You will do the same for all of my daughters.

With You, I know that I am Fearfully and Wonderfully made and I am Strong and Courageous, never terrified . . . You always keep Your promises, not like others . . . You've never lied.

With You all things are Possible and I taste and see that You are good . . . With You in my life there are no cant's, only I could.

You love me so much that You would send Your Son to die for me . . . And I love You, not only for who You are, but for who and what I have become . . . Because You love me!

Blessings for a wonderful and extraordinary day!

Michelle Reekwald
Katy, TX

January 25

I waited patiently for the LORD; he turned to me and heard my cry. He lifted me out of the slimy pit, out of the mud and mire; he set my feet on a rock and gave me a firm place to stand. He put a new song in my mouth, a hymn of praise to our God.—**Psalm 40:1-3**

We were studying the book of Exodus at church. Pastor Brad started the series talking about storytelling. He said that we are all storytellers and God is the Author of our story. We need to wait and let God write His story, but too many times we decide that our version is better—we take off and write a few chapters on our own.

In our LifeGroup, each couple was giving their testimony. For several weeks, anticipating telling mine, I made notes of the major events. My life might sound like a soap opera, or if I were writing a book, it could be classified as a trashy novel.

How could I reveal all the dirt? Can't I cut out the bad stuff? Suddenly, I just smiled as joy filled my heart when the Holy Spirit reminded me that God loves me for who I am today. I must be thankful for my previous days if I am going to be thankful for today and tomorrow. To deny any of it is to deny that God is all-knowing and all-powerful and the Lord of my life, the Author of my story.

My life hasn't been a trashy novel at all. It is a true adventure. There have been bad guys and good guys; there have been villains and thieves trying to rob me of joy. There has been tragedy and triumph, happiness and despair, poor decisions and remorse, mercy and forgiveness.

My life has also resembled a fairy tale because there was a knight in shining armor. For so many years, I longed for a handsome hunk of a man to come sweep me off my feet. Like in a fairy tale, I planned we would ride off into the sunset on his white horse and live happily ever after.

I didn't know it, but God wanted the same thing for me. While I kept on waiting for that someone, Jesus was waiting on me to realize He was all I would ever need—my Knight in shining armor. My heart no longer yearned for that handsome hunk. Yes, my Almighty Father provided the peace, love and joy that no human ever could. The ride will be bumpy, but one I will never regret. Jesus did indeed sweep me off my feet, and it wasn't a fairy tale. It was for real!

I am no longer trying to write the remaining chapters of my life story. It's not a novel at all; it's neither fiction nor a boring autobiography. It is my true adventure, written by the Author and Creator of all things, written by the One and Only.

I pray that as the story of my life continues to fill the pages, that I will allow my Father to be the author; that I won't try to add my own chapters or my own twist to the plot. For His is the perfect story, filled with trials and joy—plus I already know the ending.

January 26

The Lord your God, who is going before you, will fight for you, as he did for you in Egypt, before your very eyes.
—Deuteronomy 1:30

It's not often that I can be heard laughing out loud while reading my daily devotionals. It should be a quiet time with God, right? But this was just too funny, and I couldn't hold back.

The first book I picked up on this particular morning was my new *Daily Guideposts*. The author of the devotion, Linda Neukrug, referred to herself as a person who had a problem with clutter. That got my attention immediately because I could identify so well. She mentioned a website, flylady.net, that had changed her life because it provided helpful hints on how to de-clutter.

Then I sat down at my computer, ready to read my online devos. Glynnis Whitwer, of Proverbs 31 Ministries, had titled her story "Living Clutter-free." I couldn't help but chuckle a bit. Really, God? Two in one morning?

Referring to a friend, Glynnis wrote that her circumstances had become overwhelming and the amount of "visual mess" in her life was a source of confusion. As I read her devotion, the chuckles turned into full-blown laughter! Someone else was like me!

Oh, the "visual mess" around my desk causes me such confusion! That very morning, I had written a check, walked over to a cabinet for an envelope and when I returned, couldn't find the check. I even asked my husband to help look around my desk. I walked into the other room and came back in, hoping it would magically reappear. It didn't.

I pushed my laptop forward a bit as I decided just to go ahead and write another check. Did I ever feel silly—there it was, hidden under my computer! How did it get there? Check found, but not without a bit of confusion. All because of the clutter and "visual mess." And now God was gently telling me, through the words of two different authors, that He was going to give me some specific hints on how to de-clutter.

Here we are, at the beginning of a new year, and it seems that so many women are in the cleaning-out mode. On Facebook, one friend even posted a picture of her recently cleaned-out closet. Oh my! I wouldn't even know where to start. Some of us just need some guidance and direction.

While I got a good laugh as I read these stories, please understand that I know that the piles and the mess can be a serious matter. If anything robs me of the joy God intends for my life, it should be addressed. I am so thankful for the information I obtained from the two women God placed in my path on that morning.

Glynnis wrote that she would be featuring a 15-Day Clutter-FREE Challenge on her blog. Then, I went to flylady. net to see what she had to say. I still had my piles to contend with that morning, but I also had hope in my heart, feeling a wave of relief knowing that other women struggled with this same issue. I wasn't alone.

God understood. There are numerous daily devotionals I can choose from every morning, and He led me to two on clutter! I couldn't help but laugh at the perfect timing of the God-incidence. He just has a knack of showing up at the right time to lend His righteous hand to help me through the day

Hopefully you don't deal with clutter, but whatever is going on in your life, you aren't alone. You can be certain that God has already gone before you. He knows what you are going through today and what lies ahead. He will be there with you every step of the way.

January 27

Live in harmony with one another. Do not be proud, but be willing to associate with people of low position. Do not be conceited.—**Romans 12:16**

As a member of a conference media team, I've had the opportunity to work behind the scenes at some very large statewide conferences with nationally known speakers and state leaders. At one particular conference, I encountered some very demanding and pompous personalities.

With no intentions of passing judgment, I became puzzled regarding how some of the presenters could be so arrogant and egotistical. During this week-long event, staff—including me—displayed a lack of manners and consideration for others. I continued to ponder about self-centeredness, attitudes of superiority, unkind treatments and discourteous acts.

On the last day of the conference, I was gathering my things in my hotel room for checkout when I happened to turn on the TV to see the middle portion of a Joyce Meyer Ministries broadcast, "Enjoying Everyday Life." She was quoting the following passage from Romans 12:16 (AMP): "Live in harmony with one another; do not be haughty (snobbish, high-minded, exclusive), but readily adjust yourself to (people, things) and give yourselves to humble tasks. Never overestimate yourself or be wise in your own conceits."

My immediate reaction was that it was the answer to my recent thoughts and, better yet, it was written in the Bible. It seemed so appropriate to hear the words about living in harmony and encouraging one's self to associate with all types of people. As I continued my packing, I suddenly remembered an earlier thought I had during the week to check and see if they still placed a Gideon's Bible in the nightstand.

Sure enough, there was one there, and when I opened it, the top page corners of Romans 12 through Romans 16 were folded over. No other pages in the Bible were dog-eared and this particular Bible was in my room out of 1,500 hotel rooms! Truly overwhelmed with amazement, I cried with tears of joy as I read Romans 12:16.

After reading Romans chapters 12 through 16, it was so comforting and uplifting to realize that hearing, seeing, knowing, living and trusting the Word of God is His grace to us, and by humbling one's self, your identity can be gained through Christ, freed from haughtiness and transformed by the renewing of your mind.

Martha Bauer
Austin, TX

January 28

For God does speak—now one way, now another—though man may not perceive it. In a dream, in a vision of the night, when deep sleep falls on men as they slumber in their beds. — **Job 33:14-15**

Several years ago, I began receiving mysterious phone calls in the middle of the night. Sound asleep, one ring of my cell phone would jolt me out of bed. It was never my land line, always my cell phone ringtone. However, there was never a missed call—I simply heard one ring. Any telephone ring that comes at 2 a.m. is startling, so after that kind of wake-up call, it's hard to get relaxed and go back to sleep.

This went on for a few months. The calls came about every other week, and it was always a struggle to get back to sleep. One night, I heard a little voice tell me, *Maybe it's God calling.* I thought about that for a while. Maybe it is God calling, but what does He want and why doesn't He just talk to me? I would look at my phone and no one had called. Hmm, wouldn't that be an incredible telephone conversation if He would be on the line? Then that little voice told me *Maybe He is sending you a wake-up call because He wants to talk to you. Get up and pray to Him.*

I went to church every Sunday, attended weekly Bible study, my husband and I were part of a vibrant small group and I read my daily devotions. I would say that I had a personal relationship with Jesus. Did I pray? My husband and I prayed together at bedtime and I said little popcorn prayers during the day. But did I devote quality one-on-one time with Him in prayer daily? No, not quality time daily.

Mysterious phone calls solved! Didn't I always tell a person the best way to reach me is on my cell phone? God wanted to talk to me and He knew the best way to get in touch. He knows me so well.

Just to show what a sense of humor God has, there is more to the story. My cell phone had a different ringtone for text messages and, lo and behold, He started waking me up with the sound of a text. Know what else is cool? During this time, I was involved in two very interesting Bible studies, Priscilla Shirer's *He Speaks to Me* and *Discerning the Voice of God.* Wow, does my Heavenly Father ever speak to me! He calls and sends me text messages.

Did I start praying more intimately and more often? You bet I did! Setting aside a prayer time became a daily priority in my life. I haven't received a middle-of-the-night wake-up call in months, but I know what that means—He is waiting for just the right time and place to get my attention again, to spur me back into action in an area where I am weak. Like the Scripture above says, one way or another He will speak to me. I just need to be expectant and ready to listen.

I know my Father loves to hear my voice and never tires of me. Being in God's presence and spending one-on-one time with Him has made a huge difference in our relationship. God wants to hear from all of His children. Has He contacted you lately about your prayer life?

January 29

That at the name of Jesus every knee should bow, in heaven and on earth and under the earth, and every tongue confess that Jesus Christ is Lord, to the glory of God the Father. — **Philippians 2:10-11**

Did you read my devotion yesterday? I am not trying to make you feel guilty if you didn't, but you might want to read it quickly so this one will make more sense.

God had sent me a message, via mysterious wake-up calls, that I needed to improve my prayer life, and I made an effort to make daily prayer time a priority. I also wrote that I had not received a wake-up call in months. However, I acknowledged that if God needed to get my attention because I wasn't being obedient in my prayer time, one way or another, He would speak to me. Let me tell you what happened.

Several months after writing yesterday's story, I was listening to the last sermon in a 13-week series on the Book of James, with James 5:13-19 focused on prayer. The sermon was cleverly titled "Adieu From Ol' Camel Knees."

Pastor Brad came right out and asked, "How's your prayer life?" I smugly thought to myself that since God hadn't sent me any more wake-up calls, mine must be good. Then he threw out some other one-liners, such as, maybe we needed to do a "knee check," and "if our knees are too smooth, we aren't on them enough in prayer." (I guess that's where he came up with the title of the sermon, Ol' Camel Knees.) *Ouch!* Smooth skin is something I work at by applying body lotion daily. Prayer is a priority, but I don't get down on my knees very often.

As Brad continued, my mind wandered. God took the time to call me, waking me up from a deep sleep, just to get me to pray more. Now, He's communicating with me from the pulpit. This certainly isn't the first time He has spoken through a sermon—that occurs almost every Sunday. I recently wrote the story about the mysterious phone calls, now He's contacting me through Brad about my prayer time? Is my God on top of it or what? He knows exactly how and when to reach me. Just another example of how big and all-knowing He is.

My thoughts came back to the sermon, just in time to get more pearls of wisdom from Brad. He said, "Prayer is a direct reflection of your dependence on God. If your prayer life is lacking, then your dependence on God is too." God was speaking to me loud and clear.

I am more concerned with having smooth knees than getting down in total surrender and roughing them up. I just thought my quiet time was improving, but now He's telling me to go even deeper. Do I depend more on myself than God? Do I still not trust Him with everything? *Get to your knees, Brenda, in total surrender!*

In Daniel 6:10 we find him going to his knees three times a day in prayer, and Paul wrote in Ephesians 3:14 that he kneels before the Father. Why do I find it so difficult to bow to God in prayer? Why can't I be more consistent?

He wants me to come to Him on my knees, often enough to rough them up, in total surrender, with every aspect of my life. The big stuff and the little things. The good and the bad. The confessions and the praises. The truth, even if I must suffer the consequences. My fears and my worries. *Everything, Brenda, everything!*

January 30

"Don't let your hearts be troubled. Trust in God; trust also in me." —**John 14:1**

A few days ago, I wrote about mysterious phone calls from God in the middle of the night. I thought with great certainty God was waking me up in the wee hours of the morning so I would pray. My prayer time most definitely improved. Yesterday's story was based on a sermon that addressed the need to go down on my knees, in total surrender, during my prayers. Then the calls in the middle of the night started again. What was God trying to teach me?

In a two-week period, I had three wake-up calls. When I got the first one, I laughed out loud. The calls were back! I looked at the clock and it was 3:18 a.m. I did what I knew God wanted me to do after His wake-up call—I started to pray. At 4:18 a.m. I was still awake, but I wasn't praying. Actually, I was laying in bed worrying.

With a few too many commitments on my plate, I was overanxious about how to get everything done. I knew to ask God for wisdom, better time-management skills and peace. However, instead of asking for God's help, I was making my own plans and allowing my mind to ask all the "what ifs?" The Bible is full of verses that tell us not to worry, be anxious or troubled, but I was just flat being disobedient.

My mind was all over the place. I even asked myself if there could be any significance to 3:18 a.m. Once I had woken up at 3:16 a.m. and just smiled. I softly spoke the words of John 3:16 and went back to sleep. Was there a 3:18 somewhere in the Bible that God wanted me to focus on? At 4:18 a.m., I got my Bible, and began with Genesis. I actually came across several verses that touched my heart, but focused on Hebrews 3:18-19: "And to whom did God swear that they would never enter his rest if not to those who disobeyed." So we see that they were not able to enter because of their unbelief. Ouch!

Hebrews 3:18 referenced back to God's words to Moses in Number 14:22-23: "Not one of the men who saw my glory and the miraculous signs I performed in Egypt . . . but who disobeyed me will ever see the land I promised . . . No one who has treated me with contempt will ever see it." God might have been talking about the Israelites, but He was talking to me at that particular moment.

I have seen His glory and I have seen His miracles in my life, yet I still have moments where my faith is weak and disobedience reigns. After all the times He has carried me through trials, I still question His promises? Despite all of the occasions He has shown me the futility of worry, I still waste time and energy on my circumstances instead of His glory? Do I not think He can get me through this momentary feeling of being overwhelmed and troubled? Am I treating God, the Father Almighty, with contempt by my disobedience? I'm really not much different than those Israelites.

He had some lessons to teach me during that minor turmoil. God's place of rest and His peace will never be mine if I don't learn to totally trust Him and be obedient, even at 3:18 in the morning.

January 31

"For I know the plans I have for you," declares the Lord, *"plans to prosper you and not to harm you, plans to give you hope and a future." —* **Jeremiah 29:11**

A few weeks ago, a friend referred to her son's wife as her daughter-in-love. At a retreat I attended, the speaker introduced her family, including her "daughter-in-love." Isn't that just the most precious word! Lauren married my son Zach, and because of their love, I now have a daughter.

At that same retreat, Jeremiah 29:11 was quoted countless times within the context of the various speakers' talks. Now, I don't know about you, but that is one Scripture that I can never hear enough! This is not the only day of the year you will find it in this book either.

It was Lauren's birthday, and I had been pondering what to get her. It's tough having a birthday so close to Christmas. But I had an idea and decided to go with it. I just prayed it would be well-received by both Lauren and Zach and they wouldn't think I was meddling in their life.

My son started a new job the previous fall and his work schedule changed dramatically. Therefore, Zach and Lauren no longer had as much time to spend together. Another aspect of the position meant that Zach could be called in at the last minute on weekends; so planning ahead became more difficult. Both were thankful for the new job opportunity and knew that the unpredictable schedule wouldn't last forever, but it had been difficult for them.

I decided to get Lauren some of the "necessities" for a much-needed get-away weekend to the beach that she and Zach might take. (Now, that was the meddling part; me planning their weekend away.) I purchased a gift card from a cute little store that just sold swimsuits, because you can't go away for fun in the sun without a new suit, along with a little beach bag. In that little bag, I also included a gift card for a new pair of sunglasses and a bottle of Hawaiian Tropic sunscreen. What I was most excited about, though, was the envelope that would house this devotion.

I was very much aware that I was going out on a limb. First, I was meddling in their lives; second, a very important ingredient to this little trip was something I couldn't provide—that very precious gift of time to schedule this romantic weekend. With that job, Zach had no control over his work schedule. He and Lauren couldn't make any reservations anywhere for the future. Time was the one thing they need the most and I just couldn't buy that for them and include it in Lauren's gift bag.

Zach's lack of control in his job schedule is not much different than all of our lives. God is the One who makes our schedule. We might think we are the ones doing all the planning and juggling but, as believers, we have relinquished our lives to our Heavenly Father. We will make the plans, but God has already determined our steps (Proverbs 16:9).

In John 16:33, we are told that in this world we will have troubles. Lauren and Zach were having some trials with his work schedule. Could have been worse circumstances and could have been better. That goes for all of us. Do we have a choice in His plans for us? Of course we do! We get to choose how we will respond to the circumstances. Jeremiah 29:11 provides the hope in knowing that our future is in His hands. Now, that's a promise to keep in our hearts every minute of every day!

My birthday gift to Lauren wasn't just the material things; it was the hope of God's promise. He had plans for her future that at that time remained unseen. She would get to wear her new swimsuit; she just didn't know where, or when. In the backyard or a gorgeous beach? It could be the next month or the following year. Zach's crazy schedule would change, one day. God had incredible plans for my sweet daughter-in-love, and my son, and that was the most priceless gift of all.

I pray that Zach gets a break soon so that a long weekend won't be impossible to plan, and that the words of Jeremiah will be the most meaningful gift to both Lauren and Zach today. I also pray that all of you with daughters-in-love cherish yours as much as I do my Lauren. She loves my son dearly and I am so thankful she is part of my life.

February 1

Fix these words of mine in your hearts and minds; tie them as symbols on your hands and bind them on your foreheads. Teach them to your children, talking about them when you sit at home and when you walk along the road, when you lie down and when you get up.—**Deuteronomy 11:18-19**

My youngest son received a letter from the bank regarding a deposit he had made. The check was returned because the account had been closed, and he was being notified of the service fee being charged. I looked at the copy of the check he had deposited. It was *four* years old!

I asked Trevor if he had considered the date on the check before making the deposit. Had he even thought that since the person who wrote it had graduated from college, married and moved to Fort Worth to work, perhaps all of the information on the check might be old and no longer valid? He simply assumed that since there was no expiration date that it would still be OK. He also said that he had no idea what "account closed" even meant and that I didn't teach him about such things.

Trevor was correct. I never sat him down and had a Checking Account 101 class with him (or my older son). I simply gave him an abbreviated version. We discussed how to use the ATM, make a deposit, write a check and go online to verify his balance, but it never occurred to me to tell him that a check isn't good forever, even if there isn't an expiration date on it.

We had a good chuckle over the incident, even though the bank charge was a bit excessive. (I was pleasantly surprised when, after Trevor called, the charge was refunded since it was his first offense.) However, I did stop to consider what else I had failed to teach my children. What had they picked up that I wasn't even aware of? What had I taught them, or not taught, about living a Christ-filled life?

When the boys were younger and lived at home, God was a member of our household; church and Sunday school were part of our lives, along with reading *The Upper Room* daily devotional. With God's help, I did my best to be a good example and teach them honesty, punctuality, consideration of others, and the importance of a daily hugs, and that the words *I love you* can never be said too often. We had great fun growing up. We might possibly have played a bit too much—and that's why neither boy likes to read—but we learned the importance of communication, quality time and relationships.

There is much I would have done differently if life offered "do-overs," though. God gave us the perfect handbook on parenting, but many times I chose to do it my way instead. I just pray Zach and Trevor will remember the things I did right and that God will erase my mistakes from their memory. Even though their faith is weak right now, I know God's love is strong and I will share my compassionate God with them every chance I have, trusting that one day they will come back around.

I am still their mom and I will continue to invest in the lives of my children at every occasion possible, even though they are grown and my opportunities are limited. A mom has many responsibilities, and teaching our children is one of those never-ending joys of motherhood. As long as I am still living (and thinking rationally), I will be an example to my boys.

Just as they observed my actions growing up, they are still watching me. How am I handling this aging process? How am I loving my husband and treating others? Do I devote quality time to my own mom and siblings? Most importantly, how is my faith walk? Am I walking the walk? Do I give God the glory in all circumstances, the good and the bad?

Every day, through His forgiveness and mercy, God gives me a clean slate—a do-over—and another chance to get it right. My Father, the only perfect parent, isn't through with me yet, and He who began a good work in me will carry it on to completion until the day of Christ Jesus (Philippians 1:6).

February 2

And how can they believe in the one of whom they have not heard? And how can they hear without someone preaching to them? And how can they preach unless they are sent? As it is written, "How beautiful are the feet of those who bring good news!" —**Romans 10:14-15**

Yesterday, I wrote about parenting and what I had, or had not, taught my children. As I wrote, God intervened. Here I was writing a story all about teaching my children the lessons of life, but what about my responsibility to others? I am more than a mother, and my role in this life on earth extends beyond being a parent. God was specifically asking me how I was doing in being an example to others and spreading His Word to those outside of my home?

While I might not see or talk to my grown sons daily, opportunities to spread the Good News and share God's love and kindness to others are available every day. Just as our children learn from us and pick up our good and bad habits, we are a mirror to others outside of our home as well. That can be a scary thought.

Who was watching me today when I was at the grocery store? As I passed by the women in the motorized shopping cart, shouldn't I have asked if she needed assistance reaching something on the top shelf? My non-action certainly wasn't very neighborly.

I spend a lot of time with my sisters in Christ, in the company of other believers. What do I talk about to the others I encounter during the day? I should be treating everyone the same, and I have every right and responsibility to speak God's Word with whomever I am with. Why didn't I speak a word of encouragement to the young girl behind the counter taking my order today at lunch? All I did was say hello. My Bible study friend and I said grace before we ate, but had she been an acquaintance from the gym, would I have taken her hand and just said a blessing without asking?

Let's go a step further into being a mirror to others. What about missionary service? I used to think that to qualify for mission work, the acts of service had to be done on foreign soil, or at least within the confines of a poverty-stricken area. I have since learned that wherever God calls us to spread His Word is a mission field and that He will equip us to do His work.

Mission work can be done in the privacy of our own home. My church is involved with a prison ministry and there is a group of ladies who do Bible study with inmates via the mail. There are all kinds of relief funds set up across the nation to provide financial assistance to victims of natural disasters. With a click, we can donate online. Adopting a child in Ethiopia can cost as little as $25 a month—again, a click will do it.

We don't have to leave the United States to find volunteer opportunities. There are hungry, homeless, hurting people in every city and town right here. Perhaps God is calling you to actually be His hands and feet on foreign soil. Traveling to a far away country isn't what God has planned for everyone, but if it's what He has in store for you, be ready to say yes!

In Jesus' final words of instruction to the church before He ascended into heaven, He gave us His Great Commission (Matthew 28:16-20) to convert the world. "Go therefore and make disciples of all the nations" (Vs. 19). Jesus is calling—commanding—each of us to finish what He started when He lived on this earth in the flesh. He may call us to do that exactly where we are, to those we encounter in our daily lives. God may ask us to give our financial support to His children in need. Or He may have plans to take some of us to the other side of the world to convert people whose language we don't even speak.

No matter where we are or whom we are with, we are His hands and feet and we have an assignment. It just might be the most important assignment of our life. Don't you want everyone to know the joy that you have found? We must be ready because today just might be the day.

February 3

"And lead us not into temptation, but deliver us from evil." —**Matthew 6:13**

The question of whether or not to have intimate relations prior to marriage is a tough one faced not only by our youth, but everyone. After being shoved back into the "dating scene" following a divorce at 32, I was given a "second chance" to do it right this time. After quite a few "first and last" dates in three and a half years, I was finally introduced to "the one" by some trusted friends.

Having found a new spiritual life after my divorce, I felt very strongly about making sure each step I took was the right one. We discussed pre-marital sex and both agreed that, out of obedience to God's Word, we would not engage in this. Easily said, yet much more difficult to follow through with.

Was temptation there? Of course! Throughout months of dating, we often found ourselves questioning why we were holding out. In heated moments, the words "no" or "we should stop" did not come easily. Thankfully, at each point, at least one of us was given the strength to see that, as Eve had been tempted by evil, so were we. The act of sex comes *after* temptation. We realized that the issue was not actually vowing not to have pre-marital sex—it was resisting the enormous power of temptation.

However, on a weekend trip to San Antonio, after we became engaged, the temptation became too strong. We, as feeble humans, gave in to desires that we had so many times before vowed to deny. In a scene that we created—a fun day at an amusement park, a stroll down the river walk, a nice dinner, a glass of wine, and one hotel room—we found ourselves in an intimate moment, giving into the temptation that we had vowed to resist.

"We are engaged. We are older. We've both been married and had sex before. Why wait? We don't have to tell anyone." In just a couple of minutes, all of our promises and vows were ready to be thrown out the window of the 10-story hotel. In the heat of a passionate moment, we both agreed to give in. Without being too graphic, my now-husband described the situation well in saying that he was one small step away from entering the Promised Land!

We were almost at the point of no return when the phone rang! Startled and confused, we didn't know what to do. No one knew we were at this particular hotel. Do we answer it? We did.

"Uhhhhh, hello?"

"Hello, sir. I am calling from the hotel's front desk. I just wanted to check and make sure that everything was all right with your room."

"Yeah, it's fine."

"Is there anything you need?"

"Uhhhhh, no thanks."

"All right then, have a nice evening."

We recognized immediately that God was speaking to us: *Remember me? Why are you giving in to such weak temptation? Temptation that you created yourselves. You came here together, got one hotel room, went out on a romantic date and returned finding many ways to unjustly justify the breaking of a vow you made to me. Where do I stand in your lives right now? How can I trust your faithfulness when you so easily turn from me when it suits you? Remember, you don't have to tell any man what you have done—but I know. Do you consider the thoughts and feelings of your fellow man to be more important than mine? I have forgiven your past sins and, of course, I would forgive you of this one. But do you not find it a lot to ask, to promise and vow to be faithful to me and then go against me with each other? However, as always, I will give you the choice; it is your decision. I can't sit on the throne of your life unless you choose for me to be there.*

My now-husband and I can truthfully say that we held to our vow of not engaging in pre-marital sex. But the message to others should not be simply to stay away from pre-marital sexual intercourse. The message should be to stay away from temptation, especially that which we create ourselves. You see, our heated moment was quickly cooled and easily ended the minute God called. It was the temptation and the human desires that were the snake in our path.

To this day, we say, when God calls, you must answer.

CP
Katy, TX

February 4

*"When you pass through the waters I will be with you; and when you pass through the rivers they will not sweep over you. When you walk through the fire, you will not be burned; the flames will not set you ablaze. For I am the L*ORD*, your God, the holy One of Israel, your Savior."* —**Isaiah 43:2-3**

Lord, help me remember that nothing will happen today that we can't handle together.

On the days when I feel overwhelmed, that simple statement reminds me that I am not alone in this journey called life. It doesn't matter if it is personal or business-related, it seems that a simple approach works.

On a particularly bad day, I was having a conversation with a friend and I told her I didn't know if I could make it through the day. That is when she suggested that I just try to make it through an hour. However, even 60 short minutes, at that particular time in my life, were more than I could handle. Then we broke it down into 15-minute increments, and that I could do—with God's help.

Later, as I was searching through the radio stations for different music, I heard a preacher say that people do not pray for the right thing. Being a person who prays, he definitely caught my attention. I wanted to know what he thought I was doing wrong.

He said people usually pray for the wrong thing by asking God to take the difficulty away from them instead of asking God to help them get through it. That made perfect sense—the power to get through a difficult situation.

Lord, help me remember that nothing will happen today that we can't handle together.

C. Richard
Sugarland, TX

February 5

But one thing I do: Forgetting what is behind and straining toward what is ahead, I press on toward the goal to win the prize for which God has called me heavenward in Christ Jesus. —**Philippians 3:13-14**

Having been a nurse for 32 years, I have attended numerous seminars to obtain continuing-education credits. These programs are usually held in the ballroom of a large hotel. Most recently, I traveled to the Westin La Cantera Hill Country Resort in San Antonio. Three other nurses and I were sharing a room, and after returning from dinner we decided to stop in the gift shop.

There were many beautiful items to choose from—lacey blouses, slinky dresses, silver jewelry, and of course, magazines and candy. Since I was in a chocolate mood, I selected a Snickers bar and approached the register to pay.

There on the counter was a glass bowl filled with small beaded crosses. As I started looking through them, the clerk commented that there were larger ones on the wall behind the register and that it was OK to walk back there to view them better.

After selecting one with blue and green beads, I noticed there were many beads wired to a framework of large nails. The tag attached stated the cross was made by someone in a group of mentally challenged adults. This made the purchase even more desirable for me. I needed another cross to hang with a group on a wall at home, I would be supporting the organization that helps handicapped adults and the frame was made of nails as a reminder of Jesus' suffering.

After returning home the next day, I prepared to hang the cross on the wall by my front door. When I detached the tag, I noticed something else hanging from one of the sides. There was a tiny silver charm attached to the beads. The four letters read HOPE. How did I miss this earlier?

My friends had each picked up and looked at the cross and none of them saw the HOPE charm either. How exciting! What a discovery! What a beautiful lesson from the Holy Spirit. Because our hope is in Christ, we can let go of our past guilt and shame, and look forward to what He will help us become.

Nancy Buzbee
Austin, TX

February 6

Wives, submit to your husbands, as is fitting in the Lord. —**Colossians 3:18**

Back in my school days, homework was a dreaded chore. There was nothing fun or exciting about it. However, doing my homework for Bible study is completely different. Knowing there is something new to be learned that will be helpful in my walk with Jesus makes it a joyful process.

After saying all that, I must confess that sometimes I don't dedicate the necessary time to get it all done. Often times I am up late on Monday night before the Tuesday-morning class. Let me clarify there is no condemnation whatsoever at my church for anyone who hasn't finished or even started the assignment. There is so much to be gained in those two hours of fellowship, with the small-group discussion and the video or classroom lecture. Homework is just an added benefit!

On this particular Monday, I didn't get home and settle down to even start the lesson until about 9 p.m. After awhile, I had the most freeing thought. *I don't have to stay up for hours to complete the homework.* It was perfectly all right for me to go to class the next morning with blank pages. It was only out of pride that I would stay up past midnight to complete it anyway.

What if the lady sitting on either side of me saw my empty workbook? Would she think I was some lazy slacker? What if she thought I wasn't dedicated or committed enough to do the work?

No! I would not believe those silly lies. There would be no condemnation. I would only miss the blessing that comes from Beth Moore's extensive research. Her homework is always more than worth the time and effort. But off to bed I went.

In the wee hours of the morning, something startled me, and I jumped right up. Being completely awake, I realized I could do my homework. Not that I had to do it. No, I wanted to!

Immediately, I knew it was the Holy Spirit who woke me and gave me the extra boost of energy. It was 3:18 a.m., and I could easily complete the assignment in plenty of time. How cool was that?

As I progressed to Day Two of Week Three in Beth Moore's *James: Mercy Triumphs*, I pondered the significance of 3:18 since God has a way of speaking to me through the numbers on a digital clock. When one of the homework questions actually asked about a time that an act of obedience could only have been because of the Holy Spirit, I knew what He was up to.

A quick detour from the homework was in order. I skimmed through the New Testament on my iPad Bible app to see if there was a Chapter 3, verse 18 that was particularly significant for the day. I hit the jackpot. Four verses jumped out.

The first two "coincidentally" pertained to other questions in my homework. Another, Hebrews 3:18, was familiar because I had actually written another devotion on that verse after waking at 3:18 a.m. However Colossians 3:18 was the winner. It was the one the Holy Spirit woke me up for: "Wives, submit to your husbands, as is fitting in the Lord."

I am embarrassed to admit that I struggle with being that wife. I pray nightly for God to help me love my husband well, but I fall short. Here it is, almost Valentine's Day. I want to be the wife of my husband's dreams and the wife God wants me to be. My husband always goes out of his way to please me, but why do I selfishly find it so difficult to do the same for him?

You have no idea how pumped I was by that 3:18 wakeup call. It was such a special message from God. He knows how much is gained from participating in the written work for Bible study, so He gave me that special quiet time in the morning to complete it. I couldn't wait to share my experience with the other girls in my group, especially in response to the question about the Holy Spirit prompting me to obedience.

That wakeup call was also one of the special ways God shows His love for me. He is going to help me be the wife of my husband's dreams. By pulling me to a specific Scripture, He reinforced that doing my homework daily and consistently being in His Word, is a submissive act of obedience that can only strengthen my walk with the Lord—and my marriage.

February 7

Keep on loving one another as brothers and sisters. Do not forget to show hospitality to strangers, for by so doing some people have shown hospitality to angels without knowing it.—**Hebrews 13:1-2**

They say that opposites attract. My husband, Austin, and I exemplify that statement. He is the extrovert; I am the introvert. He loves to joke around; I am way too serious. He loves to cook; I would rather clean up his mess. He rarely exercises; I try to do it daily. But there is one "opposite" that does cause some conflict in our marriage.

I am kind of a nerd when it comes to punctuality, trying hard to be early wherever I go, or at least with a few minutes' cushion. Austin, on the other hand, is usually running late or doesn't have a minute to spare. Sometimes I get agitated by his habit of trying to accomplish too much in the amount of time he has available, and I insist there's no way he can do it all. However, he usually proves me wrong and somehow manages to get home or to where he needs to be, just in the nick of time. The stress involved with that "nick-of-time" business is what irritates me.

One Saturday, he had a list of errands. We also had a wedding to attend that evening, and needed to leave the house no later than 5 p.m. Austin promised to be home before 4:30 so he could shower and change clothes. Being the punctual nerd that I am, I called at 4 to check on him. When I found out he was at least 45 minutes from home, I wasn't happy. Hadn't I warned him he was trying to do too much that day? Some errands on his list weren't even necessities, but arriving early to the wedding was, in my opinion. He ignored my warning, insisting he could get it done.

Wouldn't you know it? He got home, showered and we were out the door straight up 5 p.m. to go to the wedding, but I was still a bit upset that I had been worried. I was probably more upset that he had actually pulled it off, especially since I had been so negative. On the way to the wedding, Austin shared the events of his day, and I was so ashamed.

He had a very valid reason for being a few minutes late—he stopped to help a woman on the side of the road. It doesn't rain much in Austin, but this was an unusually cold, rainy Saturday. A woman had slammed on her brakes and skidded into the ditch. A policeman had called a wrecker to pull her out, but Austin got there first with his four-wheel-drive pickup. His act of kindness to this woman saved her quite a bit of time and money.

After all of that, my husband had to come home to his wife, who wasn't the most pleasant since he was running just a tad late. I was reminded over and over of a verse in Proverbs about the quarrelsome, nagging wife. "A quarrelsome wife is like a constant dripping on a rainy day" (Vs. 27:15). Oh, I was that wife!

I was proud to know that my husband had gone out of his way to lend a helping hand and pleased we made it to the wedding in plenty of time. Most importantly, God taught me a humbling lesson. The time my husband gave to a stranger with a car in the ditch was certainly more important than arriving home a few minutes early or even being a few minutes late to a wedding. God's timing is perfect and I need to put more trust in His clock than mine.

God put another verse from Proverbs on my heart that I have committed to memory, for those times when that urge to nag Austin about his time schedule sneaks up. "Pleasant words are a honeycomb, sweet to the soul and healing to the bone" (Vs. 16:24).

February 8

"This is to my Father's glory, that you bear much fruit, showing yourselves to be my disciples." —**John 15:8**

Sharon Young's devotional *Jesus Calling* has made a tremendous impact on millions of people. As of August 2012, over five million Jesus Calling-branded products had been sold worldwide, and the book was ranked No. 1 on the *Wall Street Journal's* Nonfiction Bestseller list.

A few years earlier, my small group leader in Bible study gave all her girls the book as a Christmas gift. The daily devotional, written as if Jesus is speaking directly to the reader, quickly became one of my favorites. After going through it once, I started all over again. I also began sharing the book with friends and experienced great pleasure in passing along the daily treasures.

Most of the women I gave a copy to were, what I considered, strong in their faith. I wasn't introducing anyone to a daily Christian reading for the first time; I was simply sharing a book that had impacted me. Daily devotionals have played an important role in my own lifelong faith walk, and I felt led to encourage others, as I had been encouraged, by gifting them with *Jesus Calling*.

A time finally came when the person I gave a copy to wasn't so strong in her faith—she believed in God but didn't have a personal relationship with Jesus. I had sporadically shared online devotions that I felt pertained to her circumstances and thought would be uplifting. But one day I felt the Holy Spirit nudging me to give her *Jesus Calling*. Oh, I hesitated at first, not being sure of her reaction. But God was sure.

This woman also had a very close friend with whom I had become acquainted. She was wrestling with some trials, and I had sent a few online devotions to her too. Emailing a devotion was a very "safe" way for me to spread God's love and encouragement. Knowing both of these women weren't churchgoers was an indication they needed to hear the Gospel, but I was clearly playing it safe. However, I knew the Holy Spirit had urged me to share the devotions, and then the book.

They were both excited and receptive to their gift. However, one morning one of them questioned a story in the book that referenced Abraham being instructed by God to sacrifice his son Isaac in Genesis 22. She didn't have a Bible and couldn't read the Scriptures for herself so I explained the story the best I could. In addition, I immediately felt the nudging to get her a Bible.

Not one, but two Bibles were in order because neither of these ladies had one. God had blessed me—the one who was reluctant to share the Gospel—with the incredible privilege of "giving" another His Word. When I went to the Christian bookstore, I was completely overcome with emotion. Purchasing Bibles for my children when they were young or for myself was one thing, but for grown women who never had a Bible? Now, that was indeed a gift from God—for me!

One of these precious women sent me a note, and her words touched my heart deeply. One sentence in particular though pierced my soul. She said, "I have been given possessions that are far greater than so many, but I have never owned my own Bible." Perhaps this friend had just begun her journey, but she was immediately aware of the priceless value of her new Bible in comparison to her material possessions. A revelation like that only comes from God.

He kept on pushing me, challenging me to step out of my comfort zone and share more with both of these women. In my own surroundings, with my favorite book in hand and my Father by my side, Jesus called and equipped me to be His beloved disciple. All praise and glory goes to God the Father.

February 9

"Call to me and I will tell you great and unsearchable things that you do not know." — **Jeremiah 33:3**

Jeremiah 33:3 was the daily verse for one of my devotions. The author wrote a story about waiting on God's perfect timing and God's perfect answer to her prayers. Deciding the verse was one to remember, I opened my Bible to underline it and found it was already marked.

Several months ago, I purchased a new Bible to replace my 15-year-old, very ragged-looking one. But try as I might, I just haven't been able to retire it. There's something special about seeing all of the verses I have underlined over the years and reading the little notes I have scribbled throughout.

I wondered when I had read Jeremiah 33:3 for the first time—what was going on in my life that made it so significant? Perhaps I should have dated the verses as I underlined them. Oh, that would have been a great idea, but it's too late now. I could start doing that with my new Bible, if I could just get in the habit of using it. All I knew for sure was that on this particular day, Jeremiah 33:3 had a profound effect on me and it was as if I were reading it for the first time.

Thankfully my faith walk has been long, but sometimes extremely slow, almost at a standstill. I have veered off the path, only to find God patiently waiting for me at the end of that dead-end road, with a sign pointing me back in the right direction. I would seek His face once more and try to be obedient, only to fail again. It took me awhile to learn that the failures weren't the biggest obstacles—seeking Him with all my heart, soul and mind were the major roadblocks.

God is not to be fooled. He knew my heart and He knew that I wasn't giving our relationship my all. That's why I didn't remember that verse—I hadn't called out to Him with my whole heart. God finally saw a committed heart, ready to get serious about "us." He doesn't expect perfection; honest effort is enough to get us on the right road together. It was time to reveal His lesson plans, written just for me.

In this short verse, the word "you" is used three times. Three times I was reminded that my relationship with the Father is a very personal one. He doesn't write a lesson plan and make it applicable to the masses. I am not in an overcrowded classroom with an overworked professor who has one syllabus for all students. No, I am alone with my Teacher. Because of His love and mercy, I am privileged to get a private, one-on-one lesson that is meant only for me, as often as I want. All I have to do is call to Him.

I know Jeremiah 29:11 by memory and it has long been one of my underlined verses. "For I know the plans I have for you . . . plans to give you hope and a future." But the words that follow in Jeremiah 29:13-14 are just as worthy. "For you will seek me and find me when you seek me with all your heart. I will be found by you." Our future is in His hands, but unless He has our heart, we will never find Him so He can teach us and reveal His plans.

I marked Jeremiah 33:3 with the current date, even though I had underlined it sometime in the past. At that moment His Words were clear. It's so simple—the more I give of myself, the more He makes known. After honestly surrendering my heart, He will reveal the "unsearchable things I do not know," a little bit at a time. Private lessons are usually costly, and Jesus paid the ultimate price for us on the cross, so that we could have this free gift. He rejoices in our continued growth and our desire to learn His truths. Yes, He delights in His students.

February 10

There is a time for everything, and a season for every activity under heaven. — **Ecclesiastes 3:1**

If you have been reading this devotional from the first of the year, you have learned that I have a thing for number associations. I am not referring to any type of mystical concepts here. Numbers just have a tendency to jog my memory, and I feel that God uses them to get my attention at certain times.

For example, coming up on March 17, the Bible verse cited is Zephaniah 3:17. Get it? 3/17 and 3:17? The story I wrote also helped me to remember the words to that scripture. That's what I mean by number associations.

One way numbers have been significant is when I happen to notice certain times on a digital clock. I imagine there are many, when noticing the time is 9:11, think of that day in September and the lives forever changed and perhaps say a prayer. I also have a tendency to glance at the clock when I wake up during the middle of the night. If I happen to remember the time in the morning, I will look through my Olive Tree Bible app for a corresponding chapter and verse that matches up to those numbers that is noteworthy.

Recently, I woke up and noticed that it was 3:33 a.m. That's an easy one to remember. The next day, I didn't take the time to look if there was a book that contained a Chapter 3, verse 33 that touched my heart. The next night, my dog barked and woke me up. Looking at the clock, I saw those very same numbers. It was 3:33 a.m.! Waking up at the exact time two nights in a row made me think it was a God-incidence worth investigating. I actually wanted to look right at that moment but knew it was too early to get my eyes focused.

I could hardly wait to get my cup of coffee and dig through the Bible for the verse that I just knew God wanted me to find. Unfortunately, I didn't come across a 3:33 that made a significant impact. However, I got the thought that maybe I should look up a Chapter 33, verse 3. That sure did sound familiar. I quickly tuned to Jeremiah 33:3: "Call to me and I will answer you and tell you great and unsearchable things that you do not know."

That verse had been underlined and had several notes scribbled beside it. I realized that I had already written a devotion based on that Scripture. Was God telling me to go read one of my own stories?

I looked for the story in my computer, under the title I had written in the margin of my Bible. I couldn't locate it. I then checked my saved emails and found where my editor had returned it to me, but I had failed to save it in the proper file. This story could have easily been forgotten and excluded from this book without this find and seek excursion that I was on. Not that it was all that noteworthy, but I certainly wouldn't want to miss out on all the hours spent writing it.

The story was then saved in the correct file in my computer and I printed a hard copy for my binder, so it was now officially part of this book. Then I read it. Hmm. I think those words were exactly what I needed for that day. (It was the story you read yesterday.)

God not only saved that devotion from being lost forever through a minor computer oversight on my part, but He also gave me some words of encouragement for the day, all by waking me up at 3:33 a.m.

February 11

You don't even know what tomorrow will bring—what your life will be! For you are like smoke that appears for a little while, then vanishes.—**James 4:14 (HCSB)**

My husband and I were returning home to Austin from New Mexico. After boarding the second leg of the journey, a short flight from Houston to Austin, I pulled out my Bible study homework. I was on Day Five of Week Five in Beth Moore's *James: Mercy Triumphs*, which covered James 4:13-17.

Beth Moore had written an amusing story about cigarettes at the beginning of Day Five. As the doors to the plane closed and the flight attendants began the safety demonstration, I chuckled through Beth's silly narrative. Suddenly, I had the strangest sensation—I actually smelled cigarette smoke! Smoking has been banned from aircraft for years. Where was it coming from? I asked my husband if he smelled it too. He looked at me as if I were crazy.

Then I read verse 14 in the context of her homework: "For you are like smoke that appears for a little while, then vanishes" (HCSB). Even though the word that James used for "smoke" actually meant a mist or vapor, Beth Moore was fixated on the vision of cigarette smoke referenced in her story. Now I actually smelled it too.

(Before continuing, my intentions are not to be critical of anyone who is a smoker. I tried like crazy to smoke when I was in high school because I thought it looked cool. However, one day I became violently ill, and to this day, the smell literally nauseates me. That in itself was a God thing. The known serious health issues make me so thankful that I didn't succeed in my attempts. However, I have plenty of other unhealthy habits. For instance, the sun is also known to cause cancer, but I can be found soaking up the rays during the heat of the summer, plus I am guilty of not using sunscreen like the health professionals advise.)

The smell lingered for a few minutes as I pondered the God-incidence that had just transpired. I was awestruck that my nostrils were filled with the same odor that had turned my stomach since I was 16 years old.

Without going into a lengthy scientific explanation of cigarettes, research indicates there are over 4,000 chemicals found in the smoke, with over 50 of them carcinogens. Reading this verse from James in the HCSB translation, could my life be compared to a bunch of poisonous chemicals? My life is that impure and that tainted?

We "all have sinned and fall short of the glory of God" (Romans 3:23), but to think of my sinful life emitting an odor that has sickened my own stomach for over 40 years was humbling. To fathom that others could smell something that revolting being emitted from my hardened heart was embarrassing. To know my Father endured the stench broke my heart.

The focus of Beth Moore's study that covered James 4:13-17 wasn't only about life vanishing like vapor or smoke, but for those few minutes on the plane I felt polluted and repulsive as I compared myself to cigarette smoke. Thankfully there are verses 24 and 25 in that third chapter of Romans that give a sinner like me great hope: "And all are justified freely by his grace through the redemption that came by Christ Jesus." God presented Christ as a sacrifice of atonement, through the shedding of His blood—to be received by faith. There is the cleansing power of the blood of Jesus to wash away my sins and purify the poison in my life.

As the smell of cigarette smoke finally disappeared (was it ever really there?), I had another more pleasant thought: "For we are to God the pleasing aroma of Christ among those who are being saved and those who are perishing. To the one we are the aroma that bring death; to the other, an aroma that brings life" (2 Corinthians 2:15-16).

Our lives on this side of heaven may be quick—like a puff of smoke or a vanishing vapor. While we do not know what God has planned even for this day, we can certainly seek His will and do the good we ought to do (James 4:17), radiating that sweet aroma of Christ.

As all of us venture out today, how will we smell to others? Will it be the smell of stale cigarette smoke—carcinogens that can bring about death? Or will we be the aroma that brings life into the world?

Oh, my nostrils are filled with your sweet fragrance right now! There is nothing more pleasing than the aroma of Christ.

February 12

And the God of all grace, who called you to his eternal glory in Christ, after you have suffered a little while, will himself restore you and make you strong, firm and steadfast.—**1 Peter 5:10**

My husband and I have been in a LifeGroup for almost five years at our church in Austin. The first several years, there were only four other couples. We met every Sunday to share a meal, talk around the dinner table and then get serious for about an hour of Bible study. We also gathered at other times, just to hang out. I can't even begin to tell you how much I love those people. It didn't just happen instantaneously, though. It took some time.

We were actually a very diverse group, but blended beautifully over months of being together and sharing our testimonies. We all felt God put us together for a reason and were thankful for our friendships. I think my strong feelings for them stemmed from unconditional love and trust. They knew everything about me—the good, the bad and the very ugly—yet they still accepted and loved me for who I was then, not who I used to be.

Age-wise, there was a span of 20 years, with my husband and I being the oldest. There were parents of elementary-aged kids, Empty Nesters, grandparents, retirees, blended families and second marriages. Yet, despite our differences, we shared our hearts, along with lots of laughs.

We played the Newlywed Game for two years in a row the Sunday before Valentine's Day back in those earlier years. The second time there was a question concerning the number of shoes each wife had, with the answer choices being very general and easy to get correct. However, when we got home my husband still had the question on his mind.

He was literally in the closet counting—even my flip-flops—and sending out an email to everyone. By the end of the night, all the husbands had counted and we knew exactly how many pairs of shoes each of us five girls had. It was such a fun time, filled with precious laughter.

Also, that same year on Valentine's Day, I sent an email to all the girls, expressing my love for them. By the next day, I had received a reply back from everyone. I was surprised to hear from Teresa because she and her husband were off on a romantic getaway to a beach in Mexico. She sent her love to all of us girls and let us know they were having a wonderful time.

Sheji, the youngest of the group, had a much different Valentine's because her husband was out of town on business. She had spent an eventful evening with her then 11-year-old son—unclogging the toilet—and replied, "Not the memory I was looking for, but one I won't soon forget—boys!"

Even though Teresa was having fun in the sun with her hubby, she managed a response back to encourage Sheji that was priceless. *Some days are toilet days, but thankfully some are beach days.*

Oh, how true! All of us women can relate to when poop hits the fan and everything goes wrong.

But thankfully there are beach days, when life is full of sunshine, laughter, warm breezes and romantic sunsets. Everyone is healthy, the house is clean, bills are paid, food is on the table, loved ones are employed and the kids are behaving. Reality or Fantasy Island?

Maybe those days aren't as numerous as we might like or don't exist at all right now, but life doesn't come with a guarantee of more beach days than toilet days. Life isn't about *if* we face trials, it's about *when*.

It's also about restoration. Dwell on 1 Peter 5:10. Linger on God's promise for what awaits after He uses the plunger and unclogs the toilet. His light will shine so brightly upon your face you will feel as if you are on an island, having a glorious beach day. You will even be able to stand firm in the shifting sand, as the waves crash over your feet. The waves won't stop, but in Christ, nothing will knock you down.

February 13

We love because he first loved us.—1 John 4:19

My photographer son came to Austin to take some pictures the day before Valentine's. After finishing the shoot, we had dinner and he spent the night.

The following morning, before heading back home to Houston, Trevor hid a Valentine's card for me inside my closed laptop, knowing it would only be a matter of time before I discovered it. Nothing like finding a handmade card, with little hearts drawn on it, from your grown son. But what was even more special were his sweet words.

Among other things, he thanked me for showing and teaching him how to love. First, I got teary-eyed. Next, my mind began to wonder. What had I done?

Do we intentionally set out to show our children how to be sweet and to love? Especially our rough-and-tough little boys? We want our children to grow up to be polite and well-mannered, so we teach them when to say "thank you" and "please," along with "Yes, sir," and "No, ma'am." We also try to explain how and why they need to share their toys, play fair, be kind and get along with others.

We teach them how to tie their shoes, ride a bike and swim. We help them learn to dress themselves and brush their teeth. We want them to know how to read and we work on those skills, but do we actually sit down and tell them that today we are going to learn how to love?

We went to church regularly, and I taught their Sunday school classes. We prayed and read daily devotions, but honestly, I didn't know Jesus back then, so how I could knowingly share His love?

Raising two boys, our lives revolved around sports. As they became more skilled, I sought experts in the field who could fine-tune their athletic abilities. As I look back on those years, anything I did right in the parenting department was only through the grace of God. I sought professionals to help with sports, which was beyond my expertise, and my Father jumped right in to help in the parenting arena because He knew I needed His know-how.

Even when I was so undeserving, His love for me was unconditional. Little did I know His capacity to love me, no matter what, would allow me to love my own children when they messed up. Even when they broke my heart, I would stand by their side, as my Father never left me.

If you are a parent, you can identify with the indescribable affection we have for our children. How did we learn to love them so much? Where did those feelings and our actions come from?

"This is how God showed his love among us: He sent his one and only Son into the world that we might live through him. This is love: not that we loved God, but that he loved us and sent his Son as an atoning sacrifice for our sins. Dear friends, since God so loved us, we also ought to love one another. No one has ever seen God; but if we love one another, God lives in us and his love is made complete in us" (1 John 4:9-12).

For God so loved the world—that's you and me—He gave His Son as a sacrifice (John 3:16). Dwell on that thought for a few minutes. Let it seep into the bottom of your soul. Can you even imagine allowing and watching your child hang on that cross? For someone else's sins?

While I momentarily swelled with pride reading my son's tender words—thanking me for teaching him how to love—I quickly acknowledged that God was the One who taught me, and my son. Sure, all we do to help and nurture another human is an active response to loving others, but God is at the heart of it all. His capacity to love all of us so much that He would sacrifice His only Son just blows my parental efforts out of the water.

We will buy (or make) a Valentine's card for our spouse, family members, friends or that special person in our life. But what will we do for the One who loves us more than any human? Are our hearts full of tender thoughts for the One who loved us first?

No one will be without a Valentine tomorrow; we all have a Bridegroom who is longing to fill our hearts with His words of love. Let's try telling God just how crazy we are about Him. Can you imagine how ecstatic He will be to receive a handmade card from each of us?

February 14

Do everything without complaining or arguing.—**Philippians 2:14**

I always look at my digital clock when I wake up in the middle of the night and usually go right back to sleep. I have a strange connection with numbers and sometimes I just know God wants me to remember that specific time. When I do recall the numbers from the clock, I go to my Bible first thing when I get up, searching for a corresponding verse.

One morning I woke up at 2:14 a.m. I thought to myself I would certainly remember those numbers because I thought of Valentine's Day. Sure enough, when I got up the next morning, 2:14 was still fresh on my mind. So my task was then to check my Bible for a 2:14 verse that spoke to my heart.

When I read Philippians 2:14, I immediately knew that was the one. My son Zach had actually brought it to my attention years ago when he was in junior high. Back in those days, he used to read the daily devotionals I gave him every Christmas, and it was the Scripture reading one morning. He thought it was so noteworthy and timely that he cut it out and taped it on his bathroom mirror.

He and his younger brother, Trevor, argued quite a bit. Trevor had a knack for knowing which buttons to push to aggravate someone, and he pushed Zach's all the time. Zach just liked to argue, so the two of them managed to have numerous sparring matches. Zach also tended to be a bit on the negative side and was prone to complain. He felt this was a good verse for him to remember and hopefully help change his habits that weren't pleasing to God. "Do everything without complaining or arguing"—certainly words of wisdom to live by!

I remember how proud I was of him for being humble enough to admit his shortcomings and mature enough to want to change his ways for God. Unfortunately, through the years, the paper ended up tucked away in a bathroom drawer, out of sight and out of mind. However, I ran across the crumbled-up piece of Scripture one day while cleaning. It brought back such wonderful memories of when Zach was earnestly seeking Him.

The day before the 2:14 clock check, he had called. I am so blessed that he calls me several times a week just to chat. He was especially cheerful because the previous weekend was the first one in many months that he didn't have to work. He and his wife had enjoyed a rare weekend together and he just wanted to share his good news.

For the past several months, Zach had been complaining about his long hours. He liked the job he had at the time, but he didn't like spending so much time away from his sweet wife. I was glad to hear that he missed her so much, but I didn't like listening to his negativity. After all, the economy was bad at that specific time, and he should have been more thankful for his job! His extremely longs hours were just for a season—they wouldn't last forever. Oh my goodness! I was trying to start an argument with my son.

My mind jumped back to that particular morning he cut that Scripture from his devotional and taped it to his mirror. I remembered the words, "do everything without complaining or arguing," but I couldn't recall where in the Bible it was located. I think Zach and I both needed that verse.

God is so insightful to give me just what I need. He woke me at 2:14 a.m. to get those numbers in my head—to lead me to Philippians 2:14. I am going to ask Zach if he remembers taping that verse from his devotional to his bathroom mirror and tell him about waking up at 2:14 a.m. I must take advantage of every opportunity to share my God stories with him. Who knows? It just might be the very story that will rekindle his love for the Lord.

February 15

"Yet I hold this against you; You have forsaken your first love." —**Revelation 2:4**

There has been a flood of stories written about love and marriage this month throughout all the devotionals I read. I know this is the month of love, but why do I feel I am being challenged on the status of my marriage? I even read one that came right out and asked if God is trying to tell me there is something I need to change or do differently. Unfortunately, I think He is screaming at me.

I retired from work a year before Austin and I married in July 2005, so I never juggled a career and marriage too. I have had all the time in the world to devote to my husband. However, when I started writing this daily devotional, things changed. While this book had been on my heart for years, I more or less came out of retirement in 2010 when the actual writing process began.

This book isn't a job for me. I am compiling and writing God stories because I have a passion in my heart to do so. However, somewhere along the way, I fell in love with this project. I didn't fall out of love with my husband; I just have a tendency to place him on the back burner and focus on a book instead of my man. Just for the record, my husband and I have talked about this at great lengths. He is a behind me 100% in this project and has told me he doesn't feel as if he's competing for my affection with a book. God, on the other hand, doesn't feel the same because He has put this story on my heart.

All of the admiration, love, and respect that I showered on Austin before I started writing is just as important today, despite this book commitment. What about all the verses on marriage on the Bible? Here I am writing stories about His Word and yet I am not obeying them. What is wrong with this picture?

Do I really listen to Austin when he calls, or is my mind still focused on the story in the making? Perhaps some of the hours at my computer could be spent with my husband, doing life together. I hear God telling me not to devote so much time to this book that I have none left for my husband. I know God is excited that others and I are sharing our stories for His glory, but I need to make sure I don't ignore my husband along the way. God is truly glorified when I love my husband well.

Yes, God the Marriage Doctor is most definitely telling me I need to make some changes. What better time to fill me up with devotions centered on love and marriage than during the month of February? There's no better time than right now to remember the dynamics of our marriage before this book and how I wanted nothing more than to please my husband and be a godly wife. This book has brought joy beyond belief to my life and I will continue forward, but

I will also make sure that I am the wife God wants me to be, and that my sweet husband deserves. Yes, it is time to get my priorities straight.

February 16

So we fix our eyes not on what is seen, but on what is unseen. For what is seen in temporary, but what is unseen is eternal.—**2 Corinthians 4:18**

The devotion yesterday was all about getting my priorities straight. I just love how God will give me one thought for a story and then after I write it, add more to it. That's what He did with the one from yesterday. If you missed it, you might want to go back now.

It's easy to immerse myself in writing devotions. I love spending time with God, writing His stories. I didn't start this project because I was bored with life, or my husband. Quite the contrary. My spiritual passion was at an all-time high, my life was full of joy and filled with hope for the future. This book journey has actually intensified all of those feelings. With all the positives surrounding this devotional, how did I get so off-track and let it consume me?

I honestly think Satan wanted to be included in this book. I also believe that Satan can't do anything without God's permission. Just like God gave him full reign with Job, He allowed Satan to attack me too. I am not saying that the devil made me do it, but I am saying I fell while being attacked. Yes, Satan saw that God was getting all the glory through the stories that my friends and I were sharing and he just had to get his foot in the door. Had my focus been completely on God, he wouldn't have stood a chance, but I was thinking temporary thoughts—a finished book—instead of what is eternal.

What kind of eternal thoughts should I have been focused on? I feel that's the lesson God wants me to learn. Even doing something to bring glory to God, like writing a daily devotional, can become an idol, if I allow it. "Do not store up for yourselves treasures on earth" (Matthew 6:19) that are temporary. My prayer for this book is that at least one woman's life will be touched by a story she reads. That would be an eternal gift, but the book itself won't find a place on a shelf in heaven.

The time I devote to my husband and family and the time I give serving others is eternal. The deadline for this book is just a completion date on my calendar and is temporary, but being confident that He who began a good work in me will carry it on to completion (Philippians 1:6) is my hope for eternity. The book on the shelf is temporary, but the lessons God is teaching me along the journey are eternal.

"But store up for yourself treasures in heaven, where moth and rust do not destroy, and where thieves do not break in and steal" (Matthew 6:20). How is that done? The commentary in my Bible states very simply that storing up treasures in heaven is accomplished by all acts of obedience to God. Writing devotions isn't the sin in this story; my being disobedient to God's commands is. This daily devotional has many eternal qualities, but God is pointing out that I have allowed "it" to become the object of my love and affection, instead of His Word and my spouse.

For many years, I laughed at the Wife of Noble Character in Proverbs 31:10-31, but God recently led me to park myself there for a while. I think it's clear that no female could actually accomplish as much, but it is her reverence for God that makes her a wife of noble character, not her achievements. I want to be that wife, one who obeys the Father's Word, storing up treasures in heaven. Through obedience to His Word, and seeking His direction and wisdom, the choices I make in keeping my priorities in balance will be pleasing in His sight.

Are you a wife of noble character? Have you allowed anything to take priority over your husband? Children, job, friends, exercise, volunteer commitments, Bible study, Facebook? Please be honest because He already knows. God, the Father of Marriage, is here to the rescue.

February 17

But now we have been released from the Law, having died to that by which we were bound, so that we serve in newness of the Spirit and not in oldness of the letter.—**Romans 7:6 (NASB)**

I stepped out of the circle in 1988—the circle I had been in with my spouse for the last five years of our 11-year marriage. After suggesting counseling multiple times, over the years, to no avail, we agreed to separate and see if divorce was what we really wanted.

My unhappiness and bitterness in this marriage were all-consuming. After seeking advice from friends on the matter and weighing my options, I announced that I was done. I was done with the exhaustion from my trying to show up as a perfect wife and mother in spite of my unhappiness at home. I was done facing an expressionless partner who looked puzzled and oblivious when I spoke about our problems. I was done with confusion that this unloving marriage was what God had in mind for me.

The pain from the eventual divorce amplified my relationship with God. I had never cried out to Him as I did in those two years following the separation. Although I had been brought up in the church, I hadn't consistently worshipped the Lord in my college and early adult years. What I knew of God was from a legalistic approach, one of religion, not relationship. Even though my spouse and I attended a church in our community, and we even taught Sunday school for a season, I felt that I was trying to play the part of church-goer.

Something was missing. I questioned my theology and what Christ did on the cross for my sins. Would I be forgiven of my sins, my participation in the destruction of this marriage? How would I overcome the shame of divorce and making my child part of a national statistic? How could I admit that my marriage had failed in a community that knew my spouse and me through our school district careers?

In those desperate moments when fear of being a single parent and how we would survive on a teacher's salary would creep into my mind, I sometimes got an inkling of faith and peace that my daughter and I would survive. Living more independent from God than relying on Him, I forged ahead; I had a child to raise, a house to sell, a single life to pursue. Focused on the course ahead, I gave little notice to how God was directing my path.

Difficult as the next nine years were, God pursued me and showed me His loving kindness. He started by putting quality people in my life and slowly softening my hard heart that had grown callused from barnacles of anger, bitterness and unforgiveness. He gingerly removed my independent spirit and self-centeredness, and showed me the value of a servant's heart. He put me to studying His Word and gave me a hunger for an intimate relationship with Him. He used friends to introduce me to a sensitive, loving man with whom I could grow in my relationship with God. I made him my second husband that ninth year.

At the beginning of my second marriage, as we visited another church, God revealed to me what had been missing before. No longer an orphan, I had found a church home. No longer would I sit in a Sunday pew out of obligation because church was something I was supposed to do. Finding my church home, I longed to know God's Word and to gratefully worship the Lord for His redemption of my broken life. His Holy Spirit filled my spirit, as I put Jesus Christ on the throne of my life! God gave me the revelation that my renewed mind was now transformed and I could not out-sin God's ability and desire to forgive me. "And do not be conformed to this world, but be transformed by the renewing of your mind" (Romans 12:2 NASB).

From my studies of the Bible, I learned that "Christ is the end of the law for righteousness to everyone who believes" (Romans 10:4 NASB). Through Christ Jesus, God invites me into relationship with Him: "in Christ Jesus you who formerly were far off have been brought near by the blood of Christ" (Ephesians 2:13 NASB). "The veil of the Temple was torn in two from top to bottom" (Matthew 27:51 NASB).

Thank You, Father God, that You love me as Your child, and through Christ's redemptive work on Calvary, I can now have direct access to You and a relationship apart from the law. I am no longer a stranger or alien, but now a fellow citizen with the saints, a part of God's household (Ephesians 2:19).

JHH
Katy, TX

February 18

Many women do noble things, but you surpass them all.—**Proverbs 31:29**

A mini-family reunion was planned at my sister's home in New Mexico. I returned to Katy for a quick visit before flying out of Houston for the trip. My golden retriever, Holly, and I set out for a morning walk when I saw a neighbor and called out to say hello. She asked if I had come back to Katy for the funeral.

Funeral? Who passed away? The news had me in tears. A friend had died of a brain tumor only six weeks after being diagnosed. It all happened so fast; few people even knew she was sick. She left behind her husband of 36 years, who was also her high school sweetheart, and four grown boys. The funeral was in two hours.

Could I make it to the service? I was flying to New Mexico bright and early the next morning and had a long to-do list. Plus, I had nothing appropriate to wear. All I had packed was blue jeans and ski clothes. But God had made sure that I found out about Sue's death for a reason. Plus, I was overwhelmed with an incredible sadness and knew the funeral would be the place to remember and honor this lovely woman.

I called my younger son to tell him that Josh's mom had died. He immediately asked when and where the funeral would be. When I told him in two hours, at the Jewish Temple close to Katy, Trevor told me he would meet me there. *But I don't have anything to wear.* Trevor quickly put me in my place with his response back: "Mom, I can't believe you actually said that. Wear jeans. It doesn't matter."

Besides managing carpools and running an extremely busy household, Sue also worked with special-needs children within the public-school system in Katy and she was phenomenal with those kids. The words about the wife of noble character from Proverbs 31 that were read that morning fit Sue perfectly. Really. She did it all and always had time to do more for others.

Our sons had become fast friends in second grade at Cub Scouts and remained the closest of buddies until the 10th grade, when demands of their different sports got in the way. Sue had been like a second mother to my son. Not that she wanted another, but because she had a big enough heart to love one more. Trevor was included in some of their Hanukkah celebrations and Josh went to church with us on occasion. Those two boys were inseparable, and Sue and I stayed in close contact because we needed to stay on top of them.

How easy it is to lose track of friends and go our separate ways. The last time I talked with Sue was about four months before she was diagnosed. We ran into each other when I was back in Katy for another visit. As we walked our dogs around the man-made lakes, we noticed all the little boys fishing. We reminisced about the old days, when our boys were young and would spend hours doing the same. They rode their bikes back and forth to each other's house and somehow had a knack for getting into mischief. We talked about the present, too, and what was going on with our families since we hadn't visited in years. What an incredible gift God gave us with that sweet, last conversation.

Sue didn't have to be the best-dressed or trendiest mom. She *never* would have even thought about something so trivial as not having the appropriate clothes for a funeral, like I had. She was one of the most unsuperficial women I had ever met. She didn't meddle in other people's business, nor was she judgmental. Her boys weren't perfect and she never pretended that they were. She was extremely content to be exactly who God had made her to be—a godly wife, mother, friend and teacher. Yes, quoting words from her funeral, "we now all have a Sue hole in our hearts."

February 19

In his heart a man plans his course, but the LORD determines his steps.—**Proverbs 16:9**

Yesterday, I wrote about my friend Sue's untimely death. There is more I want to share with you. I am still in awe of how God orchestrated that day. God planned for my younger son and me to be at that funeral and He worked out the details. I mentioned I saw a neighbor who told me Sue had passed away. It was more than just a chance meeting; it was God's perfect encounter.

My dog and I left the house, walked through an opening in the fence and were out on a major thoroughfare. My friend was on the opposite side of that street and had just turned to go through the opening in the fence to her home. Had I been 20 seconds later, we would have missed each other, and I wouldn't have known about Sue and the funeral that was in two hours.

Trevor is a photographer and just happened to be taking photos of the grand opening at a new hospital 15 minutes from the Temple. He finished 30 minutes before the funeral and his next appointment was two hours later. Plenty of time to attend the service.

When I got in my car to drive to the Temple, I had no time to spare. I turned the key and there was a hesitation, but the ignition turned over. I got to the Temple in the nick of time, but when leaving, the same thing happened. I knew that sound and that my battery was close to its last start.

Part of my to-do list I mentioned yesterday included a hair appointment. After the funeral, there was just enough time for me to get back to Katy for that. I know some of you understand how important these appointments can be. I made it, but I knew that my car didn't have another start left in it. Sure enough, when I was ready to leave the beauty shop my car was dead. It wouldn't respond to a jump, so I got my first ride in a tow truck. Thankfully, all I needed was a new battery.

All too often I forget to acknowledge God's presence in my daily activities. You know, He's much too busy to really care if I get to my hair appointment. Is He really interested in who I encounter during the day? Did He jump-start my battery to get me to the funeral? Trevor shoots pictures all over the state of Texas. And on this day he was minutes away from the Jewish Temple? No, nothing just happens by chance, and God had His fingerprints all over the events of this day.

Trevor and Sue's son, Josh, haven't stayed in touch, but since the funeral, they have communicated via Facebook. They were too close of friends to let that friendship slip away, so the opportunity to get reacquainted was a good thing that came from a bad situation. God gave me a wake-up call to evaluate my own existence by reminding me of Sue's totally unselfish life.

God had saved two seats in the Temple that morning—He was expecting us. We never would have made it without God to handle the details. In life and in death, He is in control. Why am I so amazed that He would go to so much trouble to plan my day? He does it every day and I don't give Him the glory often enough. This time I saw Him in action. As I write this, I am shedding tears as I reflect on that day—tears of pure joy at the wonders of His mighty love for me, along with tears of sadness over the death of my friend.

Do you know the song "Shout to the Lord?" I wish I could include the lyrics here because that is the joy I feel for my Savior. If you know the words, please sing it with me.

February 20

"Therefore, I tell you, her many sins have been forgiven—for she loved much. But he who has been forgiven little loves little." —**Luke 7:47**

I first began writing poetry in high school as a creative outlet for all those confusing, frustrating feelings of being a teenager. After becoming a CPA and a mom, it just seemed there was no time to devote to my creative energies. When my younger daughter, Liza, left for college, I began to ask myself, "What was it I did before I became a mom that gave me personal satisfaction?" I love to read and have always had a desire to write fiction, but I struggled with all the details required in writing good fiction. After joining a Bible study's journaling group, God inspired me to take a Biblical image and express it poetically.

HER HAIR
(The Sinful Woman—Luke 7:37-50)

Unleashed,
Flying freely down the fabric on her back,
Scattering the crowd
As she seeks Him.

Pungent with last night's sin
Guarding the alabaster jar of perfume
Held tightly in her hands

Blanketing his feet
To the beat of her cries,
Flowing with the wash of her tears,
Ebbing as it dries them,
Taking the earth remnants with it.

Hiding her kisses
In its golden strands,
Trails of fragrance ripple over His feet,
Sacrificial gifts of herself.

Wrapping of thanksgiving,
Wrapping of repentance,
A shroud of grateful redemption,
Her instrument of worship.

Luke 7:36 tells of "the sinful woman" who crashed a party for Jesus hosted by Simon, a Pharisee. She caused quite a scene standing behind Jesus, weeping and kissing his feet, wiping them with her hair, and then anointing them with perfume.

The image of total brokenness in this story is powerful. The challenge for me in my poem was to convey the poignancy of this story in as few words as possible. Are there verses that trigger artistic or poetic images for you? I challenge you to vary your study of the Bible in new ways. Your interpretive poems or paintings or collage may just be your path to a deeper understanding of God's word.

Elizabeth Ponder
Austin, TX

February 21

"From everyone who has been given much, much will be demanded; and from the one who has been entrusted with much, much more will be asked." **—Luke 12:48**

It was an exceptionally cold day in the Texas Hill Country, with the high predicted to be 25 degrees, and a low of 16. That would be three nights in a row of below-freezing temperatures. Not the norm for us.

Before I got out of bed that morning, I had some time with God. I actually felt guilty that I was under my warm covers, knowing there were thousands, just in the Austin area, living outside in the elements or without heat. The previous night I received an email from a local organization asking for donations of coats and blankets that could be distributed to those living on the streets. I went to bed thinking about that email and woke up with it still on my mind.

The next item on my agenda was to fix a cup of coffee. I have one of those fabulous coffee makers that brews one cup at a time, and I just feel blessed every time I get a hot, fresh cup of coffee. As the last drops of coffee dripped into my cup, the electricity went off in my house. I honestly said a prayer of thanksgiving that I at least got my first cup of coffee, before the power went out.

When the outside temperature is 20 degrees, a house gets cold quickly without heat. After only an hour, my house was chilly! I had on sweats and socks, and I was still feeling the effects of no heat. I was also wishful for the second cup of coffee I didn't get.

My thoughts went back to the email requesting blankets and coats. I had extras in my houses to layer on as the temperature inside my house fell. Not so for the folks on the street. I at least had one cup of hot coffee. They had none.

It was time to get going and respond to that email!

Dear Father, please forgive my selfish ways. Please forgive my simple thoughts of Your cold, homeless children. Thinking of them isn't the action needed to make them warm. Yes, being a bit chilly inside of my home did make me more aware of their plight. However, I am called to share Your love, not just think about it; to glorify You with my actions, not my simple thoughts. I know praying for others is important but today I am being reminded of Luke 12:2. Not just on this cold, wintry day, but every day, may I be a better steward with the abundance You have entrusted to me. Amen!

February 22

"Fear not, for I have redeemed you; I have summoned you by name; you are mine." —Isaiah 43:1

A few days ago, I received an email from a friend notifying me of her email address change. I laughed all the way through it as she explained the frustrations she encountered trying to find a new username. I wasn't laughing because she had problems—it's just that no one can tell a story like Debbie. Not only was her first choice already being used by someone else, so were her second, third and fourth choices!

Her email reminded me of my own change-of-email-address story. When I upgraded to my smartphone, I had to get a different Internet service provider. After deciding which one to sign up with, I had to choose a new username. I had been using "bgerland" and, for simplicity's sake, didn't want to change. Besides, it had been *my* username for as long as I could remember. However, to my surprise, someone else in this world had already claimed bgerland with the new provider!

I didn't want to use my full name—too many letters to fool with. So, I settled with adding a "2" and came up with bgerland2. Not my first choice, but it would do.

Several months later, I was checking into the hotel for my church's women's retreat. The lady at the registration desk asked my name and suddenly exclaimed, "So, you are Brenda Gerland. I have been waiting to meet you!"

Her greeting caught me a bit off guard, but I just assumed she was exceptionally friendly. She proceeded to tell me that her best friend, who lived in another state, was also named Brenda Gerland. When she had seen my name on the reservation list, she was anxious to meet me and see what I looked like.

We chatted for a few minutes, as I learned more about her friend, Brenda. The hotel employee probably thought it was a bit strange when I asked about her friend's email address. Could she possibly be that other person in the world using the "bgerland" I wanted?

No, she wasn't the culprit who had taken my username, but it still aroused my curiosity to learn about this other woman who had my same name. Even though there are at least two of us out there, I am not worried that God will get us confused—"because I am fearfully and wonderfully made" (Psalm 139:14), and "all the days ordained for me were written in your book before one of them came to be" (Vs. 16). Yes, I am unique and special, and I am His!

February 23

"But what about you?" he asked. "Who do you say I am?" —**Matthew 16:15**

I think I am pretty easily identified as a Christian—I have all the trimmings. There is a little sterling silver fish that swings from the rear-view mirror of my car, and my radio is set on a Christian station. My iPod is full of Christian music, which, to the horror of my teenage daughter, I tend to sing along with in my "outside voice." I have cute, glitzy shirts with big ol' crosses on the front, all the latest cross jewelry, and my home—goodness!

You won't likely make it past the front door without noticing the verse plate of Joshua 24:15. Once you come in, you will see we have not left much question about our being Christ followers. I have surrounded my office with Scripture printed on pretty paper, decorated an entire wall of our dining room with crosses, and continued with scattering them throughout our home. Our bookshelves are filled with good, solid Christian reading. That's good, huh? Can you relate?

But seriously, none of that really matters. While I was looking in my Bible this morning, I came across a note I had written: "Jesus is not captivated with the here and now." I agree with that, and believe He is instead interested in our eternal perspective.

Jesus had a very simple, cut-to-the-quick question: "Who do you say I am?" That is what Jesus wants to know. He asked it of His disciples, and it was a gut check for Simon Peter, but he gave the answer Jesus was seeking: "You are the Christ, the Son of the Living God" (Matthew 16:16).

Because I am a Christ follower, I find it important to ask myself that question every once in awhile, because sometimes I forget. There are occasions where I would like to answer, "You are second in charge of my life, so I will be doing things my way today." At times like these, I need to be reminded that Jesus is my Savior and Master. Other times, I need reminding because of the comfort it brings. On both good days full of highs and bad days with their lows, it is the perfect way to start my day.

Bottom line: Good question, Jesus. Gut check time. Who do you say He is?

Teri Brown
Austin, TX

February 24

Let us not give up meeting together, as some are in the habit of doing, but let us encourage one another. —**Hebrews 10:25**

The email from Nancy's husband read: *Just a quick update on Nancy's brother Kevin. The family has decided to set Kevin free after a he receives his last rites at noon tomorrow. Kevin could be putting on his wings now and head out before noon tomorrow.* Sure enough, shortly after noon on February 24, 2013, Kevin headed home to Jesus.

Somewhat of a light-hearted message about death, but I believe that's how Kevin would have wanted it. You see, I didn't actually know him. I only knew of him from the stories Nancy shared over the years.

Nancy and her husband were in the same church home group as my husband and I when we lived in Katy, Texas. We became close friends during those years and learned interesting tidbits about each other's families. Kevin cherished his wife, kids and his LSU Tigers. He loved a good party and was devoted to his friends. Kevin had a zeal for life and enjoyed it to the fullest.

Diagnosed with a heart condition as a teenager, it wasn't until four years before his death the disease began to slow him down—considerably. Kevin had to change his lifestyle, but he wouldn't allow his failing health to interfere with his friendships and his love of life.

He got better, only to get worse. One problem would go away, but then another more serious one would pop up. By 2012, Kevin's body was ravaged with lymphoma, along with a deteriorating heart. He went to Houston in the fall for some high-tech procedures, never to leave the hospital again. It must have been incredibly painful to watch a larger-than-life personality lie almost motionless in a bed. Yet, Kevin still managed to smile and welcome family and friends to his room.

Kevin had a large circle of friends. Some of the guys he had known since elementary school came to visit him only a few weeks before his death. To have lifelong friends travel over six hours to visit an ailing buddy in the hospital speaks volumes about his magnetic personality and loyal heart.

In one of her emails to update his condition, Nancy wrote: *"I can't imagine our family without him, but have come to the realization that unless the Lord decides to do a miraculous healing (which He can) it is only a matter of time."*

"I can't imagine our family without him." Those words struck a cord on my heartstrings, especially after Nancy told me even more about Kevin after his death. Nancy shared that he was the one who made the family gatherings so special. His friends told her Kevin was the one who initiated the calls and kept those relationships going. He was the glue that kept everyone together. What a legacy to leave behind.

The funeral mass wasn't your typical service. His obituary read; "Kevin's love for the Tigers was part of his every endeavor. To honor that love, IT IS REQUESTED THAT PURPLE AND GOLD BE WORN BY ALL THOSE IN ATTENDANCE AND THAT LSU FLAGS BE FLOWN FROM ALL CARS IN THE PROCESSION." I feel certain that was Kevin's personal request.

I deeply regretted that I never met Kevin face-to-face. He sounded like such a fun guy, very much like my husband, and I just knew those two would have had a large time together. My Austin is also the one who will go to great lengths to get his old high school friends together, stay in touch with others and plan the party. Nothing is too much trouble when it comes to family and friends. Relationships were key to Kevin and still are to my husband.

Relationships were also important to Jesus. He surrounded Himself with a small circle of intimate friends and enjoyed sharing conversations about Biblical truths. With people flocking to him to learn more, He could be found among large groups at times. How else was He going to spread His message and ministry unless He was in community with them?

Jesus had a knack for initiating encounters—remember the story of the woman at the well in John 4:1-42? He went to great lengths to seek out that woman, just as He has done for you and me. Shouldn't we all follow His example and be that purposeful with our relationships?

Perhaps all of us need to reach out to a friend we haven't seen in awhile. Is there someone who just came to mind? Call her today and set a date to meet face-to-face. Be intentional about the relationships in your life. Stay attached to the community of believers who have been placed in your path. Be that glue that keeps others in your life connected.

In Loving Memory of Kevin Patrick Mahony
March 17, 1960-February 24, 2013

February 25

"My grace is sufficient for you, for my power is made perfect in weakness." —**2 Corinthians 12:9**

It was a strange meeting. I was in a shopping-mall parking lot, about to get in my car, when a lady pulled up beside me in her SUV and said, "We're about the same size, so I have something to give you." She went around to the back of her vehicle and pulled out a sack.

As she handed it to me, she asked, "What size shoes do you wear?" "9½," I replied. She smiled and said, "Well, these shoes are about the right size for you." Then she added, "I don't know why I'm doing this, except that God told me to. I even argued with Him and told Him, 'This woman doesn't know me and she'll think I'm crazy!' To which God replied, 'Do it!' So that's what I'm doing."

Well, I was just as perplexed as she was. However, I told her that if God told her to do it, then she should because He works in mysterious ways. I thanked her as we waved good-bye and went our separate ways. As I drove home, I asked the Lord, "What in the world was that all about?"

Jesus' words from John 14:21 came into my mind: "He who loves me will be loved by my Father, and I too will love him and show myself to him." I felt like God was giving me a message, and that somehow those shoes would be a manifestation—a visible sign of His love for me.

Once home, I opened the sack and examined the two pairs of shoes. The first pair was a pretty burgundy sling-back pump with black trim. They looked like shoes that I would definitely wear, except that they were a size 9. The other pair, a short brown boot, looked more masculine and was a size 10, which was too large for me. I stared at the shoes a long time, wondering why God would want me to have them.

Then it hit me that even though neither pair was exactly my size, together they averaged a 9½, which was a perfect fit. I began to sense that Jesus and I were going to be walking closely together. I felt like He was preparing me for things to come. Jesus assured me that He would be with me and I was to trust Him.

That day was February 25, 2010, and within three hours of receiving those shoes, the "things to come" began to unfold. First, there was the phone call telling me that my nephew had been killed. Next was the news that my daughter-in-law's mother had been diagnosed with cancer and wasn't expected to live. Two weeks later, the retina on my right eye detached for the third time.

On and on the trials came. Over the remaining months of that year, I faced many difficulties, including four surgeries on my eye, severe pain and physical therapy on my hip, and five close family members who died. After each trial, I wondered what would happen next. Then, I would see those shoes and remember that no matter what, Jesus was walking beside me.

He reminded me of 2 Corinthians 12:9: "My grace is sufficient for you, for my power is made perfect in weakness." His presence, His comfort and His strength kept me going. We walked a lot of miles that year. Jesus and me. Two pairs of shoes. A perfect fit. Thanks and glory to Him!

Rozelle Roberts
Fort Worth, TX

February 26

Jesus then took the loaves, gave thanks, and distributed to those who were seated as much as they wanted. He did the same with the fish. —**John 6:11**

My daughter, Lydia, and I were selling Girl Scout cookies in front of CVS on the fifth day of our cookie sale. In the midst of the cookie chanting, cheers, and silly cookie songs, a woman approached our booth.

"I would like to purchase three boxes of Girl Scout cookies to send to my 35-year-old nephew stationed in the southern tip of Afghanistan. He just loves these cookies and always shares them with others. He always says it's like 'a little taste of home.' I try to send him care packages periodically, but they can get rather expensive. His unit calls it 'Aunt Patty's Box' and they can't wait to dive into it right when it gets there," Aunt Patty said with a huge smile. (Since she said the nephew referred to her care packages as "Aunt Patty's Box, we just assumed her name to be Aunt Patty.)

"Ma'am, did you know that the Girl Scouts of America have a program called Operation Cookie?" I said. "With collected donations, we send cookies to the men and women serving in our military all over the world. And, matter of fact, my daughter and I have been praying all weekend for the name of a specific person serving overseas to be the recipient of cookies that we have already collected during this year's sale. If you give me his name and address, our Girl Scout troop would love to send some to him. This is truly an answer to prayer for us. How many do you think he might need in order to 'share'?"

"Oh," Aunt Patty blushed, "that would be so wonderful. But I don't want to be greedy. He's a captain with 300 who report to him."

"Well, I guess that means he will need eight cases. That's 96 boxes, and I would be happy to ship them out as soon as I get his address."

Aunt Patty nearly fell over.

The next day, we sent 96 boxes to Captain Alan Vargo. Later that same afternoon, I was able to share the story about "Aunt Patty's Box" and to my surprise, the person on the other end of the line said, "Then I'll need to order 200 boxes. I have two more names to give you."

That's when I nearly fell over.

In the feeding of 5,000, Jesus graciously accepted what was donated, earnestly prayed, and was able to abundantly bless the hungry crowd that was miles away from home. No donation is ever too small in the eyes of the Lord. As children of God, we are all serving on foreign soil here on earth, longing for those sacred moments when God allows us to partake in "a little taste of home—our heavenly home." Every chance He gets, God loves to take what is given from the hearts of His children serving on foreign soil and use it for His glory.

To those of you who have donated towards Operation Cookie, thank you being a part of "Aunt Patty's Box," sharing "a little taste of home" with someone who is serving in our military.

To God be the Glory! Great things He has done!

Courtney and Lydia Thomas
Austin, TX

February 27

"He will reply, 'I tell you the truth, whatever you did not do for some of the least of these, you did not do for me.'"—**Matthew 25:45**

I don't know what you call a meal eaten at 4 o'clock in the afternoon, but that's what my son and I were enjoying together. We were in Houston and stopped in a part of town that neither of us was familiar with. At that particular time of day, it certainly wasn't crowded. There was only one other table occupied by an elderly man and woman.

I was seated so that I could look directly at the couple. Out of the corner of my eye, I saw a man enter the restaurant and walk directly to their table. It was rather windy and chilly outside, so his bundled-up appearance didn't look inappropriate—until I took a closer look. He was wrapped up in a tattered, worn-out dirty blanket. I realized this man was a "beggar."

One of the waiters quickly walked over to the table and took the man by the elbow to escort him out the door. However, the elderly man sitting down called out to the waiter and asked him to bring the man back to his table.

"Are you hungry?" the elderly gentleman asked.

"Yes, sir," the beggar replied.

"What would you like to eat?"

"Oh, I really like ham sandwiches." (By the way, we were eating in an Italian restaurant known for out-of-this-world pizzas, and the smells coming from the kitchen were mouthwatering.)

The gentleman instructed the waiter to bring the man a ham sandwich. He then asked him if he would like a cup of coffee to warm him up.

The gentleman motioned for him to sit down. I looked over at that table, the three now sitting together, and felt so ashamed.

When I had realized that the man walking through the door had come inside to ask for a handout, I had felt so uncomfortable. *Oh, no! What if he comes over to my table? What will I say to him? What will I do? Is this what goes on in this part of town?*

When I see someone on the street corner with a sign, I can easily stare straight ahead and act like I don't notice, or I can roll down my window and give him one of the fast-food gift cards I keep on hand. But I am protected by my car. I can roll up my window and drive off.

Yes, those were the thoughts racing through my so-called Christian head. The gentleman sitting at that other table didn't hesitate for a minute. His act of kindness towards that man brought tears to my eyes. But then I couldn't stop crying when I realized my own behavior.

God knew my thoughts. And I knew His: "He will reply, 'I tell you the truth, whatever you did not do for some of the least of these, you did not do for me.'"

February 28

O Lᴏʀᴅ Almighty, blessed is the man who trusts in you.—**Psalm 84:12**

My son left today for a football camp in Arizona. He has graduated from college, where he played football, and now aspires to continue his career in the NFL. He's good, and I think he has what it takes. Of course, I am his mother!

Bless his heart—my son was really nervous this week. He is not punting like he wants to be, and when I have talked to him, he sounds discouraged. My mama's heart wants to pray for good success and favor, for beautiful spirals and exceptional hang time.

But I'm learning more about God and life and having an eternal perspective. Far more important than my son's success in the NFL is his relationship with Jesus Christ—his freedom to walk in the truth. And so I have begun to pray, "Whatever it takes, Lord, please make my son a godly man who loves You and follows You and loves Your Word. Whatever it takes." And I mean it!

That prayer, like one for patience, used to terrify me. But as I'm learning to trust God's heart, I can pray and know that whatever comes, it is good because God is good. And He has promised to work *all* things together for good for those who love Him and are called according to His purpose (Romans 8:28).

Perhaps my husband and I will once again have the opportunity to sit in the stands and watch our son use his gifts to punt the ball for the glory of God. Perhaps we won't. But regardless of the outcome, I trust God. He loves my son even more than I do, and His plans are good. How wonderful to trust a God like that!

Karen Gold
Palestine, TX

February 29

"Flesh gives birth to flesh, but the Spirit gives birth to spirit."—**John 3:6**

I had been asked to be a table facilitator at a women's retreat sponsored by my church—you know, just steer the conversation through the questions based upon the speaker's talk. Having attended previous retreats, I felt comfortable with the assignment. Besides, God wouldn't have asked me if He didn't plan on equipping me, right?

The second lecture of the day was based upon John 15:12-17. "My command is this: Love each other as I have loved you" (Vs. 12). One of the questions asked, "How do we deal with those who are difficult to love?" I thought it would just be a quick discussion on forgiveness. Was I ever wrong!

For some reason, God had placed several women at my table who had not only struggled with those who were difficult to love, but those people just happened to be family members. Specifically parents. The hurt still hurt and the struggle raged on.

I completely understand how our family of origin can have an effect on us. Not to belabor the fact, but just to give a few highlights: My parents divorced when I was 6, my dad ended up being married seven times and my mom three. One of my stepdads was an alcoholic, a few of my stepmoms were a bit unstable and one might have even been sent by Satan. Dad had time for all the other females in his life, but not for me.

On the positive side, both of my grandmothers were incredible, my mom persevered when thrown into the workforce, the alcoholic stepdad stopped drinking after he and mom divorced (never to fall off the wagon again), my other stepdad was a Methodist minister and before my dad's death, he and I recovered the years the locusts destroyed.

Yes, I understood that some of us weren't born into the family of our choosing. *Leave it to Beaver* and *Father Knows Best* were two of my favorite television shows, and I yearned for such families. I knew what it felt like to grow up with a hole in my heart, longing for love, but not knowing where to find it.

However, my Heavenly Father *did* choose *me*. He chose me and lavished His love and mercy upon me, filling that hole. I am one of those who can now proclaim that I have been born again.

Honestly, I never really understood the terminology "born again." In my mind it was just a flippant term that was thrown around in Christian conversations. My flesh was birthed by flesh—my earthly parents. The Holy Spirit birthed my spiritual life when I began my relationship with Christ. What a revelation to finally understand that I was indeed born again!

One question in our discussion was, "When do we walk away from a relationship that just isn't working—one that isn't healthy? Do we stick with it or leave? If the person is hateful, is that reason to distance ourselves? Due we endure the "sandpaper" people? (One crucial note—I am *not* referring to physical abuse or a situation were one fears physical harm or retaliation.)

The Sunday after the retreat, the sermon was based on Ephesians 4:1-6, titled "Fight (with each other) for UNITY." The visiting pastor from another church in Austin said we must "make every effort to keep the unity" (Vs. 3) and reconcile our relationships—that is something worth fighting for. My heart ached for those women who were not in unity with one of their parents.

Do we endure because that's what Jesus would have done? We are commanded to love just as He loved us. Jesus didn't walk away from me when I was unlovable, rebellious, defiant and spoke ugly, hurtful words. When I walked aimlessly down the wrong paths and inflicting pain upon others, Jesus stood by, patiently waiting and mercifully preventing me from self-destruction.

Way back when, I had a choice—allow the hole in my heart to grow larger or let God, the perfect Parent, fill it. I could turn my life over to the Father and forgive my earthly parents for not living up to the unrealistic portrayal of Beaver Cleaver's family or live bitter and lost.

In Matthew West's song "Forgiveness," he tells us *the prisoner that it* (forgiveness) *really frees is you.* I pray that God will release the sweet ladies at my table from the hurt caused by the flesh that bore them, allowing all to live in the freedom and joy of Christ's love.

March 1

Singing cheerful songs to a person with a heavy heart is like taking someone's coat in cold weather or pouring vinegar in a wound.—**Proverbs 25:20 (NLT)**

On this day in 2009, a dear friend of mine lost her daughter in a tragic incident. Lindsay Walters was a remarkable young woman and her mother, Lisa, surely had cause to be distraught.

As the days, weeks, months and years have passed, I've had the opportunity to observe human behavior. Please forgive me for stereotyping, but I have to be real. Based on what I saw, men generally were willing to assist on the periphery, picking up heavy things, mowing the lawn and resolving logistical matters like the sale of Lindsay's car and the like. Women were quick to jump in and make meals, tidy the house and spew flowery words in an attempt to "make Lisa feel better."

One woman came into Lisa's home and practically floated around the living room saying, "She's here. I can feel her presence. Your daughter is here." Uh, no. Lindsay knew Jesus. Her soul has belonged to Him since she was a young child. Her presence is where it should be. It's with her Creator in perfect worship! That's why it hurts for those left behind. We can no longer feel her presence. (For a season, praise God!)

A few weeks later in a flower shop, a well-meaning woman gave Lisa these words of encouragement: "Oh, Lisa! The Lord revealed to me why Lindsay was killed. He needed more young people in heaven and so He brought her home to be with Him!" Really? I mean, really? Are you kidding me?

Why do we do that? Where do we even get off thinking that we can make things better? What is it about our gender that carries the inherent need to single-handedly hit the reset button in a crisis situation?

Solomon surely was wise when he penned the Proverb above. Those flowery, unbiblical platitudes just made a bad situation worse.

Please know that there were clear moments of healing and genuine comfort that took place in Lisa's life. Those moments were precious and they will stay with me forever:

A police officer who wrapped Lisa in a bear hug, fell with her to his knees and held her as she cried.

A friend who said nothing, but sat next to Lisa for hours.

A lawyer whose first words were, "Tell me about your daughter. I want to know about her."

A news photographer who put his camera down out of respect to the family rather than pushing closer for the big emotional moment.

Do you know someone who has a heavy heart? You cannot fix it. You don't have to make it better. God won't even fix it. However, He will *redeem* whatever horrible thing it is to His glory. Just love on your friend and lean hard on the sovereignty of our perfect Savior.

Kristen Dark
Austin, TX

March 2

"Woe to you, teachers of the law and Pharisees, you hypocrites! You clean the outside of the cup and dish, but inside they are full of greed and self-indulgence. Blind Pharisee! First clean the inside of the cup and dish, then the outside also will be clean." —**Matthew 23:25-26**

Have you ever woken up in the morning and felt like you had been stuck in the same dream all night long? Try as you might, you just couldn't end it and get on to the next one? It has happened to me several times.

After this most recent occurrence, I decided to do a little research. Let me clarify, this was by no means a scientific investigation. I simply Googled "how long does a dream last" and read a few of the over 900,000,000 results that popped up in .21 seconds. Based upon the sites I visited, I came up with some very general conclusions.

Many believe that the average dream lasts about 15 minutes, with ranges from 45 seconds to 45 minutes. The National Institute of Neurological Disorders and Stroke wrote that people spend an average of two hours a night dreaming. *Newsweek* magazine said that the ability to remember dreams depends on your personality type, with introverts (like me) remembering their nocturnal adventures better than extroverts. (No wonder my husband, the extrovert, thinks I am a bit strange by my vivid recollection.)

In this dream, I had spent the whole time (for however long it was) trying to get dressed. Along with putting on makeup and fixing my hair, I tried on almost every single piece of clothing in my closet. While I woke up believing I had been in that never-ending dream all night long, it probably only lasted for minutes, according to my non-scientific research. However, I felt quite vain, thinking I had spent what seemed like endless hours trying to decide what to wear.

Once I got going on that particular morning, I started reading my online devotions. Max Lucado's story was based on Matthew 6 and the hypocrites in the synagogues. He listed some ways for us to make sure we "do good quietly," and not make a production of our faith, as the Pharisees did. That didn't hurt too much. But when he referenced Matthew 23:26, it hit home. Do I spend as much time working on a clean heart as I do on the outside of my body?

As Jesus continued taking to the Pharisees in Matthew 23:27-28, He compared them to the whitewashed tombs, outwardly appearing righteous, but within being full of hypocrisy and lawlessness. *Yes, Jesus, I know. I should spend more time on what's on the inside than what's on the outside. A pure, clean heart, clothed in acts of kindness and love for others, is certainly more important to Your kingdom than a cute dress.* I can't leave the house naked, but do I focus more on my outward appearance than my heart?

You know, that's a question that I can honestly answer. *No—not any longer.* Did I use to? *Yes, indeed.* God knows me inside and out. A cute dress and all the makeup in the world can't conceal my true character, but I sure used to think I could camouflage the real me if I looked good.

However, to write that I am not concerned with my appearance would be complete hypocrisy, like the Pharisees. I never leave the house without at least blush-on and lipstick. I get my hair highlighted to cover the gray, and I exercise and eat healthy to stay in shape. However, after finally seeking God, seeking Him with all my heart, He is teaching me how to dress myself.

"As God's chosen people, holy and dearly loved, clothe yourself with compassion, kindness, humility, gentleness, and patience. Bear with each other. . . . Forgive as the Lord forgave you. And over all these virtues put on love, which binds them all together in perfect unity" (Colossians 3:12-14). And those qualities can't be seen on the outside until my heart has been transformed.

One of my many favorite songs is "From the Inside Out," written by Joel Houston of Hillsong United. I made note of the lyrics, "never-ending, your glory goes beyond all fame." I thought of my shallow, never-ending dream where I was consumed with myself. Oh, how I want the everlasting light of the Lord to consume me. I just love that thought—to have the glory of God shining through me, glowing from the inside out—my heart being transformed into His likeness.

Am I leaving my house every day, fully clothed as a child of God, totally transformed? No, not yet, but I am a work in progress, thanks to the never-ending mercy, love and grace of my Lord.

March 3

All Scripture is God-breathed and is useful for teaching, rebuking, correcting and training in righteousness, so that the man of God may be thoroughly equipped for every good work.—**2 Timothy 3:16-17**

We were already an hour late as we started our drive to Fort Worth. The plan was to pick up my sister-in-law and her husband, then proceed to an engagement party for their son. As parents of the groom, they wanted to be there before all of the other guests arrived. That's why I was so conscious about our timing.

As soon as we got in the car, my husband handed me his TomTom GPS and asked me to type in his sister's address in Fort Worth. Couldn't *he* have done that before we started the car? He knows I have a difficult time using it. (I would rather use the GPS navigation on my phone, but he prefers his TomTom.)

After he saw the estimated travel time, he asked me if I would mind driving by one of his construction sites so he could quickly check it out. I was already aggravated because we were an hour late in leaving the house (which was his doing), then he expected me to use that TomTom, when he knows it drives me crazy. Now he's asking if it's all right if we take another hour and drive by a high school to look at the tennis courts he is building. Yes, the school is somewhat on the way out of town, but it's still another hour.

After pondering my response for a few seconds, I said what any godly wife would say. "Whatever you need to do, *dear*." I said what I was supposed to say, but inside I was fuming. You might be thinking I was overreacting a bit, but I felt justified. Every time we go somewhere, it's the same story. Time-wise, we are always down to the wire! That's just how my husband lives his life, and it is difficult for me to operate that way.

As we were driving, I sat in silence as I thought of more and more things that had just rubbed me the wrong way. I left the door wide open for Satan to come in and take over my thoughts. I could let him have full control, and blurt out everything that was going through my head, but thankfully the Holy Spirit won this battle.

I stopped listening to the Evil One long enough to hear the song on the radio. Francesca Battistelli was singing "This is the Stuff," a song about the little things that get under her skin and drive her crazy. But in the midst of her frustrations, she acknowledges the blessings in her life and that the little trials aren't the end of the world, and can actually be used for God's purpose.

I could certainly identify with her words and felt such comfort knowing that I wasn't alone with my thoughts. But at the same time, I felt a bit ashamed that, once again, I had made such a big deal out of my husband being late.

Her upbeat song got me back to a peaceful place, thinking of Philippians 4:8, my go-to verse when I happen to let my mind wander off in the wrong direction: "Whatever is true, whatever is noble, whatever is right, whatever is pure, whatever is lovely, whatever is admirable—if anything is excellent or praiseworthy—think about such things."

My husband is definitely an admirable man and I thought about his many positive character traits instead of the irritation. He works so hard and is incredibly patient. How he tolerates all of the stress and uncertainty of his business, I will never know. How he tolerates me is even more of a mystery. He is such a blessing in my life, and that I would allow myself to get upset because of his minor timing issues is something I continue to seek God's help to overcome.

I have been battling this being-on-time issue with my husband since before we got married, and believe it or not, I am actually much better at holding my tongue than I used to be. However, the negative thoughts still prevail. Thankfully God hasn't given up on me yet and is still trying to help me work through this issue.

How about you? Are there some silly things that get under your skin? Are you able to control your negative thoughts? Or do you overreact, like I did in this situation?

March 4

Your word is a lamp to guide my feet and a light for my path.—**Psalm 119:105**

Have you ever had a span of time when your heart felt empty? I hadn't in a long time, but there it was. There were no feelings of joy, no positive attitudes or thoughts. Everything just seemed to be unsettled and blah. How did it happen?

Nothing happens in life without first passing through God's hands, so the emptiness was something He allowed, but how did I allow it? Did I even have a choice in the matter?

I drove to Bible study that Tuesday morning totally worn out. The previous night had been restless. I spent much of it crying out to God. Talking with Him, pleading with Him, listening for Him. How could I go into the classroom with my small-group members and participate in our discussion when I didn't feel like I belonged in the same room? I felt so unworthy and hard-hearted.

A friend had asked if we could meet afterwards. She was depending on me to help her through a time of despair. How ironic. What words of wisdom or comfort could I offer when I was experiencing something similar?

As I sat at the stoplight, I was again overwhelmed with a feeling of desperation for His presence. However, this time there was an answer. As a memorization tool, I had written a verse on a notecard and placed it in the console for easy reference. The edge of the purple card was peeking out from under other items. The notecard in the car had done the trick, though, and the words on it quickly came to mind.

"Search me, O God, and know my heart; test me and know my anxious thoughts. See if there is any offensive way in me and lead me in the way everlasting" (Psalm 139:23-24).

I said those words over and over until I drove into the parking lot at church. As I parked my car, and opened the door, I knew that I was walking into a morning of awakening. Was there some offensive ways in me that God intended to show me that morning? I was so hopeful and expectant!

Satan had invaded my heart and I had allowed him to stay there entirely too long. There were no traumatic circumstances, nothing major going on in my life—I had surrendered to the gradual invasion of worldly, anxious thoughts and preoccupation with myself. The Evil One is a sly fellow indeed. He can just slither in and, before you know it, take up residence.

Having my Defender's Word on the tip of my tongue and ready to use as ammo at the critical moment in battle is the best defense against the deceitful ways of the Father of Lies. Do you have artillery readily available? I only have a very small one, but that morning He showed me how effective just that limited arsenal can be. Had He tested me with my memorization? I certainly reaped the reward from knowing that Scripture.

I can assure you that I always keep a notecard sitting in my console with a new verse these days. It stays at the top until those words are safe and secure in my heart—and my mind. Sometimes it might take a while, but then I add another. My Teacher has taught me I can't win the war against Satan and survive being ambushed in this dark world without the light of His Word to guide me.

March 5

As the deer pants for streams of water, so my soul pants for you, my God. My soul thirsts for God, for the living God. When can I go and meet with God?—**Psalm 42:1-2**

The deer are usually waiting on me in the mornings—expectantly waiting for me to throw out some corn. My golden retriever just loves to run along the fence—presumably to show who is boss—and cause them to scatter. After all the animals settle down, Holly just sits and watches the deer eat. It is a precious morning ritual.

As I watch the deer, I offer my praises up to my Father. He created these graceful, beautiful creatures with such precision. However, they are not household pets and I can't take care of each one of them. I throw out a little bit of corn, but it's hardly more than an enticement. The drought conditions are severe this spring of 2011 in the Hill Country, and these deer must search for water and food. Even though I live on a lake, the deer just can't walk down to the waters edge and get a drink. The water is a long ways down the steep, rocky cliffs.

Sometimes I feel like one of these thirsty deer as my soul pants for God, feeling separated from Him because of my sin. I depend on my Father, like the deer depend on water. They can't do anything about the drought, and I can't do anything apart from Him. However, I have the ability to go meet with my God and bask in His presence any time, anywhere—to quench my thirst and restore my soul.

It's a choice to trust and obey or live according to my sinful flesh. The deer have no promise of God's provisions, but I do. I can see the miracle of His creation and I know how important I am to Him. He gave me His Word and He gave His only Son for me. Why would I want to spend my days anywhere else but with my Creator, my Provider, my Redeemer?

March 6

Anyone, then, who knows the good he ought to do and doesn't do it, sins.—**James 4:17**

When we were younger, my two sisters and I used to joke about from whom we inherited our procrastination. All three of us did a great job of putting off until tomorrow what we knew should have been done that day. However, as we grew older, I excelled over the other two in being the master of procrastination.

Several years ago, it was revealed to me in one of my Bible studies that procrastination was a sin—a lack of self-control. That got my attention and I knew my tendency to put off was no longer a laughing matter. I wrestled even more with my actions (or delayed actions) because I had to admit my disobedience to God.

I made a conscious effort to make myself do something that I had at first decided could wait until the following day. I heard that small voice telling me not to allow my old habit to win over. I would think of the Nike slogan and say to myself, *Just Do It!*

Try as I might, I haven't been able to conquer this sin. Why do I think it is all right for me to keep on being blatantly disobedient to God? I tried to justify my actions as simply being a bad habit. Then God intervened to show me my iniquity through His perspective. He revealed His Word. I had seen the verse before. However, this time He wanted me to see it in relation to procrastination.

As He often does, God spoke to me through a daily devotion that began with James 4:17. "Anyone, then, who knows the good he ought to do and doesn't do it, sins." Mary Southerland's "Girlfriends in God" devotion was all about procrastination and it penetrated my soul with great force.

"We can learn to be good stewards of the time God has given us." Mary's words gave me hope—it's not too late to learn a good, holy habit. Besides convicting me that I am sinning when I intentionally avoid doing what is right by *not* doing it, the devotion also made me think of using the "moments" of my life wisely.

I just happened to be spending a few days accompanying my mother to Omaha, Nebraska, on our third trip so she could visit an ailing, aging friend. Talking with the two of them, I became even more sensitive to how important the moments of our life are—especially to someone like mom's friend who had seen a lifetime of them, and that day expressed regrets over missed opportunities.

When I procrastinate, I knowingly don't do something that should have been done. At that particular blimp in time, I wasted a moment that God intended for me to do the right thing. How many such moments have I wasted?

God has given me—and each of you—a specific number of minutes on this earth. Thanks to the Internet, I don't have to be a mathematician to figure out the number I have been alive as of this date—there is a website that will do the calculations for me. I determined, as I wrote this sentence, I have been alive 29,932,185 minutes. What was spooky was that I could look at those numbers in months, days, minutes, seconds and milliseconds and could literally watch the seconds clicking by.

God is looking at those seconds of my life too. How am I spending the time He has given me? If I am not doing what I ought to be doing, I am wasting His time that He so generously allotted. Every minute, every second, matters.

I spoke with a few of my godly friends about this issue. They concurred that I am being too hard on myself. I don't think so. I feel the Holy Spirit pushing me very hard on this.

Oh, Heavenly Father, by the blood of Jesus shed for my sins, I ask You to help me kick this enemy, procrastination, out of my life once and for all. I can't get back the moments I have wasted, but with Your help, I will be a better steward of Your precious gift of time for the future. Amen!

March 7

I praise you because I am fearfully and wonderfully made; you works are wonderful. I know that full well.
—Psalm 139:14

As my 59th birthday quickly approached, I wondered where the decade had gone. I loved my 50s—the kids graduated from college and began their careers; I stopped working and was able to be more involved in church. Life was good, so I decided to have a "Fun, Fantastic Farewell to the 50s" year.

I was going to learn something new every month and have some great adventures. I told some people about my plans, but what I didn't tell anyone about was my visit to the plastic surgeon. I'm not going to write about the pros and cons of plastic surgery. That is a personal choice. But I do want to tell you how God and I have continuous daily conversations and how He directed my life.

I booked my surgery right before my 59th birthday and told only my husband and my walking partner. However, when I went for my pre-op appointment, a few red flags flew up. I found out the surgery would be an hour longer than discussed and the cost was about $2,000 more than had been quoted. When I inquired about this, the doctor's assistant said that had never happened before. They had simply given me the wrong price. I told her I would have to think about it.

I have always said "when in doubt, wait," so after thinking about the situation, I canceled the surgery. Then I threw a big pity party because I was disappointed that my plans had not worked out. The next morning during our walk, I told my partner about the whole ordeal. On the way down my street, I was still quite upset, but I heard the words, "You are beautifully and wonderfully made." I thought it was strange for that thought to come to me. Then I heard the words two more times. I finally understood that the Holy Spirit was speaking to me.

When I arrived back at my front door, I found a present from a friend that had to have been delivered very early while I was walking. My friend thanked me for being such a "beautiful" friend to her that year. Instantly, I understood what God was trying to say to me, and I thanked Him for His loving care and asked forgiveness for my attitude. I knew canceling the surgery was the right thing to do.

The next day, my best friend's husband went into the hospital. He died that week. I was able to be with her at his deathbed and support her during the next week. That was the beginning of weekly funerals of close friends and family members for the next two months. Every week for eight weeks, someone died—ending with the death of my mother-in-law. If I would have had my surgery, I would not have been available during this time. I thanked God for His perfect timing.

I continued on with my "Fun, Fantastic Farewell to the 50s." I learned to shoot a pistol, took fly-fishing lessons, learned to make homemade pasta, and took some great trips. But during several conversations in the spring, another doctor's name kept coming up. So one day, I decided that God might have just been protecting me from the first doctor and maybe He really didn't close the door to the notion of plastic surgery. How easy it is to justify our own fleshy thoughts.

Please stay tuned for the continuation of my "Fun, Fantastic Farewell to the 50s." Tomorrow I will share with you how God's plan for my life took an interesting twist.

KH
Austin, TX

March 8

Those that look to him are radiant; their faces are never covered with shame. —**Psalm 34:5**

Yesterday, I wrote about my plans to visit the plastic surgeon prior to my 60th birthday, but canceled my appointment. After learning of a new doctor, and justifying that God had simply been protecting me from the first one, I made an appointment with the new surgeon. Surgery was scheduled for November 30, still before my 60th birthday. However, this time I did not tell anyone—not even my husband.

For the last couple of years, my husband had been talking about having surgery for a spinal fusion but said he was not ready yet, so I actually forgot about it. He was avoiding the surgery because it would involve about six weeks of recovery in a neck brace. He would not be able to drive, which meant I would be his driver and caretaker. One day, he told me he had seen his neurosurgeon, who recommended surgery and booked it for November 15.

Instantly, I thought, *How could his surgery be November 15 when I have my elective surgery booked for November 30? I can't have surgery if I'm taking care of him.*

This time I understood that God was telling me not to have the surgery, so I canceled the procedure. I thanked God for His loving care and for speaking so clearly to me. The next morning, my devotion in *Jesus Calling* said, "Instead of trying to 'fix' yourself, fix your gaze on Me. . . . Remember that I see you clothed in my righteousness, radiant in my perfect Love." I was so thankful that Jesus provided such a perfect message for me.

Soon after that, there was a meeting at church with women contemplating having plastic surgery, and I saw the struggles these beautiful ladies were going through. I was reminded of Psalm 139:14, which God had spoken to me months before—"We are all beautifully and wonderfully made." I also thought of "We are made in God's image" (Genesis 1:27) and "Those that look to him are radiant" (Psalm 34:5). With God's truths in my heart, I was able to share my story with them.

In the next few days, a friend sent me a picture of herself in the bathroom of a local restaurant. She was standing in front of a big conversation bubble that said, "I am beautiful, just as I am." I have even thought of making a sign like that for my bathroom mirror so I would read it every morning. In fact, I often say that to myself when I see the commercials for instant-beauty procedures, like a facelift during your lunch hour.

There is one final part to this story. When my husband went in for his pre-op appointment for his spinal fusion the first of November, the neurosurgeon said he had reviewed his MRI and decided that he did not need surgery at this time after all. He was told to come back in a year! This time, I just laughed at how often I make plans, but God is definitely in control.

Well, I turned 60 and had a fabulous year. I look forward to what God has in store for me this decade. I am so thankful for what He taught me during this plastic-surgery experience though. First of all, God's timing is perfect and I must trust Him. Second, I need to keep my focus on Him through daily conversations so that I will see His direction for my life. And most importantly, I am radiant in His eyes, made to worship and following His leading.

Before you go out into the world today, I ask that you ponder the following verse from 1 Peter 3:3-4: "Your beauty should not come from outward adornment, such as braided hair and the wearing of gold jewelry and fine clothes. Instead, it should be that of your inner self, the unfading beauty of a gentle and quiet spirit, which is of great worth in God's sight."

Praise God and remember that you are beautiful, just as you are.

KH
Austin, TX

March 9

*"For I am the L*ord*, your God, who takes hold of your right hand and says to you, Do not fear; I will help you."*
—Isaiah 41:13

I certainly hope you read the two previous stories written by my very dear friend, Karen. If by chance you got behind and missed those days, please go back and look over them. It's really important to read hers before you can follow this one.

Soon after I met Karen in our small group at Bible study, she spoke of her plastic-surgery experience. Then a few months later she was a speaker at the women's retreat and shared it again. In an age when there is a lot of nipping and tucking going on, and even more ladies just in the contemplating stage, I am sure there were some women in attendance (myself included) who found her story to be extremely thought-provoking.

As Karen wrote in her story, her purpose wasn't to give pros and cons of plastic surgery. She wanted to show how God, no matter how much we try to plan our days, is the one in control. Her story was such a clear example of how God steered her in one direction regarding her plastic surgery while her flesh wanted to go the opposite way. Karen wrote, "I need to keep my focus on Him through daily conversations so that I will see His direction for my life." Yes, all too often we want to go our own way.

In the second part of Karen's story she also wrote, "I turned 60 and had a fabulous year. I look forward to what God has in store for me this decade. I am so thankful for what He taught me during this plastic-surgery experience though. First of all, God's timing is perfect and I must trust Him."

Karen decided against going under the knife for a face lift, but about a year and half after she wrote that story she found herself in the operating room. Oh, this wasn't an elective surgery. No, this procedure was necessary to remove a lump in her breast. A lump that proved to be malignant. A diagnosis that would require 52 weeks of chemo. Talk about life taking an interesting twist!

As I write this story, Karen has only had two weeks of treatments. However, I can't even begin to tell you in this small space what God is accomplishing through Karen. (That might just possibly be another book in itself.) It's hard to acknowledge that a cancer diagnosis is God's perfect timing, but Karen said it about her plastic surgery experience and she will tell you her cancer diagnosis was indeed His perfect timing too.

The other day at lunch she said, "Why not me and why not now? At least I don't have small children to care for or a job to go to. I have a loving, caring husband who is capable of cooking and cleaning and will be there for me every step of the way. Plus we have health insurance so this won't be a financial crisis." In addition, she has made other upbeat comments: She will save money at the beauty shop this year—no need for highlights.

Did God take her through the plastic surgery experience to help her realize she was beautiful in His eyes just as she is? Was He equipping her with a confidence, courage and strength (that surpasses all understanding) to not fear or worry or stumble in her faith? No effects of cancer or chemo can "change the unfading beauty of a gentle and quiet spirit, which is of great worth in God's sight" (1 Peter 3:4).

Quoting from her story yesterday, "I just laugh at how often I make plans, but God is definitely in control." Of course Karen has shed some tears, but she has accepted God's path for her life. Several weeks before her diagnosis, Karen had the words of Isaiah 41:13 placed on her heart. Over and over she heard the whispers, *Do not fear*. This new decade might not be starting off the way she planned, but it's exactly what was on God's agenda. She will endure 52 weeks of chemo, not by her own strength but through that of the Father Almighty, trusting He is indeed holding her right hand.

March 10

I know, O L$_{ORD}$, that a man's life is not his own; it is not for man to direct his steps.—**Jeremiah 10:23**

I have always had a problem with directions. I can easily get turned around when driving. My husband, on the other hand, seems to have a built-in compass. He was born and raised in Houston, and I think he knows every street in the city. If there is a road closed for construction or a wreck (which happens daily in Houston), he knows how to get around it.

Sometimes when we are in the car together, I might ask him why he is taking a particular route to wherever we are going. He politely listens to my babble, then I catch myself. Who am I to be questioning him on directions?

I am well aware of my deficiency in this area. The GPS navigation on my cell phone has been a lifesaver. I just love hearing that sweet voice tell me exactly how to get to my destination. Before that great invention, MapQuest was my major source of obtaining turn-by-turn instructions. Way back in the dark ages, the ancient key map was my go-to source.

However, it's not just while driving that I can get turned around. When I walk out of an elevator, I don't know if I should turn to my left or right. When going into a building for the first few times, I must make a mental picture of where I have entered so I can find my way back to my car. Pretty pitiful, isn't it?

I have learned to compensate for my poor sense of direction so that I don't get lost when going from place to place, and it is a very concentrated effort. Before heading out in my car to a new destination, I make sure I have specific driving instructions. However, why is it that I think I can get through this intricate existence known as life without a helping hand?

Oh, I seek God off and on throughout my day, but not all the time. It's extremely easy for me to cruise through, relying on my own sense of direction when making decisions—and based on how easily I get lost, that's a very scary thought.

I start my day with great intentions. I lie in bed, talking to God, asking Him to direct my steps, asking for His will to be done in my life. But once I get caught up in the busyness of my day, I start to rely on my own judgment. If I can't drive to a new location without my GPS, how do I think I can get through a new day without my God?

There has been much progress in my daily dependence on my Heavenly Father. I think of His Words of Truth when I hear Satan knocking at my door. I find myself praying many times during the day for His guidance in my particular situation. I ask for His help to control my mouth and my temper, to give me patience and the right words to say—wisdom to know when to wait and peace when uneasy or worried. However, I have such along way to go.

I would never consider leaving home without my GPS to navigate me on a new driving excursion. My God Positioning System is always with me on my journey through life. It's my loss that I forget to use the 24-hour access that He has promised. God has my whole life mapped out, with all the correct turns and roads to follow. All I have to do is simply ask my Navigator for directions.

Oh, Heavenly Father, thank You for Your unconditional love and constant provision. I give You all the praise and glory that I am growing in my dependence on You— slowly, but surely, I am learning that this life is not my own and You are in control. I pray for wisdom to seek Your guidance daily, minute by minute, instead of trying to navigate through this new day by myself. Taking the words from Carrie Underwood's song, I cry out, "Jesus, take the wheel 'cause I can't do it on my own." Amen!

March 11

Ears that hear and eyes that see—the Lᴏʀᴅ has made them both.—**Proverbs 20:12**

It was going to be a busy Sunday. When the alarm went off, I needed to linger in bed for a few minutes of alone time with my Father.

God might not have gifted me with a tolerable singing voice, but He did give me a love for a wide variety of music. One of the many ways God speaks to me that I seem to notice the most frequently is through songs. On this particular morning, He was at it again.

As I was trying to focus on praying, the Holy Spirit, began singing to me. It was one of my favorites—"From the Inside Out," written by Joel Houston and originally recorded by Hillsong.

What a great way to start the day! To be serenaded by the Spirit of God. I don't think the Holy Spirit forgot the words, but all I kept on hearing were the same lyrics over and over—*I give you control, consume me from the inside out.*

Hillsong must have also been on the worship team's mind because the first song that Sunday morning was "Blessed," written by Ginny Owens and Cindy Morgan, and recorded by Hillsong. *Hear our prayer oh, Lord, God Almighty. Come Bless our land as we seek You.* Haven't I been praying for several years for the Lord to bring the rain and heal this drought-stricken land? Don't my husband and I pray every night for our nation and our leaders, for economic recovery and rebirthing of God back into our society? Oh, He does hear my prayers, and now the whole congregation is asking Him to bless our land.

Knowing that God is the ultimate Worship Leader, I was simply overwhelmed that He picked such a perfect song for all of us to sing. Oh, please, Lord Jesus, bless our land.

I am not the only one who becomes emotional during our praise and worship. Many times after church, as I talk to a friend or say hello to a new face, I see some black mascara smeared under her eyes. Yes, the music gets to lots of us girls. And this morning was just one of those mornings.

There weren't any Kleenex in my purse and the tears were flowing freely. However, when the next song started, the tears stopped just as quickly as they started and the laughter began. *A thousand times I've failed, still your mercy remains.* In case you don't know, that's the first line of "From the Inside Out."

Mornings like that—times when God just goes out of His way to fill me with love songs—I am overwhelmed with joy. He knows how to tug at my heartstrings, how to bring me to tears and back to laughter. He let me feel just how indescribable it is to be consumed from the inside out with His love.

No wonder I kept on hearing those same words over and over before I got out of bed that morning. *I give You control, consume me from the inside out.* God was preparing me for what was to come later at church. I had to relinquish control and allow my Father into my heart. How can He consume me from the inside out if I don't allow Him in in the first place?

The art of losing myself in bringing You praise, more lyrics from the song, was exactly what happened as I sang my heart to God. I find myself holding back so often, afraid to let go and let God have His way with me. Not that morning. Not after all He went through to get my attention.

Does God know your love language? Of course He does! The question really becomes: Do we know how to listen and observe when He's reaching out to us? If you don't feel you and God are communicating well, ask Him for discernment to hear that small voice of the Holy Spirit that lives within you. Ask for eyes to see His glory all around you. He is there, just waiting to be noticed. You don't want to miss Him.

March 12

For thus says the One who is high and lifted up, who inhabits eternity, whose name is Holy: "I dwell in the high and holy place, and also with him who is of a contrite and lowly spirit, to revive the spirit of the lowly, and to revive the heart of the contrite."—Isaiah 57:15

An old college roommate confided recently that she had hit rock bottom. Well, she didn't just confide in me, but rather to the masses that are "out there." She is a blogger, a writer—one seeking to influence the world through her observations and insights. Her wit is catchy, her intellect sharp, but as she attested, her life was broken.

Self-employed for two years, things weren't working out like she hoped. Until this point, her life had been a long litany of outward success. And when she hit a crossroads in the past, she would make a major change to shake things up: a move or a new job. But this time, instead of seeking to vary her environs, she realized that it was she who needed to change. *Brava.* This dear friend's honesty surprised me.

Brokenness has a way of leveling the playing field. It's a good place to be. No matter what has driven you to the end of yourself, it has the power to capture your attention. It's a place where you can finally surrender the vestiges of yourself.

But this is the point at which my friend and I diverge. Her path is not one of faith in her Creator but rather of faith in herself. Her solution is to look inward, not upward, to pull herself up by her bootstraps and try harder. "Come to me, all who labor and are heavy laden, and I will give you rest" (Matthew 11:28).

She had decided to read positive affirmations to start each day, believing meditating on them long and hard enough will make them true in her life, leading her to success. "But his delight is in the law of the LORD, and on his law he meditates day and night" (Psalm 1:2). David wrote in Psalm 19 that it is the law of the Lord that revives the soul; it is His precepts that rejoice the heart. He wrote from a position of personal brokenness in Psalm 51 that the Lord doesn't delight in sacrifices—He doesn't want or need our self-effort. What the Lord desires is a broken spirit and a contrite heart.

As I read her blog, I was struck by the inadequacy of my friend's efforts to improve herself, and I was reminded that it is the Gospel that is the power of God for salvation. She is seeking positive people and thoughts to influence her toward fulfillment and success. While she may reform some of her habits, there will never be true transformation apart from the Lord.

I applaud her longing for change; I grieve her shunning the very One who is able to give her the desire of her heart. Oh, that she would see, *that I would see and know*, that He who dwells in the high and holy place also dwells with him who is of a contrite and lowly spirit.

Carrie Runn
Austin, TX

March 13

"You did not choose me, but I chose you and appointed you to go and bear fruit—fruit that will last. Then the Father will give you whatever you ask in my name."—**John 15:16**

The radio was playing as I drove to the airport, but I wasn't listening closely. However, my ears tuned in at one point and I heard the words "fly to Jesus and live." (From Chris Rice's "Come To Jesus.") I thought those words were quite appropriate for my journey that day. Yes, I would literally be flying in a matter of hours. And, I would be going up in His direction.

Mom and I were headed to Omaha, Nebraska, to visit her friend. It also just happened to be Spring Break, and many families and college kids were taking the week off. When we arrived, the terminal at Houston Intercontinental was packed!

There was a group of young people wearing matching T-shirts hanging out at our gate. On their backs were these words: *Today is a Day of Serving—John 15:16*. I naturally assumed they were a Christian group, most likely returning from or going on a mission trip.

Thirty-four students from Northwestern College in Orange City, Iowa, were returning from a 10-day service trip. (Their Spring Break had been the week before.) They were not the least bit worn out either. Oh my goodness, they were on fire for the Lord! They were full of laughter, joy and fun! The whole plane was electric with their energy.

There was so much chatter once we became airborne that the flight attendant politely asked everyone to please be quiet as the safety instructions were announced. There was immediate silence on that plane! Those college kids were so respectful and obedient. Once finished, she announced that everyone could get back to "partying," which they promptly did.

The young man across the aisle had a green rubber bracelet with "Hebrews 12:11" on it. Another male a few rows up was reading a book on prayer. I heard their conversations, explaining to the passengers in the adjoining seat about their trip. There were hugs and high-fives and endless smiles. I thought of the words to the song I heard that morning. I wasn't flying *to* Jesus—He was there with me in each of those students.

I had never heard of this college, so when I had the opportunity, I went to the website. Quoting from the mission statement, "Northwestern College is a Christian academic community engaging students in courageous and faithful learning that empowers them to follow Christ and pursue God's redeeming work in the world." I also read that during the break, 200 faculty and students were sent to 13 different sites for service projects. With an enrollment of only 1,200, that is an impressive number.

I reflected on the verse noted on their T-shirts. Those young leaders had been chosen and appointed by the Lord to go out and bear fruit, the kind of fruit that would last. Not only did they do that on their mission trip, but they continued during the flight home. They were examples of Jesus with skin, and there was no doubt Who these kids served and Who held their hearts.

On this trip to Omaha, Jesus was alive in folks everywhere! It was so exciting to see Him working in and through so many, not just the group from Northwestern. What is even better, I know those I observed, those who had been called to bear fruit, had no clue that I was watching. God placed these people in my path so I could share how they touched my life—and He was glorified! Certainly they had no idea they would be the main characters in some daily devotion.

March 14

Be wise in the way you act toward outsiders; make the most of every opportunity. Let your conversation be always full of grace, seasoned with salt, so that you may know how to answer everyone.—**Colossians 4:5-6**

Yesterday, I wrote about the delightful flight from Houston to Omaha with the students from Northwestern College. They were returning home after a 10-day service project, and they were overflowing with love for the Lord. But they weren't the only ones on the plane who God chose and appointed to bear fruit—He showed me two more.

There seems to be much talk these days of how prevalent infidelity is among married couples, especially with spouses who travel. Some seem to think that no one sees their behavior when they are away from home. Possibly no one but God!

Sitting behind me and across the aisle were two married men. Both of them were sitting beside a student from Northwestern. Both of the students were very talkative, more than anxious to discuss their trip, and get to know their seat companion. I actually think they were hoping to witness to anyone who might not be a believer.

Please don't think I am an eavesdropper, but I couldn't help but overhear these conversations. I didn't listen intently to every word, but I did catch much of the discussions. The young man behind me was flying home after being away for four days. It was his first time to be away from his 6-month-old son and he couldn't wait to get back home to hold him, and his wife.

He had pictures on his phone to share with the college student and stories to tell about his precious baby. He couldn't stop talking about his wife and son. I thought of a recent sermon when my pastor spoke of the temptations faced by traveling spouses. This man didn't fall into that category. He was testifying to the unmarried student that husbands can be faithful and stand firm in their marriage vows. They also talked about God and their churches.

The man across the aisle had been married a little longer and had two children. He traveled extensively with his job and was honest with the young college kid about the strain of being gone so much. However, he too knew God and wanted to be obedient. I was so thankful I had the opportunity to hear those two men proclaim their commitments to their spouses and children. Most importantly, they served as positive examples to the unmarried students.

Here the ones working in the mission field, away from home, were being ministered to on their flight back home. How sweet of God to bless those two with seat companions who were equipped to express their love of God and family.

Seeing Jesus in these people was what I found so exciting. I hear so much about the demise of God in our society and the decline in morals and values. I know the world is full of sin and deceit. However, I was on a plane of God's chosen children—chosen to bear fruit. I honestly felt like I was flying with angels!

We never know who is listening to our conversations and what an impact our words can make on someone else. But God knows and He will use us and He will also place us in the perfect situation to do His work.

It was no accident those folks sat beside each other and that I sat close enough to hear their conversations. The married gentlemen sharing the importance of a Godly marriage to two single students, giving me the opportunity to retell the incident—for the purpose of giving God the glory!

As you go through your day, think about the words from today's Scripture. How will God use you today in your conversation and encounters with others? Like with the two married men on the plane, you will never know who is listening and retelling your story. Who knows, your words and actions might even be recounted in someone's book.

March 15

You were taught, with regard to your former way of life, to put off your old self, which is being corrupted by its deceitful desires; to be made new in the attitude of your minds; and to put on the new self, created to be like God in true righteousness and holiness.—**Ephesians 4:22-24**

The week that mom and I spent in Omaha during Spring Break of 2012 was delightful. On this particular gorgeous spring day, Mom was with her friend, and I had the afternoon to myself. I walked across the street from my hotel to the quaint, historic Old Market area to eat lunch.

I stopped in at a little bakery/deli where I had eaten the last time I was in Omaha. The lunch crowd was long gone, with only one other occupied table. Soon after I ordered, two young girls were seated in a booth near by. They might have been old enough to be in college. They were dressed like typical students—shorts, tank tops and flip-flops—and looked darling.

The waiter brought my salad in only a matter of minutes. I bowed my head, ever so slightly, and said a hurried blessing. They received their order quickly as well. Why was I surprised when they bowed their heads to pray? Did I assume I was the only holy person in the room?

The one facing me began the prayer—out loud. I couldn't hear what she was saying, but I knew it wasn't silent. Nor was it speedy like mine. She talked to God much longer than I did and with great passion and joy. The expression on her face was intense. The time spent with God was important to her and He was worthy of her best.

Here were two more people God had placed in my path during this trip to Omaha. Two people chosen by Him to bear fruit. Two young girls to show me how special a prayer should be. If I was touched by this sweet young lady and her sincere reverence to God, how must the Almighty One have felt?

They were unaware that I had been blessed by their blessing that afternoon. I was not only humbled by their prayer time, but I was also encouraged. For the previous two days, God had been making sure I saw reminders of His presence through the actions of His chosen ones.

God is alive in so many. His presence is so real, but how often do I fail to notice Him in people? It's easy to see God in a sunrise or sunset or in the beauty of nature. But do I see Him as others perform random acts of kindness or say words of encouragement—or simply go about their daily lives?

If we were created in God's image (Genesis 1:27), I should be seeing a glimpse of God in everyone. Too often I just fail to notice. Paul reminds us in Ephesians 4:22-24 of our new selves, created to be like God in true righteousness and holiness. I want to recognize those attributes of God in others. It is obviously something He wants me to see also. He used that little Spring Break trip to set me up with His appointed children, as they filled my life with His spiritual fruit.

Two young girls, going for an innocent lunch on a sunny afternoon in Omaha. Do you think they had any idea I watched them pray, then wrote a story about how God spoke to me through *their* actions?

March 16

"In the same way, let your light shine before men, that they may see your good deeds and praise your Father in heaven."—**Matthew 5:16**

Spring Break 2012 in Omaha was over, and it was time for Mom and I to leave and head back to Texas. I prefer to leave for the airport plenty early. Arriving two hours before departure is my idea of perfect timing.

Eppley Airfield in Omaha must be one of the most convenient airports in the United States. It is only a 10-minute drive from downtown (where our hotel was located), the rental car lot is directly across the street from the terminal and I have never waited in line to check my bags or get through security.

On this morning, Mom and I were ready to leave the hotel three hours before the flight. For once in my life, even I thought it was way too early. Mom was the antsy one, and I finally gave in.

Sure enough, it took 10 minutes to drive there. We got the rental car checked in and it was still two and a half hours before the scheduled departure. We walked into the terminal, expecting to proceed directly to the check-in counter with our bags. But wait. What is the deal with all the people? There must have been 75 waiting in two very disorganized lines—all in front of our airline carrier's counters.

Asking around, I found out that two earlier flights had been cancelled and all those folks needed to be re-routed. Two airlines carriers had recently merged and that very morning was the day they went from two computers to one. Apparently all the kinks hadn't been worked out and airports around the country were experiencing problems.

In Omaha, there just aren't that many flights coming in and out of Eppley to accommodate two extra planeloads of displaced folks. Second, there weren't enough live bodies behind the counters to handle the situation. The airline personnel didn't have control and the crowd was restless.

As I stood in the line that seemed to be going nowhere, I looked around. Most everyone appeared anxious, agitated or disgusted. But someone stood out in the crowd—the man casually reading his Bible.

He actually had a pleasant, peaceful expression on his face and didn't seem the least bit concerned about the large crowd standing around. Then I noticed others looking at him too. Some were trying to camouflage their pointing fingers and their nonchalant whispers, but I also saw sweet, thankful smiles.

I was thankful because his actions prompted me to re-evaluate my attitude and reaction to the confusion. What a wonderful example this man was for all to see. Where else should we turn when our plans don't quite go our way?

Perhaps the airline personnel had lost control of the crowd and were not prepared for the task of helping all those displaced passengers—but not God. He is always in control, and nothing is a surprise to Him. He was also right there in line with us in the form of one gentleman, reading his Bible, in the middle of utter chaos.

By the way, Mom and I managed to bypass all of those stranded passengers who needed to speak with a live person to find other flights to their destinations. Because of modern technology and self-check-in, we were able to get our bags checked and arrive at the gate with a full hour to spare.

March 17

The LORD your God is with you, he is mighty to save. He will take great delight in you, he will quiet you with his love, he will rejoice over you with singing.—**Zephaniah 3:17**

Sometimes God has a way of placing a verse on my heart, and Zephaniah 3:17 was one of those. I was first introduced to it through a homework question in a fall Bible study lesson. We were asked to select our favorite Scripture that spoke of God's love for us. One of the ladies read this particular one and a few of the others had the same verse. Not me. I had never heard it before.

First, I had to find Zephaniah in the Old Testament. After reading 3:17 several times, the words penetrated my soul. How much more would a girl want from a relationship? I had this vision of God as a mighty warrior by my side, ready to fight for my heart and soul. I felt total acceptance, knowing that He delights in me, exactly as I am. I could feel His loving fingers stroking my head, to relax me, calming my fears and filling me with His peace. Then, because of His desire to win my heart, He would burst out in a song, just for me! To have it resonate that God would sing to me was overwhelming.

I recall one of the praise songs we sing to God, "Mighty to Save," written by Ben Fielding and Rueben Morgan and recorded at Hillsong Church in Australia. I wonder if they were wowed by the words from this verse too. If you don't know the song, you can listen to it on YouTube. I can't get the song out of my mind now and simply thinking of the title helps me remember the verse.

The following spring in Bible study, Zephaniah 3:17 was referenced in Beth Moore's *Stepping Up: A Journey Through the Psalms of Ascent*. She wanted to emphasize the Psalms as being songs, but also point out other verses that referenced singing. More specifically, God singing. Once again, that mental picture of God singing a praise song over me touched my heart and soul, sending goose bumps all over.

The day *after* the Beth Moore video, the key verse in one of my daily devotionals was Zephaniah 3:17. OK, God, I get the message. This is another one You want me to remember. How did I go all these years and never hear such tender words of love?

Besides being a day to focus on Zephaniah 3:17, I just remembered it is also St. Patrick's Day. In case you don't know the story behind all the green you are seeing today, I will give you a three-sentence history lesson. In 432, Saint Patrick said that he was called by God to bring Christianity to the Irish. Folklore claims that one of his teaching methods included using the shamrock (a three-leaved green plant, not to be confused with a clover) to explain the doctrine of the Trinity to the pagan Irish people. He died on March 17, 461, thus the celebration on this date.

I personally don't do anything special for St. Patrick's Day, nor am I wearing anything green today. However, I am wearing a smile knowing my Lord God intentionally placed this verse on my heart. In obedience to Him, I will memorize this Scripture. I can use St. Patrick's Day as a helpful tool. (Work with me here.) When I think of the three-leaved shamrock and St. Patrick's Day being 3/17, maybe my mind will think of the three words *mighty to save* in Zephaniah 3:17. That should at least get me started. If you don't already know this verse, let's see if this little trick helps you too.

March 18

And I pray that you, being rooted and established in love, may have power, together with all the saints, to grasp how wide and long and high and deep is the love of Christ, and to know this love that surpasses knowledge—that you may be filled to the measure of all the fullness of God.—**Ephesians 3:17-19**

One of the sweetest days of my life was March 18, 2010. That was the day my precious grandson Ryen Jr. came into this world. With the first glimpse of that tiny little baby, I knew my heart was forever changed!

Since that day, I've had many wonderful times with him. One memory that rises to the top of the list was when he was about a year old and just learning to walk. My extended family had gathered for a big dinner. Afterwards, all the ladies were settled into the living room chatting while little Ryen sat on the floor playing with his toys. All of a sudden he stood up, steadied himself and started to take a step forward.

Immediately, all four of us ladies widely stretched out our arms towards him and simultaneously said, "Come to me!" Ryen looked a bit confused, but started walking toward one of my sisters who was standing closest to him. He had almost reached her arms when he heard my voice coming from the other side of her saying, "Ryen, come to me! Come to Gigi!"

He glanced over towards me and when his eyes met mine, he turned and wobbled those chubby little legs right over to *me*! Oh, what joy filled my soul! It was a wonderful feeling as I scooped him into my arms and told him how much I loved him!

In reality, I knew why Ryen Jr. had come to me. It was because he knew me better. He recognized the sound of my voice. He remembered the love and warmth he'd found in my arms before. We had a closer bond because of all that time we'd spent together. But it was still a precious moment!

That very next Sunday, I was in church, praising God in worship. It was one of those times that I felt so close to the Lord. We were singing "Forever Reign," as recorded by Hillsong. As I sang the words in the chorus, *Oh, I'm running to Your arms, I'm running to Your arms*, that scene of Ryen Jr. running to me flashed in my mind. Once again, that incredible joy flooded over me. And that's about the time when I sensed the Lord whisper clearly to my heart, *That's how I feel when you come to me.*

Tears rolled down my face as I lifted up a sweet "Thank You, Lord" and sang with a renewed heart. Yes, Lord, I want to run to Your arms and be filled to the measure with Your love, because *nothing compares to Your embrace.*

Teresa Maldonado
Austin, TX

March 19

If one falls down, his friends can help him up, but pity the man who falls and has no one to help him up! —**Ecclesiastes 4:10**

I love this season of life I am in right now. I have been an Empty Nester for eight years now, so I feel I should be beyond referring to it in those terms. I am not a grandmother yet, but am anxiously awaiting that stage. So, exactly where am I in life? I like it, but I don't know what to call it.

When my sons were young, life was fast and furious. I worked outside of the home, yet still managed to be involved with their activities. I was blessed with an exceptional childcare giver who made it all possible. Her assistance made a tremendous difference in those hours after work until bedtime. However, I had little time for anything else. Close friendships with other women just never developed. If I didn't know "her" through sports or a school activity, the relationship wasn't ever going to happen.

It wasn't until I moved to Lake Travis in Austin and my youngest was in his second year at the University of Texas and my oldest about to graduate from LSU that I learned how special "girlfriends" could be. Without kiddos to open the door to a social outlet, I was forced to venture out and make friends, all on my own.

I started at my church. Through Bible studies, I met the most incredible women, forming some godly, transparent relationships. Through small groups, the women with whom I was sharing life became role models and sources of inspiration and wisdom. For the first time since my high school days, I found just how special girlfriends could be.

One day I was particularly distraught about my sons. I want nothing more than for my boys to walk with Jesus—for Him to be their Lord and Savior. They used to be seekers and followers, but not during this time of their life. I understood where they were because, unfortunately, I walked their same path at their age. That's why I was so concerned. I didn't want them to do as I did and live in years of darkness and despair. I want my sons to have the joy of Jesus *now*. My friend Teresa sensed my feelings of helplessness and reached out. She gave me a book to read, *The Power of Praying for Your Adult Children*, by Stormie Omartian.

Teresa realized I was down and needed encouragement. She had read the book and knew it would be helpful. I can assure you, it was exactly what I needed! My dear Father used Teresa to give me just the right tool to guide me through my difficult time. Omartian's words of wisdom gave me hope and a plan of action through more meaningful prayers. However, if Teresa hadn't been my friend and knew the intimate details, would she have been so bold as to give me a book to read? Would she have dared to speak such truths and share her own journey through a similar situation?

Dear Father, thank You for this season of life. Thank You for the time to form relationships with godly women and for the women You have placed in my path here in Austin. What a special gift, that You provided a sweet friend to pick me up when I was down. I look forward with anticipation every day to what You have in store for me in this season. Amen!

March 20

Now all glory to God, who is able, through his mighty power at work within us, to accomplish infinitely more than we might ask or think. —**Ephesians 3:20 (NLT)**

My husband and I went to early church, and then planned to run some errands before our LifeGroup met after the second service. However, before we left the sanctuary, Austin was asked to stay and usher because someone had just called in sick.

During the second service I decided to visit a women's LifeGroup. Walking into the room, I looked around for a good friend of mine who attended regularly. Not seeing her, I sat at the first empty seat I came to. The sun was glaring straight through a large window right at my chair. It was seriously blinding.

A few of the ladies at the other tables motioned for me to come join them so I wouldn't be in that bright sunlight. I couldn't see a thing because of the glare, but I also felt compelled to stay there. I squinted; I shaded my eyes, but felt no urge to move.

The visitors in the room were introduced and one woman at my table was welcomed back after being gone for a while. She was with her daughter and both were strikingly pretty. I just assumed the teenage daughter had been dragged to church against her will though because she didn't look very happy and the mom looked a bit stressed. Teenagers can do that to a mom.

After the lecture, we had table discussions. Our table leader asked each of us questions, but purposely skipped the mother and daughter. We all had a lively discussion, but I was puzzled why those two were not engaged in the conversation. Out of the blue, or so I thought, I asked the young girl how old she was.

Next, I asked what high school she attended. The school she mentioned was completely across town and didn't have the best reputation. Then I quizzed the mom about other family members. When I heard the ages and the where-abouts of the kiddos, I decided it was a blended family of some sort.

The high school years can be difficult for young girls with all the peer pressures to be pretty, thin and popular. Soon all the ladies at the table were talking to this teenager and filling her with praises and encouragement. We were all Empty Nesters and also shared helpful advice with the young mom.

Monday, I received a call from the table leader. While I felt blessed to receive a call from my very special friend, I wondered what she wanted with me. The purpose of the call was for her to thank me. Before I could even ask for what, she explained. She knew that mother and daughter very well, and because she knew their story, didn't want to make them feel uncomfortable by asking them questions. She was just thankful they were at church.

The story was a tragic one and because I wasn't a regular in that LifeGroup, I was unaware of it. The mom (and dad) had spent years in and out of prison, and the young girl spent most of her life in foster homes, only recently being reunited with her parents. They looked like any other people at my church, and I never would have imagined the magnitude of struggles they face everyday. And I had bombarded them with one question after another?

The family was desperately trying to fit the broken pieces of their lives back together and my friend was actively involved, but had been praying for others to lavish some godly attention and love on that precious young girl.

The purpose of the call was to thank me for reaching out to the mom and daughter.

I explained the story behind my attending that LifeGroup in the first place. I didn't know why I couldn't move out of the sun to another table or why I blurted out those questions. But we both knew Who had orchestrated the events of that Sunday morning.

God sent me to that LifeGroup, kept me in that sunny seat, had me initiate dialogue and allowed all of us to pour out our love and encouragement on some broken, shattered hearts. Then to top it off, He led me to Ephesians 3:20—just to remind me that He works behind the scenes more than we could ever imagine. Today just happens to be 3/20. Perhaps His purpose is to put Ephesians 3:20 in my memory bank.

By the way, the daughter is helping with the special needs children at church and is blossoming. Indeed, all glory goes to God!

March 21

Many are the plans in a man's heart, but it is the Lord's purpose that prevails.—**Proverbs 19:21**

In June 2010, our lives were full, busy and good in Austin. We loved our home, friends, church, and were very involved. We had even just begun leading a wonderful small group of families a few months earlier from our church. As the group started meeting, my husband boldly asked the couples present to commit to two years of meeting on a regular basis so we could all effectively live life, and learn and grow spiritually together for an extended period of time.

Funny how things can change—very quickly. My husband stumbled upon a new job opportunity that would take us nearly 2,000 miles away. This would be many miles away from my oldest son and his wife and my youngest son (all still living in Texas). But it would also take us much closer to my husband's widowed mother in New Jersey and to a part of the country we've always loved.

Within just a few weeks, it was final. The Lord was telling us to go. How did we know? Every detail of the job and move fell into place seamlessly. In the middle of a recession, our home sold in less than a week. The job was perfectly suited to my husband's talents and experience. We pulled into a small town north of Charlotte, with our little U-Haul trailer just two days before school started for our second-grade daughter. Everything was going smoothly, according to plan. We would be living in temporary housing in an apartment complex for two to three months max — or so we thought.

Let me back up a bit. Just a couple days before leaving Austin, a dear friend of mine said out of the blue, "I am praying for you. You may be in your apartment longer than you think and I'm praying for God to provide you with specific purpose while you are waiting for a permanent home." I thought that was interesting and comforting. She's an amazing, godly woman. Her words rang almost daily in my mind as we went past that three-month mark in our apartment.

The very day we drove up in front of our temporary living space, out on her front porch stood a tiny, frail, hunched over little lady of about 70 years. She called out to us. "I would help you with your boxes, but I have back issues." That same day we met her husband. He was wheeling around the complex in his motorized wheelchair; with two fewer legs than most of us are blessed to have.

In visiting with them over the next couple of weeks, we discovered that she would soon be scheduled for back surgery — a very extensive surgery that would require a long stay in the hospital, many months of rehab and many more months of healing. She was her husband's primary caregiver as he struggled through the effects of years of diabetes, three visits per week to a dialysis clinic and, ultimately, the amputation of both legs. What was God unfolding here?

It would be another six months before we moved into our new home. A full year in the apartment at that point. But our sweet neighbor finally had her surgery and God gave me the ability and time to help them by taking her husband to dialysis during the week, giving him rides to the hospital and rehab center to see his recovering wife and also to share my faith with them in the process.

A sweet friendship grew and now that a trust has developed, they call when they need me. About the time we moved into our new home, she was back in hers and well on the road to recovering and regaining her more active lifestyle.

Isn't the Lord amazing? I'm so thankful for the "purpose" He provided during that season of my life.

Amy C
Charlotte, NC

March 22

Your beauty should not come from outward adornment, such as braided hair and the wearing of gold jewelry and fine clothes. Instead, it should be that of your inner self, the unfading beauty of a gentle and quiet spirit, which is of great worth in God's sight. — **1 Peter 3:3-4**

My friend and I were on our way home from having dinner with a group of girlfriends, and she began to share something that had been troubling her. It was nothing major — she was just very much aware of a spiritual battle raging in her mind. Feeling the Holy Spirit urging me to be honest, I confessed my own struggle with the same issue.

How does one age gracefully? That was the question both of us were wrestling with.

My husband and I are close in age, going through this season together. He is absolutely incredible in how beautiful he makes me feel. His words of adoration and compliments flow freely and abundantly, and I know he loves me unconditionally. God looks at my heart, and could care less about the wrinkles, plus I am aware of what the Scriptures say about outward beauty, with the words from 1 Peter 3:3-4 above being my favorite.

God has placed some amazing "older" women in my life who have exemplified "aging gracefully" at its best. These role models have shown me true beauty at 60-, 70- and 80-plus years of age, and have aided in my acceptance of the outward changes. The old cliché, "it's what on the inside that counts," has been imbedded in my heart, thanks to these ladies. Truthfully, I had become quite comfortable in my less elastic and not-so-smooth skin, but was wrestling with the physical and mental downhill spiral.

In my attempt to be totally honest with my friend, I confessed that I was actually pondering my sons' reactions to their aging mom. The mom who had been very active and in good shape. The one who was always on top of things and knew what was going on. The person they would go to when they had a question about anything. I was already struggling just to stay above water in the technology department so I could remain in communications with them. With my mental and physical limitations becoming more visible, how were they viewing me?

Could they accept the memory lapses and the fact that I moved a bit slower? While I was used to the person I viewed in the mirror daily, what did they think of the mom they saw? Was the condition of my heart the most important thing to them, as it was to God?

It's very clear that I was consumed with pride—I didn't want my sons to stop being proud of me. Was I fearful they would turn their backs on me when I wasn't as sharp or useful? Would it not be cool to hang out with me anymore? I confessed to being worried that I would lose the affections of my sons as I entered this new phase of the aging process. Shouldn't the love and acceptance of my Heavenly Father be enough? And why did I have such little faith in my own children?

God has the most incredible knack for gently teaching me what He wants me to hold dear to my heart and what is of great worth in His sight. One of His beautiful lessons came the very next day after my friend and I had our pity party about trying to age gracefully. Tomorrow I will tell you what He revealed.

March 23

And God will generously provide all you need. Then you will always have everything you need and plenty left over to share with others.—**2 Corinthians 9:8 (NLT)**

Yesterday, I wrote of a pity party I had with a friend as we questioned how to age gracefully. The following morning, my sisters and I took my mom on a day trip to visit her sister suffering from Alzheimer's. Our trip had been planned for weeks. I wonder how long ago God planned our pity party the night before, because it sure wasn't a coincidence.

Aunt Jean was the first person close to me who was plagued with the progressive, memory-loss disease. Witnessing the effects on her, and on her close-knit family, was devastating. My uncle visited her faithfully twice daily at the nursing home. My oldest cousin and his wife also lived close by, and one of them went every day as well.

Gathered together in the visiting area, reminiscing and catching up on all the family news, I gazed at my aunt. She looked back, with completely blank stares. She had previously been full of spunk, never without something witty and funny to say. Now, seeing the once tall, stately woman slumped over in a wheelchair, gazing silently and aimlessly, I was overwhelmed with sadness.

The only time she smiled was when my cousin walked into the room, kissed her forehead and spoke directly to her. He was the only one she responded to or appeared to remember. After 62 years of marriage, my uncle was still filled with love for a woman who didn't even recognize him. He still cared deeply, despite the fact that her witty personality was gone, along with her sweet smiles for him. She didn't even look like the same person, but his heart was full of fond memories of his beautiful bride.

The love between my cousin and his mom was what touched my soul. Her eyes lit up when she saw him, and his gentle touch and voice brought tears to my eyes. The bond between those two was still there. While Aunt Jean's memory will continue to fade, I have no doubt her son will remain steadfast and by her side for as long as necessary, and so will my uncle.

Once again, God did what only He could do by using the trip to visit Aunt Jean as a teaching moment and revealing some of His promises to my uncertain heart. My faith was renewed and my hope soared when I saw how naturally my cousin showered his mom with attention and how my uncle's eyes still glistened with love. If such a day were to come, one of my boys (my husband or sons) would do the same for me. I know all three of them love me unconditionally—and my Father loves me even more.

I can just hear Jesus saying to me, "You of little faith, why are you so afraid?" (Matthew 8:26). How could I ever have doubted my loved ones and imagined they would put me out to pasture and forget about me? As I arrived back home from our trip, one of my sons called, just to chat. Asking what I did that day, I filled him in on my visit with Aunt Jean. What a loving gift from God—a phone call reminding me of my son's love and genuine interest in my life.

If I am faithful to my Father and His commands, He will provide my every need, as promised in the daily verse above. Early on in the Bible (Genesis 22:14) we are introduced to Jehovah-Jireh, the Lord my Provider. "So Abraham called that place The Lord Will Provide. And to this day it is said, 'On the mountain of the Lord it will be provided.'"

Because of my Jehovah-Jireh, there is no reason to question what He has in store for my days to come. He will provide, according to His perfect plan.

March 24

No discipline seems pleasant at the time, but painful. Later on, however, it produces a harvest of righteousness and peace for those who have been trained by it.—**Hebrews 12:14**

The gym where I work out has a four-week competition that coincides with March Madness. There are four teams, with participants choosing their favorite "coach," and earning one point for every hour they work out. Each week, two teams are pitted against each other, culminating with the top two competing for the championship title.

Points can also be earned away from the gym, so time spent at golf, tennis, walking, running, skiing and biking are included. I particularly like that because I enjoy walking. The only exercise I do at the gym is Pilates two or three days a week. To be useful to my team, I must be faithful in my walking.

At the suggestion of my doctor, I started walking almost ten years ago. After moving to Lake Travis in the Texas Hill Country, I was introduced to the many hilly streets, and walking became much more of a challenge, compared to the flatlands of Katy.

Walking on windy, cold days is brutal, so the past winter, I took my annual hiatus. However, this year I quickly got in the habit of not walking, even when it wasn't so cold. I found that I would rather spend my time writing than walking. Before I knew it, four months had slipped by. When I finally started back, I was totally out of shape. To make it up some of the hills was a chore, and I was exhausted.

It was the final week of our March Madness competition, with my team being in the top two. Our coach encouraged everyone on the team to step it up for that final week so we could take on the title of "repeat" champion.

On Monday morning of that final week, I planned to walk. However, I procrastinated all day, not having the energy or the desire to put my body through a five-mile walk up those hills. If I could just take a leisurely walk along a nice flat road, it wouldn't be such an effort. But I couldn't do that—how else was I going to build up my endurance and get stronger without tackling the hills?

As I begrudgingly tied my tennis shoes, the Holy Spirit decided I needed a pep talk to get me ready for the competition. Some very convicting thoughts filled my head.

Where would I be if life had been easy? I wouldn't know what it felt like to be discouraged, weak and broken, leaving me without compassion or empathy for others. I wouldn't have known what it felt like, in my desperation, to cry out to God and acknowledge it was His mercy and grace that pulled me out of that pit.

God allowed me to go down the hard roads of life so that I would see His glory. Yes, it was the hard times that made me stronger in my faith, in my relationship with God. In my weakness, I saw His might. I committed my life to my Lord and Savior, trusting in Him to change my heart. With His help, I would have the perseverance to face the other hills in the journey of life—all for the prize of eternity in heaven.

Just as I trained my spiritual body, I must train my physical body. I can't always take the easy road if I want to increase my endurance and make my body and heart stronger. The difficult paths in life were building blocks in my faith walk, and these hills around Lake Travis have a purpose too.

As I walked, which by the way ended up being a seven-mile journey along the most challenging route I had mapped out, I kept on thinking of the words to the song "Mountains" by the country group Lonestar that refer to an image of God giving us mountains in our life so that we can learn to climb. There is a big difference between a hill and a mountain, but God wants us to get over whatever He puts in front of us, but always with a dependence on Him—all glory going to our Father when we succeed.

"He has raised us up for this very purpose, that He might show us His power and that His name might be proclaimed in all the earth" (Exodus 9:16).

March 25

*The L**ord** himself goes before you and will be with you; he will never leave you nor forsake you. Do not be afraid; do not be discouraged.*—**Deuteronomy 31:8**

I moved out to California in my mid-20s. I also moved away from the church because I thought I knew everything. I was living large.

A few months earlier, I had recovered from jaw surgery that had my mouth wired shut for two months. I was feeling a little depressed, so my mom suggested that we meet each other in Mexico for a girls' vacation. I was flying in from California and she was coming from Texas. She had made all the plans, so all I needed to do was jump on a plane and meet her at the airport in Puerto Vallarta. Sounds easy, but things went very wrong.

Little did I know, but my mom's plane in Texas was delayed. By the time she arrived in Mexico, I had been at the airport for several hours and did not know why she hadn't arrived. Being very naïve and not knowing how to reach my mother (cell phones did not exist at this time), I trusted a young man to help me and left the airport with him.

To my good fortune, he was not a serial killer, but I was missing for 24 hours. I made my mother worry for no reason, other than my bad judgment. The young man did help me find my mom by calling all the hotels until we found the one where she was staying. I think of this story every time I hear about a young girl who wasn't so lucky.

I know God had other plans for me and protected me, even though I made all the wrong decisions. I thank God every day that I am here and was able to get married and have children—and get to worry about them, just like my mom worried about me.

Susan
Friendswood, TX

March 26

"Why do you look at the speck of sawdust in your brother's eye and pay no attention to the plank in your own eye? How can you say to your brother, 'Let me take the speck out of your eye,' when all the time there is a plank in your own eye? You hypocrite, first take the plank out of your own eye, and then you will see clearly to remove the speck from your brother's eye."—**Matthew 7:3-5**

It was tax time, so I made my annual visit to the CPA. There is a surface parking lot between two office buildings, and my CPA firm has three reserved spots. I consider myself very fortunate when I find one of the three empty. It is much more convenient to park in one of them, instead of dealing with the huge garage.

When I arrived back to my car after the appointment, a car pulled into the empty space beside me. I waited for the couple to get out of their car before backing out. I watched as they walked across the lot—they were walking into the opposite building from the CPA office.

Oh, how I wanted to shout out to them, "Hey, wait! The space you just parked in is reserved for clients of my CPA firm. You can't park there!" How could they even think of taking up that coveted parking space when they weren't clients?

As tempted as I was to say something tacky, I kept my thoughts to myself.

The silly incident kept popping into my head. How can people blatantly disregard a sign? Don't they know we are supposed to follow the rules? Finally, the Holy Spirit must have heard enough because that small voice start questioning me.

How many times have you totally disregarded that speed limit sign, Brenda? 70 mph doesn't mean 74, even if everyone else is driving 80. OK, I am guilty of that. What else?

What about the message before the movie starts that clearly reads NO TEXTING? Didn't you decide, more than once, that when your sons sent you a message it was all right to respond back? Yes, I did that too, but it was important.

We went back and forth for a few minutes. Then the subject kind of shifted as an interesting thought came to mind. What about the parking spaces at church? Are those reserved just for the good, non-sinning Christians? Of course not—the parking lot would be empty if it was for non-sinners only.

Sure, I consider myself a Christian, but I deliberately disregard His rules, making me a sinner. I am (obviously) judgmental, quick to anger, selfish, guilty of worshiping idols (like my kids, my house, my stuff, rain) and my procrastination is due to lack of self-control—just to name a few of God's rules that I fail to follow.

God still allows me into His house of worship. He welcomes me with opens arms, wherever I am. However, I must confess my sins (all of them), and I trust He will hear my cries. I may suffer the consequences, like receiving a speeding ticket (or worse), but He will never fail me, "for with the LORD is unfailing love and with him is full redemption" (Psalm 130:7).

When I glanced in my rear-view mirror, I missed the plank(s) in my own eye. I am so thankful the Holy Spirit kept me from speaking my mind to the couple that failed to respect the words on a sign that day. I was certainly the one who needed the reprimand.

March 27

In all things God works for the good of those who love him.—**Romans 8:28**

"How do I keep my eyes on Jesus when they are full of tears?" This was a question I asked myself many times from March 7, 2004, to November 5, 2009.

In the early hours of March 7, 2004, our family was forever changed through an unimaginable tragedy: Our beloved Eileen had a brain aneurysm that would leave her in a coma for nearly six years. Eileen was full of the fruit of the Spirit: love, joy, peace, patience, kindness, goodness, faithfulness and gentleness (Galatians 5:22). Eileen was more to me than my young aunt—she was a best friend! My daughter Sage put it best when she wrote a college entrance exam that started, "She never saved someone from a burning building. She never had super strength or the ability to fly. But Eileen was and always will be a hero to me." These were the words that were read by our pastor at the beginning and the end of Eileen's memorial service on November 5, 2009.

How does a very young daughter cope with the horror of her mom being in a coma in the bedroom next door? How does a husband cope with taking care of his daughter, their home, running a business and caring for his wife throughout the night? We all have different ways of coping with tragedy. For me, I believed that with Christ all things are possible.

The Lord carried me through inconceivable hours, days, months and years. I learned nursing skills to help care for Eileen. She had to be turned every two hours, fed through a feeding tube, changed, washed and watched when she suffered a seizure. To add to that, my husband and I were going through a financial crisis that caused us to come within a few days of foreclosure on our home.

Through all of this, I learned to believe that when I am weak, then I am strong in Christ (2 Corinthians 12:10). The Lord sustained me in peaceful sleep after long, traumatic days and He rescued me when I could not cope anymore. He gave me times of joy, perfect peace and great strength in the face of adversity. The Lord matured me, helped me grow up and then gave me a new family in Christ.

Now I understand how we can have joy in our suffering (Romans 5:3). I know that God's ultimate goal for my life on earth is not comfort, but character development! God works all things out for our good. He doesn't do it by making a bad situation good, but He will strengthen and enable us to get through a tragedy or crisis a better and stronger person—if we trust in Him.

These days, I am greatly comforted by the knowledge that those who love God never meet for the last time. I will see you soon Eileen.

Michelle Reekwald
Katy, TX

March 28

Where is God my Maker, who gives songs in the night, who teaches more to us than to the beasts of the earth and makes us wiser than the birds in the air?—**Job 35:10-11**

God blessed Austin with some heavenly rain in the spring of 2012 to ease the pain of the ongoing drought. Lake Travis had many feet to go before being back to the normal level, but thankfully she was receiving a little bit of help from the thunderstorms—this one even causing flash-flood alerts. (The storm fizzled out before that happened, though.)

While I rejoice at the reverberation of booming thunder, marvel at the sight of brilliant lightning and literally shed tears of joy at the sound of rain pounding on the metal roof, my sweet golden retriever, Holly, doesn't share my same emotions. I don't remember ever not having a dog, but she is the first to have an adverse reaction to thunderstorms.

All dogs are supposed to be able to sense the change in pressure as inclement weather approaches, and Holly starts to display her strange behavior long before the storm arrives. She paces back and forth and pants noisily. The closer the thunder, the louder she pants. She will stand, trembling, with her face to the corner, as if she is in timeout, staring at the wall. While outside going potty, she has actually stopped mid-stream as thunder roared, only to race quickly indoors for shelter. However, even in the security of the house, she continues to pant, pace and shake with fear.

One day my husband came home with a present for Holly—a Thundershirt. It resembles a dog sweater, but connects with Velcro snuggly around the dog's abdomen and neck. Like swaddling soothes a baby, the gentle pressure of the Thundershirt is intended to provide calming relief to dogs during anxious moments, such as thunderstorms.

Holly looks quite cute in her Thundershirt and it does alleviate her anxiety—during a normal rain shower. However, during this particular ferocious storm, from 12:30 a.m. to 5:30 a.m. the two of us were wide-awake. The thunder roared relentlessly and nothing could calm Holly.

I watched as she paced around the house. I felt her trembling body as I lay on the floor with her trying to soothe my precious girl through words of assurance. I listened helplessly as she panted with her head turned towards the corner of the room. Holly is a dog and, unfortunately, I have not discovered a way to verbally reason or comfort her.

Stretched out on the hardwood floor with my 85-pound, quivering golden retriever, I was reminded of the times I also refused to listen to the voice of reason. God has given Scriptures to assure me there is no need to be anxious, but yet I am. How about all the *fear not* verses? I tend to ignore them too. Time after time, I have felt the peace of His presence, but how easily I forget when He carried me through that previous storm—then wonder how I will survive the current trial.

There I was, thinking that it was so unfortunate I couldn't speak words of truth my dog would understand, and the Holy Spirit led me to see myself.

Holly was dressed in her Thundershirt, but still trembled with fear as the storm raged all night long. The intensity of the loud noises took away her sense of security. My Savior has covered me with His love, mercy and grace, yet sometimes the storms of life overwhelm me. All I hear is the evil lies clamoring in my head instead of the Voice of Truth.

It was rather humbling to realize I am capable of demonstrating the same mentality as my dog! I don't know if I can ever be as sweet as my Holly and love as unconditionally as she does, but I should be wiser. I took a picture of Holly wearing her Thundershirt and have it by my computer, along with the words from Job 35:10-11—just as a reminder. My Maker has taught me, and I should know better!

March 29

In him we have redemption through his blood, the forgiveness of sins, in accordance with the riches of God's grace that he lavished on us with all wisdom and understanding.—**Ephesians 1:7**

After a women's event at church, I was asked to help wash the tablecloths. As I was removing the dirty ones, I realized they had no wrinkles. So I not only needed to wash them, ironing was part of the process too?

The other, experienced tablecloth-washer assured me that there was no ironing involved. Just dry on low heat, pull them out of the dryer and they would be wrinkle-free. That sounded better. You know, I don't iron much anymore. I have very few things that require it. My husband sends his shirts to the cleaners and most everything else is simply wash and wear—or worn with a few wrinkles.

My church isn't just down the street—it's about a 50-minute round trip. To save time and gas, I planned to deliver the tablecloths back to church a few days later on Tuesday, Bible study day. They were washed and dried as instructed. However, when I pulled them out of the dryer, they were anything but wrinkle-free. What had I done wrong?

Let me be totally honest here. While I was more than happy to bring those tablecloths home and wash them, the thought of ironing them didn't sound too inviting. Especially since it was now the night before Bible study, and I still had plenty of homework to finish. There was no extra time on my agenda for the evening, or more specifically, ironing time.

When I started on the first one, I had anything but a servant's heart. The Holy Spirit saw that I needed an attitude adjustment and got to work. By the time I was finished, I wished there was more to iron.

As those first wrinkles disappeared from the heat of the iron, God immediately let me see how He had done the same thing with my life. Every time I have messed up, each time there was a wrinkle or a sin, God was there to take it away. Yes, I went through some heat as He took me through the refining process. However, because of His mercy and love, that sin, that wrinkle, was forgiven and forgotten by my sweet Savior. Soon it became a great joy to see those wrinkles on the tablecloths disappear and it was a true labor of love.

Not only did God take my sins away, like the heat from the iron was taking away the wrinkles, but He cleansed me with the blood of Christ, making me white as snow, like the white tablecloths. As often happens, a song came to mind as I was ironing: *Nothing But the Blood of Jesus.* I thought this was a relatively new song because it had been recorded by several contemporary Christian artists, but discovered it was written in 1876 by Robert Lowry.

What can wash away my sin? Nothing but the blood of Jesus. What can make me whole again? Nothing but the blood of Jesus. Oh! Precious is the flow that makes me white as snow; no other fount I know, nothing but the blood of Jesus.

I had no idea that washing and ironing tablecloths would be such a spiritual experience. I will never look at a white tablecloth quite the same again. Oh, dear Father, that You would so lovingly change my heart as I do Your work during the day. You allowed Your Son to die for me! How can I *not* glorify You in all that I do—even something as simple as washing and ironing.

March 30

And do not forget to do good and to share with others, for with such sacrifices God is pleased.—**Hebrews 13:16**

Surveying a very large, newly hand-tilled and mulch-covered planting bed, I felt mild panic to see it dotted with tiny green shoots. *Already?* I thought. The bed was turned and cleaned out just a little more than a week ago.

Most of the shoots had no roots. I easily brushed them out with a little hand trowel. With others, I had to dig down into the soil to find the root; some required a good bit of patience and persistence. All of it was work. With each root ball or tap root I untangled from the earth, I felt a great sense of satisfaction.

"I win," I said out loud after the particularly stubborn ones came out, smiling at my little victory. Each time, I also remembered the faces and hands of those whose backbreaking sacrifice had created the opportunity for all these little victories.

That bed had been neglected for a very long time. The Bermuda grass had overtaken the soil even as my discouragement had overtaken the plans I had for this particular space that encompasses and frames the front of my home. For those who don't know, Bermuda grass is as invasive and difficult to control as a weed. I despised how it looked every time I came home.

Only a week earlier, I thought a dear friend was bringing her family to enjoy pancakes with mine. As I stood on the front porch waiting for the kids to meander up the grassy, overgrown walk, I noticed a landscaping trailer pulling up in front of our house. "What is this?" I suspiciously demanded. My friend just smiled.

Knowing how much I wanted to be able to create beauty in that space, and how the circumstances of my life kept me from it, my friend had enlisted her neighbors and showed up at our house on this particular Saturday morning to work. The pancakes had been nothing more than a ruse.

These strangers became our friends as they spent the better part of that day trimming trees and bushes and turning the soil in the planters and beds. The particular one in which I stood that morning was **huge**. It had made my back hurt to watch them, bent over, using picks to break up the grass as others raked out the clumps to leave the fresh dirt. When they left late in the afternoon, the beds were prepared and covered with dark, rich-smelling mulch, an empty canvas readied to hold the beauty I saw in my mind's eye.

I could not let this grass win. *I will not neglect to honor their sacrifice and work,* I thought. So humbled, neither could I toss aside the gift my friend had given out of her love for me. I still can't comprehend why.

With each root ball, my thoughts tumbled toward God's goodness; the rich smell of His earth, the cool breeze of the day; the gift of this friend in my life. Then came the tears—undeserved, love, sacrifice.

Oh, that I would daily remember His love-driven sacrifice. That I would not neglect His gift, but would persist in digging out the roots of my sin that crop up with each new sunrise. Even as I had determined to honor the labors of these new friends, how much more should I—should we—diligently work to honor God with our hearts and our lives?

Terri Carriker
Austin, TX

March 31

And my God will meet all your needs according to his glorious riches in Christ Jesus.—**Philippians 4:19**

It was the Monday morning before Easter Sunday. The weekend had been exceptionally busy. My husband's nephew got married, there had been many fun wedding festivities, and for two nights in a row, I didn't get as much sleep as I was accustomed to. As the sun was inching through the blinds, I was resisting the need to get up and start the new week.

Snuggled under the covers, gathering my thoughts and speaking to God, I heard the words from Casting Crowns' "Glorious Day (Living He Loved Me)" in my head. I silently sang along, thinking of what a special way to start my day—hearing Casting Crowns serenade me!

In case you don't know the song, it basically tells the story of Jesus' birth, life, death, resurrection and second coming. Through the words in the chorus we hear of what all Christ did—he loved us, saved us, took away our sins, and one day, He will return.

The word "glorious" was stuck in my head. Just a few days earlier, in Sarah Young's *Jesus Calling* devotional, I read, "Before you arise from your bed in the morning, I have already arranged the events of your day." If God had arranged for my day to revolve around "glorious," I was anxious to discover what He had in store for me.

The daily reading for *Jesus Calling* that Monday started off with Philippians 4:19, written as if Jesus were speaking: "I have promised to meet all your needs according to My glorious riches." I immediately thought of what we had discussed the night before in our LifeGroup—stepping out in faith through sacrificial giving (both of our time and money), going out of our comfort zone to serve and be a light to others, being obedient in our daily walk, even when we find it difficult. If we do what we are called to, God knows our needs even before we do, and He will provide, according to His will—according to His glorious riches.

I was inspired. Not only was our discussion from the previous evening reinforced through that verse, but also my musical morning message made me extremely aware of that special word. I found it again moments later when I went online to read devotionals received via email and saw there was an article written by S. Michael Craven at crosswalk. com entitled, "The Glorious Power of the Resurrection."

Here it was, almost Easter, so the title sounded very appropriate. However, to be honest, the only reason I clicked on it as fast as I did was because of the word "glorious." I already accept that Christ was resurrected from the dead and He is still alive, seated at the right hand of God. However, Mr. Craven also pointed out, as Christians, we have been called to "bear witness to the glorious power of the resurrection." We have been called, and have the power, to spread His light and love.

How can I bear witness to others if I don't sing at the top of my lungs of how much Jesus loves me and how He endured the excruciating pain on the cross for my sins? I woke up with a worship song in my heart, but I must leave my house with those same words on the tip of my tongue, for others to hear and see through my actions. God didn't just wake me up to a praise and worship song again because He knows how much I love music. No, He woke me up with words He wants me to spread to others right now.

I pray for the boldness to go forth on this glorious day and give Him all the praise. I pray that others might see the risen King through me and know that Jesus is indeed alive—here, today, in my heart. I wasn't blessed with a pleasant singing voice, but may all I encounter today hear the love of Jesus pouring from my soul.

April 1

It is because of the Lord's mercy and loving kindness that we are not consumed, because His [tender] compassions fail not. They are new every morning; great and abundant is Your stability and faithfulness. The Lord is my portion or share, says my living being (my inner self); therefore will I hope in Him and wait expectantly for Him. The Lord is good to those who wait hopefully and expectantly for Him, to those who seek Him.—**Lamentations 3:22-25 (AMP)**

One of the churches in Austin has a billboard that I drive by frequently. The message changes often, and it is always creative and witty. Prior to Easter, the special worship times were listed, along with the words "The Boss is Expecting You." I know that Bruce Springsteen is nicknamed The Boss, but I had never heard God referred to that way.

God has many names. Alpha and Omega, Master, Counselor, Creator, Rock, Abba, Jehovah, Yahweh, Defender, Redeemer, King, Father—just to name a few of my favorites. However, I wasn't so intrigued by what God was called on that billboard as I was the wording of the question.

Certainly God must smile when He sees us walk into His house of worship. However, if I were to erect a billboard, instead of stating that God was expecting us to be at church, I would ask, "Are You Expecting God?"

Do you begin each morning with the hopeful anticipation of seeing the Creator? Is He your daily Companion? Are you earnestly seeking the Lord? Do you have faith that the Deliverer will carry you through the current trial? Do you expect to see God's fingerprints all over the events of your day? Are you in awe of how the Master just shows up everywhere?

If you can't answer "yes" to those questions, may I offer a suggestion? Start writing a daily devotional. Seriously!

Before I started this book, I already had many God story ideas jotted down in a journal or stored in my head. But, after those were written, I was overwhelmed—not because I didn't have anything more to write, but with too many stories to tell and not enough time to write them all.

My Heavenly Father has been training me how to be expectant. He has coached my eyes and ears to see and hear Him at work in my life. Every day has evolved into a "God-story seeking day," and I never come up empty-handed.

I don't have a billboard, but I do have this page to pose my question: Are you expecting God today?

April 2

*And Jesus said to him, "Truly, I tell you, this very night, before the rooster crows twice, you will deny me three times." —***Mark 14:30**

My church began an online devotional called "Time With God," starting in the Book of Mark. The Wednesday before Easter, the reading covered Mark 14:26-42.

The next day, Maundy Thursday as some denominations call it, I set out for an early morning drive from Austin to Houston. For those not familiar, Maundy Thursday is described as the beginning of the three-day celebration of Easter, commemorating the Last Supper.

After all the coffee I drank before leaving home, I needed a potty break. Hruska's, a yummy bakery/deli on Highway 71 between La Grange and Columbus, Texas, is my favorite pit stop. It's kind of "country" and really cute, plus the restrooms are super clean.

When I got out of my car, I noted that it was only 7:45 a.m.—very early for me to be two hours away from home. As I started my walk across the parking lot, I stopped dead in my tracks because of the noise I heard. *Cock-a-doodle-doo.*

I hadn't heard a rooster crow in years. But there he was, strutting behind the cars and doing his job of making sure everyone was awake. My mind immediately flashed back to the Time With God reading the day before. Jesus, speaking to Peter, said "before the rooster crows twice, you will deny me three times."

Prior to continuing my drive to Houston, I re-read the devotion on my phone. One of the comments by that day's contributor, Carrie Runn, really grabbed my attention. "The disciples were subject to temptation when they were prideful and not spiritually alert and on watch. In their weakness they failed."

Was this a warning for me? I heard one crow. Would there be two? If so, what would happen in the meantime before that second one? Would I be like Peter and deny Jesus three times?

Hearing a rooster crow isn't a common occurrence for a city girl like me. I have stopped at Hruska's countless times on my drives back and forth between Austin and Houston and can't recall ever hearing one.

Was the Holy Spirit giving me a warning to watch out and be spiritually alert? Was He preparing me for something? In my heart, I knew this rooster was no coincidence and was there for a reason. The rest of that day I thought of nothing else.

Little did I know what was in store for me the next day. The *cock-a-doodle-doo* I heard was indeed the Holy Spirit calling out to me to be careful, to stand firm. I was going to be tested to either defend my Jesus or deny Him, like Peter. Would I fail also?

Tomorrow, I will tell you what happened.

April 3

Be on your guard; stand firm in the faith; be men of courage; be strong. Do everything in love. — **1 Corinthians 16:13-14**

Yesterday, I wrote about my encounter with a rooster on my drive to Houston. Hearing that *cock-a-doodle-do* wasn't an accident. His purpose that morning wasn't just to wake up the neighborhood, but to alert me to be on my guard. I just didn't know why.

The day after my rooster sighting was Good Friday. I was anticipating a fun-filled day at my daughter-in-law's parents' annual crawfish boil. At some point during the evening, my oldest son and I, along with a family friend, were engaged in a conversation that somehow drifted to religion. (I have written in several stories that both of my sons have strayed in their faith. Both had walked with the Lord in their younger years, but as they entered college their direction changed.)

I was more than exuberant to share some of the amazing truths from my Tuesday morning Bible study, the Beth Moore lecture series on Revelation, along with the current sermon series at my church on Daniel. However, Zach didn't have that same enthusiasm.

He quickly turned my world upside down with his remarks. "Mom, I feel sorry for you." I looked at him in bewilderment and asked why. Both of my boys have done certain things that hurt me deeply, but I don't know if I have ever felt as if I had been stabbed in the heart with a dagger before—until his next comment.

Mom, I feel sorry for you because you believe the fairy tale. That's all the Bible is. It is nothing but a fairy tale. Stories that were passed down from generation to generation. You know, there wasn't even the written word yet, so how could the Bible be factual?

I knew his faith was wavering, but I wasn't prepared for that outright denial. I was shocked, and my first reaction was to cry. I cried because I felt sorry for my son. I cried because he had denounced my Lord and Savior and the God-breathed Scriptures. Yes, his words cut me to the core, and I was hurt, but I was also mad. I knew I needed to walk away or else I might say something I would later regret.

The only verse I could remember at that moment was James 1:19: "Everyone should be quick to listen, slow to speak and slow to become angry." I had listened to his words quickly, but I had failed and was already angry. The only thing left for me to do was to be slow to speak, so I told my son that I needed to remove myself from the conversation and went inside to gather my thoughts and composure.

When I actually had time to reflect, I realized a very sad fact. When I was Zach's age, I felt the same way about the Bible! I had gone to church, believed in God, but there was so much more I didn't know. Yes, I too had those same misconceptions.

Only after I began attending Bible study and delving into His Word, earnestly seeking the Lord and asking for wisdom and direction, did the Bible become real and my relationship with Jesus personal. I discovered that all those kings in the Old Testament were also found in history books. All the names weren't just make-believe characters created to spice up the story. The events were real and so were the people. Facts cannot be fairy tale.

I realized why the rooster had alerted me. I couldn't allow this conversation to be swept under the rug. I couldn't deny Jesus, like Peter, and the God-breathed Scriptures. Out of love for my son and wanting him to know the Truth, I would have to stand firm and speak from my heart.

I had walked away from the conversation because I was unprepared, but I knew I would have to go back with facts and truths, and stand up to the Father of Lies who had taken up residence in my precious son's heart. Please read tomorrow's story to find out how it went.

April 4

But in your hearts set apart Christ as Lord. Always be prepared to give an answer to everyone who asks you to give the reason for the hope that you have.—**1 Peter 3:15**

My family has been gathering the Saturday before Easter at the family farm in Weimar, Texas, for over 30 years. Family members have come and gone, but it is always a blessed and fun day, spending time with loved ones. However, after the conversation I had with my son Zach the day before on Good Friday (yesterday's devotion), I had a very heavy heart.

After leaving the crawfish boil the previous night, I was devastated by his comment that the Bible was nothing more than a fairy tale, along with his comment that there weren't even records of the printed word at the time the Bible was written. Where had my son heard such a lie?

The words from 1 Peter 3:15 rang in my ears: "Always be prepared to give an answer for the hope that you have." In my heart, I felt that I was just as guilty as Peter of denying Jesus. I wasn't prepared to respond to the falsehoods my son proclaimed about my Heavenly Father.

I was totally amazed years earlier when I discovered the Bible was an actual accounting. I had also harbored thoughts that the Bible was just a nice storybook. The current sermon series at church on Daniel was my third time to study that book and I am still fascinated with the rich history I have learned each time. However, I wasn't sure about the history of the written word, nor had it ever really mattered to me. Thanks to Google, I found more information than I had time to read.

Once again, this book took me on a great research adventure. On one website, the very first question was, "How could the first five books be by Moses, since people (allegedly) could not write back then?" I found that archeologists once thought the practice of writing began in ancient Mesopotamia (modern-day Iraq) around 3000 B.C. However, in 1998, a German archaeologist discovered writings on pottery and clay tablets at the tomb of King Scorpion the First near Luxor in Egypt that dated back to 3400 B.C. The Book of Genesis was written around 1400 B.C. Anyone wanting to use that myth as a reason to dispute the Bible is truly out of luck.

I prayed for God to give me the words to speak to my son. I asked for wisdom and discernment. However, I never questioned whether I was supposed to confront him or not. I knew I had to stand firm and give reason for the hope I have because of my belief in the Lord and His Word.

God provided the perfect opportunity for Zach and I. The first thing I told him was how I could identify with his way of thinking since I also had my doubts about the Bible at his age. Then I shared some of the fascinating "facts" I had gathered in my research the night before, along with some I had learned along the path of my spiritual journey.

In a college class, Zach understood the professor to say that since there was no history of the written word, the Old Testament was only hearsay. After that, he dropped the class, along with his faith. So, that's what he had been basing his disbelief on these past years?

Zach was very attentive to hearing the "historical facts." However, he also heard about my faith. None of us were around when God created the earth, but I am living proof of the wonder of His creation. All that He has done in my life truly is a miracle, almost like a fairy tale. But my testimony of redemption and restoration is all the evidence I need to explain the magnificence of God's grace and His power of salvation.

There are so many mysteries in the Bible, but it also full of indisputable truths. We have the privilege to read the Bible, study commentaries, conduct our own research, pray, spend time in His presence—whatever it takes—to cover ourselves with the armor of God's Word.

The next day would be Easter. The empty tomb, the risen King—the reason for my hope and my belief in the promise of eternity.

The day I wrote this story, I received a blog post from a friend on a year-long mission trip that included the following verse and just what I needed to close this story:

"The secret things belong to the LORD our God, but the things that are revealed belong to us and to our children forever" (Deuteronomy 29:29).

April 5

For you did not receive a spirit of slavery to fall back into fear, but you received the Spirit of adoption, by whom we cry out, "Abba, Father!" The Spirit Himself testifies together with our spirit that we are God's children.—**Romans 8:14-16**

On April 5, 2003, my dad passed away. I have written several stories about my dad and our dysfunctional relationship, but to sum it up, Dad was a womanizer and had time for "them" but never for his own daughters. For much of my life, there with a longing in my heart for what I thought I had missed out on.

A few days before the anniversary of his death, there was a devotion in *Daily Guidepost 2011* written by Roberta Messener who longed to have one-on-one time with her daddy, but never had it either. (Her circumstances were much different than mine though.) She decided that instead of remembering what she didn't get to experience with her dad, she would store memories in her heart of all the things her dad did right. I want to do the same.

The one most important trait my dad had was his compassion for the underdog. He always wanted to provide for the underserved and the underprivileged. That was the concept behind the grocery store he opened in Houston in 1972 that served the inner-city Hispanics—a unique concept back then. He had previously worked in grocery stores in South America for over eight years and had great insight in how to market to that ethnic group. But in addition to having a business plan, he had a sincere heartfelt desire to provide a higher quality of service to a group that had been ignored.

Before my parents divorced in 1961 and Dad moved to South America, we lived in Corpus Christi, Texas, where he owned and operated grocery stores. Back in those days, all retail stores were closed on Sunday. Sometimes after church, we stopped by the closed stores so he could check the refrigeration. On one occasion, my sisters and I grabbed a handful of candy on our way out. Dad asked where that candy came from. I replied that since he owned the store, we thought it was all right to take it.

That was one of the few childhood memories I have of my dad, and even though it wasn't a pleasant memory, the lesson was huge. Dad let us know quickly that just because he owned the store, we had no right to take anything without paying for it. I felt "privileged" being the boss' daughter, but I learned at a very early age that I wasn't entitled.

I started working for Dad in 1975 when the second store opened in Houston. Even though we worked together for over 25 years, we never had a close father-daughter relationship, but looking back, I know he was still proud of me. His desire to treat all of his employees fairly kept him from showing me favoritism. At the time, it hurt my feelings because I thought by working harder, he would notice me, but now I understand.

My dad was a good man with a heart of gold. Along with the thousands of employees and customers who benefitted from his desire to serve the underserved, he also shared his financial gain through his many philanthropic donations. I was born the boss' daughter, with a blessed life materialistically. Perhaps my sisters and I missed out on a daddy, but thousands of others were blessed because he was such a successful, innovative and generous businessman.

I was the boss' daughter, but I was never daddy's little girl. That intense longing I had to feel my daddy's love took me down a road of sin, heartache and despair as I searched for that love. But it was out of that desperation, out of total brokenness, that I found my Heavenly Father—the only One who could fill that hole in my heart, a Savior who loves me like no other. While I certainly didn't feel it as a young girl, today I am so thankful for the desperation that brought me to know my Heavenly Father. Yes, I embrace it.

My dad was a caring, generous, brilliant man. He just didn't have the capacity to be a loving daddy because he also spent his life searching for that perfect love to fill the hole in his heart. The Father of perfect Jesus, adopted us as His children, giving us the privilege to call Him "Abba, Father." It took my dad his entire life, but in the end, I know he found perfect love in his Heavenly Father too. Tomorrow I will share that incredible story with you.

April 6

"There will be more rejoicing in heaven over one sinner who repents than over ninety-nine righteous persons who do not need to repent." —**Luke 15:7**

The devotion today is a continuation on the death of my dad. Even though my dad lived a very colorful life and our relationship was strained, I had some sweet thoughts of him that I shared yesterday. Now I have the opportunity to tell you an incredible story about the perfect ending to his life.

Dad grew up in the Methodist Church. He was active at church when we were little, but behind the scenes he lived a life of sexual sin. He attended the Unity Church the last 15 years of his life, but even before the Unity Church, Dad didn't believe that his sin was punishable by spiritual death or that heaven and hell were actual places. He didn't believe that the only way to the Father was through the Son or that he was in need of a Savior. No wonder he led such a sad life.

In June 1995, Dad suffered cardiac arrest and was clinically dead for 10 minutes, resulting in a short-term memory loss. Then, to make matters worse, he suffered a stroke on November 3, 2001.

At first, it appeared to be a minor stroke, and by Thanksgiving he was talking and walking and his prognosis was good. But then he began having mini-strokes and his condition deteriorated. He could no longer speak and developed wounds on his feet because of poor circulation. He had around-the-clock care in his home from some loving, caring, qualified nurses, yet the wounds wouldn't heal. He eventually had a leg amputated because the infection on his foot and ankle was so severe.

In October 2002, he entered the hospital. His body just seemed to be shutting down. I received a call in the middle of the night that the doctors thought he would die within 12-24 hours. His wife, my sisters and their husbands and I were all together at the hospital. My sisters and I we were so afraid that he would die and go to hell because we knew he didn't consider Jesus Christ to be his Lord and Savior. We began to pray with him, shared the gospel and told Dad the simple steps to being saved.

Dad would open his eyes and the look of terror was horrific. He had the look of a crazed animal. To this day, I believe he saw Satan and a glimpse of hell and he didn't want to go! He fought, his condition improved, and by the next day he was back home.

After that incident, Dad was different. He couldn't verbally communicate, but his eyes spoke volumes. There seemed to be a glimmer of peace and happiness. The doctor informed us that his days were numbered and that we should prepare for his death. We had heard that before and knew that they really had no idea how much longer he had.

Early in the morning of April 5, 2003, I got the call from my stepmother. Dad had passed in his sleep. I rushed over to his home and it was one of the most profound scenes I had ever witnessed. His wife, who was very "spiritual," had soft music playing, and Dad's body was positioned in the middle of the bed with the most peaceful, almost angelic glow on his face. Thinking back to that morning, I am getting goose bumps all over as I write this. I have no doubt that he met with Jesus before his final breath. The expression on his face said it all!

Dad was a lost sheep, and the Good Shepherd wasn't going to give up until he was found. God wasn't going to allow one of His children to fall into Satan's hands. Strokes can be very cruel, and my dad suffered immensely, but God had a purpose. He knew Dad had to be totally broken before he would surrender, so He waited. He waited on this lost soul to repent and accept Christ.

It took my dad his whole life to find his Lord and Savior, but I feel there was rejoicing over this lost sheep who found his way home. I also found peace in Dad's death—there is hope of salvation for our friends and loved ones whose faith we aren't sure of. The Good Shepherd in heaven doesn't want any in His flock to perish.

April 7

"For if you forgive men their trespasses, your heavenly Father will also forgive you. But if you do not forgive men their trespasses, neither will your Father forgive your trespasses." —**Matthew 6:14-15 (NKJV)**

In 1963, in a small town in Minnesota where I was related to half of the residents, the unthinkable happened: My father walked out on my mother and me. After numerous affairs—a rumor linked him to the minister's wife! A tumultuous 25-year marriage was over. As a self-absorbed teenager, I didn't appreciate how my mother managed to pick up the remnants of her life and forge ahead. She rented out the ground floor of our two-story home to make ends meet. We moved upstairs. She clerked in a drugstore for minimum wage. We survived.

How could my father do this to me? No one else in our little town had divorced parents! I railed into the darkness and prayed for God to strike him dead, preferably in a compromising position. Would he be with the minister's wife when he met his doom? What had gone wrong? He'd seldom hurt me intentionally. I wasn't abused or neglected. But now he'd cut me to my core and he didn't seem to care. When the parochial students, who hadn't heard the truth because little gossip passed between Catholics and Lutherans back in 1963, transferred to the public high school that same year, I told them he was dead.

For all practical purposes, he was. But it was me who had withered inside, harboring my hate and my anger, allowing it to fester and grow. When he returned momentarily a few months later to retrieve some things he'd left behind, our terrier went delirious with joy. I wanted to react the same way, but instead I locked my bedroom door and refused to talk to him. After all, hadn't he left *me* behind?

A decade later, when I began having my own children, I made a conscious effort to forgive him. It wouldn't be fair to deprive my kids of their grandfather, I reasoned. But I remained quick to point out his faults and our relationship remained tenuous.

In the spring of 2011, I published my first novel, *The Enigma Journal*. (Odd how its main characters are a precocious young girl and not one, but two, deeply flawed fathers!) Margaret, my 90-year-old former teacher and lifelong mentor, while lauding my efforts said, "Linda, you harbor *such* a father fixation. It's time you get over it. Don't you realize that you've had another Father all these years, one who will never disappoint you?"

For five decades, the obvious had escaped me! I'd always longed for the epiphany—the aha moment when my dad would turn to me, discuss his shortcomings, and beg my forgiveness. He lived past 90. I was his caretaker for the final three years of his life. But the epiphany never happened.

Suddenly I realized it no longer mattered that he'd never justified himself to me. Who was I to demand such a thing? He would answer to God. And I would answer to God too. It was imperative for me to relinquish the hurt of my childhood and truly forgive my human father as I wanted my Heavenly Father—my Perfect Father—to forgive me—immediately!

Corrie Ten Boom, a Christian who survived a Nazi concentration camp during the Holocaust, said, "Forgiveness is to set a prisoner free, and to realize the prisoner was you."

Here I'd been wallowing in a self-made prison, mulling over how I'd been wronged, writing about it, and waiting. But waiting for what? My father had been dead for seven years by 2011. Had he received forgiveness from God before his passing? I sincerely hope so. And my Heavenly Father had been waiting too—waiting for me to forgive the past and forge ahead as my mother had done so many years ago.

"Then Peter came to Him and asked, 'Lord, how often shall my brother sin against me, and I forgive him? Up to seven times?' Jesus said to him, 'I do not say to you, up to seven times, but to seventy times seven'" (Matthew 18:21-22 NJKV).

Jesus understands that forgiveness is not easy for us. It goes against our human inclinations. But it is a necessary choice that we must make, acknowledging the wrong done us but letting the matter go for God to judge, if we desire His mercy and grace to apply to our own lives. We must continue along the path toward forgiveness until our wounds are healed, and our hearts are at one with Him.

L.A. Kantor
Katy, TX

April 8

Finally, brothers, whatever is true, whatever is noble, whatever is right, whatever is pure, whatever is lovely, whatever is admirable—if anything is excellent or praiseworthy—think about such things.—**Philippians 4:8**

How is your day going so far? Did you wake up singing praises to Jesus, with an expectant heart filled with anticipation of an intimate encounter with the Father? Were you rejoicing in the day made by our Lord? How about the first words spoken to another human being this morning? They were sweet and kind, filled with encouragement, right?

What? Your day didn't start out like that? Perhaps the alarm went off or the baby started crying, you jumped out of bed and haven't had an extra minute for some alone time with God. The boys fought during breakfast and your daughter couldn't find anything to wear. There wasn't any bread to make sandwiches for lunch and that homework assignment that should have been completed the night before was now jammed in the printer. In the chaos the kids missed the bus and now you must drive them to school. But wait—you have a meeting and you will end up being late too.

Perhaps your husband has been the wonderful man he always is, helping with the morning routine, but you both know that life will be different soon since he was just laid off from his job. The bills are already piling up and the car needs new tires. Or perhaps you don't even own a car and there's no way to drive the kids to school now that they have missed the bus.

Wayward children, illness, homework, jobs, deaths, troubled relationships, divorce, single parenting, unemployment, traffic, deadlines, broken appliances, not enough sleep—and on and on. There is so much happening in our lives that can rob us of peace and joy if we allow our minds to become entangled in the busyness and messiness of life. We are humans living in a fast-paced world and it's difficult to escape.

It's difficult, but not impossible, to enter into God's peaceful kingdom. Jesus did it. "I have told you these things, so that in me you may have peace. In this world you will have trouble. But take heart! I have overcome the world" (John 16:33).

"But take heart," He tells us. Our Lord and Savior overcame this world! Right now, ponder those words of triumph. Through Jesus' victory on the cross, we also have victory in our everyday struggles. We can begin with Scripture to meditate on instead of allowing our minds to be infested with Satan's lies. Words that fill our hearts with hope and get our minds focused on the Father's truths.

Today, I started us off with a verse that has been my saving grace time after time. For those times when I just wanted to throw up my hands and quit. Oh, the countless occasions I wanted to lash out and verbalize the horrible thoughts that were spinning in my head, the Holy Spirit held my tongue and put this verse on my heart instead.

A single verse can't replace quality time with the Father, but it's a place to begin when it's just one of those days. When your head is spinning with worry, frustration, fear, anger and doubt, think about the words of Philippians 4:8 (or the go-to verse of your choice). If this is a stormy, blustery season or simply a rough start to the day, I pray that you will find your way into God's peaceful kingdom—even if it's one verse at a time.

Since Philippians 4:8 is one of my favorites, I felt it only appropriate to give it this special day of 4/8.

April 9

Though the fig tree does not bud and there are no grapes on the vines, though the olive crops fail and the fields produce no food, though there are no sheep in the pen and no cattle in the stalls, yet I will rejoice in the Lord, I will be joyful in God my Savior.—**Habakkuk 3:17-18**

As I was walking into the grocery store shortly after moving to Austin, I noticed a woman entering at the same time. She clutched the hand of her son, who wore headphones over his ears. Something told me he wasn't a typical little boy, but I also knew immediately this was no ordinary woman.

She moved quickly through the store, gathering only a few items. She never let go of her son's hand or took her eyes off of him, nor did he take his off her. I only had a few things to get as well, and we ended up at the checkout together. I wasn't staring; I was just in awe of this woman who was lovingly attending to the needs of her son, while taking care of the necessities in life.

She had smiles for other people—she even smiled at me. She also spoke kind words to the cashier. But in her eyes I saw an intent look. This woman had a child requiring some type of extra care, yet she moved with such flawless grace. I saw God in her heart. Even in the busyness and stress of her life, she glowed with a certain joy. Weeks later, at a church we had been attending, I saw her again. Later, I discovered she was the pastor's wife.

Several years have passed, and we are members of that church. I have learned details about their special-needs son and the unending trials they had already endured—the unanswered questions, the countless hospital visits, the sleepless nights, the challenges of maintaining a "normal" home life with a child having a condition that remains undiagnosed. Yet, this pastor and his wife love their Lord and Savior, and their faithfulness is for all to see.

My first impression of Courtney when I saw her in the grocery store was that she was a godly woman. Now that I know her personally, I realize she is that—and so much more. Courtney is God's instrument. He uses her to sing His praises, as she lives her life for His glory in the middle of her daily storms.

Courtney is a living testimony of a woman who still praises God and finds tremendous joy in Him, despite the unusual trials in her life. I am moved through music, and when I see her, I think of the song by Casting Crowns, "Praise You in the Storm." (If you aren't familiar with it, please Google the lyrics and you will find encouragement.) She touched my life, even before I knew her, and she still does—reminding me of what it looks like to sing His praises in the storms of life; to find joy in the Lord, a joy that surpasses life's circumstances.

Tomorrow, you will read a poem written by Courtney. Be prepared to be encouraged!

April 10

Blessed be the God and Father of our Lord Jesus Christ, the Father of mercies and God of all comfort, who comforts us in all our tribulation, that we may be able to comfort those who are in any trouble, with the comfort with which we ourselves are comforted by God.—**2 Corinthians 1: 3-4 (NKJV)**

"Great is Thy Faithfulness!"
Song sung many times,
Only words, not much meaning.
April 10, 2003,
Brad preaches: David and Goliath
Children growing, family happy, future hopeful!
One day later, son's life falls apart.
Can't explain it, can't understand it, can't stop it!
Still singing, only words, not much meaning.
Journey begins. Five states traveled, lots of doctors, too many medications.
Nothing changes!
Still singing, voice faint, only words, meaning questioned?
Therapy starts, battling insurance, bills stacking up, still not sleeping.
Where are you, God?
Right here, Courtney!
I'M paying your bills, providing meals, training therapists, guiding doctors, setting up special programs, scheduling faithful babysitters, sustaining your marriage, and protecting your every step.
Still singing, voice louder, becomes personal.
All prayers answered? Not yet, maybe never, Thy will be done!

But, never lonely, not forgotten, never in need!
Great is Thy Faithfulness! Not words . . . Reality!

We all have a story to tell of God's faithfulness. Some that encourage others, some that encourage us alone, but all that praise God! Who needs to hear your story today?

Courtney Bennett Thomas
Austin, TX

April 11

Be joyful always; pray continually; give thanks in all circumstances, for this is God's will for you in Christ Jesus.
—1 Thessalonians 5:16-18

Mitch and I celebrated our wedding anniversary yesterday. It's hard to believe we have been married since 1971. And it seems like only yesterday that I was walking down the aisle. Looking back on all the years we have been together, I know that the Lord has been with us on this long journey. I have tried to live out 1 Thessalonians 5:16-18 in my marriage, and with God's help I am learning every day to look to Him.

When I was only 24 years old, we moved to Batman, Turkey. I had rarely left Meridian, Mississippi, and here we were leaving all our family and friends, going to a country where I would not even be able to make a phone call much less be able to go home for two years. To tell you the truth, I was not looking forward to my first Christmas away from home and family. With God's help, it was a Christmas that I will never forget.

The time that we spent in Turkey taught me how to appreciate everything in life, not only material things but just being able to be together with Mitch. When we left the U.S. to go overseas, we said it would be for only two years. Well, after 11 years and four countries, we returned with two beautiful daughters, ages 6 and 4. (One conceived in Sudan and born in Mississippi, and the other one born in Tunis, Tunisia.)

I can tell you that the Lord was with me every minute of every day, showing me all the wonders that He had for me in this world. It did not matter where we were and how difficult the hardships in the country we were living in at the time, He always showed me the good of the place. I will always thank Him for the people and the experiences that we had while living overseas.

After coming back to California for four years, we moved back overseas to Kuala Lumpur, Malaysia. Angela and Ashley learned about other cultures and how to appreciate all that the United States has to offer. I pray that they will never forget their experiences they had while living in Tunisia, Egypt and Malaysia. In our second tour overseas, we lived in Malaysia for about three years and then moved to Pittsburgh for nine months. In 1995, we moved to Houston.

Mitch had always told the girls that when they got in high school, we would stay in one place to let them finish. Guess what? That is what we did. Then the Lord had different plans for us. As soon as Ashley graduated in 2001, we moved to Saudi Arabia. He knew that was what we needed to start our empty-nesting and get us ready for Mitch's retirement. I love and treasure our children and how they have enriched our lives, but I am thankful for the alone time Mitch and I have enjoyed.

I believe and know that the Lord knew we needed that time together to grow and learn to be one. Since Mitch retired, we have been able to take many motorcycle trips, enjoying all of God's wonderful and amazing works. His most amazing wonder is our grandson, Aiden. What a blessing, getting to know and help take care of him. In the last few months of 2010, Aiden's little sister Chloe was born and his cousin Aaron. God is so good.

I am so grateful the Lord put Mitch in my life. We have had our bad times, but with God's help, we have had more good ones. I give Him all the praise and glory for everything. I pray that God will give us many more years together, and that we will be a blessing to everyone that He puts in our path. I want to live every day being joyful, a prayer in my heart, giving thanks in all our circumstances, for this is God's will for us in Christ Jesus.

We had a special anniversary celebration! Mitch, thank you for all the love you have given me each and every year. What a wonderful life you and God have given me.

Syble Tillman
Houston, TX

April 12

I press on towards the goal to win the prize for which God has called me heavenward in Christ Jesus.—**Philippians 3:14**

On Easter Sunday 2012, Pastor Brad began his sermon by saying, "I love underdogs—love them. I love pulling for teams that no one else thinks are going to win." Knowing how much of a golf enthusiast Brad is, I wonder if he was pulling for Bubba Watson to win the Masters Tournament that very afternoon?

I am not a golfer nor do I enjoy watching the game. However, my husband was right in front of the TV, and, even though I was in another room, I could hear the comments and the cheers. The announcers were offering little tidbits of information about a particular player. I learned this man had never had a professional golf lesson, his father died of cancer two years earlier and he and his wife had just adopted a baby boy.

The golf pros of the world were probably cringing at those comments about never taking a golf lesson, but I thought it was very interesting and inspiring! Being one of those moms who took both of her sons for private pitching, batting, goalie, kicking and punting lessons, as well as sending them to all kinds of sports camps, I felt a bit foolish.

When I overheard that it was a sudden-death playoff, I was intrigued. The curiosity in me prevailed, and I went into the other room just in time to see Bubba Watson sink the putt that made him the champion of the 2012 Masters. As he hugged his caddy tightly and openly wept, I cried along with him. I had never even heard of the man until that afternoon, but I somehow knew that he was considered an underdog, an unlikely candidate to win such a prestigious tournament.

The next morning, I received an online devotional from the Austin Fellowship of Christian Athletes. The Austin FCA online message is called "Inspired" and offers information and quotes from Christian athletes and coaches, both college and professional. This story was about Bubba Watson.

Steve Vittorini with the FCA said, "Bubba's the real deal, folks. He uses his PGA platform to bring God into the mainstream conversation." I decided to dig a little deeper into this new celebrity—this man who thanked his Lord and Savior Jesus Christ after he slipped into that green jacket.

There was a radio interview on CBSsports.com in which Tim Brando referred to Bubba as a "golfing accident" because of his unorthodox swing and YouTube videos. He asked Bubba if there was some type of "higher force" that was with him during the Masters. Bubba responded that as a Christian, he had to believe that God was in control and he was to let God's will happen.

Bubba openly wept on many of the post-tournament talk shows that I saw. He was most emotional when speaking of his newly adopted son, Caleb. There was one show, Morning Drive, I saw on GolfChannel.com where Bubba made a surprise visit. He said that it was more of an honor to have his son in his arms (after arriving home from the Masters) than to wear the green jacket. And, on speaking of the timing of the adoption, he said that it was all in God's planning.

The mainstream media isn't very receptive to speaking about the Christian religion, but even ABC News with Dianne Sawyer mentioned the "golfing accident," and reporter Josh Elliot called Watson a "man of deep faith." (On the flip side, ESPN somehow developed "technical difficulties" just as Watson mentioned Jesus.)

Because of his win, Bubba can no longer be considered an underdog, though, can he? Being the 2012 Masters champion is currently his claim to fame, but only time will tell how God will use this now-famous golfer for His purpose. Long after the bright green jacket fades, the bright light of Jesus can continue to shine through him, God willing.

On Easter Sunday, Christians celebrate the resurrection of Jesus Christ and His victory over death—"the last enemy to be destroyed is death" (1 Corinthians 15:26). Winning the Masters must be an indescribable experience, and only one can take home that prize. However, each and every one of us can claim the prize that God has promised. Plus, we have opportunities every day to share the incredible Good News.

After the sermon, we sang one last song—the timeless hymn "Victory in Jesus." Amen!

April 13

I can do everything through him who gives me strength.—**Philippians 4:13**

If you have been walking with Jesus for years or just started your journey, you are most likely familiar with Philippians 4:13. For many, it is one of those "go-to" verses we keep tucked in our hearts and refer to in the moments we need immediate motivation. According to Biblegateway.com, the popular online site for researching Scripture, it was the third top verse for 2012.

There are two online sites I subscribe to that send me a verse every day, and I have tried to make it a practice to look up the passage in my Bible, reading the verses before and after the one I received. Those few extra minutes in my Bible every morning have opened many new doors in my relationship with Christ and my knowledge of Him.

The morning that Philippians 4:13 was the daily Scripture, I pondered what Paul wrote to the Christians at Philippi (and all believers) prior to those popular words: "I am not saying this because I am in need, for I have learned to be content whatever the circumstances. I know what it is to be in need, and I know what it is to have plenty. I have learned the secret of being content in any and every situation, whether well fed or hungry, whether living in plenty or in want. I can do everything through him who gives me strength" (Vs. 11-13*)*.

Paul was writing this letter while in prison. Earlier in verse 3:10, he told the church that he wanted to know Christ and the power of the resurrection. He needed that power to get him through the trial—his circumstance. Even earlier in Romans 8:11, Paul told all believers, "If the Spirit of him who raised Jesus from the dead is living in you, he who raised Christ from the dead will also give life to your mortal bodies through the Spirit, who lives in you."

Could that be Paul's "secret" to being content in any and every situation? If we have accepted Christ as our Lord and Savior, we have that same Spirit that raised Jesus from the dead living in us. Doesn't that thought just give you all kinds of hope and encouragement? That same indescribable power that resurrected Jesus lives and operates in the body of every believer!

Allocate some time to explore Paul's letters. There, he will unlock the mysteries to overcoming all obstacles that will be encountered in this life on earth.

"In reading this, then, you will be able to understand my insight into the mystery of Christ (Ephesians 3:4). I pray that out of his glorious riches he may strengthen you with power through his Spirit in your inner being, so that Christ may dwell in your hearts through faith "(Vs. 16-17).

"Now to him who is able to do immeasurably more than all we ask or imagine, according to his power that is at work within us, to him be glory in the church and in Christ Jesus throughout all generations. Amen" (Vs. 20-21).

Go forth today knowing that you *can* do all things through Christ who gives you strength. By the way, did you notice the correlation of the date, 4/13 with the verse 4:13?

April 14

Once God has spoken; twice have I heard this; that power belongs to God.—**Psalm 62:11 (ESV)**

God is powerful! I've known that all my life. But what does it really mean?

Exodus 15:6 tells us, "Your right hand, O LORD, is majestic in power, your right hand, O LORD, shattered the enemy." And Daniel 2:20: "Praise be to the name of God forever and ever; wisdom and power are his."

Powerful means controlling the outcome! Whether it's a battle with guns in the Middle East or an arm-wrestling battle in your home, the one with the power controls the outcome! I worked in a business where the most powerful man was not the president, but a manager. If he decided that he didn't like you, whether you reported to him or not, you would soon be gone. He controlled the outcome. In sports, the most powerful team wins the game. It controls the outcome. But does it really?

Our Powerful God is the One in charge of the outcome! He is sovereign. He controls the outcomes of office politics and national politics. God controls the outcomes: physical, emotional and spiritual. I don't go to battle with a sword or a gun, but I do battle in personal ways. When I am battling disease or fatigue, God controls the outcome. When I am battling the bills, or am betrayed by a loved one, God controls the outcome. When Satan taunts me with lies about my worth or about God's love for me, God controls the outcome.

Because of that, I can trust in His power and His ability, rather than my own. I can trust because I know that He is good, that everything that He does is ultimately for my good and His glory.

I don't have to worry! I make it a practice to not worry about things that are not in my sphere of control. There is no point in being concerned about something that I have no control over. It only serves to drag me down. If I do have control, then I must do what I can. Then, I leave it in God's hand, and not worry about it. That is freeing!

Powerful God, I thank You for controlling the outcomes. I rest in that knowledge!

Fran Upton
Austin, TX

April 15

So if you faithfully obey the commands I am giving you today—to love the LORD your God and to serve him with all your heart and with all your soul—then I will send rain on your land in its season, both autumn and spring rains, so that you may gather in your grain, new wine and oil.—**Deuteronomy 11:13-14**

March winds, April showers, bring forth May flowers. It is April, but there haven't been too many rain showers here in the Hill Country. But on this particular April morning, I woke up to the heavenly sound of thunder and rain beating down on my metal roof.

Yes, rain, glorious rain! God knew I would be delighted with His gift. Here we were in the middle of *another* serious drought. Back in July of 2007, lake levels were seriously low and there was a major flood along the Highland Lakes. Unfortunately, many along Lake Travis suffered severe damage. We had been praying for rain at that time, but failed to be more specific and ask for smaller increments instead of a total lake refill all in one night.

After that flood, there was no measurable rain for over two years. Lake Travis recorded the fourth-lowest level in history during that drought of 2009.

Beautiful Lake Travis looked like a creek. Marinas that had been located in quiet coves were forced to totally relocate out to the main body of water because the coves were dry. All but one of the public boat ramps was closed for almost the whole summer of 2009. It was a sad sight indeed, along with being a financial disaster for businesses located on the lake.

Water rationing was strictly enforced and green lawns turned into brown fire hazards.

The farms and ranches in central Texas were severely affected by the drought, not just the residents in Austin areas. Ranchers had to sell off their cattle at record low prices because there was no hay to feed the animals, and if hay could be found to buy, it was too expensive to afford. Farmers lost their entire crops.

Lake Travis isn't just a pretty face. She plays a very important role, serving as a reservoir. Lake Travis supplies water to hundreds of thousands of homes in the greater Austin area, as well as water for industry and energy.

Water is released from Lake Travis when springs and tributaries that feed into the lower Colorado River do not provide enough water to meet the needs downstream, including irrigation for the agriculture crops and the need for fresh water in Matagorda Bay on the Gulf Coast. Fresh water from Lake Travis is needed to maintain a healthy habitat for fish and other aquatic life way down on the coast. The water in this lake is crucial to the food supply and livelihood of millions!

In the fall of 2009, there were some soaking rains and the lake actually rose about 10 feet. Then slowly over the next few months, there was more rain and by the spring of 2010, Lake Travis was back to the normal level. No major flooding, no damage, no deaths. What a blessing.

Unfortunately, there has been no significant rain since 2010, and 2013 surpassed the lowest levels from 2009. This April shower only lasted for 15 minutes, but every drop is a special gift. The previous drought taught me an important lesson in trust—only God can bring the rain.

Deuteronomy 11:13-14 states *we* must obey His commands, then He will send the rain. I do realize that we must be very specific for the location and the amount of rain we ask for because parts of our world are receiving devastating amounts right now, but clearly prayers are needed for much more than rain. Prayer is needed for all of the people affected by this drought, similar to what David prayed in Psalm 122 for his brothers and sisters in Jerusalem. He prayed for peace and prosperity, the kind of peace that can only be found through faith in God and obedience to His commands.

Oh, Jehovah-jireh, I pray 2 Chronicles 7:13-14 right now for all residents in this drought-stricken area of central Texas. You have shut the heavens and there is no rain. May we, who are called by Your name, humble ourselves and pray and seek Your face and turn from our wicked ways. In our true repentance, in our obedience, may there be forgiveness and healing of our land. Amen!

April 16

"I will make you a great nation." —**Genesis 12:2**

Father, forgive me for my pride, my impatience and my self-sufficiency in attempting to live my life apart from total trust and dependence on You.

Lord, in Your Word, You give us examples of those who followed You with unwavering patience and trust. Abraham never doubted You as the years went by and he grew to a very old age. In Genesis 15:5, when promised descendants too numerous to count, Abram was 75 years old and childless. *"Look up at the heavens and count the stars—if indeed you can count them."* Then you said, *"So shall your offspring be."*

Abram waited; he and wife Sarai remained without a child. When Abram was 99 years old, You appeared to him again and said, "As for me, this is my covenant with you: You shall be the father of many nations. No longer will you be called Abram, your name will be Abraham, for I have made you the father of many nations. I will make you fruitful" (Genesis 17:4-6).

Finally, when Abraham was 100 years old and Sarah (formally Sarai) 90, You did for Sarah what had been promised. Sarah became pregnant and bore a son to Abraham in his old age, at the very same time You had promised him (Genesis 21:2). Abraham waited for 25 years for that promise to be fulfilled.

Moses waited many years for Your calling, and served You in the wilderness for 40 years. Joseph trusted You in prison, and went on to lead a mighty nation. Paul glorified You while in chains, and led multitudes to You. John wrote Your brilliant book in exile.

They and countless others served You while waiting in total patience and faith for Your perfect timing. They trusted and obeyed You, Lord, and You blessed them. I am humbled by what You accomplished through them, and for their waiting, their trust and their patience.

Lord, I thank You that patience was given to us as a gift from the Holy Spirit: "But the fruit of the Spirit is love, joy, peace, patience, kindness, goodness, faithfulness, gentleness, and self-control" (Galatians 5:22).

Help me, Father, to live in patience, totally loving and trusting You in every area of my life.

Judy Wickham
Dripping, TX

April 17

For the LORD is the great God, the great King above all gods. — **Psalm 95:3**

I flopped down on the couch, totally exhausted. I don't watch TV much, but went ahead and turned it on, flipping through the channels. Upon seeing Chris Tomlin, I stopped to listen as he sang "How Great is Our God." *Sing with me, how great is our God.* Oh my goodness, did I ever agree with those words after the events of that hectic day!

It started out with me in Austin and my husband working in Houston. It was a Wednesday, so I went to Java Dive for my weekly coffee time with a group of friends. Before saying our good-byes, we went around the table sharing our plans for the rest of the day. I was looking forward to an afternoon of writing, sprinkled with a Pilates class and a long overdue pedicure. Sounds lovely, doesn't it?

In a split second, those plans changed. Before leaving the group, I checked my phone and noticed a missed call and text from my husband. He was at the ER in Houston and being admitted to the hospital—for a possible heart attack. I went home, grabbed some clothes and my dog then headed that direction.

Austin is a bit overweight, doesn't exercise, works extremely hard and has high blood pressure, making him a prime candidate for some heart-related health issues. However, during the three-hour drive, I was in a state of shock by the unexpected news and my mind was racing. What if my husband died?

We were too young for that. Our year-long house remodel was almost complete. I couldn't handle the house and big yard by myself. Summer was around the corner. We had so many plans, which by no means included a heart attack. His two children, even though they were grown, depended on him. What in the world would they do without their dad? What would I do without my husband—my very best friend?

I prayed. I pleaded. However, deep down I knew that all the days ordained for my husband were written in God's book (Psalm 139:16), which offered me a sense of peace. God was in control, but I still prayed big and bold.

Thankfully, it wasn't a heart attack. Austin's problem wasn't even heart-related. He needed to remain in the hospital for additional tests the next day, but I was able to leave for the night, knowing he was out of immediate danger. Before I left though, we prayed. As my husband began to give thanks to the Lord, I looked down at our hands, tightly clasped together.

Our pairs of hands looked a bit seasoned. We certainly weren't as young as we used to be, and there were well-defined signs of wear and tear, along with some arthritic, crooked fingers. We have only been married since 2005, but I thought of couples that have celebrated 50-60 years together. My husband and I will never make that mark, but what a special gift to be able to grow old with your spouse. We are all going to die one day, but we are not all given the privilege of reaching the golden years with the one we love still by our side. Our hands might have looked a bit aged, but I sure was thankful for God's gift of another day to grow more "mature" with my man. I prayed that when the day comes for one of us to depart this earth, that our hands would look *extremely* decrepit, with knotty, crooked fingers intertwined together.

I was curious about the concert on TV and discovered that it was *Night of Joy*, a contemporary Christian musical festival sponsored by Disney that has been going on since 1983. Wow! I had no idea. I was watching a taping of the event that had previously occurred on September 7, 2012, at Cinderella's Castle in the Magic Kingdom and featured Needtobreathe, Chris Tomlin and Casting Crowns.

As Chris Tomlin finished "How Great is Our God," I was overwhelmed with thanksgiving for my Father's love and mercy. Not only was my husband still alive, and actually very healthy, but God had arranged for me to find that specific channel—so I could sit back and enjoy my own night of joy, listening to some of the most powerful worship music ever, singing my own praises to our great God.

April 18

Then the word of the LORD came to Jonah a second time. —**Jonah 3:1**

Yesterday, I wrote about my husband's unexpected trip to the ER because of a suspected heart attack. After a short hospital stay to run tests, he was released with a clean bill of health for his heart. Other, less serious issues would be addressed later. I drove back home to Austin, and my husband stayed in Houston to finish some work.

As I merged onto I-10 west towards Austin, the song on the radio was Jason Gray's "Good To Be Alive." After driving to Houston two days earlier, thinking my husband had suffered a heart attack and expecting the worst, it was a definite hallelujah for him to be alive.

About a third of the way to Austin I lost the Houston station so I switched over to The Message on satellite radio. Within a few minutes, I heard it again. *I wanna live like there's no tomorrow. . . It's good to be alive.* As I approached Austin, I turned to a local Christian radio station to stay on top of the traffic situation. About a mile from my house, I heard those now familiar words for a third time in three hours: *It's good to be alive.*

My husband wasn't actually close to dying, but I didn't know that at first, nor did he. We were both terrified. But I know God gives us those little wake-up calls for a reason—to get our attention so we focus on Him, not our own agenda. God was working in other ways too.

Pastor Brad had been preaching on Ephesians for several months, and the Sunday before the trip to the ER, the sermon was based on 5:22: "Wives submit to your husbands as to the Lord." Oh, how I needed a sermon to help me be a better wife! I had been trying to control my husband, trying to transform him into the image I wanted, instead of praying for him to be transformed into the image of Christ. My husband is a unique, God-created man. Why did I expect him to think like me and do things my way?

If the husband is to be the head of the wife, as Christ is the head of the church (Vs. 23), we want our husbands to be like Christ, don't we? We should be praying daily for them to be consumed from the inside out with more of Jesus. As Christ served His disciples and loved on others, we want our husbands to do the same for his family. There's great responsibility in being the spiritual leader, and we need to be covering our husbands in prayer every single day, for God to equip and protect them.

After Brad's sermon, I was filled with excitement and great anticipation of how God was going to help me become that Ephesians 5:22 wife. God breathed His instructions to Paul on how to do marriage, and I had read them many times before. Although I had good intentions in the past, God was giving me another chance, telling me again what He expected of a godly wife. I felt He had been preparing my heart so *this time* I was better equipped for obedience.

I had a thought when I was paralyzed with fear that my husband had suffered a heart attack: What if he died and I didn't get another chance? Yep, I pleaded with God for a do-over, and He so mercifully answered my prayer.

God gave Jonah a second chance to allow for faith and obedience to work. God didn't put me in the belly of a whale, like Jonah, to get my attention for being disobedient. However, He did create a possible life-changing situation that opened my eyes to His message.

We only get so many chances and have so much time in this life. If you are reading this page right now, this very minute is a gift from your Father. Right here, right now, you have been given that second chance to do life God's way.

I pray we will live like there's no tomorrow. And love others, especially our husbands if married, like we're on borrowed time—because we are! It's all God's time. Let's live and love well for His glory.

April 19

"Remember not the former things, nor consider the things of old. Behold, I am doing a new thing; now it springs forth, do you not perceive it?" —Isaiah 43:18-19 (ESV)

A few years ago, when I told my then 6-year-old son Noah that we would be moving from our tiny Texas town to Austin, he had mixed emotions, and so did I. We would be moving away from our family, from good friends, from a church family that knew our songs, our cries, our petitions and our praises. We would be saying good-bye to the familiarity of a home whose walls held lots of preschool art projects and listened to countless moonlit prayers.

Everyone knew us by name. People I didn't even recognize approached me along the cobblestone sidewalks downtown to share with me that they hunted bucks with my brother, that they saw Noah play soccer, that my mom makes the best chocolate rum cake in the world. Teachers, coaches' wives, pastors' wives, grocery-store clerks, ranch hands, the local billionaire, the county judge . . . all of our kids played together, and we all served the one true God together.

As God has been known to do, He was prompting me to leave behind these wonderful comforts, and move us forward into the next chapter: Austin, Texas, where good schools, live music, lots of kid activities, autism resources, and wonderful friends—old and new—awaited us with open arms. *But where will we live, God? Where will Noah go to school? Where will we worship? How will it all work?*

You know, the servants of biblical times moved a lot. The Israelites moved from barren desert to barren desert; the New Testament disciples followed Jesus up and down the shorelines of the Galilean Sea. God often calls us to move, whether it's from one location in the world to another or from one space in our hearts and minds to another. One of my favorite sayings is this: "Jesus will meet you wherever you are; He just loves you too much to let you stay there." God tells us in Isaiah 43:18-19, "Remember not the former things, nor consider the things of old. Behold, I am doing a new thing; now it springs forth, do you not perceive it?"

So, writing of new things, at my church in Austin we're learning the creation story in Sunday school. When I read to my very literal son, " . . . and the spirit of God *moved* upon the face of the waters" (Genesis 1:2), he wrinkled his nose and asked, "What did God move like? Like a monkey? Like a pterodactyl?" I laughed with him and decided to look up the Hebrew word for *moved*. *M'rahaphet* means "to flutter or shake."

Flutter. I instantly thought of butterflies. Have you ever seen a flutterby of Monarch butterflies? Each fall, these amazing creatures migrate over 2,500 miles from east of the Rocky Mountains to the Oyamel fir trees of Mexico.

I'll bet those butterflies don't spend a single wing flutter thinking about where they'll stay along the way, how difficult the journey might be, or how much effort it will take to get there. They just sense the winds of change, grab a friend or a hundred, and move! Scientifically, they shouldn't have enough fuel to make it that far, but they do—year after year. Some believe that they glide along the wind currents to conserve energy. Sounds a lot like that old adage "go with the flow," doesn't it?

What if, when God calls us to move, we make a flutter? What if we spread our wings and ride along the current of the Holy Spirit, trusting God to provide exactly what we need to get there? If God loves us even as much as the butterflies, we know this—the journey is going to be amazing, we're going to be in beautiful company, and we're going to have everything we need to reach our destination. Allow God to soar you, fuel you, love you, and move you. I will if you will. Meet you on the next fir tree.

Kristen M
Austin, TX

April 20

As iron sharpens iron, so one man sharpens another.—**Proverbs 27:17**

On the drive home from LifeGroup that Sunday afternoon, my husband and I were still talking about our lively conversation. From the homework assignment through the open conversation at the end, I had been inspired and enlightened. I just cherish the six other couples God assembled for us to share life with and am so thankful for each and every one of them.

I confessed to my husband that I "needed" to be with our LifeGroup. I yearned for the truthful biblical discussions. I appreciated that there was never any condemnation to a response, but if it wasn't biblically based, there would be sound correction. We were challenged to dig deeper and the discussions were always thought-provoking and stimulating. The quality and quantity of theological wisdom and knowledge in the group, when pulled together, was incredible.

There was always great encouragement, lots of laughter, a few tears along the way and priceless Christian fellowship. But most importantly, I felt it was an opportunity for refinement. Everyone in the group had unique, special gifts and all contributed to the process of sharpening each other. The Holy Spirit put the words of Proverbs 27:17 on my heart as I told my husband I needed those folks each week to sharpen me, to make me stronger in my faith. To put me into the fire and test me, as God refined silver (Psalm 66:10).

The very next Monday morning while reading my online devotions, I came across the one sent from the Austin Fellowship of Christian Athletes titled "Inspired" and written by Steve Vittorini. Monday through Friday, Steve highlights a coach or an athlete (from all levels of the playing field) and shares how faith has impacted their life in sports. This day the focus was on John Harbaugh, head coach of the Super Bowl champion Baltimore Ravens.

Steve always begins with a quote. In this one, Coach Harbaugh stated that competition is like the fire that refines us. He wrote, "Coach Harbaugh loves God and is passionate about weaving his faith into how he coaches." Steve went on to share that in an ESPN.com interview, Harbaugh told the reporter he often referenced Proverbs 27:17 in team meetings because he believed it encompassed what is true of football. He also felt a team must incorporate devotion and fellowship to be successful.

The Holy Spirit put that Scripture in my heart twice in less than 12 hours. What is God telling me? My LifeGroup is like a successful football team? We both come together in fellowship. We challenge each other; push each other to be all that we can be—on the football field and in God's kingdom?

No, I don't think that was exactly God's message. As I pondered what it could be, I sensed the Holy Spirit asking me a question. We had a great adventure together searching for the answer, and tomorrow I will tell you all about it.

April 21

So in Christ we who are many form one body. We have different gifts, according to the grace given us.—**Romans 12:5-6**

Yesterday, I wrote how the Holy Spirit put a verse on my heart twice within a 12-hour period: "As iron sharpens iron, so one man sharpens another" (Proverbs 27:17). As I pondered what God's purpose might be, the Holy Spirit responded by asking me a question: *How is iron sharpened?*

Good question. Since I was writing a story based upon that Scripture, perhaps I should understand how iron was actually sharpened. I thought a quick trip to the Internet would provide the answer. Wrong. I spent an entire afternoon reading a handful of the million-plus results, trying to understand the process.

According to Wikipedia, sharpening is defined as the process of creating or refining a sharp edge on a tool. Sharpening is done by grinding away material on the tool with another abrasive substance harder and stronger than the tool itself.

When I first Googled "how is iron sharpened" I read several current, scientific, high-tech articles. However, Proverbs was written during the Iron Age, which was the early part of King Solomon's reign. I read that during the Iron Age, a steel file was the most common tool used to sharpen blades.

According to eHow.com a standard metal file is still used today to file the edges of iron. The filing is done in "slow, measured strokes," resulting in a jagged edge. This rough edge is then rubbed back and forth against the surface of a hard water stone or whetstone, which will rub the jagged edge smooth. The last phase of the process involves running sandpaper along the sides of the iron blade edges, to blend the edge with the rest of the blade, while also adding one final dose of sharpness.

In my research of how to sharpen iron, it was clear that the material used to sharpen the other must be stronger, of a different material or alloy. My LifeGroup is made up of individuals of different strengths, along with an assortment of weaknesses, gifts, triumphs and baggage. For example, there are certainly some in my LifeGroup who I consider to be significantly stronger than others in their knowledge of Scripture and in their understanding of God's Word. Still others who once lived in a pit of darkness are now radiant with Jesus' glow of salvation. The sum of the personalities is what makes the group so beneficial as a whole.

The filing and grinding is done in "slow, measured strokes." Isn't that what the whole sanctification process is about? It happens a little bit at a time and it's not complete until our time on this earth is finished. The sharpening process also includes rubbing of the sides of the blades with sandpaper. How fortunate to be surrounded by other believers who are willing to say the difficult things, knowing their views just might be that friction needed to smooth another's rough edges.

The conclusion I gathered from my afternoon of research was whatever is used to sharpen a piece of iron, or another person, cannot be exactly like that piece of iron. That's why my LifeGroup can do what it does—because of our differences. We all came to the group with diverse strengths, gifts and personalities.

We grow stronger from the stronger ones. We flourish by being with those who aren't afraid to rub us the wrong way in the spirit of truth and love—even craving that sandpaper person to smooth away the rough edges so that our lives might be a shiny reflection of Christ.

God might have put this verse on my heart not once, but twice to emphasize the importance of the folks in my LifeGroup. We need the differences, the strengths and the abrasive surfaces to sharpen each other. We can't grow in our faith by only hanging out with others who think exactly as we do or have the same gift of knowledge. Being pushed towards stricter obedience to the Lord, nurtured in love, challenged to stretch our minds and go deeper into God's Word by a close community of believers is how man sharpens another.

Are you sharing life with a group of believers where you feel safe, challenged and encouraged—where both criticism and praise is given in the spirit of affection and received as a gift of love? Are you in a community with other God seekers, where the strength of the body is established by the sum of its diverse parts? Perhaps you can ponder those questions today and see where the Holy Spirit leads you.

April 22

God's blessing makes life rich; nothing we do can improve on God.—**Proverbs 10:22 (MSG)**

The Women's Ministry at church offered a wonderful community outreach program. Several times a year, during normal Tuesday-morning Bible study time, we had Service Day. Instead of going to church, we went out into the community. There were numerous projects to sign up for, so there was something for everyone in various parts of the city.

For one Service Day, I signed up to work at a non-profit social service organization on the outskirts of downtown Austin. The mission statement of this organization reads "to provide a service continuum for those experiencing poverty that begins with a safety net and links them to resources to achieve self-sufficiency." One of the safety nets is a community kitchen that serves lunch to 300-400 people Monday-Friday, no questions asked. My commitment for that Tuesday was to help prepare lunch.

I had volunteered at this organization before and was impressed with the services provided and the kitchen's efficiency. I signed up again, knowing that my time would be utilized for a meaningful task and that I would be blessed by the time spent there.

But this particular Tuesday, I was focused on all the other things going on in my life. I was more concerned with my own selfish needs instead of serving others. The temptation to stay home and work on my own to-do list was overwhelming, but not going wasn't an option. God had something in store for me, and I knew that. The Holy Spirit had whispered several times that morning that God had a surprise waiting for me.

The kitchen supervisor greeted me with a smile and an apron, along with explicit instructions on sanitary procedures. At 9 a.m., the kitchen was in full swing, filled with volunteers from several walks of life. There were interns from a local culinary school chopping vegetables for soup, and a few other interns making the soup in a huge industrial-sized pot. One woman from another church was slicing donated cakes into serving sizes, others from my church were peeling carrots to be used the next day for soup and salad. My job, along with two others from Bible study, was to make ham sandwiches—400 of them.

During the summer at our lake house, we often have large groups of our children's friends come out, and we fix sandwiches to take out on the boat. There is always a wide assortment of options: turkey or ham, wheat or white bread, American, Swiss or jalapeno jack cheese, regular or light mayo. Plain mustard, honey mustard or Dijon? Lettuce and tomatoes? Yes, sandwiches are made to order before being carefully placed in a Ziploc and labeled with a name.

This sandwich assembly line was a bit different. We set out 100 pieces of white bread on the counter (the very clean, sanitized counter), placed one slice of ham on each, topped it with another piece of bread and piled the 100 sandwiches in a large plastic tub. Then we repeated that procedure three more times. Large bowls of plain mustard and regular mayo were placed on a table as the only choices for condiments.

After making these 400 sandwiches, I will never make sandwiches at the lake house again without being reminded of this experience. There were no individual Ziploc bags with made-to-order sandwiches. There were no names designated for these ham sandwiches, but God knew exactly who would receive each and every one of them.

My 1½-hour time slot went by quickly. Then the kitchen manager asked if any of us could stay longer and help serve lunch because they were short volunteers for that Tuesday. So this was the surprise God had waiting for me!

God blessed me beyond measure for the next two hours. Over 350 people were served ham sandwiches, fruit salad, hot soup and some yummy-looking desserts, no questions asked. I thought I was just going to help prepare a meal, not get the honor of serving God's precious, hungry children. And to think that I almost missed out on receiving God's surprise that morning.

April 23

For from him and through him and to him are all things. To him be the glory forever! Amen.—**Romans 11:36**

Singer/songwriter Matt Redman released "10,000 Reasons" in the summer of 2011. However, it wasn't until the following spring that I heard it frequently on the radio. When it played on the drive to Pilates class one afternoon and then again on the way home less than two hours later, I felt the Holy Spirit nudging me to pay closer attention.

After singing it in church one Sunday, I finally decided to print out the words and do some research. It's a powerful song, proclaiming 10,000 reasons to praise and worship His holy name, but the lyrics that kept going through my head were the very first ones: *Bless the Lord, O my soul.*

One website revealed that Psalm 103 was the inspiration behind "10,000 Reasons." I opened my Bible and read and re-read that Scripture. "Praise the LORD, O my soul; all my inmost being, praise his holy name. Praise the LORD, O my soul, and forget not all his benefits—who redeems your life from the pit and crowns you with love and compassion" (Vs. 1-2, 4).

A few days later, Sharon Jaynes wrote a story titled, "It's Not About Me," for the Girlfriends in God online devotional. Her point was that true worship is all about putting the focus on God, not ourselves. She cited Psalm 62:5-8: "Find rest, O my soul, in God alone: my hope comes from him" (Vs. 5). There were those words again: "O my soul."

What exactly is a soul? Coming up with my own definition is beyond my limited expertise, so I will not go there, but I will use the words from The Message to help explain: "God formed man out of dirt from the ground and blew into his nostrils the breath of life. The Man came alive—a living soul!" (Genesis 2:7). I am blown away by that visual (no pun intended)—God blowing his life-giving breath into a lifeless body. All that I am is because of His breath and just as easily, He can take it away. God Almighty is the one with all the authority and power.

My life on this earth is certainly not about me because I wouldn't be here without God, but I sure tend to focus on myself. How easily I forget all the reasons to praise His holy name and all that He has done for me. I may sit in my quiet time and thank Him for the gorgeous sunset or for providing me with food to eat and a roof over my head, but Matt Redman writes of finding *10,000* reasons to sing praises to the Lord. WOW!

So, was that why the Holy Spirit kept on singing *Bless the Lord, O my soul* over and over in my head? Did He take me to those Scriptures to tell me to stop thinking so much about Brenda and to praise the One and Only more? Aren't I supposed to give the One who redeemed me from the pit all of the glory? How have I become so self-centered?

With an existence consumed with iTunes, an iPod, iPad, and my constant companion, the iPhone, it is easy to see how "i" has become so predominant. But, I just took a double look at that little "i"—a spec above a simple vertical line. I need to remember just how small i am and how big my God is.

Thank You, dear Father, for placing such a sweet song in my heart. Forgive me for thinking so highly of myself that I have failed to give You the glory and praise that You alone are worthy of. May I not forget all of Your benefits—Your very breath that brought me to life and redeemed me from the pit of darkness. Hallelujah and Amen!

April 24

"I form the light and create darkness, I bring prosperity and create disaster; I, the LORD, do all these things."
—Isaiah 45:7

One fall, my mom and I went to Omaha, Nebraska, so she could visit a friend. It was such a fun, easy trip for her that we decided to do it again six months later. While I didn't anticipate any problems, having made the trip before, I was still a bit nervous. I don't like to fly and I get very anxious. The morning of our departure was no exception.

My husband gets exasperated with me when we travel because I insist on arriving at the airport at least two hours before the scheduled departure. Since it was just Mom and me going on this trip, I could leave as early as I wanted. We were flying out of Houston Intercontinental Airport, and just the thought of battling Houston morning-rush-hour traffic is enough to get me out of the house extra early.

To make the traffic conditions even more unpredictable, it was raining. Rain and rush hour can be a nasty combination in Houston, but on this particular morning we got to the airport in record time. So far, so good. We got our luggage checked, I took Mom into the terminal, and actually found a parking spot in the garage right by the elevator. We made it through security without Mom getting too flustered with all the rules. There was even time (plenty of it) for a sandwich before the flight. I was almost peaceful.

Once at our gate, I saw that our flight was still on time, but many others had been delayed due to the weather. I smugly thought to myself how lucky we were that ours would still depart on time, which it did. Sort of. We pulled away from the gate—but wait. Why are all those planes just parked on the runway? As our plane taxied by the parked ones, I once again thought how lucky we were that we didn't have to wait. But then the plane came to an abrupt halt and the pilot announced there would be a slight delay. We were number 20 in line for takeoff, the backlog caused by the weather. Estimated wait: 25 minutes.

That turned into an hour. As we sat, I couldn't help smiling. As carefully as I planned our morning—what time we woke up, when we left for the airport—and no matter how smoothly the check-in process had gone, I had no control over the weather. There was never any "luck" involved whatsoever in any of the flight takeoffs or delays. I am sure the One Who Is was smiling too—pleased that I acknowledged His control and relinquished some of mine.

Notice I said "some" of mine. Tomorrow, I will address the control issue.

April 25

I do believe; help me to overcome my unbelief.—**Mark 9:24 (NASB)**

Yesterday, I wrote about a flight delay on a trip with my mom to Omaha. I had already experienced anxiety just getting to the airport, but all had turned out better than I anticipated. Then the takeoff was delayed by an hour, which didn't help my uneasy feelings.

Because of bad weather, we were in a backlog of planes for takeoff. As we were waiting on the runway, I started thinking about why I get so anxious about flying. It didn't take me long to realize it is a control issue. I try to control the few things I *think* are controllable, like getting to the airport in plenty of time. However, when in that plane, I know I am totally out of control.

I have surrendered every ounce of me to that pilot. I can't even see where the plane is flying; I can barely see out one side of the plane or the other. I can't control the weather, the mechanics of the plane, the guys in the control tower—nothing! While I have surrendered all, I don't trust all the circumstances. Thus, the feeling of anxiety.

My life is the exact opposite of flying. I am full of anxiety in the plane because I don't have total trust, yet I have surrendered my life away. On the other hand, I have a hard time surrendering every part of me to God, even though I actually want to. I trust Him and know that His way is always the best, no matter what! I long for that feeling of total surrender, which can only come through complete obedience, but I stop short. What am I so afraid of?

There is beautiful hymn written by Judson W. Van DeVenter in 1896 that I often sing to myself, in hopes that God will hear my longing and help deliver me to such a place of joy.

All to Jesus I surrender; now I feel the sacred flame. Oh, the joy of full salvation! Glory, glory, to His Name! I surrender all; I surrender all. All to Thee, my blessed Savior, I surrender all.

Oh, my blessed Savior, I long for You to be Lord of my life. Take away the stubbornness I harbor in my heart and help me to come to a place of complete obedience and surrender. I want that joy that can only come through giving You every ounce of me. I feel so close, yet I am holding back part of myself. In my heart, I know You are the only One I can trust completely and You are the only One in complete control. I long for the day when I can say with great joy, *Father, I have surrendered all.*

April 26

He makes me lie down in green pastures, he leads me besides still waters, he restores my soul.—**Psalm 23:2-3 (NASB)**

Over the past few days, I have written stories about a trip to Omaha with my mom. We stayed in a beautiful hotel in downtown Omaha, right across the street from the historic Old Market. It was my third time to stay at that hotel and I just love the area. (By the way, if you are a baseball fan, the new stadium for the NCAA College World Series is just down the street!)

During our stay, we had a daily routine. Mom and I ate breakfast at the hotel and then I took her to spend the day with her friend, Charles, at his retirement home. She had the chance to meet his new friends and just hang out. (Even older people just like to hang out with their friends.) I picked them up in the evening, we went out to dinner, I took Charles home, and mom and I returned to our hotel. She went to bed and I stayed up late, writing devotions.

Mom woke up early, which meant I did too. One day, while I was by myself at the hotel, I had a real sinking feeling after lunch. My days and nights were spent writing, with little sleep, and I was just tired! I did something I never, ever do—I took a nap! Really, I never even napped when I had a new baby in the house. I closed those wonderful blackout curtains and just crawled into the soft, cushiony bed, with all the extra pillows and blankets that I don't have at home, and just snoozed for almost two hours. When I woke up, I almost felt like I had done something wrong, but I sure felt rested, renewed and ready to write a new story God had placed on my heart.

That evening, on my way to pick up the "kiddos" for dinner, I was listening to K-LOVE, a contemporary Christian music radio programming service. The DJ was talking about Sharon Young's devotional, *Jesus Calling*, and the specific story for that day. I have that book at home and read from it daily, but I didn't have it with me on the trip. (This was also prior to the app being available for my iPhone.) What a gift to hear the devotion on the radio.

The on-air DJ said Sharon Young wrote we should take little breaks from the chaos during the day. OK, maybe my two-hour nap was more than just a little break, but I felt as if God had just told me I hadn't done anything wrong at all. Didn't I wake up totally refreshed, with a new story on my heart?

How comforting to know that I can leave home without my devotionals, but God will be with me and His Word will reach me wherever I am. Even as I nap, He will restore my soul. "Surely [Your] goodness and love will follow me all the days of my life, and I will dwell in the house of the LORD forever" (Psalm 23:6).

April 27

Therefore, as God's chosen people, holy and dearly loved, clothe yourselves with compassion, kindness, humility, gentleness and patience.—**Colossians 3:12**

When a day starts out really crazy, when everything seems to go wrong, I keep my eyes wide open. Besides trying to stay positive, even though the circumstances aren't what I anticipated, I don't want to miss what God is doing. If He has totally reconstructed the day, He has my full attention. I have finally learned that when I encounter a roadblock, I need to look for the lesson in the detour.

While with my mom in Omaha, I had a major catastrophe—my computer crashed. Certainly not what I planned for the day. My computer is crucial to this book. Ideas may start in my journal, but through the magic of delete, cut and paste, and insert, the final story emerges.

After running some tests at the Apple Store, the diagnosis was worse than I expected. Based on the cost of repairs vs. a new computer, I decided to go with the new computer. Even though I was in Omaha, I decided to purchase it there, since I was already at the Apple Store.

My oldest son is a computer whiz. He had been the one to pick out my previous computer, transfer the data from my old one and teach me what to do. He is amazing! However, without Zach to help, I had to trust the people at Apple. Much had changed in the five years since I purchased my other computer, so a complete stranger was going to give me a crash course on the new one. Oh, how I resist change!

The Apple Store can be a very intimidating place if you are an older computer-illiterate, like me. A twenty-something person started asking me all kinds of questions I couldn't answer. Then she started racing through this and that on the computer. *Whoa, wait a minute. What did she say? How am I supposed to remember all that? I wish Zach were here. He would go slower because he knows my limitations.*

The twenty-something computer genius was actually very compassionate, totally aware of my apprehension to something new, and was extremely patient with me. Suddenly, I just started laughing. She was startled by my outburst and asked what was so funny. I told her my story.

I had spent several days with my aging mom and her friend, who has dementia. It was necessary to repeat myself numerous times, just during the course of a dinner. Though I tried to demonstrate some of the features on my smartphone, I was met with blank stares. I thought Mom finally grasped the idea of a text message only to have her ask why I was typing on my phone. I even tried to explain about blogs and what I do with my iPad, with no success. A new concept was difficult for either of them to understand. At times, I had been completely exasperated with both of them, as if I were just talking to myself. Now, the tables were turned.

I suddenly felt how my mom must feel. So inadequate, so ill-equipped to comprehend all the new, high-tech information I was receiving. How difficult it is to accept our slower minds and embrace change and unfamiliar circumstances. This twenty-something computer genius was demonstrating to me how to be gentle and patient with an "older," slower person. That "older" person was now me, not mom.

I knew there was a reason for my less-than-perfect day. Something good was to come from my computer crash. God wanted me to feel how my mom must be feeling these days.

In those situations when I start to get a bit frustrated with her, I need to remember how I felt that day. Had that computer genius become exasperated with me, I know I would have cried! I am so thankful that I kept my eyes wide open to see that I was at the Apple Store for much more than a new computer.

April 28

Weeping may remain for the night, but rejoicing comes in the morning.—**Psalm 30:5**

After my husband, Foster Whittaker, died, there were so many days I just wanted to give up. However, being left to raise three little boys, ages 3, 7 and 9, that wasn't actually an option. My parents died when I was young and my natural aunt and uncle raised me. They were wonderful Christians who took me to church and I knew of God. I prayed, but didn't actually know what it meant. With my husband gone, I felt so all alone.

At the age of 33, I didn't know if the pain of living without Foster would ever go away. Honestly, I wanted to stay in bed and just sleep and never get up. God let me wallow for a little bit, but then He spoke to my heart and said, "That is enough! This is what faith is—depending on Me when you don't know what to do."

Ladies, you may feel like you want to give up, but please press on with the Word of God, prayer and praise and worship songs. When I asked God what I should do, His answer was clear: "Trust Me, raise your boys, and I will take care of the rest." Then in my heart I heard the words from Matthew 6:33: "Seek ye first the kingdom of God"(KJV).

I aligned my life with God's directions, reading His Word with my sons and actively working in God's kingdom. I started seeing my life in a different light, knowing that God really would take care of my sons and me. I discovered many things outside of the church that I could do with my family that glorified God's kingdom as well.

My three boys are grown men today. Grown, godly men. Thanks to their Heavenly Father who did indeed take care of us. So when you feel down and out, don't give up or in. As Matthew 28:20 says: "And surely I am with you always, to the very end of the age."

Gloria Whittaker
The Woodlands, TX

April 29

Do not let any unwholesome talk come out of your mouths, but only what is helpful for building others up according to their need, that it may benefit those who listen.—**Ephesians 4:29**

The editor of this book, Rick Weber, and I have butted heads a few times during this journey, and other times he has made me laugh when he told me he just "didn't get" one of the stories he was reviewing. However, all in all, it has been a delightful experience working together.

We actually met at my previous church in Katy where Rick led the DivorceCare program and I was a volunteer. Rick's son, Austin, attended the program for the children, so I got to know him as well. It's hard to imagine that Austin is already a senior in high school and maturing into a fine young man.

One day, Rick shared with me that he helps Austin memorize Scripture. At the end of each year, he'll pray for God's direction in picking a Passage of the Year that Austin will memorize and commit to following. In 2004, he felt God calling him to Ephesians 4:29, perhaps because Austin seemed to be struggling with some back-talk issues, but also because a Christian rock band called Building 429 had formed in 2000 and was rapidly gaining in popularity.

What a great parenting tool! God's holy Word can arm our children with the best defense against all the evil that is found in our world and in their schools.

I think most of us are aware when "unwholesome talk" comes out of our mouth. On this date of 4/29, let us all focus on Ephesians 4:29. Perhaps if we commit this verse to memory, we too will be better equipped to monitor the words we speak. Being able to refer to specific Scripture is extremely effective in battling the evil we encounter daily. Come on, you are never too old or too busy to commit a verse to memory.

April 30

"Enter through the narrow gate. For wide is the gate and broad is the road that leads to destruction, and many enter through it. But small is the gate and narrow the road that leads to life, and only a few find it."—**Matthew 7:13-14**

My quiet time with God, before I ever get out of bed, is very special, unique, personal and intimate—most of the time. Unfortunately, there are some mornings that I just fly through my greetings. But on this particular one, I lingered and listened.

It was one of those days when everything just seemed right with the world. I woke up, full of anticipation of what God had in store for me. I had no problem with remembering my abundant blessings and telling Him all that I was thankful for. I didn't even think of asking my Father for anything. It was the day that the Lord had made, and I was rejoicing and being glad in it! (Psalm 118:24).

Truthfully, I dozed back off to sleep, being at such peace in His presence. All of a sudden, I shot up in bed, with the sound of my own voice waking me up! But I was puzzled because I wouldn't have thought of those specific words, not that morning. I hadn't planned on asking for anything. I thought it was a perfect day and I didn't need a thing.

Guide me rang loud and clear in my head. As hard as I was trying *not* to petition God that morning, I had asked Him to guide me? Why had the Holy Spirit put those words in my mouth? I was soon to find the answer.

I couldn't stop thinking of *guide me* as I fixed my coffee and gathered my daily devotions. I knew there was something special God wanted me to learn, and I thoroughly expected to find a message through one of my daily readings. Nope, there was nothing in any of the books I randomly picked out. I fixed my second cup of coffee and sat down at my computer. That's where I found the special devotion God had prepared just for me, written by one of His faithful servants.

Dr. Charles Stanley writes one of my daily online devotionals, and on this morning it was titled, "Two Gates, Two Ways," and the selected Scripture was Matthew 7:13-14, found above. To sum up his message, we can either walk along the wide path of destruction, without God in our life, which most people tend to like because it is easier. Or we can travel through the narrow gate that is guarded by the Lord.

Those who enter through the narrow gate, because of their faith in Christ and their intimate relationship with Him, find true peace and joy. Those who chose the wide gate, and conform to the standards of the present-day culture, are on the path to a disappointing life without God.

I know which path I want to travel. And even though I thought I didn't need to petition God for anything that morning, He knew I needed to ask for help. That's why He got my attention with *guide me*. I certainly can't stay on the path to heaven on my own strength and power. Yes, dear Father, guide me along that narrow road, through that small gate. Don't let me stray.

My quiet time with God, even before I get out of bed, now includes those special words. *Guide me*. I am so thankful He has taught me to linger and listen for His words of wisdom.

May 1

And we know that in all things God works for the good of those who love him, who have been called according to his purpose.—**Romans 8:28**

There is no hiding it: I am not the tidiest person. I have already written a few stories about trying to overcome being messy. As of yet, I haven't succeeded.

After living in our lake house for almost five years, my husband and I decided to remodel—a major endeavor requiring moving out of the house into our garage apartment. The home was in need of a re-do when we moved in and I knew the day was coming, but had put it off.

The thought of packing up the whole house, just for a short period of time, was the main reason the construction had been postponed for so long. What an ordeal. Yes, it is a blessing that we could proceed with a remodel in this tough economy, and it will certainly be wonderful to have more room and an updated kitchen when it was complete. However, boxing up just isn't my idea of fun.

One positive result from the process, however, was that my piles of stuff would get cleaned up. As I packed, I also tried to get organized and throw away any clutter. There was a stack of papers inside a cabinet that I looked through quickly to determine if they were important. To my surprise, I found two hidden treasures.

My sons write me letters for special occasions, like my birthday, Christmas and Mother's Day, and I have saved them in a folder. (I do try to keep important papers in a safe place.) In this stack, I found a Mother's Day letter from the previous year and one for my birthday written four years earlier from my younger son. I don't know how they got there, instead of the safe folder, but in the midst of the packing and all the mess, they were a delightful surprise.

I sent Trevor a quick email about what I had found: "Once again, I am sifting through piles of stuff and wondering how in the world they ever grew so out of control. However, there is some good that came out of the piles—like finding two letters you wrote. Had I been super-organized, I wouldn't have the pleasure of finding these hidden treasures to brighten up my day. I cherish your words and they always bring a smile to my face, along with some tears to my eyes."

Included in my email were also some motherly words of wisdom. Trevor had been going through a period of trials and I thought he could use encouragement, so I tried to weave Romans 8:28 into my message. The good out of packing and my messy piles was that I ran across his sweet letters. There would be good out of his situation too. I wrote, "Sometimes God lets us get so desperate that we have nowhere else to go but to Him." If it took this dark corner for Trevor to seek God with all his heart and then find Him, then it would be worth every minute he spent there—and an answer to my daily prayers.

The following morning, the online devotion from "Girlfriends in God" cited that very same verse in Romans, so I sent an excerpt to Trevor. Sharon Jaynes wrote, "What does God really mean by "all things?" Most likely He means all things—the good, the bad and the ugly. In every dark circumstance of life, I believe that there is a nugget of gold or a hidden treasure just waiting to be discovered."

Later, I received a text message from Trevor, thanking me for my two emails. Then he added his own words of wisdom, aimed at the messy, ugly corners of my life. "And those piles, though they contain treasures (lost letters), are only dust in the way of what God has in store for you." Could Trevor have seen a glimpse of God in his own dark corner that morning? Did all this talk about the good that can come from trials ignite a spark of hope in his heart?

Do you start your day eagerly waiting to see what God has in store for you? Open your eyes, in the midst of your circumstances, and wait expectantly. Today—every day—be on the lookout for His nuggets of gold to shine through the good—and the bad.

May 2

"Who of you by worrying can add a single hour to his life?" —**Matthew 6:27**

When we moved to our lake house, my husband and I had two preconceived thoughts. We would do lots of entertaining with family and friends, sharing our little piece of paradise. Second, somewhere in the future, the old house would get a facelift.

The thoughts about remodeling were on the backburner for several years. Besides being costly, it would be such an inconvenience. The house was old and almost every room needed some TLC, and a few required a major overhaul, so it would be necessary to move out during construction.

Another thought to consider was the timing. We didn't want the house torn up during the summertime "peak season." How could we enjoy the lake with family and friends if we didn't have a place for everyone to stay? That's part of the fun—having a houseful for the whole weekend!

After many months, the design plans were finished and there was a timeline. We would move to our garage apartment while the remodel took place in the "off season" so we wouldn't miss out on the warm-weather activities.

The planning might have been perfect, but nothing went according to that so-called perfect plan. Besides some normal construction glitches, we encountered unforeseen structural issues that resulted in a huge delay. Before long, it was late spring and there were no sounds of hammers and saws. We had moved the furniture into storage and our bodies into the small apartment; the demo work was completed, but construction was on hold.

It was too late to turn back now and there was no rushing the process. It was a sad fact, but we would basically miss out on a whole season of fun in the sun. No moonlit dinners out on the balcony overlooking the lake—the balcony had been demolished. No family/friend reunion weekends—there were no extra bedrooms. Even a large gathering around the pool would be awkward because the only functioning bathroom was in the apartment, way up the hill (not counting the port-o-potty).

The previous September, we had the young professional singles from church over for a social gathering, and we wanted to do it again. I reluctantly explained to one of the young ladies in the group that we wouldn't be able to accommodate them because of the construction. She told me not to worry; we always had next summer for another party.

Next summer? As much as we wanted to have the house remodeled, we sure didn't want to miss out on "this" summer at our lake house. But what really stuck in my head was the realization that, at my age, every season is precious. To the young single girl at church, she probably never thought about getting older and her summers being numbered.

Then I caught myself. There is no guarantee of tomorrow, so why was I worrying about the following year? Last year, had I known of the construction delays we would encounter, would I have done anything differently? Would I have had more people over for dinner or for the weekend? Would I have marveled at the beauty of God's creation *every time* I walked by the windows that overlooked the lake? From the apartment, I couldn't even see the water and now regretted those times I took the view for granted.

Paul had such great words of wisdom for the church at Ephesus—be careful how you live, be wise, make the most of every opportunity (Ephesians 5:15-16). His words still hold true today.

I can't go back and have a do-over, and worrying about tomorrow or next summer certainly won't add any days to the ones God already ordained for me. But today I can go forward, with God walking beside me, and have the time of my life—with or without a lake house full of company.

Are you ready? Make the decision right now to make the most of this day so tomorrow you have no regrets. Trusting God will be with you, there is no reason to worry about anything.

May 3

Now we know that if the earthly tent we live in is destroyed, we have a building from God, an eternal house in heaven, not built by human hands.—**2 Corinthians 5:1**

My golden retriever hadn't been her normal self for almost a month. After several rounds of antibiotics, blood work and X-rays, the vet suggested an ultrasound to determine if there was some type of cancer in her young body. Needless to say, I was overanxious.

Holly's appointment was at 7 a.m. The builder and the job superintendent for my home remodel were quite surprised to see us up and at 'em so early, since we were preparing to leave just as they arrived. However, I was probably more surprised to see them. At that point in time, the demo work had been completed, but the job had been on hold. No workers, or anyone connected to the job, had been around. Now, on this very traumatic morning, they showed up.

I totally understood the reasons for *some* of the construction delays because of the structural problems encountered as the old walls came tumbling down. But, seriously, after a whole month of nothing—not one thing—being done, I was more than frustrated. I had been given a timeline, and we were already several months behind schedule.

As I was trying to get Holly and myself ready to leave, the builder started giving me what I thought were extremely lame excuses. Poor guy, he had no idea what horrible timing it was or the situation he had walked into. I was on the verge of tears because I was so worried about Holly and there he was, trying to appease me. All I heard were excuses for work that hadn't been completed as promised—I felt I had been lied to and taken advantage of because I was too timid to voice my concerns.

Silently I prayed for the right words. I needed courage to respond, but I wanted what came out of my mouth to be kind, yet firm. "Set a guard over my mouth, O Lord; keep watch over the door of my lips" (Psalm 141:3). I didn't want to be the raging homeowner, yet I had the right to voice my feelings on how I had been treated. Didn't I?

Words flowed as I was trying to be tactful, honest and gracious—all at the same time. Suddenly, I was silent and I heard that still small voice telling me, *Brenda, it's only a house.* Yes, it is only a house, my temporary residence, at that. With that warning, I excused myself from the conversation.

Back at home from the vet, I had my quiet time with God. It had been too rushed prior to taking Holly and now, more than ever, I needed to be in the Word. The daily reading for the first devotion came from Psalm 103:8: "The Lord is compassionate and gracious, slow to anger, abounding in love." Why didn't I read that before ever walking out of the house? How gracious was I with my builder? And anger—it came on all too quickly. No matter how "justified" I thought I was, thinking I had been wronged, was I speaking out of love or pride?

Had it been love, I wouldn't have felt so guilty.

Another devotion led me to Philippians 3:20: "But our citizenship is in heaven." Is that why the Holy Spirit reminded me it was only a house—an earthly tent, a temporary dwelling place on earth? Oh, I prayed for the right words and for the Lord to guard my mouth, which He did. But God knew my prideful heart, and thankfully the Holy Spirit intervened and told me to zip it up.

I will end by telling you that Holly was fine. After my conversation with the builder that day, we still encountered problems, but the work progressed in a timely manner. From that point forward I prayed daily, no matter how perturbed I became with the whole remodeling process, I would never forgot the warning from the Holy Spirit—*it's only a house.*

May 4

Then Peter got down out of the boat, walked on the water and came toward Jesus.—**Matthew 14:29**

The winter of 2012 was unseasonably warm in the Texas Hill Country, and there was actually some desperately needed rain in the early spring. Those two unusual weather phenomena contributed to another marvel—an abundance of butterflies. According to Wizzie Brown of the Texas AgriLife Extension Service, the mild winter and the extra rain meant more vegetation and, therefore, more food for them.

My front and side yard is full of huge, tree-sized ligustrums, and they were covered with tiny white flowers that served as a butterfly's all-you-can-eat nectar bar. I have always noticed the ligustrums in bloom every spring, mainly because the aroma of the flowers makes me sneeze like crazy. However, this time, I almost forgot about the sneezes because the butterflies were simply amazing!

Then I had a really blonde moment and realized something profound. My husband and I had moved into the garage apartment to avoid the dust and mess of remodeling. Sitting at my desk, I now looked out behind the garage and to the front of the house, instead of towards the lake. The new scene was of overgrown vegetation, ligustrums and trees, compared to a very unobstructed view of the lake from my office in the house. It was my new office set up in the apartment that allowed me to gaze at what has probably been a haven for these beautiful flying creatures for years.

One afternoon, I found myself sitting at my desk, just staring at the literally hundreds of butterflies fluttering from branch to branch. I decided to Google this butterfly invasion. Were there really more than usual this spring, or had I just never noticed? I found an article that had been posted to the Internet just 30 minutes prior to my search from the Austin-based newspaper at statesman.com: "Butterflies, caterpillars are swarming this year." Wow, what perfect timing. Did God just put that posting there for me?

From the article, I discovered that what I thought were Monarchs were actually Red Admirals. That article was also where I found the information from Wizzie Brown that I wrote in the first paragraph. I asked a question pertaining specifically to butterflies in the Austin area and, lo and behold, there was the answer freshly posted to the Internet. God got the glory for that quick answer.

The Holy Spirit also nudged me to think about what the change of scenery had done to my awareness of the butterflies. How much more do I miss because of my limited point of view?

If I never talk to others who are different than me and don't share my same thoughts on Jesus, how will I ever spread His good news? If I don't go to the other side of town, how will I reach out and help those in need? If I don't get out of the boat I am in, how will I see all that God has in store for me? By simply looking out of the same window every day, I will never see all the riches of my Father's creation. How can He use me if I don't move?

I don't know about you, but I am not much of a risk taker. Taking a leap of faith doesn't come easy for me. When Peter got out of the boat and walked towards Jesus, he was doing fine—until he started focusing on the wind and his fear. That's when he began to sink and cried out to the Lord, "Save me."

"Jesus replied, 'You of little faith, why did you doubt me?'" (Matthew 14:31).

God has a plan for me, this girl of little faith. But I will miss it if I don't change my comfortable point of view, get out of the safety zone and move!

But what if I mess up and sink or stumble and fall? Prior to His words in Matthew 14:31, Jesus reached out His hand and caught Peter. He will be there for me too—to pull me up, with His righteous right hand. He's got me covered, no matter what. So, what am I waiting for? How about you?

May 5

Set a guard over my mouth, O Lord; keep watch over the door of my lips. —**Psalm 141:3**

There had been much hype about the Supermoon on May 5, 2012—the closest and largest moon of the year. My husband and I scheduled our evening around the event. First, we would watch the sunset over the lake, go inside to prepare dinner, then go back outside to eat and watch the moon.

Plans started to fall apart early in the evening. We were too tired from a very busy day to fix the meal, so we got takeout. As we made our way to the sunset deck, there was another change of plans. This time, it was due to the weather. Clouds had invaded the previously blue sky and the sun was hidden, which meant the moon wouldn't be visible either. So much for well-made plans.

My husband and I still enjoyed our dinner and our time together. Missing the Supermoon wasn't so bad, especially after we realized that the clouds signified potential rain. Off in the western sky was some very intense lightening. Could rain actually be coming?

I woke up at 3:30 a.m. to the sound of booming thunder and a well-lit room from the lightning. It was awesome! Severe drought conditions were still looming over the Hill Country and rain was always a welcome interruption to sleep or other plans. Surely, we were in for some heavy showers with all that noise.

After an hour, I got up to look out the window—searching for signs of rain. Nope, there was nothing. When my dog woke me up at 6 a.m. to go outside, I checked again. Still no puddles on the ground. OK, God, all the hype about rain—all the noise and all the indicators of a big storm—and nothing!

As hard as I have tried not to dwell upon the lack of rain, I failed again this time. With all that thunder and lightning, surely, God wouldn't just tease me like that. I was mad! Instead of being thankful for all that God had provided, I was stuck on the one thing I thought He had purposely withheld. I just lay in bed and let God know my thoughts.

As much as I wanted to acknowledge that His ways are higher than mine (Isaiah 55:9) and that God will meet all my needs according to His glorious riches in Christ Jesus (Philippians 4:19), I still wanted what I wanted—rain. But, no. He was holding it back. Really, God? Again?

After what seemed like forever of pleading with God and lashing out at Him, I got out of bed to let Holly back inside. Was I ever in for a surprise! There were puddles of water, the ground was soaked and I could smell that glorious aroma of rain. How did I miss hearing it? While I had been complaining to God, He had been busy bringing some heavenly rain.

Did I ever feel foolish! First, for having the audacity to complain to God Almighty about not providing what I wanted, and second, for making accusations without thoroughly checking out all the facts first. Had I looked closer or listened more intently, I would have seen and heard the rain, and saved myself the embarrassment of saying something I later regretted.

Unfortunately, that was hardly the first time I allowed my unruly, prideful mouth to take over. How many times have I been upset and blurted out something ugly, only to regret my lack of self-control? How about the occasions I voiced my opinion, without knowing all the details? Not just to God, but also to others I know and love. The words of Psalm 19:14 are imbedded in my head—"May the words of my mouth and the meditation of my heart be pleasing in your sight"—but they don't do any good stuck there!

Thank You, sweet Jesus, for this little lesson in being more careful with what is in my heart and comes out of my mouth. And, thank You for the rain!

May 6

"And I, the Messiah, have authority even to decide what men can do on Sabbath days!"—**Mark 2:28**

Growing up, my family always went to church on Sundays. Afterwards, we went out to eat or over to my paternal grandmother's house for lunch. When I was 6, my parents divorced and the schedule changed a bit. We still went to the same church, but we stopped going out for lunch.

Instead, my mother cooked a roast. She would stick it in the oven before we left and when we got home, the house smelled so yummy. My mother went to work after the divorce and didn't have much spare time, but she never let up on the church attendance.

I liked Sunday school and thought communion was fun, but other than that, church was boring, and I found it difficult to sit still for an hour. We never talked about God or religion at home that I can remember, nor did we say the blessing before a meal. We just got up like clockwork on Sundays and knew the routine.

At my grandmother's house, we did say the blessing and she read from the *Upper Room* daily devotional and Bible every morning. God and His truths became real. Between my mother's insistence on church attendance and my grandmother's readings, my faith grew.

I am sorry to admit that once I went off to college, Sundays changed. College life for me consisted of studying hard during the week and partying hard on the weekends. Making time for church or God wasn't part of my college scene.

I am so thankful for what my mother and grandmother taught me. When my first son was born, somehow I knew he was to grow up knowing God. Getting back in the habit of going to church was difficult; however, memories of my childhood made it feel like home. It's a miracle that God changed my heart, and now I can't wait to walk into the sanctuary every week. I am living proof of His unequaled redemptive power.

Today, my husband and I are members of a Bible church in Austin. If we have to miss for any reason, there is an app on my phone so I can watch the sermon. I am inspired by the unbelievable music and fellowship. Our pastor tells us if the only time we open our Bibles is on Sundays, we are missing out on His blessings. I feel my church experience is my pre-game pep talk from the Coach, getting me ready for the game of life each week.

After church, it's on to LifeGroup—a small group of adults with whom we share life. We have lunch then dive together into the Word. Our Sunday is anything but a ritual—God has made the day a blessed event.

Unfortunately, my two boys took the same route I did in college and church wasn't on their agenda either. I pray when they have families (or hopefully before), they will look back to their Sundays and be filled with the desire to get back in the routine—not just of going to church, but of being filled with His Word and seeing it as the best day of their week.

May 7

Children are a heritage from the LORD, offspring a reward from him.—**Psalm 127:3**

Nine months after I sent out my first emails requesting other women to share their God stories for this devotional, I celebrated because I was officially one-third of the way done! I was so encouraged, feeling I had made significant headway.

It had also been Mother's Day week and the nine-month milestone reminded me of a pregnancy; however, my baby wasn't quite ready for birth yet. My baby, my book, was only one-third of the way finished. However, I sure didn't want to think of those first nine months as only a trimester. My goodness, that would be a 27-month pregnancy! I had the strangest thought as I celebrated—perhaps I could liken this book to birthing an elephant and envision a 22-month gestation period. At the time, I believed that was an attainable goal for 366 devotions. I would later discover that wasn't the plan either.

I honestly loved being pregnant. It took several years to conceive, so when I finally heard the doctor's confirmation, I was overjoyed and thankful. Never experiencing even one day of morning sickness, I felt wonderful; so very special, so very beautiful. Even the birthing process was a delightful memory. Labor was extremely short with both of my boys and their birth was completely "natural." It all went so fast there wasn't even the opportunity to use those silly breathing techniques learned in Lamaze class. Yes, I absolutely loved those nine months.

When the goal of 366 stories was finally reached, I far surpassed the gestation period for an elephant: I even went past the 27-month marker. This baby took three years to be born. However, I clearly remember that day when I had written and/or received 123 devotions. Much like the sigh of relief women feel when they reach the end of the first trimester, I also felt encouraged with how the book was going. I felt like, one day, it was actually going to be a reality. It was exhilarating!

What a sense of humor God has to put that thought in my head of equating this book to the birthing process! He knew how much I loved being pregnant. My child-bearing years are long gone, so this might be the next best thing to having another baby. Birthing His book.

It is God's book, just like my children are His too. My children were truly a gift from my Heavenly Father, not from myself, and this book journey has also proven to be a special blessing from Him as well.

I still think the idea of comparing this book to birthing an elephant could only have come from God, just to make me laugh. I never could have thought of the elephant connection on my own. Where does He come up with this stuff?

May 8

So God created man in his own image, in the image of God he created him; male and female he created them.
—Genesis 1:27

Deer are plentiful in residential neighborhoods around Lake Travis. When we first moved here, I was surprised at how bold the deer were, just wandering up and down the streets, grazing on whatever they could find to eat. Even though my yard is completely fenced, I learned all about the "deer-resistant" plants and to always be on alert when driving, especially at night.

Starting in May, one must be extra careful when out on the road. The babies start arriving the first of the month. I may be a bit prejudiced thinking there is no cuter baby animal than a golden retriever puppy, but little fawns rate right up there. Neither of my neighbors has a fenced yard, so the deer congregate there—sometimes as many as 15-20 can be seen lounging in the grass. Come May, there may be five or six fawns added to the group.

May is always associated with Mother's Day. I know the animal kingdom doesn't celebrate that day like us humans, but I find it very sweet that the deer have their offspring at that time. When I see those fawns scampering around and I see the mommies nursing their babies, I can't help but think about the miracle of new life and the joys of motherhood.

"Are not two sparrows sold for a penny? Yet not one of them will fall to the ground outside your Father's care. And even the very hairs of your head are all numbered. So don't be afraid; you are worth more than many sparrows" (Matthew 10:29-31). These words assure us that, as humans, we are valued more by God than the sparrows, and, presumably, more than the other animals too—even more than the beautiful, graceful deer. The wonder of all creation is incredible, but the fact that we are worth more than any of His other creatures makes our lives so special and unique. Surely if God created us in His image, He had something extraordinary for us in mind.

I pray that you *do* feel amazingly special today. Stop for a few minutes and just relish that thought. Take it captive and be in awe.

May 9

Her children rise up and call her blessed; her husband also, and he praises her. **—Proverbs 31:28**

My mother and I have a special bond, a bond that most girls don't have with their mothers. I feel blessed to have a wonderful relationship with my mother, Connie.

As I am getting older, I am beginning to realize that our bond is rare. I consider my mom to be my best friend. I know some may think that it is weird or unrealistic to call your mom a best friend; however, I truly can say that she is mine. My mom knows how to make me feel loved. She loves me unconditionally and makes me feel important in her life. She did not have the greatest relationship with her mother and tries to give me the love and compassion that their relationship lacked.

Here is a little background about my mother. She was born in a small town in southern Louisiana—one of six children born to a Korean War veteran and a mother who suffered with mental illness. She was the oldest daughter; therefore, she grew up quickly to help her family. She cooked, cleaned, helped her siblings and attended school. My grandmother suffered with manic depression throughout her life. Due to my grandmother's illness, my mom never had a typical mother-daughter relationship.

During my mother's college years, she had many struggles. She attended college, worked part-time, and took care of her younger siblings. She always acted like the "mother hen" of the children and tried to keep them all out of trouble. Her three brothers were very outgoing and liked to live on the wild side. This unfortunately caught up with her middle brother, Dwight. One night, Dwight was out with his friends and got into a horrible car accident. He was the passenger in a van that his friend was driving when they hit a tree.

Dwight suffered a neck injury that paralyzed him from the neck down. My mom took this very hard and she stayed by his side while he was in the hospital. During that time, my mom was working towards her teaching certification. She was student teaching during the day and visiting Dwight at night. Dwight came home from the hospital months later. He was bound to a wheelchair and he lived for 17 years until his passing in 1998.

My mom is a courageous woman who is always there for her family. Not only was she there for Dwight when he needed her, but she has always been there for her sister Beth, who is mentally handicapped. My mom has worked with Beth and cared for her throughout Beth's life. She has been there when no one else has been. She is the caretaker for Beth and to this day looks after her like a mother.

My mom had a great relationship with her father, who was a Prisoner of War. I did not know my grandfather, however; every time my mom speaks of him she smiles and sings him praises. Due to my grandfather being a POW, he suffered from shell-shock and drank to ease his mind. He was a stubborn man with a difficult past. He died when my mom was in her twenties of an asthmatic attack. He never wanted to go to the hospital and unfortunately it took his life. I am sad that I never had the opportunity to meet my grandfather because he loved my mother just as much as I do.

With all of the hardships in my mom's life, she has grown to be a strong successful woman. She is married to a wonderful man and she has two children, my amazing brother, Ben and me. She not only is an outstanding mother but she also is a preschool teacher. Due to the tragic moments in her life, she cherishes every moment with her family. She is continually telling me, "Be careful" and "I love you." She is always concerned about my well-being and my safety. I still have to text her when I get home even though I am married. I love my mother for who she is and only hope that I can be half the mother that she has been to me.

I am truly blessed to have my mother. Mother's Day is right around the corner. Take a few minutes and think of all the reasons you are blessed to have—or were blessed to have had—your own mom.

Lauren Becnel Gerland
Houston, TX

May 10

God is our refuge and strength, an ever-present help in trouble.—**Psalm 46:1**

Growing up in a home with a scarcity of affection, I craved the love I saw expressed in my first boyfriend's family. At age 19, we married, and the first seven months seemed fine. Then, the bottom dropped out when I learned that my beloved husband was caught up in the whirlwind of cocaine addiction.

The next eight years were stormy as he went in and out of rehab. Yet, through this unhappiness and uncertainty, the Lord blessed me with three wonderful children, who became my motivation to search for steadfast love I'd been missing. Through a Bible study, I finally found that love in Jesus Christ.

As the relationship with my husband continued to deteriorate, my walk with the Lord became closer. I felt such a conflict between my abounding love for the Lord and my growing hate for my husband, who had become physically and emotionally abusive.

The turning point came during a worship service when a woman, seeing my tears, touched my shoulder and told me everything would be OK. With her encouragement, I went home and told my husband that I loved and forgave him, that we were both unclean and needed the forgiveness of Jesus.

But the abuse raged on. Although I loved my husband, I hated what sin had done to him. I was so confused. I wanted to be a godly wife and honor God in my marriage, yet I was enabling my husband's addiction by giving him money and lying to his employer. Worst of all, I was putting my children and myself in physical danger. I prayed for

God's protection and help. When I finally decided to leave, my husband's reaction was so violent, that it led to his arrest for domestic abuse.

When the nightmare ended, I could look back and see God's protection. He showed me that being a godly wife does not mean living with abuse in any form. God carried my children and me through the storm and set us in a loving, caring family.

Esther Newcomb
Katy, TX

May 11

Therefore encourage one another and build each other up, just as in fact you are doing. — **1 Thessalonians 5:11**

The woman behind the counter at the Christian bookstore told the manager she really needed to take a break. She looked to be about 75 years old, and said her back was hurting and her feet were tired. The first time I was in the store, the same woman was at the cash register. I wondered if she would remember me.

That previous visit, I had purchased quite a few Bibles, and the sweet, older woman was excited about my purchase. The Bibles were to be given away through a program at my church that provides mobile meals to folks out on the streets of Austin. The store was running a special on them and I went to take advantage of the discounted price. The woman was interested in why I was buying so many, so we chatted about the Bibles for a few minutes. The store was busy and she had to call for the manager to come help her at the register.

The woman apologized for not working faster and for needing to call for help, but the manager was so kind and told her it was no problem. She actually was a little slow, but it was because she spent so much time talking with each customer. She was delightful and her interest in each person was refreshing.

This visit, she had to call the manager again because she needed a break, and once again apologized. The manager was quick to reassure her it was no problem; it was time for her to take 30 minutes to get off of her feet anyway. However, the sweet woman said she wanted to wait on one more customer before her break — me.

Yes, she did remember! I was the lady who bought all the Bibles a few weeks ago and now I was back for more? She wanted to know all about the mobile meal program at my church, and we had an interesting conversation as I learned about her personal involvement with a similar program at her church. You know, everyone just seemed so pleasant and full of kind, uplifting words at this Christian bookstore.

I looked up towards one corner of the store where the greeting cards were located and there was a banner hanging from the ceiling with the words from 1 Thessalonians 5:11 written on it. How appropriate, I thought. The employees were encouraging each customer through thoughtful conversation and genuine interest in their purchases. The manager showed compassion to the older, slower cashier. And that "older" cashier had a pretty good memory because she recalled my last visit, which sure made me feel special. I could just hear the Holy Spirit, telling them to keep up the good work, to encourage all customers and each other, "just as in fact you are doing."

And what was even more noteworthy, the date was May 10. That verse would be the perfect memory verse to include in this book for the next day, May 11. Isn't it nice though, that in this Christian bookstore, one can find encouragement and inspiration on any date. It was certainly the place to see people living out 1 Thessalonians 5:11.

As you go out into the world today, think how you can "do" this verse. Just storing the words in your memory bank isn't the purpose of learning it — you need to know it so you can show it!

May 12

"And surely I am with you always, to the very end of the age." —**Matthew 28:20**

When I was a little girl growing up in Corpus Christi, Texas, I lived about five minutes from my grandmother. Going to her house to spend the night on Friday was the highlight of my week.

Everything was extra special there, especially the food. No matter what we had to eat Friday night, I would get a big glass of chocolate milk, made with Hershey's syrup from the can—Grandmother's house was the only place I got chocolate milk. Saturday-morning breakfast was the best meal *ever*! She cooked bacon and white-cream gravy—to this day I have never had better gravy—and Pillsbury biscuits. Plus, I had my very own pot of coffee! It was actually served in a teapot and probably about 25% coffee and the rest milk and sugar.

After breakfast, Grandmother would get her half-frozen little bottle of Coca-Cola, her black Bible and *The Upper Room* daily devotional, and she would read to me. When I was six, my parents divorced and we moved to another part of town where the homes were more affordable. I was devastated because I was no longer five minutes from Grandmother's house. I don't really remember how, but my mother managed to get me there on Friday nights and, thankfully, within two years we moved closer to her.

When I had children of my own and they were old enough to listen and understand, I started reading *The Upper Room* to my two sons at breakfast. As they entered the teenage years, I gave them their own daily devotional every Christmas. They kept it in the bathroom, and it was their favorite reading material during those important times when nature called.

I also bought myself a daily devotional every Christmas. So many times I read from it exactly what I needed to hear for that day. Even though we attended church regularly, those daily inspirational stories were what actually opened my ears to hear God, my heart to feel His presence and my eyes to see Him working in my life. He still speaks to me through the devotions I read (and countless other ways), and I eagerly begin each morning reading several from the stacks I have collected through the years, knowing that God has a special message for me.

I still have the teapot used to serve my coffee, and I think of Grandmother every time I have a glass of chocolate milk, but most importantly, she is the reason for the devotions that I read daily. What an incredible legacy she left me with her example of spending time in God's word at the breakfast table! Little did I know that God was there with me at Grandmother's on Saturday mornings, directing my path and showing me how to plant seeds for my own children.

One day, like Grandmother, I will no longer be on this side of heaven. I pray my two sons will look back at those quiet times we shared with God—our investment in eternity—as being the most valuable gift they ever received from me.

May 13

"You brood of vipers, how can you who are evil say anything good? For out of the overflow of the heart the mouth speaks. But I tell you that men will have to give an account on the day of judgment for every careless word they have spoken. For by your words you will be acquitted and by your words you will be condemned." —***Matthew 12:34-36***

My grandmother had a plaque in her yard that was displayed in her prettiest flowerbed. Dorothy Frances Gurney (1858-1932) was the author of "The Lord God Planted a Garden," which included the popular verse found on my grandmother's plaque:

The kiss of the sun for pardon
The song of the birds for mirth
One is nearer God's heart in a garden
Than anywhere else on earth.

Grandmother loved working in the yard and was very active in the Corpus Christi Garden Club. Since I spent so much time at her house when I was a little girl, I often helped her. She usually gave me a hose and asked me to water the plants. I assume that kept me occupied while she did the serious stuff like weeding and pruning.

Some incidents just stay in our hearts forever, like this one. I was watering and grandmother asked me to give her the hose. She was always so gentle and loving with her words, and when she wanted me to pay close attention she would say, "See there? Lookie here." With those words, I knew to watch closely and listen up.

She directed the flow of water upwards to the leaves of the bushes, away from the ground where I had been holding the hose. Then she said, "See there? Lookie here." And pointing the nozzle towards the leaves she told me that *sometimes they just like to have their little faces washed.* Grandmother told me the plants were special to God because He created them. And then she personalized them even more by saying we needed to wash their little faces.

Did grandmother know I would keep her words in my heart for over 50 years? What she did know was that her words mattered and she chose them wisely and spoke them lovingly. She also knew how important God was in our life and included Him in the conversation. I know that she was closest to God in her garden and her yard reflected her adoration for Him and His creation.

My garden has never looked like grandmother's. Honestly, I don't expect it ever will because I don't have the same passion for yard work as she did or her green thumb. But her words still resonate in my heart. Do you ever notice how happy the plants look after God washes their little faces with a nice rain shower?

Unfortunately, my words don't always sound as sweet as hers either. Will anything I said to my boys as they were growing up remain in their hearts for a lifetime?

As I have written before, I try to begin each day with the words from Psalm 19:24, and I find myself repeating it as often necessary throughout the day. However, no matter how much I want to please my Father, there are times I still blurt out the evil thoughts overflowing from my heart.

Let's say Psalm 19:24 together now and let God know our intentions to glorify Him as we go out into His world. *"May the words of my mouth and the meditations of my heart be pleasing in your sight, O Lord, my Rock and my Redeemer."*

May 14

A woman of noble character who can find? She is worth far more than rubies. — **Proverbs 31:10**

"Every mother needs a daughter, and I'm so glad you are mine." My mother said this to me all my life. My mother and I had such a special relationship. How many daughters can say they *never* fought with their mother? I can! Our love for each other was so special.

My mother earned the nickname "Proper Tish" when I was a teenager. She taught by example and tried her best to make sure we behaved properly. What lessons I learned from her! I'm so thankful God blessed me with my precious mother! What a fun-loving and kindhearted person she was.

She also was an accomplished musician and shared with me her love for music. Thomas Edison once said, "My mother was the making of me. She was so true and so sure of me. I felt that I had someone to live for—someone I must not disappoint. The memory of my mother will always be a blessing to me." How true those words are.

In 2002, my mother had a stroke that left her paralyzed on her left side. It was so difficult for her, and she was so courageous. Even though her quality of life wasn't good, she continued to make a person feel better being with her. Mother's health continued to decline and eventually she was unable to speak. But oh, how I read what she felt by looking into her beautiful brown eyes that always had a smile for me.

She was in a wonderful facility named Marian Place, surrounded by fabulous caregivers. The evening she died, the caregiver who was a little superstitious said, "Ms. Tish, you are not going to pass during my shift." My mother shook her head as to say, "Yes, I am!" Then mother smiled and winked at the caregiver and quietly went to be with our Heavenly Father.

Grief is different for all of us. I was so relieved that my mother no longer suffered, but I missed her terribly. I went through the motions of life but I was really struggling with the loss. One day, I came home from teaching school and was really down. I walked into my bathroom and found a poem sitting on top of the counter. It was exactly what I needed to read!

Thinking my husband had left it for me to read, I called him at his office and began thanking him for sharing the beautiful poem. He told me he didn't leave me a poem to read. We are Empty Nesters and there was no explanation for how the poem got there. Well, maybe there was! The Lord works in mysterious ways and knew I needed this. The poem, "When I Must Leave You," by Helen Steiner Rice, helped me to pull myself back together. If you need such comfort right now in your life, please find this poem. It will help!

Penni Parker Mitchell
Kilgore, TX

May 15

"You are my friends if you do what I command. I no longer call you servants, because a servant does not know his master's business. Instead, I have called you friends, for everything that I learned from my Father I have made known to you. You did not choose me, but I chose you and appointed you so that you might go and bear fruit—fruit that will last—and so that whatever you ask in my name the Father will give you."—**John 15:13-16**

Mother's Day was on May 8 in 2011. My mother's birthday was the following Sunday, May 15. There was actually nothing so special about the two being exactly one week apart that year. What struck me as unusual was reading a devotion written by a woman whose mom was also born on May 15.

The stories for the first few weeks in May were about moms and Mother's Day in this particular book. As I read the story, I felt a bond to the author and her mom. You probably know someone who has your same birthday; I can name three with whom I share mine.

I read my devotions in the morning, knowing I will find one that hits the spot for that day. I can relate to what the writer is going through and see God in action in her life, showing me how to handle the situation or that emotion. Even though we might be sharing a similar circumstance or trial or joy, and I identified with the story, I never actually thought much about the author herself.

This story was different. This writer and I have been celebrating our moms' birthdays together on May 15 for our whole lives. We have had to combine Mother's Day and her birthday or decide how to celebrate each one separately for all these years. However, something that was very different about our moms was that hers was deceased and mine was still very much alive, celebrating 83 years in 2011. This woman was mourning the fact that this was the first Mother's Day and birthday since her mom had passed. I felt sadness for this woman I didn't even know.

I started thinking about all the stories I read and how all of us women really do have so much in common. Perhaps it's not moms born on the same date, but we have issues with husbands and children. We have friends who have passed and births to celebrate. There have been weddings and divorces. I can identify with the Empty Nesters, but I can also remember the plight of a tired, new mom.

Whether married or single, we struggle with finding prayer time and quality time for our family and friends. The concern of not having enough hours in the day to get it all done is a recurring subject. We worry about finances, health, employment, war, what to cook for dinner and having a clean house. Yes, we are all sisters in Christ living life. That's what makes reading other's stories so special—we can find someone else who understands what we are going through and experience this life crisis or joy together, with God being with us every step of the way. I want to embrace that most significant thread that binds us all—our sweet Heavenly Father—and thank Him for this delightful sisterhood of women.

Besides just reading their stories, are you living life with other women too? I do hope you have a group of godly women who will walk with you on your journey. The time spent visiting, disciplining, learning from other women, has been instrumental in my faith walk. Every person God has placed in my path is there for a reason. I also want to embrace her, along with the One who brought us together.

No matter what year you read this, Mother's Day in the United States is celebrated on the second Sunday in May. Not every female is a mom, but all of us have been called to plant God's seeds of hope, love and promise into the lives of others. We have been chosen and appointed by our friend Jesus to bear spiritual fruit. Now that's something to celebrate!

Happy Mother's Day week and Happy Birthday to my dear mom!

May 16

Be joyful always; pray continually; give thanks in all circumstances, for this is God's will for you in Christ Jesus.
—1 Thessalonians 5:16-18

My golden retriever fractured her foot and had to wear a splint—a splint that had to stay dry. She just loves to float in the pool (no, she doesn't swim, just lounges on a large float) and that became off-limits. Holly loves to play in the water sprinklers, and that also became a no-no. Plus a heavy plastic bag wrapped around her splinted foot was required every time she went out to potty after the grass had been watered. She wasn't very happy with her situation and it made me sad just looking at her.

I was actually able to capture a picture of her that was the epitome of frustration and sadness. There she was, stretched out on the floor with that hideous "cone of shame" around her head so she wouldn't bite at her foot, looking up at the camera with the saddest eyes. I sent this picture via email to my dog-loving friends, looking for some sympathy, knowing they would share in our plight.

I got a response from Vickie, a friend from Katy whose 27-year-old son, Nick, was killed in a tragic, freakish accident on September 16, 2006. This is part of her email:

"This picture takes me back to my last conversation with Nick. He sent me a picture of Gracie (his dog) with the cone around her neck because she had an infection. Seeing Holly with the cone on brought back the picture of Gracie and my conversation with Nick. We laughed at how pathetic Gracie looked. I actually made a copy of the picture to remind me of that last conversation and how special it was. I think I see that same look in Holly's eyes. Make sure you write on her cast, *God loves you.*"

While Vickie still misses her son beyond words, she celebrates his extraordinary life and finds joy in her memories. How very typical of Vickie to bring out the good in any situation. She has certainly experienced the worst trial any mother could endure, yet she continues to praise God. Her unfailing love for Him, despite her loss, has been my inspiration.

My picture of sad Hop-along Holly, as we lovingly nicknamed her, brought back a joyous memory of her son. Through Vickie, God showed me there was something positive in Holly's pitiful gaze and circumstance. After Vickie's comments, I no longer looked at Holly and saw sad eyes; I saw a glorious reminder of Nick. I was so thankful for the new perspective.

How about you? Do you need a new outlook on a situation in your life today? All you have to do is look up to our Father in heaven. 1 Thessalonians 5:16-18 are truly a few of my favorite "go to" verses when I need an attitude adjustment. I hope you find them helpful too. Since it's 5/16, let's keep 1 Thessalonians 5:16 in our memory bank: "Be joyful always."

May 17

*"Therefore say to the Israelites, 'This is what the Sovereign L*ORD *says: It is not for your sake, people of Israel, that I am going to do these things, but for the sake of my holy name, which you have profaned among the nations where you have gone.'"*—**Ezekiel 36:22**

Several years ago, I read Ezekiel 36:25 in a Tuesday-morning Bible study: "I will give you a new heart and put a new spirit in you; I will remove from you your heart of stone and give you a heart of flesh." The words resonated over and over within my hardened heart, until one day I actually had an encounter with Jesus. Since that experience, I have smiled inside and out, knowing I was a living testimony to God's miraculous transplant surgery.

To briefly explain, one morning I "felt" Jesus' warm embrace envelop my whole body. It was truly one of those aha moments in my faith walk. I had felt Jesus' presence before—you know those times when you just knew He was there. But to feel the warmth of His embrace flowing over my body literally changed my life! My heart was not in a very pliable, healthy condition at the time, and I was a prime candidate for a transplant.

Telling others about my new heart and giving God the glory for what He did for me has been a great joy. Yes, I felt that my new heart was a gift just for me. So, a few years after the described incidence, I was enlightened when I read more of Ezekiel 36.

A homework question for Priscilla Shirer's *One in a Million: Journey to Your Promised Land*, led me back to Ezekiel 36:25-27. I have tried to incorporate reading more than just the verse of a homework question or the daily reading in a devotion in order to gain a better understanding. This time, I decided to read all of Ezekiel 36. God gave the Israelites a new heart and new spirit not because they deserved it, but for the sake of His holy name.

Why do I try to make everything all about me? I know better. It's all about God. It's all about bringing glory to the King. Not for my sake, but for His. However, reading God's very own words spoken to the prophet Ezekiel helped me to visualize God in a much more profound, magnificent light. His words also made me sad. Sad because I saw the similarity between the Israelites and our culture today.

Haven't we also "profaned" His name? Churchgoers act so pious on Sunday, but Monday-Saturday can display behavior similar to non-Christians. Why do some say the biggest obstacles to going to church are the folks who go to church? The hypocrisy of those who want to call themselves Christians repulse those who are wondering who to follow.

The divorce rate for Christians is the same as those who don't follow Jesus. Pornography is just as widespread inside the church as outside. Many proclaiming Jesus as their Lord and Savior also lie, cheat, steal, lust and/or gossip. Yep, today we still fall short of bringing glory to the Father, and there is no way we can rise above our sinful nature on our own.

Like the Israelites, we don't deserve to be forgiven of our sinful behavior, but the Lord Almighty will not share His glory with Satan and other false gods. If left to wander in the darkness, we would not be set apart from the others. When we are rescued from the wilderness, others will know that God, and God alone, was the power behind the transformation.

"Then the nations around you that remain will know that I the LORD have rebuilt what was destroyed and have replanted what was desolate. I the LORD have spoken, and I will do it"(Vs. 36).

As we go out into the world today, let's be mindful of how we represent God. Remember, our salvation wasn't just for us—it was for His sake. To bring Him glory. Show the love, honor, respect and reverence due His most Holy name.

May 18

"For where two or three come together in my name, there am I with them." —**Matthew 18:20**

Throughout the Bible, we find many different names for God, each one pointing to one of His characteristics. Have you ever thought of him as God, the Event Planner? After a recent turn of events at a dinner, I had no doubt in my mind that God had planned the entire evening!

My church has a wonderful quarterly program within the Women's Ministry called Guess Who's Coming to Dinner? On the dinner sign-up sheet, you indicate the night of a designated week that is most convenient, but no one knows who else will be attending. When I first started attending the church, I went to a GWCTD and it was the perfect opportunity to meet other women.

A member of my Tuesday-morning Bible study had recently moved to Austin from California. I suggested she attend the upcoming GWCTD so that she might meet some new faces. She not only signed up, she also volunteered to host a dinner. The week before, I got an email informing me I was assigned to attend the dinner at her home, along with six other surprise guests.

For various reasons, only two other ladies and I were able to attend, with the other ladies needing to cancel at the very last minute. So instead of eight, we had a small, intimate dinner with just the four of us. What was really noteworthy is that we all just happened to be in the same Tuesday-morning Bible study small group, and it was such a wonderful opportunity to visit on a more personal level.

The table was already set and the food prepared. I was sorry our hostess had gone to so much trouble and that there was so much extra food. She was expecting to meet some new faces, and that didn't happen. However, all of us knew that God had purposely arranged our small dinner party.

In Bible study, we have some incredible conversations but we don't have enough time to get off the subject of our lesson very often. That night, I discovered that one of the ladies has a sister who lives about two minutes from my old house in Katy, with our kids graduating from the same high school only a few years apart. Two have daughters in their first year of college. The hostess got to educate us Texas girls about California, and we had the chance to brag on the city of Austin. Of course, we talked about our favorite restaurants and how we each ended up at our church.

We learned about each other's children, and talked of their trials and praises. We shared stories of our faith walk and some of the specific God stories in our lives. There was certainly no doubt in any of our minds that the dinner was exactly as God planned, and that He was sitting there at the table with us. I know He was pleased that we were able to spend this intimate time together, sisters in Christ, learning more about each other and sharing some of the details about our walk with God.

God, the Event Planner. I will definitely consult Him the next time I plan a party.

May 19

Do not be anxious about anything, but in every situation, by prayer and petition, with thanksgiving, present your requests to God. And the peace of God, which transcends all understanding, will guard your hearts and your minds in Christ Jesus. —**Philippians 4:6-7**

Until recently, I never truly knew what it meant to submit my life to God's plan and to fully trust in the Lord. As my family and I suffered a loss earlier this year, I was tested and taught. I was given the opportunity to grow in my faith, surrender to God and realize He is completely in control.

Ever since I was a little girl, I knew I wanted to be a mother. I have memories of carrying my doll in my shirt, pretending to be pregnant, pushing her in a stroller and taking care of her like she was my own daughter. In April 2009, my dream became a reality and I gave birth to our precious baby girl, Sophia Rose. She brought so much joy, hope and love to our lives. God had blessed us, and life was wonderful and going according to plan.

Just before Sophia turned 1, my husband Alan and I were surprised to find out that I was pregnant again. I was overwhelmed with emotion. I felt so much excitement but also fear of having our babies so close in age! We prayed about it and each day we grew more comfortable with the idea. After all, having two kids so close would be hard work, but we knew many joys would come of it as well.

I was six weeks pregnant the first time Alan and I saw our second baby on an ultrasound. At eight weeks, we saw a very clear picture of the baby and heard a strong heartbeat. We took pictures home of our growing little one and started to spread the exciting news to our family and close friends. Sophia's brother or sister would arrive December 2!

When I went to see the doctor for my routine 12-week checkup, I planned on hearing the heartbeat, getting my vitals checked and being out the door in minutes. God had something else in store. The nurse came in to do a preliminary ultrasound and a quick checkup before the doctor visited me. She was having a hard time finding a heartbeat or seeing the baby but she didn't seem too concerned; she said that my uterus must be tilted. But I knew from my pregnancy with Sophia that this was not the case. After a few minutes, which felt like an eternity as I anxiously waited for confirmation that everything was fine, the doctor came in and did the ultrasound herself.

She looked and looked and eventually the dreaded words that were written all over her face came out of her mouth: There was no baby. It had been taken from us. How could this be happening? The doctor explained that when a miscarriage occurs early in pregnancy, sometimes the baby absorbs into the uterus lining. As I sat on that table and the endless tears rolled down my face, I felt God's presence. I knew there was something bigger to all of this and the only thing I could do was look to Him.

The nothingness that I saw that afternoon broke my heart into a million pieces. I felt completely helpless and I realized just how much I already loved this child. Hearing the news without Alan by my side was devastating and I dreaded having to tell him. I didn't think I would be able to speak the words. We cried a lot that day, and that week. I had a D&C a couple days later, and the pregnancy was over. We said our goodbyes and I began the emotional and physical healing process. Sophia and Alan gave me so much courage and motivation, but I completely relied on God for the strength to recover.

At my post-operation appointment, I learned more distressing news. The doctor reported that my miscarriage was caused by an extremely rare occurrence called a Partial Molar Pregnancy, where two or more sperm fertilized the egg. While I was relieved to have some answers, the aftermath of this condition was very stressful. The pregnancy sent my body and hormones into overdrive, and it would take time to get everything back to normal. I would undergo many blood tests and months of monitoring, and we would have to wait six to 12 months to get pregnant again. Our faith and trust in God and His plan would be the hope that Alan and I relied on to get through this nightmare that never seemed to end.

As I write this today, I can joyfully share the "nightmare" is over. Sophia has a little brother and our third baby is on the way. We are stronger as individuals and our marriage is in an incredible place. But most importantly, we have gained an extraordinary respect for God's divine plan. Not only have I discovered the meaning of fully trusting the Lord, but I am so much more aware of His blessings that surround us. Not a day goes by that I don't thank Him for the incredible gift of our family. My eyes and heart have been opened to His abundant love and blessings and I look forward to what He has in store for us in the future.

Xiomara Goss
Austin, TX

May 20

You were taught, with regard to your former way of life, to put off your old self, which is being corrupted by deceitful desires; to be made new in the attitude of your minds; and to put on the new self, created to be like God in true righteousness and holiness. —Ephesians 4:22-24

One of the books we studied in Tuesday-morning Bible study at my church was Liz Curtis Higgs' *Bad Girls of the Bible*. The book began with the original bad girl, Eve, and ended with the Sinful Woman who anointed Jesus' feet in Luke 7:36-50. I was able to identify with every Bad Girl she wrote about. However, the story of the Woman at the Well (John 4:1-38) and the Sinful Woman really spoke to me. To be truthful, those two lessons literally transformed my life!

I had been living with such shame and guilt because of my sinful past. I knew that God had forgiven me, but I had not forgiven myself. What if others knew what a "Bad Girl" I had been? I haven't had five husbands like the Woman at the Well, but I had more than one. The Sinful Woman who anointed Jesus' feet was scorned by Simon because he knew her past, like I have been so fearful of being scorned by others if they only knew mine. She was my hero, though, because her faith is what saved her and for that, Jesus totally forgave all of her sins. All of them!

Jesus pursued the Woman at the Well. He went out of His way to meet her, right where she was. He has done the same for me. He has met me on my own turf over and over all these years, to offer me the same living water he offered her. It just took me awhile to accept it and leave my old water jar, my old self, behind and go forward, basking in his mercy and forgiveness.

The Sinful Woman sought Jesus. She knew Jesus was going to have dinner at the home of Simon, the Pharisee, and went there. She was totally broken, had nothing to lose and didn't care if those in attendance disapproved of her presence. Besides that, she poured a whole bottle of expensive perfume on His feet, which Simon thought was wasteful.

Oh, I remember being that woman. So broken, so desperate, that I sought God's presence—I had nowhere else to go. He was there waiting on me. He knew I would come. He orchestrated all the events of my life that led to that exact day when I would admit I was in need of a Savior.

I so desperately needed a refresher course on forgiveness, and the story of the Woman at the Well and the Sinful Woman were perfect. The need to forgive myself and stop focusing on my sin was what I needed most of all, though. How could I glorify God if I was so concerned with myself?

He wiped my slate clean. I needed to move on and let others know what He had done for me. God deserves all the glory for a life that has totally been transformed through His great mercy, love and forgiveness. I knew all those truths; I just hadn't allowed myself to believe them. After I finished that Bible study, I felt different. I was ready to let go of who I used to be.

Do you feel unworthy because of your past sins? Don't let Satan's lies steal your joy. You are forgiven. It's done. Let others see how God has transformed your life. Before you leave home today, make sure to put on your new self so everyone can see Jesus in you.

"Your faith has saved you; go in peace" (Luke 7:50). Yes, go out in peace today!

May 21

Delight yourself in the LORD and he will give you the desires of your heart.—Psalm 37:4

It was May 21, 2010, and I could hardly believe that I was about to get my first glimpse of Israel— God's Holy Land. My friend, Margaret, and I had been studying together weekly for this trip during the past six months. We knew this would be a spiritual pilgrimage like none other, and we were ready for what the Lord had to show us!

Every day of our journey brought incredible experiences as we traveled from place to place, following in the footsteps of Jesus. It was surreal to open up the Bible and read the very words of God in the place they were spoken.

Our days started early and ended late. It was every bit the physical, emotional and spiritual journey that we had anticipated. One of my favorite memories of the trip was finding surprise and delight at the Western "Wailing" Wall.

Both Jews and Christians from all over the world come to the Western Wall of the Temple to reach out and touch these sacred stones, in hopes of feeling the presence of God as they lift up their prayers. I couldn't wait to do the same! The night before our scheduled visit, I spent hours writing out heartfelt praises, Scripture prayers and important requests to place before my Abba Father.

It was late in the day when we arrived at the Western Wall, and I was surprised how busy it was. I had a hard time focusing on the historical facts our tour guide was sharing with us because there were so many people to watch. I saw little boys with curly locks dangling at the side of their faces, men dressed in long black coats, boots and tall, furry hats, and a beautiful bride in her long, white dress. After soaking up the scene, I turned my attention back to our guide just as he said we had 12 minutes to pray before we had to leave.

What? Could I have possibly heard him right? It would take at least 10 minutes to get through the line of people waiting to get to the wall! My heart raced as Margaret and I ran to the women's area and waited and waited and waited. With only a few minutes left, I approached the stones for my big moment. I frantically looked for a spot in the mortar to slip in my *Tzetel*—my big prayer written on small paper.

I reached out, touched the wall, prayed some short prayers and quietly backed away. A sense of disappointment enveloped me as I walked back to the bus. Did I do something wrong? Did I place too much emphasis on this Wall and this moment?

It was then that the Holy Spirit gently reminded me that it's not about the where, but the who. I knew that because of the blood of Jesus I did not have to go to a certain place or through a certain person to pray. I could boldly approach the throne of grace anytime and anyplace. It wasn't about the wall, it was about the Lord! My spirits were lifted as I thanked God that He is not limited to one place.

The next morning, our first stop was the Rabbi Tunnels beneath the Temple Mount. To enter the tunnels, we went past the Wailing Wall again. It was 7:30 a.m. and the Wall was quiet, with only a few people there praying. I couldn't help wishing it had been like that during our visit. I turned to Margaret, who had that same look of longing on her face, and said out loud. "It's not about the where, but the who." We laughed and headed on to the tunnels.

Part of our group went into the tunnels immediately, while the rest of our group waited for the next available guide. A few minutes later we were informed it would be about 20 minutes before we could go, so we were free to walk around or go to the wall and pray. I couldn't believe it! Tears filled my eyes and gratitude filled my soul as I realized that God had specifically answered my heart's longing. This time, I confidently approached the stones and joyfully lifted up praises and prayers because I knew, without a doubt, that my sweet experience here would not be about the Wall, but about God delighting one of His children!

Teresa Maldonado
Austin, TX

May 22

And don't forget to do good and to share with those in need. These are the sacrifices that please God.—**Hebrews 13:16**

My church in Austin has a program called iServe. Instead of worshipping in our sanctuary on a designated Sunday, the church goes out into the community to spread the love of Jesus. For instance, there would be folks going all over the city of Austin doing home repairs, cleaning up parks and public areas, preparing meals for the homeless and collecting and distributing necessities of life for struggling families. Of course, that is only a partial list of what goes on during an iServe Sunday.

My LifeGroup of five couples took on a rather simple project. We were to provide 60 bags of food to residents of a trailer park in the Lake Travis area of Austin. If you have ever been to Lake Travis, you might be thinking there couldn't possibly be "needy" people there. I can assure you there are.

This wasn't a trailer park of doublewides or big motor homes. These trailers were quite small and very old. We were told that some people were unemployed and others had jobs. There was no question that the people lived on very limited incomes and would surely appreciate our provisions.

The day before iServe, the daily word of encouragement from K-LOVE was Hebrews 13:16, which I thought was very appropriate for our project. We were going to serve our neighbors in need and share our blessings with them. However, I couldn't really call it a sacrifice. Buying the requested items for 12 families didn't cost much and was not a financial burden. It wasn't even a sacrifice of time. My husband and I would normally be in church on Sunday morning, so we didn't have anything else planned for that time.

I had the preconceived notion that we would knock on a door and talk to each person about the love of Jesus. I would feel warm and fuzzy inside because of the good we were doing. We would be Jesus in the flesh and have the opportunity to change lives. Surely God would be pleased with that. Well, it didn't quite go that way.

Of the 12 trailer doors my husband and I knocked on, only two were answered. We simply left a bag at the other 10. So much for talking about Jesus. But along the way, Jesus spoke to us.

At the second trailer, a person peered through the curtains after we knocked on the door. OK, someone knows we are here, but doesn't want to answer. After a minute or so, we simply left. Just as we walked back to the dirt road, a man yelled for us to stop. He came around the trailer, hurriedly buttoning his shirt and apologizing for taking so long.

I told the man about our church and iServe. He knew where the church was located because he worked for a lawn service that mows lawns for homes nearby. He thanked us for the food, but said he really didn't need it. He had a job and so did his wife—they were the lucky ones because most of his neighbors were unemployed. He didn't need the food, but the folks across from him sure did, and he would give his bag to them.

From the appearance of his trailer, I thought he needed help. From the looks of his vehicle, I wasn't sure he would be able to make it to work the next day. Yet he didn't feel he deserved our help, placing his neighbor's needs above his own. We were there to share the love of Jesus and this man shared it with us instead.

We were at the trailer park to do good and help those in need. We were there to serve our neighbors. What happened? I didn't take me long to figure out the missing component—sacrifice. What I was doing that morning was not a sacrifice at all. But this man, he knew what sharing was all about. He had a job and his neighbors didn't. He would take our gift and give it away to someone else who needed it more than he did.

That was a sacrifice. That was showing the love of Jesus.

May 23

Who, O God, is like you? Though you have made me see troubles, many and bitter, you will restore my life again; from the depths of the earth you will again bring me up. You will increase my honor and comfort me once again.
—Psalm 71:19-21

Yesterday, I wrote about a project called iServe in which my church went out into the community on a designated Sunday to share the love of Jesus, instead of holding worship inside of our sanctuary. My LifeGroup went to a trailer park to take food and to introduce ourselves, in hopes of establishing a long-term relationship.

While driving from one side of the trailer park to the other, my husband had a minor accident with one of the residents. He had the right of way, when a young girl backed her car into the street—right into mine. My husband honked, but she failed to stop.

The terrified driver jumped out of her car in horror. I walked over and saw the frantic look in her eyes. I knew this girl came from a very low-income family. Everyone in the trailer park was struggling—that's why we were there.

When I saw the damage to the front passenger door, I really wasn't upset. Probably because only a few weeks earlier I had run into my own garage and my front bumper was smashed in. I hadn't been in any hurry to get that dent repaired; now I know why.

These two minor mishaps weren't the first for my car. She's older, with over 150,000 miles, and I can't remember how many fender-benders she has been through. It was only nine months earlier that she had been in the body shop to repair three minor bumps—another garage-door incident, a collision with a deer and a serious key job done by an anonymous person in a parking lot.

When I saw the look in the young girl's eyes, the first words out of my mouth were to assure her there was nothing to worry about. I already had a damaged bumper, so a crunched door wasn't a big deal. I couldn't put the financial burden on this person, who I later found out was a high-school-aged, unemployed single mom, living with her mother and grandmother in a tiny trailer.

Weren't these fender-benders very much like my own life? Haven't I been in one mishap after another, with God coming to rescue and restore me? But then, I turn back to my sinful ways, only to find myself with another dent in my fender? I have been a total wreck at times in my life, and have been in and out of the repair shop. What if God had told me to fix the damage myself? Sure, I didn't deserve it, but only He could restore me through His love, mercy and forgiveness.

Francesca Battistelli recorded a cute, fun song titled "Free to Be Me." The words to the chorus kept on going through my head: *'Cause I got a couple dents in my fender, got a couple rips in my jeans.* She goes on to sing that she can't fit the pieces of her life together on her own, but only with God's help. And through it all, God lets her know that He loves her, just as she is.

It was very humbling to compare myself to a wrecked car. However, the human-operated paint and body shops can never out-do my Father's restoration and salvation business. Oh, God, there is none like You!

May 24

"And I will ask the Father, and he will give you another Counselor to be with you forever—the Spirit of truth. The world cannot accept him, because it neither sees him nor knows him. But you know him, for he lives with you and will be with you." —**John 14:16-17**

The reservations were complete. It was actually going to happen. We were taking a family cruise vacation. It was going to be an "expanded" family trip. My daughter-in-law's parents and younger brother would be going too. What a blessing that we could all travel together as one family.

Since we wanted our rooms close together, I spoke with a reservation agent. When she asked if there were any "senior citizens" traveling, I told her no. Later she went down the list of names, asking for birthdates. When I gave her my husband's and mine she burst out, "Oh, you do qualify for the senior discount! You are both over 55."

When did being over 55 get classified as a senior citizen? I am very appreciative of the discount for the cruise, but being a "senior" does have some downsides to it. For example, I have already noticed how forgetful and easily sidetracked I am these days.

One Thursday morning, I took my golden retriever outside just as the sun was rising. It was a gorgeous sunrise and all of the birds were singing their praises. I decided to sit on the porch, drink my coffee and visit with God. As I sat down, I saw Holly chasing the deer along the fence. Seeing the deer reminded me that I didn't feed them the night before, so I decided to do that before I prayed.

Going into the garage for the deer food reminded me that the 40-pound bag of dog food I had purchased on Tuesday was still in my car. So, instead of getting the deer food, I opened the back of my SUV to take out the dog food. When I picked up one corner of the bag, I saw my car keys, hidden underneath the bag. Had I been looking for my keys, I would have been overjoyed to find them, but I didn't even know they were missing.

When I came home Tuesday from buying the dog food, I had to have unlocked the house to get in. Why in the world did I take my keys back out to the car and put them in with the dog food? How did they get there? Wednesday I didn't drive anywhere, so I didn't miss them. I was indeed puzzled.

I totally forgot about feeding the deer that morning, but at least I remembered to pray. I just chuckled out loud at my memory lapse with the keys, but then I had a sweet thought. God knew my keys were lost and in a few hours, when I was rushing out of the house for my meeting, I would have frantically searched for them. I would have never thought to look in the back of my SUV.

Without even asking, He provided for me. "For your Father knows what you need before you ask him" (Matthew 6:8). Do I really think God keeps tabs on such minor details of my life? The Holy Spirit lives in me and knows my every move. Finding my keys was just God's way of providing a glimpse of Him in action.

I think it is great fun to look for God's touch throughout the day. It is not a game, though—it is a joyful pursuit that comes from being confident I will see Him. Even "senior citizens" aren't too old for that kind of fun.

May 25

Now faith is being sure of what we hope for and certain of what we do not see.—**Hebrews 11:1**

Getting out and about before sunrise doesn't happen too often for me. But on this particular morning, I was driving into Austin from Lake Travis to meet a friend for coffee as the sun was barely peeking over the horizon. It's lovely to venture into town and watch the skyline emerge as I drive through the rolling hills of my rural area to the urban freeways and thoroughfares. Then, to have the big ball of orange rising up behind the tall downtown buildings is a beautiful sight to behold.

As I was driving along Southwest Parkway to Loop One in Austin, I was enjoying my Christian praise and worship songs, along with the gorgeous early-morning sky. "Open the Eyes of My Heart," as recorded by the legendary Michael W. Smith, filled my car and I joyfully sang along. There were actually a few clouds in the sky and when I heard the lyrics requesting to "see" God, I glanced up in the sky.

Did I expect the clouds to form a silhouette of Jesus? Was I hoping to see a chariot drawn by horses and Father God standing up in all of His glory as He steered them down to earth? I don't know exactly what I was looking for, but I definitely had this longing to "see" an image of God Himself.

This wasn't the first time I had looked for Him to appear before me. Why wasn't the sunrise enough to satisfy my yearning? My thoughts quickly went to Hebrews 11—the faith chapter. As I spoke the words from the first verse out loud as I drove—"faith is being sure of what we hope for and certain of what we do not see"—I was ashamed of my wish to see a figure in the sky.

On my drive back from the big city of Austin to my house on the lake, Michael W. Smith kept on singing that song to me in my head. Perhaps I had focused too much on wanting to "see" God, instead of the song's title itself. "Open the Eyes of My Heart." I don't need my physical eyes to see my Father. Isn't faith defined as being certain of what we do not see? Yes, Lord, open the eyes of my heart so I can see the love that radiates from You and is the essence of Your being.

When I arrived back home, I sat at my computer to write about my early-morning visit with my friend. She asked me what I was struggling with the most in my walk with God at that moment. I had a quick answer: obedience. I know exactly when I am not obeying His commands, and it happens too often. If I loved God more, would I be more inclined to obey Him faithfully?

In John 15:9-12, Jesus left His instructions to the disciples: "As the Father has loved me, so have I loved you. Now remain in my love. If you obey my commands, you will remain in my love, just as I have obeyed my Father's commands and remain in his love. I have told you this so that my joy may be in you and that your joy may be complete. My command is this: Love each other as I have loved you."

My eyes can't love; only my heart can do that. Was that revelation the reason why the song had been stuck in my head all day, playing over and over? The more intimate of a relationship I have with my Father—the deeper my love for Him—the more I will want to please Him and follow His commands. May the love that radiates from my Master also fill my heart and overflow through my acts of obedience.

May 26

The heavens declare the glory of God; the skies proclaim the work of His hands.—**Psalm 19:1**

I am a morning person. I love the cool air, the smells, the quietness that is broken only by birds singing.

But what I love the most is the sky. I often walk at Lady Bird Lake early in the morning. Driving there from my house, I crest a hill and see a spectacular view of the Austin skyline silhouetted against an expansive sky. Some days, it's crystal clear; on others, there are big, puffy clouds overhead; on others, a light haze sets in.

On those clear days, it almost takes my breath away. The colors look as if God took a broad brush, dipped it in beautiful paint colors and just drew it across the horizon. I see colors that I've seen in paintings that made me think, *Very pretty, but the artist must have just added those to make a captivating picture.* But, no, right there in front of me are lavenders, peach, pinks, blended in with every shade of blue you could imagine. All I can think is, *Thank You, God, for the beauty You have created! Thank You for letting me live in a place where I am surrounded by such beauty.*

Where is it in your day that *you* see God declaring His glory? Where is He showing you the work of His hands? If an answer doesn't quickly come to mind, be on the lookout today. He's there; just look for Him.

Marilyn Ingram
Austin, TX

May 27

O Lord, you have searched me and you know me.—**Psalm 139:1**

In August 2007, I moved from Katy, where I had lived since 1982, to Austin. Moving to a new town was an adjustment, but not too painful. My husband and I found a wonderful church in Austin, and formed a close bond with the couples in our new LifeGroup. The new doctor I go to is extremely smart and I now know the grocery store like the back of my hand (until they reset the aisles again.)

However, I haven't even considered changing my dentist or hairdresser. I recently made the 160-mile trip to Katy for my six-month dental checkup and my six-week hair appointment (plus have dinner with my grown kids).

When I walked into the dentist's office, I felt like I had never moved away. While the practice has grown tremendously since my first visit in 1982, both in the number of dentists within the office and the new state-of-the-art facility, the friendly faces behind the desk are the same, including my dentist.

They know me there. The ladies at the desk asked how things were going in Austin. One of them told me how nice it was to see one of my sons, who went in for his six-month checkup a few weeks earlier. When I saw my dentist, we exchanged kid stories because she knows both of my boys and their mouths very well. She is younger, with three children, and I can still remember when she was pregnant with her first.

After taking care of my teeth, I was off to take care of my gray hair. My friend Esther has been my hairdresser for 20 years. I know so much about Esther, and she knows all about my life too. We were members of the same church in Katy before I moved and we have shared some very intimate conversations—about the Bible study we are doing or how God is working in our daily lives. We talk about the hopes and dreams we have for our children and their trials and praises. I could find someone in Austin to cut and highlight my hair, but I don't know if I could find someone to highlight my life like Esther.

I have made some very special new friends in Austin, but sometimes it's a bit sad knowing we don't have a history together, but we are working on that. It is comfortable to be with people who knew my children and where they went to school. Since I haven't moved much in my life, I must admit that leaving my familiar surroundings was difficult.

My short trips back to Katy are enjoyable, but I don't have to go back there to find someone who has a history with me. I don't have to go anywhere at all! *"O LORD, you have searched me and you know me"* (Psalm 139:1). Those words are so sweet and loving. David continued in Psalm 139 to tell us that God is omniscient (all knowing) in verses 2-6 and omnipresent (present everywhere) in verses 7-12. My God knows all, sees all, is all-powerful, and I cannot flee from His presence (Vs. 7).

I love my old friends, and my new ones, but the relationship with my Heavenly Father is the most special of all.

May 28

"Greater love has no one than this: to lay down one's life for one's friend." —**John 15:13**

For several days, I have pondered what Memorial Day means to my family and me. I've thought about my husband, who for nearly 20 years has proudly served this country. I think about his brother, their father, and their grandfather and now the next generation in our nephews. I think about my dad, uncles and grandfather, all who have at one point worn that uniform with pride.

I think about the wars that most of these men have experienced—the horrors they've seen, the fear they must have felt and the loss of life they had to deal with. I think of my husband's grandfather, who received a Purple Heart, or my great uncle, who picked up the dead so that no man was left behind during the dark days of World War II. I wonder about the secrets my father-in-law keeps about his days in Korea and the pain he felt losing his friend.

Then I stop and tearfully remember my husband's deployment—the 15 long months he was gone. I remember the days leading up to that day and all the preparation that had to be done. But the worst was having to sit down and seriously discuss the "what ifs."

What if he didn't return? Most military wives know this talk all too well; it is the one where you have to plan his funeral, just in case, because he does not want you to worry with the details. It's the talk that he gives you about moving on, being happy and relying on God, and that if God calls him home, he is ready. I remember the day I kissed him goodbye, then slowly turned to walk away, and the look in his eyes of being torn between service to a greater cause and his family.

Then there are the sleepless nights, living by the phone. And the jokes to the neighbors that I was married to the computer because that was the only way I could see my husband. And kissing the girls goodnight and knowing that when they would ask if Daddy would be OK, I couldn't promise them anything and just had to pray God would protect him. And watching our girls swell with pride when someone would ask them, "What does your daddy do for a living?" and they would answer, "He is a soldier."

Then I remember the four men who did not return with my husband's unit—men who gave their lives for this country. I think of the wives and kids they left behind to carry on, and how they feel that sacrifice every day. I think of all the men and women who have given all so we could have the freedom to get an education, to choose our careers, to vote, to enjoy a day at the lake or a good meal with friends, and most importantly, to worship without fear.

On this Memorial Day, you will find us camping at the lake near our hometown with my husband's family. Oh, it will be a lot of fun, laughter and time with God. Yet, I know of a few men who will ponder some memories. They will quietly think of their fallen comrades and understand the sacrifices that have been made for the freedoms we enjoy every day in America. But they also have a unique perspective on how Jesus made the ultimate sacrifice so that we may be free for eternity. Those men understand freedom is not free.

One of the greatest gifts you can give a solider and his family is a simple handshake and a thank you. I can say from experience that those moments have meant more to our family than words can express. And it's that simple gesture that can show the love of Christ in a huge way. And while you are at it, do not forget to thank God for sacrificing His Son.

Shanna Jacobson
Brownwood, TX

May 29

But if we walk in the light, as he is in the light, we have fellowship with one another, and the blood of Jesus, his Son, purifies us from all sin.—**1 John 1:7**

God has a way of placing a song in my heart, and I hear it at different times during the day. Sometimes it comes in the form of a wake-up call. I wonder what God is up to and ponder how that song will impact my day.

A Christian rock band that was popular in the late 1980s, dc Talk, recorded "In the Light." My two sons loved dc Talk, and the band, along with Michael W. Smith, were my own introduction to contemporary Christian music. I hadn't heard "In the Light" for years and now I was waking up to it?

The words to the song could have been written for my own life. (Google "In the Light dc Talk.") Perhaps that's why God used it that morning for my wake-up call. In the chorus, songwriter Charlie Peacock referenced wanting to walk in the light, as He is in the light, wanting to shine like a star in heaven. Over and over, the lyrics that were inspired by 1 John 1:7 echoed in my head. Yes, Lord, on this day, may I walk in Your Light, as You are in the light. Where else would I want to be?

"God is light, in him there is no darkness at all" (1 John 1:5), but sometimes we step out of His light and try to live on our own, apart from God. We may think we are out there by ourselves in the dark, but His light never goes out. We are the ones who left Him, not the other way around.

Trying to visualize total darkness reminded me of the blackout curtains that, when tightly drawn, can "almost" block out all the light from the outside world. There must be some trick to pulling both ends of the curtains together though. Try as I might, I can always see rays of sunshine right in the middle or at the top or the bottom.

Early one morning, while still in bed in our hotel room on a get-away weekend with my husband, I saw glimpses of the morning sun peeking through, right in the middle of the drawn, blackout curtains. I was reminded of both the words from "In the Light" and 1 John 1:5. His light shines, no matter what! We can draw the curtains or try to run and hide. We might even refuse His invitation to come close and try to live on our own, but we can never completely block the brilliance of His glorious light.

My sweet sisters, I know all too well about being on that gloomy road that leads to nowhere. Oh, the years I spent fumbling around in the darkness! I felt totally isolated from God, but looking back, I see time after time my Savior was there, rescuing me from complete self-destruction.

Yes, there were consequences for my sinful actions, but there was also the promise of redemption when I found my way back to His glorious Word. "But if we walk in the light, as he is in the light, we have fellowship with one another, and the blood of Jesus, his Son, purifies us from all sin."

Oh, Blessed Redeemer, I am still a sinner, in need of a Savior. There is nowhere else I would rather be than with You—in Your Light. Thank You for sending such a sweet song to start my day.

May 30

"I am the way, the truth and the life. No one comes to the Father except through me." —**John 14:16**

I can get extremely anxious before a flight. One such experience that will remain etched in my mind was when I had an early-morning flight to California. I believe you can never get to the airport too early, so I got up at 4:30 a.m. to walk my dog, hoping to get ahead of the Houston rush-hour traffic for the drive to the airport.

It could be spooky being out at that time of the morning, but I felt safe in my neighborhood, so I really didn't give it much thought. After leaving my quiet cul-de-sac, I was on the sidewalk of a major street I have walked many times, but this morning it was different. No cars, no noise, just my golden retriever and me.

On one side of the sidewalk is a grassy area lined with large trees, then a brick wall that is actually the back fence of homes. On the other side is more grass and streetlights, then the street. Even though it was well lit, I had a feeling that I was no longer alone, and I was actually frightened.

I had the most overwhelming sense that "something" was in the trees. Suddenly there was a rustling, and a whole flock of birds flew out of the tree I was walking under, making a very loud noise. That really spooked both my dog and me; I laughed at myself. However, I still felt something hovering over me. What I saw stopped me in my tracks, and I was completely overwhelmed.

As I watched the birds fly off, my eyes glanced at the brick wall. There I saw the most perfect silhouette of Jesus—His profile was a shadow on the brick. His long, flowing hair seemed to be blowing softly in the gentle breeze and His righteous hand was pointing straight down the sidewalk. I could hear Jesus whispering to me, *I am the way, the truth and the life. Follow Me.*

I honestly couldn't move. Others have said they have seen Jesus or have heard Him, but I couldn't really imagine that whole scenario in my head. But at that moment, I felt His presence. I knew "someone" was with me on that sidewalk. I heard Him in the trees and then I saw His face on the wall, and He was motioning to me. Then He spoke to my heart and His words permeated my soul.

Seeing and hearing from God is a personal experience, and He is extremely creative in the ways He reaches out to us. This particular encounter was totally indescribable, and I can still see His beautiful profile on that brick wall. I was walking closer with God than I ever had, but He was there, inviting me to come even closer. I was filled with such an incredible peace and suddenly all anxiety about that flight disappeared. Oh, how He loves me and pursues me again and again.

He loves and pursues you, too, my sweet friend. Listen for His invitation—*Follow Me!*

May 31

So whether you eat or drink or whatever you do, do it all for the glory of God.—**1 Corinthians 10:31**

Songwriter and recording artist Stephen Curtis Chapman's song "Do Everything" is based on the Scripture above. Before it was released, I watched a video clip where he explained the story behind the song.

Chapman spoke of growing up, wrestling with the spiritual aspects of life verses the secular and finding there was actually no distinction between the two—that *everything* we do in life should be done as an act of worship to glorify God. So, whether we are cleaning house, driving carpool, changing diapers, cooking dinner, presiding over a corporate meeting or going on a date with our spouse, it all matters. It matters "just as long as you do everything you do to the glory of the One who made you."

The words and the tune have been stuck in my head every since I heard it for the first time back in August 2011. I knew that God was reaching out to me through this song—He knows how I love music! He was reminding me no matter how big or how small, it's important to Him. He wants my actions to bring Him glory.

The stronger my relationship grows with my Father, the more I am truly aware of all I say and do, and I *want* to honor Him. One area in particular that I must pay attention to is how I treat others who might have irritated me just a wee bit. For that reason, every morning I start out with Psalm 19:24: "May the words of my mouth and the meditations of my heart be pleasing in your sight."

You know what I am talking about when I mention being irritated by others. The driver in that car who just cut in front of me and didn't even use her blinker. Or how about the person in the parking lot who took the open space that I saw first? The telemarketer on the phone just doing her job, but called for the third time in a row. What about the gal talking on her phone who just sat through the green light? Oh, I must also include the times my husband kind of gets under my skin.

All these little irritations can bring out the worst in my behavior, and I could say something ugly (audible or silently) if I am not careful. That's when I think about this song and the Scripture. However, sometimes the old me resurfaces and the ugly words blurt out. That's what happened just the other day. I snapped at the customer-service person on the phone. It wasn't her fault. She didn't make the rules.

Later, when in my car and feeling very disappointed in myself, "Do Everything" played on the radio. I have listened to that song countless times, but why haven't I ever paid attention to these specific words: He made you to do every little thing *"to bring a smile to His face."* I had never imagined God smiling because of something I had done. I bet He wasn't smiling while I was barking at that customer-service person, though.

Just to imagine the Creator of the universe smiling down at me gives me goose bumps. I can actually bring a smile to His face when my actions glorify Him? But what does He do when I say something cruel, think bad thoughts, worship idols like money and my children, spend time on the computer instead of in prayer? How often does He frown at my behavior?

I know my Father's love for me is unconditional, and when I mess up, I am forgiven. However, the thought of God smiling because of my acts of obedience is so cool. I am so thankful that at just the right time, God spoke to me through the words of a song. With His help, today I am going to do my very best to keep that smile on His face.

June 1

This is the day the LORD has made; let us rejoice and be glad in it. — **Psalm 118:24**

Yesterday, I wrote about a song recorded by Steven Curtis Chapman. While looking around on the Internet about his song "Do Everything," I found a YouTube video of Chapman singing "Morning Has Broken," which is on the same album. Turned out to be another God-incidence in my life.

I remembered a song by Cat Stevens, an English pop musician and folk singer, from my college years by that title. Could this be the same one? Sadly, in those days I wouldn't have intentionally been listening to Christian music.

I watched the video and, sure enough, it was the same. So I delved into the subject further and found some interesting facts. "Morning Has Broken" was written in 1931 by English author Eleanor Farjeon and is a well-known English hymn. Cat Stevens was looking for a few more songs to include on his album, *Teaser and the Firecat*, and happened to find a hymnal in a bookstore while looking for ideas.

"Morning Has Broken" was in that hymnal. Stevens' recording of it came in at #6 on the U.S. pop chart and #1 on the U.S. easy listening chart in 1972. I had the eight-track tape of *Teaser and the Firecat*, and I sure didn't know I was listening to an English hymn when "Morning Has Broken" played. Hmm, God knew.

The words to this hymn are so appropriate to start a new day. If you were into music in the '70s, you might remember Cat Stevens' version of this. If not, you can Google "Morning Has Broken" and find both his and Chapman's recording on YouTube, and sing along.

Morning has broken, like the first morning
Blackbird has spoken, like the first bird

Praise for the singing, praise for the morning
Praise for the springing fresh from the word

Sweet the rain's new fall, sunlit from heaven
Like the first dewfall, on the first grass
Praise for the sweetness of the wet garden
Sprung in completeness where his feet pass

Mine is the sunlight, mine is the morning
Born of the one light, Eden saw play
Praise with elation, praise every morning
God's recreation of the new day

I grew up knowing Jesus. However, somewhere along the way, while in high school and on through college, I didn't have much to do with Him. I shudder at the thought of those dark days. I had no idea He was there during that wild, turbulent period—even singing hymns to me like "Morning Has Broken." Looking back, I know He was protecting me from even worse situations.

I lived in fear when I actually rekindled my relationship with God, and became a mom. Involved at church and with school activities, I wanted to hide from the past. What if they knew?

It took time, but God released me from that fear. I finally came clean and talked with some trusted friends about those dark clouds that hovered over me all those years. He knew, yet loved me anyway. And my friends? They still loved me too.

My Redeemer has transformed me from a confused girl, seeking love in all the wrong places, to a woman finding her true love in the arms of Jesus. Those years had a purpose—to make me desperate for God. I never want to be locked up in those chains again. I still make mistakes and I seek His forgiveness daily, but I can walk in freedom. I am a continuous work in progress, and each day I am so thankful that my God is with me, showering me with His love, mercy and grace.

I am so happy that He led me to this great old hymn. Yes, a new morning has broken, springing fresh from the Word. Let us rejoice in this day!

June 2

For we must all appear before the judgment seat of Christ, that each one may receive what is due him for the things done while in the body, whether good or bad.—**2 Corinthians 5:10**

During Memorial Day weekend several years ago, my younger son made a poor decision that led to his arrest. His case wouldn't appear before the judge for several months because of the massive backlog, so the incident loomed overhead.

The attorney gave my son some advice on what needed to be done "in the meantime." He provided Trevor with a to-do list, which included some mandatory classes, so that when the court date arrived, he would be a few steps ahead. The attorney said it would demonstrate he was acting in good faith and was a responsible young man, willing to do whatever it took to right this wrong.

A few weeks after visiting the attorney, I asked my son if he had started any of the items on the list. He had not. The second time I asked the question and received the same negative response, I was a bit upset. Our conversation went something like this:

You have been given an opportunity to do what is right. When you appear before the judge, he is going to ask you if you have completed any of the classes. He is not going to be impressed if he looks at the dates of completion and sees that you have just finished (or haven't even completed them). He wants to see that you made the most of the time you had and did what was required. He wants to know that you were willing and motivated to do what was right.

That very evening, I had dinner with a friend and we discussed our children, or, should I say, our young adults. Both of us had kiddos making some bad decisions. I relayed the conversation I had with my son. After I finished with my story, I felt a heaviness on my heart and began to tear up.

One day, I too, will appear in judgment before my Heavenly Father. He will have some questions for me. What did I do with what He gave me? Is He going to tell me He was pleased? Did I make the most of the time I had been given? Ashamed and humbled, I could only cry.

I was so upset with my son for not doing what the attorney had asked. This parent was totally disgusted with her child for his blatant lack of responsibility that got him into the mess in the first place. He knew what he did was wrong and he endangered other lives. However, he didn't have remorse for his actions, only thinking he was just the unlucky one who got caught doing what everyone else did all the time. Now, he had the opportunity to take advantage of the time before his court appearance and he wasn't using his time wisely. Plus, he was trying to justify his actions.

Oh, my goodness! I do the same thing! My Heavenly Father must have been wringing His hands in exasperation with me, just as I was with my son. I am over twice his age and still hadn't learned my lesson. How many times have I turned and gone the opposite direction when God was calling me? How many times have I done exactly what I wanted instead of being obedient to His commands? How often do I worship an idol—money, my children, clothes, my house—instead of God? What am I doing "in the meantime" with my life, in the time between birth and death, before going to my permanent home in heaven?

I was so distraught when my son got in trouble. My heart ached! Believe me, going to bail your child out of jail at 5:30 a.m. on Memorial Day is not a mother's proudest moment. But how many times has God bailed me out of a jam? I can assure you, too many for me to count! I had to suffer the consequences, but He was always there with me.

When I saw my son walking out of the jail, I thought I would hit the floor. I had some flashbacks of him walking, in both sad and happy moments—walking down the aisle at graduation, walking up to the podium to receive his first place medal at the state track meet, walking out of the locker room after a poor performance in a football game, walking into the house to report that he had aced the test, walking into my bedroom and flopping on my bed to chat after a date—I was always there for him. I couldn't let him down at that horrible moment, but I was so incredibly sad. This wasn't something I had prepared for as a parent.

How must God have felt all the times I let Him down? That was the reason for my tears. I had such remorse for the heartache I have caused the One who truly loves me more than anyone else in this world.

While I love my son dearly, God loves him more. He is more disappointed than I am. While not being pleased with his actions, God wasn't caught off guard like I was. Could this be part of God's plan to bring my son to his knees in surrender? Or perhaps, could it be His plan to bring me to mine?

June 3

I am carrying on a great project and cannot go down.—**Nehemiah 6:2**

After spending 48 years as captives in Babylon, the Jews returned to Jerusalem in 538 B.C. Their city had been destroyed and the southern kingdom of Judah defeated by King Nebuchadnezzar. Once there, under the leadership of Cyrus, the King of Persia, they began the task of rebuilding the temple that had been demolished by the Babylonians in 586 B.C. The temple was completed in 516—20 years after it was started—but the walls surrounding the city remained in shambles.

When Nehemiah heard the devastating news, he asked permission from the Persian king to leave his distinguished post as the king's cupbearer so he could travel to Jerusalem and organize the reconstruction of the wall. "And because the gracious hand of my God was upon me, the king granted my request" (Nehemiah 2:8). God placed the vision on his heart and Nehemiah proceeded with great fortitude. God provided every detail he asked for in prayer and Nehemiah proclaimed, "The God of heaven will give us success" (Vs. 20).

Nehemiah didn't jump blindly into this construction project. He mourned, fasted and prayed for days, seeking wisdom and guidance. He used his organizational and leadership skills to motivate and guide the Jews during the process. He worked alongside them and the wall was finished in a record 52 days. What seemed like an impossible task was accomplished through God's servant who prayed continuously and walked faithfully with his God.

When doing the Lord's work we must be aware of the enemy lurking behind the scenes, bent on thwarting our endeavors. He will attempt any devious scheme to get us sidetracked from God's plan. Nehemiah experienced opposition from enemies and had to be on guard against their sneaky moves, but he never faltered or doubted that God would bring success. When all other attempts to stop construction of the wall failed, Sanballat and Geshem, stooped even lower and went after Nehemiah's character. Part of the scheme was to lure him to a remote location and ambush him along the way.

"Sanballat and Geshem sent me this message: 'Come, let us meet together in one of the villages on the plain of Ono.' But they were scheming to harm me; so I sent messengers to them with this reply: 'I am carrying on a great project and cannot go down. Why should the work stop while I leave it and go down to you?' " (Nehemiah 6:2-3).

No, Nehemiah wasn't going to be tricked, and he sure wasn't about to stop the work he had been entrusted by God to complete. He was in the middle of "a great project" and he would not be deterred. Now, that's a faithful servant! The two of them had a very special, intimate relationship. Everything Nehemiah did was out of the love he had for the Father and to ultimately bring glory and honor to His name. No wonder God chose Nehemiah to be the one in charge of rebuilding the wall.

Nehemiah was not only selected to rebuild the physical wall around the city of Jerusalem, but also to restore the crumbled hearts of God's chosen people—to strengthen and renew their faith. What at first seemed like an impossible task was seen to completion because Nehemiah never strayed from God's plan. Through prayer and perseverance, he remained obedient. Nehemiah was totally dependent on God to fulfill His purpose, and he was able to bring others to that place of dependence as well.

God knew He could rely on Nehemiah to go out and do His work. Are you a doer for God? Can He depend on you to follow through on the plans to grow His kingdom? We are all called to be Nehemiahs. We are summoned by God to go out into the world and bring hope and renewal to the broken and crumbled hearts we encounter.

When Satan tries to wiggle his way into your life and knock you off God's course, are you strong enough to defend your heart with the armor of God's Word and stand firm against his advances? Nehemiah not only fended off evil influences, but he also persevered through those difficulties, refusing to come down and stop work until the job was done.

Are you whispering to yourself that Nehemiah was probably some supernatural person? Nehemiah was a mere human, who did the "seemingly" impossible, and so can you and I. How? For starters, we can read the Book of Nehemiah and learn by his example. Yes, I am serious. Nehemiah is a present-day hero.

God has a specific purpose for each of us as we come together to expand His kingdom. Now, let's go get ready for work.

June 4

"No one can come to me unless the Father who sent me draws him, and I will raise him up at the last day." —**John 6:44**

Bible study was over for the summer months. Many women gathered in neighborhood homes for informal study, but a few of us decided to simply meet for coffee once a week and talk. No agenda—simply sweet, godly fellowship.

There were two commonalities between us. One, we were all about the same age with adult children. Two, we all expressed the desire to spend time with other women our age since we all ministered in some form or fashion to "younger" women. So, that's how our group started.

Because of summer vacations, the group fluctuated each week, and it was actually great fun getting to know each other in such a small, intimate setting. What was said in the group stayed there, and our discussions were incredibly open and honest.

In the group, there were three of us who had kids who were floundering in their faith walk. Needless to say, the conversation often reverted to our trials with our wayward kiddos. Yes, they were all adults, but still our children.

The most reassuring comment heard was that if they once believed, they will come back to their faith in God's perfect time. A few of us could relate to those years in our twenties that we were also lost and a bit unruly, and we got back on track once we had our children. There's something about becoming a parent that will get us back to church. However, we all agreed that the most effective tool we had, as moms, was to pray for our children.

On one particular morning, I rushed out the door to meet the girls before taking the time to read all of my daily devotions. When I returned home, I sat down to finish. John 6:44 was the daily verse for one of them. How appropriate for the conversation we just had about praying for our children to return to God.

Some of us moms tend to want some control of our children, even when they are living on their own. The empty nest season of life is actually very nice, but some of us still try to manipulate the parts of their lives we feel needs tweaking. We would like to think that somehow we could bring our unbelieving sons to Christ—somehow, we could be the force behind their faith walk. (In this group, it was all boys who were the problems.)

John 6:44 makes it very clear that we can pray all we want, we can share the Gospel all day long, we can live a righteous life and be a good example, but it is up to God to open the hearts and eyes of the non-believers to accept Christ as their Lord and Savior.

I have no problem giving up control on this issue. It's a tremendous relief knowing that bringing others to Christ is not up to me. I certainly won't stop praying and presenting the Gospel, but I will find peace acknowledging it is God's decision on the when and where eyes and hearts are opened to accept His free gift of salvation.

I couldn't wait to share this verse the following week with the girls. Perhaps you know of another woman to share it with also. That woman might even be you.

June 5

Therefore, there is now no condemnation for those who are in Christ Jesus, because through Christ Jesus the law of the Spirit of life set me free from the law of sin and death.—**Romans 8:1-2**

When our small group of women from church started meeting on a very informal basis one summer for coffee, we had no plans or agenda. There were no reminder emails, just a standing date at 9:30 every Wednesday morning at the Java Dive, and the table was open for discussion.

Our group of six knew of each other—we just didn't actually know everyone well. One of the ladies and I were close friends, being in a LifeGroup together. Two had been in my small group the previous year in Bible study, and the other two I had only met a few times at church. I would say that's more or less how it was for all in the group.

God gets the credit for organizing our "Java Time" and being the facilitator of our group. I can't explain how it happened, but our hour or two on Wednesday turned into an almost sacred time together. When we sat down at that table, it was as if we bared our souls to each other.

There was the freedom to say what was on our heart—to be open, honest and transparent with the assurance of no condemnation from the others. Our conversations covered a range of topics, and there were times we laughed so hard we cried. There were also a few occasions we shed some tears of sadness and found comforting words and loving arms.

One particular morning I shared a dilemma I had been holding back from speaking to anyone about, leery of what others might think. Lo and behold, one of the other ladies chimed right in behind me. Oh, it felt so good to have some company on this one. It was so incredibly freeing, and hilarious at the same time. When I got up from the table to go home, I felt as if a ton of bricks had been lifted off my shoulders. There hadn't been any condemnation, only a round of supportive wisdom from the others.

Funny, I knew the words from Romans 8:1 by memory. I have spoken them over and over in my head to experience the peace and comfort of Jesus' love and forgiveness. But here I was, worried about fessing up to a group of women about harboring my silly thoughts? Then I was reminded of the words from Galatians 1:10: "Am I now trying to win the approval of human beings, or of God? Or am I trying to please people? If I were still trying to please people, I would not be a servant of God."

These women helped me think through my plans, they shared their wisdom with me and offered their unfailing love and support. They didn't all necessarily agree with me, but still provided godly guidance. God spoke through this group of Spirit-filled women and gave me a gift of peace and grace. If it weren't for our Java Time, I might still be carrying this burden around, but God provided an answer to my dilemma through these wonderful ladies.

I do hope that you have a friend or friends with whom you can bare your soul. Keep in mind, intimate relationships with others should never be a substitute for time with God or your spouse, if married. But it is so helpful to have some godly women to do life with, women who will truthfully and honestly share their wisdom. It is also important to have relationships with ladies who love you enough to let you know if the direction you are headed might take you away from Jesus instead of closer to Him. True love is about pursuing authenticity in a relationship, not seeking worldly approval.

Your enemy the Devil prowls around like a roaring lion looking for something to devour (1 Peter 5:8), just waiting to entice anyone who takes their eyes off Jesus, even if only for a few minutes. In addition to being in God's presence and in His Word, staying in touch with some godly girls helps keep the Evil One out of our life.

If you don't have such a circle of women, pray for God guidance. There's no way our Java Time could have come together like it did through any efforts of our own. God brought us together, and He can do the same for you.

June 6

"Remember Lot's wife." —**Luke 17:32**

Have you ever made a bargain with God? Have you promised if He would just get you out of the mess, you would never again do whatever it was that got you there in the first place? If you made such a promise, was it your first time or your umpteenth time to be tangled up in that same sin?

Jesus told the disciples to "Remember Lot's wife," but the Bible doesn't provide much information about the woman. We do know when the two angels led Lot, his wife and two daughters out of Sodom and Gomorrah, they were told: "Flee for your lives! Don't look back, and don't stop anywhere in the plain!" (Genesis 19:17). "But Lot's wife looked back, and she became a pillar of salt" (Vs. 26).

The Bible does give information about the culture of Sodom and Gomorrah. When the angels arrived in Sodom, Lot invited them to his home. Before the end of the night, all of the men in the city surrounded the house demanding: "Where are the men who came to you tonight? Bring them out to us so that we can have sex with them" (Genesis 19:5). From Jude 1:7 we read "Sodom and Gomorrah and the surrounding towns gave themselves up to sexual immorality and perversion. They serve as an example of those who suffer the punishment of eternal fire."

We can't single out sexual immorality as being the only reason for destruction. In Ezekiel 16:49-50, the Lord gave Judah even more insight into the sins of the city: "Now this was the sin of your sister Sodom: She and her daughters were arrogant, overfed and unconcerned; they did not help the poor and needy. They were haughty and did detestable things before me. Therefore I did away with them."

The culture of Sodom and Gomorrah doesn't sound much different from the one we live in today, does it? Ours is a sinful society and even those of us who call ourselves Christians struggle daily not to fall into temptation. But what if we do? How many chances do we get? When is "enough enough" for God?

Was looking back Lot's wife only sin, or had she found great pleasure in the immorality of the culture? Did she look back because she was remorseful of leaving her former way of life? Before His *"Remember Lot's wife"* statement in Luke 17, Jesus told us on the day the Son of Man returns, we must be spiritually ready, not taking time to go back for anything left behind (Vs. 31). "Whoever tries to keep his life will lose it, and whoever loses his life will preserve it" (Vs. 33).

God knows our heart and if we are truly repentant for our sins. A child tries to pull the wool over a parent's eyes, but there's no way we can do that with the Father. Though we try and make a deal, pleading for our lives if we can just get off the hook this time, He will punish the one who doesn't mean it. We do not know Lot's wife's true heart, but God did. However, we are told she disobeyed and got what God promised: "For the wages of sin is death, but the gift of God is eternal life in Christ Jesus our Lord" (Romans 6:23).

Some sinners are turned into a pillar of salt, while for others the consequences are less severe. I was one of those who tried to make a deal with God back in my younger days. I promised Him one too many times I would change my sinful ways if He would just get me out of the jam I was in. He knew my heart wasn't truly repentant, so why should I not suffer the consequences?

My Father is full of mercy and grace and has used those incidents to transform me and use me for His purpose. "I sinned and perverted what was right, but I did not get what I deserved. He redeemed my soul from going down to the pit and I will live to enjoy the light" (Job 33:27-28).

If you are reading this today, you have not received what you deserve either. "He is patient with you, not wanting anyone to perish, but everyone to come to repentance" (2 Peter 3:9). Though undeserved, we have been redeemed. Hallelujah!

June 7

Where can I go from your Spirit? Where can I flee from your presence? —**Psalm 36:7**

The clock struck midnight and I was still up and at 'em. My husband and I had been out of town for a week and there was so much to do in order to catch up. Just one more load of clothes to put in the wash, and I would go to bed.

There was a pair of jeans that I had worn for the first time that caught my eye as I was tossing the other items into the machine. Burnt orange straight legs purchased in Omaha, Nebraska, of all places. No wonder they were on sale. Those Cornhuskers up there aren't very fond of anything Texas Longhorn burnt orange.

Since the jeans had never been washed, I checked the instructions before throwing them in. There were two labels on the inside. The first was a cute black tag with the brand name and size. I lifted it up to read the second one underneath that was a smaller, white label with the washing instructions.

After reading how to properly wash these new jeans, I happened to glance at the backside of that first label. It also had the laundry information, but below the instructions was something else. In the wee hours of the morning, as I yearned for my bed and sleep, I received a very special gift that revived my weary soul. There were the words "God Loves You" printed on that tag.

Yes, I know God loves me. However, in this day and time when there is such a roar over the use of "God" in the public schools and public buildings and so many denouncing Christianity, I was inspired that a company that manufactures trendy jeans would include such a sweet hidden nugget.

For someone who had recently felt sleep-deprived, I was now wide-eyed and raring to go. Are you old enough to remember a gasoline commercial that referenced putting a tiger in your tank? That's how I felt at that moment. I wanted to rush and tell my husband about the message, but he was fast asleep.

My own physical exhaustion had been coupled with a spiritual low, and my tank needed to be re-fueled. My heart is full of holes that can only be filled with God's gifts—His love, forgiveness, joy and peace. He is the only one who can fill me up when I am running on human fumes.

Because of human frailty, those gifts can leak out, get used up or even dry up, resulting in a continual need for God's replenishment. He is always ready to equip me with all the necessary components to live each day for His purpose, but He wants more than a quick pit stop. He wants me to come in for full-service, quality one-on-one time.

The God who loves me was waiting. We hadn't spent much time together the previous week. He longed for an extended visit, and so did I. That little message found in a pair of jeans was just the spark I needed to perk up the conversation between us. I know that label is found in thousands of pairs of jeans, but for me, at that particular time, it was very personal. It was just God and me, alone together. There is nothing like intimate prayer time with the Father to jump-start a weary soul.

God's knows everything about us. We can't flee from His presence. No matter where we go, He's there (Psalm 139:1, 7-8). He misses us so much when we don't stay in touch that He will go to any length to get our attention. And He knows just where to find us. God found me at midnight in my laundry room, ready to refill the holes in my tank.

Perhaps you won't find a message hidden in a pair of jeans today, but you will find it right here. Let it sink in—God Loves You!

June 8

Carry each other's burdens, and in this way you will fulfill the law of Christ.—**Galatians 6:2**

I was standing in the Express checkout lane at the grocery store when a lady with one item came to wait behind me. I offered to let her go before me, but she said, "No." I noticed that she seemed agitated so I asked her again. She shook her head and refused. Because she was not standing still, I said, "You seem to be in a hurry. Don't you want to go before me?"

As she was moving ahead of me, she said, "It's just that my 18-year-old nephew has to go back to M.D. Anderson (Cancer Center) again, and we don't think he is going to make it." I expressed my sympathy and she replied back to me, "You can pray."

So I put my arm around her and prayed. When I finished, I noticed that all the people in front of us were gone, but the cashier was standing there with her head bowed and eyes closed.

As I watched this caring aunt leave the store, I realized I would never know the outcome. But even today, I thank God for giving me this opportunity to speak His words of comfort to her.

May the Holy Spirit make us sensitive to a time that God places in our path a special someone who is burdened and needs words of comfort and relief.

Marylee Barnard
Austin, TX

June 9

"I took you from the ends of the earth, from its farthest corner I called you. I said, 'You are my servant'; I have chosen you and have not rejected you."—**Isaiah 41:9**

One of the first Bible verses I recall memorizing was Isaiah 41:10: "So do not fear, for I am with you; do not be dismayed, for I am your God. I will strengthen you and help you; I will uphold you with my righteous right hand."

I had been asked to give the invocation at a business-related banquet when I was 20something. Having recently read Isaiah 41:10 in my *Upper Room* daily devotional, I decided to use that verse in my prayer. Because I only had religion at that time in my life—not a relationship with Jesus—glorifying Him through the prayer wasn't even on my mind. My goal was to speak eloquent, religious words that made me sound like a committed churchgoer. There were many favorable comments about my prayer, and I was extremely proud of myself.

Despite my selfish ambition, God used it for His glory anyway. After that invocation, Isaiah 41:10 was imbedded in my memory bank. Little did I know, as I grew in spiritual maturity, how many times that verse would come back to help me through a difficult situation. God became so real in my life as His words calmed my soul time after time, making an overwhelming impact. God taught me that His Scriptures were more than just pretty words written on a page or to be spoken in prayer. "For the Word of God is living and active" (Hebrews 4:12). Yes, His Word is full of power and is alive.

Thinking back, Isaiah 41:10 was instrumental in the early, formative years of my faith walk. But what is so much fun about the journey is how God continues to woo me, day after day, with little surprises and glimpses of His love.

Recently Isaiah 41:9 was highlighted in "The Daily Verse." To be honest, I have no recollection of how I discovered the online site, but I delight in receiving a daily Scripture, sometimes one I am acquainted with, but in this case, one that opened my eyes to God's amazing power. At first I didn't realize the significance of it, but later I put 2+2 together. For close to 30 years, I had Isaiah 41:10 memorized, but somehow I failed to notice the verse before it. "I took you from the ends of the earth, from its farthest corner I called you."

The senior pastor of Grace Church in New York City, Dave Whitehead, writes the commentary for "The Daily Verse." Of this Scripture he said, "Isaiah prophesies that even though Israel is rebellious, God is with her. This shows that no matter what past mistakes haunts you, God will not forsake his children."

How did I go all those years and not know what preceded my memory verse? God pursued the Israelites from the farthest ends of the earth, telling them not to fear, because He, God Almighty, was with them. Wow, that is the story of my own life! God pursued me too. Through all of my rebellious years, despite my sinful nature, He did not forsake me. There was forgiveness and redemption. However, only in the past few years have I been able to forgive myself for being such a wayward child.

"*Be not dismayed,*" He told me in 41:10, yet, I was in awe. I still find it amazing how His Word, written thousands of years ago, remains relevant to my life. But how come others seem to understand everything they read in the Bible perfectly? Why does it take me longer to grasp the meaning of His truths?

In 1 Corinthians 2:9, Paul said, "What we have received is the Spirit who is from God, so that we may understand what God has freely given." I probably skimmed over Isaiah 41:9 numerous times, but wasn't ready to receive it yet. But the Holy Spirit knows exactly what I need and when it will change my life.

Through that verse and commentary, the Holy Spirit revealed something profound—I had to learn to trust God's promises in 41:10 as I matured in my faith walk *before* I could receive or understand His power of redemption in 41:9.

There is peace knowing that's God's wisdom is made known by the Spirit that lives within, and He speaks to each of us personally. The Holy Spirit opened my eyes to Isaiah 41:9, in His perfect timing. I wonder what's on His agenda today? For me and for you.

June 10

"*You did not choose me, but I chose you and appointed you to go and bear fruit—fruit that will last. Then the Father will give you whatever you ask in my name.*" —**John 15:16**

Don't ever go grocery shopping on an empty stomach. Surely, you have heard that same warning before. It can be tempting, when your tummy is growling, to toss all sorts of items into the cart, whether you need them or not.

That afternoon when I walked into the produce department and smelled the huge display of peaches, I couldn't resist. It was already after 3 p.m. and I hadn't eaten lunch. The peaches were perfectly ripe, so one of them would be an immediate fix on the drive home. I don't know why I loaded up with four. Oh, the grapes looked really delicious too. They were large and firm to the touch. I couldn't decide between the red or the green, so I grabbed both.

By the time I checked out, I had more than necessary to alleviate my hunger, and had far exceeded the six items on my list. I actually ate the California Roll I picked up from the in-store Sushi bar on my way home. When I was putting the groceries away, I was no longer hungry and all that luscious fruit simply went into the fridge.

There were good intentions to munch on the fruit over the next few days, but life got busy. When I finally did grab a peach, it was shriveled up and mushy. The nice firm grapes had turned soft. That fresh fruit certainly didn't last long.

As only God could do, He put John 15:16 right in front of me in one of my online daily devotions. I chuckled out loud with the words "fruit that will last," thinking about my sad grapes and peaches. Those little pieces of fruit didn't choose to go home with me, to be put in the fridge, only to be forgotten. Surely they had hopes of being appreciated, savored to the very last bite by some thankful person.

Those peaches were ripe and ready when I picked them—unlike myself when God picked me. He saw my unformed body and all the days ordained for me were written in His book before one of them came to be (Psalm 139:16). God knew what He had to work with and He chose me anyway! He appointed me to go and bear fruit that will last. A sinner like me to do His work?

After reading John 15:16, I re-read the entire chapter. With new eyes I saw the incredibly beautiful visual of our dependence on a life spent with Jesus Christ: "No branch can bear fruit by itself; it must remain in the vine. . . . I am the vine; you are the branches. If you remain in me and I in you, you will bear much fruit; apart from me you can do nothing. This is to my Father's glory, that you bear much fruit showing yourselves to be my disciples"(Vs. 4-5, 8).

When plucked from the vine (or tree), the fruit I purchased only remained viable for a few days before it began to wither away. Separated from the Son, I would do the same. As a chosen child of God, I have been given the honor to share in His truths, grow His kingdom and do His will on this side of heaven, with a promise of an eternity spent with the Father. All that can only be accomplished by abiding in Him.

To bear His fruit. Fruit that lasts. For His glory and purpose. And He chose me *anyway*, knowing what He would make of me. I don't think I will ever look at a piece of fruit again without thinking of Jesus' words in John 15:16. Just as I carefully picked out those peaches, Jesus chose me—and He chose you too. Let's go out today, as His disciples, and accomplish what He appointed us to do.

June 11

And he carried me away in the Spirit to a mountain great and high, and showed me the Holy City Jerusalem, coming down out of heaven from God. It shone with the glory of God, and its brilliance was like that of a very precious jewel, like a jasper, clear as crystal.—**Revelation 21:11**

The Texas Gulf Coast beaches aren't known as the most beautiful in the world, but our short vacation to Port Aransas, Texas, was still a fabulous week. For me, there is nothing more peaceful and soothing than the sound of the waves rolling into the surf, over and over. Along with being mesmerized by the tranquility of the sounds, I have found time spent at the beach can be full of God-lessons.

First, the unceasing waves remind me of God's love—unending, powerful, consistent, unconditional. Those waves are going to keep on coming in, no matter what. Looking out into the Gulf of Mexico at the vast expanse of water, it appears to go on and on. Just like God's love—forever.

One morning, I was walking my dog along the nearly deserted beach at sunrise, with the rays streaming down behind the lofty clouds. The water resembled a sea of sparkling jewels, shining with the glory of God. I could just imagine Jesus calling out to me: *If you think this is pretty, just wait 'til you see heaven.*

I thought back to the description of the New Jerusalem in Revelation 21, with the foundations of the city walls decorated with every kind of precious stone (Vs.19). The first foundation was jasper and the second sapphire. At one precise moment, as the rays of the early-morning light reflected on the water, it did indeed look like a sea of brilliant blue sapphires.

In the beginning, our Creator made the heavens and earth, the land and the seas. In the book of Revelation, we read how He concludes with the creation of a new heaven and a new earth. "There will be no more death, or mourning or crying or pain, for the old order of things has passed away" (Vs. 4).

The Creator can even make His Gulf of Mexico look gorgeous, but I know that the place He has prepared for us in heaven is even more spectacular. Why? Because God Himself will be with us and be our God (Vs. 3).

Dancing in the Drought

As the sun rose higher in the summer sky that morning in Port Aransas, the beach became a busier place. However, I was alone with God, lost in the sound of the waves, being reminded of His unending love—and imagining Jesus calling out to me: *Just wait 'til you see heaven!*

June 12

*"Therefore go and make disciples of all nations, baptizing them in the name of the Father and of the Son and of the Holy Spirit." —***Matthew 28:19**

While vacationing in Port Aransas, I spent countless hours on the beach. That's the reason most people go there, right? However, rain dampened the first two days, so I didn't even go out to the water. How ironic is that? I live on Lake Travis, where the lake is over 50 feet below normal and it hadn't rained in months. I started driving to Port Aransas, and two hours from home, it started pouring and didn't stop for two days.

For me, rainy days make for perfect writing conditions. I wrote several devotions while sitting at the window, watching and listening to the heavenly sound. I also discovered some fun souvenir shops in the quaint little town and started hunting for a poem, "The Legend of the Sand Dollar."

There are several poems about the special shell, but I specifically wanted the one I recalled from a plaque at my grandmother's house. I thought surely in that little beach town I would find a plaque of some sort with the poem. I saw others, but it took awhile before I finally found what I was looking for. The author is unknown, so I can't give the proper person credit for these sweet words, but I would like to share "The Legend of the Sand Dollar" with you, just in case you haven't ever heard this lovely story.

There's a pretty little legend
That I would like to tell
Of the birth and death of Jesus
Found in this lowly shell

If you examine closely
You'll see that you find here
Four nail holes and a fifth one
Made by a Roman's spear

On one side the Easter Lily
Its center is the star
That appeared unto the shepherds
And led them from afar

The Christmas poinsettia
Etched on the other side
Reminds us of his birthday
Our happy Christmastide

Now break the center open
And here you will release
The five white doves awaiting
To spread good will and peace

This simple little symbol
Christ left for you and me
To help us spread his gospel
Through all eternity

Take a few moments today and ponder the truly magnificent story God created in this one lowly shell. (If you have never seen a sand dollar, look at one on the Internet.) My next goal was to find an unbroken one on the beach (after the rain stopped), which I thought would be a simple task because I used to find them all the time when I was a little girl. Tomorrow, I will tell you where that search led me.

June 13

Thanks be to God for his indescribable gift.—**2 Corinthians 9:15**

The souvenir shops in Port Aransas had baskets and baskets of shells for sale. Sand dollars the size of a quarter sold for only 30 cents. However, I had this silly notion that to find an unbroken shell on the beach would be like a sign from God. Surely He would place one right in my path as I combed the beach on my sunrise or sunset walks.

After a week on the beach, I hadn't found one whole sand dollar. On our last evening there, my husband and I had an early dinner with my sister, Rhonda, and her husband, Randy, who were also visiting the beach for a few days. Rhonda mentioned a project she was getting ready to start—Randy had made her a wooden cross and she was going to "adorn" it with bits of broken shells she had collected.

As I listened to her, I heard the Holy Spirit's small voice: *Broken shells. Brenda, do you get it?*

Yes, I get it. Broken shells, just as I am broken—I thought to myself as Rhonda continued to explain she planned on gluing the shell fragments to the cross, to represent the sins and the brokenness of her life that Jesus asks all of us to hand over to Him.

After dinner, I couldn't wait for our final sunset stroll on the beach. I eagerly looked for some broken sand dollars—ones like I had passed over on previous walks—passed over because they weren't whole and perfect. When I scooped up that first half of a sand dollar, I was overwhelmed with love for my Father as I thought of how He has done the same for me my whole life. Thankfully He never passed by me—a crumbled mess—but picked me up, brushed off the sand and dirt, then washed me clean.

The Lord wants me to hand over all the shattered parts of my life—the shame, hurt, pain, insecurities, greed, jealousy, guilt—to be nailed on the cross in total surrender. Because of Jesus' completed work on Calvary, all my past, present and future sins have been forgiven. He will take everything I lay at His feet and transform and restore me into His perfect workmanship. While the transformation won't be complete until I meet my Savior face to face, I have the hope in knowing that on that day I will be His perfect, complete child.

"The Legend of the Sand Dollar," cited in yesterdays' devotion, tells a perfectly true story of the only perfect man to walk this earth; however, "legend" is defined as a "fable, myth or fairy tale." I think that wonderful poem should be renamed "The Legacy of the Sand Dollar," since two of the synonyms for that word are "inheritance" and "gift."

All of the bits and pieces of that magnificent shell depicting the story of Jesus are irreplaceable parts of His legacy. Jesus' birth, death and resurrection were all necessary to complete God's plan for all of humanity—the gift of His Son to die for our sins so that we may live with Him forever.

Every portion of my tarnished life and every merciful act of redemption has been and will be vital to God's plan and purpose for my life as well. It all adds up to *my* story. Will mine be a silly *legend* or a lasting *legacy*?

Never again will I look at a fragment of a sand dollar, or anything broken, and be disappointed because it's not whole. I will remember my sister's cross of "imperfect" shells and be thankful for God's indescribable story that He—and He alone—will create from the shattered pieces of our imperfect lives.

June 14

And pray for us, too, that God may open a door for our message, so that we may proclaim the mystery of Christ, for which I am in chains. Pray that I may proclaim it clearly, as I should. —**Colossians 4:3-4**

Unceasing Prayer for Austin is a citywide initiative to cover the Austin area in prayer 24 hours a day, 365 days a year. My church was one of over 30 participating, and there were enough volunteers for each of us to take a 30-minute time slot for the 24-hour period. The vision was to unite local churches with one prayer focus each month for our city.

One month, the theme was the growing population in Austin. The email sent to all participants read, "According to the U.S. Census Bureau, from 2000 to 2010, Austin was the fastest-growing metro area in Texas and the eighth-fastest in the United States. Along with this growth comes responsibility for the faith-based community. We don't have to go to a foreign country or a different city to reach out, extend grace and share the Gospel."

We were given a suggested prayer guide; however, we were also encouraged to allow the Holy Spirit to lead us during our time. One of the suggestions was to pray for opportunities to share the Gospel with our neighbors and others we come in contact with daily and lead them to accept Jesus Christ as their personal Lord and Savior. Honestly, I had never had that privilege, so I prayed for the Holy Spirit to guide me so that, as Paul said, "I may proclaim it clearly," when given the chance.

After my prayer time, I was still thinking about sharing the Good News. Providing Scripture references would be the first step, emphasizing that Christ's death on the cross was the payment for our sins and His resurrection the guarantee of eternal life. The more exciting part of the conversation would come when emphasizing that Christianity is actually a personal relationship with Jesus, and sharing how my personal bond has developed over many years, and grows stronger every day. To share my testimony, to give my Savior the glory for rescuing a mess like me from the pit of hell, would be so much fun!

However, the challenge would come if someone were to question my faith and the Bible. I know because it happened to me when my own son expressed his doubt in the validity of the Bible. I was totally unprepared to defend the Word and the hope I had through my faith in Jesus Christ.

Prior to that month's Unceasing Prayer, I read an article on Crosswalk.com by Josh McDowell and Bob Hostetler titled, "The Top 10 Defenses Youth Can Give for Their Beliefs." The content was valuable and based upon a book the two men co-authored, *Don't Check Your Brains at the Door*, a book of Christian evidences geared to high school students. Deciding I should be able to understand high school level, I ordered it through amazon.com.

A few days after my Monday night prayer time, I was still pondering defending my beliefs when I found a package sitting on top of my mailbox. "Know What You Believe and Why" was written above the title of the book I unwrapped, *Don't Check Your Brains at the Door*. Obviously that's where I left mine because I had totally forgotten ordering it. It was exactly what I needed to not only share the Gospel, but to help provide answers if challenged regarding my beliefs. God was opening more doors for me, in preparation of proclaiming the Gospel.

When He arranges the opportunity for me to declare His message to a non-believer, I can't wait to share the story of God's providence in our pre-determined encounter. That will certainly be some Good News!

June 15

"For this reason a man will leave his father and mother and be united to his wife, and the two shall become one flesh." —**Matthew 19:5**

My boys were born in 1984 and 1986. How times have changed! What's even more mind-boggling is what has transpired since I was born way back in 1954. One such noticeable difference is the presence of dads in the delivery room.

In the 1950s and 1960s, dads were allowed into the "labor" rooms (although few actually went), but once it was time to deliver, they were whisked away to the waiting room. In the 1970s and 1980s, hospitals slowly opened birthing rooms—the combined labor and delivery rooms. The atmosphere was more relaxed, and dads were definitely part of the birthing process.

Now there is another "sign of the times" emerging—extended family members showing up at various stages of the birthing process, with many hospitals allowing up to three "coaches" in the room. The new birthing centers, also indicative of the times, allow even larger numbers during normal deliveries.

Also growing in popularity is the presence of the grandparents and other immediate family members hovering around the newborn *immediately* after birth. Before the baby or mom has a chance to look presentable, the iPhones and cameras start clicking away.

Perhaps I am just modest, but I can't imagine a roomful of family members hanging around as I made those first attempts at breastfeeding my son. That time right after the birth of my children was an experience I will never forget. I was filled with more emotions than I can ever explain, and I am thankful for the privacy we had. Just Mom, Dad and baby!

I was perfectly happy to share my happiness a few hours later, with clean sheets and a clothed newborn resting peacefully in my arms. After a few hours of bonding and gazing at the wonder of God's creation, I was ready to communicate and show off my baby. (Please know that I respect the individual differences relating to this situation.)

Recently I was speaking with a friend who was pregnant with her first baby. She and her husband had just attended their introductory Lamaze class and were told that the two hours after birth were very crucial to the bonding experience between parent and child. She and her husband had talked and prayed and felt they wanted those two hours to themselves.

Knowing the grandparents already expected to be invited into the delivery room soon after birth, since that's what had been done with the other grandchildren, how would she and her husband break that news to them? Did they actually have the right to take that experience away from their own parents? This sweet mother-to-be was worrying about something that was months away from happening, but still very troubling.

Several of my close friends are now grandparents and in asking their opinions, I received mixed reviews about either being in the delivery room beforehand or going in immediately following the birth. However, they were all in agreement that the baby's parents must make the decision that is most comfortable and right for them, establishing the delivery-day "ground rules" before the baby is born.

Whew! That was the advice I gave this pregnant friend, so I am thankful the experienced grandmothers felt the same way. Someone reading this story might be in total disagreement and think I am very old-fashioned, but I stand firm in my belief. Even though practices change with the times, what doesn't change is our responsibility as parents to allow our children to grow up, marry and make their own decisions.

God's Word doesn't change either. In Matthew 19:5 above, Jesus gave His instructions on marriage. In reading numerous commentaries, the verse can be summed up as meaning that the commandment to honor one's mother and father (Matthew 19:19) doesn't cease with the union of a husband and wife. However, biblically, with the union, obligations to one's spouse supersede loyalty to parents.

Sometimes it is difficult for us moms to let go of our married kiddos, but we must help them be obedient to God's Word, not hinder them. As far as what goes on in the delivery room, allow your married child and spouse to make their own decision together—and then be 100% supportive.

June 16

Stand firm then, with the belt of truth buckled around your waist, with the breastplate of righteousness in place, and with your feet fitted with the readiness that comes from the gospel of peace.—**Ephesians 6:14**

"The captain has advised that there is extremely rough weather ahead and has turned on the *fasten seatbelt* sign. All passengers are asked to remain in their seats until further notice. You can look out the window and see for yourself the dark clouds we are approaching."

I didn't need to fasten my seatbelt because I never undo it when flying. I don't actually think it would do much good in the event of a crash, but in turbulent weather, it is probably a good idea to be buckled in. And from the looks of the ominous clouds, a bumpy ride was imminent.

As I gazed out my window, I pondered the flight attendant's warning. Gee, wouldn't it be nice if before climbing out of bed in the morning I could get a forecast for the day, so I would be prepared? *Brenda, be extra patient today because people are really going to aggravate you. Especially the guy at the tire store. Oh, yeah—you shouldn't have procrastinated so long about getting new tires because you will have a flat and miss that afternoon appointment.* (Not that such a thing ever happened to me.)

Silly girl! God *has* provided a forecast. He has forewarned all of us what to expect in this world. He didn't sugarcoat His words either. No, He was upfront and honest. It was as if He spoke over the intercom and made an announcement to us all.

"Be very careful, then, how you live—not as unwise but as wise, making the most of every opportunity, because the days are evil. Therefore do not be foolish, but understand what the Lord's will is" (Ephesians 5:15-17). Did you catch that? *The days are evil!*

"I have told you these things, so that in me you may have peace. In this world you will have trouble. But take heart! I have overcome the world" (John 16:33). Jesus Himself told us we will have troubles in the world. Not maybe—*we will.*

"Consider it pure joy, my brothers, whenever you face trials of many kinds, because you know that the testing of your faith develops perseverance. Perseverance must finish its work so that you may be mature and complete, not lacking anything" (James 1:2-4). When you face trials of *many* kinds? That's laying it all out on the table, isn't it?

"Dear friends, do not be surprised at the painful trial you are suffering, as though something strange were happening to you" (1 Peter 4:12). Yes, we are told to expect trials as being the norm.

"And the God of all grace, who called you to his eternal glory in Christ, after you have suffered a little while, will himself restore you and make you strong, firm and steadfast" (1 Peter 5:10). He didn't tell us how long "a little while" was, did He?

Oh, but even though He warned us to expect the trials, He prepared and equipped us to handle whatever comes our way. He provided positive words of assurance to help through those times when the black, ominous clouds loom overhead.

In my opinion, Ephesians 6:10-18 supplies the most explicit, hopeful instructions on how to protect ourselves against the trials and evil of the world—for the bumps we will face each day:

"Therefore put on the full armor of God, so that when the day of evil comes, you may be able to stand your ground, and after you have done everything, to stand. Stand firm then, with the belt of truth buckled around your waist, with the breastplate of righteousness in place, and with your feet fitted with the readiness that comes from the gospel of peace. In addition to all this, take up the shield of faith, with which you can extinguish all the flaming arrows of the evil one. Take the helmet of salvation and the sword of the Spirit, which is the word of God. And pray in the Spirit on all occasions with all kinds of prayers and requests."

We have heard the warning from the Captain, and we know the reality of the forecast. As long as we keep that belt of truth around our waist—our safety belt—we will be prepared to face the turbulence.

In case you were wondering, the remainder of that plane ride was incredibly smooth. Not even one bump! Honestly.

June 17

"My grace is sufficient for you, for my power is made perfect in weakness." —2 **Corinthians 12:9**

Being a product of divorced parents who remarried, I have been the stepchild, living and being around a stepparent. Now I am the stepparent. I can tell you that neither situation had any resemblance to the popular Brady Bunch television program from years ago. Did such a family actually exist?

I do know of blended families who make it look easy. Those families have overcome the obstacles and aren't much different than any other. However, I will shamefully admit that ours is not one of those.

While dating, my husband-to-be and my two sons had the opportunity to get to know each other since the boys lived with me. Austin's two children lived with their mom; therefore, I didn't see much of them. His kids were in high school and beyond, and mine were middle and high school age.

At first, neither his kids nor mine were thrilled about our dating. It is a very weird situation, seeing your mom or dad with another person. I know because I had been there myself with my own parents. However, my boys soon felt less apprehensive because they got to know Austin and realized he was a good guy. That's not exactly how it went with Austin's daughter and me. She and I encountered some difficulties along the way.

Adding to the tension between the two of us was the discord between the four kids. They had all graduated from high school by the time we married, had never spent much time together and had totally separate lives. When it came time for family gatherings, we all tried to be one happy family, but it didn't always work out that way.

My husband was the glue that held us all together, though. Everyone loves Austin. He is the fun-loving practical joker. He is very slow to anger and has an unbelievable amount of patience. He is a wonderful stepfather, and has done an incredible job of showing fairness and love to my boys. I, on the other hand, have had a very difficult time not showing partiality to my own children and loving his children well.

The disparity reached a point that it was causing a rift in our marriage and with the kids. No one was happy and we were all pointing fingers at who was at fault. Sarah Young said it so well in "Jesus Calling" when she referenced coming face-to-face with impossibilities—situations totally beyond one's ability to handle. On the day I read those words, I had reached that crossroads. It had definitely escalated to what felt like an impossible situation and too much for me to handle.

I know all too well that when I am desperate, there is only one place to go. When I am weak, I am only able to stand because of my Heavenly Father's strength. There was something else so very clear to me—my disobedience to love as God commands was the reason for the problem.

In our sin, it is so easy to feel distant from God. We are embarrassed and ashamed for our behavior. He is so amazingly loving and quick to shower His mercy and grace, though. During my days of despair, I clung to Him, searching and crying out for help, and He delivered.

First, through the words of one of my online devotions, another woman shared her own struggles in step parenting. That's one reason I read daily devotions—to find someone else who is going through the same situation and can provide hope and encouragement. God let me know that He was there with me; He wasn't going to let me go through this alone. I must suffer the consequences for my disobedience, but He would never leave me or forsake me. Even in the midst of my sadness and despair, I felt so loved by my Father because of her story.

Second, through the perfection of His Word, I gained knowledge into the purpose of this trial. I will explain that tomorrow.

June 18

To keep me from becoming conceited because of these surpassingly great revelations, there was given me a thorn in my flesh, a messenger of Satan, to torment me. Three times I pleaded with the Lord to take it away from me. But he said to me, "My grace is sufficient for you, for my power is made perfect in weakness." Therefore I will boast all the more gladly about my weaknesses, so that Christ's power may rest on me. That is why, for Christ's sake, I delight in weaknesses, in insults, in hardships, in persecutions, in difficulties. For when I am weak, then I am strong.
—2 Corinthians 12: 7-10

The daily verse from yesterday's story is also included in the verses above. When I sat down to write that devotion, I wasn't sure what Scripture to use, but 2 Corinthians 12:9 just happened to appear right under my nose in one of the devotions I read that particular morning. "My grace is sufficient for you, for my power is made perfect in weakness."

My family disharmony had reached what felt like an impossible situation, and I needed help. From past experience, I knew that the only One to help in a desperate situation is Jesus. Yes, I must admit that I have been desperate enough times in my life, and rescued enough times, to be in awe of His power. When I read those words, they were exactly what I needed to hear that morning. I picked up my Bible and went straight to 2 Corinthians 12 to read the entire chapter.

Oh, my goodness, was I ever blessed by God's perfect Word. I had written other stories about God revealing Himself to me, and perhaps I was feeling a bit smug. In *most* areas of my life, God and I were doing well. Could God actually have a purpose for this major family issue, this thorn in my side? I had been pleading with God to take it away, but it only festered and got worse. In my sin and my weakness, the great Teacher did indeed have a purpose for allowing it—for me to draw closer and surrender my selfish ways.

In Matthew 22:39, Jesus tells us that the second most important commandment is "to love your neighbor as yourself." Picking and choosing what I want to obey isn't an option, yet I continue to battle these selfish desires that get in the way of dying to self and surrendering my heart completely. And in this situation, it was more than a thorn in *my* side. My act of not loving my stepchildren well had allowed the thorns to grow in the whole family.

I couldn't control the actions and feelings of others, but with God's help, I could change my own. The Holy Spirit urged me to seek guidance from two very special women in my life. One was also a stepmother, so we had a common ground. The other was another godly mom who didn't have stepchildren, but would be open and honest with me.

The stepmom understood my struggles of showing partiality to my own children, and she could identify with the problems facing blended families. Once again, God let me know that I wasn't alone in my trial. He was there, providing another sister in Christ to share her own situation with me. Through the other mom, God shared specifics on what to pray and how to work at reconciliation. By the end of our time together, I felt such love—not only from my two friends, but also from my Heavenly Father.

How wonderful it would be if I could tell you that all is well in our blended family now, but I can't say that. Not yet. Just as it took years to get to the boiling point, it will take time for all to simmer down. However, I do know that there is a purpose for this conflict, for this thorn. God wants all of my surrender—*most* of it is just not enough. Only through the power of He who is strong and working in me will I overcome this messenger from Satan who is determined to destroy my family. I completely trust in the perfect power of the Holy One to equip me, and also walk with me, on the path to restoration.

Will you please pray for reconciliation in my family and for God's will to be done in our lives? Thank you, my sweet friends.

June 19

I rejoiced with those who said to me, "Let us go to the house of the LORD." —**Psalm 122:1**

My husband and I spent Father's Day weekend a few years ago with some delightful friends at South Padre Island. On Sunday morning, all four of us visited the local First United Methodist Church. My husband and I are members of a contemporary Bible Church in Austin, and I honestly can't remember the last time I attended a traditional church service. Being raised in the Methodist Church, I was looking forward to the visit.

We walked in a few minutes late and the morning announcements were in progress. I looked around and counted heads. There were fewer than 100 in the sanctuary, and that included the choir. Also, most of the folks were older, and I would guess there wasn't one person under the age of 50. Much different from what I am used to at our church in Austin, where each of the services is packed. Plus families with young children make up the majority of the congregation.

However, when I looked at the church bulletin, I saw that the order of worship looked much the same as it did the last time I attended a traditional Methodist church. And the very first song we were to sing was "How Great Thou Art." My mind was flooded with memories of times spent in church as a little girl.

Soon after sitting down my friend sneezed, rather loudly I might add. She instantly received a roomful of "bless yous." I don't know that I have ever heard an entire congregation extend a verbal blessing like that. This church might be small and it might be old-fashioned, but the people were extremely friendly and thoughtful, even to a stranger.

How easy it is for me to get caught up in my little routine of attending my own church, totally oblivious to the world around me. Church goes on outside my large sanctuary; it goes on at the beach and even while on vacation. I must admit, that I haven't always *rejoiced* when going to church, especially when I was that little girl growing up. I went to church because my mother gave me no other choice. But here I was, away from home, at the beach, in the house of my Lord, and full of joy. God has certainly changed my heart over these years!

The sermon this particular morning was on the Ten Commandments and more specifically the first one. "You shall have no other gods before me" (Exodus 20:3). We have only one true God, our Lord and Savior. However, He has many houses of worship. It is such a blessing that we are free to worship Him anywhere in our United States. We can receive His message and sing Him praises on any given Sunday, no matter where we are in America.

What a special Father's Day—worshipping the one and only perfect Father in this little Methodist Church at the beach.

June 20

"Let him who is without sin among you be the first to throw a stone at her." —**John 8:7(ESV)**

As I approached one of the busier intersections in Austin during the morning rush hour, I began braking for the red light. The motorcycle that had been dangerously weaving in and out of traffic stopped at the same time next to me. The driver looked all around—then just sped right on through the light. "Are you crazy?" I yelled.

Of course, he couldn't hear my outburst, but I sure felt better for screaming at the guy. Really, no one does something like that. Not only did he put himself in danger, but what about the other vehicles? And there wasn't a policeman in sight to dish out the punishment he deserved for his action.

No sooner had the words spewed out of my mouth than I felt convicted. Who was I to judge that motorcycle driver? I have never blatantly cruised through a red light, but I have broken a few other traffic laws. Speeding? Even though I try to obey, I can't honestly say I adhere to the posted speed 100% of the time.

Besides being opinionated about his lack of good judgment, I knew absolutely nothing about his personal situation that morning. I just assumed he was in a hurry or just a daredevil or speed demon. But perhaps there was a real emergency, and after assessing the situation, he deemed it safe to run the red light.

After those comments to myself, a very decisive thought came to mind. Perhaps I never purposely ran an actual red light, but what about the stop signs that God has placed in front of me? How many times did I know in my heart and mind that what I was doing was flat-out wrong or sinful, against the will of God, but did it anyway? What about all *those* red lights that I just cruised on through? Oh, goodness, I couldn't even begin to count all of *those*!

My earlier years, before my relationship with Jesus, were filled with running one red light after another. Unlike the guy on the motorcycle, however, I seemed to always get caught in my reckless acts and endured the consequences for my actions. Looking back, God was there all along, keeping His shield of protection around me that prevented something worse from happening though. I have faced those years and know of God's forgiveness.

What about now that I do have a relationship with Jesus—and I still run His stop signs? The times I just kept on going when I knew I should have stopped the gossip or being judgmental. How about when the Holy Spirit told me to hold my tongue, but I said something tacky anyway? I wonder how many hours I've wasted worrying about money or my kiddos, placing those gods before my God? I knew better, but did it anyway.

I could write a whole book about all the red lights I have just whizzed right through, instead of listening to my Father's words to stop. But I could also fill the pages with examples of the green lights He gave me that I ignored just as well—times He encouraged me to go forward, but I resisted.

There was the opportunity to offer my garage apartment to the young lady from church needing a place to stay for a few months. Oh, I couldn't do that—and give up my privacy for that length of time? God put the offer in front of me several times and I kept on saying no. Months later after I got to know her, and after she had moved in with a "hospitable" church member, I realized what a blessing I missed out on. All because I refused to observe His green light to open my home to a person in need.

God never loses sight of me, and could dish out any punishment He wants when I am disobedient. But what does He do (in addition to the necessary punishment)? He gives me something I totally don't deserve. He blesses me with forgiveness and His love, mercy and grace.

If you have time today, please read the whole story of the adulterous woman in John 8:1-11. I am not insinuating you are an adulteress, but please note this woman has no name—she could be any one of us and her sin isn't the point of Jesus' story.

"And Jesus said, 'Neither do I condemn you; go, and from now on sin no more' " (Vs. 11 ESV).

June 21

Though outwardly we are wasting away, yet inwardly we are being renewed day by day. For our light and momentary troubles are achieving for us an eternal glory that far outweighs them all.—**2 Corinthians 4:16-17**

My husband and I were driving back home to Austin from Houston. Reaching into the back seat to grab my *Jesus Calling* devotional, I twisted my back. Nothing severe, just enough to warrant a verbal "ouch." Turning back to face the front, I leaned too far on my left leg and a sharp pain shot through my body.

After a nasty fall while water skiing, my left leg had yet to mend. That's why I felt the sharp pain when I put too much weight on it. For the past few years, I had been noticing more aches and pains in this aging body. More recently, arthritis had settled into my right elbow, becoming a real nuisance, especially when exercising. I could go on, but I am sure you get the picture.

Aging is an inevitable process if we are living on this earth. I voiced my displeasure to my husband about my body parts that weren't functioning like they used to and became quite disgruntled about this getting-older business. Thankfully, I heard Jesus calling me to stop the complaining. Picking up *Jesus Calling*, I turned to the reading for that day. I honestly couldn't believe the words on the page. How did Jesus know?

The human body is wonderfully crafted, but gravity and the inevitable effects of aging weigh it down. As I continued to read, my husband wanted to know what was so funny. Yes, my laughter was almost uncontrollable. Jesus was speaking directly to me through the pages of Sarah Young's devotional. How awesome that I had been speaking about my aging body, and this devotion dealt with the same issue.

The laughter suddenly turned to tears as I was overwhelmed by the love of Jesus Christ. How many times does He reach out to me through the written word of others? Why am I still in awe of the way He loves on me? For as long as I can remember, He has spoken to me through devotions, and I should be used to it by now. Yes, the LORD's love never ceases and His mercies are new every morning (Lamentations 3:22-23). On this particular morning, He was being exceptionally merciful.

God willing, we will grow older, and at some point the inevitable effects of aging will set in. I can't control the fact that I will not be as strong and physically resilient on the outside, but with God's help, my spiritual health can continue to flourish, at any age. My bones will become brittle (I have already been diagnosed with osteopenia) and my skin thin. I can no longer lift as much at the gym as I used to. But as Nehemiah wrote in verse 8:10, "The joy of the LORD is your strength."

David told us in Psalm 16:11 that being in God's presence—having a relationship with Jesus—is where we find that joy. The pleasure of that joy is for now—and forevermore. "You make known to me the path of life; in your presence there is fullness of joy; at your right hand are pleasures forevermore" (Psalm 16:11).

Aches and pains or "light and momentary troubles" can weigh us down. However, we will receive daily spiritual renewal from our Father, as long as we remain in His presence, "achieving for us an eternal glory that far outweighs them all." Where else would we want to be?

June 22

The LORD will guide you always; he will satisfy your needs in a sun-scorched land and will strengthen your frame. —**Isaiah 58:11**

June 21 is the Summer Solstice, the day that marks the beginning of summer and is the longest day of the year. For the city of Austin, the spring of 2011 was the hottest on record, so this day could only mean more of the same.

During the month of June 2011 (the days preceding June 21), Camp Mabry, a military installation in Austin that houses the headquarters of the Texas Military Forces, recorded 15 days with a temperature of at least 100 degrees. June 17 and 18 shot all the way up to 106 degrees! The time from January to May 2011 was also the 10th-driest since 1856 at Camp Mabry. Many parts of the country had to contend with floods and there had been a record number of deadly tornadoes during that spring. Austin, and all of central Texas, had high temps and a drought. The weather had certainly been a major issue all over.

So why am I writing this story for today instead of June 21? In the wee hours of the morning on June 22, something very unusual happened, and I thought it was an event worthy of recognition. About 12:30 a.m., we experienced thunder and lightning, which didn't happen often. At 1:15, I heard raindrops. At that point I had almost forgotten what that sounded like!

I quickly turned on the television to the local channel and saw the weather radar. There were some serious thunderstorms moving slowly to the southeast of the state, and my sister's ranch near Weimar was in the line of storms. I was so excited! I wanted to call her, wake her up, and tell her to get ready for a heavenly event.

Almost two inches fell at my lake house, and my sister had over four. Once again, God came through with His special gift from above. Certainly not enough to change the lake level, but enough to brighten spirits. The rain is such a sweet reminder of our dependence on our Sovereign Lord.

He is the only one who can do anything about the heat and drought in this sun-scorched land. And wouldn't you know it, Isaiah 58:11 above was the Scripture reading from one of my devotions on that morning of June 22. I thought it was only fitting to use it here.

The high for that day was predicted to be only 91 degrees. The weatherman jokingly referred to it as a "cold front." So, here we were, the first few days of summer, and God had blessed us with a reprieve from the heat. The forecast was for triple digits by the end of the week, but what a difference the cooler air and the rain had made. Thanks be to God!

June 23

For the wages of sin is death, but the gift of God is eternal life in Christ Jesus our Lord. —**Romans 6:23**

Every written story has a beginning, middle and end. Right? At least that's what I remember from English class. Perhaps I should have taken some writing classes before I decided to go forward with this book, but I obviously didn't.

One of my biggest problems in writing my stories has been the ending. Sometimes I have a very hard time tying it up. A story might sit in my computer for days because I just can't come up with the words to finish. I get a kick out of God's sense of humor. The other day in church, He revealed something to me.

We were singing "From The Inside Out," as recorded by Hillsong United, and a few of the lyrics just jumped out at me. The song reminded me that God's love is "never-ending."

The Holy Spirit then prompted me to remember something that Billy Graham once said. "Life doesn't end at the cemetery" for those who believe in Christ Jesus. Our earthly bodies will perish, but our soul lives for eternity with our Heavenly Father.

I felt God cutting me some slack and trying to help me find some humor in this writing process. There is no ending to His love for me. My death won't actually be the end—it will be the beginning of eternal life in heaven. Having an ending isn't always part of the greater plan.

Today, I am going to focus on God's gift of eternal life and His never-ending love. There is no end to that story!

You might have noticed that the daily verse for today is Romans 6:23 and the date is 6/23. It just might be one of those Scriptures you want to store in your heart.

June 24

"If you love me, you will obey what I command." —**John 14:15**

I receive a Bible verse from K-LOVE's Encouraging Word via email every day. Most of the time, it is one I have heard before, but just don't think of often. I enjoy being reminded of the Scripture, but I also like to read a verse I am not familiar with so I can learn something new about God's Word.

Before getting out of bed in the morning, I have a quick conversation with God and always pray Psalm 118:24: "This is the day the LORD has made. Let us rejoice and be glad in it." I even wear a bracelet with the Scripture engraved on it. I don't just say the words as a ritual. I sincerely want to embrace each day as a gift and to find joy in whatever God has planned. I want to begin each day in a spirit of thanksgiving and praise, not with a heavy heart. Sounds like a great start, doesn't it?

One morning the K-LOVE verse was Psalm 118:24 and I was actually disappointed. I was hoping for a "new" Scripture—one I wasn't familiar with, one that would teach me something I didn't already know. I was hoping for one of those WOW mornings when all the online words of inspiration and devotions I received would just rock my day and be exactly what I needed to hear. God's message would be so loud and clear there would be no mistaking that He was talking directly to me.

Really? Psalm 118:24 again? I just prayed it back to God before I got out of bed. *I don't need to pray it again, do I?* Now, is that a crummy attitude or what? Here, I had told God before I ever got out of bed that I was going to rejoice in His day and make the most of it. Now I was complaining about the verse He sent. Did I ever need an attitude adjustment!

As you can imagine, my morning was anything but joy-filled. I was even grumpy with my precious dog, and all she wanted was to go on her morning walk. I got in the car, hopeful that going to Pilates might help boost my spirits.

God had something else in mind. He was going to speak to me through a song. I had heard it before, but never listened closely to the words. Isn't it interesting how that happens? When God has a message, the Holy Spirit just encourages me to tune in. Suddenly a song is being directed straight to my heart and the words are louder and clearer than ever before.

Slow down before today becomes our yesterday. It happens in a blink. The song, simply titled "Blink" and recorded by Revive tells the story of how we need to make each moment count, before it's too late, and the one thing that matters at the end of life is how we have loved.

Isn't that what Psalm 118:24 tells us to do? Enjoy *this* day God has made, before it becomes our yesterday. If we are to embrace each day, rejoicing and giving honor and glory to God, what is the one command we have been given that is the most important to achieve our purpose? "Jesus replied: 'Love the Lord your God with all your heart and with all your soul and with all your mind. This is the first and greatest commandment. And the second is like it: Love your neighbor as yourself ' " (Matthew 22:37-38).

Sounds like it's all about how we love, doesn't it? It's not just about rejoicing in the day, it's also about being obedient to God's greatest command to love. To love Him and our neighbors.

How can I not love Him with all my heart and all my soul and all my mind after He plans such a perfect daily lesson for me? Oh, how easily I forget the most important commandment of all, and yet I want K-LOVE to send me "new" verses, not the same ones I already know. Ones I know, but don't obey.

I think God wants me to *do* more with what I know. Head knowledge isn't what's important. What's in my heart and what am I doing with it? How am I loving God and others?

It actually ended up being one of those WOW mornings after all. His message was loud and clear.

June 25

Then he took the Book of the Covenant and read it in the hearing of the people. And they said, "All that the Lord has spoken we will do, and we will be obedient." —**Exodus 24:7 (ESV)**

Please notice where in Exodus the Scripture above is found. Chapter **24**, verse **7**. I have stated several times in this book how numbers kind of catch my eye and this one sure did. Why? Wouldn't it be incredible if we all did what the Lord said and obeyed His commands **24/7**? I can easily put this one in my memory bank, and even remember where in the Bible to find it. But will I actually do it? The Israelites didn't so such a good job. Will I do better?

We are of the flesh and are going to mess up. No human can be perfect **24/7**. However, our lives will be transformed the more that God consumes our thoughts and our behavior. As one who was once stuck at the bottom of the pit, I am living proof of that statement. I know my Lord and Savior, the only One who could claim perfection **24/7**, is overjoyed with the growing intimacy of our relationship.

He's with me every second of every day, even when I am caught up in the world. My disobedience cannot separate me from Him. My constant Companion has reassured me of that truth in Matthew 28:30: "I will be with you always."

Always! In today's terminology and on this side of heaven, that equates to **24/7**.

June 26

"Fear not, for I have redeemed you; I have called you by name and you are mine. When you walk through the fire you shall not be burned and the flame shall not consume you." —**Isaiah 43:1-2**

When in Houston, I listen to Christian radio station KSBJ. One trip, the on-air DJs were talking about the station's 30th anniversary coming up in July. Wow! Thirty years ago I didn't have a clue that Christian radio even existed.

It happened to be late in the afternoon when the music being played was the "golden oldies" of the 1980s. The DJ spoke about the recording artist for the upcoming song, Dan Peet of America. *America?* It was one of the prominent bands back in my 1970s college days with such songs as "A Horse with No Name," "Lonely People," "Ventura Highway" and "Sister Golden Hair."

What I didn't know was that in 1977, Peet renounced drugs and alcohol, became a Christian and left the band a few years later. He rewrote one of his songs made famous by America and re-recorded it, along with many others, on a Christian label.

Peet had originally written "Lonely People" with his wife after their marriage in the early 1970s. It was a song to give hope to other lonely people searching for true love. When I heard the Christian re-recording that afternoon, I was intrigued.

The first few lines were the same, *This is for all the lonely people, thinking that life has passed you by. Don't give up until you drink from the silver cup,* but then came the new lyrics: *and give your heart to Jesus Christ.* (The original words were *and ride the highway in the sky.*) The song even referred to Jesus coming back someday. It was so sweet!

After listening to the new version of "Lonely People," I knew I had to Google more information about Peet. While searching, I discovered an interview between Peet and "The 700 Club," a Christian Broadcasting Network show. He said, "Sex, drugs and rock 'n' roll: It was the whole cornucopia of fleshy material. I tried everything. I tasted every possible thing. I had a spiritual compass, but I abandoned it completely."

Peet published a book about his life, *An American Band*, and wrote, "I'm baring my soul in this writing to help someone/anyone out there who is going through life and stumbling over the same rough spots as I've done. If I sound foolish, so be it. I truly pray that what I write will bless all who read it."

He said that as his life began to "spiral upwards spiritually," economically he was pushing rock bottom. In his cry for help, he had challenged the Lord to test him, which He did. Peet wrote, "Faith is essential, yet faith that isn't tested doesn't count for much. As a boy of 12, I had been baptized with water; very soon I was to be baptized by fire . . ."

I also made that trip back from a spiritually empty existence. When reading how others were able to climb out of the pit of darkness and despair, it reinforces that no one is beyond the saving grace and redemption of Jesus' blood. God just has a way of using the least likely for His glory, and I am encouraged when I hear others' journeys of redemption and new-found joy.

If you are thinking that there is no way God can forgive your past, please know He already has. "I, even I, am he who blots out your transgressions for my own sake, and I will not remember your sins" (Isaiah 43:25).

We must also know that just because we are worth saving, doesn't mean we will be spared from the fire. Hold tight to the promises made in Isaiah 43:1-2 above. We will go through the fire, but not alone. Perhaps you can spend time reading the whole chapter for some real God-breathed inspiration before you venture out today.

Upon going to Peet's website, I read the simple words at the top of the page: "Dan Peet went to heaven on July 24, 2011."

Living by his own words, *Don't give up until you drink from the silver cup and give your heart to Jesus Christ*, Peet received God's most precious gift—a life spent with Him in eternity.

June 27

"Call to me, and I will answer you, and tell you great and unsearchable things you do not know." — **Jeremiah 33:3**

Of all mornings to not get cleaned up or even dressed, why did I choose this morning?

"Lord, use me to grow Your kingdom and share Your love. Take me outside my comfort zone," I prayed.

So after a prayer like that, why wouldn't I get ready for the day? I should have been prepared, waiting expectantly, for God's call to work.

I had just put my newborn daughter down for a nap and was about to take a nap myself when I saw two police cars and a hysterical woman in front of my house. I was almost certain the woman was my neighbor, but sadly I had never even met her, so I couldn't be sure.

Now if this was the neighbor I thought it was, her family had been a nuisance since they moved into our cul-de-sac. I instantaneously called my husband to gossip. Before he could answer, I felt a tugging on my heart to go.

Go? I protested. *I don't even know her and I'm sure there's a law against interfering when police are present.* I let God know what I thought of His crazy idea. Besides, wasn't the rest of a new mom more important that talking to some stranger?

Go! God's voice was clear as spoken words. God was unmistakably telling me to help her.

I obediently walked out of my house (yes, still in my pajamas) and straight to my neighbor, praying as I went, "Lord, give me Your words."

God used me that day to care for and love on my neighbor. My home became her place of shelter. My cell phone became her lifeline to family and friends. I put gas in her empty tank so she could have the means to leave her situation. I prayed with her and told her about God's love, all the while still wearing my pajamas.

Next time I ask God to use me, I'm going to get dressed and get ready to do God's work.

Janelle
Austin, TX

June 28

"I am the Lord *your God, who teaches you what is best for you, who directs you in the way you should go."*
—**Isaiah 48:17**

When my husband and I reached the security line at the airport, the sign read: *Maximum Wait 15 Minutes From This Point*. Knowing how testy I had become with flying, and the whole airport experience in general, he knew to keep the conversation light and airy.

Upon reading the sign, Austin stated he was going to conduct a test and time how long it would actually take to get through the line. The couple in front of us heard his comment, thought it was amusing and chimed in on the conversation. It was now a game and a test to determine if the airport personnel were correct with their 15-minute wait time.

There was nothing amusing about the situation to me, however. My husband realized that the experiment wasn't helping to keep my mind off the fact that we were running a bit late for our flight, and changing the topic of discussion might be best. He glanced up at the ceiling and started talking about the huge piece of artwork hanging above us.

The structure probably cost a considerable amount of money, and presumably someone thought it was worthy of being displayed prominently above the security line. Obviously we didn't have the same eye for beauty, because we both agreed it was more of an eyesore.

It was very modernistic, made of metal, draped in colorful fabric. It resembled a lengthy box kite, with three bow-like attachments for the tail. In the middle, or the string of the kite, was more fabric draped over a pointed metal frame that looked like a very long arrow.

As we were critiquing the structure, my husband made a very interesting observation. The three bow-like formations on the tail had taken on a different appearance. In his eyes, he saw three crosses and a beautiful, colorful arrow pointing upwards to heaven.

Because of my typical, anxious behavior prior to flying, the reminder of what happened on the cross quieted my soul. How sweet that my husband saw Jesus in that strange-looking piece of art hanging above the heads of travelers bound for destinations all over the world. There were people of all races, all walks of life, and, most likely, all religions. I pondered how the thought of a cross would settle with the crowd. Would all find the same peace that I had just experienced?

I am actually much more relaxed about flying than I used to be, and I am thankful for the calmness I have found while soaring 35,000 feet in the air. The main source of anxiety I currently experience is rooted in my fear of being late for departure, along with all the heightened security measures and long lines. On this particular morning, I was nervous that the wait would be longer than 15 minutes and we might miss our flight.

If that were God's plan for my day, who was I to think that worrying would make any difference? In the whole scheme of things, it certainly wouldn't be the worst change of plans I could experience. Don't I trust God enough to know that nothing happens unless it passes through His hands first? All I need to do is stay focused on what happened on the cross and the promises found in following His Word.

Just as we were testing the validity of the airport sign, it occurred to me that I was also testing my Lord on His ability to direct my life and help me handle whatever comes my way.

Sure enough, it took exactly 15 minutes to get through that line. I guess whoever posted the sign knew their business. We got to the gate with plenty of time to spare. I even had time to read the online devotions on my phone before takeoff.

When I read Max Lucado's devotion titled "Peace for Anxious Days," I felt God's strong arms of comfort embrace me. What I found especially reassuring were the words from The Message: "Give your entire attention to what God is doing right now, and don't get worked up about what may or may not happen tomorrow. God will help you deal with whatever hard things come up when the time comes" (Matthew 6:33-34).

June 29

For from him and through him and to him are all things. To him be glory forever. Amen.—**Romans 11:36**

It was Sunday morning, and I was preoccupied, trying to decide what to wear. I hadn't heard a knock at the door, but there he was. Oh, is he ever the bold and clever one—sneaking in like that while I am getting ready for church. No, he wasn't invited but just assumed it was the perfect time to plant some seeds of doubt into my mind. That way, I would go to God's house troubled, instead of with a peaceful, receptive heart.

The Evil One had made his way into my unarmed mind. Out of the clear blue I had a random thought about this book. *I just can't do it.* I asked myself, *What can't you do?* That's when all the negatives started pouring in, all the what-ifs and all of the doubt. Yep, he just hit me broadside.

Previously, I had reservations that my goal of 366 stories was actually attainable. But once I reached 266, with only 100 left to go, I could see the finish line. I felt more enthusiasm than ever, so where did this cause for doubt suddenly come from? Did Satan see me as an enemy that needed to be stopped?

OK, Brenda, so when you get your 366 stories, then what are you going to do? You don't have the technical skills to compile them into the necessary format to submit to your publisher. You are in way over your head at that point. You are so unorganized and inefficient, plus you lack the knowledge; you will never be able to do it.

I went to church with those thoughts swirling around. Why did he have to show up so early on Sunday morning? In hindsight, it is probably the best time to attack so that before we are armed with God's truths, the Father of Lies can ambush us with *his* deceptions.

Our former youth pastor, lovingly nicknamed T.A., had come back to preach for the entire month. His sermons series was "Insomnia"—the things we lose sleep over because of worry and doubt. On this Sunday the sermon was titled, "Do I Have What It Takes?" So that's why Satan tried to destroy me before getting to church. He certainly didn't want me to gain strength from that message.

The sermon was based on 1 Samuel 17, the well-known story of David and Goliath. David was the very unlikely one to face the giant, Goliath. Saul even told David, "You are not able to go out against this Philistine" (Vs. 33). But David, a shepherd who had experience protecting his sheep from a lion and bear replied, "The LORD who delivered me from the paw of the lion and the paw of the bear will deliver me from the hand of the Philistine" (Vs. 37).

We know how the story ends. David never doubted that he had what it took to win, saying to Goliath in verse 47, "The LORD saves not with sword and spear. For the battle is the LORD's, and he will give you into our hand." T.A. posed the question, "Do I have enough with what I have?" He then answered, "No, but the One who has me does." Put another way, T.A. said that we can be self-sufficient, placing our trust in what we think can be accomplished on our own or we can trust in the One who has us. Then he asked, "What Goliath are you battling today?"

Did Satan think I would be so overwhelmed with his lies that I wouldn't even hear God's truths spoken through T.A.? First of all, Satan gave himself way too much credit. Secondly, he totally underestimated the power of God's message spoken from the pulpit.

Of course, I don't have what it takes to get this book into print, relying on myself. I have never done it before and lack the knowledge and experience. However, I can completely trust that if it is God's will, He will provide me with the necessary resources, whatever it takes, to see it through to completion.

I went into church with my Goliath being this book. However, the battle still belongs to the Lord, and He prevails every time. *"For from him and through him and to him are all things"* (Romans 11:36).

June 30

Woe to those who go down to Egypt for help, who rely on horses who trust in the multitude of their chariots and in the great strength of their horsemen, but do not look to the Holy One of Israel or seek help from the Lᴏʀᴅ. —**Isaiah 31:1**

This verse became my "motto" during a season in my life, and I am deeply grateful for how the Lord drew me close to Him so I could rely on *nothing* but Him.

Our first two children were born 18 months apart during my husband's residency and fellowship. I struggled with postpartum depression after my second child was born. I truly just "got through" each day while they were toddlers. Once I was healthy and my oldest began kindergarten, I longed to have another baby. I wanted an opportunity to savor each moment with a little one. I felt like I had missed that sweet experience.

Over a five-year period of time, we tried to have a third child. I did not get pregnant very easily nor did I stay pregnant with ease. Three miscarriages later and an unexpected period of unemployment left me with a longing for a baby and no maternity insurance. (We finally dropped it from our policy because it didn't seem to be wise to pay for it month after month.) The Lord used all these circumstances to bring me to a place of surrender with Him. I no longer held onto my dream tightly. I was finally able to walk in a place of freedom that no matter if this tiny baby was not meant to be, Jesus was enough. I celebrated my 38th birthday in the summer and I distinctly remember thinking, *I am getting too old for this to happen. I will choose to be content.*

Imagine my delight to discover one October afternoon that I was pregnant again—and then my immediate fear of no insurance. With my other unsuccessful pregnancies, I got blood tests every few days, went to the doctor constantly and took doses of progesterone to try to sustain the pregnancy. Our agent told us we could add the maternity back to our policy but I could not go to the doctor until he was able to make these adjustments.

For seven weeks, I clung to the words of Isaiah. I cried out to the Lord to please be mighty on behalf of this unborn child. I knew that He *alone* would have to sustain this little life. I could not trust in the "ways of man."

Never will I forget lying on that table in early December with such a sense of the Lord's presence as my doctor confirmed that there indeed was a heartbeat and I was already days into my second trimester! What a humbling and sweet time this was—complete and total dependence upon a God who chose to show Himself mighty for His beloved. Looking to Him each day deepened my faith in His provision for me. I merely needed to set my eyes and heart on Him.

Amy K
Austin, TX

July 1

You have made known to me the path of life.—**Psalm 16:11**

Following a recipe has always been difficult for me. I have the mindset that if a little bit of my favorite ingredient is good for whatever I am cooking, a tad more will be even better.

My first experiment with recipes began when I was in college. My dad loved carrot cake, and because I felt I had to work extra hard to capture his love and attention, I baked him many! I personally love cinnamon, so instead of the two teaspoons on the recipe card, I added three or four or even more. Adding more cinnamon meant more sugar, and extra grated carrots made it moister.

Folks have said my cake is the best they have ever eaten and ask for the recipe. I never hesitate to give the original one, with an asterisk beside a few of the ingredients because I just don't know for sure how much cinnamon, sugar, carrots and vanilla actually ends up in each cake. I add and taste—when it tastes just right, I know it's enough. "If a little bit is good, a little bit more is better."

Looking back on those years I tried so hard to get my dad's attention, I marvel at the way God filled that hole in my heart with His love and affection. No amount of carrot cakes was going to make my dad shower me with the love I craved. But my Heavenly Father was there, just waiting for me to finally accept His love and acknowledge He was the missing ingredient in my life.

Just like trying to win my dad's affections with carrot cake, how often do I think I can earn God's favor by my works? If doing a few good deeds is good, will doing a few more be even better? The more I strive to do, the more I will be rewarded, right? Of course not, but those thoughts still linger in the back of my mind at times.

How often have I said, "yes" just because I was afraid of saying "no"? What would the person think of me if I declined to teach that Sunday school class or lead Bible study? If I didn't offer to bring food to the meeting or sign up for the new committee, would I be perceived as being a hypocrite—wanting to be considered a Christian, but not willing to do the work?

Thankfully, as God has led me to this new season of life, I have learned that "more isn't always better." Doing more tasks will not put me in better standing. Christian women often get overly stressed and burnt out because we try to juggle too much. It's all good stuff, but has thoughtful prayer gone into the decision?

God has provided a recipe for living—one where He is the first and main ingredient. "Taste and see that the LORD is good" (Psalm 34:8). In following His recipe, I don't think there can ever be too much of God added to my day. More *is* better—more time spent in His presence, in prayer and in His word, pursuing Him and being more obedient. More time devoted to loving others and seeking to do His will, not my own. More time working *for* His glory, not trying to win His favor.

What are you going to add more of to your day? More activities—or time with God?

As I spend time with my Father today, I will thank Him for my dad's life—today is his birthday. God restored our lost years and healed my brokenness before his death back in 2003. Girls, I know there are many of you out there who also feel like you missed out on being daddy's little girl. Please know God can fill that hole in your heart, like He did mine. He has all the perfect ingredients to bring restoration to your soul so you will see that you are indeed His special prize-winning recipe.

In honor of my dad, I think I will bake a carrot cake today—just because. Wish I could share a piece with you—it's so yummy!

July 2

The LORD gave, and the LORD has taken away; blessed be the name of the LORD.—**Job 1:21**

Have you ever heard anyone comment about the mess associated with home construction and remodeling? I've heard people say, "I should have had my head examined" or "Whatever could go wrong, did." And now I understand how such thoughts originated.

From start to finish, from the planning stage to moving back in, our remodel project took over two years. We lived in the apartment above our garage for 14 months and the bulk of the heavy construction took place in the heat of the summer. Was it ever a long, hot summer! However, it was one of the more fruitful times of my life.

God used the time to humble me and bring me to my knees—over and over. Specifically, there were two situations that He wanted to put on my heart.

My emotions associated with the drought in the Hill Country of central Texas were some of the predominant inspirations for many stories in this book. However, I found it very interesting that God continued to emphasize the lack of water during the remodel (along with little to no rain). One young friend pointed out He must indeed be out to teach a very profound lesson regarding water shortages, not just in my little world, but also in the far corners of the earth.

God used other losses of everyday conveniences to make me more aware of how easily He can give and He can take away. Why did He do this? What point was He trying to make by the absence of water and the loss of taken-for-granted amenities? It didn't actually take me too long to figure out. *Break my heart for what breaks Yours.*

At the time I wrote this story, there were three Christian songs that contained those words: "Hosanna" recorded by Hillsong United; "My Own Little World" by Matthew West; and "Jesus, Friends of Sinners" by Casting Crowns. Repeatedly, I heard them on the radio and in my head. My Father wanted to make my heart more sensitive to what mattered most to Him.

Many of the lyrics found in Christian music are taken from Scripture. However, there isn't a verse that reads verbatim "break my heart for what breaks yours," though some reference Matthew 25:34-40 as being the Scripture back-up.

Jesus went out of His way to minister to the least, the have-nots, the sick, the lame and the unlovable. He expects all of us to do the same. "The King will reply, 'I tell you the truth, whatever you did for one of the least of these brothers of mine, you did for me' " (Matthew 25:40).

Matthew West said it so well in "My Own Little World": *Father, break my heart for what breaks yours. . .let me see, that my own little world is not about me.*

God allowed a few minor inconveniences in my cushy lifestyle to illustrate what millions of His children have done without their entire lives. He wanted me to have new eyes and a softer, more concerned heart for the severity of living conditions that others endure, around the world and in our own United States of America. In my next two stories, I will let you see how easily my privileged little existence was rattled as the Lord took away some of those comforts that I take for granted.

July 3

Turn my eyes from worthless things. — **Psalm 119:37**

Living in the garage apartment during our remodel was very convenient. Thankfully, the apartment had its own separate electric and water sources, so when power and water had to be cut off to the house for almost the entire duration of construction, the apartment was unscathed. But the yard suffered.

Not only was access to water an issue outside, but also more than half of the irrigation system was damaged because of broken pipes due to digging and the weight of heavy equipment. When water was available, it was necessary to haul hoses all around the property. (Just for clarification, I live in a slightly rural area, and don't use "city" water for outdoor purposes, relying on a pump.)

By mid-June, the temperatures were already into the high 90s, with the heat indexes into the 100s, plus no rain in the forecast. I could handle moving hoses, and the fact some of the grass and plants were going to die. But one evening when I was prepared to do some heavy-duty watering, I was in for a rude awakening. After spending more money than I should have to re-route pipes, fix broken irrigation lines and make sure there was water available for the yard, I discovered there was none.

That's only a minor little glitch, right? It's not a life-or-death situation for humans—it's only plants. But I spent all that money that very day and the watering woes were supposed to be over. Yet, I couldn't get one drop of water out of the outdoor faucets. A privilege taken for granted had been taken away.

As I plopped down in frustration on the driveway, the Holy Spirit sang to me. It had to have been the Holy Spirit singing Matthew West's "My Own Little World," because I sure don't have a voice like that. When I heard the lyrics, *Put Your light in my eyes and let me see that my own little world is not about me*, I realized there was a reason for this minor inconvenience. When He finished singing, I heard the soft whisper: *Get a grip, Brenda. It's only some grass and trees. Think about all the people dying of thirst in this world.*

God knew my obsession with rain and how focused I had been on the drought. If He wasn't going to bring the rain to water the yard, by golly, I would take care of it myself! I had the repairman come out to fix the problem, and

165

all I needed to do was turn on the faucet. Once again, God proved who was in charge, and at the same time showed me what was truly important.

I should be more concerned with supplying *drinking* water to people who have none instead of worrying about my plants. The money I spent that day with the sprinkler guy could have gone towards something much more useful and eternal than the yard at my temporary home. It's not that I didn't care about the needs of others—I had just been consumed by the problems of "my own little world" instead of His.

God has used water and a drought to teach me countless lessons throughout the course of this book. The water that I take for granted to come out of the faucet—to drink, bathe, wash clothes, cook, even water my yard—is a precious commodity, yet nearly one billion people lack clean water.

As I write this story, I don't know exactly where God is leading me on this issue, but He has opened my eyes to what is breaking His heart. I am still ashamed that providing my yard with a drink took priority over even thinking of His millions of children longing for some clean water to quench their thirst.

The big calamity of no water was a quick fix the next morning; it was simply a wire to the water pump that had been severed by a backhoe. If only others in this world could be blessed with such a speedy solution.

Dear Father, please help me get my priorities straight and stay focused on the heartbreaking issues of Your world, not what I think is important to mine. Give me eyes to see where You are leading me in this worldwide crisis of access to clean drinking water. Amen!

July 4

"Then he will say to those on his left, 'Depart from me, you cursed, into the eternal fire prepared for the devil and his angels.'"—**Matthew 25:41**

Yesterday, I wrote about the problem I encountered trying to water my yard during the remodel of our home. It was simply a minor inconvenience that opened my eyes to the plight of the millions in this world who don't have access to clean drinking water.

God wasn't finished with trying to raise my awareness of His less fortunate children. He had another everyday luxury in mind to take away—air conditioning—when the heat index was over 100 degrees. My husband and I attended a neighborhood party that Saturday night and were a bit clammy by the time we walked back home. When we opened the front door to the garage apartment, where we were living during construction, we were greeted with a blanket of warm, sticky air.

It wasn't hot air, at least not yet. The AC could only have been broken for a few hours and the thermostat read 84 degrees. We turned on all the ceiling fans and the two floor fans, opened the windows and enjoyed the unusually pleasant summer night.

One of our friends owns an HVAC business and has been a lifesaver more than once. The following morning, I felt confident that I could call him, leave a message and he would be right over after church. When my husband and I returned from the early service and lunch, he still hadn't called back. We watched helplessly as the temperature in the apartment crept up to 93 degrees.

By mid-afternoon, I called around to some other companies, hoping to find someone who would be willing to come out on a Sunday. The best I could find was first thing Monday morning. To escape the heat we went to a movie and to hang out at a recently opened grocery store.

It was actually cooler outside than inside by nightfall. I was hot, sweaty and grumpy. Because of our golden retriever, going to the local motel or staying with friends wasn't an option. My husband, who doesn't get upset over much of anything, never complained, but quietly listened to my whining and grumbling. The Holy Spirit must have heard enough and gently reminded me of how I was really over-reacting.

During the summer months, I do thank God daily for air conditioning, and, likewise, in the winter I thank Him for heat. Yes, I am thankful for the comforts I have; however, what about those who don't have such luxuries? Every so often, when I see someone working outdoors in extreme hot or cold weather, I say a quick prayer for that person, but then continue to go about business as usual in "My Own Little World." (There's that song again I mentioned yesterday by Matthew West.) But on this particular Sunday night, as I lay in bed feeling extremely uncomfortable because of the heat, I knew there was a purpose in God taking away the comforts of my daily life.

After spending a while with God in prayer, I finally dozed off, but didn't sleep long, waking up drenched in sweat at 3:16 a.m. I silently spoke the words from John 3:16 and thanked God for waking me up at such a perfect time, to remind me that God so loved the world that He gave His only Son so that, through believing in Him, I would have life eternal in heaven. I figured God wanted me to focus on what He had given me—the promise of eternal life—instead of the temporary earthly pleasures that could easily be taken away.

At that moment, an interesting thought flashed through my head. The alternative to eternity in heaven would be eternity spent in hell. My vision of that place was of a fiery furnace. Here I lay, in a house without air conditioning in the summer, and I was complaining about the 93-degree heat? The sweat I was presently wallowing in was only a small inkling of the misery of *the eternal fire prepared for the devil and his angels.*

Was God sending me another message? Did He not only want me to think more about those less fortunate, who never have the luxury of heat or cooling, but also the real aspect of hell and the Evil One?

Hmm. I pondered that question for a while before dozing back to sleep.

July 5

"I know your works: you are neither cold nor hot. Would that you were either cold or hot! So, because you are lukewarm, and neither hot nor cold, I will spit you out of my mouth." —**Revelation 3:15-16 (ESV)**

Yesterday, I wrote of waking up at 3:16 a.m. I don't know too many Bible verses by memory or their exact location in the Bible, but John 3:16 is one that I memorized years ago. Instinctively, when I notice that the time is 3:16 (a.m. or p.m.), I think of that Scripture. A few days after writing yesterday's story, I came across an entry in my journal with the words from Revelation 3:16: "So, because you are lukewarm, and neither hot nor cold, I will spit you out of my mouth."

The first time I heard that verse while studying Beth Moore's Revelation study, I was mesmerized with the force of Jesus' statement. *"I will spit you out of my mouth"* stayed in my mind every since I heard it in her lecture. Even though I had forgotten it was also located in Chapter 3, verse 16, I did recall how real the eternal punishment would be for non-believers.

While I still find Revelation difficult to understand, there are two words that Beth Moore said that, in my mind, summed up the whole book. No matter what we do or don't understand about the Book of Revelation, the most important thing to remember is that "righteousness matters." It matters because all of God's prophecies have come true, except for the end of times. But when it does occur, it will be exactly as John recorded.

Just to get an idea why righteousness matters, let's look at Revelation 14:9-11:

"And another angel, a third, followed them, saying with a loud voice, "If anyone worships the beast and its image and receives a mark on his forehead or on his hand, he also will drink the wine of God's wrath, poured full strength into the cup of his anger, and he will be tormented with fire and sulfur in the presence of the holy angels and in the presence of the Lamb. And the smoke of their torment goes up forever and ever, and they have no rest, day or night, these worshipers of the beast and its image, and whoever receives the mark of its name."

Sounds horrific, but we have the choice—to follow Jesus or not. All the way or not at all. We can't be lukewarm, part-time Christians. That's how Jesus found the church of Laodicea, and He warned them: *"I will spit you out of my mouth."*

When I woke up at 3:16 a.m. on that particular morning, my body was hot and sweaty. The air conditioner was broken and it was over 90 degrees in our house. But I felt God asking if I was on fire for *Him*. Did I love all of His children as much as I loved "My Own Little World" and myself? (I still had that song by Matthew West playing in my head.) Was I totally committed to living for my Savior, in complete submission? Was I all in or just lukewarm?

I didn't spend more than one second pondering those questions. No, I wasn't living a life totally devoted to Jesus. In God's own special, unique way, He was speaking to me, just as He spoke to the church of Laodicea, sending me a warning. If I remain lukewarm, He *will* spit me out.

After seeing Revelation 3:16 in my journal, I felt the Holy Spirit urging me to read the rest of the chapter. Even though Jesus rebuked the church of Laodicea for their indifference, He didn't pass judgment and forget about them—He lovingly gave them grace to repent. *"Those whom I love, I reprove and discipline, so be zealous and repent. Behold, I stand at the door and knock. If anyone hears my voice and opens the door, I will come in to him and eat with him and he with me. The one who conquers, I will grant him to sit with me on my throne, as I also conquered and sat down with my Father on his throne"* (Vs. 19-21).

The Holy Spirit didn't wake me up at 3:16 a.m. just for the fun of it. He led me to Revelation 3:16—and beyond—and lovingly reprimanded me with His perfect words of discipline. I have a choice. I can be spit out of the mouth of Jesus or I can repent. Yes, repent, and fellowship with the King on His throne.

Now comes the act of *daily* surrender to accomplish what my heart and my Father desire—because righteousness *really* does matter.

July 6

And the peace of God, which transcends all understanding, will guard your hearts and minds in Christ Jesus.
—Philippians 4:7

We were finally off on our family cruise vacation. It started off a bit stressful, though. We arrived at Houston Intercontinental Airport in plenty of time that Saturday morning—two full hours before our 7:30 departure for Fort Lauderdale, where we would board the ship. However, it took well over an hour to get our bags checked.

Most of the airlines had started charging a fee for all checked bags. This airline did offer a little perk, however. If the airline tickets were purchased with their credit card, the fee for the first checked bag would be waived. Since that fee was $25 and there were 10 of us traveling, saving $250 was a big deal.

Because of the group, I had to speak with a live person instead of just making reservations online. The customer service person I spoke with was extremely helpful and very patient. She seated us all together and I just knew it would be a fun flight. She did alert me to some of the specific details of the check-in process in order to make sure the bag fee was waived.

Part of that process included that we all be at the airport to check in together. Just getting five different households to the airport at 5:30 a.m. was a major feat in itself, but everyone actually showed up on time. The problem was that the little procedure was more time-consuming than anticipated.

After spending an hour at the bag counter, we still had to make it through the security line, and by 6:30 the airport was busier and the line was long. Plus all 10 of us had expected to get our bags checked and through security in less than an hour with plenty of time to get coffee and a bite to eat. Without coffee or food in our tummies, there were going to be some grumpy folks!

Thankfully, we made it through security and everyone had a chance to grab a cup of coffee and a bagel before boarding the plane. However, we didn't have a minute to spare. The door to the plane was closed immediately after the last of our group boarded.

Whew! Not exactly the way we planned to start our family vacation. I breathed a sigh of relief as the plane pulled away from the gate. I also said some words of thanksgiving to God.

Were those the first words I said to Him all morning? Had I been so wrapped up in the excitement and confusion and stress of the morning that I totally put God on the backburner? Did I just jump out of bed at 3 a.m. when the alarm went off and never stop to have my morning talk with my Father?

He allowed me to communicate with Him, like I had done nothing wrong. He was there, patiently waiting to hear from me. Oh, how peaceful it was to be in His presence. And to think, I was more concerned with free bags then the free gift my Father had to offer.

July 7

But I call to God and the LORD saves me. Evening, morning and noon I cry out in distress and he hears my voice.
—Psalm 55:16-17

I am amazed at the changes that have occurred on cruise ships since my first trip in 1987. Even in the five years since my last trip, the differences are surprising.

If you have had the opportunity for such a vacation, you know that communication with folks back home can be somewhat of a problem. Back in 1987, the only way to call home was by using the very expensive satellite service on the ship, with calls costing $15 a minute. Once the ship docked in a port, there would be lines at the pay phones to call and check on the kids or work.

Here it was July 2011, and technology had made its way to the cruise ships. However, it was not as advanced as most were used to. On this trip, Internet service was available for a fee and cellular phones worked—most of the time. It was during those days when there was no Internet connection or cell phone usage available that I realized my unhealthy dependency on technology.

On two consecutive days, while the ship was in Costa Rica and Panama, I felt like I was cut off from the world. So, what was the big deal? My husband and two sons were on the cruise with me, so I wasn't expecting calls from the three most important people in my life. Being retired, I wouldn't be needed at the office. However, I was in the middle of selling my home and communication with the realtor was crucial, or so I thought.

At first I was extremely stressed out that I couldn't make or receive calls, or access my email. But then I realized there wasn't one thing I could do about the situation. For those two days, life would have to go on without carrying a cell phone around, without depending on constant communication with the world.

As I became used to my new-found freedom of not having my phone in my pocket or purse 24/7, the ship traveled back into waters where there was Internet service and cell phone coverage. Life was back to normal. Besides realizing my reliance on technology, those two days also raised my awareness of another very important truth.

Communicating with God isn't dependent on how many bars I have on my phone or if there is Internet connection. He is so much bigger than technology. I will never need to ask God, "Can You hear me now?"

July 8

May the God of endurance and encouragement grant you to live in such harmony with one another, in accord with Christ Jesus, that together you may with one voice glorify the God and Father of our Lord Jesus Christ.
—Romans 15:5-6 (ESV)

My newly married daughter and her husband entered the realm of outdoor grilling. Strat, coming from a strictly indoor cooking family, participated reluctantly. Caroline was totally committed to the grill. Caroline confided in me that because of their different backgrounds, the grill had become a bit of a source of stress in their marriage.

She called recently to enthusiastically describe a meal they had prepared the previous evening—on the grill.

"How did it go?" I asked.

"I'm learning to let Strat manage the grill," she said. "No more questioning his judgment about timing or doneness."

"I taught you well—how *not* to manage the outdoor cooking!" I said.

I remembered chicken breasts pulled off the grill before my husband/chef was ready to pronounce them done—often followed up with a microwave fix and meals eaten in shifts!

What a blessing to see my daughter, so early in her marriage, have Christ-like encouragement for her spouse in a matter as seemingly insignificant as grilling. Encouragement in everyday tasks, endurance of a few overcooked meals, may be one often-overlooked ingredient in a life of *glorifying the God and Father of our Lord Jesus Christ together with one voice through a life well lived together.*

In the name of the Ultimate Provider of all our sustenance, Amen!

Elizabeth Ponder
Austin, TX

July 9

Finally, brothers, whatever is true, whatever is noble, whatever is right, whatever is pure, whatever is lovely, whatever is admirable—if anything is excellent or praiseworthy—think about such things.—**Philippians 4:8**

There are many times in my life when I realized that my faith took a step forward in trusting and believing God. The most significant growth generally followed a very difficult or dark time in my life. One of these times was when my children went off to college and I felt like they had checked their upbringing at my front door.

I was appalled and quite frankly hurt by some of their decisions and actions. Since I knew about some of the rebellious things that they were doing, I feared the things that I didn't know about. My thoughts and imagination began to believe the worst possible scenarios and I was fearful of the consequences of their decisions—or at least the decisions I *thought* that they were making. I felt I had lost control, and that gave me a sick, hopeless feeling. I was on my knees praying and asking God to lead them back to the straight and narrow way.

God and I talk a lot. Actually, I talk a lot and God does a lot of listening, but I know that He is a good listener. We have been in the trenches before and things work out; maybe not like I thought they should, but actually better in the long run. Funny thing about God—when I ask Him to fix someone else, He usually starts by fixing me. He wanted me to realize that I did not have control over other people. I only had control over myself and my thoughts and actions.

He made me aware that some of my thoughts were not based on truth, that they were based on my imagination and fear of what I didn't know. He brought me to Scripture that told me what I was to think about and if I kept my mind on these things, I would not feel sick or become hopeless. The verse has many examples of what to think about, but at this time in my life I needed to stop at the first one: *whatever is true . . .* think about such things. Those words were freeing for me. I no longer dwelled on what-ifs or what might happen to my children. I no longer let my mind stay on what I didn't know to be true. Instead, I filled my thoughts with what I knew to be true.

God is love and He loves my children more than I do. God is in control and I don't have to be. God is sovereign and whatever happens, it will be all right. I love a God who sees beyond my pain and requests and gives me peace and understanding to live in this world. Finally, sisters *"whatever is true, whatever is noble, whatever is right, whatever is pure, whatever is lovely, whatever is admirable—if anything is excellent or praiseworthy—think about such things."*

Cathy Hale
Katy, TX

July 10

I thank my God for every time I think of you.—**Philippians 1:3**

My daughter, Molly, was married on this date. She looked like Cinderella—she was so beautiful. She chose to have her wedding and celebration at a wedding venue at the Atlantic shore in New Jersey. Everything was perfect, just as she had envisioned and planned. My husband, Scott, wrote the music for the ceremony and sang. I was glowing (as I was told) that my baby was getting married. The entire evening was an affair to remember, as Molly's personal touches made for many intimate moments with laughter, tears and joy.

Well, the day was *almost* perfect. We were missing someone we loved so dearly—my son and Molly's brother, Nicholas, who lost his life in 2006 due to a tragic accident. He was 27 years old, married and just months away from obtaining dual degrees in medicine and law.

We were experiencing great joy and great pain on the day of Molly's wedding. Molly made sure Nicholas was a part of her wedding. He was listed as one of the groomsmen in the program and one of her bridesmaids walked solo with a University of Michigan (his favorite school) Mardi Gras necklace wrapped around her bouquet. There was a picture of him next to a poem about growing up with a big brother who was now watching over Molly. The guests wore green bracelets supplied by Gift of Life Family House in Philadelphia, for which we made a donation in remembrance of Nicholas. Heartstrings were tugged, ever so sweetly and gently.

We made sure that the focus was a celebration of Molly's marriage and not a memorial to Nicholas. He needed to be remembered and included, and he was. But for me, the most difficult and painful part of the wedding was the mother/son dance. I have attended many weddings since Nicholas' death. When it was time for the mother and son to dance, I would very discreetly and quietly leave the room until it was over. The pain of watching was overwhelming and no one could know, except Scott and Molly. I would go outside, breathing deeply, swallowing hard and holding back tears. I would talk to God and ask Him to hug my son. It had become my ritual.

When it was time for my new son-in-law, Brandon, to dance with his mother, I couldn't leave as I had done all those times in the past. I was mother of tthe bride, and my place was front and center to witness this dance. I couldn't hide. Watching and trying not to make eye contact with anyone, I felt my eyes burning and my heart beating hard and fast. Scott held my hand tightly and Molly slipped her arm in mine. I kept praying for God to help me stay strong. *Everyone's watching, no one can know. Please help, God. I can't let these tears spill over.*

Brandon and his mother were a precious sight, dancing to "Somewhere Over the Rainbow." Halfway through their dance, they parted and Brandon turned towards me and opened up his arms. Oh, my. I felt this gentle push to go to him. Brandon knew what I was feeling and how much I was suffering. What an incredible gift he and his mother gave to me. I went to his arms and we danced to the remainder of the song. Scott said that there was not a dry eye watching.

And dancing to "Somewhere Over the Rainbow": Brandon did not know that I had told people I would see Nicholas on the other side of the rainbow. Thank You, God, for Your perfect plan.

A few weeks after the wedding, I was walking with my neighbor, Jeri, sharing with her about Molly's wedding. I told her about the details, especially the dance. She and I both shed tears, at this most loving gesture and moment. We talked about the glory of God and His unending love. We continued walking and sharing until we reached her home.

As I was preparing to say goodbye, I looked up to the western sky. There it was. A rainbow! I told Jeri to turn around and look up. She looked up and saw it too. She was in awe. She said that there had not been any rain. I stood gazing and smiling. I knew why it was there and who sent it. It was a gift of love from God, reaffirming that He has His hand on me and He is with me, always. Thank You, God! I love You!

Vickie Sayles
Katy, TX

July 11

Jesus went up on a mountainside and called to him those he wanted, and they came to him. He appointed twelve—designating them apostles—that they might be with him and that he might send them out to preach and to have authority to drive out demons.—Mark 3:13-15

The sermon was based on the Scripture above where Jesus selects the 12 disciples. We were in the middle of a series titled, "Follow Into a Relationship with God," and this particular Sunday our Pastor of Spiritual Development was speaking. I had never met Brian, so it was delightful to hear him for the first time.

I just love how the pastor dissects a Bible passage, bringing it to life and explaining each line so clearly. Since the series was about having a relationship with God, Brian focused on the relationship between Jesus and the disciples. He emphasized that Jesus called them so they could be with Him, being in constant contact with Him. Brian said that for the disciples, living life with Jesus was "a constant reality."

I don't know why, but when Brian used those words, "a constant reality," my mind immediately thought of "Reality TV."

Reality TV, as we know it, began back in 1992 when MTV first broadcast *The Real World*. It was a show that took seven strangers, placed them in a house to live together for several months and had their interactions aired for all to see.

Today, there is a wide variety of reality television shows ranging from a cast of people exiled to a deserted island to survive and undermine each other to win the grand prize of $1 million, to folks trying to get their big break through singing and dancing competitions or even find a spouse. There are other reality shows that depict ordinary people, and even movie stars, living their daily lives, as it is filmed for millions of viewers.

I know that writing about Reality TV in a daily devotional is rather odd—I don't even watch Reality TV, except for *American Idol*. However, Brian's words made me envision a Reality TV show where Jesus is the star and the co-star is me—or you. The Holy Spirit already lives in us, so we don't go through life alone, but just imagine getting up in the morning and Jesus is in your house! He will come back one day, but what if, for today, He was at your house in the flesh and the TV cameras were rolling?

There you are, sitting with Jesus on the back porch, drinking coffee together. What would be the topic of conversation? Just picture being with Jesus at the grocery store and having Him help pick out the ripest cantaloupe. Do you think He could just look at it and know or would He pick it up, thump it and smell it? Can you imagine chatting with Him as you drive to work or having Him proofread your resume, hearing Him tell you all the good stuff you left out. I wonder how He is in the kitchen? Would He be the cook or the dishwasher or both?

How would I act if I knew my life was being televised and Jesus was right there with me, live and in person? Would my behavior be totally different or the same? Would I be more considerate and kinder to those we encountered during the day? Would I use my time more wisely? Would my house be cleaner and not so cluttered? I know I would certainly pray more.

How popular would this show be? Would folks today really want to watch Jesus living His life in the flesh again with a normal person like you or me? As of this writing, Jesus hasn't made His return, but I don't think this is such a far-fetched idea.

Shouldn't we live our life in the "constant reality" of being in His presence? Even though this TV show might not ever hit the airwaves and there won't be millions of viewers tuned in, He is watching *us* 24/7. Our constant Companion, that constant Audience of One, is all that matters.

July 12

To every thing there is a season, and a time to every purpose under the heaven: A time to be born, and a time to die; a time to plant, and a time to pluck up that which is planted; A time to kill, and a time to heal; a time to break down, and a time to build up; A time to weep, and a time to laugh; a time to mourn, and a time to dance; A time to cast away stones, and a time to gather stones together; a time to embrace, and a time to refrain from embracing; A time to get, and a time to lose; a time to keep, and a time to cast away; A time to rend, and a time to sew; a time to keep silence, and a time to speak; A time to love, and a time to hate; a time of war, and a time of peace. —**Ecclesiastes 3:1-8 (KJV)**

Back in 1965, the song "Turn, Turn, Turn," recorded by an American rock band, The Byrds, quickly became my favorite. I heard the lyrics came from the Bible, which I found very intriguing at the ripe age of 11. The thought of a long-haired band singing a religious song made it that much more of a reason to like it.

In 1965, "Turn, Turn, Turn" reached #1 on the Billboard Hot 100 chart, making it the #1 song with the oldest lyrics. The writer(s) of the song are listed as Pete Seeger and the Book of Ecclesiastes. So, King Solomon, with words inspired by God, wrote the song! Even though the verses were rearranged a bit, Pete Seeger put his music to words that were adapted almost entirely from the King James Version of the Bible, except for the very last line of the song.

Several years ago, I purchased a plaque with Ecclesiastes 3:1 written on it. *"To every thing there is a season, and a time to every purpose under the heaven"* hangs in my laundry room, where I see it several times a day. I knew eventually I would write a devotion about the song and the verse. However, little did I know what I would discover along the way.

Across the board, the consensus was that "Turn, Turn, Turn" was a protest song and plea for world peace (during the Vietnam era), because the last line referenced the fact that it was not too late for peace. While many recognized the words came from Ecclesiastes, very few wanted to acknowledge that God or King Solomon deserved any credit for the #1 hit. It was also surprising that many folks were totally unaware the lyrics came from the Bible at all.

In a 1988 interview for Paul Zollo's book *Songwriters on Songwriting*, Seeger explained: "I don't read the Bible that often. I leaf through it occasionally and I'm amazed by the foolishness at times and the wisdom at other times. I call it the greatest book of folklore ever written. Not that there isn't a lot of wisdom in it."

Folklore! I realized that for Pete Seeger, "Turn, Turn, Turn" was never intended to be a religious song. It was simply his version of a protest song.

When I was young and didn't have a relationship with Jesus, I was very much a part of the world and influenced by the pop culture. While I am not trying to rationalize my love for music, I don't think there's any harm in listening to secular music. (I enjoy country, good ol' rock 'n' roll, classic rock, oldies and contemporary Christian.) However, I do think it's important to have the wisdom to discern what is "of God" and what is "of the world." "Turn, Turn, Turn," even though inspired by King Solomon's words, was never a song written to be "of God." I still like the song. I'm just glad I got my facts straight.

The footnotes in my NIV for verses 1-8 read: "The secret to peace with God is to discover, accept and appreciate God's perfect timing." I think it was God's perfect timing that, through writing this story, I actually realized I wasn't listening to a contemporary Christian recording back in 1965. I was a foolish little girl who just thought it was a religious song. I have learned that simply using all the right words—God's words—doesn't make it right. There's got to be that all-important relationship with Jesus first.

July 13

Humble yourselves, therefore, under God's mighty hand, that he may lift you up in due time. Cast all your anxiety on him because he cares for you. —**1 Peter 5:6-7**

Learning to trust God is one of the hardest things we can do, and at the same time, it is one of the most freeing things we can do in our lifetime. In trusting God, we let go of our own forms of control. But who wants to do that? I sure don't.

After realizing how much I like to control things, I became very aware that I wasn't relying on God. I was relying on my own strength to get things done. When in reality, I can choose to believe that the God of the universe does have it all under control and I get to lay my worries and my cares at His feet. When I do this, God's strength is perfected in my weaknesses and in my admission of how much I desperately need Him every day.

When I let this control go, I am free to love. I am free to give, because God is my provider and He satisfies the desires of every living thing. I am free to forgive, because I realize that I am fully forgiven in Him and I can rest in His abundant grace. When I rest in His will, that is where I find true peace, true joy and true life. That is the life I want to live.

Ashley Lyn Pruitt
Katy, TX

July 14

This is the day the LORD *has made; we will rejoice and be glad in it.*—**Psalm 118:24**

On July 14, 1987, God blessed me with a precious daughter. She brought boundless joy to my life every day. She was my reason for living. I worked to provide for her needs. I juggled my schedule to support her activities. I planned my future based on her dreams. She grew into a young lady who loved the Lord with all her heart, and it was evident in how she lived her life and treated people. She was my best friend. I was and am delighted to be known as Lindsay's mom.

Never did I think that on what would have been Lindsay's 24th birthday, I would address her killer in court and actually forgive her for brutally killing my daughter in her negligence. On my own, I could never have done this. *Never.* As in, not ever! But knowing that God forgives me and instructs me to forgive, I had to do this.

It was not easy. In fact, it took years for God to bring me from blinding rage to genuine compassion. And I won't lie; there are days that I have to forgive again, but this is what I am led to do to keep bitterness and evil from having control in my life. This way, Jesus is in control of my life each day—it is through the "Amazing Grace" of the Lord that I am sustained.

My daily joy is in being a child of the King. I now work for different reasons but always to glorify Jesus. I juggle my schedule to support other mothers who have lost children and share my faith in Jesus with them. I plan my future based on God's promise that through the sacrifice of His perfect Son and my belief that He died in atonement for my sin, I'll live with Him in Heaven for eternity and worship alongside my precious daughter.

Happy Birthday, Lindsay. Mama misses you, but only for a while.

In Loving Memory of Lindsay Dian Walters
July 14, 1987-March 1, 2009

Lisa~Lindsay's mom
Georgetown, TX

July 15

For as high as the heavens are above the earth, so great is his love for those who fear him; as far as the east is from the west, so far has he removed our transgressions from us.—**Psalm 103: 11-12**

The sunrise was in progress, but because of the trees in the front of my house, I didn't have a clear view. However, I could tell God was in the mood to show off His glory. The colors in the sky were spectacular. The sunsets here in the Hill Country tend to favor the University of Texas Longhorns in shades of burnt orange, but pink seems to be the color for the mornings. And what brilliant pinks adorned the eastern sky this particular day!

I walked around to the back of the house and was quite surprised to note that the western sky also was full of color instead of the normal grayish hues. The clouds were big and fluffy, and the sky just looked fun! The lake even seemed to take on a pink aura. I was wowed with this sunrise. The view from the back porch usually isn't this colorful in the mornings and I felt like God was giving me a special gift.

I can't carry a tune, but love music and am often moved to tears by the words God speaks to me through songs. Scripture memorization or remembering where verses are found in the Bible doesn't come easy for me, but I can remember song lyrics. Since many of the contemporary Christian songs contain verses from the Bible, I have been able to learn more Scripture through them.

As I was admiring the beauty of this sunrise, which encompassed the whole sky, a song by Casting Crowns, "East to West," was playing in my head. The lead singer, Mark Hall, previously explained in a radio interview that the inspiration for it came from one of the Psalms. At that sunrise moment, I couldn't remember which one, but I did remember the lyrics to "East to West." Oh, how I needed those words of assurance!

My past is so full of sin that shame and guilt can consume me. Even though I know there is forgiveness, I can't always forgive myself. How can I glorify God, though, if my focus is on the sin instead of Him? Yes, sometimes "the chains of yesterday surround me," but thankfully "in the arms of Your mercy I find rest."

My sins are removed by an immeasurable distance, as far as the east is from the west, and God has gifted me this glorious, clean-slate day. I have the assurance of His words from Psalm 103:11-12, and I have the words in the song by Casting Crowns to remind me of God's amazing mercy and forgiveness. Plus, I witnessed the most glorious sunrise ever this morning—God's special gift to remind me of His abundant love. Oh, dear Father, thank You for loving me—who I was, and just as I am today.

July 16

Be wise in the way you act toward outsiders; make the most of every opportunity. Let your conversation be always full of grace, seasoned with salt, so that you may know how to answer everyone.—**Colossians 4:5-6**

One summer, my two sons played on a softball team together in Houston, where they lived and worked after graduating from college. While both of them played organized sports since they were 4 years old through college, they only played together one year during the high school football season of 2002, when Zach was a senior and Trevor a sophomore.

The boys mentioned they were going to be playing together in a tournament, and I might enjoy coming to watch them play. Since I lived on Lake Travis in the Austin area and didn't see them as often as I liked, it sounded like fun.

The softball complex was on the other side of Houston and was an incredible facility. There was a huge indoor seating area, complete with tables, chairs and a restaurant. One could sit inside, in the cool air-conditioned room, and watch all three of the fields. Plus outside, the stadium seats were covered and there were additional tables with overhead ceiling fans.

The players on the teams were much different than the school-aged boys Zach and Trevor used to play with. These were grown men (like them). There were a few wives and girlfriends on hand to watch their guys, but it looked like I was the only mom.

Our team left the complex for a few hours to go eat lunch before the second game. It was an extremely hot summer day and there was a long wait in-between games. (Many of the players did drink a beer or two while they waited.) When we got back from lunch, our team went outside to warm up for the second game, and two of the girlfriends and I settled right under one of the outdoor ceiling fans where we had a clear view of home plate.

Our team was first at bat and when Zach walked up to the plate, two players from another team were standing directly in front of us, obstructing our view. Unfortunately, it was very clear that these two men had consumed more than just a beer or two. They were quite loud and very obnoxious. I politely asked if they could sit down or move out of our way. After all, I had driven four hours that morning so I could watch my sons play.

These two men took one look at the two very cute girlfriends sitting beside me and decided it was flirting time. The scene went from bad to worse. We just wanted to watch the game and these slightly tipsy guys had other ideas. However, help was on the way. Another team had just arrived on the scene to watch the game, but this wasn't just any team. These men were from a very large church in the Houston area. They had their church name and website on the back of their jerseys—and they weren't drinking beer. They saw what was going on and came to our rescue.

Several of the church ballplayers gently ushered the two men away from our table. They sat down beside them and just started talking. Every so often I could hear little bits and pieces of their conversation, and I heard "Jesus" mentioned numerous times. The players from the church team took the opportunity not only to rescue us girls from these two men who had consumed a few too many, but also to be bold in their faith. And, as I saw later, they also prayed on the field before their game.

As I watched the incident, I recalled one of the daily devotions I had read that morning. When I got home that night I went back to look at it again. Dr. Charles Stanley with In Touch Ministries had given instruction on beginning your day alone with God, in His Word. He went on to encourage those who read the Scriptures to share what God had revealed with others. Dr. Stanley said, "Be bold and remember that the authority of your message comes from Him."

I don't think this was the first time members of that Church team were bold in their faith. I got the impression that those ballplayers knew their opportunity to witness to others was God's game strategy all along.

July 17

I have fought the good fight, I have finished the race. I have kept the faith.—**2 Timothy 4:7**

Have you ever heard of a professional organizer? Someone who is actually so efficient that she organizes for a living? I am an absolute mess and just can't imagine what it would be like to have an uncluttered life. I am not saying I wouldn't want my life to be like that—I just don't know how to get it that way.

Procrastination and piles have been my way of life for as long as I can remember. I am not proud of my lack of self-control and have done an extremely good job of hiding it. I always get things done—at the last minute, of course. However, no one else is aware of just how fast I worked at the end. I have also become a pro at camouflaging my piles. I know every empty nook and cranny where I can stash something so it's out of sight when company comes. The real trick is to remember where I put things when it comes time to uncover what was hidden.

Mary, a fellow church member, is a professional organizer. I had read about her on the blog site for the Woman's Ministry. We met at a going-away party for a mutual friend (and later ended up in the same small group for Bible study).

Mary is a bundle of energy and just delightful. My first impression was that she was a no-nonsense kind of girl, quick and to the point. It was easy to understand how Mary could easily decide what to keep, what to discard and how to stay on task because of her energetic, decisive personality. I am the total opposite. Before the party was over, I had some of Mary's helpful hints, plus her business card, just in case I felt the need to use her services.

The very next morning, I woke up feeling overwhelmed, buried under all the clutter. I think I had been totally intimidated by Mary. The piles on my desk were overflowing and I could barely see my closet floor. Besides the stuff I could see, there was all the clutter in my head. I had stories waiting to be written, but felt I didn't have enough time. I had errands to run, but felt I would rather write than drive around town. I hadn't read my morning devotions yet, and I was looking for some encouraging words of wisdom as I sat down to escape the mess and dive into God's Word.

God was on my case. The very first devotion I read was from Proverbs 31. Glynnis Whitwer had titled it, "Why You Should Hang Up Your Robe." Glynnis had a habit of not finishing her tasks and she referenced the words from Acts 20:24: "However, I consider my life worth nothing to me, if only I may finish the race and complete the task the Lord Jesus has given me." At the end of her story, Glynnis wrote, "So I guess I'll take the extra step and actually hang up my robe. It's one more stitch in this tapestry of finishing well that God is trying to create in my life."

Once again, my God spoke to me through the written words of another sister in Christ. How comforting to know I was not alone with my mess. My mind was flooded with all the times I just tossed clothes on the chair in the closet instead of hanging them. (Hint: never put a chair in the closet.) While I would love to be like Mary, I can't compare myself to her. But I can sure try to finish the tasks that God has given me, like Glynnis. Taking a few extra steps during my day is an attainable goal.

God sent me Mary and Glynnis for a very good reason. He also used Paul to give me some words of encouragement to incorporate into my daily prayers. I will try using God to help me organize my life. I can't think of anyone with more experience.

By the way, I want to inform you that I may be messy, but my house isn't "dirty." On a very regular basis the floors are mopped, the carpet is vacuumed and the bathrooms are cleaned. Clothes are washed (almost) daily and there are no piles of dirty dishes in the sink. If you paid an unexpected visit to my house, you would find it presentable. Just don't look at my desk and never, ever, go into my bedroom closet—until God and I get it cleaned up.

July 18

"Watch out! Be on your guard against all kinds of greed; a man's life does not consist in the abundance of his possessions." —**Luke 12:15**

After moving to Lake Travis, it took awhile to put the house in Katy on the market. After deciding to sell, we did some updating before listing the house. My contractor was a family friend, and his wife helped when she could. She did such things as taking the knick knacks off the built in shelves or the dishes out of the cabinets when he painted.

The realtor was also a friend. She was very frank when telling me what I should do to sell my home. Besides the minor remodel, she suggested putting away all the clutter, all the knick-knacks and, most certainly, all of the family photos. Basically, she said I needed to stage the house so it would look more like a model home and very impersonal.

Since I would have to eventually box all those things, I went back to Katy for a few days to get to work on de-cluttering. My lake house was already full of more "stuff," and decisions would have to be made on what to do with this clutter. In my den were several shelves jam-packed with collectible items like Hummel figurines, family photos, some crystal items and shells—lots of shells. I love the beach, so my house was decorated like I lived there. These shelves had also been freshly painted so everything had already been removed once, and then put back, by the contractor's wife.

As I was boxing up, I knew that many of the items weren't where they had originally been. I finally made it to the top shelf, where I picked up a large framed picture of my two sons in their cute Little League uniforms. When I got through reminiscing about those baseball days, I happened to notice two ceramic figurines that had been placed behind that large photo. Now, they weren't costly pieces of sculpture, but they were certainly priceless. They were handmade ceramic treasures—works by my two sons.

Back when they were young, one of the popular spots for birthday parties was the ceramics shop. The kiddos could pick out the piece of plaster, paint it and take home their work of art. My two sons had each picked fish-related pieces to add to my "beachy" decorations. One was three dolphins, painted very carefully and neatly. The other was three ferocious-looking sharks, with blood coming out of their mouths, and a not-so-neat paint job. I thought it was very ironic that my contractor's wife had purposely placed them behind the large photo, probably thinking they weren't as pretty as the other items on the shelf and should be hidden.

I sat and pondered the treasures. I felt so silly for boxing up all those other things in the bubble wrap, like they were priceless, when all of those collectibles were now meaningless. The two items that were gifts from my boys were the items of real value, and they had been hidden from view. I was overwhelmed with joy for discovering them all over again.

I couldn't remember who did which one, though. I texted the boys (who were then 24 and 26), and we had a delightful time going back and forth about the sharks and dolphins. The boys had fun thinking of the day they gave them to me and the birthday party they attended. I thought about the expensive Hummel figurines I had collected over the years and the other pieces of glass and crystal that had been carefully wrapped up and put in boxes. I could hardly remember when I received them and who gave them to me. None of the pieces had the same significance as the dolphins and sharks.

How often do we get caught up gathering "stuff" and cluttering up our homes with collectibles, gadgets, shoes, cute jewelry and clothes? We want a new car and a bigger house. Then we wonder, how did life get so messy? I am thankful for those ceramic treasures I found on that top shelf. It was certainly God's way of letting me know what's important—what possessions are priceless and what I can easily get rid of. With His help, de-cluttering will be easier than I expected.

July 19

Our citizenship is in heaven. And we eagerly await a Savior from there, the Lord Jesus Christ.—**Philippians 3:20**

My house in Katy was on the market for less than three weeks when I got a contract on it. I had known for several years that the house would eventually be sold and Lake Travis would be more than just a part-time home. However, I wasn't prepared for the emotional impact the actual move would have on me.

When we moved to the house in 1997, my son Zach was in seventh grade and Trevor was in the fifth. We had moved from a house only five minutes away, where the boys had lived since they were born. Neither had to change schools and all of their friends were still close. Even after my divorce in 1999, life went on for me and I met the man who is now my husband. Zach and Trevor graduated from the high school that was less than two miles down the street. There were countless, wonderful memories packed into that house and the entire neighborhood.

I don't know how I became such a pack rat, but I saved everything my two boys brought home from school. There were special boxes with compartments for each grade level, even pre-school, to keep those priceless works of art and stories, report cards, notes, etc. Scrapbooking became an obsession for a while and I had a whole work area designated for that, with folders filled with pictures and memorabilia, just waiting to go onto a colorful page, with all the fancy frills. Boxing all of that was quite emotional and time-consuming—I couldn't just place all those memories in a box without looking and reminiscing.

Besides the schoolwork and pictures, I came across other treasures. As I have mentioned previously, every year for Christmas I gave both boys a daily devotional or inspirational book. Inside the cover, I shared my own words of inspiration. I also wrote them letters on special occasions like birthdays, graduation, big sports competitions, leaving for college, Christmas—you get the picture. As I came across those books and the letters that had been stuffed in drawers and placed on shelves, I read the words written from the depths of my heart, poured out to my sons.

After reading the letter I wrote to my oldest son just days before he left for college back in 2003, I was overwhelmed with emotion. How could I leave this house, this little neighborhood and all of these memories? The move to Lake Travis in Austin wasn't a necessity; it was just because my husband and I wanted to live on the lake. As long as I had the house in Katy, I felt like I could hold on to the past, but now it was time for closure on that chapter of life.

I finished packing for that day, and with my eyes still swollen from crying, I got in my car to drive back to Lake Travis. The radio was set to my favorite Christian station in the greater Houston area. The beautiful voice of Laura Story filled my car as she sang "Blessings." The message of the song is that we should consider our hardships as blessings in disguise. The words that I heard as I started my car were reminding me that the pain is only momentary because this place on earth isn't my home.

This temporary home of mine in Katy had become a shrine to my children. I cherished all of the memories, the stories, the letters, the trophies. My sweet Jesus wanted to let me know He was with me in my sadness, and that there would be healing through my tears. However, He wanted me to focus more on my home in eternity than on that house at the end of the cul-de-sac in Katy.

There comes a point in my drive where I lose my Houston station and must switch over to my station in Austin. The song that was playing when I made the change was "Blessings" once again. God was reminding me, one more time, that I was just driving from one temporary home to another. While I am here though, I will look for all the blessings that my Lord has provided in the little trials on the journey to my permanent dwelling place with Him.

July 20

Please accept the present that was brought to you, for God has been gracious to me.—**Genesis 33:11**

A while back, I wrote a devotion about being overcommitted and having too much on my plate. I knew I needed to cut out something, but what? I didn't want to be a quitter, but I also knew that God wasn't able to work through me if I was on overload. I prayed about what to do, and I want to share how God answered.

My friend Linda and I worked together doing data entry for a prison ministry. We simply entered the date an inmate finished a Bible study lesson, with the information found on the envelope that he/she returned the lesson (to another group of women for their review). Linda did half of the envelopes each week and I did the other. The task itself wasn't the problem—for me, it was the time commitment. Plus, when one of us was out of town, the other would need to double up and do all of the envelopes. Sometimes Linda felt sorry for me, knowing I was a bit stressed, and would do all of them anyway.

Soon it was summertime and both of us had vacations planned. In addition, I had recently sold my home in Katy and knew I would have to spend time packing and moving. I felt bad asking Linda to do my half, but I also was worried about the time I would need to do her part. If I felt doing half of them each week was time-consuming, certainly the full load would make my plate overflow!

My dear sweet friend sensed my feelings of being overwhelmed and responded with the most beautiful email one evening:

"I know you have been so busy and I've been concerned about you feeling overburdened. Please consider reducing your load by giving up this responsibility, at least for the summer, then you can reconsider doing it again. If I feel I can't handle it all, I'll find someone else to help. Right now I am getting caught up at work, etc. Please accept my grace and the good timing the Lord has supplied to be released of this so that you can feel some freedom."

Her words, *please accept my grace*, touched my heart. What an incredible act of unselfish service she was offering me! Just the Sunday before, Pastor Brad had said that as Christians, we shouldn't have to be asked to serve. I didn't ask her; Linda just offered this free gift to me. In that same sermon, Pastor Brad said some of us struggle with allowing others to serve us. Yep, I am one of those. I often refuse someone's offer to help—I am polite about it, but my unspoken reason is that I feel I can do it myself. That is being prideful at its worst, thinking I can do it on my own. Brad pointed out that a refusal, besides being an act of pride, also takes away the other persons' opportunity to fulfill one of God's blessings.

When I read Linda's email, I didn't even think of refusing her offer, though. Perhaps it was her sweet words, but I also think God had prepared my heart. I had previously prayed for wisdom to know what to prune and peace to know when it was time. I knew instantly that my prayer had been answered through Linda's offer to temporarily release me from this particular commitment.

This isn't the first time Linda has reached out to me. I sure hope you have a friend like Linda in your life who lovingly gives of herself, without even being asked. Please don't let pride keep you from accepting God's blessing. It just might be the answer to one of your prayers.

By the way, today is Linda's birthday. God is using her in a mighty way for His kingdom. And to think that she was born to be a special gift in my life! Happy Birthday, my sweet friend!

July 21

And Jesus grew in wisdom and in stature and in favor with God and man.—**Luke 2:52**

I have learned about the Lord in baby steps throughout my life. One of the biggest steps for me was to learn to claim verses from the Bible for myself and for my family. Luke 2:52 is my favorite for my children. I have claimed this verse for them for as long as I can remember.

I have claimed it for them because I was not wise. For that reason, my greatest wish for my children is that they love the Lord and gain His wisdom. I made many mistakes, most avoidable. I carry scars around, and I pray that my children will not have those burdens. I want them to be the best people they can be. That's why this is so dear to my heart.

This verse speaks clearly to me about the things I want for my children through the Lord. I want my children to know that wisdom comes from seeking God's plan for their lives, not their own. I want them to have an extraordinary life filled with godly opportunities and things that they will look back on with godly pride; to avoid making bad choices that bring deep scars, both seen and unseen, into their lives forever; and to ask the Lord every day for wisdom.

It is my prayer that they have the wisdom to be friendly because Jesus was; to choose friends wisely; to know God's commandments are freeing and not binding; to know that helping others makes one happier than self-centeredness. Always.

I pray they have the wisdom to know that even if they have all the world has to offer, if they don't have the Lord, they have nothing. And finally, I want them to know that even when they make a mistake, the Lord is there to pick them up.

I hope you will find the verse in the Bible that speaks to your heart as this one did to mine. Claim it and claim the Lord's promises.

Keri Bonner
Katy, TX

July 22

The boundary lines have fallen for me in pleasant places; surely I have a delightful inheritance.—**Psalm 16:6**

My golden retriever is a strange girl. I love her to pieces and she brings great joy to my life, but she does some weird things. For instance, she doesn't particularly like treats. There is no way to bribe this dog with biscuits. And what dog doesn't get excited about going for a ride in the car? Plus, you don't hear of too many retrievers that don't like to swim, do you? My sweet Holly doesn't like any of that.

I am really thankful for most of her amazingly "good" behavior. Holly has never destroyed, torn up, devoured or damaged anything of value. No furniture, shoes, books, plants, food from the table, or wild critters. She will dig in the trashcan and is an incredible paper shredder, but, hey, I can live with that. If I give her a box to tear up, she will entertain herself for hours. But the other day I witnessed something that just amazed me.

Holly loves to go outside on the upstairs back porch and just chill. If she goes down the steps, she is safely confined to a small, fenced-in yard. However, since the porch circles to the front of the house, she could easily walk around and then have access to the entire yard. To keep her from venturing into the unsafe territory, I placed a baby gate between the house and a column. Perhaps I should have installed something sturdier, but the baby gate has always worked.

One day, after an incredible windstorm, I looked out the window onto the porch where Holly was. I saw her walk to where her gate should have been and just stand there. As a result of the high winds, it had blown down. Holly could have simply walked right around the baby gate and escaped, but she didn't. She looked at it, then plopped down right in front of it.

Holly knew her boundary lines and for some reason, respected and obeyed. She could have easily knocked that baby gate over at any time—she weighs 85 pounds. She has never even tried, that I know of. She has learned that it is there to keep her confined, and she accepts it.

God has erected boundaries for us too. He has warned us of areas in life that we should steer clear of. However, there are times when we think it looks more appealing on the other side of that fence and decide to give it a whirl. We know better, yet we give into the allure of Satan's lies and our selfish flesh.

Parents have controls on the home computer to keep kiddos from going to websites they shouldn't, but what about the places that we parents shouldn't go? For you married gals on Facebook, did you stop before looking up that old boyfriend, or did you listen to that smug whisper that urged you onto that slippery slope?

I didn't need those expensive shoes. The no-name brand would protect my feet just fine. And that purse? Just because they have a higher price tag, am I suddenly worth more? That credit card makes it so easy. Just a little swipe here and a little swipe there. Before long, I've gone over my limit. I could go on and on, but I think you get my point.

Oh, I just wish I could be as obedient and content as my Holly. Instead of going off into forbidden territory, why can't I just lie down and rest at the feet of Jesus and be happy where He wants me and with what I have? The restrictions He has established for my life are for my safety, not for my harm. He has promised me a delightful inheritance—why should I ever venture outside His protective gate?

I didn't put up Holly's baby gate to be cruel. I love that girl and want to shield her from danger. And to think, my Heavenly Father loves me more.

July 23

When times are good, be happy; but when times are bad consider: God has made the one as well as the other.
—**Ecclesiastes 7:14**

Mud happens. It just does. And it can happen a lot. If it rains long enough or hard enough, or both, and if you're at the right place at the right time, it will happen. There will be mud.

My husband Rob and I, along with our three kids, moved to Sabine Creek Ranch in the spring of 2009. Sabine Creek Ranch is a summer preteen/youth camp and a year-round Retreat Center, as well as a working, 330-acre ranch with cattle, horses, chickens, sheep, pigs, dogs, cats, coyotes, skunks, etc. Rob was to become the director of a ministry program there, as well as the program director for the camp.

Now, I'm a city girl, so living on the ranch was quite educational for me in many ways, but especially when it came to "mud-avoidance." The first day we arrived at the ranch, my lifelong friend, Monica, who has three boys and lives on 30 acres in the country, gave bright, yellow John Deere T-shirts to my three kids, which read, THERE WILL BE MUD! Cute and fun. That's all I thought. I had no idea there was a deep ancient truth that spoke through those shirts, nor did I know that this truth would try to thoroughly change my life.

Over the next few weeks, I would fall apart on the inside every time my children walked out the door, knowing that no matter what they did, they would come back in the house with that dark north Texas mud that surrounds us. I created almost a "Border Patrol" feel at the back door to ensure no mud would enter the house. I had used a massive amount of Shout stain removal and detergent, and most people that came by noticed my washing machine was always running. I had supplied rubber boots for my entire family that stayed by the back door, which were to be taken off BEFORE entering, and there was an in-depth inspection that took place before "crossing over."

But this was tiring. And truly, it was a hopeless battle. After only a few months, those bright yellow shirts that were presented to my kids were dingy with faded mud spots carelessly splotched all over the front and back. I was growing feeble of "patrolling" the back door, and the rubber boots were falling apart. There were some places I could not allow mud to go, but I began to soften on other places.

I know that mud is actually a good thing for many situations. I know that nothing could replace the fact that my kids were running, playing, romping and roaming around the ranch with their Davy Crockett and Batman gear on, or just simply digging the deepest mud hole around. This is good and right. Actually, it was a blessing.

It was with this realization I started see it a little differently. We can either try to avoid the mud over and over again, working effortlessly to stay "clean and stain free," or we can let it change us. You know, I'm just talking about what life brings us—some of those situations that are just dark mud. It stains. It even kind of stinks, but it does something to us when we just go ahead and receive it, learn from it, and even suspect that maybe God might be the one who brought it, or at least allowed it.

I think God likes mud. He made it. He even used it to heal a blind man. However, that blind man allowed the mud to go somewhere I'm sure I would not be very welcoming to at all—his eyes! Yet he was wiser than I, and he received it. I know. He probably didn't know Jesus was making mud for his eyes. He was blind. He couldn't see Jesus doing anything! But God makes the mud anyway, and then He lets us choose to receive it. Or not.

I want to be healed of anything that is blinding to me. I want to be free of attitudes and thoughts that hinder my perception. *I don't want to be a stick in the mud.* I just want to see mud the way God sees mud. That it's actually a tool of change, a healing agent.

So now, sometimes begrudgingly and sometimes invitingly, I receive the age-old message from the words of the great, wise John Deere: THERE WILL BE MUD! And because of this, if listening closely, one might even hear *me* say, "Let there be mud!"

Misti Matchett
Montgomery, TX

July 24

May the God of hope fill you with all joy and peace as you trust in him, so that you may overflow with hope by the power of the Holy Spirit.—**Romans 15:13**

My house on Lake Travis sits on a peninsula, bordered by water on the north, east and west. The south end is the only access in or out via land. Right past the last cross street is a yellow road sign that reads "No Outlet." I actually never paid much attention to that sign until recently while walking my golden retriever.

It was one of those blah Monday mornings and there was a heaviness weighing on my heart. My husband had just left to return to Houston for work and I already felt lonely. I was also worried about my youngest son and his girlfriend situation. Was he about to get his heart broken? The house remodel was wearing on me and my patience was running thin. Instead of counting my blessings and being thankful for all I have, I was focused on all the negatives I could round up.

I looked at the "No Outlet" sign and thought of some additional words that could be used for it. "No Way Out" or "Dead End" came to mind. The Holy Spirit jumped right in at that point and reminded me how blessed I was to not be stuck with a permanent case of the Monday-morning blahs and believing there was no way out.

Because of my hope and faith in Christ and our special relationship, I have all I need to get me through every situation encountered. I know that. However, there are just certain times that I allow the battle to rage in my mind and the Evil One to do his work. Before I accepted Christ the war went on for days, causing me to feel defeated and discouraged, not knowing how to find my way out of the dismal fog of uncertainty.

Now, with God's help, I have learned how to resist the Devil, making him flee from me (James 4:7). He may hang around for a bit, but his stays are getting shorter and shorter. I look back at all the streets I ventured down in my life that only led to emptiness, pain and despair—dead-end streets providing no way out of my mess.

Life with Jesus and His promises is different. He has provided a way out of every trial, every situation imaginable through His Word. I know all too well what it feels like to have that desperate feeling of not knowing what to do or where to go and am so thankful to have those promises in my heart.

Right after the Holy Spirit got involved in my pity party, my morning began to change. I looked down the street and saw a mama deer and her baby crossing from one side to the other. (I think a little fawn is almost as cute as a golden retriever puppy.) My sweet neighbor waved as she drove by on her way to pray at the Catholic Church—something she does every morning.

My cell phone rang and it was my husband—calling to tell me he loved me and to let me know his drive was going well. I could feel the Monday-morning blahs slipping away as I allowed God's blessings to fill my heart. Then I started to think about some of His promises stored in my memory bank. The heaviness of the doubt, negative thoughts and worry that had invaded my mind slowly started to dissipate. Was that Satan on his way out?

Even though I was walking down a street with a big yellow sign telling me there was "No Outlet," the Holy Spirit did His job of filling me with hope. Satan tried to be my walking partner that morning, but the promise found in James 4:7 proved to be a more suitable companion: "Submit yourselves, then, to God. Resist the devil, and he will flee from you."

July 25

In him we have redemption through his blood, the forgiveness of sins, in accordance with the riches of God's grace that he lavished on us with all wisdom and understanding.—**Ephesians 1:7-8**

Do you ever have a hard time deciding what to wear? Sometimes I just stare into the closet, expecting a dress or blouse to jump right off the hanger into my hand. Almost without fail, I face my biggest dilemmas on Sundays.

One morning, as I was trying to decide what to wear to church, I kept on looking at a white dress—one I didn't particularly like. For starters, it had to be dry-cleaned. I try to avoid buying anything that requires being sent to the cleaners, but every so often one slips by. As much I was resisting that dress, I felt like I was being urged to pick it.

Is the Holy Spirit trying to tell me what to wear to church? Does God really get *that* involved with my life? On *that* Sunday morning, I knew, without a doubt, I was supposed to wear *that* white dress.

We had been out of town the previous Sunday and I was so happy to be back at church. I jumped to my feet as soon as the praise and worship music began. The first song we sang was "Grace Like Rain" by Todd Agnew. If you aren't familiar with the song, it includes verses from the traditional hymn, "Amazing Grace," sung to a different tune, with a chorus of new lyrics. The chorus refers back to the song title—grace falls, like rain, washing away our sins.

The next song was "All Because of Jesus" by Fee. This upbeat tune is just pure praise to Jesus! One of the lines that stuck in my head refers to the blood of Jesus being the reason we are alive.

"Jesus Paid it All," as recorded by Kristian Stanfill (although originally written in 1865 by Elvina M. Hall), was our third song, with the chorus going like this:.

Jesus paid it all,
All to Him I owe;
Sin had left a crimson stain,
He washed it white as snow.

I was suddenly quite aware of my white dress—my white as snow, white dress. All my sins have been washed away, because of the blood of Jesus Christ. Had I been wearing blue or yellow, it wouldn't have changed the truths found in the lyrics. However, would the words of those three songs have penetrated my hard heart if I hadn't been wearing that particular white dress?

Sometimes this old heart of mine just needs softening and my sweet Jesus knows just how to do it. He wanted me to wear a white dress to allow those words to reach the depths of my heart and soul, which explains why it was hand-picked for me that morning. More lyrics from that old hymn sum up what was going on that Sunday morning as I stood, praising my Lord, in my white as snow, white dress.

I hear the Savior say
"Thy strength indeed is small;
Child of weakness, watch and pray
Find in Me thine all in all."
CHORUS
Lord, now indeed I find
Thy power and thine alone,
Can change the leper's spots
And melt this heart of stone.

July 26

One thing I ask from the LORD, this only do I seek: that I may dwell in the house of the LORD all the days of my life, to gaze on the beauty of the LORD and to seek him in his temple.—**Psalm 27:4**

As a young girl, I longed to be beautiful. As an adult, I seek beautiful things. But I never thought of God as being beautiful. However, there it was, plain as day, right on the page in front of me: "Beautiful LORD," one of the names of God in my study of the 200 names, attributes and titles of God.

In Isaiah 53:2 we read: "He had no beauty or majesty to attract us to him, nothing in his appearance that we should desire him." Now I had to think about it. God is beautiful! It is hard not to translate that into the human dimension that we are comfortable with. But as God, He is so much bigger, so much grander and more beautiful than a beautiful person.

Then I thought about nature. Nature is beautiful, and I love and enjoy its beauty—the power and grandeur of mountains, the tenderness of a mother deer caring for her fawn. I see beauty in the sunset and in the lightning storm. While nature is beautiful, it is created by the Creator.

Beauty is a gift from God. He created it. He also created the "eye of the beholder" to appreciate the beauty He created for Himself, and for us, to enjoy. We appreciate beauty with our eyes, and our other senses as we see, touch and smell the beautiful things around us. We appreciate beauty with our minds, understanding a complex plan or design, seeing wonderfully kind things done. We can see the beauty in the plan that God put together from the time of creation—to send His Son Jesus to pay the penalty for our sins, so that we can worship Him with clean hearts and spend eternity in His temple.

So what have I learned about God? That He *is* Beautiful. We are drawn to beauty. It is one of the ways we are drawn to God! We cannot see God, but we can see the beauty that He created. We know that He is perfect, so I believe that when I do see God in heaven, He will be beautiful to look at!

Thank You, Beautiful LORD, for allowing me to glimpse Your beauty.

Fran Upton
Austin, TX

July 27

"Forget the former things; do not dwell upon the past." —Isaiah 43:18

The day arrived to close on my house in Katy. The time between putting the house on the market, receiving a contract, packing up and this final day seemed like a blur. All the moving and cleaning wasn't actually finished until the night before. That had been a frantic, hot, grueling day, and when I left the empty house to go spend the night in a hotel, I knew I would be back the next day to say my final good-bye.

So, here it was. I had it all planned out. My agenda consisted of going to the house early in the morning to journal my thoughts. The closing was set for 1 p.m., and I would have plenty of time to say my good-byes and write about the emotions I was feeling. It would be a special time with just that empty house and all the memories — plus my computer, to document the experience.

However, I didn't get that early start. I piddled around in the hotel room and before long it was 11 a.m. I wouldn't have time to write, but I could at least walk through the rooms, remembering the past. It had actually been quite an emotional morning for me. I even sent a prayer request to my Bible study girls in Austin asking they pray for God's peace to consume me, instead of the sadness I was feeling.

As I approached the house, my realtor called to inform me that the buyers and their realtor were also headed there for a final walk-through at 11:30. Yikes! It was 11:35 as I pulled into the driveway. I didn't want to run into the buyers before the closing. We had never met and I didn't want to be there as they conducted their final inspection.

I ran inside, grabbed the computer modem I had forgotten the night before, jumped back in my car and drove off quickly. Thankfully, I missed them. However, as I was driving to the cable store to return the modem, I realized I also missed saying my final farewell to the house! I missed all the drama, all the sadness, all the tears I planned on shedding. But wasn't that a blessing in disguise?

Did I really need a final, staged farewell? I just burst into laughter when I realized that God wasn't going to let me wallow in the memories or cry over an empty house. It would belong to new owners soon and it was time for me to move on. How clever that He arranged for the buyers to schedule that walk-through at the same time I had planned my gut-wrenching good-bye.

While I was standing in line to return the modem, my realtor called to apologize. She had told me the buyers were going to the house at 11:30, but she looked at the text message incorrectly and the time was actually 12:30. She was sorry I had rushed out of the house when I could have stayed for a while after all.

I laughed again. No apology was required. Her mistake had also been a blessing. I was so relieved that I didn't put myself through that unnecessary, drawn-out final adieu. As I stood in that line, I felt God's peace engulf me as I reflected on His perfect planning.

Memories are stored in my heart and mind, not in empty rooms. No need to be sad about the past — I can smile and be thankful that it happened. I am so blessed that God put me in Katy to raise my children, belong to a Christ-centered church and meet my husband. Oh, the years there were so joyful.

God had protected my sentimental heart that day. He didn't want me stuck in the past because He has plans for my future. I arrived back home that evening just in time for Bible study. When the girls asked how my day went (since I had asked for their prayers), I was only too eager to let them know what God had done for me.

Yes, the closing went fine — not only on the house but also on that chapter of my life.

July 28

"If you obey my commands, you will remain in my love, just as I have obeyed my Father's commands and remain in his love. I have told you this so that my joy may be in you and that your joy may be complete. My command is this: Love each other as I have loved you." —**John 15:10-12**

If you have been following this book, you have read about the trips my mom and I have taken to Omaha, Nebraska. Mom's friend moved there to be closer to his family because of poor health. We had just returned from our fifth trip in two and a half years, and I couldn't wait to write this devotion—to give God the glory for what He did in my life.

When mom expressed a desire to go visit Charles the first time, I didn't hesitate to offer my assistance. At her age, there was no way she could travel by herself, and many friends told me what a good daughter I was to accompany her. Let me be totally honest and assure you that my actions had nothing to do with being a good daughter. No, I did it out of guilt.

Mom and Dad divorced when I was 6 years old, and she was forced into the workplace, while attending night classes. My two older sisters and I were also forced into a lifestyle completely foreign to us —we had to fend for ourselves. We had lived in a privileged environment and our world was turned upside down by the divorce. There was no mother-daughter time—no girly shopping trips, no painting our toenails together, no warm-and-fuzzy late-night talks. Looking back I don't know how she did it all, but with her being gone so much, my sisters and I missed out on having a mom (and a dad). Please understand that I am in no way insinuating she was a bad mother. Quite the contrary—she sacrificed everything to provide for us. It was just unfortunate circumstances.

During my high school years, I was overly rebellious, but I never felt the least bit guilty for the hell I put her through. We weren't close, and I felt no remorse. After I became a mom and had my heart ripped out a time or two by my boys, I was consumed with guilt for what I did. To accompany her to Omaha to visit Charles, a trip she could never make on her own, helped ease the years of guilt. Good daughter? I don't think so.

Those previous four trips we took weren't exactly what I expected. I had the mindset that I would have hours to myself while mom spent the day with Charles at his retirement home—time to write, exercise and shop or whatever my heart desired. I would drop her off in the morning and pick them up in the afternoon. We would go to an early dinner, I would take Charles home, then mom and I would go back to the hotel. The next day, we would start all over again.

Very quickly I found that our time in Omaha had nothing to do with me, and everything to do with what Mom wanted. Being the "it's all about me" person I am, I didn't adjust well to those plans. I was there to serve mom, but I didn't like my time being so constricted, and unfortunately my heart was bitter. The really sad part was that I knew the condition of my heart, but wasn't willing to empty it of myself and fill it with God and others.

I have also written about being a late bloomer in my spiritual journey. All along the path, I encountered one roadblock after another because of my pride and selfish nature. The Holy Spirit has been giving me all kinds of signs indicating that I wasn't making the correct turns on the road that would lead to loving myself less and loving God more. Through sermons, devotions, Scripture, circumstances, events, I have seen God directing my steps down His path to surrender. When would I ever make the turn?

Finally, God blessed me with a sense of what it felt like to go down that road. Perhaps it was only in one situation, but it was a start. Isn't it absolutely incredible when we see His miracles in our life?

The words from John 15:10-12 spoke so clearly to me, and I can't wait to tell you tomorrow about the joy God poured into my heart as a little bit of self trickled out. It can happen!

July 29

But because of his great love for us, God, who is rich in mercy, made us alive with Christ even when we were dead in transgressions—it is by grace you have been saved.—**Ephesians 2:4-5**

While driving to pick up Mom for our fifth trip to Omaha, something felt different. First of all, I woke up with an excited pep in my step. I hadn't been too excited about another trip, and here I was suddenly looking forward to it. What's up with that? I even woke up before my alarm and was out the door 30 minutes ahead of schedule.

The drive from Austin to Mom's house in Schulenburg is two hours, with the second hour extremely picturesque along Highways 71 and 77, with a short spurt of a country back road. As I poured out words of praise and thanksgiving for the glorious scenery, I also questioned why I was feeling so exuberant.

Traveling with mom has been stressful. Time to myself was limited on these trips. There wouldn't be much time to write, and I would spend my days being a chauffeur. Despite all the negatives I could think of, there was no heaviness in my heart.

Mom has the habit of asking me to repeat 50% of what I say, and that had really irritated me. If she was hard of hearing, I would understand, but it's only me she doesn't seem to hear. I am ashamed to admit that I have lost my patience more times than I can count and responded with a very snappy tone. Sure enough, we hadn't been in the car more than a few minutes and she asked me to repeat myself.

I was literally blown away with the thought that went through my head. Perhaps having the opportunity to repeat my words was a second chance at making sure that what came out of my mouth was pleasing to God (Psalm 19:24). If not, I got a shot at a do-over if necessary—to re-phrase my statement, or not say it all. I could also make sure my tone was sweet and kind. That second chance wasn't so bad after all.

Whoa! Where did that come from? Immediately, I knew. Only God could put that thought in my heart.

At the Houston airport, surprisingly Mom didn't get upset when the flight to Omaha was delayed. I even enjoyed our time together over lunch and during the extended wait at the terminal. For some reason, I was seeing my mom with an entirely new set of eyes and with a more compassionate, loving heart.

Once in Omaha, I assumed we would have the same routine as before, but, out of the blue, I suggested taking them out to lunch each day as well, instead of having Mom and Charles eat at his retirement home. I mentioned that the extra outing might be fun for him since he doesn't get out much anymore. In the past, I complained to myself about having to drive so much, and now I was adding another round trip? What is happening? God was doing some mighty chiseling on my hardened heart.

When I realized I actually wanted to make sure Mom and Charles enjoyed their time together, and was thankful for the opportunity to do everything possible to make their time together special, I was awe-struck. I wasn't concerned that I had no time for myself. There was no time for a long walk along the Missouri River or to go across the street to the quaint Old Market and browse the cute shops and eat at one of the delightful, trendy restaurants. The only time for writing was after Mom went to bed, but that wasn't time enough to get my thoughts on paper. And I wasn't resentful?

After years of praying for God to help me to love Him more, to surrender my selfish desires, I saw Him answering that prayer. Oh, I was by no means free of myself, but just to enjoy my mom was a special gift that could only have come from my Father. I was forgiven for those years I tormented her, and God showed me how to act out of love for her instead of that bitter, ugly darkness of guilt.

I can't tell you how wonderful it felt to know that I was treating my mom out of love—love, not obligation. If God can chisel away at this selfish, it's-all-about-me girl, there's hope for everyone. To God be the glory for His wonderful act of mercy and grace.

July 30

The LORD replied, "My Presence will go with you, and I will give you rest." —**Exodus 33:14**

I arrived back home on a Friday night from taking my mom to Omaha for the week, and I was pooped! The week had been busy and spiritually uplifting, but the trip home zapped me. The flight delay meant arriving later than scheduled into Houston—on a Friday afternoon. If you know Houston, you know rush-hour traffic can be horrific, and on Fridays it starts long before the five o'clock whistle blows.

Mom waited in the terminal while I wheeled both suitcases through the sweltering parking garage. As I approached the car, my heart sank. The back end was lower than the rest of the car. The right rear tire was completely flat. The parking lot security arrived within minutes of my call. He informed me he couldn't change the tire but could fill it with air, in hopes that I could at least make it to the nearest Discount Tire.

Thankfully we made it, but that was just the beginning of the ordeal. We had to wait over an hour while they removed not one, but two nails. Then it was off to face the traffic—and it was then close to five. By the time I got Mom back to her retirement community in Schulenburg, Texas, and drove home to Austin, it was almost 10 p.m.

Saturday, there were all kinds of household chores to catch up on. All I really wanted to do was catch up on my writing, but I was extremely tired. I went down to the deck overlooking the lake, sat in the shade and read some of the daily devotions I missed while I was gone, hoping that quiet time would rejuvenate and jump-start my soul. The whole time I was waiting for God to perk me up. Nothing happened. The next step was to pray and just be still, hoping to hear something from Him, but it remained a one-way conversation.

Later in the day, I was still dragging and even attempted a nap but sleep never came. I talked to my husband about feeling so down and out. He did his best to cheer me up and ease my burden by going to the grocery store, cooking a wonderful dinner and even washing the dishes. I knew there was some type of spiritual attack going on, but never did I delve right into the Word for help. I had diagnosed my problem, thought I had the solution to fix it and went about it my way.

No wonder nothing was happening. Maybe I was spending time with Jesus, but how could I rest if I was in the war zone and not defending myself with His Word? That's a losing battle. Certainly it is human nature to be tired, but I knew evil forces were invading, to keep me from writing my God stories. God hadn't left me to fight alone, but it was my choice to cover myself with His promises and shield my soul from attacks by the Enemy—or be defeated. So I chose His Word. What better place to go than to the Psalms to see what David had to say?

The theme for Psalm 6, as written in my NIV stated: *Deliverance in trouble. God is able to rescue us.* Oh, I needed to be rescued from Satan's attack. "My soul is in anguish. How long, O LORD, how long?" (Vs. 3). "I am worn out from groaning" (Vs. 6). That's exactly how I felt. My soul longed for rejuvenation, but how long would I have to wait for an awakening? "The LORD has heard my cry for mercy; the LORD accepts my prayer"(Vs. 9). The Lord *accepts* my prayer? It's already done!

The last song we sang the next morning in church that nest day was Chris Tomlin's "Awakening." *For You and You alone awake my soul, awake my soul and sing.* I will hear His voice and He will awake my soul. What perfect timing to hear that message.

If you are in need of rejuvenation today, Google "Awakening" and listen. Come on, let's belt it out together: *Awake my soul and sing!* Keep on singing and choose to allow the mighty power of Jesus to perform what only He can do—His awakening in you.

July 31

We love because he first loved us.—1 John 4:19

It was a special sign sent just for me. I can't say it was a sign directly from God, but I believe it was sent through His messenger.

The past few days, I have written about a trip my mom and I took to Omaha and the miracle God performed in me. He softened my heart in a dramatic way towards my mother, in a way that only God could. He allowed me to feel love for her instead of guilt and obligation. Obviously He wasn't through with His love lesson.

God's messenger came in the form of my husband. Now, Austin is always going out of his way to shower me with affection, so he is actually God's love messenger every day. However, I needed some regeneration in my role as a wife because I was taking his love and kindness for granted.

I have been praying for years that God would help me think less of myself. My husband and I joke about life being all about me, but deep inside, I know it's no laughing matter. I earnestly seek God's power in not being so self-consumed.

During the remodel of our home, I moved my car out to the street every day so I wouldn't get boxed in when construction workers were in the driveway. I had a certain place I liked to park (in the shade, of course) and was very possessive about it. Some of the workers had the same idea about not wanting to get stuck in the drive and also wanted to park out front. I pulled into my spot and noticed a sign had been placed for all to see: "Parking reserved for Brenda's car only. All others towed away at owner's expense."

I laughed so hard I cried. I thought it was so funny that Austin would actually make a sign and put it in my spot. That's just like him to do something thoughtful and silly. But then I cried because I was so overcome with love—for him and Him. It's just like God to send me a message of love—to be thoughtful and have as sense of humor too.

Out of the blue, He sends me a song, a thought, a butterfly, a fawn, an email from a dear friend, the perfect daily devotion, a phone call from one of my sons, a text from my husband, a hug from him too. You get the picture. God is always showing me His love, and I tend to take it for granted—like I also take my husband for granted.

On the day Austin put the sign up for my parking spot, God rekindled my heart. It was a rejuvenated, refreshed love. It was truly a special moment as I sat in my car, laughing and crying.

It was also a special day that my husband posted that No Parking sign—our wedding anniversary. Being married to Austin has been so incredibly wonderful and fun, but the best part has been having God in our marriage. How blessed to have a husband and Heavenly Father who shower me with love daily, in all kinds of ways.

My prayer is that every day my soul is awakened with a deeper love for them both. As the passion for my First Love strengthens in my heart, soul and mind, may the love for my husband (and others) intensify as well. Hopefully one day there will be no more spots in my heart reserved for Brenda only.

August 1

He who dwells in the shelter of the Most High will rest in the shadow of the Almighty. Surely he will save you . . . and under his wings you will find refuge; his faithfulness will be your shield and rampart.—Psalm 91:1-4

At 3 a.m. the nurse on duty came to me and asked if we wanted to have our 8-month-old daughter baptized. Alone in the intensive care unit, panic flooded through me. It struck me then that they thought Courtney might not live through the night.

Just the day before, I had taken her to our pediatrician after she had fallen out of her crib onto the hardwood floor. One moment she had been happily dancing in the crib as I got her pajamas and in just a split-second turn of the head, she had toppled over the side. The doctor assured me she was fine.

The next day, her head began to swell greatly, her crying, though subdued, was constant, and her fever soared to 104 degrees. After waiting on hold for what seemed an eternity for the doctor, I hung up and rushed her to the emergency room.

We were soon transferred by ambulance to the hospital downtown that was better equipped to deal with her injury. It was painful to watch the intern struggle with repeated sticks to get an IV going. So difficult to see her tiny body wheeled away for CT scans that revealed a fractured skull and bleeding on her brain. And rock bottom to have the nurse ask about a middle-of-the-night baptism.

For a week, we didn't step outside Northwestern Memorial Hospital in Chicago. It was during this time that an encounter with the Lord marked me profoundly. The days were filled with more scans, testing, a horde of doctors coming by (it was a teaching hospital) and lots of waiting. And as a side note, CPS was investigating us.

All these things didn't leave much time for a breakdown that was brewing. Sure, there had been tears, but as I sat in the small hospital shower one night, I was finally able to pour out all my emotion before the Lord. And He asked me for her. Would I release my precious first child into His hands? His presence assured me there was no safer place for her to be.

For the next year, she faced ongoing medical issues and we had to continually trust Him with all of the "what ifs." There have been many subsequent moments of surrender in my life as I have dealt with fear and wanting to control situations so nothing bad happens again. He has met my fear with peace. He has loosened my grip with His gentle rebuke. Pain and suffering are a part of this world, but He has walked through the valleys at my side, His gracious strength carrying me along.

Seventeen years have passed and Courtney is heading off to college. And I find Him coming to me once again, asking me to release her, His small, still voice reassuring me that she is covered by the shadow of His wings.

Carrie Runn
Austin, TX

August 2

The great dragon was hurled down—that ancient serpent called the devil, or Satan, who leads the whole world astray.—**Revelation 12:9**

The temperature was expected to reach 108. Another scorcher. It was also a Monday—one of my walking days. Since the summer had been so brutally hot, I tried to get an early start. However, as I was driving to the park where I would start my five-mile route, I noticed the temperature had already reached 100 degrees. I was usually out walking before it hit 90, so this was going to be a test of endurance.

I have several different five-mile courses mapped out. During the heat of the summer, I chose the one that is predominantly shady. The streets are narrow and the huge oak trees offer welcome relief from the direct sun. This particular course is about 80% along the shady trail and 20% totally in the sun. That 20% is along a street named Dragon—to get to the top and come back down, I feel like I have worked hard enough to have slain a dragon. The steep grade, along with the direct sun, makes for a treacherous climb!

As I made the turn to start the trek up Dragon, I was pleasantly surprised to see that the sun was behind one lone, large cloud. It is crazy when I get excited about a cloud or two in the sky. Day in and day out, there had been nothing but a clear blue sky that radiates heat. At least this time, my walk up the hill would be less strenuous because of that cloud.

I have walked up and down this street countless times over the past years. Why did I feel led to write about it now? At first, I was just so elated about the cloud cover I felt the story would be about God's timely provision to shield me from the heat. But I couldn't get my mind off of "slaying the dragon" and I didn't understand why. After I got home, God gave me the answer.

A few days earlier, a friend had loaned me a book of short inspirational stories, *The Stained Glass Pickup* by Cathy Messacar. After starting this story, I came to a standstill, wondering where God was taking it. I picked up the book and just flipped through, hoping to be blessed with some divine inspiration. Low and behold, there was a story titled "Slaying Dragons," and underneath the title were the words from Revelation 12:9.

I looked up the verse, starting with 12:7, and continued reading through Revelation 13:1. The word "dragon" was underlined numerous times with the word "devil" written out to the side. How had I forgotten about the dragon and the devil association?

After the Dragon had been hurled down to earth, he pursued the woman who had given birth to a male child. The Dragon tried to destroy the women with torrents of water, but the earth helped her by swallowing up the water. "Then the dragon was enraged at the woman and went off to make war against the rest of her offspring—those who obey God's commandments and hold to the testimony of Jesus Christ" (Vs. 17).

I had been waging a war against Satan all week. He had been pursuing me with his lies and, in my weakness, was gaining a foothold into my life. I had walked up and down Dragon numerous times and had felt victorious afterwards, but not because I had won a spiritual battle—it was a personal, physical conquest since I had scaled the hill.

This time was different. God knew I was vulnerable. Satan had been beating me down, and I was weary and discouraged. God not only sent a shield of protection, that one lone cloud to keep the ferocious heat off of me, but also led me to His Word. My Protector was strong and mighty, covering me with His grace, mercy and love.

I will never walk up and down Dragon again without feeling victorious over the Enemy. Remembering the one day that God protected me from the Dragon's fire because I was powerless on my own, the truths from Revelation will be my armor for future encounters with the Father of Lies.

Satan is just waiting for the opportunity to wage war against those of us who try to hold tight to our Lord Jesus. Are you prepared to defend yourself?

August 3

*"For I know the plans I have for you," declares the LORD, "plans to prosper you and not to harm you, plans to give you hope and a future." —***Jeremiah 29:11**

Well, I finally did it. I just replaced my old set of trusted dishes that I've had since I began college. It's interesting how updating certain parts of your life can carry so much significance. Those plain, beige dishes have sat in my cupboards so faithfully over the years as I have seen dozens of close friends and relatives get married and register for their own new dishes; each time sending me into a world of wonderment over what kind of "stuff" Mr. Right and I would pick out to start our life together.

Realizing that I'm now in my thirties and still single, I decided that it's time to go ahead and pick them out myself. It was a bittersweet experience, really—getting something pretty and colorful and new while at the same time letting go of the timeline I had anticipated for my life.

As I took the old dishes out of the cabinet and replaced them with the new, God so sweetly reminded me of Jeremiah 29:11: "For I know the plans I have for you . . ."

A future as bright and colorful as my new Fiesta dinnerware? I think so. After all, Jesus came to give life and to give it abundantly. Whether that is life as a single woman or as a married woman, I will choose to trust that His plan for my life is a good one.

Jamie H
Austin, TX

August 4

Trust in the L<small>ORD</small> *with all your heart and lean not on your own understanding. In all of your ways acknowledge him and he will make your paths straight.* —**Proverbs 3:5-6**

Today is my son Trevor's birthday. Like most moms, my mind is just whirling with flashbacks. I woke up at 4:30 a.m., just like I have every year since that Monday, August 4, 1986, when my water broke. I can still hear those words, "It's another boy!" I can still feel his little head resting on my shoulder as I rocked him to sleep night after night. And I will never forget the sound of him singing "The Lord's Prayer" at bedtime. Oh, that was really precious!

Both Trevor and my older son, Zach, said their prayers every night. They both attended Pine Cove Christian Camps in Tyler, Texas, and told me their week at camp was the best week out of the whole year! Trevor was active in youth group and Young Life, plus he read all the daily devotionals I gave him for Christmas.

I thought Trevor's faith was strong. But then he went off to college, and the devotionals and his strong faith stayed at home. He did attend church occasionally while in Austin at the University of Texas, and I know he prayed. He listened when I talked about the wonderful sermons at my church, and he would occasionally read the inspirational emails I sent, so I knew he still believed. Unfortunately, obedience and surrender were not part of his lifestyle.

I pray every night that Trevor will allow God to be Lord of his life. I even pray for God to do whatever it takes to bring him to his knees in total surrender. The spring after college graduation, Trevor tore his ACL, during a potentially important step in his athletic career. I actually thought God had answered my prayer—that He had literally taken Trevor down to his knee for the purpose of showing him exactly who was in control. Afterwards, I prayed that in his despair and frustration he would see God working in his life and cry out to Him. That didn't happen.

My birthday blessing for my son is the same today as in the years past:

Trevor, my precious pun'kin pie, I pray that you will open your heart in complete surrender to God. You have been searching for the perfect "everything," never quite satisfied with what you have and wanting something better. I can tell you from experience that you will continue to search and feel like "Desperado" until you surrender to His calling. When you do, you will find the joy and peace that you have been longing for.

There is no person or material object that can ever fill the hole in your heart. Only God can do that. Seeing God, feeling His presence, hearing His words, is the greatest joy I know. But you must seek Him with all your heart and be desperate for Him. I want you to enjoy Him now, not later. There is nothing better. I know that in God's perfect timing He will open your heart, but my birthday prayer is that you will seek His free gift today. It's your birthday—please open His present. Amen!

I love you so very much, my dear one, and I find it almost inconceivable that God loves you even more. Happy Birthday, Trevor.

August 5

Many will say they are loyal friends, but who can find one who is truly reliable? —**Proverbs 20:6 (NLT)**

I have three "bestest" friends. We've been the Four Musketeers since 6th grade. Three (gulp) decades later, we're still tight, and our annual girls weekend is sacred. We grew up together in our church youth group. We whooped it up at lock-ins, roller rinks, slumber parties, car washes and softball games. We're kids of the '80s: Reaganomics, big hair, parachute pants, friendship pins and Duran Duran blaring from our cassette decks.

We all attended separate colleges and ended up as a stay-at-home mom, a paralegal, an environmental engineer and a TV producer. We're running full steam in different directions, bonded by our faith and our childhood together.

I know all about these amazing women. I know how they were raised because their parents helped raise me too. I know what broke their hearts before the first boyfriend did. I know who gave them their first kiss. I know what hacks them off. I know who is a terrible driver, who will pee if you make her laugh too hard, who can't ever drink vodka again and who still sleeps with her "little pillow."

We've all married honorable men who adore us and who encourage us to remain close. In fact, our husbands boot us out the door for girls weekend because they know we'll come back euphoric!

I realized several months ago that there's one thing I hadn't been doing with or for my "besties"—praying. Who better to intercede for them than me? I know the personality flaws that will drive their mates batty. I know which insecurities will need loving attention. I know which quirks are absolutely hilarious and make life with them so much fun. I should be praying for their marriages, for their kids, for their careers. And now, I am.

Tomorrow, I will go to lunch with one of the Musketeers. She's anxious to tell me about a break-through in her marriage. She's anxious to celebrate God's blessings and to take a look together at how He orchestrated certain really yucky events in her life to bring about abundant joy. I can't wait to tell her about a hard time I have looming over me right now. I cherish her advice. She knows me to my very core and she's not afraid to call me out when it's necessary.

Thank You, God, for good girlfriends! Give yours a call today and tell her you prayed for her! And then go get a cupcake together. It's OK. You can say your devotional book told you to!

Kristen Dark
Austin, TX

August 6

Let us not give up meeting together, as some are in the habit of doing.—**Hebrews 10:25**

My husband, Greg, and I were returning from a week-long vacation. My mother was taking care of our two children. Colette was 4 and MacGregor 18 months.

We had moved to Friendswood from the Montrose area of Houston when our daughter was 1 because Montrose was not a neighborhood where we wanted to raise a family. My mom was driving the kids back to Friendswood from her house in nearby Pasadena, when Colette asked her why there was so much traffic.

My mom, being the storyteller she is, told her there was so much traffic because families were returning home from church services. Colette was so excited. She told her grandma that her mom and dad took her to church too.

Mom thought, *Oh, thank God, my daughter has finally started taking her kids to church.* Colette then began to tell Grandma that's where the family gets chicken and french fries.

Needless to say, Greg and I decided the Lord was pulling at us through "Church's Chicken!" We heard the message and found a great church and church family.

Susan
Friendswood, TX

August 7

Dear children, let us not love with words or tongues but with actions and in truth.—**1 John 3:18**

Living on Lake Travis is like being on vacation every day. The view from the back of the lake house is amazing, especially in the evening because of the spectacular sunsets. The morning is equally enjoyable. I get my cup of coffee, sit on the back porch with my golden retriever, Holly, and just gaze at the water and listen to all of God's creatures. There is something so inviting about that early-morning lake. When it is as smooth as glass and there are no boats in sight, it just seems to be calling out to me, *Come on, Brenda. Let's go skiing.*

I am retired and can go skiing anytime. My dear husband, Austin, (who is my boat driver) is still part of the working world and on weekdays has places to go and much to do. Weekends, when he's home, are extremely busy on the lake and just not as inviting because the water gets so rough. I guess I complained one too many times to Austin about not being able to get on the lake when the conditions were "perfect."

One Sunday night, without my knowing it, he got out of bed to do paperwork for bids due the next day. He woke me up early Monday morning with a cup of coffee and told me to hurry up and get ready because we were going skiing. I was so excited! He had totally reworked his Monday-morning schedule so he could stay home and we could hit the lake while it was still smooth.

Going outside to drink my coffee and check the conditions, I was hugely disappointed! It was cloudy and breezy, the lake wasn't smooth as glass, and I knew I would be chilly. However, as selfish as I can be, I couldn't tell Austin that we should wait for another time, when it was "perfect." Especially after he had been up half the night doing work so he could stay home to take me skiing.

I jumped in the water and was pleasantly surprised by how warm it was, and it really wasn't so rough after all. I looked up at the sky and noticed a few rays of sunshine streaming through the clouds. While these weren't the "perfect conditions" I had been longing for, it was still wonderful to be out there skiing.

I looked into the boat and saw something better than "perfect conditions." Holly was in the back, watching me ski while wearing the biggest smile on her face. She had become quite the "boat dog" and was happy to be out there. She certainly didn't care that it was cloudy and a bit choppy.

Then I saw Austin's face. He looked so peaceful as he glanced back to watch me ski. He loves being on the water, no matter what the conditions. Then I saw God! I saw God in the perfectly unselfish act of love Austin demonstrated that morning. I was overwhelmed by the sacrifice he made, knowing that he did it not only because of his love for me but because of his love for God and his desire to be obedient to Him. Today is Austin's birthday, and I am so thankful and appreciative of my godly husband.

Happy Birthday! I love you!

August 8

"If you believe, you will receive whatever you ask for in prayer." —**Matthew 21:22**

I wish I could count all the times I sat through a sermon about the power of prayer. I've learned that sometimes we are told the answer is "no." And I've learned that sometimes we are told the answer is "not now." Here's a story with a different twist about the power of prayer.

When my triplets were very young, we lived in Austin. My mother lived alone in Dallas—my dad had passed away many years earlier. I knew from visits to Dallas, and from the frequent phone calls, that she wasn't really coping very well. I felt deep in my heart that she needed to sell her house and move to Austin to be closer to me. In every conversation, I would bring up the subject and ask her to consider selling the house. In every conversation, she would say "no." She'd usually get mad and tell me to mind my own business. But I knew that she was not healthy either mentally or physically and she shouldn't be so far away from family. I'd beat myself up after each phone call for not being more forceful and for being, frankly, a pretty bad daughter! In psychology, I guess I was called an "enabler."

At that time, we had a routine on Sunday. My husband and I would take our children to church. We'd come home, eat a light lunch, and then put the kids to bed for an afternoon nap. As soon as the house was quiet, I'd always call my mom. I'd talk to her at other times during the week too. But she always knew to expect a call from me on Sunday afternoon around 1 p.m.

I had another routine on Sunday. That was my prayer. Each Sunday during prayer time in the service, I'd raise the same prayer to God: "Please, God, give me the strength to stand up to my mom. Make me a better daughter. Let me find the words to convince her to sell her house. Change my mom's heart so that she would understand what I am asking is the right thing to do."

Nothing. Zilch. Nada. Each Sunday afternoon phone call was the same. I'd plead (some days more than other). She'd get mad. We'd end the phone call, and I'd call her a few days later. This went on for months!

Finally, one Sunday, I just gave up. Instead of my usual request, this is the prayer I lifted up to God: "OK, God, I give up. I turn the situation all over to You. I know this is in Your hands, to be fixed in Your time. Just promise me one thing. Do not let my mother die alone. Get me there in the nick of time."

That day, we got home from church, ate lunch, and put the kids to bed for their nap. I called my mom. This time, the phone rang, and rang, and rang. I knew that she wouldn't leave the house because she expected my call. In a panic, I called her neighbors and asked them to go check on her.

They found her sitting in her usual chair, semi-conscious and unresponsive. They called 911. I jumped in the car and drove to Dallas.

Eventually, I was able to transfer her to a hospital in Austin. I called my brother, and we made arrangements to sell her house. When she was ready to come home, she came to live with me, while we looked for an appropriate place of her own in Austin.

I look back at this circumstance and see a different lesson about the power of prayer—different from any I had heard in a sermon. The answer wasn't "yes," "no" or "not now." The answer was, "When you ask the right question . . . " God was waiting for me to turn the problem over to Him. Rather than asking God to make me stronger, I needed to tell God, "I turn this problem to You, because You have the strength of the universe."

Kathy W
Austin, TX

August 9

He makes me lie down in green pastures, he leads me beside quiet waters, he restores my soul.—**Psalm 23:2-3**

When I sat down to write this story, I struggled a little bit. Not because of the story—it will write itself. I couldn't figure out what the theme would be. At first, I considered "the power of prayer," but that didn't seem to fit. Finally, I thought about the previous church service. One of our "20-somethings" read Psalm 23 to the congregation, and the theme became apparent: quiet waters.

Yesterday you read about my mom—how she was widowed and finally moved from Dallas to Austin, where I live. This story happened a year later, when she was living in an apartment in an assisted-living complex. Her health continued to deteriorate and she finally had emergency surgery. The surgery went as expected (after all, she was a very sick woman by this time), and we were waiting for her to wake up from the anesthesia. She didn't wake up the first day or even the second or third. The doctors didn't know why, and at first they said she just needed more time. Eventually, she was placed on a respirator—not because she couldn't breathe on her own, but because the doctors said it would be easier for her to recover if she didn't have to work so hard.

Close to two weeks passed with little change. When I was with her each day, every ounce of my body would scream prayers to God to make my mom better. But then, I would go home, and I would think, *This is cruel. Why doesn't God just let her go?*

One evening, the phone rang and it was my mom's older sister. "We just had a family meeting," she said. "All of us (my mom's brothers and sisters) got together to talk about your mom. We have a concern that, at some point in the future, you will have to make some very difficult decisions. We just want to let you know that whatever you decide, we are behind you 100%."

The next morning, I went to the hospital as usual and got into the elevator to take a ride down to the ICU. When I got into the elevator, it was filled with doctors. They were whispering quietly about a patient. I was focused on my own concerns, so I paid little attention to their conversation. When the doors opened, the doctors got off first and began to walk briskly down the hall. One of the doctors turned back to look at me.

"Are you Mrs. Hawes' daughter?" he asked.

"Yes," I said.

"We have been talking about your mother. We have diagnosed her problem as a brain tumor. That's why she hasn't awakened from the anesthesia. Her brain waves are totally erratic, and we do not believe that she will get any better. We want to disconnect her from the respirator. We expect that she will pass away."

Immediately, I thought about the phone call that I had gotten from my aunt the night before. God had control of the situation—there was no doubt about it. And He wanted me to be at peace with the difficult decision that I was about to make.

At noon, they disconnected her respirator. She did catch her breath and began to breathe on her own. But she struggled for each breath. The nurses did everything they could to make her comfortable. She passed away seventeen hours later.

I look back at that time in my life, and I realize with all certainty that God truly did lead me to the green pasture and show me where to find the quiet waters. I've never had a moment of doubt that I made the right decision to remove her from the respirator.

As my children have grown, we've had the opportunity to talk about decisions that they have had to make. I'll ask them, "What do you think God is telling you to do?" So many times, they will answer, "I don't know. How do you know when He's telling you something?"

The circumstance of my mother's death is the perfect answer to the question. First, you go to God in prayer, asking for wisdom. If, after making the decision, you feel totally at peace, then you know that God was leading you to the still waters.

Kathy W
Austin, TX

August 10

And you also were included in Christ when you heard the message of truth, the gospel of your salvation. When you believed, you were marked in him with a seal, the promised Holy Spirit, who is a deposit guaranteeing our inheritance until the redemption of those who are God's possession—to the praise of his glory.—**Ephesians 1:13-14**

While waiting for the oil to be changed in my car, I decided to check the emails on my iPhone. It was one of these extremely hot Texas summer days, and the AC in the little waiting room was very much appreciated. I had been out walking prior to the oil change and still had on my very sweaty workout shorts.

My phone was in the palm of my left hand, which was propped on my bare left thigh that was crossed over my right knee. I must have spent 15 minutes responding to some emails and reading the online devotions I missed earlier in the morning.

If you are from Texas, you have probably heard of James Avery Jewelry. I wear one of his Ichthus hook-on bracelets on my left wrist. In Greek, the first letters of the words "Jesus Christ, Son of God, Savior" spell *ichthus*, which is the Greek word for fish. Early Christians used the fish symbol as an "underground" means of identification. Thankfully, today in the USA we don't have to be secretive and can boldly display symbols of our faith.

With the top of my left wrist resting on my left leg while I held my phone, the little bit of pressure exerted by typing and scrolling resulted in a fish imprint on my thigh. When I got back into my car, I noticed it was still there. However, by the time I arrived home, it was gone.

When I first noticed the fish on my leg, I thought it was really cool. It was as if I had been marked as a Christian, for all to see. But then as quickly as the fish made its mark, it disappeared. I don't know why I felt let down when it was gone. The little fish disappeared, but wearing a visual symbol of Christianity doesn't make me more of a Christian. My relationship with Jesus and what is imprinted on my heart is what matters.

Then I had another thought. What if I did have a large cross or fish etched on my forehead, for all to see? When I was in the Word—doing God's will, thinking good, righteous, honest, pure thoughts—that mark glowed brightly. And what if I harbored sinful thoughts, it disappeared—again for all to see? Would that change how I lived daily?

Certainly, that visualization is rather far-fetched. God is a merciful God, and I can ask Him to forgive my sinful thoughts and actions and help me be more Christ-like. Isn't that part of the sanctification process—to be transformed into His image?

When I find myself slipping, or my Christ-like imprint fading, I can refer to the God-breathed Scriptures He provided for teaching, rebuking, correcting and training me in righteousness (2 Timothy 3:16). Ephesians 1:13 guarantees I have already been marked with the seal of the Holy Spirit. His Truths and that seal of the Holy Spirit will bring glory to the Father—so that all may see the miracle of my transformed life.

"And we, who with unveiled faces all reflect the Lord's glory, are being transformed into his likeness with ever-increasing glory, which comes from the Lord, who is the Spirit"(2 Corinthians 3:18).

August 11

"You have covered yourself with anger. . . . You have covered yourself with a cloud so that no prayer can get through."—**Lamentations 3:43-44**

The heat wave during the summer of 2011 had been relentless throughout the state of Texas. On August 11, the city of Austin experienced its 25th straight day of triple-digit temperatures. Only one of the previous 39 days had been under 100, and that was a chilly 99 degrees. By this date, there had been a total of 57 days in 2011 over 100. To add to the heat wave, only.05 inches of rain had been measured in the previous 49-plus days. The drought had plagued the state for over a year.

In addition to the physical drought and heat wave in the summer of 2011, I was going through a personal spiritual drought. Intense negative waves of emotions were pulling me under and I felt like I was drowning in an ocean of boiling water. There was no relief from the scorching hot days of summer, and I couldn't escape Satan's heat either.

I was caught up in the hectic circumstances of life. I was desperately trying to dig my way out from the pit of hell to no avail. There wasn't anything traumatic about the circumstances, nothing horrific whatsoever. You know what the problem was? Life wasn't going my way and I was just fed up! It seemed that nothing had been going right and I was angry. I was completely wrapped up in my selfish pride!

When I first felt the joy slipping away and the anxiety and anger creeping up, I started saying Philippians 4:8 over and over. "Finally, brothers, whatever is true, whatever is noble, whatever is right, whatever is pure, whatever is lovely, whatever is admirable—if anything is excellent or praiseworthy—think about such things."

I knew I had to focus on that verse and not Satan's lies. It wasn't working, though. How could it? I was simply saying the words, but not feeling them in my heart. Satan kept on whispering that I was entitled to have things go my way. Instead of agreeing with God's plan for the day, I tried to re-work it my way. Satan was ready and willing to help convince me that God couldn't be trusted and His ways were not the best.

Where was God's voice? Where were the pure, lovely, righteous thoughts? I knew there was a battle going on. I had to get the Evil One out of my head. I kept on repeating that verse every time I felt the Enemy lurking around, praying for the words to permeate my heart and soul. Finally God blessed me with relief from the heat of Satan's fury.

I was flipping through a daily devotional and the words from Lamentations 3:43-44 jumped at me. The devotion wasn't even for August 11. God, through His mercy, led me to the exact page with the healing words He wanted me to read. "You have covered yourself with anger. . . . You have covered yourself with a cloud so that no prayer can get through."

There had been nothing but blue skies all summer long—rarely any clouds in the sky. But I had covered myself with a cloud of anger so that none of my prayers was getting through to God. He knew exactly what the problem was. Moments later, God led me to the words in another verse. "The LORD is far from the wicked, but he hears the prayer of the righteous" (Proverbs 15:29). Oh, I wanted to be back in the presence of my Heavenly Father, among the righteous ones. He was waiting so patiently for me to return to Him.

I know my merciful Father disciplines His children. We must go through the heat and parched land to appreciate the refreshing spring of living water Jesus spoke of to the Samaritan woman at the well in John 4. My merciful Father ended my spiritual drought for that period, lifting my cloud of anger. If He cares enough about me to bring me through my personal dry spell, in His perfect timing He will bring the clouds—clouds full of rain—to heal this drought-stricken land.

August 12

But I trust in your unfailing love; my heart rejoices in your salvation. I will sing to the LORD, for he has been good to me.—**Psalm 13:5-6**

On August 12, 1981, I gave birth to our second child—a boy. We already had a daughter, so now we had one of each. Our family was complete. All was good. Plans were on track. Only things did not go like they had with our first child.

He could not nurse well. He sweated terribly. He was like a washrag. He did not sit up when he should have or turn over on his own. We had him evaluated and found out he was developmentally delayed. I then pushed my doctors to find out why he sweated so much and why he was often sick. After an EKG and chest x-ray, we learned he had two heart defects that eventually needed to be corrected by surgery.

For the next year, I did PT with him to get him to sit up on his own, turn over and eventually walk. The same month he learned to walk, we had his heart fixed. He was 21 months old, and I knew all would be good again. He would catch up, and I would have my perfect family back. However, I discovered the only thing the surgery fixed was his heart. The delays were still there.

Into the world of "early intervention" we went. By nearly three years of age he had not spoken. At the first of many evaluations, he was diagnosed as "language-impaired." So we learned to sign. One night, I heard from the top of the stairs "Maaama, Maaama." When I realized it was him, I cried like a baby.

Many years of speech therapy followed, but he was talking. Now his diagnosis was "learning-disabled." I could do this. Lots of people with learning disabilities lead very productive lives. When he was 9, they wanted to change his diagnosis to EMH: "educable mentally handicapped." I went to pieces.

Barely able to get out of bed, all I wanted was to pull the covers over my head and stay there. This was not my plan. I had hopes and dreams about this child. I did not deserve this. I had done all the right things. My son did not deserve this—he was just a little boy. It was NOT FAIR!

I had prayed over this child nearly every night for almost all his life and God answered many of those prayers. Why didn't He answer this one? I thought of Job and got angry. I saw God and Satan playing checkers with my life. I railed against God. I shook my fist at Him. I told Him I did not want to have anything to do with Him if this was how He would treat me.

Then I did the only thing I knew to do. I went to my pastor. I talked and I cried and he listened. He gave me books to read and we talked more. I'd like to say I had an epiphany, but I did not. There was no aha moment.

God, in His incredible love for me, allowed my temper tantrum. He understood how much I hurt. He let me grieve the loss of all the dreams and plans that were tied to this child. He listened to all my angry words at Him and just loved me. And then He set about restoring me to Himself. He has shown me over and over again during the last 20-plus years that He is trustworthy.

I cannot count the number of prayers He has answered with a resounding "Yes!" I do not know why He said yes to so many but not to this "one." But it is OK. This has not been a quick journey; as a matter of fact, I am still on it. I see friends with lots of grandchildren, and I can still have a "what if" moment.

There are also times I have another kind of "what if" moment. What if God had given me exactly what I wanted? I would have missed this journey with Him where I got to see and truly experience His love for me. I know Him so much better now than if this had not happened. Knowing my Father is of greater value than anything I can think of. I would not trade that knowledge for anything.

Lou Ann
Austin, TX

August 13

I have led you through the desert for forty years. Your clothing has not worn out nor have your sandals deteriorated—all so that you might know that I am the LORD your God!—**Deuteronomy 29:5-6 (NET)**

Deteriorating sandals! Two pair in one summer. Um, both were gold sandals, but then I'm partial to metallic shoes. Both let me down in a bad spot. The first pair broke on the way to an important business engagement with my husband. We detoured back to buy super glue and managed to salvage the evening, but the shoes were finished.

The second pair disintegrated two weeks later while walking across a university campus. Exploring the possibility of entering a doctoral program, I heard that now-familiar flop-flap on a sole disengaging from a strap. I was there to revisit my dream of 25 years ago and see if that desire was still alive. The dream seemed to have disengaged itself too. No thanks, I like my current life much better than the one described to me that evening.

What was God telling me? Two pairs of my favorite sandals rejecting me at inconvenient times—coincidental? Perhaps, but I don't think so.

Sometimes I feel like my life could only be about remedying deteriorating things. My daughter made a personal list labeled "Things That Don't Work." My husband and I still laugh over that label when our fix-it list starts getting long again; it seems the list of things that work might be easier to compile.

At times like these, I remind myself that a God who can make clothing and sandals last for 40 years trekking through the desert can certainly make what is meaningful and worthy in my life last as long as I need it to last.

Maybe my favorite sandals deteriorated that summer, but not my marriage, my health, my relationships. God gives me what I need to get through this trek I'm on, just like He gave the Israelites the means to reach the Promised Land. He doesn't make the journey easy or without incident, but He provides so that we know that He is the Lord our God, traveling right there beside us.

Heavenly Father, remind me on a daily basis that You provide for my needs. Focus my thoughts on what works in my life thanks only to Your grace and goodness. In the name of the One who made sandals last for 40 years. Amen!

Elizabeth Ponder
Austin, TX

August 14

God has put all things under the authority of Christ and has made him head over all things for the benefit of the church. And the church is his body; it is made full and complete by Christ, who fills all things everywhere with himself.—**Ephesians 1:22-23 (NLT)**

My church had been growing by leaps and bounds. Growth is always good in God's kingdom. However, when there are not enough seats for folks, the visitors might not come back. The staff and elders had a tough decision to make about expansion.

The church had already been through several expansions in its 31 years, but the current sanctuary was no longer large enough, even with three Sunday services. The solution making the most economic sense was to keep the current worship center and remodel an existing building on campus (thus adding an additional worship center), and offer live, video streaming.

The plan was for the pastor to preach in one of the venues and the sermon would be streamed live, via fiber optic network in high definition, to the other. The teaching pastor would be seen life-size, center stage, and also on two side "image magnification" screens. While one site would see the sermon on video, both would have live worship music with two separate bands. The number of seats would basically be doubled for the 9:15 and 11:00 services, and the third service would be discontinued, all for a fraction of what a new 1,200-seat sanctuary would cost.

I totally understood the economics. The money saved by not building a new sanctuary could go towards other needs in God's kingdom. However, I wasn't real excited about watching a sermon on video. There would be no way of being sure which venue would feature the "live" pastor each week. I even questioned if perhaps the church was just getting too large for my personal preferences. Especially since church, as I had known it, would be different.

Negative attitudes like mine were anticipated. In the weeks before the going-live date approached, the congregation was kept updated about the construction progress, all of the changes in parking, nursery and Sunday school locations, *plus* the need to be patient with the newness of it all. But most importantly, the congregation was reminded that our church is being led by God to reach more of His children though teaching His Word. A very poignant reminder that church was not about my comfort and me; it was about being obedient and expanding God's kingdom.

Despite all the words from the pulpit, I still harbored skeptical thoughts. I was aware that my selfish feelings were totally out of line with God's plan. Technology is great—I love being able to watch a sermon via an app on my iPad if I miss a Sunday—but don't change my Sunday church experience.

The week before the go-live date, I had told myself that this would be my last Sunday of "normal" church. However, before leaving that morning, I read the verses from Ephesians 1:22-23 in one of my daily devotions: "The church is made full and complete by Christ." A person preaching a sermon isn't what church is about. It's all about Him! Why did I feel so pessimistic about this change?

As I sat down after the last praise and worship song, I reached for my purse and fumbled through it, searching for my reading glasses. *OK, this is it. The last sermon of church as I have known it.* I heard a strange noise as I was looking in my purse for my readers, but didn't pay much attention. But when I looked up, there was T.A., the Student Ministry Pastor at the time, center stage, announcing he was appearing via video streaming in HD.

Oh, my goodness, someone pulled a fast one! While I wasn't looking, the big screen had lowered (the noise I heard) and, sure enough, there was a larger-than-life T.A. on the stage. The new building wouldn't open until the following Sunday, but he was over there preaching and the congregation in the older venue was getting its first taste of video streaming. I didn't even have a chance to get all huffy about watching the sermon on the big screen. It was happening a whole week early.

A funny thing happened—I became so enthralled with T.A.'s message that I never even thought of him not appearing in person. That's how church is supposed to be, right? We go to hear God's message— as He speaks through a human—not to watch or worship an earthly person.

I just love my *new* church! Having two venues, watching the sermon on video or seeing the pastor live—it's all wonderful. I just never know what surprises God has in store for me. He is so clever and so much bigger than a large, center-stage screen.

August 15

Dear friend, I hope all is well with you and that you are as healthy in body as you are strong in spirit.— **3 John 1:2**

It was time for my annual well-woman checkup, including the mammogram and bone-density check. OK, I assumed it was my "well-woman" checkup. After all, I can't go through life expecting bad things to happen.

For all of the women who have had a mammogram, I know you can relate. You sit and wait for your name to be called so you can go into a room to have your boobs squashed. Then you go back to the small waiting room and sit and wait some more while the technician looks at all the pictures.

You sit and wait to hear that everything is all right so you can get dressed and go home. Those few minutes seem like hours, don't they?

Several years ago during my annual well-woman checkup, when I was waiting to hear those reassuring words, I was startled by the news that I needed to go back for a few more pictures. At that moment, I was overcome with fear.

I asked what was wrong. Had she seen something terribly disturbing or had the pictures just been blurry? Of course, those technicians are highly trained. They know exactly what *not* to say. She simply told me she would have to take a few more.

So, it was back into the room, then back to sit and wait again. Only this time my mind was all over the place. I had come for my well-woman annual checkup. *I feel wonderful. I exercise and eat well. I do my monthly self-exams. There's no history of breast cancer in my family. This isn't supposed to happen!* I immediately thought of my friends with breast cancer. Is this how it started for them?

"Ms. Gerland, everything looks fine. You can get dressed and go home now. Sorry for the delay." To say I felt a huge surge of relief when I heard those reassuring words is an understatement.

For this visit, technology had advanced since the previous year, and as each picture was taken, it was viewed immediately, to make sure it had come out clearly and that I didn't breathe at the inappropriate time. I had the urge to turn around and look at the screen, but I quickly realized that was futile—I didn't know what I was looking for. I assumed that the technician would be able to tell me before I left the room if everything was all right or not. Nope, it was back to the waiting room.

As I was waiting to hear those encouraging words again, I was so aware that in an instant, my life could change. My thoughts were interrupted by the technician's voice: "Everything is fine. You can get dressed and go home now."

Go home and continue with my life. No interruptions today. No, not this time.

My Father has blessed me with incredibly good physical health all these years. But how's my spiritual health? Just a few days ago, I wrote about a time of spiritual drought, a time of spiritual warfare with Satan. I feel that the enemy is constantly on the lookout for Christian bodies to invade. While I am trying to live a healthy lifestyle, I also need to make sure I am taking care of my relationship with God, so I am prepared to stand strong against the attacks from the Evil One.

I take my vitamins and supplements, eat my fruits and veggies, watch my cholesterol and remain committed to my exercise routine to stay physically fit. Am I being as proactive with my spiritual well-being?

As King Solomon said, "Do not be wise in your own eyes; fear and respect the LORD and shun evil. This will bring health to your body and nourishment to your bones" (Proverbs 3:7-8).

August 16

"Come to me, all who are weary and burdened, and I will give you rest. Take my yoke upon you and learn from me, for I am gentle and humble in heart, and you will find rest for your souls. For my yoke is easy and my burden light."—**Matthew 11:28-30**

While driving on the freeway, I noticed the traffic ahead slow down, and all cars merging over to the left-hand lane. I soon saw the problem. There was a large tractor-trailer, loaded down with a massive piece of machinery. Across the back, was a large yellow banner—STEER CLEAR, OVERSIZED LOAD.

The truck could barely fit in the right-hand lane, and it was moving slower than the other traffic. The cars behind it wanted to get around and the cars beside it were trying to stay a safe distance away. Yes, the truck was certainly something all the other vehicles wanted to avoid.

I thought about that yellow banner. Sometimes I feel like I am wearing one too. I carry all of my worries, problems, sins and concerns around with me. There are times the weight of the world gets me down. God didn't intend for me to carry my burdens alone, so why do I?

"Come to me" are three simple words. However, I will never receive the "rest" until I totally, honestly, wholeheartedly give all of myself to Christ. Why do I have such a hard time surrendering all to Jesus? Why do I pray about my trials, but try to fix them myself?

I don't simply carry all that extra weight with me; I also let the feeling of being overwhelmed consume me. Worry and frustration are written all over my face. Who wants to be around a person like that? Just like the cars trying to avoid that truck, people will avoid someone like me.

On the other hand, what about the woman who has trials, but has totally surrendered her life to the Lord? The woman who doesn't let her circumstances consume her, the woman who knows that Christ will help carry her load and allows Him to. This woman can go through her day with such peace and grace that no one else would ever know her difficulties. Others even flock to her because they sense she has something special.

Big trucks were built to carry large loads. God made us in His likeness, to depend on Him to help carry our heavy burdens. "Take my yoke upon you and learn from me." Jesus commands us to take His yoke. OK, but exactly what is a yoke?

The word isn't used much in our society today, but a yoke is a piece of wood used to hold two animals together (usually oxen) so they can *share* the load of pulling something heavy. Many times an older, more experience ox is paired with a smaller, younger one to teach it and to carry the heavier weight.

Jesus calls us to Him, so we can walk and work together. He is the Leader and we are to follow and learn from Him. The yoke Jesus spoke of isn't a physical piece of wood, of course. It is a symbol of being one with Him, through our obedience and submission.

Being yoked with the Lord, walking daily with Him, allows us to become more like Him—to know His Word, to love and trust Him completely. We learn to depend on His strength, not just our own. Although the weight may be lighter because we are sharing the load, the circumstances don't change. However, we will find His peace reigning in our hearts, instead of the anxiety, the stress, the feelings of hopelessness.

I want to be in total surrender to my Heavenly Father, so when I hear that whisper, "Come to Me," I am already there, yoked with my Savior, as we share the weight of life's trials. I want His glory and peace and rest to be written all over my face—not a bright yellow banner reading STEER CLEAR, OVERSIZED LOAD.

August 17

You will keep in perfect peace the mind [that is] dependent [on You], for it is trusting in You.—**Isaiah 26:3 (HCSB)**

Trying to beat the heat, my golden retriever and I went for an early morning stop-and-sniff. I can't call it a walk because she does more stopping and sniffing than walking. Holly is in no hurry; she has no deadlines or worries. Nothing distracts her from following her nose. She has all the time in the world to stop and smell whatever is in her path.

As we approached a curve, I heard a loud engine noise—much louder than one might expect on a quiet neighborhood street early in the morning. Next thing I knew a big yellow bus was coming around the corner. Oh, yes, the school buses must be practicing their routes because classes will start next week.

Those days are long gone for my boys and me, but even those of us without school-age kiddos can't totally block it from our minds. All of the stores have been advertising Back to School sales for weeks. There are school zones we must watch out for—not only so we slow down, but also so that we stay off our cell phones. And whether we have kids in school or not, we must all stop for the school bus picking up or letting off.

When my boys were still at home, the end of summer was a sad time for me. I just loved the slower paced summertime schedule. No homework, no school-related meetings. At least one, if not both, of the boys had some type of sports going on in the summer, but thankfully without the stress of classes. We could stay up late and sleep in. There was always a houseful of their friends and life was fun. Best of all, we just got to spend more time together.

The few weeks before the start and the first month of school always seemed so hectic. Michelle, a sweet friend who is mom to young boys, posted on Facebook: "Starting to feel like the faster I go, the behinder I get. Gotta love the days that lead back to school."

How easy it is to get distracted by all of the hustle and bustle of a new school year. As one who is no longer in that season of life, might I suggest that you stop what you are doing right now and take time to pray? Pray for a peaceful transition. Pray for the teachers and the bus drivers. Be thankful that you can afford the necessary supplies and a new pair of tennis shoes. If you can't, pray for God's help locating organizations that can offer assistance.

Take the time to focus on the wonderful world around you and all the many blessings God has provided. Don't get so caught up in your to-do list that you forget to worship the One who blessed you with your precious children in the first place. I know for many that the whirlwind associated with the start of school is nothing compared to all of the other storms in your life. However, there isn't anything that should take precedence over the time spent with your Lord.

My precious Holly has taught me many lessons on life. The way she enjoys her walks, taking time to stop and sniff is one example—so totally focused on the many enticing smells, she pays no attention to anything else, and not even another dog can divert her. I want to be so centered on Jesus, that the distractions of this world can't catch me off guard or take me away from His holy presence. There will always be storms in this life (or even spiritual droughts), but in my Lord's presence there is a peace and calm that surpasses all understanding.

"And he arose, and rebuked the wind, and said unto the sea, 'Peace, be still.' And the wind ceased, and there was a great calm" (Mark 4:39 KJV).

August 18

Let us fix our eyes on Jesus, the author and perfecter of our faith, who for the joy set before him endured the cross.
—**Hebrews 12:2**

There is an abundance of deer here in the Hill Country. Even though I live in an established community, there are deer everywhere. It's not uncommon to walk out front and find a street full of deer. And it's unusual to drive most anywhere without seeing a deer or two (or more) along the road.

While driving, being on the alert for deer is a must! And so is maintaining the speed limit of 30 mph. It's tough going that slow on a flat street, but it's even harder driving down a hill, riding the brake. It's not called the Hill Country around here for nothing, and there are plenty of them. Also, the local police do an excellent job of enforcing that posted speed.

I have become so leery of speeding that I often use my cruise control. However, when going down a certain hill one-half mile from my house, my speed inches up to about 36 mph (even with cruise control set on 30). One of the favorite places for the police to sit and wait is right at the bottom of that hill.

One hot summer afternoon, for some unknown reason, I decided to drive slower than the posted 30 mph and set my cruise control at 25. I did make sure no one was behind me though because I personally get a bit irritated when other drivers go slower than the posted speed.

As I was going down the little hill, I "glanced" down at the speedometer. I was curious what my speed would be with the cruise control set at 25. In that instant, I saw a something out of the corner of my left eye—and then, WHAM!

My side-view mirror suddenly slammed against my window, my car jolted and my knee smashed against the dash. I had obviously hit something, but what? Was it a deer, a buzzard, a dog? (I quickly felt a sense of relief, realizing a dog wouldn't be tall enough to collide with the side view mirror of my SUV.)

I got out of the car and looked around. There were no feathers. There was nothing in the street. There was no blood anywhere—only broken glass and pieces of my mirror. It was as if "something" came out of nowhere, crashed into my car and then disappeared.

A man out for a walk saw the whole thing. He said a deer simply ran across a yard, onto the street, jumped at my car and ran off. At the instant it jumped, I must have taken my eyes off the road and glanced at my speedometer. Thankfully, I didn't see the deer because my natural instinct would have been to swerve to avoid hitting it, even though I have been told repeatedly that's extremely dangerous.

Experts say it is better to hit a deer head on, and damage your car, than to swerve, loose control and run into another car or tree or ditch. However, I instinctively veer to one side or another to avoid a squirrel, and I know I would do the same for a deer.

Just as in my daily life, I try to escape from the trials, heartache or problems. I want to dodge the difficult times, but that's not possible. Just as experts say it is better to hit the deer head on, I must face my challenges head on. I can't turn and avoid reality. Only with my thoughts fixed on God's promises and truths can I get through the trials of life.

It only takes an instant for something to come along and blindside us. As long as we abide in Christ and keep His Word close to our hearts, we will be equipped to handle that sudden jolt. He is here to equip us with all we need to endure the daily challenges. There is no need to swerve off the road to avoid life—just keep your eyes fixed on Jesus and let it hit you head on.

August 19

Those who sow in tears will reap with songs of joy. He who goes out weeping, carrying seeds to sow, will return with songs of joy, carrying sheaves with him.—**Psalm 126:5-6**

On a recent trip to Home Depot, I purchased a variety of seeds for an herb garden. My husband, who is the gourmet cook of the house, always needs fresh basil, thyme, rosemary or cilantro, so I decided it would be fun to get it fresh from our own garden.

Driving home, I listened as two disc jockeys chatted. One of them had the opportunity to visit with her non-believing brother about God and share the Gospel with him. She expressed her heart's desire to see him accept Jesus as his Lord and Savior, but on that particular day, he didn't.

The other disc jockey commented that at least she had planted the seeds in the brother's heart. Perhaps she would see the harvest soon—he might chose to follow Jesus in the near future or it might take awhile.

Jesus said to His disciples in Mark 16:15, "Go into all the world and preach the gospel to all creation"(NASB). He didn't ask them to do it if they felt like it—it was a command. We don't have to stand on the street corner to preach the gospel, but if we are to obey His word, we are to plant the seeds in non-believers whenever we have the opportunity.

But what about those of us who know His Word, but fail to spread the gospel? What about those of us who spend years in Bible study, memorizing Scripture or reading daily devotions, but never put what we learn into action? What good is knowledge of the Word if we don't do something with it?

In Luke 8:4-18, Jesus told the Parable of the Four Soils, a story of a farmer who sowed seeds in four different types of soil. Jesus stated that "the seed is the word of God," and the seed that is planted on good soil represents "those with a noble and good heart, who hear the word, retain it and by perseverance produce a crop." If we have received the word of God and have it planted in our heart, we will never see the harvest unless we share it with others and apply it to the reality of everyday life through our obedience.

My husband won't be able to gather fresh herbs from our garden unless I get those seeds out of the packets and plant them. If I follow the instructions on the back of the seed packet and I am obedient in caring for them, there will be a harvest of fresh herbs in our garden. I must be patient, though, because it takes time for the seedlings to emerge.

Just as the seedling has to push through the soil as it grows, we must persevere in our journey through life with our Lord. I find it fascinating that an itty-bitty seed has the strength to rise up through the dirt, transformed into a growing plant. Read Matthew 13:31-32 about the Parable of the Mustard Seed. The smallest of seeds produced the largest of garden plants. Never underestimate the power of one seed, one new creation, emerging as God's precious work of art. God will pull us up out of the mud and dirt, to emerge as a new creation in the love of Christ Jesus.

There are no promises that life on this side of heaven will be easy, but God's steadfast promise of eternal life with Him is worth every tear we shed. The joy will come to those who are faithful to His commands and patiently wait on His promises to be fulfilled in their lives, and in the lives of others where we have planted seeds.

My dear sisters, let's all go out today and sow His seeds, shine His light, share His good news—all for the glory of our King. Sing your praises and your songs of joy to all you encounter today. May your harvest be abundant!

August 20

But he said to me, "My grace is sufficient for you, for my power is made perfect in weakness."— **2 Corinthians 12:9**

Whether your child is going off to kindergarten or college, there is a whole range of emotions for moms when it's back-to-school time. My oldest son's senior year of high school was the weepiest for me. Actually, it could possibly go down as the saddest year of my life.

It was inconceivable to imagine life without Zach. The thought of him being gone day in and day out was unbearable. I loved his company and our conversations. I enjoyed watching ESPN with him and talking about all the sports events, especially baseball. I treasured our life—together.

Zach was only going to college 2½ hours away from home in Katy to Austin. I could jump in the car and go have dinner with him on the spur of the moment if I wanted. I knew this separation anxiety I was experiencing was out of line. A single parent at the time, I focused way too much on my children.

Since my sister lived in Austin, we spent the night at her house so we could get to campus early for move-in day. When I went downstairs to get my morning coffee, Rhonda was in the kitchen sobbing. Her son's very close friend, Chris Ashmos, had been killed in a car wreck in the wee hours of the morning while returning to Austin from a baseball game in Houston with his dad.

I didn't know the young man, but it didn't take long for me to discover what an outstanding person he was—fun-loving and much loved. He was a few years older than my own son, a college student playing baseball at another university in Texas. Chris' death changed my life—forever.

I had the privilege of taking my son to college that morning, helping him unpack and arrange his dorm room. Chris' mom had the unthinkable task of making funeral arrangements for her son.

I cherished every minute of that move-in experience with Zach. I was amazed at the joy I felt. Over and over, I kept on thinking what a blessing it was to take my son to college. When all was unpacked and put away, it was time for me to go. I had been dreading that very moment for months, but God had prepared my heart. We said our good-byes, had a wonderful long hug, and I was off with a peace that surpassed all understanding.

But as I sat in my car, I sobbed. However, my tears weren't because I had left my son at college—my heart was broken for the mother who had to leave her son at the funeral home.

Visualizing her pain allowed me to see the blessing of my circumstances. That mom's loss led to a complete change of attitude for me. Not just for the day when I took my son to college, but also for every trial I have been through since. His grace is sufficient to help me endure my weakest moment. In my weakness, His power alone is what has and will carry me through.

That incident had another profound impact on my life. You see the events of that day were the reason for this book.

I felt the Holy Spirit urging me to share life changing, God-incidences with others. I had no idea what I was supposed to write, but that day was the beginning of this journey in my heart. Seven years passed before I wrote the first entry for this devotional, and 10 years after Chris' death, it was finished.

Chris' mom shared with a friend she feared her son would be forgotten. My hope is that this story will be another avenue for his memory to live on. I pray any mom who has been anguishing over a child leaving for kindergarten or college or anywhere in-between, will be on her knees in thanksgiving she has a son or a daughter to hug when it's time to say good-bye on that first day of class this fall.

As you pray for protection over your kiddos heading out the door, please also lift up parents who have endured the most painful event of all—the death of a child. And to think that our Father in heaven watched His only Son die on that cross, for your sins and mine. All the more reason to be on our knees in thanksgiving.

In Loving Memory of Christopher Reed Ashmos
June 28, 1983-August 20, 2003

August 21

Where can I go from your Spirit? Where can I flee from your presence? If I go up to the heavens, you are there; if I make my bed in the depths, you are there.—**Psalm 139:7-8**

God amazes me in so many ways—every day. He just meets me wherever I am, in whatever circumstance, and most times, I'm not even aware of His presence. He knows what I need before I even ask, making it easy to miss His fingerprints in my life.

Let me give you an example. I have written stories on the condition of my heart—a hardened heart, full of self. God has been carefully chiseling away at my selfish heart, but just a little bit at a time. I wasn't aware there could be "partial" organ transplants, but that's how God has chosen to work on mine.

When it came time to sign up for the upcoming fall Bible study at church, I wasn't too excited when I heard that the fall series would be based upon the Book of Nehemiah. It sounded boring. However, when I read the blurb in the church bulletin, I was sold:

Restoration Heartware: A study of the book of Nehemiah; Nehe. . . who? Not one of those weird Old Testament books! How can it be relevant to you today? Because the book of Nehemiah is about restoration of the heart. Standing on the rock-solid foundation of an intimate relationship with God, Nehemiah tackles an intricate restoration project. He is not afraid to attempt great things for the Mighty One as he partners with God in the work of restoring walls and hearts that have been in ruins for many years.

What a catchy title. I have never shopped at Restoration Hardware, but received their huge catalog, full of rather pricey items. I wondered what it would be like to go through a catalog, pick out a new heart, order it online and receive it in the mail? It would be less painful and faster than God chiseling away, little by little, at this old heart of mine.

Restoration Heartware sounded like it might accomplish the same thing, though. Only instead of searching through a huge catalog, I will be reading the tiny Book of Nehemiah, stuck in the middle of the Old Testament. Having God in charge of my new heart is certainly the better way to go—experience has proven that I am in much better hands with Him.

Psalm 139 is one of my favorites! In my NIV Bible, the theme is described as "God is all-seeing, all-knowing, all-powerful and everywhere present. God knows us, God is with us, and his greatest gift is to allow us to know him." Knowing that I can't flee from Him, knowing that He does know everything about me—those are the most incredible, comforting thoughts ever.

I have a feeling God plans on chiseling a little bit more of my old hardened heart each week during the lessons. *Restoration Heartware*. A Bible study He designed with me in mind. I can't wait!

August 22

There is a time for everything, and a season for every activity under heaven. . . . A right time to hold on and another to let go.—**Ecclesiastes 3:1, 6 (MSG)**

We have all moved in our various seasons of life, so we know about deciding what is a necessity to pack and what to discard. Even if only going away to college, more than likely you didn't take all of your belongings, especially if moving into a tiny dorm—there wouldn't have been space. At first you might have saved the high school keepsakes in your bedroom at your parents' house, but as the years went by, it became easier to discard those homecoming mums and prom dresses.

For a period of time, we want to hold on to those old memories, but then there comes a point when we are ready to make room for new ones—as we move from one season to the next. We don't forget the past, we just don't hold on as tightly. After all, it's not altogether healthy to live in the yesterdays or long for days gone by. God provided some helpful words in Isaiah 43:18: "Forget the former things; do not dwell upon the past."

Since my youngest son graduated from high school in 2005, the beginning of the school year has been a time of reminiscing. What a whirlwind of busyness those days were! Oh, but I loved it. However, the thought of my boys leaving home and going off to college used to be more than I could bear. Without my boys, I wasn't sure what I would do. I had allowed my identity to be wrapped up in being Zach and Trevor's mom. How could I let go and go forward?

Here it was, 10 years after my oldest son left for college. Ten years since I thought my world had come to an end. Oh, the thought of him going off to college just ripped my heart out. Lo and behold, with God by my side, I made it through to another season of life. As I was walking my dog that August morning, I realized it was the first day of the new school year. (That big yellow bus rolling around the corner to pick up all those kiddos was a definite indicator.) I felt a sense of relief that those school days were over, and I had graduated to this next stage.

While I cherish the memories, there came a point when I was ready to let go of school days and move on. At first, I was overwhelmingly sad on that first day without a child to take a picture of before he ran out the door. Amazingly, as only God can do, He offered up new opportunities and doors for *me* to run through. Through earnestly seeking His guidance and provision during that time, He answered my prayers for purpose and direction.

After my encounter with the school bus, I ran into a woman I hadn't seen in months. By the look on her face, it was evident that something was troubling her, so I just asked. The woman's daughter was now a senior in high school. This was it! One more year and she would be gone. That mom couldn't bear the thought of letting go.

Immediately my mind went back to my own struggle with letting go of my two boys, especially the first one. How sweet for God to arrange for us to meet that morning since I had walked her very same path. Hopefully, by sharing encouraging words of how God walked alongside of me I could help comfort her heavy heart.

Paul's words to the churches in Galatia hold true for us today: "Carry each other's burdens, and in this way you will fulfill the law of Christ" (Galatians 6:2). All that love we poured into our own children doesn't need to stop because they no longer live at home. One doesn't have to look too far to find some vessels that could use a hug and a listening ear—and a voice of experience.

Just think for a minute about the many seasons you have already been through and where you are right now. God got you through those, didn't He? If this is a time for sending a child off to college, don't hold on too tightly—let him/her go. Cherish what was, but know there are many more memories to be made. Strain toward what is ahead; press on towards that heavenly goal (Philippians 3:13, 14). God has a great adventure in store for you.

Someday, sharing your own experience of moving from one season to the next just might be the words of comfort another woman is waiting to hear.

August 23

And the God of all grace, who called you to his eternal glory in Christ, after you have suffered for a while, will himself restore you and make you strong, firm and steadfast.—**1 Peter 5:10**

Throughout the Bible, we read of all the "unlikely heroes" God used for His purposes. One might assume if God wanted to use anyone as a main character in His Book, that person would possess such characteristics as being highly esteemed in the community and of good moral character. Therefore, "unlikely" sounds appropriate because many of these heroes lacked such traits.

Let me remind you of some God used who wouldn't have been considered to be pillars of strength in their neighborhoods. Noah was a drunk, Abraham was extremely old, Jacob was a liar, Moses a murderer, Sampson a womanizer and Rehab a prostitute. David committed both adultery and murder, Jonah ran from God, Peter denied Christ, the Samaritan woman at the well was divorced numerous times and living with a man who wasn't her husband—just to name a few.

Despite obvious weaknesses, God used those, and many more, in His Book for His glory and His purposes. Have you ever considered being worthy in your weakness? Have you ever wondered how God would use your past hurts and mistakes in His master plan? Have you ever pondered how God plans on weaving your redemption story into the life of another? I have.

I spent so many years in darkness, trying to hide from God's glorious light, but one day I realized that He was going to use all those hurts and all my poor decisions so that I could reach out to someone else—to share His radiant forgiveness, mercy and grace with somebody else. That one day would be in His perfect timing.

A young friend called, asking if I could meet with her that afternoon. She is a planner, so I knew this was important to be so spontaneous. I thought I knew what was troubling her because we had talked previously about a situation. I asked God to give me His words of wisdom to share with her, I prayed for the Holy Spirit to guard my mouth and give me listening ears. I actually thought I was prepared, but her story caught me totally by surprise.

My friend's sister was in a bad relationship and made some poor choices. That was the root of the problem. The whole family was frantic, their life had been turned upside down and my young friend was overwhelmed. As I listened to her, I realized that one of her immediate concerns was that her sister had reached a point of no return and there was no hope for her present or her future.

I knew it was time—this was what God had prepared for me. This was the purpose of my years of darkness and shame, my road to salvation and my ultimate victory in Christ.

I shared how I could relate to her sister—I had in fact been just like her back in my younger years. The Holy Spirit filled my mouth with words of encouragement, suggestions on what to do next, truthful facts about the trials ahead, but most importantly, my story of redemption. If God was able to transform a wretch like me, His mighty act of "Amazing Grace" is available for everyone. That story of my redemption gave my young friend hope for her sister's life as well.

Why did I become such good friends with this young lady in the first place? I am old enough to be her mother, yet God orchestrated this relationship so that one day He would use my story of salvation to minister to her while so distraught about her sister? I am in awe that my Father loves me so much that He would use me for *His* purpose.

Big Daddy Weave's "Redeemed" could actually be a 2000s version of "Amazing Grace." I would love to include all of the lyrics because they touch my soul and speak so clearly of what God will do for each of us. You will need to Google them yourself, but just know that we are all redeemed and God has set us free. *I'll shake off these heavy chains, wipe away every stain. Now I'm not who I used to be. I am redeemed.*

None of us is who we used to be. However, we can thank God for who we were, for who we are becoming and for who we will be one glorious day when He takes us home.

August 24

Finally, brothers, rejoice. Aim for restoration, comfort one another, agree with one another, live in peace; and the God of love and peace will be with you.—**2 Corinthians 13:11**

In Boston, school summer vacation is eight weeks long. It wasn't that way when I was growing up—it was the whole 12 weeks of June, July and August. When we were still living there, I remember thinking, *Man, these poor kids. As if the lives they lead aren't demanding enough, now the only chunk of real down time they have to be kids is cut short.* It seemed to me that the children were being robbed.

In Texas, summer vacation is the whole 12 weeks, which seems *way* too long when you're the parent. So if I'm ever polled, I'll be sure to reply that somewhere around 10 weeks is probably just right.

So the anticipation for the first day of school builds up the longer the summer is, right? When the summer is short, you barely have time to dread/celebrate back to school. But when that 11th week rolls around, you've dismissed any nonsensical flirting you've ever done with home-schooling and you know there is indeed a light at the end of the tunnel of summer.

Then the first day of school arrives. After the whirlwind of getting breakfast on the table, making sure everyone was dressed and all the hair combed, teeth brushed, snacks packed, socks on both feet, shoe laces tied, photo-op cinched, it hits. You look around and abandonment sets in. The house is so quiet, the silence grabs ahold of you, squeezes your upper arms and it hurts a little, doesn't it? You look around the corner waiting for one of them to screech in on two wheels. But the house is empty and so are you.

So is this to brace me for what it's like when they really leave? For you Empty Nesters, I wish I could send you a bear hug. My solitude is from 7:40 a.m. to 2:40 p.m., and I can hardly stand it. I hope I don't become one of those crazy cat ladies when they all really leave for life, not just for learning.

It's amazing how much thinking you can do when five kids aren't all in the house at once. So I thought about God. He designed us with a blueprint that only He can fill. He wants us to want Him in all parts of our lives, especially the lonely ones. Is this first-day-of-school blues how He feels when we don't turn to Him in our lives? Does He await our time together as eagerly as I sometimes yearn for the clock to just hurry up and turn to 2:40? Does He ache? I have to guess it's no coincidence that we all have a level of separation anxiety, because maybe He does—on a God level.

Imagine that our Heavenly Father, up there in paradise, feeling so excited to spend time with us every time we turn to Him. It just never gets old. Maybe He taps His watch sometimes because He longs to have us near.

That second day they left for school seemed easier on my fragile emotions. So I met a friend for coffee. She told me that her son drove himself to school for the first time and it hit her like a ton of bricks. Terror set in as I was processing her story. Oh man, it gets harder, not easier? So I asked her how she was doing this second day of school and she half-chuckled, "Oh, I'm totally over it now."

I shared a full belly laugh of relief with her because I think I was too. Day 2, and we were over them leaving, but tickled pink when they walked back in the door. Even if we're just human and frankly need a break, ultimately we long to have them near too.

I'm sharing this with you because I want you to recall that gut-wrenching feeling of emptiness that first day and do something about it. Go sit with God and then make plans to have lunch with your single friend or elderly neighbor, write your college girlfriend who just lost her husband or make time to go to the hospital to cheer up your brother-in-law with a bag of gourmet jellybeans.

We all get lonely, but some of us don't have 2:40 to look forward to. Many folks are on a desert walk, and I have to guess sometimes it's more than they can bear. It's a lot like the parallel I drew earlier about the anticipation being relative to the length of summer. Think about those people in your life who have been lonely for a long time. Your time means more to them than you could ever know. What would Jesus do? He would connect, right? So what are you waiting for?

Lori Prehar
Austin by Boston

August 25

O Lord, you are my God; I will exalt you and praise your name, for in perfect faithfulness you have done marvelous things, things planned long ago. —**Isaiah 25:1**

The *Daily Guidepost* from 2010 was the first devotional I pulled off the shelf that morning. Author Debbie Macomber wrote, "As I grow older, I've come to recognize God's hand in my life more and more." It was 2011, but those words from 2010 were so appropriate. It was my birthday, so I was definitely getting older. And without a doubt, I saw God's hand in my life all the time.

I couldn't wait to read what Sarah Young had written in *Jesus Calling*. Yep, she was right on target too. She wrote about Jesus living inside of us, being involved in all aspects of our lives. But when she wrote, "your mind goes off in tangents . . . but do not be alarmed by your inability to remain focused on Me," I was stunned. Tangents? I had just used that exact word a few days earlier when describing to a friend my inability to stay on task. The dictionary on my computer defined tangents as, "to change quickly and suddenly to a different subject or line of thought." That was me for sure!

God was speaking to me faithfully in my devotions; what a nice way to start my day. Later that morning, I met my friend Linda for coffee. As often happens when moms get together, we talk about our children, both our joys and our concerns.

Linda and I had spent time together in Bible study and knew much about each other's lives, but there were some gaps. Since I had expressed anxiety about my grown sons, I filled her in.

I told Linda all about the boys attending Pine Cove Christian Camp every summer. They listened to Christian music, prayed and were active in church. We read our daily devotion every morning and had open conversations about Jesus. But when they left for college, all that changed. Now, I longed for their return back to God. I prayed for Him to do whatever it took to bring them back in total surrender. By faith, I believe they will return. However, because I know how much better-equipped they will be to handle the trials of life with God's help, I am anxious for the return to be sooner rather than later.

My younger son and I talk about God often and he prays—sporadically. He reads the devotionals I give him each year—some of the time. But one thing that Trevor does consistently is write an annual birthday letter. Later in the day, when I checked my emails, there it was in my inbox.

Talk about God having a hand in my life! This email was an answer to my prayers! It was as if Trevor had been listening to my conversation with Linda and was reassuring me that the Holy Spirit was active in his life. God certainly had his fingerprints all over Trevor's life too.

I had given Trevor a copy of *Jesus Calling* for his birthday and had mentioned to Linda that I was skeptical that he had even opened it. To my surprise, Trevor sited the reading for August 25 in his letter to me. He was so moved by what Jesus had to say to him that morning, he wanted to share it with me. Trevor goes off on tangents too, and all morning God kept on telling him to slow down and read his devotion. He had finally picked it up and more or less challenged God that it had better be some good stuff, since He had been bugging him all morning to read it. Trevor said the words on that page were direct answers to his prayer the night before.

Trevor also referred to his time at Pine Cove in his email and longed to get back to those days when his faith was strong. While reading, with tears streaming down my face, I felt God had just given me such an incredible birthday present. He had answered some of my own prayers and shown me in a powerful way His mighty hand at work—not only in my life, but my son's as well. And to think, God had this birthday gift planned all along. He is so amazing!

August 26

For the word of God is alive and active. — **Hebrews 4:12**

For my birthday in 2012, my husband, Austin, gave me two extremely meaningful presents. The first one I unwrapped was a box full of Sarah Young's *Jesus Calling* devotionals. God had placed it on my heart to share that book with others I encountered who didn't have a copy. To save me some trips to the Christian bookstore, Austin just got me a bunch of them. I was so excited!

The other present would only have significance to me. It was a clipboard with 66 white cards attached, each one with a number printed on it, counting backwards from 66 to zero. Why was that such an incredible present? Allow me to explain.

After working on this book for over two years, there were 300 devotions—only 66 to go. The timing of this milestone just happened to occur around my birthday. I often questioned if I would ever reach 100, so Rick Weber, my editor, and I rejoiced when he returned the edited #300 story to me.

Austin had been a tremendous source of encouragement during this project. He lifted it up to God every night in our prayer time. Then he made this creative gift for me. The premise was that as I received an edited devotion back from Rick, I could celebrate by tearing off a page from the clipboard. Thus, a final countdown to 366!

The 5x7 clipboard was large enough that I shouldn't have lost it on my desk, but I did. That weekend, I looked everywhere for it. My only conclusion was that I had accidently knocked it into the trash can beside my desk, and it was long gone with the weekly garbage collection.

Monday morning rolled around, and I was still pondering the mystery of the disappearing clipboard. However, it was time to write, and I started looking through some of my old journals. I came across one written back in 2007, when I "attempted" to read the Bible in a year. (I never got very far, though.) The entry I looked at covered Jeremiah 10-12 and John 14. John 14 was familiar, but I didn't remember Jeremiah 10-12, so I proceeded to look it up.

My new ESV Bible was still in the car from church, so I reached for my old, worn-out NIV Bible that had been semi-retired to my desk. As I unzipped the protective cover, I thought something didn't feel right. (It was quite tattered and detached from the binding; therefore, it was lovingly protected with a sturdy cover.) At that moment, to my utter delight, I saw my bulky clipboard in the very back of my Bible!

There are several possible explanations for how that clipboard made it to the back of that Bible and got zipped up inside the cover, but I will never know for sure. At that point, how it happened didn't matter as much as where I found it. Zipped up in my Bible? Really, God?

The homework assignment from LifeGroup the day before had been to record how God revealed Himself during the upcoming week. In my opinion, finding my clipboard inside my Bible was a significant revelation from God.

I just thought I had looked everywhere for that clipboard, but failed to look in the most obvious place—I failed to look to my Father. Jesus told us God knows what we need before we ask (Matthew 6:8), so I shouldn't have been so surprised when God had the answer the whole time. Even after I boasted to myself that I knew John 14, I hadn't recalled Jesus' words from verses 6: "I am the way, the truth and the life. No one comes to the Father except through me."

Jesus is the only way, and God's perfect Word provides all the answers—but we must open it for His truths to change our lives. My newer ESV went to church and other public places, but that old NIV just sat on my desk for a few days unopened. God meant for His Word to be read, shared and active in our lives, not neatly zipped up.

God is patiently waiting to share His word and reveal His promises with anyone who chooses to seek it. Is your Bible closed, sitting on the corner of your desk or table? Open it up! Allow the Father to reveal His treasures and be amazed today at the revelations you find in His Word.

August 27

As for God, his way is perfect; the word of the LORD is flawless. He is a shield for all who take refuge in him. For who is God besides the LORD? And who is the Rock except our God? It is God who arms me with strength and makes my way perfect. —**2 Samuel 22:31-33**

Life takes us on amazing journeys. As a young expectant mother, I worked feverishly to prepare for our upcoming child. A bit of a perfectionist and planner, I wanted our new baby's nursery to be just perfect. Not knowing if we were having a boy or girl, I pondered over what would be just the right fit. I decided to go neutral—green and white gingham, a definite '80s theme—and to decorate with Noah's Ark and rainbows.

The day our new baby boy arrived, my *Upper Room* daily devotional contained a prayer: *Thank You, God, for the many different kinds of rainbows You send to say "I love you."* What a testimony to God's greatness and love. He had delivered to us a perfect son in His likeness.

This son has grown into a wonderful, God-fearing young man who loves the Lord with all his heart, mind and soul. Throughout the years, I have continued to look at rainbows differently, as a definite gift from God, as a reminder that the God who created us is always with us and loves us. He is a God who made us in His likeness and has plans for us to prosper and honor Him. He is a God who promises us the ultimate gift: eternal life.

Fast forward 27 years, six months, and 17 days. Our son, born under the rainbow of our Lord, was given the gift of a son, our first grandchild. He and his wife were blessed with a baby boy. And the *Upper Room* devotional for *that* morning was entitled, "A Love That Knows No Bounds."

Wow, that is so powerful. It is just another reminder that God is almighty and continues to bring us unexpected blessings. The prayer on our grandson's birth was, *Oh, Jesus, Your love knew no bounds as You willingly sacrificed Your own life for our betterment. Touch our hearts this day with Your compassion. Amen.*

And, as we should only expect, in the early-morning hours following our grandson's birth, we were in a neighborhood park and yet another rainbow appeared before our eyes! I just pray that in spite of all life's unexpected turns and detours, we will continue to search for God's rainbows and know that each one reflects God's love and promise in our lives.

Pam
Katy, TX

August 28

When Pharaoh let the people go, God did not lead them on the road through the Philistine country, though that was shorter. For God said, "If they face war, they might change their minds and return to Egypt." —**Exodus 13:17**

The end of the journey was near. My daily devotional was about to become a reality. I looked back to the beginning, August 2010, and laughed out loud at the lofty plans I had once envisioned.

The idea was so simple. Everyone had God stories tucked away in their hearts. If I sent email requests to the wonderful women God had placed in my path, surely they would share at least one or more, resulting in 366 stories within six months. That is actually how I expected this book to progress.

My six-month time frame stretched to the three-year mark. In the beginning, it was a common occurrence to find a story in my inbox, sent from one of those ladies. However, within a few months, that changed. I don't remember exactly when the light bulb went off, but one day I realized God's intentions. He didn't plan a book compiled of stories written completely by others. No, His purpose was for the two of us to grow closer as I spent time writing my God stories.

The devotions I received from other women were such a blessing, but, honestly, I was mad at God. Why didn't He encourage more women to participate in my idea? He led me to this project, just to leave me floundering? Besides, I wasn't a writer!

God might not have blessed me with the gift of eloquent composition, but He gave me salvation through the death of His Son on the cross. I could compose volumes of all the miracles He performed in my life. The three-year book project was an opportunity to reflect on my own years of wandering aimlessly through the wilderness in search of a Savior, to remember the miracles He performed and to grow closer to my Father as we spent precious time together.

With devo 366 right around the corner, my Tuesday-morning Bible study started Priscilla Shirer's *One in a Million: Journey to Your Promised Land*. Each week I was more in awe of God's handiwork as I related the lessons to my own life. God deliberately led the Israelites into the wilderness; He purposely took them on a 40-year trek that could have taken less than a few months.

Where would we be today without those 40 years? How much of our Christian faith is based upon the miracles God performed to save the Israelites? The parting of the Red Sea, the Ten Commandments, the daily manna from heaven, to name a few. Don't those miracles serve to encourage us and place our hope and trust in God? Didn't we learn the importance of obedience to His commands?

God planned those 40 years, not only to demonstrate to His chosen people He alone would provide for all their needs—He alone is God, worthy of all glory—but He also knew that even today we would need the reassurance of those Biblical truths and the miracles He performed. The journey wasn't just for the Israelites; it was for you and me as we struggle through our own wilderness.

Had I known God's plan was for me to write so many devotions, I would have changed my mind early on. I wasn't prepared for that task, just as the Israelites weren't equipped to fight against the people who resided along the Mediterranean coast. God took me down the longer, more difficult route to prepare me, to strengthen me and to demonstrate what He alone was able to accomplish. I am thankful beyond words that God and I developed such an intimate relationship during those three years. Had this book happened my way, I would have missed out on the joy of the journey. Oh, my Father deserves all the glory for His perfect plan!

From those 40 years in the wilderness, we gained proof of God's unwavering character, so we need not fear the road He leads us on, even when the uphill battle makes no sense. "By day the LORD went ahead of them in a pillar of cloud to guide them on their way and by night in a pillar of fire to give them bright light. Neither left its place in front of the people" (Exodus 13:21-22).

As Christians, we are on the same journey to a promised eternity in heaven—we simply travel different roads to get there. Regardless of the hardships and trials we encounter, we have the opportunity to live in victory of that ultimate prize. He's walking in front of us, leading the way. Will you follow?

August 29

The grass withers and the flowers fall, but the word of our God stands forever. —**Isaiah 40:8**

While doing some house cleaning, I saw a Bible on the shelf that belonged to my youngest son, Trevor. He no longer lived at home, so it shouldn't have been there either. (As I already mentioned, when he left for college, he also left his faith behind.) I am not real sure why I felt the impulse to open it. I assume the Holy Spirit was urging me on, knowing I was about to find a treasure.

I opened it to the page where you can write the date it was given. The words from Isaiah 40:8 were printed across the top of the page. It was presented on August 4, 2001, and I had written, "On the occasion of your 15th birthday and your 8th trip to Pine Cove (Christian camp). On the way home from camp you wanted to stop and get a new Bible for your birthday present." I had forgotten all about that stop at Lifeway Christian Bookstore that Saturday afternoon.

Also, tucked in the Bible were some notes he had written, apparently from a Bible study, either at Pine Cove or Young Life in subsequent years. I felt like I had found a priceless hidden treasure! What a comforting reminder that in the past, God's words had been alive in his life.

My sons absolutely loved their week at Pine Cove every summer. Their first time to go was in July 1994. Trevor had just completed the first grade and Zach the third. Both went every summer after that until they graduated from high school. They would come home on such a spiritual high, just on fire for God!

I know Zach and Trevor will never forget their time at Pine Cove, even though their lives now don't reflect it. I am thankful to have been financially able to send them to camp. What a blessing that my sister Rhonda suggested they go because her three children attended and she knew the spiritual experience they would have. What a God-incidence that two spots opened that first summer for them to attend and He continued to lead them back every year.

It was no accident that they attended Pine Cove. God was present in their lives back then and I know He's still there, waiting patiently for Zach and Trevor to seek His presence again. God planted His words in their memory bank, not only at camp but also in church, Sunday school, and through the devotions we read together. Someday they will recall His truths.

My treasure hunt didn't stop there, though. That very same day, still cleaning, I opened a drawer in Trevor's room and found another Bible—a Thinline NIV that was easier for him to carry around. When I opened it, I found it had been presented "to Trevor by Trevor" on September 25, 2001. In a six-week period, he had acquired two new Bibles, purchasing one himself! I thumbed through and found a bookmark at the first page of James. He had several verses underlined and little notes written on the pages throughout. What a powerful place in the Bible to hang out!

I will stand firm in my faith and comforted by the promise: "*The grass withers and the flowers fall, but the word of our God stands forever.*" God was doing some mighty work when Trevor was 15 and I am so thankful for the hidden treasures I found that day. Satan will try, but he cannot take away what we read and store in our hearts. God's truths are more powerful than Satan's lies, and His will be the words that prevail throughout all eternity.

August 30

To the Jews who had believed him, Jesus said, "If you hold to my teachings, you are really my disciples. Then you will know the truth, and the truth will set you free." —**John 8:31-32**

Sometimes I wonder what I did before the Internet. How did I ever live without Google? All too often I find myself searching how to do something or asking what something means. Back when I was a little girl, the encyclopedia was my go-to reference. But that meant going to the local library for the most current edition. Now, I just go to my phone or computer. It seems that the standing response for an unanswered question is "just Google it and find the answer."

What other resources, besides the Internet, are readily available to find out how to do something? One that comes to mind, perhaps because I recently needed it, is the owner's manual for our cars. Have you ever read it cover to cover before driving your vehicle? Most of us don't pull it out until we see a weird icon on the dash.

My son and I switched cars one weekend because he needed my larger SUV to move. I was forced to drive his small foreign car from Houston to Austin. I wanted to set the cruise control on the highway, but didn't know how. I had to pull over, get the manual out of the glove box and search "how to set cruise control." Perhaps if I had read the book before driving, I might have remembered how to do it, but that obviously didn't happen.

What about the Bible? Isn't it the manual on "how to do life"? For years, my Bible spent more time on the shelf than in my hands. Back in those days, I would wait until I had a problem, then pull out my Bible, cry out to God and search for help to get through the most current crisis. But slowly, ever so slowly, my Bible found its way into my hands more often. It has been a lifelong process, but His lessons are being etched into my daily thought process.

If we want to be prepared for living, we need to know the Master's instructions. We need to know what God has to say before the crisis. When we have His word stored in our heart, we are better equipped to handle any situation as

214

it comes along. When we know His truths ahead of time, we are free to live and make decisions, knowing His will. Oh, the freedom in having answers and knowing what to do!

John 8:36 says "if the Son sets you free, you will be free indeed." Jesus freed us from the consequences of sin and showed us the way to eternal life with God. When we know God's Word, when we follow Jesus' teachings, when we do His will, we will know the truth He desires for our lives. He wants us for eternity and He clearly has left us His manual on how to live life here on earth, in preparation for that great reward.

August 31

"A new command I give you: Love one another. As I have loved you, so you must love one another. By this everyone will know that you are my disciples, if you love one another." —**John 13:34-35**

Today marks the feast day of St. Aidan. I didn't grow up in a Christian tradition that celebrated the heroes of our past through such feast days, but when I first heard the story of Aidan I recognized that his was a story I wanted to remember. It was during the summer of 2000 when I was traveling through England that I visited the ruins of an old monastery on a tiny island on the eastern cost. There I first heard the story of Aidan and fell in love with all he represented—so much so that eight years later, I even gave my newborn son the name Aidan.

Aidan lived in the 7th century and served as a monk in the small Celtic Christian community of Iona off the western coast of Scotland. The Roman Empire had attempted to spread Christianity across England, but had met with little success. So in the 7th century, the Iona community started sending missionaries to England to convert the people there.

The first missionary they sent was a harsh man who attempted to bully the people into following Christ. Needless to say, he had no success and left the mission field full of bitter contempt for the people he had tried to reach. Aidan was chosen as his replacement, and from the very beginning, Aidan did things differently. He made it a point to learn the local language (English), which was something his predecessor hadn't done. He took the time to discover the needs of the local people and used his church on the island of Lindisfarne to serve the poor and the orphans of the land. He didn't stay in his church either, but went to the people and got to know them as friends. And he saw the church in England start to grow.

Aidan is credited with bringing Christianity to England, but he did so through acts of charity and love. Where others had despised the people, Aidan became their friend and so demonstrated the love of Christ to them.

His story reminds me of the hymn that states, "They will know we are Christians by our love." Often we can become so convinced of the rightness of our faith that we expect others to simply see things as we do and join us. We can even develop attitudes of contempt for those who don't abandon their sinful ways and follow Christ. But as Aidan's story reminds us, it is not through contempt and condemnation that people see Christ most clearly. Aidan served the people's needs, he got to know them for who they were, and he loved them above all else. And that is what changed the course of a nation.

I wanted my son to carry a name of such a great hero of the faith like Aidan. For I think his story is one that Christians of any time who desire to spread the word of Christ in this world can look to for encouragement and guidance. For it will always be through our acts of love that people will see Christ most clearly in us.

Julie Goss Clawson
Austin, TX

September 1

Better is one day in your courts than a thousand elsewhere. —**Psalm 84:10**

Back on August 25th, I wrote a story about my son Trevor. He had written me a birthday letter that made my heart jump with joy because he shared how God was working in his life. I was so excited that Trevor had actually read a daily devotional that I had given to him and was seeking God again after a long dry spell. What an incredible gift—a message that the Holy Spirit was pressing Himself on Trevor's heart.

My editor, Rick Weber, and I exchanged a few emails about our kids and their spiritual journeys after he had read that story. I told Rick that while I was thankful Trevor had read his devotional one day, I wasn't so naïve to assume he would read it consistently. As I wrote my thoughts to Rick, a song came to mind that left me with a warm feeling of peace.

I could hear Chris Tomlin singing "Better is One Day" to me. For that one day, Trevor had been communicating with God, praying, reading His Word, seeking His presence, asking to renew their relationship. Perhaps Trevor won't read from his devotional again for months, but I will be thankful for the one day he spent with his Lord. I will continue to pray for Trevor's spiritual renewal and return to his Savior, and I will keep the words of Psalm 84:10 singing in my heart.

Without a doubt, "*better is one day* [that Trevor spent] *in His courts than a thousand elsewhere.*"

September 2

"For your Father knows what you need before you ask him." —**Matthew 6:8**

Best-selling author and preacher Max Lucado wrote a devotion publicly acknowledging an unnamed man for being influential in his faith walk during his college years. His story made me think about my own journey. When was my turning point? Was there someone I could thank?

My grandmother and mother were certainly instrumental in laying the foundation in my childhood. Mom made sure I went to church every Sunday and my grandmother introduced me to devotions and the Bible, but I didn't develop a relationship with Jesus until years later. Fast-forward to being 30 years old and giving birth to my first son. A friend mentioned I should start thinking about Mother's Day Out and pre-school. Looking back, her suggestion was a turning point.

This friend was a darling stay-at-home mom of two precious boys, had a beautiful home and a seemingly happy marriage. In my eyes, she had it all. I followed her recommendation, and when Zach was old enough enrolled him in the Early Childhood Development Center (ECDC) at a Methodist church near my home in Katy, Texas.

Little did I know what a huge step that was in my spiritual walk with Jesus. Being a church-affiliated program, I discovered that members received priority registration. Since the pre-school was the only accredited one in the area at the time, it was extremely tough to get in. So, of course, I joined the church.

The journey continued. After a few years, I was chairperson of the ECDC Council, similar to a PTA president, just on a much smaller scale. I was a Sunday school teacher and on a few committees at church— playing all the right parts, but missing Jesus, the main character.

All this reminiscing prompted me to think about my friend. I had lost track of her, and I am positive she had no idea what an influence she was in my faith walk. She was also an unlikely candidate to be a hero, but isn't that just like God? Throughout the Bible, He used the most imperfect people to do His work. I say my friend wasn't the most perfect candidate to be influential in another's faith walk because she was also desperately struggling with her own.

She didn't have the perfect life that I assumed she did. Her marriage was crumbling during those years and later ended in a nasty divorce. However, God still used her to open the door that led me to His throne. We never know whose life we may influence, but I think it's so amazing that God can and will use anyone for His purpose.

Reflecting on this spiritual awakening, I realized something else profound—I wasn't even aware I was on a journey searching for a relationship with Jesus. What little bit I knew about God was enough, or so I thought. I was able to pull off being a Christian on the outside, but on the inside there was a total void. The feelings of emptiness were overwhelming, but I didn't have a clue what to do about it. Jesus was missing and I didn't even see He was waiting to be invited in.

But God knew. He knew exactly what I needed and how I would find it. I wasn't capable of planning the journey on my own, so He did it for me. All the twists and turns, each dead-end, every peak and valley— He was aware what I would face along the way and who I would encounter. He had it planned perfectly before I ever had the wisdom to ask.

How am I to thank my Heavenly Father for all the turning points in my life? I can start by giving Him all the glory for even being here today. Why He didn't take me out at the height of my disobedience and sin, I will never know. What I do recognize is that He has been unrelenting in His pursuit, and He knew exactly what was required to bring me to the throne of mercy and grace.

September 3

(Wisdom) has sent her servants to invite everyone to come. She calls out from the heights overlooking the city.
—**Proverbs 9:3 (NLT)**

Several years ago, in a Tuesday night Bible study, we were discussing our prayer life. One of the ladies, who was very soft-spoken and always had something worth hearing, made the comment about how important it was to kneel when praying. She asked us all to consider, for just one second, to whom we were praying. I will never forget Sandra's words, so soft and sweet, yet so emphatic, "We are praying to *God,* for goodness sakes! Don't you think He deserves for us to bow down before Him?"

Maybe it was what she said or perhaps how she said it, but that night before going to bed was the first time ever I went to my knees in the quiet of my own home. I remember it so well. Being on my knees did make a huge difference. It was a powerful time with God. I was struggling and pleaded with Him. I called out to Him, feeling an intense closeness and positive He was listening.

My husband and I had recently moved to Lake Travis from Katy, Texas. Now, that's not a huge move, only about 160 miles, but it was significant because I had lived in Katy since 1982. I wasn't exactly sure why we had uprooted; it wasn't a move of necessity, totally of choice. Who wouldn't want to live on beautiful Lake Travis in the Texas Hill Country? But why had we come and what was I to do here? I honestly didn't know the answer and I was floundering in confusion. God was on to a new chapter for my life—recently re-married, retired, and an Empty Nester. I had left my familiar surroundings for this new, lonely, beautiful location on the lake.

There was no question that God was up to something, but I still felt like I was lost in the wilderness, or actually lost in paradise. That night, on my knees, I cried out to God for wisdom. Wisdom to discern His will for my life. Wisdom to follow His direction. It was such an incredible time we spent together. I still didn't have answers but I did have peace, knowing I had finally turned my dilemma over to God.

The next morning, I was reading from *The One Year Book of Proverbs,* and the devotion for that day started out with the words from Proverbs 9:3. I read on, in total amazement. Wisdom is available to anyone; all we need to do is ask for it. Better yet, God wants us to have that wisdom. "Wisdom is calling, have you sent your RSVP to Wisdom's invitation?"

The night before, I was on my knees in total reverence of God. Yes, I had sent my RSVP to Wisdom. I was there before God, giving up any control I thought I had in my circumstances and seeking His gift of wisdom. I had felt such peace after praying because I had done what God asks from each of us—to surrender our worries to Him. Total surrender, though. He knows our heart and He can't be deceived.

God didn't give me a calendar of events that night, but He did provide me the assurance that wisdom was mine, because I surrendered. Today, years later, my life is rich and full—God did fill my calendar in His timing.

I look back to that night in Bible study and that devotion as one of those "markers" for my life. First of all, ladies, never underestimate how God will use us. He spoke through Sandra to get me to my knees in prayer that night. Then God gave me such a clear affirmation that He will provide the wisdom I so desperately pleaded for, after earnestly asking.

On this date of 9/3, please re-read Proverbs 9:3. Commit it to memory. We are all invited to Wisdom's party. You have the invitation. All you need to do is send your RSVP!

September 4

"The man who has two tunics should share with him who has none, and the one who has food should do the same."—**Luke 3:11**

Finally, there was a break in the triple-digit temperatures! When I went out to feed the deer that morning, there was an ever-so-slight coolness in the air. My boys, daughter-in-law and some of their friends were expected after lunch for an afternoon out on the boat. The air was breezy though, signaling a rough time on the water.

My husband and I went to church and by the time I walked from the parking lot into the sanctuary, my hair was a mess. The wind had really kicked up, but at least with the lower temperature, the breeze wasn't so blistering hot.

I was excited as we drove home after church. It would be the last outing on the lake with the kiddos for the summer. As we got closer, I noticed what looked like clouds on the horizon hovering around the top of the hills. It couldn't be rain clouds though—we hadn't seen those in months. When we had to stop for the fire truck going through the intersection, reality set in. We were seeing clouds all right—smoke clouds! With the high winds and extreme drought, the conditions were perfect for wildfires.

We immediately turned on the local news channel when we arrived home and saw what was going on. Wildfires were popping up all over central Texas. There was one six miles down the road from the house. Another across the lake to the west. Looking to the north or south from my back porch overlooking the lake, there were huge clouds of smoke, and the smell of destruction was in the air.

The once-blue sky was now hazy with smoke and there were whitecaps on the lake because of the high winds that were gusting to over 30 mph. The festive mood was gone as we listened to the reports of home sites around Lake Travis being threatened by the fire.

The city of Bastrop, a historic small town east of Austin, had three separate fires burning. Homes were being evacuated all over the town and in the rural areas. We sat glued to the TV, watching the infernos engulf homes and trees.

The following morning, Labor Day, conditions deteriorated. The three Bastrop fires had merged into one massive wildfire and over 400 homes had been destroyed. The flames were raging out of control. Schools were being used as emergency shelters for the people who had fled their homes with whatever they could grab as they ran out the door.

By late Monday night the winds died down, but by Wednesday there were a total of 33 fires across the state, 120,000 acres had been burned, over 1,500 homes destroyed and four people had lost their lives. Before the week was up, the Bastrop fire of 2011, which was the largest and most destructive, would end up going down in the record books as the most catastrophic wildfire in Texas history.

But folks who lost their homes expressed their thankfulness to be alive and safe. People unaffected were reaching out to help. There were collections sites all over Austin for such items as diapers, non-perishable food, socks, underwear and household items. Meals were prepared to take to emergency shelters and firefighters. People rallied to help their neighbors whose lives have been forever changed by the horrific tragedy.

This was certainly one of those times that we had nowhere else to go but to God. He is the only One who can provide peace and comfort at such a time. This was also the week leading up to the 10th anniversary of 9/11. Folks rallied together in unity back in 2001. Yes, God does bring good out of every situation. *And we know that all things work together for good to those who love God, to those who are called according to His purpose* (Romans 8:28).

September 5

You keep track of all my sorrows. You have collected all my tears in your bottle. You have recorded each one in your book. — **Psalm 56:8 (NLT)**

Several years ago, if anyone had told me that one day I would be pleading with God to bring rain, I would have laughed right in their face. Not this sun-worshipping girl! There is nothing better than a warm day, feeling the rays of the sun shining on my face.

Then I moved to Lake Travis in Austin and the drought began. Watching my backyard oasis retreat daily, seeing the boat docks rest on dry land instead of the crystal blue water, watching the yards turn brown and the trees die, seeing cows trying to drink from dried up ponds, driving by fields of crops burnt to a crisp . . . those were all signs of too much sun and too little rain.

I longed for dark clouds and the sound of rain pounding on my roof. Days of such dreary weather sounded like a heavenly forecast. It took a destructive drought for me to yearn for a deluge. I never thought rain could lift my spirits until I witnessed what devastation the lack of it caused. The rain that I used to loathe became the desire of my heart.

During the years of drought on Lake Travis and the surrounding Hill Country, the few days of measureable rainfall were unbelievably delightful. There were actually times I sat outside and cried with joy as I watched, listened and smelled the showers from heaven. I also wept in complete disbelief that something so dreary as rain would brighten my day, restore my soul and fill my heart with thanksgiving for the One who gave the precious gift.

The prolonged drought and its devastating effects have forever changed my perception of the beauty, joy and necessity of rainstorms. I have a plaque that reads: *Life isn't about waiting for the storms to pass; it's about learning to dance in the rain.* I certainly rejoice at even the prospect of rain, but what about the everyday storms of life, such as death, divorce, unemployment, wayward kids, sickness, car repairs, rising gas prices, shattered dreams?

Do I welcome those kinds of storms into my life? Did I dance and cry with joy when I received the call informing me my son had been taken to jail on a DWI charge? Or how about the call that my dad had passed away? When I saw the fiery inferno of the World Trade Center, I trembled in fear. The devastating news that my friend Vickie's son was killed or that my friend Pam's son had MS certainly didn't have me jumping up and down. Watching my children endure hardships has probably been the toughest of all trials and the buckets I have cried for them definitely weren't filled with tears of joy.

No, I didn't dance through those storms of life, but I have learned some valuable steps. God has used every trial and every tear to bend and shape me to who and what I am today. The sanctification process will not be complete until Jesus calls me home, but I am thankful God loves me enough to continue the refinement procedure.

I have only just begun to see His glory in the rain and appreciate the storms. While I don't wake up every morning praying for devastating news, I do begin the day by asking God to equip me to handle whatever call I receive. As I walk out into the storms of everyday life, I pray to see His umbrella of love over me. He won't keep me out of the bad weather, but He will offer His protection in the sun or in the rain.

My dance lessons with Jesus have been breathtaking! Just to be held close in His arms and be twirled and guided—as He leads.

September 6

He has showed you, O man, what is good. And what does the Lord *require of you? To act justly and to love mercy and to walk humbly with your God.*—**Micah 6:8**

The morning of September 6, 2013, was going to be a milestone of a day. After three years of working on this book, I was prepared to hit the send button and let her go.

Walking to my study, I was almost giddy with excitement. I had anticipated this day for so long. I didn't know what to expect after I sent it to the publisher—I was just focused on the moment. The previous three years had been life changing, and I felt God holding my hand as we walked from the kitchen to my desk, to take this huge step together. Little did I know He was upholding me with His righteous right hand for the shocking news I was about to hear.

The ringing of my cell phone interrupted my thoughts. Why was Pam calling so early? Oh, no! Something must be wrong. My heart leaped with anxiety. Unfortunately, some very unsettling news had come via the phone years before about Pam's sons. The first time was the news that her oldest son had been diagnosed with leukemia. The second time was to inform me her other son had Multiple Sclerosis. Thankfully both are doing well now, but for some reason I expected to hear alarming news about one of her boys.

This call was worse than alarming. A very close friend had died the previous night during open-heart surgery. A routine procedure with very unexpected results.

Not Keith! As I talked to Pam, I put the call on speaker and went to my husband so he could hear the conversation. We held each other and wept. *Not Keith!*

It is hard to imagine life without Keith Ulatoski. He was just one of those "one-of-a-kind" kind of guys. He was the glue that kept us all together. He was a God fearing man and there was no doubt some rejoicing went on in heaven upon his arrival home. But back on this earth, tears of sadness were flowing.

Last June I sat next to Keith at a wedding. He asked how the book was coming—something he always did when we saw each other. He genuinely cared about my project and looked forward to receiving a finished book. Keith shared that he was currently going through *Grace for the Moment Daily Bible,* with devotional writings by Max Lucado. He found it to be very inspirational and thought I would too, suggesting I get a copy. Less than a month later, a book arrived.

Honestly, I had forgotten about our conversation and wondered where this book came from. There was no indication who had ordered or paid for it. After doing some research, I discovered the sender was Keith, and the book, of course, was *Grace for the Moment Daily Bible.* That's just who Keith was. Doing random acts of kindness out of the overflow of God's love from his heart.

During the funeral, all three of Keith and Debbie's grown children shared their hearts. Daughter Jen read what Keith had written in a Bible he gave her on May 12, 2013. *"I hope this helps you on your faith journey. Faith is indeed a journey and not a destination. The destination is eternal life in heaven and I look forward to spending that with you. Love, Dad."*

Keith lived life to the fullest. Perhaps his attitude had something to do with a near-fatal car wreck during his college years. On December 8, 2012, Keith shared this post on Facebook: *Forty years ago today I laid in a snow-covered corn field coughing up blood while passing in and out of consciousness. I made my peace with God and expected to pass on to the next life. At times since then, I ponder for what purpose He chose to leave me in this world. At other times I think it may be simple. . . "to act justly and to love mercy and to walk humbly with your God"* (Micah 6:8). Keith lived by those words.

When someone dies, it is expected for the family and close friends to be filled with sadness over the loss. However, Keith's passing impacted countless people. Keith was loved by so many because he loved so many well. He might have had a diseased heart, by human standards, but his spiritual heart was healthier than most. Keith's heart was God's instrument, used for the Father's glory. Keith was indeed his Lord's faithful, humble servant and his legacy will live on.

My plans for the morning of September 6 certainly went a different direction. I re-opened my final edit for this book that Friday, trying to decide how I could honor Keith without making too many changes to the finished product. God led me to something within the pages of this manuscript as I glanced through and revealed it wasn't just quite ready to be sent.

I know in my heart God so lovingly pointed out the oversight so I could take the time to make those little changes—and write these words. Yes, Keith was genuinely interested in this book and being able to include this tribute to honor such an incredible man is a privilege. Thank You, Heavenly Father, for blessing our lives with Keith's.

My prayers go out to the family and all his friends as we now must go on without him in this life. But we can look forward to seeing him again in heaven. Debbie shared John 14:27 with me several years ago and I will close with Jesus' promise for Keith's family: "Peace I leave with you; my peace I give you. I do not give to you as the world gives. Do not let your hearts be troubled and do not be afraid."

In Loving Memory of Keith Raymond Ulatoski
October 5, 1955-September 5, 2013

September 7

Then the LORD said to Moses, "I will rain down bread from heaven for you. The people are to go out each day and gather enough for that day. In this way I will test them and see whether they will follow my instructions.—**Exodus 16:4**

My prayer life hadn't been very consistent, *again*. Previously I made the commitment to spend more time on my knees and actually felt much closer to God. But something happened—my quiet time with God had been very limited and I hadn't been on my knees at all.

One of the devotionals that I randomly picked off the shelf spoke directly to me. The devotion for the day dealt with getting priorities in order, not allowing the busyness of life to get in the way of our time with God. Nothing should take precedence over Him. What I read wasn't anything I didn't already know. It was, however, just what I needed to be reminded of.

I went outside, thinking I could connect more intimately with God. There was a fine drizzle coming down, and I looked up and smiled at the precious gift. Just a few days ago I wrote about the severe drought in this part of Texas, and I was just sure God had heard my very short popcorn prayers pleading for rain.

However, my smile quickly faded. Suddenly I was furious with God! Out loud, I announced my disappointment. *Really, God? This is it? We need rain so badly and all we get is a little drizzle? Why can't you just open up the sky and bring the rain? You are the only one who can do it, and You just won't give us a soaking downpour?*

God probably laughed at my little temper tantrum. He created this earth and knew very well there was a drought. Today, God gave us drizzle, and that's enough. The Holy Spirit quickly reminded me of the words from 2 Corinthians 12:9: "My grace is sufficient for you."

For some strange reason, I looked up at the fine drizzle and thought of the manna God provided for the Israelites in the desert. They were to gather only what they needed to eat for that day. It was God's way of testing their obedience and it also kept them dependent upon Him to provide. A simple lesson in trust and obedience.

Was that the meaning of the drizzle? The bread of life coming down from heaven, providing just enough of what God wants to give at the moment? If He gave us everything all at once, would we still depend on Him and seek Him? My one-on-one time with God had been anything but sufficient lately. If I didn't need anything from Him, how much worse would it be?

God wants us to present all of our requests to Him, through our prayer and petitions (Philippians 4:6). He wants to hear from us, He wants to have a relationship with us. But he knows our human weakness of self-reliance—if life were perfect, some of us might not reach out to Him.

There is nothing more important to the quality of my relationship with God than the quality of my prayer life. I have read that fact, I have heard sermons on the subject, and I have experienced it. On this morning, I was reminded once again.

That little drizzle was just a gentle reminder to start my morning off with God and to be thankful for His provision, no matter how large or small. His grace is enough. All I need will be found in His word, in His presence.

"Very early in the morning, while it was still dark, Jesus got up, left the house and went off to a solitary place, where he prayed" (Mark 1:35). Want to be more like Jesus? Find more time to pray like Him.

September 8

Submit to one another out of reverence to Christ.—**Ephesians 5:21**

My sister and I had been on the phone for almost an hour when I heard that familiar beep. "Call waiting" was at the bottom of my phone and at the top, my husband's name. I don't like switching calls, putting the person I am talking to on hold, so I just ignored it.

After talking for so long, one might think I could easily end our conversation and take Austin's call. Had I been speaking with Austin, and my sister or one of my sons was to call, I would most likely have told him I "needed" to take it. How easily I can put my husband on the back burner.

My husband seems to always be on the phone. Being a small business owner, he doesn't have an office assistant to take his calls, and he rarely sits at a desk during normal office hours. He conducts much of his business on his cell phone out on the job site. I am accustomed to being told he needs to take the call from whomever it is calling. Sometimes it's like I am the one being placed on that lonely back burner, but try to understand that his work is very important, especially in this economy.

Austin was driving back home one night from Houston while I was having dinner with some girlfriends. Before leaving the restaurant, I called to see how far away he was. I wasn't surprised when I heard his voicemail—he's always on the other line.

Fifteen minutes later I tried again, but still no answer. It was almost 9 p.m.—not very likely a business-related call. He was probably chatting with a friend and had decided he could talk to me later. For some reason, being ignored irritated me this time.

When he finally answered on my third attempt, he told me he was on the other line with someone and would call me back. I never ask who he's talking to, but this time I did. Only his old friend Bob? My feelings were hurt even more. If it had been a customer questioning a job, it would have been OK. But Bob was more important than me? Yes, I totally overreacted, but it was the principle of the matter.

He did call back after his conversation ended, and knew I was a bit upset. "What if it had been an emergency?" I asked.

While I waited for Austin to get home, I thought about the situation. I do the same thing to him. I decide that it's all right to *not* answer his call when I am talking to someone else. What has happened in my marriage that my husband is no longer the most important caller? If it just happened every so often, it wouldn't be such an issue. However, it was becoming the norm. For both of us. That worried me.

We later had a heartfelt talk about our phone manners. I wasn't trying to make a big deal out of our not taking each other's calls—I just felt we needed to make sure we weren't ignoring the importance of our marriage. Cell phones have made instant access an expected way of life and constant communication a part of our busy days. But do we overdo it? Do we let the ways of this ever-changing world consume us? Girls, we must keep our husbands toward the top of our priority list in this hectic life of ours, and not on the backburner.

We have all experienced what happens when we get too far out of His Word and too far into the world. We are commanded to put God first above all else, to love Him with all of our heart—not once, not twice, but four times in

Deuteronomy 6:5, Matthew 22:37, Mark 12:30 and Luke 10:27. That won't happen if He's simply an afterthought in our daily lives.

Out of reverence to our Lord, we are also commanded to submit to our spouse. Placing either our husband, or God, on the back burner isn't the role of a godly woman. Isn't it sweet that God cares so much about our marriages that He's right there, in the middle of a potentially threatening situation, to help us keep our priorities straight?

The Evil One will do all he can to destroy a Christian marriage, but God is the Protector of the relationship He created between a husband and a wife. "Therefore what God has joined together, let man not separate" (Matthew 19:6).

September 9

You God, are my God, earnestly I seek you; my soul thirsts for you, my body longs for you, in a dry and weary land where there is no water.—**Psalm 63:1**

I have written many stories about the drought in the Texas Hill Country. In July 2010, Lake Travis was actually considered "full," and that was also when I began this book project—full of excitement and on fire for the Lord. In only two year's time, the lake level dropped 50 feet below that full mark. Unfortunately, at that two-year mark, I was dealing with another type of drought—a spiritual drought.

There have been several stories written about praying for rain, trying to be patient and thankful for God's provision of drizzle and being mad at God for withholding the rain. In one devotion, I confessed to having the audacity to lash out at the Lord because I longed for a deluge and He didn't deliver. In another, I felt the Holy Spirit was leading me to rejoice in the difficult circumstances or storms of life—teaching me to dance in the rain.

I reflected on that story for a while. Wanting the rain so badly would actually make learning to dance in it easy. I felt the Holy Spirit nudging me and then I heard His whisper. *How about dancing in the drought, Brenda?*

The low lake levels, the stringent water restrictions, the dead trees and crops; those were the worldly by-products due to the lack of physical rain. But the Holy Spirit was prodding me to think of my own spiritual drought. I was craving rain more than Jesus.

Allowing Jesus to fill my jar with His living water and not looking to other sources for fulfillment is the only way to end the drought in my spiritual life. I can identify so well with the Samaritan woman Jesus encountered at the well in John 4. Jesus purposely sought her out, knowing she thirsted for His promise of living water to fill her empty jar of life. He has done the same for me.

Just as I have longed for torrential downpours to fill the lake, there has also been a craving in my heart for fulfillment in other areas. I have been looking for "something"—if not rain for the lake, more cute clothes, a job for my son, additional stories written by other women for this book, better organizational skills, inclusion within certain groups, fewer wrinkles, youthful muscle on this aging body, rekindled romance in my marriage—I am sure you get the picture.

There is no coincidence about the timing of this book and the physical drought in the Hill Country. God purposely sought me out on Lake Travis and led me to this book project to spend precious time in His presence! What better location for me to learn complete dependence on His living water? He knew the best place to teach me about the spiritual drought was to put me right smack dab in the middle of a physical one.

Just as it's impossible to miss the cracks in the soil and the dried-up coves and creeks, there is no way to hide my empty heart from God. Nothing can satisfy the thirst of my soul but God. Until His love is enough, nothing else will be—not even a deluge of rain to fill the lake.

The Lord provided such perfect words in Jeremiah 17:7-8: "But blessed is the man who trusts in the Lord, whose confidence is in him. He will be like a tree planted by the water that sends out its roots by the stream. It does not fear when heat comes; its leaves are always green. It has no worries in a year of drought and never fails to bear fruit."

You sought me in this dry parched land and I feel Your presence. The love I longed for is seeping into the barren crevices of my heart and I wait expectantly to be filled to the point of overflow as I learn to trust in You and You alone. Amen!

September 10

"I have heard the Israelites' complaints. Now tell them, "In the evening you will have meat to eat, and in the morning you will have all the bread you want. Then you will know that I am the LORD your God." —**Exodus 16:12 (NLT)**

"Wow, it's really cold in here!. . . . My hair is so darn thick. . . . That waiter didn't put very much ice in my drink. . . . I didn't get enough sleep last night. . . . She is always so rude on the phone. . . . All I got in the mail today is a bunch of bills. . . . I hate cooking every night. . . . There's absolutely nothing good on TV."

I complain *a lot*. It's an easy thing to do. It really takes no amount of ingenuity or creative thought. It's so common, it's cliché. You'd think the fad would eventually get old, but instead, it seems to just get a sharper edge. I hate to brag, but I'm an exceptional complainer. I'm so good at it that I do it without even thinking about it.

When I think of all the complaints I launch in a day, I shake my head in wonder that God tolerates me for even a second. I can't imagine how putrid my words are to His glorious ears or how the ungratefulness behind those words turns His stomach.

I am a woman, born in an era of extraordinary advancement. I'm a woman born in the United States of America, where I'm free to vote, to worship, to wear whatever clothes I choose, to be educated and to choose whom I will marry. I sleep in a warm, soft bed next to a man who would never strike me. I never worry that I will go without food. My home, office and luxury vehicle are kept at a consistently pleasant temperature. I could go on, but the guilt is starting to get too heavy. . . . Ooh, another complaint!

I used to read about the Israelites following Moses through the wilderness and roll my eyes at their ungratefulness for manna and quail. I'm worse! I complain about having to eat leftover casserole for lunch! I would throw a tantrum if I had to eat it for lunch every day!

How dare I? I mean, seriously!

Thank You, Father, for pouring out Your favor on a filthy sinner such as me. Thank You for allowing me to know You. Thank You, Father, for each and every one of the little things that I take for granted. Please bless and protect my sisters who live in fear, poverty, abuse, neglect and squalor. May they know that You are God and may they feel Your precious comfort this day. Please make me aware and sicken me when I complain despite the abundance You have poured out on me. May I be a woman who is salt and light among others and may my words be music to Your ears.

Old habits are hard to break. Here's to kicking this one to the curb!

Kristen Dark
Austin, TX

September 11

He who dwells in the shelter of the Most High will rest in the shadow of the Almighty. —**Psalm 91:1**

Have you ever discovered that God had you on a detour, totally unaware, until you could see His work in hindsight?

That happened to my husband, Jay, and me 10 years ago when Jay was in the process of selling the company he partnered. Through God's blessing, the sale of the business was successful and the appointment was scheduled for Jay to meet with the attorneys and sign the closing documents. That was to occur on a Monday. Jay had planned to attend a technology conference on Tuesday and Wednesday, then come back home.

He had asked me to go with him on his trip, but caught up in the busy life of three elementary kids who had just started the school year and a 2-year-old at home, I totally forgot to get a babysitter arranged. Highly unusual for me because I loved to join Jay on business trips—a "mini-vacation" from my hectic mommy world!

Things didn't go as planned. Sound familiar? While I was waiting in the carpool line at school Friday afternoon, Jay called to tell me that the attorneys needed more time to finalize documents, so the closing meeting was rescheduled for Wednesday. Jay decided that he would not attend the two-day technology conference since he couldn't be there for the final day's presentations, so he would only travel to New York on Tuesday evening, returning late Wednesday evening.

That Tuesday morning was a beautiful fall day in New York City.

That Tuesday morning was September 11, 2001.

That Tuesday, Jay had planned to be attending the technology conference on the top floor of the World Trade Center.

That Tuesday, Jay had wanted me to be with him on his business trip.

That Tuesday, there would be no survivors from the conference—all attending died.

As I watched the events of 9/11 unfold on the television at home in Austin, I grieved about the terrible tragedy and loss of life. I was also amazed beyond comprehension that God had orchestrated a detour that protected my husband, and kept me from joining him on the trip.

While I don't fully understand why God didn't orchestrate that same plan for everyone there that day, I do know that His plan for Jay and me while on this earth isn't over yet. I can live in confidence, and not fear, because He ordained my days before I was even born (Psalm 139:16). I know that God will never forget me because He has engraved me on the palms of His hands (Isaiah 49:16) and that nothing can separate me from His love (Romans 8:39). I don't have to worry, or be anxious, or live paralyzed by fear about the yet unknown tragedies that I will have to face because I live and walk daily in the shelter of the Almighty and I can *rest* in His shadow (Psalm 91:1).

And I will be eternally grateful for a detour that I didn't realize I was on.

Where are you on your journey? Do you need to look in your life's rear-view mirror? Have you thanked Him for the detours He's put you on, even the tough ones? Does the Enemy torment you with fear and worry? Have you accepted God's invitation to walk with Him and rest in His shadow?

Lisa McEntire
Austin, TX

*Note from Brenda:
When Lisa sent this story to me, I couldn't help but notice the connection between the Scripture she include, Psalm 91:1, and the date 9/11. Just might be the perfect words of hope to hold in our hearts on this date.

September 12

God does not judge by external appearances.—**Galatians 2:6**

As I have grown in years, I have filled my head with all kinds of myths. I thought as long as I exercised, I would never get cellulite in my legs or gain weight. Plastering on expensive facial moisturizers would prevent lines and wrinkles from forming. Covering up my gray hair would keep me looking youthful. Also, if I dressed like a youngster, I would feel like one.

Thankfully, as I have grown older, I have also filled my head with God's truths. "Being a wife of noble character is worth far more than rubies" (Proverbs 31:10)—or even expensive facial creams. God commands me to love my neighbor in Matthew 22:39 and to seek Him in Matthew 7:7, not search for the newest techniques to get rid of cellulite. To walk humbly with my God (Micah 6:8) and be honest and transparent is more essential than covering up my gray hair. That the words of my mouth and the meditations of my heart are pleasing in His sight (Psalm 19:14) is far more imperative to focus on than the numbers on the scales. Being filled with the Fruit of the Spirit that Paul writes of in Galatians 5:22 should be my goal, not mastering the advanced Pilates movements. I know all that, but still have this desire to look in the mirror before I leave the house.

While waiting for my Pilates class to start one fall morning, a blind woman walked by. I watched as she went into the weight room and began her workout with a personal trainer. I was quite humbled at that moment. What if I couldn't see myself in the mirror? Would I still be so concerned about my weight and my wrinkles? Most importantly, why do I even worry about the Brenda I see in the mirror? What about the characteristics I can't see? What does God see?

There's nothing wrong with being concerned with getting enough exercise or wanting to take care of myself. But I must make sure I know God's truths and not focus on the lies of the world. I want to keep my eyes on Him and His purpose for my life and not allow exercise or trying to capture my fleeting youth become idols. "I am fearfully and wonderfully made" (Psalm 139:14), and if that means I am a woman created to nourish both my internal and external being, I can embrace that.

Through the God-breathed Scriptures, I am assured that I am His. I pray to seek the approval of God as I go out into the world each day, not the mirror. I am His workmanship, created in Christ Jesus to do good works, which God prepared in advance for me to do (Ephesians 2:10). Inside and out, He created me, and you. He is enthralled with our beauty (Psalm 45:11).

I give my praise to El Roi, the God who sees me. He sees my heart and all that I do. I can't conceal anything from Him. I can't put on moisturizer or wrinkle cream and hope my sins disappear and go undetected. He sees all the wrinkles in my life and still loves me. Jesus' death on the cross removed all those transgressions, not some magic cream or surgical procedure.

I don't plan to stop any of my anti-aging practices, but as I grow older, I pray that through God's grace and mercy, I will continue to grow in wisdom and obedience to El Roi—the God who sees.

His eyes are on me. I feel His gaze, along with His righteous right hand, guiding me through this journey of life. I pray that all I do, all I am, my total essence, is pleasing in His sight.

September 13

The LORD himself goes before me and will be with me; he will never leave me nor forsake me. — **Deuteronomy 31:8**

After reading my daily devotions, it was time to pray. It looked like another beautiful morning on the lake, so I decided the back porch would be the prayer spot.

The sun rises in the front of my house, but I don't have a good view because of all the trees. However, I knew it was slowly peeking over the horizon because of the different colors in the sky. The back of my house looks out on Lake Travis, and today was one of those "smooth-as-glass" days on the water. The western sky was still gray, with some very slight shades of pink going on. What caught my attention, though, was a bright round circle of light in the water close to the boat docked across the lake.

I soon realized the mysterious light was the sun rising in the east, reflecting off of the aluminum on the boat. As the sun rose, another circle appeared on the surface. In my little imaginary mind, these two round circles of bright light on the water could have been two eyes. I have become so used to seeing and hearing from God, so I just decided that perhaps an image of Jesus was going to appear out of these reflections of light.

In *Discerning the Voice of God*, Priscilla Shirer said that we need to "expect" to hear from God, and I do. I also "expect" to see Him. So I patiently waited for the face. *The nose is forming, and look, I think I see a mouth!* I just knew the Holy Spirit had sent me outside to pray so that I would see the image of Jesus on the water. Really far-fetched, I know, but I was expectant and anxiously awaiting for Him to appear.

Within a few more minutes, the circles of light disappeared. I realized that there wasn't going to be the face of Jesus in the water formed by the reflection of the sunlight, and I just laughed at myself. I was trying so hard to see His face; could this be a story in the making? Oh well, I decided to just get on my knees and pray. As soon as I shut my eyes and quieted my soul, I heard the Holy Spirit whisper: *Instead of trying to make me appear, just TRUST and know that I am here!*

Why do I seek "proof" of God's presence? Why do I keep on trying to make Him appear, like a magic act? Sure, it is a moving experience to have that happen, but that doesn't make Him more real. He is with me, even if I don't see a reflection of His face on the lake. He created the water and the sun. Isn't that enough proof? He is with me, even if I don't hear His voice every minute. Through the God-breathed Scriptures, I have His precious words that I am free to read and listen to at any time. In Psalm 46:10, I have the simple instructions to be still and know that He is God.

He is God. He is with me. He *is*, and that's enough!

September 14

Train up a child in the way he should go, and when he is old he will not turn from it. —**Proverbs 22:6**

What parent hasn't prayed and pondered on this scripture? I sure have! My husband and I lovingly refer to our children as the first batch and the second batch as 15 years separate our oldest son from our triplets who were born when I was 43 years old. We've been through the teen years with our two oldest sons, the first batch, and I can honestly say that we are not in any hurry to get to the teen years with our second batch!

Train up a child. . . . Well, that sounds pretty simple to me. Live by the Ten Commandments, go to church regularly, be actively involved in the lives of your children, know who their friends are, say "no" when the situation calls for it, lead by example and on and on. So why is it that kind-natured, sweet loving children do really stupid and dangerous things that are completely contrary to the "training" we have given then? I don't have that answer, but I can attest to my personal experience and my *revelation*!

Each of our children is so different from each other and from their dad and I. Sure, there are similarities, but the differences far outnumber those that are the same. With that observation, it only stands to reason that each child will act and react to life situations differently and by the same token, rewards and discipline for each child are unique to each child. In a nutshell, what works for one child will not work for the other. I found that out by trial and error, as I guess all parents do.

During the teen years of our "first batch," I prayed a lot. I cried a lot. I laughed a lot and I worried a lot. Over and over, Proverbs 22 kept going through my head. *"Train up a child in the way he should go; and when he is old he will not turn from it."* Train, teach, discipline—like a broken record sometimes, but that is where I found my strength. Just keep training. Just keep training. As hard as the teen years can be on parents, we sometimes forget how hard it really is on our children.

Now, finally to my revelation! Have you ever felt like God just thumps you on the head sometimes? Well, that happened to me during one of the teenage crises we were going through. I can't tell you which one it was as they all tend to blend together and my memory sure isn't what it used to be. *"Train up a child in the way he should go: and when he is old he will not turn from it."* It hit me! The key word here was not "train' but *OLD!* I'm over 50 now and I still make wrong choices. I know better. God has told me, but I don't always listen.

No matter what the teen drama may have been, my husband and I always made sure that our children knew that we loved them and would always forgive them, just as our Father in heaven forgives me now when I disappoint Him. Am I "old" yet? Well that question can be debated as I sure haven't reached my spiritual maturity. The "training" never really ends for God's children does it? Lay the foundation down for children. It really did stick with our "first batch." *Dear Lord, please give me strength to get through the "second bath." Amen!*

JSN
Sanford, FL

227

September 15

The Lord *is the everlasting God, the Creator of the ends of the earth. He does not faint or grow weary; his understanding is unsearchable. He gives power to the faint, and to him who has no might he increases strength. Even youths shall faint and be weary, and young men shall fall exhausted; but they who wait for the* Lord *shall renew their strength; they shall mount up with wings like eagles; they shall run and not be weary; they shall walk and not faint.*—**Isaiah 40:28-31**

Tuesday-morning Bible study was back in full swing for the fall. Taking Holly on her walk was amazingly pleasant this particular morning because unlike typical September days, God had blessed the Texas Hill Country with some unseasonably cooler temperatures.

The deer also seemed to be enjoying the brisk, early-morning air. They were out and about, up and down the street, frolicking and grazing in the yards. As plentiful as they are in my area, I never tire of seeing the Lord's graceful creation. The deer don't seem to mind seeing my dog and me either—they never even budge as we stroll by on our morning walks.

I noticed one deer standing all by herself at the corner of a house. (All the male deer had their antlers at that point, so I could easily distinguish male and female.) She wasn't moving, and at first that didn't strike me as being unusual since these deer aren't intimidated by humans. However, this one looked as if she were waiting on something, as she glanced from side to side. Sure enough, moments later another deer ran from behind the house to catch up with her friend, and the two trotted off together.

That scene struck me as being incredibly sweet. Just as we girls wait on each other in the restroom, this deer waited on her friend to catch up with her. All right, I know there is no proof to this theory, but that's the thought that flashed through my mind—this doe was waiting on her girlfriend.

After our small group time in Bible study later that morning, we gathered in the sanctuary for praise and worship prior to the lecture. The first song was "Everlasting God," written by Brenton Brown and Ken Riley and recorded by Lincoln Brewster. Many of the lyrics came from Isaiah 40:28-31, which are the daily verses above.

As we sang *"Strength will rise as we wait upon the Lord,"* my mind immediately raced back to the early-morning scene with the deer as she waited for her friend to come meet her. We are supposed to patiently wait on our friend Jesus too, but why is that so difficult? When we rush ahead, not trusting in His plan and timing, we demonstrate our lack of faith in God's sovereignty.

We wait for our children in the carpool line, we sit and wait through track and swim meets, recitals and graduations. We wait for a table at a popular restaurant and we even wait months to get an appointment with a particular doctor or hairdresser. And whether we like it or not, it's the norm to sit in traffic at rush hour, stand in the security line at the airport or the checkout lane in the grocery store. But wait on God?

Many times we don't think twice about the wait in our secular world. Other times we do it because we have no additional choice. Waiting on God is always a choice, though. We can run ahead and live life our own way. Or we can wait as our friend Jesus comes and meets us wherever we are. Lingering patiently certainly has more advantages than going solo because those "who wait for the Lord shall renew their strength; they shall mount up with wings like eagles; they shall run and not be weary; they shall walk and not faint" (Vs. 31).

The choice is ours. Will we wait for our friend Jesus to lead us today? Will we wait, even if it takes weeks, months or years, to hear the answer to prayer? Strength *will* come from our everlasting God and every minute of the wait will be worth it.

September 16

Love is eternal.— **1 Corinthians 13:8 (GNT)**

Remember to always say, "I love you."

The phone rang. My husband, Scott, and I were still at the dinner table, just finishing our meal. Neither of us made the effort to get up to answer the phone. We played our game, saying, "It's not for me." We waited for the answering machine to record a message. The caller's voice on the answering machine was nearly unrecognizable.

It was our son's father-in-law. Scott and I froze listening to his message. Something bad had happened, and by the sound of his voice, it was very, very bad. We did not pick up the phone, instead reaching for my cell phone to call him back. I stood directly in front of Scott as he made contact. The color drained from Scott's face as he listened. I stood there begging for him to tell me what was going on. Scott pulled the phone away from his ear, looked at me and said, "Nick's dead."

My Nicholas. My precious son was dead, having lost his life in a tragic accident. I remember running around the house, looking for him. I had to find him, even though Nicholas lived in New Jersey and I was in Texas. A cinder-block wall seemed to be in front of me. I knew Nicholas was on the other side, and if I could get to him, I could fix him because I was Mom. In my mind, I tried to go over the top of the wall, but it was too high. I tried to go around, but it was too long. I tried to go under, but it was too deep. Finally, I looked up and said, "Help."

God was waiting. The rush of emotions that I felt—shock, confusion, pain and fear—was overwhelming. I moved aimlessly around the house, not knowing what to do. I wandered into the kitchen and stopped. There before me was a vision. It was a vision of Jesus holding Nicholas. My precious son was in the arms of the precious Son of God. I felt indescribable comfort. I knew then where Nicholas was and that he was safe. Thank You, God.

Still not knowing what to do, I continued to wander around the house. Scott was already on the phone, trying to reach family members, all residing long distance. I came to that place in the kitchen again and stopped in my tracks. God was again waiting. He had something to tell me. God whispered to my soul, *You have no regrets.* Oh, my. Nicholas knew I loved him and I knew he loved me. And now it was revealed to me how much God loved me by touching my heart with His loving and compassionate presence. God knew what I needed and when I needed it. Thank You, God.

We flew to New Jersey the next morning to gather with family and friends. We needed to plan a service to celebrate Nicholas' life and to say good-bye. Scott and I chose to speak at the service. People were desperate for healing. They would look to us to see how we were coping. We felt that healing needed to begin with us.

Scott spoke first, telling everyone that we knew where Nicholas was and it was going to be OK. We would see Nicholas again as he awaited us in heaven. Then I spoke. I wanted all to know Nicholas from an early age on. So I shared "Mom stories." People told me that they could feel the anguish slipping away. There was even laughter through tears. The last thing I shared was the closeness Nicholas and I shared. We always said, "I love you," to each other, no matter the situation or conversation. My last words to all in attendance were, "Remember to always say, 'I love you.' " Many have told me that it was imprinted on their hearts. Thank You, God.

It is also imprinted on my heart. I ask Jesus to tell my Nicholas how much I love him, how much I miss him and that I can't wait to see him again someday, when God calls me home, and we will have our reunion day. I say, "I love You," to God and to Jesus many, many times during my day, no matter the situation or conversation. It flows from my heart so freely. By the grace and love of God, I can go on loving. Thank You, God!

Remember to always say, "I love you."

Vickie Sayles
Katy, TX

In Loving Memory of Nicholas Christopher Sayles
December 12, 1978-September 16, 2006

September 17

Praise be to the God and Father of our Lord Jesus Christ, the Father of compassion and the God of all comfort, who comforts us in all our troubles, so that we can comfort those in any trouble with the comfort we ourselves have received from God. For just as the sufferings of Christ flow over into our lives, so also through Christ our comfort overflows. —**2 Corinthians 1:3-5**

Hopefully you read yesterday's devotion, and had the opportunity to meet my friend Vickie. I am certain you would agree that she is an incredible woman of tremendous faith. While the story of her son's death is tragic almost beyond comprehension, she remains committed to proclaiming her love for her Lord and Savior.

Throughout the years since Nick's death in 2006, I have witnessed my friend grow into one of the most enthusiastic cheerleaders for God ever! When I first met Vickie in Bible study in 2005, she and her husband had just moved to Katy, Texas, and she was very shy. She will be the first to admit that Nick's death changed all of that.

The tragedy strengthened the bond between Jesus and Vickie, and God began growing her for His purpose. There were so many grieving parents out there, and Vickie was handpicked by God to be His tool to comfort them. She became a leader for Grief Share at her church and has ministered to many hurting people enduring the loss of a loved one. She is open and honest about the trials she still faces, but she is also ready to give God all the glory for using her to comfort others. I am in awe of how Vickie has accepted her role, and is her Father's faithful servant and cheerleader.

God has not only used Vickie to reach out to those mourning a loss, but also to help the rest of us know what to say and do to comfort those who are hurting. She has emphasized the importance of remembering the ones who have gone home to heaven, not just the first year, but for years to come, and to accept that all people grieve differently. Simply being present with an ear to hear our friend is huge; we aren't expected to have magic words, just loving hearts.

One day we were having lunch, eagerly sharing how God had been working in our lives, and Vickie just blurted out "Yeah, God!" To this day, when I think of Vickie, I can just see her radiant smile and hear the love and devotion she holds in her heart for the Lord. She is His cheerleader and ready to share her V-I-C-T-O-R-Y yell at any time.

There is no way I can have a pity party for very long because Vickie always comes to mind. Just thinking of her changes my attitude. If she can maintain her unwavering strength, faith and love for God, if she can be joyful despite experiencing a mother's most tragic moment—if Vickie can still cheer *Yeah, God*—then I certainly can too. There is nothing that could be more heartbreaking than to lose a child, yet Vickie's heart has remained firmly in God's hands. I want to be like her. I want to have the same joyful spirit, no matter what else is going on in my life.

Oh, my sweet friend is truly an inspiration, and I just wanted to share her with you. How she handled her tragedy truly impacted me, and countless others. Her presence in my life is such a special, intentional gift from God. *Yeah, God, for Your servant, Vickie!*

September 18

If anyone speaks, he should do it as one speaking the very words of God. If anyone serves, he should do it with the strength God provides, so that in all things God may be praised through Jesus Christ. To him be the glory and the power for ever and ever. Amen —**1 Peter 4:11**

Early one morning, I was on the back porch drinking my coffee with my golden retriever. One lone fishing boat had just raced by, and I listened as the sound of the motor grew softer and softer. It was so quiet that I could hear the creaking coming from our boat going up and down on the lift as the fishing boat's wake rocked our dock.

Slowly, God's creation began to wake up. First, I heard the leaves rustling in the gentle breeze, followed by the birds warming up their vocal chords. Maybe someday I will be able to discern the specific sound emitted by each one, but that morning it was just a song-bird jam session. Next I heard a noise coming from the roof of the house, and I looked to see what it could be. There was one lonely dove making her way across the red aluminum roof, and I could hear each little hop as she sang her solo.

Of course, the bird had no idea I was watching or could even hear her, but in the quiet of the morning I was listening and watching her every move. How much does a dove even weigh? I didn't know so I Googled that question and discovered that the average weight is four ounces

Since I am much heavier than a bird, I wondered how loud my own footsteps might be? Does someone hear me stomping around and watch where I go and what I do? Do people look at me when I am unaware? Is there some stranger listening to what comes out of my mouth? That little dove was impacting my morning. Do I impact others' lives too?

I love the words from Matthew 6:25-34, the don't-be-anxious verses. Surely, if God takes care of the birds, He will provide even more for His children, created in His image. "Are you not of more value than they?" (Vs. 26).

If I am of more value to God than a bird, He surely longs for me to act as His valued child. God is always watching, but who else might be questioning, *So that's how a Christian talks and behaves?*

I pray that today, I will represent God well. Through His power, may the reading from 1 Peter 4:11 above become a reality in my life and not just words on a page.

September 19

*Then the Lord said to Moses, "Write down these words, for in accordance with these words I have made a covenant with you and with Israel." —***Exodus 34:27**

My son had a small skin irritation below his right ear lobe that was diagnosed as a basal-cell carcinoma. The dermatologist assured me that the surgery would be quick and easy and that there would be nothing to worry about. So, as I sat in the waiting room, I actually had no reservations.

I felt so much at peace that I did something I rarely ever do—I watched TV. One of the morning talk shows was on, so I tuned in. Had I been worried or concerned about the procedure, I would have been off in a corner praying or listening to my iPod. I am so thankful that God gave me that time because the segment covered the completion of the Saint John's Bible, which I knew nothing about.

My ears perked up when I heard that it took 12 years to complete. Since this book has taken longer than I anticipated, I felt a great sigh of relief that someone else had endured a lengthy time-line for their project. However, once I found out exactly what the Saint John's Bible was, I sheepishly had to admit there could be no other comparison between the two.

The segment that aired was very short, and I wanted to know more. SaintJohnsBible.org was full of valuable information, and I spent much of the afternoon reading about this fascinating masterpiece. (I just love how God put devotions in my heart, and I spend hours researching for a story in the making.)

"*The Saint John's Bible* is a work of art and a work of theology. In 1998 Saint John's Abbey and University (in Minnesota) commissioned renowned calligrapher Donald Jackson to produce a handwritten, hand-illuminated Bible. This work of art combines an ancient Benedictine tradition with the technology and vision of today, illuminating the Word of God for a new millennium." (SaintJohnsBible.org)

The Saint John's Bible is separated into seven volumes, written in the New Revised Standard Translation. Each page is two feet by three feet, and the combined weight of the books is 165 pounds. It is the only handwritten and illuminated Bible created in the past 500 years, for a total of 1,150 artful pages sparkling with gold leaf and jewel-toned colors. Jackson started the project in 1998, with the first volume completed in 2001 and the final volume, the Letters and Revelation, finished on September 16, 2011. (That explains the television coverage on that Wednesday morning, September 19.)

There is one other interesting tidbit of information I found when reading an article written by Mary Abbe and printed in the Minneapolis Star Tribune on September 16, 2011.

Abbe wrote, "He (Donald Jackson) is not a Catholic nor even a religious man by temperament, but writing the Bible was a lifelong dream whose completion has obviously been enormously satisfying, friends say."

"When you have the whole Bible wash through you and then write it out, you are transfigured by it too," said Eric Hollas, a St. John's official and longtime friend of Jackson. "He may not have been particularly spiritual in the beginning, but the words take over at the end, so in that respect he is a changed man."

Hmm. At that particular point in time, I had only been working on this book a little over a year. While I acknowledge that I was a Christian and had a relationship with Jesus Christ before I started, I was certainly a changed woman as a result of the time spent with God while writing my stories. This book project had transformed my life in only one year's time. I wonder: What will 12 years of writing do to me?

September 20

Rejoice always, pray continually, give thanks in all circumstances; for this is God's will for you in Christ Jesus.
—1 Thessalonians 5:16-18

Can you really rejoice always, pray continually, and give thanks in *all* circumstances? I learned that you can. At least that's what I felt like I was doing with every breath in my being for eight months. My then 16-year-old son was going through horrific pain every minute of his life with a condition called Reflex Sympathetic Dystrophy, or Complex Regional Pain Syndrome. It's a rare nerve disorder usually following a minor injury where the nerves get stuck on sending the painful signals to the brain even though the injury has passed.

Think about stubbing your toe over and over again all day long, even though you only did it once. Now try walking with that painful stubbed toe getting stubbed over and over again, and driving and acting normal. He had been to the best doctors in Houston and had tried several medical procedures, but nothing lasted longer than a few days. Some had made it worse. He was on heavy-duty painkillers and going to a counselor for depression. God was literally carrying us through every minute of every day. Like I said, I felt like I was breathing prayers in and out all day.

I went through all kinds of stages of grief. When I got to the stage of acceptance, I decided that I couldn't give up hope that God would heal our son, but I could thank Him for every good thing, every blessing that He gave us. I could even thank Him for our son going through this.

I started by thanking God that He had kept our son here with us instead of taking him through a fatal disease or accident. I believed and gave thanks that the Lord was saving our son from something much worse than what he was going through now. I spoke to my son of the days when God would heal him, of the blessings he would have someday—a girlfriend, college, a wife, his own children, and smiles and laughter. I reminded him of how many blessings he had to be thankful for now—"wonderful" parents, a loving sister, his sweet puppy, his friends, his car that he could still drive, and an amazing God who loved him enough to give His only Son.

I thanked God for: my husband, who was going through this with us; hundreds of friends who prayed for our son faithfully; Karen, who dropped off a wonderful book, *The Red Sea Rules;* and Sherrie, who called me every single day to check on me, to encourage me and to pray for us. I began to thank God for so many things He sent my way every day to tell me that He loved me—for flowers and the sun and funny emails, and especially for my almost-grown children.

The more I thanked God, the more it seemed like I had more to thank Him for. Even after a painful and discouraging medical procedure, I saw God's Spirit break down the walls of my son's anger and defiance, replaced by reliance and submission to the Lord in prayer. And I thanked and praised Him for that.

And then our weeping that had lasted for an eight-month nightmare was turned to rejoicing one morning! I had been on the Internet every day researching RSD, joining on-line support groups, looking for a cure. God answers prayers His way. The Lord sent one of my husband's friends, Scott, an email from his financial guy about a promising new medical device for pain that he wanted him to consider investing in. Scott forwarded the information to my husband, who forwarded it to me.

The successful clinical trials had just been released that week. Before a month was up, we were in Providence, Rhode Island, at the Calmar Pain Relief Clinic. Dr. D'Amato explained how this machine had been intricately encoded to teach the nerves to send a "no-pain" message instead of the pain message they'd gotten stuck on. We were also glad to learn that Dr. D'Amato is a fellow Christian and believes that God is answering many prayers through this new treatment.

After the first three minutes of treatment, our son felt no pain for the first time in eight months! After 10 days of treatment, our son was completely pain-free! And we thank Him for all the other people who have also been set free from pain. I'll always be grateful to God for His healing for our son, and I hope that no matter what, I'll remember to rejoice in all of God's blessings.

Kim
Katy, TX

September 21

Then the LORD reached out his hand and touched my mouth and said to me, "Now, I have put my words in your mouth." —**Jeremiah 1:9**

Throughout my 22 years of life, I have felt God's presence many times, but never thought I heard Him speak to me. My mom would tell me countless stories of times when she heard God's voice giving her directions or reassurance, but I never personally had that experience. I knew that He was around me and I could often feel His presence, especially when I was sad or scared. It was like a warmth spread through my body until I felt safe and more hopeful than before.

I started having anxiety attacks when I was 17. For a while, I would have at least one a day, and it was awful. It felt like a heart attack and I would shake for hours afterwards, praying that I wouldn't have another one, only for it start up later that night. Feelings of intense fear and hopelessness became the daily norm, and it was exhausting. I was about to go back to school for my sophomore year of college, and I was even more terrified of having these continuous attacks where no one could understand me or comfort me the way my family and friends at home could.

One day, while sitting in church, I felt a panic attack coming on. My arm started tingling and the irrational fears started creeping into my mind. My first instinct was to leave immediately. I needed air, water, space—anything but sitting in a crowded group of people. I tried to calm down, but nothing seemed to work. I said prayers to myself for some kind of reassurance that I was OK, that I had no need to fear and that God was protecting me. I was worried that something bad was going to happen to me, which was always the seed of my anxiety.

I felt a calm come over me and a verse I had known for a long time popped into my mind: "For I know the plans I have for you, plans to prosper you and not to harm you." I instinctively wrote it on my bulletin, followed by Jeremiah 1:9. I looked at it and knew that Jeremiah 1:9 was not the same verse I had just written. (The scripture I wrote was Jeremiah 29:11, of course.)

I was stumped, so I looked it up in my Bible, and there it was—the first time I had ever felt God "speak" to me. Jeremiah 1:9 says, "Then the LORD reached out his hand and touched my mouth and said to me, 'Now, I have put my words in your mouth.' " I started tearing up and felt elated. Not only did God completely reassure me and take away my fear, but He also beautifully crafted this intimate experience that I will remember forever.

My anxiety did not completely dissipate with that experience, but it did give me the hope and comfort I needed to go on and live my life with a little less fear. I know God is on my side and He doesn't want me to feel anxious, and I love how, when I'm feeling hopeless, He does amazing things to fill me with hope. I know He has a plan for me, and I can't wait to watch it unfold and live the life He created for me.

Stephanie
Katy, TX

September 22

You have received the Holy Spirit and he lives within you, so you don't need anyone to teach you what is true. For the Spirit teaches you everything you need to know, and what he teaches is true—it is not a lie. So just as he has taught you, remain in fellowship with Christ.—**1 John 2:27**

Several years ago, I made a decision to make God my first priority in the mornings. We usually have a little good-morning chat before I get out of bed, I fix my coffee, and then it's devotion time. I am always anxious to read from my collection because I find a special message, just what I need for that day. I am much better equipped to handle my worldly circumstances after soaking up the word of God.

One morning my husband and I were having a little disagreement before he left for work. It was early and I hadn't even had my coffee yet, much less my devotion time. My husband builds tennis courts and recreational facilities, so he deals with the construction world. That includes not only the workers who set the forms and pour the concrete and paint the courts, but also engineers, architects and inspectors.

On this particular morning, Austin was on his way to meet with a building inspector and was not anticipating a cordial meeting. There had been a few disagreements between the two, and my husband was a bit frustrated. He shared with me what he planned on saying to the man. I was concerned that he was overreacting and that his frustration would escalate to anger, resulting in an unnecessary argument with the building inspector. My lack of faith in how Austin would handle the situation was the reason for our disagreement.

He left for his meeting; I got my coffee and pulled out my devotionals. The first one I opened was one I hadn't looked at in months, *The One Year Book of Proverbs*. The scripture verse for the day was Proverbs 20:3: "Avoiding a fight is a mark of honor; only fools insist on quarreling"(NLT).

Before Austin left, I suggested he cool down and be careful with his words. The Scripture agreed with me! God had led me to the exact words I needed to share with my husband. So, what did I do with this confirmation? I immediately sent him a text message that included the verse.

When I had made it a priority to put God first in the morning, I had hoped I might avoid incidents like that one. My purpose was to be filled with God's truths so I wouldn't say or do something that would be displeasing to Him. But this morning I couldn't wait to finish my God time. I only read one devotion and fired off a text message. I actually felt very convicted that I had just sent Austin some very valuable words of wisdom, while gloating in being "right." I don't imagine God was very pleased with me at that moment.

I continued reading about five more devotions, with the last one being one I subscribe to online. It was about women who try to play the role of the Holy Spirit in the lives of our husbands, especially when we think they aren't as spiritually mature as we are. One of the ways some women try to do this is by quoting Bible verses to them. Yikes! I had just done that exact thing, via a text message, and it wasn't the first time!

Yes, I have a way of preaching to my husband. This very timely devotion spoke right to my heart and helped me see that I was trying to be the small, quiet voice within my husband, instead of the Holy Spirit. Perhaps if I had read that one first, I wouldn't have sent the text, but I couldn't take it back now.

I did send my husband another message; this one was an apology. He has been in the construction business for many years and is respected for being fair and honest. Perhaps he doesn't have the same amount of time as I do to delve into the Word of God, but he is a godly man and seeks his Father daily.

Austin didn't need me to preach to him that morning—he has the Holy Spirit to lead him.

September 23

"Come to me, all who are weary and burdened, and I will give you rest. Take my yoke upon you and learn from me, for I am gentle and humble in heart and you will find rest for your souls. For my yoke is easy and my burden is light." —**Matthew 11:28-30**

Are you currently in a Bible study or small group? I sure hope so. My life totally changed when I enrolled in my first one back in 1997 at the age of 43. I had been doing church my whole life, going to Sunday school, even teaching it for many years when my boys were young. However, it wasn't until I became part of a small group of women, digging into God's Word together, that I actually began my relationship with Jesus—and other Christian women.

One fall, the Women's Ministry at my church selected a study written by Nancy Barton and Anne Garnett, members of another church in the Austin area, entitled *Keeping Company with Jesus* for the Tuesday morning group. The second week's lesson was based on Matthew 11:28-30.

As we went through the pages, answering the questions, the conversation in our small group of 10 women kept on going back to the difficulty we had in actually "resting." I'm not referring to taking-a-nap resting—it is the peace, comfort, joy, healing, encouragement and learning we can only find by spending time in God's presence.

What I found most interesting was that in this group of 10 diverse women, we all shared the same dilemma—a difficult time responding to Jesus' call to "come" to Him with all we have and sit at His feet in total surrender. To take His yoke would require that we let Jesus have our heavy load and we would have to relinquish our control. And rest? Really? We are women—wives, mothers, volunteers, friends, grandmothers, employees, sisters. We don't have time to linger very long in solitude. We have way too much to do.

I have previously written about my struggle with procrastination and disorganization. I am not the most efficient person, and I tend to be messy. If I ever had a to-do list, I would probably not be able to find it or would forget to look at it. On the complete other end is Mary from my small group. Mary is a professional organizer. Yes, she loves for everything to be nice and neat and orderly. She is so good at it that she gets paid to help others do the same.

Mary tends to grow anxious when she is spending time with God because entries on her to-do list aren't being crossed off and she feels guilty. Mary jokes that she is the extreme Type A personality, where constant "achieving and doing" is a must, with a sprinkling of OCD; feeling that everything must be orderly and perfect. While I can't identify with her way of living, she certainly isn't tolerant of my do-it-tomorrow attitude either. Between our two distinct ends of the spectrum, everyone else in the group had a place.

Despite our differences, we are all longing to sit at the feet of Jesus and just hang out. Yet Mary doesn't want to get anxious about not accomplishing all that she has on her list for the day. I don't want to worry about trying to do what should have already been finished the day before. How do we let go of ourselves and grab hold of Jesus' yoke that He is offering?

That's the beauty of Women's Bible study. We come thinking we are so different from everyone else. But when we are willing to be transparent and honest, when we allow others into our lives, we learn so much from each other, especially our similarities. All ten of us wrestled with sending our RSVP to Jesus' call. All in the group had struggles that kept us from His place of rest. Every one of us was resisting that ultimate surrender to our loving Father.

I left our group study that morning feeling such comfort. Even the person I longed to be (that super-duper, efficient, organized woman) had the same difficulties as me—the messy procrastinator—in her quest of a quiet time with God. Ten different women in my small group, with a total enrollment of about 140, and only one Bible study selected for all us on Tuesday morning. Yet the One and Only knew exactly what each of us needed and how to reach our hearts. He is so amazing!

September 24

Then he said to them all: "If anyone would come after me, he must deny himself and take up his cross daily and follow me." —**Luke 9:23**

Yesterday, I wrote about the small group time in my Tuesday-morning Bible study. After our classroom time, all 140 of us gathered for a lecture based on the homework we had just discussed in our group. I was especially excited about Teresa's talk—this was her first. Teresa had recently been selected as the new co-leader of the Tuesday morning Bible study, and I just knew that her presentation would be incredible. It was!

Her talk was based on Matthew 11:28-30 (that was the scripture from the story yesterday) and she made an acrostic from the word REST. For the letter "S" her word was surrender. Hadn't my small group just discussed the difficulty we had in surrendering to Jesus? Oh, I talk to God daily about that word. I struggle with it so.

Teresa said that we need to "surrender the hurry" to Jesus. As women, we have the tendency to get overly anxious with "finishing" tasks, when all He wants is to spend time with us; to walk with us.

I got lost in her lecture at that point. Oh my goodness! Her words just pierced my soul. That was me all over. Ever since I started this book I had obsessed over the finis∆235hed product! My plan to have others submit the majority of the stories hadn't materialized. I was only halfway to my goal of 366 devotions. There was no way I could ever rest at the feet of Jesus with such a task looming over me. I needed to hurry and write more stories so I would be finished.

Please understand one very important fact.—this book transformed my life. I absolutely loved the project and the journey. I had so much fun looking for God every day, expectantly waiting on Him. Sitting at my computer was what I consider resting at His feet. But wait. I was working. I was writing. I don't think that's really resting.

I had a goal of 366 devotions and as I wrote this one, I was only at #192. I was more concerned with quantity than quality time spent alone with the Author of my faith. I felt like all my time *must* be spent writing. If I was not writing, I would never reach my goal. Thus, the self-induced anxiety.

I prayed daily for God to place stories on the hearts of women and that they would share them in this book. I prayed for specific women who said they would write something but just needed encouragement. Several times I audibly cried out to God for help and in His true faithfulness, I received an email with a devotion within a day or two. (As I wrote that previous sentence, I actually received a story from my friend Meghan. How is that for a faithful God!)

While I say this book is God's, I still claimed it as "my" project. I said it would be finished in His perfect timing, but I was consumed with the numbers. No, I hadn't surrendered the need to hurry up to God. While I loved every minute spent with Him, I was overly anxious about the finish. Teresa hit the nail on the head for me!

This word "surrender" pops up all the time, doesn't it?

I re-read Luke 9:23 several times and found great encouragement in the word "daily." It's not something we do once, and then it's a done deal. Surrender occurs on a minute-by-minute basis. We can never be in such a hurry that we don't take time to pray or seek His guidance.

As Christians, we are in complete dependence on the strength of God, and that requires us to walk with Him, hand and hand. We are all sinners in need of a Savior. Each day we have the choice to follow our Lord or the Evil One. Who will you choose today?

September 25

In your presence there is fullness of joy. —**Psalm 16:11**

For the past two days, we have read words like "rest" and "surrender." Today, I would like to share the words of a beautiful hymn written by Charles A. Miles in 1913, "In the Garden." (If you have access to a computer, you can Google "In the Garden" and actually listen to Elvis Presley or Alan Jackson sing it on YouTube for a special treat.)

When you get to the refrain, notice the word "tarry." We don't hear it too often these days, but it's such a sweet way to suggest that we slow down and linger. Perhaps even rest a spell. So before you get started on your busy day, spend some time alone with Jesus. You don't have to be in a garden—He will meet you wherever you are.

Cherish these few minutes with your Lord and Savior. Relish in the fact that He loves you and wants to spend this time with you more than you could ever imagine. Listen for His tender voice. Oh, He's waiting on you. Don't tarry any longer. Go meet Him and linger in His presence. Just you and Jesus!

I come to the garden alone
While the dew is still on the roses
And the voice I hear falling on my ear
The Son of God discloses.

Refrain:

And He walks with me, and He talks with me,
And He tells me I am His own;
And the joy we share as we tarry there,
None other has ever known.

He speaks, and the sound of His voice,
Is so sweet the birds hush their singing,
And the melody that He gave to me
Within my heart is ringing.

Refrain

I'd stay in the garden with Him
Though the night around me be falling,
But He bids me go; through the voice of woe
His voice to me is calling.

Refrain

September 26

In your anger do not sin. Do not let the sun go down while you are still angry, and do not give the devil a foothold. —**Ephesians 4:26-27**

Dennis Rainey and his wife, Barbara, are the founders of FamilyLife, a branch of Campus Crusade for Christ, and have a radio broadcast called "Real FamilyLife." I don't know exactly where in his talk I tuned in, but I was shocked by one of his statements.

I quickly pulled out my journal I keep in the console of my car and jotted down, "Less than 8% of all married couples pray together." Did I hear that correctly?

Later, I Googled "Dennis Rainey" and found an abundance of information about his and Barbara's ministry, along with the words I heard on the radio.

In 2001, Dennis and Barbara published *Starting Your Marriage Right—What You Need to Know and Do in the Early Years to Make it Last a Lifetime.* Chapter 11 was titled "The Secret Ingredient in the Happy Marriage Recipe."

There it was in black and white: "Surveys from FamilyLife Marriage Conferences show that less than 8% of all couples pray together regularly." That's not very many!

They went on to write "prayer can be the most intimate encounter between a husband and wife (other than sex) that builds and strengthens a marriage." The chapter also drew a correlation between the increasing rate of divorce and the lack of prayer between spouses.

My husband and I do pray together every night before going to sleep (when he is not working out of town). I can't tell you exactly when or how we started the nightly routine, but it was definitely the Holy Spirit at work in us. Having been divorced, we were earnestly seeking to have God in our marriage and that small voice led us to the bedtime prayer. (My editor, Rick Weber, offered another interesting statistic with me that he shares in the DivorceCare program he leads: "Only 0.4% of marriages end in divorce if both partners pray together every night.")

It's easy for me to cry out to God when it's just Him and me, but being so vulnerable with my husband there beside me wasn't comfortable at first. Both of us have learned much about each other's heart through our bedtime prayer, and I must agree with the Rainey's that it is definitely an intimate time spent with my husband.

Phyllis Diller was quoted as saying, "Never go to bed mad. Stay up and fight." The first sentence is good advice, but I don't think that staying up to fight are words to live by. Paul's words in Ephesians 4:26 are probably the better ones to follow. "In your anger do not sin. Do not let the sun go down while you are still angry." He even gives us a reason why in verse 27. "Do not give the devil a foothold."

Take it from the voice of experience: It is very difficult to pray with your spouse—face to face in bed and holding hands—while angry with one another. I have done it though, asking for God to help us resolve our conflict. After praying, the wall between us starts to crumble, though sometimes only one brick at a time.

Unfortunately, I can't say that my husband and I have *never* gone to bed without praying. (I was reassured when I remembered Mr. Rainey said less than 8% of couples prayed together *regularly*.) Paul didn't say not to become angry; he said to deal with it quickly. In my anger, it is easy for Satan to get his foot in the door of my marriage, to twist the truth and fill my mind with lies. I know because it has happened.

He worked to conjure up all the what-ifs in my mind, then reinforced the silly notion that I was justified to feel hurt and my spouse should be the one to apologize first. Once Satan was in, the doubt, worries, lack of trust, irritations, loss of intimacy and conflicts started to mount. If you and your spouse can commit to that time of intimate prayer, you have the opportunity to shut the door on the lies before they ever enter the relationship.

If you are married, are you and your spouse among that 8%? If so, let's make sure that our girlfriends and their husbands are too. If you aren't praying regularly with your spouse, I want to encourage you to try it. There is no better way to ensure God is at the center of your marriage than to have Him there with you as the three of you pray together.

September 27

Many are the plans in a man's heart, but it is the Lord's purpose that prevails.—**Proverbs 19:21**

After I started this little project of mine, I spent many sleepless nights worrying. My original plan had been to solicit the fabulous women God had placed in my life to contribute stories to this book. I wanted to show the incredible ways He had worked in the lives of just plain, ordinary women. Just as He picked many ordinary people to do His extraordinary work in the Bible, I wanted to illustrate how a bunch of everyday women could glorify the Father through our God stories and provide encouragement to others. I had prayed so much about this book and felt I was doing what He wanted me to do. But what if the stories didn't come from all those women I solicited? Was I prepared to write hundreds myself?

I was so excited and passionate about compiling this devotional and just assumed everyone else would be too. God soon helped me realize that He put the passion and excitement in my heart, not in everyone else's. He already knew who was going to submit a story and what it would say. If this book were going to be filled with 366 stories—which was the desire of my heart—it would only happen because that's what God also wanted. This book is for His purpose, to let His glory prevail, not my selfish desires.

Slowly, I received a devotion here and there. I still longed to know what the finished product would look like. Would I have a whole year's worth of stories? I wondered what my feelings would be when it was finished, with all the God stories compiled together and sent to the publisher.

I started sending stories/devotions one at a time to my friend and "editor," Rick Weber, when I only had a total of 40. I had a question about which Bible translation my friend Kellie had used in her story and sent her an email, and I also mentioned I had started sending devotions to Rick. I obviously didn't explain myself clearly because she thought the book was finished and that's why Rick was actively engaged.

Kellie sent the most awesome email back to me! She used such pumped-up words as *Congratulations! Way to go, Brenda, for following your project all the way to the end! Let me know when it's available!*

As I was writing a response back to her, explaining that I wasn't quite finished with the book, I just started laughing! Hadn't I just been worrying if there would be 366 devotions, enough to fill the book? Hadn't I just spent time pondering what I would feel when it was done? It was as if God sent me a secret message through this dear friend. (Was that why You placed her in my life, to be Your messenger?)

After reading Kellie's email, I felt such excitement and peace. It was as if I had been allowed to get a glimpse into the future, just a tiny peek. God had given me the task of gathering the stories He had already written on the hearts of other women, plus writing the countless stories He would put on in my heart. He had it under control. I didn't need to waste my time worrying. I just needed to trust and obey and follow God's instructions all the way to the end. The finished book would be exactly as He planned.

This daily devotional is for God's glory, and He is just as passionate and excited about it as I am. Together, we will get it done. I was thankful that God spoke through my friend and sent His sweet words of assurance. I just needed to persevere, staying focused on His plan and purpose, and not worrying about mine.

September 28

"Be holy, because I, the LORD your God, am holy." —**Leviticus 19:2**

Ever read those words and cringe because you think you can't emulate God's holiness? Does that cause hopelessness that threatens your tender faith walk? If so, take another look.

It is God who bestows holiness upon us, by His grace and mercy, for His always and forever perfect purpose. We often find ourselves in an internal war over this very verse. Satan and the world system accuse us of being unholy, pointing out our every failure to live up to the standard of perfection that this word implies and we, in our frustration and confusion, shake our heads in agreement, all too willing to focus on our sinful humanity. Isn't this where we often live?

Friend, this was never intended to be so. The One who gave the command, "Be holy," did not stop with those words. He went on to say, "because I am holy." Maybe it makes more sense to us if we read it from 1 Peter 1:16, where it is transliterated as "You shall be holy, *for* I am holy" (NASB).

God does not expect perfection from us. In fact, quite the contrary. He sees and lives in the perfection of Himself. As unworthy recipients of His Holy Spirit, we are enabled, by virtue of His presence, to walk in the holiness that He brings in His person.

He has, in fact, bestowed holiness upon His people because it is the character of the Holy Spirit who gives life and understanding to our ways. Since, according to Galatians 2:20, we were crucified with Christ and we no longer live, but the Spirit of Christ lives in us, we can depend upon Him to live a life worthy of our calling. It is not up to us. The minute we shift our gaze from Him to ourselves, our countenance becomes downcast and we begin to doubt the very truth and validity of our lives. When we live in condemnation, we are self-focused rather than God-focused.

Holiness is a byproduct of our inexpressible joy in the presence of an all-loving and holy God. It is such a paradox to our human thinking that we can do nothing but fall down before Him in our regenerated hearts, thus finding fulfillment of the commandment, "Be holy, because I am holy."

Anonymous

September 29

Therefore encourage one another and build each other up as you are already doing. — **1 Thessalonians 5:11 (HCSB)**

It hadn't been one of my better days. Nothing in particular, just everything in general. I let my focus stray from God, and I was wallowing in my earthly circumstances. My Heavenly Father knew I needed a spiritual boost and came to my rescue.

Before closing my computer for the night, I received a response to an earlier e-mail from my sweet friend Linda. She wrote such godly words of encouragement that humbled and totally uplifted me. I went to bed thankful for having such a special friend in my life and gave God the glory He deserved—instead of pouring out my selfish concerns because of my crummy day.

The following morning when I began my quiet time, I expectantly opened my first devotional and was totally in awe of God's timing. The Scripture reading was 1 Thessalonians 5:11. God not only commands us to spread the Good News of the Gospel, but also to also spread words of encouragement.

Isn't it just too cool that God wanted me to read that verse about encouragement? He wanted me to know that my friend Linda had been both a blessing to me and to Him by honoring that command. Linda didn't know I needed some sweet words; she just offered them anyway.

After reading my other devotions, I proceeded on to my emails. I had sent my editor, Rick Weber, one of my stories, and he returned it with his corrections. Only this time he had a few personal comments. His words were incredibly encouraging to me, especially after my bad attitude the day before. It is so uplifting to get some feedback that I am going in the right direction. He had no idea that he was also reinforcing the Scripture God had just placed on my heart, along with being faithful in his obedience.

Needless to say, I felt so loved that day and had such a huge smile on my face. My Father provided that specific verse for me, along with two special people to offer their words of encouragement! Be on the lookout: He has tidbits all around for us, just when we need it. Also, be on the lookout for opportunities to offer your own tidbits of love and encouragement to those God puts in your path. You just never know who needs your kind words and what a blessing you will be.

Tomorrow, my friend Kathy will share her story of being encouraged.

September 30

But encourage one another daily, as long as it is called "Today," so that none of you may be hardened by sin's deceitfulness. — **Hebrews 3:13**

Barnabas is one of my favorite Bible characters. I learned in Bible study recently that Barnabas is not his birth name—it was given to him because of the way he treated his friends, and means "son of encouragement." This story is about someone who was a "Barnabas" to me.

After my husband, Mike, and I had been married for four years, we decided that it was time to start a family. But for us, like so many couples, it was not so easy! We connected with a well-respected fertility specialist and eight years later, we were thrilled with the news that we were pregnant. A few weeks after that, we had a sonogram and learned that we were having triplets.

The doctor who helped us was a man of character and great faith in God. Shortly after the birth of the babies, he came to visit me in the hospital. "I work with hundreds of women who are so desperate to have a baby," he said to me, "but I can think of only a small number of them who I truly believe can handle the challenges of a new family such as this. You are strong, and you will be a great mother."

The babies spent two weeks in the hospital, then we took them home. Once home, we had our share of hard days. (Generally, days were hard when there was a lot of crying and not much sleep!) Whenever we ended one of those, I would think back to what Dr. Vaughn told me in the hospital. I felt so much encouragement from those words, because I know he spoke them from his heart, and his heart was filled with the love of God.

Kathy W
Austin, TX

October 1

"I will not forget you. See, I have engraved you on the palms of my hands." —**Isaiah 49:15-16**

On a gorgeous fall morning in October, I pulled out a stack of devotionals to read. One was *Daily Guidepost 2010*. It might have been a few years old, but I enjoy re-reading stories and thinking about what I underlined or wrote in the margins.

For that day, author Fred Bauer wrote a story about the fall and winter months not being his favorite time of the year. He mentioned that others think fall is special because of football. The legendary coach at Penn State, Joe Paterno, who just happened to be Mr. Bauer's neighbor at the time, told him that the college football season was his favorite. Penn State. Those words got my attention. (Please note that this story was written before the heartbreaking scandal at Penn State was revealed and has nothing to do with that situation.)

I will be honest and tell you that when I think of college football, I do not immediately think of Penn State. I live in Austin, where the University of Texas Longhorns reign supreme. My son Trevor was on the football team and graduated from there as well. My oldest son, Zach, and his wife, Lauren, are LSU grads. During their college years, both schools made two trips to the national championship, so we have talked a lot of football at our house, but I don't recall Penn Sate ever being part of the conversation.

So, why did I take special note of Penn State in that devotion? Actually, it was the association I made with the university. You see, my editor, Rick Weber, is a grad and a die-hard fan. He had made a difficult move from Texas to Florida and had been in my thoughts and prayers. I immediately thought of him as I read the devotion that mentioned his beloved alma mater, and I said another prayer for him.

Later that day, I noticed Rick had posted some pictures on Facebook of his recent vacation to Pennsylvania. There he was, at a Penn State football game with his son! Oh, he looked so very happy. Praise God for the wonderful vacation and time spent with his family.

Do you see or hear something and have a person come to mind? It happens quite often with me and is such a blessing to lift him/her up in prayer. However, that hasn't always been a habit of mine. Now that I want to be more consistent in praying for others, I have become more alert to the "reminders" during the course of the day that trigger a conversation with God about a precious friend. Below is just a sampling of one morning:

When I was sitting on my back porch, drinking my morning coffee, a barge that is used to work on boat docks passed by on the lake. The man who has been called more times than I can recall to come fix our dock just went through a divorce and needed some words of comfort.

After my coffee, I went to feed the deer and saw my neighbor pulling out of her driveway. Yes, it's 8:10 a.m.—time for Patty to go to the Catholic Church down the street and pray. (Patty is 80 years old and drives to the church almost daily.) I am so honored to ask God to get her to the church safely.

Later on in the morning, I went for a walk. I saw the vacant lot where our recently engaged friends want to build a home after they get married. Oh, but Janis just found out she has breast cancer and is having a double mastectomy in a few days. She is 60 years old and this is her first marriage! I pray that Jeff and Janis' wedding day will be a glorious time and that they celebrate many happy, healthy years together as husband and wife.

I am so thankful that God places special friends on my heart through a subtle reminder. It sure is comforting to know that He doesn't need a reminder to think of us, though. No, He won't forget about me or you. We are engraved on the palms of His hands!

October 2

"All this I have spoken while still with you. But the Counselor, the Holy Spirit, whom the Father will send in my name, will teach you all things and will remind you of everything I have said to you." —**John 14:25-26**

Yesterday, I wrote about reminders that led me to lift up friends in prayer. A few days after writing that story, the Holy Spirit did it again. He prompted me to think of a friend I needed to pray for and to call.

Driving from Austin to Houston on Highway 71, I pass by a little airport in Smithville. There are usually a few small planes around the hangars, but this time there was helicopter directly in the middle of the runway. I made that trip countless times, and I had never seen a helicopter at that tiny airport. Immediately I thought of Susan. Her husband, a pilot, had been killed in a helicopter crash four months prior to this particular trip.

I couldn't attend the funeral because of our family vacation. I called Susan as soon as I heard, but could only leave a message on her answering machine. Then I sent a card and made a donation in lieu of flowers. I still had the copy of the obituary sitting on my desk. I had thought about her countless times, but never followed the promptings of the Holy Spirit to call and send my love. This time, I didn't hesitate.

Susan sounded like herself. I was so happy to hear her sweet and cheerful voice. Why did I expect her to "sound" different? She is still the same person, only her circumstances have changed considerably. Susan had all kinds of questions about my boys and what was going on in my life. Typical Susan—always expressing an interest in others.

After we chatted for a bit, I finally apologized for not calling sooner—for not letting her know how much I had been thinking of her and hurting for her. I was extremely embarrassed for being such a crummy friend and told her so. Susan was full of grace, reassuring me several times that it was OK. She understood that conversations at such a time could be difficult.

Even if I had called and simply told her I loved her and that I was sorry, that would have been enough. I didn't need to know ahead of time what to say. God would have given me the words if I only asked Him for guidance. Ignoring the many reminders that the Holy Spirit gave me over those past months was certainly *not* the right action to have taken.

I am so thankful that I have learned to recognize the Holy Spirit within me. It has taken many years to get to this point and I am overwhelmed with joy. I have also learned to identify the occasions I chose to ignore that quiet voice and go about life on my own. The times I didn't call Susan were such instances. I am not trying to beat myself up for my behavior. I pray, with God's help, I will be more obedient to the teachings and reminders my Counselor gives me in the future.

Before Susan and I ended our conversation, we set a date to meet for dinner. I knew not to casually suggest that we get together soon—a firm commitment was best. If you know someone who has recently (or perhaps not so recently) endured the death of a loved one, take a few moments to pray about her. Is the Holy Spirit urging you to call, just to say hello?

October 3

"But when they arrest you, do not worry about what to say or how to say it. At that time you will be given what to say, for it will not be you speaking, but the Spirit of your Father speaking through you." —**Matthew 10:19-20**

My friend Susan and I met for dinner at one of my favorite Italian restaurants in Austin. I will be honest: I was a bit apprehensive about our time together. I hadn't seen Susan in a couple of years. I should have been excited about all the catching up. But her husband had only been deceased for four months. I didn't know what was in store for the evening.

Driving to the restaurant, I prayed for the Holy Spirit to fill my heart and mind with just the right words. I repeated Psalm 19:14: "May the words of my mouth and the meditations of my heart be pleasing in your sight, O Lord, my Rock and my Redeemer." I wanted to be a source of comfort to Susan. I certainly didn't want to say something inappropriate or stupid.

My good friend Vickie's son was killed in a tragic accident back in September of 2006 and we have shared some very special times together. God has used that relationship to better equip me when talking to someone who has lost a loved one, but would I know what to say or not to say to Susan?

I talked to her a few times before our dinner and she sounded great. When she walked through the door at the restaurant she looked as sweet and pretty as ever. When we sat down, the conversation flowed freely. I don't know exactly what led Susan to bring up Steve's accident, but the door just opened naturally.

She talked about her husband's death, his funeral and what the past four months had been like; I talked about my dad's death back in 2003 and Vickie's son. I also told Susan about others God had placed in my path who had lost loved ones. We weren't having a morbid conversation. Quite the contrary. It was an open and honest discussion—a remembrance of God's powerful, healing hands at work in the midst of sadness and tragedy. He was truly glorified.

We lingered at our table long after the plates were cleared and the water glasses refilled several times. I am thankful the restaurant wasn't busy, so I didn't feel like we were keeping the waiter from having more customers come sit in his section. He sensed we were there for the conversation and encouraged us to stay as long as we wanted. It was truly a special time spent with a dear friend.

On the drive home, I thought about my earlier concerns and my specific prayer. I praised God for giving me the words to speak and the ears to listen. He knew what both of us needed and His provision was such a sweet gift. Of course, He already knew all about our evening—He was right there with us at the table.

October 4

Do not neglect the gift that is in you; it was given to you through prophecy, with the laying on of hands by the council of elders.—**1 Timothy 4:14 (HCSB)**

The Scripture reading for my morning devotional was: *Do not neglect the gift that is in you.* The story was about the unique ways God created each of us, giving special "gifts" to be used for His glory. Later, I pondered the many godly women God had placed in my path who are living that verse—who are using their talents to grow His kingdom and glorify Him in the process.

Many of those women have been my small-group leaders in Bible study. I can't think of a one I haven't grown to adore, even though each had her own distinct personality and strengths. Despite the differences, each has loved on me, challenged and nurtured me. Every year, God purposely placed me alongside a godly woman who used her gift of facilitating and teaching for the glory of the Father.

As I had my quiet time with God that morning, thinking about those women, I honed in on my current facilitator. It doesn't take a rocket scientist to identify the spiritual mentors in women's ministry at a church—they just stand out because the love and light of Jesus shines through them. When Susan called me one fall day to tell me she would be my small-group leader for the new session of Bible study, I was ecstatic! Though I didn't know her personally, I knew of her and had seen her radiant Jesus glow.

To radiate the love of Jesus indicates an intimate relationship with Him. There is not only knowledge of His Word, but also God-given wisdom to know how and when to apply that knowledge. God gave Susan a distinct passion for women and she shares that wisdom with incredible authenticity, compassion and integrity. Because she has experienced her own horrific pain, she is extremely intuitive and empathetic when she senses other hurting souls.

Those special qualities overflow from her heart because of her husband's sudden death—an example of God using our greatest hurts for His glory.

Oh, to hear Susan pray! She starts off so softly, but as the Holy Spirit works in her, Susan's voice becomes incredibly passionate, and there is no doubt Who is speaking through her. I promise you, to hear Susan Smalling pray is a one-of-a-kind experience. You will most likely be in tears when you hear that *Amen*—and so will she!

"Each one should use whatever gift he has received to serve others, faithfully administering God's grace in its various forms. If anyone speaks, he should do it as one speaking the very words of God. If anyone serves, he should do it with the strength God provides, so that in all things God may be praised through Jesus Christ. To him be the glory and the power for ever and ever. Amen" (1 Peter 4:10-12).

Hopefully you also have a special friend or mentor come to mind who is living the verses above. Let her know how much you love her. Let her know that her authentic walk has not only impacted yours, but also glorified the Father.

Allow me to share one more tidbit: After that year of Bible study, Susan and I figured out there was another connection between the two of us. In casual conversation about our teenage years, we discovered we attended the same high school in Corpus Christi, Texas—at the same time! Here we were 40 years after the fact, chatting over coffee, and we found we knew more about each other than we thought. Now, does God have a way of orchestrating relationships and connecting people or what? Remember, nobody walks through your life by accident.

Our Heavenly Father created Susan with a distinct passion to love, minister and connect to women. Tomorrow, you will have the opportunity for an encounter with Susan yourself.

October 5

Trust in the Lord with all your heart and lean not on your own understanding; in all your ways acknowledge him, and he will your direct your paths.—**Proverbs 3:5-6 (KJV)**

It was my first big trip since my husband died. I would be meeting my two sisters-in-law in Aspen to celebrate all of our birthdays on the 4th, 5th, and yes, 6th of October. Not wanting to miss leading my small group in a difficult Bible study on the 4th, I decided to take an afternoon flight to Denver, but that meant I would have to drive to Aspen alone. I was nervous about the plan, having never driven in the mountains and knowing it would be tight trying to get there before dark.

While checking out the navigational system on the rental car, I asked the attendant about the two possible routes. He said not to worry—just go west on I-70. So off I went and soon encountered Denver traffic at a near standstill. I prayed, "God, I have done what I can to get in this car by 4, but I can't do anything about this traffic. It's up to you to get me there tonight *when* you want me to arrive."

Outside of Denver, it began to rain. I hadn't calculated that in my travel time, so the plan to make the first birthday dinner seemed less likely. I finally came to the base of a mountain, which appeared to be the last leg of my journey. It began to rain harder and darkness fell. Warning signs of hairpin curves and 10 mph speed limits appeared—and then it began to snow.

I put a white-knuckle grasp on the steering wheel and leaned forward, straining to see the road. Ice formed on the windshield. I couldn't identify the sides of the road. The GPS calculated another 20 miles. I tried my cell phone, but had no service. I prayed, "Lord, I don't think I can do this for another 20 miles."

I made it to the hotel in time for dinner. Everyone asked about my drive. As I related the story, their eyes got big, and Jeanne choked up with tears. They couldn't believe that I had come that way. I had just gone through one of the most dangerous stretches of road in the country, in the dark and with it snowing.

Earlier that day, they had taken that route to view the 12,000-foot drop and were nervous doing it in the daylight with dry conditions. Mike said, "That's Independence Pass." I shuddered to hear its name. That didn't seem right at all, because for me, it had been a total dependence on Him. I quickly replied," No, it's In HIM Dependence Pass."

I had begun the trip nervous about driving alone up mountain roads in the dark. That night, God showed me that even if my situation is worse than I fear, He would always be with me and would always be in control.

Susan Smalling
Austin, TX

October 6

This is the day the LORD has made; let us rejoice and be glad in it.—**Psalm 118:24**

In late October 2011, Lake Travis, one of the highland lakes in Central Texas, had surpassed the drought of 2009 and was at the third-lowest level in history. My daily prayers were filled with pleas for God to show mercy on the drought-stricken land and to bring the rain. I looked at the lake, and asked Him to please fill it up again. I saw the dead leaves on the plants and trees and asked Him to please bring the water to restore them back to life.

God endured my rage as I lashed out in frustration when the thunder and lightning brought nothing but a beautiful light show on the horizon. He patiently listened to my broken-record request for moisture-filled clouds to appear, instead of the constant, gorgeous blue sky. I know He heard me, yet He wasn't ready to bring the deluge that was desperately needed.

I had developed such a negative attitude that I no longer spoke Psalm 118:24 when I sat on the back porch, drinking my morning coffee. Instead, I sang a very sarcastic rendition of the Mister Rogers theme song, "It's A*(nother)* Beautiful Day in the Neighborhood!" And I wondered why God refused to answer my prayers? With an attitude like mine, why should He?

One morning, I woke up with a song blaring in my head—however, this time it wasn't the Mister Rogers theme. "Grace Like Rain" by Todd Agnew was playing over and over. The song includes the timeless words from "Amazing Grace," with a chorus that refers to grace coming down, falling down like rain! Was God telling me that He *had* been answering my prayers, that He had been showering me with His abundant and undeserved grace every day?

Oh, but the song in my head didn't stop with that one. I got in my car and heard "Song of Hope" by Robbie Seay Band. The chorus mentions singing a song of hope, asking God in heaven to come down.

Asking God to come down from heaven? What had I been so obsessed with lately? I had been more consumed with rain coming down than anything else. I was seeking the benefits of God rather than God Himself. I was literally transformed with that realization of where my true passion had been focused.

I have a feeling that God wasn't very pleased with my constant begging and pleading for rain. What if I longed to hear His voice as ardently as I longed to hear the sound of rain on my roof? The song tells me that having God near me is all I need, yet I cry out for rain. Day in and day out. Like a broken record.

Shouldn't I long for His presence, not for what He can give me? I know He listens to my supplications, but my whining for rain must be getting old. God wants to know how much I love Him and am thankful for His daily provisions, instead of bombarding Him with my honey-do list. He knows how low the lake is and how dry the ground is and how thirsty His plants are, but does He know how much I love Him? I can ask Him for anything, but have I taken the time to acknowledge what I have already received?

Father God, Maker of the skies. Every day You provide me with showers of love, mercy and grace, and "Your grace is sufficient for me" (2 Corinthians 12:9). Please forgive my obsession with worldly desires instead of Your eternal love. May *I long for You, God, as a deer longs for streams of water* (Psalm 42:1 HCSB), finding joy and contentment in simply knowing that You are near, You are here, and that is enough!

October 7

The Lord has sent me...to bestow on them a crown of beauty instead of ashes, the oil of gladness instead of mourning, and a garment of praise instead of a spirit of despair.—**Isaiah 61:3**

Can you recall or are you going through a tough time when you question God or circumstances? Do you feel in deep despair and alone? I have been there and I understand how you may be feeling.

About 10 years ago I started my day much as usual and mid-morning I got a call from my husband. His tone and his question of where I was started the alarms to sound. He wanted me to meet him at home as soon as possible. Now the alarms were sirens.

My mind went all over the place imagining the worst scenarios—so much for the previous Bible study to take captive every thought and think of whatever is true! Well, my husband met me at home and told me he had just heard from our daughter, then a junior in college. She was pregnant.

He wept on the couch and questioned his parenting. I had seen my husband down and hurting, but never like this. Surprisingly, at first, I was relieved. I had imagined even worse. Of course, those feelings were quickly replaced with the feelings of hurt, despair, fear, shame, anxiety and guilt.

My daughter moved back home; rejected by her boyfriend, isolated from her peers and displaced by her school. She finished college locally (and that is another amazing story of God at work!) and gave birth to a son.

Fast forward (and here again we have to skip quite a few amazing stories of God at work!): My husband and I have the most beautiful and wonderful grandson and he is the light of our lives. My daughter married the father of our grandson (and that is another amazing story of God at work). You know, you hear this all the time, but I truly would not change things even if I could.

My entire family has not just endured this season. We have not just gotten through. We have not just accepted. We have been blessed and changed and grown all for the better. Oh, yes, we have had difficult times, but we have learned humility, trust, patience and faith. We have been supported by a loving church body and surrounded by real Christian friends who have supported us with their kindness, acceptance and love.

We are so blessed and this "season of despair" has been turned into "a garment of praise." If you are going through a "season of despair," I pray that my story will encourage you. God can lift your burden, lighten your load, brighten your days and truly change ashes for beauty!

Carol
Texas

October 8

And the church is his body; it is made full and complete by Christ, who fills all things everywhere with himself.
–Ephesians 1:23 (NLT)

When I was in high school, I would drive my Aunt Dorothy about 15 miles to another part of Ft. Worth to attend a church pastored by a man who had been a family friend for many years. The church was well-received in that community, even by those who lived in the neighborhood but did not attend the services. Everyone seemed so happy to be there; I know that I was. I felt God's presence in my everyday life, but not as much as when I was there in that little church. Something wonderful was going on there, and I knew that God must be pleased with us.

One day, our world there on Galvez Street was changed forever. A teenage girl from the neighborhood accused the pastor of assaulting her in his study.

The pastor and his wife left town for a few days after that. At the Wednesday evening service, as one of the deacons was reading from the Bible, the pastor and his wife came in and sat at the back of the church. After a few minutes, it seemed that their emotions had gotten the best of them and they left. She was crying out loud, and he was trying to comfort her and lead her out at the same time. My aunt, who was really close to the wife, left right behind them. Then a few others from the congregation left. The deacon who was leading service said, "That wasn't a very Christian thing to do, walking out of service." One of the boys down the pew from where I was sitting leaned forward, looked at me and said, "Well, I guess you won't be coming back."

He was right. We did not go back there or attend church anywhere else. I missed being there so much and felt an emptiness that I had never experienced before. Up until then, I had attended church my whole life. I knew that something was missing. It was several years later, after marriage and the birth of my daughter, before I attended worship services regularly.

As I was writing this, I kept thinking, *Why did God want me to write about this incident? Certainly my life was not impacted as much as those who were directly involved.* Then I realized He wanted to remind me that He is always with us, not just in church. Yes, Christians are to come together and to encourage one another, but we are to take Him with us in every part of our lives. He is present every moment; He never leaves us. I know now that He is present at my kitchen table when I am doing my Bible studies just as much as He is present on Sunday morning at my church.

Wanda L. Rosello
Austin, TX

October 9

But you, O God, do see trouble and grief; you consider it to take it in hand.— **Psalm 10:14**

What a stressful day it was. No, actually, what a stressful month it had been. Have you ever had to fight City Hall? Have you ever had to fight to keep what you thought were your indisputable rights, until someone tried to take them away? If you have, you understand it can be extremely frustrating.

My little piece of heaven on earth—my home on Lake Travis in the Hill Country outside of Austin—is situated on a very eclectic street on the outskirts of a well-established lake community. To put it in a nutshell, the little community (I will refer to as the City) wanted to annex my street of 18 home sites. I am not going to go into the details of the annexation in this little space, because that's not what's important. The way that God revealed Himself to me—the way He spoke to me—is what gave me happy fingers as I sat down to write that morning in October.

Each homeowner had the opportunity on two occasions to speak for three minutes before the City Council, to voice our concerns. Previously, we had gone through the same procedure with the Zoning and Planning Committee. After hearing us, they reversed their stance and voted unanimously to recommend that we *not* be considered for annexation. But that was just the first hurdle, and now we had to face the City Council, the ones who have the final vote. The first meeting was oppositional and now we were on to meeting No. 2, expecting much of the same.

Our united front presented emotional, heartfelt appeals for the second time, trying to convince the City to leave us alone. It is difficult when there are two distinct views to an issue, and there are actually compelling arguments for each. However, some of the comments from both sides weren't exactly the most appropriate, and at times the tension in the room was thick—so dense that I actually left the room to go out in the foyer. I just couldn't handle the adversarial atmosphere.

Before both meetings, I prayed without ceasing. I prayed that when it was my turn to have my three minutes that the words of my mouth would be pleasing to the Lord (Psalm 19:14). I prayed for God to soften the hearts of both parties and that all would seek His guidance and wisdom. Did I pray for the Council members to see things "our" way? Not exactly, but I did ask that they would hear our pleas and listen to our concerns. Did I really think that God was in control? Of course!

So, why all the turmoil if I really believed God was the one sitting on the bench, not the mayor? God already had determined the outcome of this annexation. But we couldn't just sit back and not stand up for what we believed was right or fair, could we? Even Jesus got angry in the temple. But I had to ask myself if all of us in the room kept our words under proper control and if our focus was always on God's will, as Jesus' were. Were our own personal agendas, those of both parties, at the center of this controversy?

As I sat out in the foyer, away from the adversity, my mind was racing. *God, what is going on here? This meeting has gone from bad to worse. Words were spoken that shouldn't have been. God, where are You? These are our homes and our way of life. I don't think those people sitting at the front of the room are hearing us. I don't think they care one bit about the fears we have concerning this issue. Please intervene.*

This particular morning, the day after the second, combative and argumentative, yet emotional and genuine meeting, God had a private encounter with me. To this day, I still smile when I recall the way He spoke to me. Yes, through the words of the daily devotions I read that morning, His presence became so very clear. He did answer my prayers and He was there. Please, don't ever doubt that He hears our pleas and responds, in His perfect way. Tomorrow, I will have Part II of this story.

October 10

Know therefore that the LORD your God is God; he is the faithful God, keeping his covenant of love to a thousand generations of those who love him and keep his commands.—**Deuteronomy 7:9**

As I wrote yesterday, it was the day after the second City Council meeting regarding the annexation of my neighborhood on Lake Travis. It had been a highly argumentative, emotionally charged meeting. I got a bit upset with God because the situation seemed to soar out of control.

I had specifically prayed that my words would be pleasing to God. I was so concerned about what would come out of my mouth during my three minutes to voice my thoughts that I carefully wrote my speech. I actually spent many hours putting my words on paper. During the first Council meeting the previous week, I did the same thing, however, by the time my name was called, I knew that what I had written wasn't what I needed to say. I spoke for three minutes from my heart, not from the paper in front of me.

For this second meeting, I had a specific area of concern and I wanted all my facts correct, so writing my speech would be helpful. Sure enough, by the time my name was called, I knew that what I had spent hours writing wasn't what God wanted me to say. I didn't know exactly what I would say to the City Council, but somehow I knew He did.

Three minutes goes by quickly, especially when one is nervous. I don't remember my exact words, but I several times I said that all of us needed to avoid making this annexation an "us" (the residents of the street) versus "y'all" (the City) issue.

The day after that meeting, I opened one of my online my devotions and the very first one written by Dr. Jack Graham, a pastor from Plano, Texas, was titled, *Avoiding an "Us" Versus "Them" Mentality*. I couldn't believe almost the exact words I had spoken the day before now appeared before me on my computer screen. God gave me those words to say at the meeting and today, via my online devotion, He was reinforcing that thought. I had wondered where God was the day before. Well, He had been there with me in front of that microphone, giving me that catchy phrase.

Another prayer of mine had been for hearts to be softened. The City has every legal right to annex, so the only chance of changing their minds would be to change their hearts. If only they could understand our passionate reasons for wanting to remain a rural, eclectic street, without City rules and regulations to follow, then perhaps they would vote against annexation.

Before the meeting was adjourned, one of the Council members spoke with so much emotion, his voice even broke several times. This person had listened to our passionate pleas and was convinced that annexation wasn't the answer for us. Another said there were issues that the City needed to research further before he could form an opinion.

The second devotion I opened from Proverbs 31 Ministries was titled, *I Wanted to See God's Faithfulness*. That's exactly how I felt. I just wanted to know where God was in this whole process. The author, Holly Good, was writing about her son's soccer game, not a City Council meeting, but we had the very same thoughts. She so eloquently said that winning isn't the only way God shows His faithfulness. How true! Getting our way with God doesn't prove He is with us.

There had definitely been a change of heart from two Council Members. Two votes aren't enough to win, but their change of heart was enough to show me that God answered my prayer.

At the meeting the day before, I had been too upset to see God in action. After reading these devotions, I saw His faithfulness so clearly. What a perfect reminder of what happens when we take our focus off of God and get caught up in the circumstances. We will miss seeing and hearing Him. Once again, I heard from God, through reading my daily devotions.

The outcome of this annexation is yet to be resolved, but this day I already felt like a winner. I had God on my side—He always has been.

October 11

You intended to harm me, but God intended it for good to accomplish what is now being done, the saving of many lives.—**Genesis 50:20**

For the past two days, I have written about the issue of annexation. I don't want to wear out the topic, but I had another thought to share. We know that God can use all circumstances to fulfill His purpose. Genesis 50:20 tells us God brought good from the evil and trials Joseph endured. Romans 8:28 tells us, "And we know that in all things God works for the good of those who love him, who have been called according to his purpose."

As frustrating as the annexation issue was, there was something very good that came out of it. The residents on my street became very close, bonding together for a common goal. I had lived on the street for four years and never met all of the other homeowners. Suddenly we were emailing back and forth. We had each other's cell phone numbers. There were neighborhood gatherings in our homes so we could meet and greet each other and discuss the issues.

The threat of a forced annexation, something that none of us favored, brought a very diverse group of people close together. I heard delightful stories of family outings on the lake that took place over 50 years earlier when there were only dirt roads leading to the waterfront cabins. There were stories of floodwaters that filled up homes throughout the years but could never destroy the spirits of the folks inside of them. My little street was full of some rich history and strong people.

One sweet young lady down the street lives in her family's home that has flooded (up to the roof) 15 times since 1951. Yet, they cleaned it out and life went on. She recently had back surgery, forced to lie flat much of the time. However, she wrote letters to the City Council, did research on her computer, and visited folks at the Capitol in Austin to discuss this issue once she was able to get out and about. She also reads her daily devotions to stay encouraged. I never would have formed a relationship with this young lady had it not been for this ordeal.

Older people live on both sides of me who have been here for almost 40 years. One couple is delightful and we visit often, but I assumed the other was just a grumpy old man. Was I ever wrong! Come to find out his wife was seriously ill and he was her caretaker. For one gathering at my house, he fixed homemade hummus and brought it over in the cutest little dish.

One of my 80-year-old neighbors drives to the Catholic Church once a week at 2:30 a.m. to pray (in addition to the daily trips she makes during normal hours). When she gets there, she relieves a Spanish speaking couple who also live on this special street.

Jesus is part of my life, but I can't guarantee that all my neighbors have a relationship with Him. However, I learned more do than I expected. While all might not have a relationship with Jesus, I saw God all over this street. I am thankful for the close friendships that resulted from this adversity. We started off as a group of neighbors coming together to fight City Hall, but we emerged as close friends, sharing a special bond. No matter what the final vote is concerning the annexation, good has been accomplished.

October 12

But you were washed, you were sanctified, you were justified in the name of the Lord Jesus Christ and by the Spirit of God. — **1 Corinthians 6:11**

The 2012 Presidential campaign was in full swing. Unfortunately, so were all of the allegations of wavering positions against both major political-party candidates on such important issues as healthcare, the economy, energy and social values.

There are times I feel somewhat like a politician. I write a devotion and later compose another one that more or less contradicts the first one — just as those running for office are often accused of being contradictory. I assumed they just changed their story to suit the crowd they were talking to, but perhaps, like me, they really do see a circumstance from a different perspective, which changes one's thoughts and attitudes.

God never changes, but, being human, we do. As my relationship with Jesus develops, I can't help but notice positive growth in my life and a new outlook on the world around me. Once I accepted Jesus Christ as my Lord and Savior, the Holy Spirit entered my life to start that progressive sanctification process — that inward spiritual journey to bring about holiness and change in the life of a Christian.

I have spoken many times about this book being a journey. Since God didn't provide an entire book of stories written by other women, which was the original desire of my heart, I needed to seriously evaluate His plan that began to unfold. I looked up "journey" in the dictionary on Microsoft Word, and read one of the definitions as "process of development." Yes, this three-year journey has indeed been a process of spiritual development in my life.

Reading stories that I wrote in the beginning, then progressing through the months that followed, I could be accused of wavering in my stance, just as some of the political candidates are. I said one thing, but never actually followed through. I made promises to God about how I would do life differently, but never kept them.

In addition, I had totally different perspectives on the same circumstance at different points in this excursion. Hmm, sounding more and more like a politician. As a reminder to self, sanctification has nothing to do with living in sinless perfection, but everything to do with growing in holiness. In an effort to not be judgmental, I must be hopeful those candidates, accused of being wishy-washy, might also be going through a similar spiritual transformation.

As a Christian, I am continually being transformed into the likeness of Jesus, through the power of the Holy Spirit — one day at a time. I still falter, but my Father will be my strength in my weakness. I will look forward with great anticipation as the events of this day unfold, and the Holy Spirit reveals something new to me, so that I can look less like the old me and more like Jesus.

October 13

"When Jesus had called the Twelve together, he gave them power and authority to drive out all demons and to cure diseases, and he sent them out to preach the kingdom of God and to heal the sick. He told them: "Take nothing for the journey — no staff, no bag, no bread, no money, no extra tunic." — **Luke 9:1-3**

My husband had a business-related conference in Boston, and since it was spouse-friendly, I went along. Being a homebody by nature, traveling — especially by plane — isn't one of my favorite pastimes. Packing for the trip is the most stressful part, though, and I succumb to packing anxiety weeks before the day of departure.

Thanks to weather.com, accessing a 10-day advance forecast is where it starts. As soon as possible, I was online checking the temperature. It was extremely frustrating, though, because every day it changed. At one point, the upcoming weekend weather was sunny with a high of almost 80 degrees. A few days before departure, the high was all the way down to only the mid-50s with an 80% chance of rain. That made a big difference in what to pack.

Traveling lightly has never been easy for me. I will pack what I think I need and then add extras for "just in case." On this trip to Boston, I came back with more clothes that I didn't wear than whatever touched my body.

This trip to Boston was more challenging than most for me. Not only because of the erratic weather predictions, but also because the afternoon sightseeing excursions were subject to change. In addition, I had no idea I would become ill and spend so much time in bed. I thought I was prepared for anything, clothes-wise, but had I known how crummy I was going to feel, I would have taken a suitcase full of chicken noodle soup instead of so much clothing.

When I read the words from Luke 9:1-3, I thought how I would react to such a command. Leave home and *take nothing for the journey*. No moisturizers, makeup, cell phone, computer or battery charger? *No extra tunic*. I wanted something nice to wear for dinner, but comfy shoes and casual clothes were a must for touring the incredibly historic city.

My sister Rhonda and her husband were planning a trip to Turkey tracing Paul's footsteps the same time we would be in Boston. They would be changing planes several times and to make all the transitions easier, they were instructed to take only carry-on luggage. My sister explained to me how she would pack all she needed for two weeks into one small suitcase and a backpack. Yes, they would be able to wash their clothes, but still—only two bags? She didn't know exactly what to expect, and I am sure the weather in Turkey was just as unpredictable as Boston.

Rhonda has had a much longer relationship with Jesus than I have—she is my role model, and I admire her completely. To actually pack for two weeks in two small bags speaks volumes of her trust and dependence on God to provide and take care of her in any situation. My packing almost twice as much as I needed was a reflection of my absorption with myself—my appearance, my comfort, my worldly desires. Rhonda's main focus was walking the same path as Apostle Paul. I was more concerned with the weather in Boston and having enough clothes.

She was so excited about that trip, I feel quite certain she would have gone empty-handed if that's what she was instructed to do. I am thankful that I have my sister to set an example for me. She has her priorities straight, and she walks faithfully with her God. I hope you have such a godly role model in your life as I have in Rhonda. You will meet her tomorrow as she shares one of her stories.

October 14

*He has showed you, O man, what is good. And what does the L*ORD *require of you? To act justly and to love mercy and to walk humbly with your God.*—**Micah 6:8**

When I had my children, I made the decision to be a stay-at-home mom. This went against the popular women's-liberation philosophy that was going on in the '70s, but I didn't mind. I was extremely busy taking care of three children, and I loved my job! When they started school, I had some free time for myself. I quickly got involved in volunteer work at their schools, in their activities, and at our church.

Over the years, I became more and more involved in the programs at our church and several other Christian ministries outside our church. This cycle of getting involved in ministries only escalated when my youngest child graduated from high school and I was in the "empty nest" stage of my life. I had daily and weekly commitments that I honored as if they were paying jobs. My volunteering in all these ministries was consuming me, costing me time with my husband, time to do things with friends, and my time with the Lord. I focused on several verses, particularly Ephesians 2:10, which describes how we are created to do good works. I could never do enough. The second chapter of James—which talks about how faith without works is useless—was imprinted on my mind. This seemed to reinforce my need to do more.

James 3:13 spoke to me in another way. That verse tells us to show our wisdom by our deeds done in humility that comes from wisdom. I started asking myself some serious questions about my life and my faith. Was I truly walking in humility in the wisdom of the Lord? Was there only busyness in my doing the good things I was involved in? Where was my joy in serving the Lord? Where had the closeness with my Savior gone? Was I ever still (Psalm 46:10) to be able to hear His voice drawing me nearer to Him? No, I wasn't. I had been going in my own strength and agenda for years.

Two years ago, I laid all I was doing on the Lord's altar. He led me to give up all I was doing "for Him." This was very difficult, as I painfully realized that my self-worth and the justification for my life were based on my ministry work, just as many people define their lives around their career choices. It took me a whole year to stop all I was involved in and another year to stop feeling guilty for not doing enough for the Lord. I was truly tempted during this time to get "busy" again.

In my season of being still, I have come to know peace and the awesome power of the Holy Spirit in my life. I have been ministered to deeply by the power of God's word in the Bible as never before. God has taught me that He wants my heart, not my sacrifices, as it says in Mark 12:33. The good works I was created to do, I will be led to do through my closeness with Him. What amazes me most is that after nearly 40 years of walking with my Lord, I can be confident in the message of Philippians 1:6: "He who began a good work in you will carry it on to completion until the day of Christ Jesus."

I have chosen Micah's mandate or command as a guiding Scripture for my life.

Rhonda Bonham Goss
Austin, TX

October 15

Anyone who lives on milk, being still an infant, is not acquainted with the teaching about righteousness. But solid food is for the mature, who by constant use have trained themselves to distinguish good from evil. Therefore, let us leave the elementary teachings about Christ and go on to maturity.—**Hebrews 5:13-6:1**

The day had arrived. I finally made the decision to do what I had been pondering for months. It was time to buy a new Bible!

My old one was purchased on October 16, 1996. That is significant in itself because that's my older son's birthday. Besides being purchased on a special day, my Bible and I had spent countless hours together, and I felt a sense of attachment. The underlined verses and notes throughout were extremely important to me.

I never considered a new Bible until the pages started breaking away from the binding. First, it was just those pages in the front where marriages and deaths could be recorded. Since those were still blank, I wasn't concerned. But then Genesis Chapters 1-3 fell out, then the maps from the back. When the rest of the Bible broke away from the binding (the whole thing), I decided it was time.

After over an hour of browsing, I thought I had made the perfect choice. However, when I arrived home and took it out of the box, I made a crucial discovery: I had accidentally picked up the one without the reference tabs indicating the Books of the Bible. When searching for one of those little Books in the Old Testament, I wouldn't be able to just glance at those tabs and flip right to it.

My first thought was to take it back and exchange it. Then I thought for a minute. I wouldn't have any difficulty finding anything in the New Testament. In the Old Testament, I could find about half of the Books. With a little effort, I should be able to master the whole thing.

I thought back to the days when all I could easily locate were Genesis, Matthew, Mark, Luke and John. It was only through consistently delving into the Word, seeking to locate specific Scriptures, and thumbing through the pages that I became more comfortable. It had taken some effort, but through Bible studies, devotions and sermons, God's Word had become familiar and easier to navigate.

How silly of me to be concerned that my new purchase didn't have little tabs. My grandmother's didn't have them and she could flip to any Scripture (Old or New Testament) when she read her morning devotion in a matter of seconds! Now that I had a tab-less Bible, it was time that I study it more diligently and become as proficient as she was.

It was no accident that I picked that particular Bible. Could it be God's way of telling me the time had come to study a little harder? Had I been using the excuse of being a "baby Christian" for too long? Was it now time to start acting like a mature child of God? I think so!

October 16

"I will put my laws in their hearts, and I will write them on their minds." —**Hebrews 10:16**

The digital display on the clock read 10:16—again. For the third time in less than a week, that's what I saw when I casually glanced to check the time. Actually, it is uncanny how, week after week, that habitual glance results in either a 10:16—or a 9:11 reading.

Very soon after the 9/11 terrorist attacks, I found myself checking the time and it was 9:11. Feeling that was God's way of making sure I didn't forget to pray for the victims and all affected by the horrific events of that day, I did indeed stop whatever I was doing and have a quiet time with my Father. The Holy Spirit still makes sure I look at the clock several times a week just at that moment.

You may be wondering about the significance behind 10:16. Thankfully, October 16 is a joyous day. It is my oldest son's birthday.

Several years ago, soon after I started this book, I began noticing when it was exactly 10:16 (a.m. or p.m.). I never glanced and saw a display of 8:04, my other son's birthday, or 8:07, my husband's. No, three or four times a week, that casual turn towards a clock reminded me of that glorious 16th day of October, 1984. What a wonderful opportunity to lift my son up to the Lord in prayer.

When Zach was in fifth grade, he received the Presidential Fitness Award at the end of the year. The P.E. coach commented that Zach always contributed 110%. I will clarify that remark by saying that he contributed 110% to anything sports-related.

He was a very good athlete and posessed an incredibly passionate heart for whatever sport he participated in. In high school he was on the varsity baseball and football teams his sophomore through senior years, but baseball was his first love. He lived and dreamed it. He received all kinds of private hitting lessons, played on select teams and attended numerous baseball camps. We also watched hour upon hour of ESPN baseball when he came home from a date (with Lauren, now his wife.)

I must confess that I was just as passionate about sports. Who do you think paid for all those private lessons and camps? When it came time for Zach to go to college, it was all about baseball. He opted for a small Division III school to pursue his dream. However, after one semester, he was ready to give up baseball and transfer to LSU to be with Lauren, and to pursue academics. Suddenly, without sports in his life, all of that competitive energy went into the classroom. My son, who never made all A's in his life, earned a spot on the Dean's List every semester and graduated magna cum laude!

I am often in the company of younger sports-enthusiast moms, and, unfortunately, I see myself in them. How easy it is to idolize our children and their sports. We worry if they will make the team. Will another student move in who is more talented? What if they get injured and lose their spot? All that wasted time and energy worrying about a future over which we have no control. We just never know the plans God has for our children.

My Zach is now gainfully employed, happily married and has an incredible work ethic. I couldn't see a life for him that didn't involve sports, but look what God did! He is a financial analyst and still giving 110% of himself towards something non-sports related. Intellectually, he has certainly excelled! I am so thankful for the mature, hard-working, efficient, business-minded man he has become.

253

It has been so sweet to watch him grow in his relationship with my daughter-in-love. The night before their wedding, he professed his love for Lauren at the Rehearsal Dinner and it was as if my son emerged into a man right before my eyes! It's crazy how our children "grow-up" to be such fine men and women! Honestly, I am still in awe of what Zach has accomplished and give all praises to our Father.

I have written several stories about my two sons leaving for college, and leaving their faith at home. However, I cling to the promise of Hebrews 10:16, Zach's birthday verse.

Father God, by faith I trust You will put Your laws in Zach's heart and You will write them on Zach's mind. Amen!

When I was Zach's age, I was in much the same place, though. It is miraculous how Jesus reached down into that pit, pulled me out and changed my heart. The Lord has great plans for my son too, and I will continue praying Hebrews 10:16 for him—especially every time I notice the time is 10:16.

Happy Birthday, Zach-A-Roo! I love you!

October 17

And now these three remain: faith, hope and love. But the greatest of these is love.—**1 Corinthians 13:13**

Beside my stack of daily devotionals is a pad of mini neon Post-It notes. No matter which books I choose to read in the morning, I invariably find one devotion, or more, that is just what I need for that day. Or the Scripture might touch my heart and is one I want to remember. I like to mark the page with one of those little neon notes and write myself a message on it.

On this particular morning, it was the Scripture that touched my heart: "The one who follows instruction is on the path to life, but the one who rejects correction goes astray" (Proverbs 10:17 HCSB). Actually, I wanted to jot it down and send it to my son, thinking God was speaking directly to him. I reached for my pen and underlined the verse, and then I picked up the little stack of Post-It notes. Right before I tore off the top one, I glanced down and saw a message had been written on it: "I Love You."

My husband and I used to leave notes for each other all the time. Just sweet little messages like "I Love You" or "Have a Wonderful Day." When he traveled, he would stick a note under my pillow before he left home or I would put one in his suitcase. But life had been kind of hectic and neither of us had written each other a sweet message in months.

Here I was, thinking I needed to make a note of Proverbs 10:17 to send to my son and I found those precious three words from my husband on that Post-It. Immediately, some other words from Scripture came to my mind—"but the greatest of these is love." What could be more important than that verse?

"For God so loved the world that he gave His one and only son" (John 3:16) might be equally important. There is no greater love than the love of our Heavenly Father for His children. If not for that incomprehensible love, what else could have led God to send His son to die for us?

The love my husband has for me is as close to God's that I could ever hope to find this side of heaven. It is unconditional, he loves me just as I am, he is patient and kind, and he never keeps a record of my wrongs. There is nothing he wouldn't do for me and he would protect me until the very end (1 Corinthians 13:4-7). He always places me, and others, above himself. Have I shown my husband that same love? Have I loved others I encounter every day that way?

Were those words from Proverbs 10:17 meant for me, instead of my son? Was God telling me to follow His instructions on how to treat others and how to be a good wife? Perhaps I needed to concentrate on making sure my husband felt the same about my love for him as I do of his love for me. Isn't that the Golden Rule—treat people the same way I want them to treat me? (Matthew 7:12).

Life shouldn't get so busy that I forget to love the people well in my life or to follow God's instructions on how to treat them. To obey God's commands, the most important words for me to remember are the ones my husband left on that Post-It note. Yes, *"the greatest of these is love."*

October 18

Let us then approach the throne of grace with confidence, so that we may receive mercy and find grace to help us in our time of need.—**Hebrews 4:16**

After praying daily that I would not lose my temper again with the whole remodeling process, I blew it. Yep, I totally lost my cool with the building superintendent. Since an ugly episode at the beginning of the project, I continually asked God to set a guard over my mouth (Psalm 141:3) and to help me remember that "it was only a house." I couldn't believe the venom that spewed from my mouth that morning. It was as if I were possessed by Satan!

My first little tantrum had occurred six months earlier. I was so embarrassed and ashamed of my behavior then. How did it happen again?

Easy. I had simply allowed myself to become completely wrapped up in the busyness of life and the complications of construction. I had become more focused on my circumstances and my little world than on Jesus.

In addition to my commitments, that had become duties instead of blessed opportunities to grow God's kingdom, I had grown weary of the building process. And the most dominant frustration was that my writing time was being infringed upon. Now, how ironic is that? Without being in God's holy presence, I have no words to write, even if I had the time. And I obviously wasn't abiding in Him.

You might be wondering what happened that caused such an outburst. Believe me, it was nothing that couldn't be fixed. Had I not been so absorbed with circumstances of the world, if Christ had been my focus, I could have controlled my mouth. However, that morning, I hit the floor running and never looked to Him.

After I apologized profusely, the building superintendent was incredibly kind. I immediately went to my husband, who had witnessed my explosion, and burst into tears. As he held me, I spoke to God in humble confession. I knew at that moment that my Father extended His grace, mercy and forgiveness, but I just couldn't forgive myself.

I continued to beat myself up the rest of the day. Instead of accepting God's mercy, I held on to my shame. The next morning, it still weighed heavy on my heart. I wanted to be in God's presence. I knew there was no better place to be. I didn't want to be separated from Him, but I was.

Picking up my "Jesus Calling" later that morning, I found words for my weary soul. I was told not to be discouraged by my inability to keep my focus on Jesus 24/7. Reading two phrases— "Don't let feelings of failure weigh you down" and "I am delighted by your desire to walk closely with me"—filled me with encouragement. I was reminded that I achieve a victory every time I reach out to Jesus during my daily disruptions and to rejoice in every step of growth.

After reading that daily entry, I was overcome with my Father's love. Accepting His forgiveness and forgiving myself, I returned to His peaceful presence. Oh, it felt so wonderful to be back.

How easily we women beat up on ourselves. We can focus on our shortcomings and completely miss out on what God had in store for us. We often allow our sin and shame to be bigger than He is, and that guilt burdens our hearts. Those burdens will cast a shadow that block out His magnificent light, and we miss the opportunity to walk in His radiance and glorify our great God. He wants us to grow His kingdom, not our guilt.

No matter where you are today, no matter what you have said or done that you think brings displeasure to God, just know that He is waiting to welcome you back to His holy presence. "Those who look to him are radiant; their faces are never covered with shame" (Psalm 34:5).

What are you waiting for? Don't focus on your failures—focus on being in your Father's presence.

October 19

Be self-controlled and alert. Your enemy the devil prowls around like a roaring lion looking for someone to devour. Resist him, standing firm in the faith, because you know that your brothers throughout the world are undergoing the same kind of sufferings. —**1 Peter 5:8-9**

Yesterday I shared a story about yelling at the building supervisor of my remodeling project. I compared myself to someone possessed by Satan. Shamefully, I must admit that as hard as I tried to focus on God's presence, the Evil One set up residence in my heart for several weeks and there was some serious warfare going on.

During this period of time, I didn't write a single devotion. In addition to the writing frustrations and the construction woes, other circumstances in my life were causing anxiety. My husband and I rarely get cross with each other, but during this time we had several ugly disagreements. My youngest son was going through a difficult time in a relationship, and I was filled with sadness because he was so distraught.

The Presidential election of 2012 was also on my mind. I knew that God was in control and that He was my leader, not the man in the White House, yet I was anxious about the spiritual climate of our country.

Over coffee with my Java Dive girlfriends, I discovered that Satan had invaded *all* of our lives and was thriving. We shared stories and were amazed at the similar battles raging in our lives. Later on, as one of these precious ladies and I exchanged text messages, she wrote, "I think you are able to identify the Enemy's attack faster than I can."

I pondered that comment for a while. I thought about her life and mine. I knew her testimony and she knew mine. I compared our two extremely divergent pasts and came up with a very simple conclusion.

Perhaps, since I used to hang out so much with Satan, I could indeed identify his attacks easily. Yep, we used to run in the same crowd and spend time together. We know each other well. He is acquainted with my weaknesses, insecurities and tendency to worship false idols, like my children and possessions. He knows the shame and guilt that I used to harbor, and does his best to rekindle those emotions. The Evil One is aware of what makes me stumble, lose my temper and spit venom from my mouth.

The guy has a very good memory too. Even though I had distanced myself from him long ago, he still remembers everything about me. Maybe with all the new technology, he has a sophisticated database filled with all that info.

Previously, I lived in a constant state of warfare and just accepted it as the norm. After learning there was a better way, after accepting that Jesus died so I didn't have to endure a life of continual strife, everything was different. Coming from such a dismal existence, the disparity between the new and old is so obvious that it can be difficult for the lurking shadow of the Evil One to slip by unnoticed.

That is the good that came from all those years of stumbling in the dark. Now it's easier for me to see that sly fox attempting to invade my circle of light. Knowing that I was under attack, I armed myself with truth, prayed feverously, told the Devil to flee and cried out to God for protection and for wisdom. Satan persisted, but so did I. Desperately! After falling for his tricks before, I will resist his advances with every ounce of strength God gives me.

God also persisted in this war. He was silent for a while—waiting to see how passionately I would cry out. In my heart, I accepted that He was allowing Satan's actions, but with the intention of having me grow closer to Him and more dependent on His presence and protection. For as easily as I think I can identify satanic infiltration, I cannot fight the battle without my Savior.

God let me suffer a bit, but then revealed Himself as the One in charge of the battle. I am slowly learning what it means to be thankful for these trials in life. If this was the plan, for me to seek Him more passionately and depend more on His power to resist the evil of this world, He succeeded—again!

"And the God of all grace, who called you to his eternal glory in Christ, after you have suffered a little while, will himself restore you and make you strong, firm and steadfast. To him be the power for ever and ever. Amen" (1 Peter 5:10-11).

October 20

Jesus Christ is the same yesterday and today and forever. —**Hebrews 13:8**

The temperature soars to 99 outside and your AC goes out. Who do you call? Do you Google "air conditioning repair," read the reviews and select the one with the most positive comments? Or, perhaps you call the neighbor down the street, remembering she recently had a repair truck in front of her house. Was she happy with the service? Would she recommend the company to you?

You move to a new city and you need a new everything—dentist, OB-GYN, and most importantly, hairdresser (I still haven't even looked for that yet). Where do you start? When I moved to Lake Travis, I certainly didn't just Google "doctors." I wanted word-of-mouth referrals first.

Oh, what about car repair? As women, we certainly want to know if we can trust the service technician or even the guy at Jiffy Lube when he tells us we need a new air filter. We are quick to repeat the stories of feeling like we were taken advantage of just because of being a female and not being astute in the car-repair department. We ask around and go to the place where others feel the employees were honest.

Which laundry detergent is the best? Does that moisturizer really prevent wrinkles? Can you believe what *Consumer Reports* says about the most fuel-efficient car? Is that babysitter responsible enough to watch your children? Will that contractor do a good job remodeling your home or would the other guy be better?

Can we actually be 100% sure of *anything* "in this world"? We want to read the reviews, we want to hear what others have to say, we want affirmation that we have selected a reputable, qualified person for the specific work we need. One negative comment might be all we need to skip that number and call another. But even after all that, we can never be totally sure, can we?

Have you ever asked for references on whom to worship? Since you are reading this devotion, I assume you are a Christian and you believe in God and that the only way to Him is through His Son, Jesus Christ. You might have shopped around for a place of worship, but Who to bow down to wasn't the question.

Think about it. Have you ever received a negative review or comment about God? Has He ever *not* delivered one of His promises? Has He ever been proven wrong? Can you trust Him? When you moved, did you have to search for a new God? Can you look back and remember a horrific trial in your life—one you thought you couldn't survive, but now, years later as you look back, you are thankful for the One who carried you?

God has no record of failures. He has never made a mistake. He is the same yesterday, today and forever. I can't think of anything in this world that I can be that sure of, but I can hold fast to the words of Jesus in John 16:33: "I have told you these things, so that in me you may have peace. In this world you will have trouble. But take heart! I have overcome the world."

Our Father in heaven is my Rock. He is faithful. His promises never fail. I don't need to ask for referrals, reviews or Google "who is my Savior." I have the *blessed assurance* that Jesus is mine!

If you would like to Google something though, try "Third Day Blessed Assurance." My favorite Christian band sings the 1873 hymn, and it is enchanting! You can even watch the YouTube video and sing along.

October 21

Be careful not to forget the covenant of the LORD your God that he made with you; do not make for yourselves an idol in the form of anything the LORD your God has forbidden. For the LORD your God is a consuming fire, a jealous God. —**Deuteronomy 4:23-24**

My husband and I have an amusing time discussing the details of my dreams. In my waking hours, I live a very ho-hum life without too much excitement. Oh, but when I go to sleep, it's a different story. The dreams I remember are kind of crazy and don't make much sense, but I find it interesting the details I recall so vividly. But every so often there is one that gives me a jolt when I wake up, because I am convinced that dreams are one of the ways God communicates with me.

We were finally seeing a light at the end of the tunnel with our remodeling project. The builder had actually given us a move-back-into-the-house date. We had been under construction over a year! But you know what—the year had flown by. However, I must shamefully admit, that during that period I spent more time thinking, worrying, daydreaming and focusing on the project than anything else. Yes, more than *anything* else.

The first two Commandments said it very clearly: "You shall have no other gods before me. You shall not make for yourself an idol" (Exodus 20:3-4). In one of Pastor Brad's sermons—one that I have listened to numerous times—he said that the things we care about most become our idols. God has given us good things to enjoy, but we must be careful not to let those things become the source of our joy and our focus. My house had definitely become an idol.

In this particular sermon, Pastor Brad spoke on Genesis 22, the testing of Abraham. Would he give up his long-awaited son to prove that he loved God more? God didn't want Isaac to die, and His testing was for the purpose of strengthening Abraham's character. God knew his weak point. God knew what the hardest thing in Abraham's life would be to give up. Brad asked the congregation: *What is your Isaac?* What would each of us fear losing the most?

My dream was literally a wake-up call for me to examine what my Isaac had become. As I slept, I saw my completed house. It was finally done and all the furniture was back in. The power was on, and it looked like someone lived there, but no one was home. In my dream, I was at an unknown location, taking a live, virtual tour of the house on my computer.

Suddenly, I saw flames shooting out of the windows and through the roof. Our newly completed house, filled with all our worldly belongings, was on fire! I had visualized exactly where the furniture would go and how the rooms would look. I had rearranged the family room in my mind and had my new office arranged just so. On that virtual tour, everything looked exactly as I had planned. But in one quick glance, it was up in smoke.

To make the situation even worse, the insurance company told me the fire was my fault and they wouldn't pay a dime. I saw our newly remodeled home burn, along with all of our possessions, with no hope of reimbursement.

My weakness was no secret to God. He commanded that I not make an idol for myself, but I did. Yes, He blessed me with good things to enjoy, but I got so wrapped up in those "things" I didn't give God the time He deserved. I thought of the Bible verses about God being a jealous God, and searched a few. Deuteronomy 4:24 immediately grabbed my attention: "For the Lord your God is a consuming fire, a jealous God."

Jealousy is a sin when it is a desire for something that doesn't belong to you. A holy jealousy can be described as being appropriately possessive of something that is rightly yours. Our God burns with a holy jealousy—our love and adoration belong to God and to God alone. We are His. He will do whatever is necessary to remove whoever or whatever stands in the way of His enjoyment of those He loves. It was just a dream, but too real for me to ignore.

You now know *one* of my Isaacs. Tomorrow, I will tell you another idol I worshipped far longer than my house.

October 22

You shall not make for yourself an idol. —**Exodus 20:4**

Yesterday's story is a prerequisite for this one. If you didn't read it, I will wait a few minutes for you to catch up. Or you can go back and skim it, just so the topic of idols will be fresh on your mind.

Pastor Brad was speaking about Genesis 22 and the testing of Abraham. The long-awaited Isaac, born to the aged Abraham and Sarah, had become an idol in their life. Brad asked the congregation: *What is your Isaac?* I wonder how many moms squirmed in their seat and had the same answer as mine. Brad proceeded to announce he would be speaking about the idolatry of children.

"Whose schedule runs the schedule of your family?" Brad inquired. My boys are out of college, but back in their younger years, their extra-curricular activities controlled mine. I hear young moms comment that their husbands have been placed on the back burner because the kids consume all their time and energy. Mine did too. Please be careful. Obsession with the kids can destroy a marriage. I know from past experience.

I think the most significant lesson Isaac learned from God testing his dad was that Abraham demonstrated he loved God more than his son. Our kids need to rest assured of our unconditional love; however, they should never question who is No. 1 in our life. They must know Mom's first love is God, and, if Mom is married, Dad ranks second, not them. We know better, don't we? But somehow our hearts become, as Brad coined it, "an idol factory" for the things we care about the most.

Brad noted that many parents take extreme measures to protect their children from the dark corners of life. We try to manipulate life circumstances to make their life comfy. I squirmed in my seat again, silently acknowledging doing just that for my boys. When Brad declared those dark corners could be part of God's plan to grow our child and make faith happen, I realized I might have hindered my sons from experiencing God's perfect plan. However, at the moment, God was clearly speaking to my heart about a specific situation, and I was very uncomfortable.

My younger son attended the University of Texas on a football scholarship. He was a standout high school athlete—any young man awarded a football scholarship to a Division I school has to be. However, once he got to the University of Texas, he was only one of over 100 exceptional athletes on the team. His college football career didn't quite materialize as planned, and no matter how much I worried and prayed for more playing time, it just didn't happen. Add two torn anterior cruciate ligaments (ACLs) to the picture, and it was a difficult five years.

After graduation, the job market was particularly tough, and he couldn't find a job in his field of advertising. He pursued his real passion of photography, which wasn't very lucrative or full-time at first. I agreed to "subsidize" his monthly income. Yes, I agreed to enable my son. I felt that was the least I could do to help make his life easier—to shield him from those dark corners.

I knew it wasn't the right thing, but I wanted to protect him for the cold, cruel world. He wasn't overzealous in his job search for full-time employment; why should he be? Mom was making life manageable without a full-time job. But then Brad's sermon knocked some sense into me and changed everything. God didn't spare His own Son, why was I overprotecting mine?

Why did my child's success in life somehow become the determining factor for my own joy and happiness? Yes, I worried way too much about his less-than-perfect circumstances. Isn't God supposed to be the one I look to for my joy? Time was long overdue for me to lay my Isaac on the table.

The first step was to stop enabling my son. I tearfully wrestled with that decision, but God helped me through the process. A few weeks after I cut him off financially, he confessed that was the best thing I could have done to help him take responsibility for his own life. Most importantly, after all those years of allowing my children to reign, God was showing me how to take them off the throne and place Him as Ruler of my life. Please pray for a permanent closing of my "idol factory."

"Therefore speak to them and tell them, 'This is what the Sovereign LORD says: When any Israelite sets up idols in his heart, I the LORD will answer him myself in keeping with his great idolatry. I will do this to recapture the hearts of the people of Israel, who have all deserted me for their idols'" (Ezekiel 14:4-5).

October 23

"I will give you a new heart and put a new spirit in you. I will remove from you your heart of stone and give you a heart of flesh." —**Ezekiel 36:26**

There were just a few more days left of Daylight Savings Time. I will admit I don't like it when we "fall back" to regular time, but the prolonged darkness in the morning sure made sleeping in very enticing. However, my golden retriever has a built-in alarm clock, no matter what the sunlight situation. If it was 6:30 a.m., everyone needed to be awake.

As I listened to her whining at me to get out of bed, I lingered for a few minutes to talk to God. I finally threw off the covers and walked towards Holly to give her the good-morning hug she was waiting on. Then I did something I never do: I crawled back in bed. Honestly, I never do that! I even asked myself, *What in the world are you thinking?*

As I snuggled back into my comfy bed and pulled the covers close to my face, I was overcome with the most incredible feeling. For a few seconds, I physically felt the love of Jesus covering me as I pulled the sheet and blanket back over my body. Yes, I "felt" the love of Jesus! I knew it was Him!

I know in my mind that Jesus loves me—that was one of the first songs I can remember singing as a little girl. I know His tender words of love that He has spoken in the Bible. I know that He is Love and He commands me to love. But to physically feel Him covering me with the warmth of His embrace was a first for me—and basically indescribable.

As a mother, I can identify the strong feelings of affection I have for my sons. When they were babies, the physical touch of their little bodies next to mine was the most precious feeling I knew. As they grew older and larger, the strength behind their hugs spoke volumes of their devotion to me. Something inside of me longed to feel that same closeness with Jesus.

What made the moment even more remarkable was that I had actually been praying to "feel" God's love. It seems I had blocked Him out—my heart was hard and full of scar tissue. I wasn't close to my earthly father, and that has been one of the hurts I have battled all my life. I have wondered what it would have felt like to curl up in my daddy's lap and feel his warm embrace? What would it have been like to be daddy's little girl? Longing for the affection I never received from him kept me from knowing what it felt like to be adored by my Heavenly Father. For years I have been pleading with God to soften my heart so that I would surrender myself to Him and "feel" His adoration for me.

God sent His only Son to die on the cross for my sins over 2000 years ago. I accepted that as fact when I was much younger. That morning, He sent His Son to cover me with that blood He shed, to cover me with His love. It was as if He was saying to me, *This is what you have been praying for. I am going to give you a taste of just how strong my feelings are for you.*

He removed my heart of stone so that I was able to receive His love—a gift that has been there all along. With my new heart of flesh, I felt His presence. Yes, I actually felt His physical presence, and my life will *never* be the same after my Jesus hug.

October 24

*But they that wait upon the L*ORD *shall renew their strength; they shall mount up with wings as eagles; they shall run, and not be weary; and they shall walk and not faint.*—**Isaiah 40:31 (KJV)**

A sweet friend invited me for a belated birthday lunch. We had spent time in Bible study together and she had already written a poem for this book. When I arrived at her house so we could ride together to the restaurant, she had a very special gift for me—a gift that was an answer to a heartfelt plea to God just the night before.

As I have mentioned previously, the response from other women to submit their God stories for this book didn't materialize by the numbers I had envisioned. While I knew the journey was His purpose, I still got frustrated. I thoroughly cherished my time with Him, spending hours on end writing these stories. However, without the response from others that I had anticipated, the challenge of writing the devotions necessary to fill this book was overwhelming at times.

So when doubt clouds my mind and Satan gets his foot in the door, I easily get entangled in my little world. The previous night I pleaded with God and begged for help. This book would only be completed by His hand, not mine. I asked Him to open the hearts of other women to submit their stories. I know He heard the frustration and impatience in my voice. Because of my doubt, I wondered if He heard the plea from my heart.

That morning I had randomly selected a few devotionals for my quiet time. Inside *Take my Heart, Oh God*, written by a long list of godly women, the bookmark was placed at a date way back in June, so it had been a while since I had read from that one. I grumbled to myself. That's what I wanted for this book—for it to be written by a long list of godly women. Why, of all the options on the shelf, had God led me to that one?

The title on the top of the page, "Waiting with God," grabbed my attention immediately. I read that sometimes God arranges a time of waiting to obtain His goal of a "life-altering" bond with Him. When do we spend the most time with God? Usually while waiting for an answer to a specific prayer request.

All right. I thought God's purpose for me all along had been the journey. Could the wait be His goal? Either way, it all comes down to the fact that I was spending more time with Him, which had certainly produced a "life-altering" bond between us.

Back to the special gift I mentioned previously. My sweet friend Elizabeth gave me a card with a personal note inside that just took my breath away. "My birthday gift to you is a promise of three more devotions. Please hold me accountable for these." She even had the stories in her heart already and went so far as to list the three she planned to write!

As my eyes welled up with tears, I explained to Elizabeth that just the night before I had called out to God, pleading for more women to submit stories. I told her about my daily devotion on waiting with God. I thought about the bond God and I were making in the wait, but I also felt the life-altering moment—a moment of knowing a prayer had been answered.

The rest of the day I played a song over and over in my head. Do you know "Everlasting God" by Lincoln Brewster? If not, you might want to watch the video on YouTube. Listen and allow the words from Isaiah 40:31 to renew your weary soul.

Tomorrow, Elizabeth shares one of her gifts.

October 25

You've been given insight into God's kingdom. You know how it works. Not everybody has this gift, this insight; it hasn't been given to them. Whenever someone has a ready heart for this, the insights and understandings flow freely. But if there is no readiness, any trace of receptivity soon disappears. That's why I tell stories: to create readiness, to nudge the people toward receptive insight.—**Matthew 13:10-12 (MSG)**

I had been praying for a nudge from God for my daughter, Liza. A sophomore in college, Liza had her share of transitional struggles: roommate issues, boyfriend breakups, sorority cuts, just to name a few.

Especially homesick after being home over a long weekend, she called with yet another roommate issue. *God please just give Liza some encouragement today, just a nudge to let her know You're there, that You care for her even more than I do as her mother. God, You gave me these feelings of compassion and empathy for my daughter, feelings so strong that I would take on the pain for her if I could. Something only Your Son could do for us.*

I then remembered a time when I felt so overwhelmed by God's care for me, almost as if God were physically wrapping His arms around me in a huge hug. Coincidentally, the setting was Liza's college town.

We had driven her back to school the previous fall on a scorching-hot day. Tired after driving six hours, unloading cars and finding a motel, we faced what should have been a pleasant enough decision: Where are we going to eat dinner? We pulled into and out of several restaurant parking lots. Not surprisingly, with many families doing the same thing we were doing, the restaurants were packed.

Finally, we committed to one of my favorite chain restaurants and asked if we could eat in the bar. Mercifully, the hostess said yes and we were seated and eating in no time. As we were eating, I noted a family leaving the seating area—several kids, a grandmother, husband, and wife. The man was extremely polite to the hostess, who was obviously stressed with the crowd, telling her how good everything was. I thought to myself, *I am so glad that my husband often does the same thing when he knows someone could really use a word of encouragement.*

Then, to my surprise, that same man looked right at me. "You're Mrs. Ponder, aren't you?" he said. Dumbfounded, I quickly said, "Yes," mentally trying to place the face. "You were my accounting professor at Tech many years ago. You sure were a good teacher," he said, disappearing out the door, leaving no time for a response.

My husband and daughter were as stunned as I was—first that someone would remember me from having taught in a city that I had not lived in for over 25 years, and second that a sincere compliment was laid at my feet when I so desperately needed to hear one.

A nudge when needed! That's all I could think of. *Dear Jesus, thank You so much for real-time insight into Your kingdom. Thank You for caring about me, right here, right now. Thank You for a glimpse of reassurance that what I do matters.*

Elizabeth Ponder
Austin, TX

October 26

The LORD answered Moses, "Is the LORD's arm too short? You will now see whether or not what I say will come true for you." —**Numbers 11:23**

Flying in a plane puts life into perspective for me. I love to look out of the window during takeoff and watch cars. Where are all these people going? What are they thinking? Do they look above them and wonder the same of me? I suspect the answer to that question is no!

What about God? Is that how He sees the world? He has a much bigger perspective than I do out of my little view of the world from seat 7A. He has millions to watch. Does that make you feel insignificant? Maybe you are feeling intimate with Him in your relationship today. But do you see Him as big as He really is?

Moses, a man who had one of the closest relationships with God in recorded history, underestimated God's bigness. As he was leading the Israelites through the desert, they began to crave the things they had left behind in Egypt, and complained miserably about wanting meat to eat instead of the manna God laid down for them each morning. Moses, worn out from all the complaining but not knowing how to get the people off his back, went to speak to God about fulfilling the people's desire for meat. God told him that He would give the people meat, and not just as an appetizer. He would provide so much that the people would have enough for a whole month.

Moses was skeptical about the ability to pull off such a feat, so he asked God how He was going to make that happen. Moses knew he had 600,000 foot soldiers (plus women and children), and God was going to suddenly come up with enough meat for a whole month? In Moses' eyes, even if all the flocks and herds were slaughtered and all the fish in the sea were caught, the people would not be satisfied because there would not be enough.

To that, God responded, *Is the LORD's arm too short? Is there any limit to my power?* (Numbers 11:23 NASB). He brought a wind that drove quail in from the sea, and let them fall into the camp to about three feet above the ground, extending "as far as a day's walk in any direction." Think about that for a moment.

That is how big I want to see God each and every day, because He is that big. Nothing is impossible for God, and there isn't a place where He is not. Praise be to Him!

Teri Brown
Austin, TX

October 27

Consider it pure joy, my brothers, whenever you face trials of many kinds, because you know that the testing of your faith develops perseverance. Perseverance must finish its work so that you may be mature and complete, not lacking anything.—**James 1:2-5**

When it comes to listening to music in the car, I am in the dark ages. It seems as though everyone else I know plays CDs, has Pandora on their smartphone or an iPod. I just prefer the good, old-fashioned radio. However, I am not totally out of date because I do have Sirius Satellite, even though I prefer a local station.

On this particular day as I was driving back to Austin, I couldn't get my Austin or Houston station to come in clearly, so I punched the button for The Message (satellite Christian music). Just as I switched over to it, I heard the disc jockey say something that I thought was quite profound, and I jotted it down.

When I arrived back in Austin, I had a visit scheduled with a sweet young friend from my church. As we shared what had been going on in our lives during the week, she mentioned some of the hurdles she was facing. I immediately thought of what I heard on the radio.

My memory isn't as good as it used to be, so I am glad I wrote down what the disc jockey said because I never would have remembered it word for word: "God won't protect you from what He can per-FECT you through."

Think about those words for a few minutes. Then think about any trials you feel God is taking you through right now. Can you see perfection on the other side? It's there. Stay focused on Him and He will make sure you get through whatever it is—all the while growing you into the woman He intends for you to be. Someday we will be mature and complete, not lacking anything!

October 28

You were taught, with regard to your former way of life, to put off your old self, which is being corrupted by its deceitful desires; to be made new in the attitude of your minds; and to put on the new self, created to be like God in true righteousness and holiness.—**Ephesians 4:22-24**

Sometimes while sitting in traffic or at a stoplight, I play a little word game. I look at the license plate on the car in front of me and try to think of a phrase that the letters could possibly stand for. I have also done the same thing for my own license plate, just to help me remember it.

Years ago I drove a Suburban with a license plate of 243 OEC. Three and C rhymed, so that helped, and coming up with a phrase for the OEC was even easier—Over Every Curb. Those Suburbans are long, and I had a very bad habit of turning corners too sharp and running over the curb (thankfully not *every* one of them).

My last license plate was 02BTM4. Once again, I had no problem coming up with a catchy little phrase: O, 2 Be Their Mother 4ever. Yes, I did idolize my two boys and to be their mother forever was my idea of true joy and contentment.

When I received my registration renewal notice in the mail, I noticed in big bold letters "New Plates Required." In the state of Texas when a license plate is seven years old, it must be "retired." I was shocked to realize that my car was that old, but new plates? Oh, no! I wanted 2 Be Their Mother 4ever, and now the state of Texas was going to strip me of my title.

Honestly, I battled child idolatry for years. At first, I didn't realize my problem, but as it progressed, it became very clear. Over the past few years God has gone to great lengths to help me see that I had placed the boys at the top of my priority list. Even though it was painful, He opened my eyes, through skillfully orchestrated sermons and Bible studies, to the reality of my misplaced worship. My Father then patiently waited as I slowly took the boys off of their pedestal and put Him on the throne where He belonged.

The thought of taking off that old license plate made me a tad bit sad. On the other hand, the more I thought about it, the more I realized how healing it was—part of the sanctification process. As the Scripture reading for today states, I must take off my old self and put on the new me in order to be more like God. Part of my old ways was that silly phrase I attached to that license plate. It was time to let it go too.

Of course, as long as I am living, I will be their mom. And I love my boys more than words can describe. However, I found that lasting joy and contentment comes from my relationship with Jesus Christ. To surrender my boys to God instead of making them the objects of my worship was an action I never could have done in my own power.

The new plates came in the mail, and I couldn't resist coming up with a little phrase for the letters BMT—Brenda's Major Transformation. My Heavenly Father had indeed begun some mighty work in the attitude of this son-worshipper's mind.

October 29

This is the day that the LORD has made. Let us rejoice and be glad in it.—**Psalm 118:24**

Several years ago, my mom wanted a travel buddy to go with her to Omaha, Nebraska, so she could visit a friend. I volunteered. Mom lives in a retirement community in Schulenburg, Texas, which is just a couple of hours from me. I see her often, but usually for quick, one-day visits. Spending five days together would be a wonderful opportunity for both of us.

Mom was 82 years old at the time of that first trip in 2010—26 years older than me. My older son, Zach, had just turned 26, so I was very much aware of just how quickly 26 years can fly by! Of course, time is relative. I had just listened to a sermon from church on my iPod, and Pastor Brad made a comment referencing the time frame between October and Christmas. He said that for a small child, those two months can be a lifetime, but for the mom who hasn't even started thinking about shopping, Christmas is "just right around the corner." For my son, 26 years *had* been his lifetime up to that point, but for me, turning 82 was just right around the corner, God willing!

Mom goes to the gym five days a week, eats healthy, drives her car all over the place, plays bridge, works lots of puzzles, is active in her church and community, and looks good "for her age." However, her mind just isn't as sharp as it used to be. While in Omaha, she asked the same questions several times and got disoriented easily, especially in the unfamiliar surroundings. She has no idea what a text message is and, even though I have tried to explain it to her several times, she just can't comprehend.

What's scary is that I can already see myself in her. How many times do my sons try to explain new technology to me and I just can't quite grasp it? I am still trying to understand all of the fancy things I can do with my "smart phone" and my iPad. I am forever forgetting where I have put something and will waste countless hours searching for the lost item. I work out four to five times a week and hear that I am in good shape "for my age," but the old brain just tends to deteriorate anyway.

God willing, 82 is just around the corner. Am I going to waste time worrying about growing old while in my temporary home or am I going to think about my eternal life in heaven? Shouldn't I be more concerned about what I can do to glorify God today?

Dr. Jack Graham said in his PowerPoint message that the question isn't, "Am I going to die?" It's, "How am I going to live?" Am I going to get stuck on what life is going to be like in 26 years, or am I going to focus on the words of Psalm 124 and rejoice in this day that God has already planned for me? While on this side of heaven, I want to be filled with the joy that is found in the Lord's presence—glorifying Him today, tomorrow, and, if God's willing, 26 years from now too.

October 30

Speak to one another with psalms, hymns and spiritual songs. Sing and make music in your heart to the Lord.
—**Ephesians 5:19**

While in Omaha with my mother, I listened to K-LOVE on the rental car radio. For those of you not familiar with K-LOVE, it is a Contemporary Christian Music radio network available throughout the United States.

The on-air disc jockey was telling a story about a car dealer in Baton Rouge, Louisiana, who would pre-set all the radio stations to K-LOVE whenever a car was made ready for delivery to a new customer. I thought that was such a cool idea. At the next stoplight, I pre-set all six stations to 88.1, the K-LOVE station in Omaha.

After adjusting the seat and all the mirrors in a rental car, I search for a Christian station. Now, I don't know if finding a radio station is what everyone does before they drive off in a rental car for the first time, but I have a feeling that the next person who rented that car wondered why all six stations were set to the same one.

God willing, the music made a difference in that person's life.

October 31

So whether you eat or drink or whatever you do, do it all for the glory of God.—**1 Corinthians 10:31**

Sharon Jaynes, one of the three contributing writers for the online devotion "Girlfriends in God," had recently published her book *A Sudden Glory*. As I headed out the door to get a pedicure, I grabbed it to take along with me.

Chapter Three was titled "Living in Sacred Union" and covered the subject of erasing the dividing lines between the secular and sacred world in order to live in union with Christ. From what Paul said in the daily Scripture for today, God never intended for us to live in two separate worlds. Everything we do—whether it's cleaning, cooking, working, volunteering, studying the Bible, singing praise and worship songs, driving carpool —should all be done for the glory of God. It sounds simple, but is it?

Writing devotions for this book has actually made the division line less noticeable for me, but far from invisible. I am in awe of how God orchestrated this journey and placed it upon my heart to look for Him throughout my day. It started out so that I might fill a book with God stories, but it became a daily, joyful way of life. While I won't succeed in being focused on God every minute this side of heaven, the more I am in His presence, the more I want to stay there. I can't bring glory to God if I am not abiding in Him.

While my toes were soaking, I listened to the song that was playing through the speakers above my head. In his distinctly raspy voice, Rod Stewart was belting out the famous love song, "Have I Told You Lately." As I have mentioned before, I enjoy all kinds of music, and I knew this one well.

(Just for clarification, this song is not to be confused with "Have I Told You Lately That I Love You," written by Scotty Wiseman and first released in 1945. You might want to Google the lyrics to both, if you aren't aware of the distinction.)

"Have I Told You Lately" was written by Van Morrison, but made famous by Rod Stewart. It is an extremely popular selection for the first wedding dance and is on the list of the 100 greatest love songs.

I imagined Mac Powell of Third Day, with his own raspy voice, praising God with the song. *Have I told you lately that I love you? Have I told you there's no one else above you?*

As I thought about Third Day singing that song to God, taking a secular song and turning it into Christian praise and worship, I had my own personal sacred encounter with the Holy Spirit. *Brenda, have you told God that you love Him—lately?*

My prayers are full of words of thanksgiving, confession and lots of supplication, but I slack off in the adoration department. "No," I replied back. "I haven't."

In a secular nail shop, in the midst of random secular conversations, I had a very sacred time with God. I turned that Rod Stewart song around and made it my own love song to God. As Tammy was applying my polish, she looked up at me and asked if everything was all right. Through my tears, I assured her all was simply wonderful.

Did you notice that today is **10/31** and the Scripture comes from 1 Corinthians **10:31**? It might be one we need to keep handy for quick reference as we go about our lives in this world, trying to erase the dividing lines between the secular and the sacred.

November 1

Now faith is being sure of what we hope for and certain of what we do not see.—**Hebrews 11:1**

On a rare occasion when I was in a cleaning-out-the-storage-closet mood, I stumbled across a box packed full of books and knick-knacks that once belonged to my grandmother. She was everything a grandmother is supposed to be, and so much more.

I couldn't believe the lost treasures I found as I sifted through. There was her big, black Bible with her name engraved in gold letters that she used to keep by the kitchen table—the one she read in the mornings along with the daily devotion from *The Upper Room*. When I was young, that Bible looked huge, but I realized that the one I now use is actually larger.

There were also about a dozen very small prayer books. The copyright dates ranged from 1935 to 1943—they were some old books! Two of them jumped out at me. One was entitled *God's Minute—A Book of 365 Daily Prayers Sixty Seconds Long for Home Worship* (1943) and the other was *God's Purpose—A Book of 365 Daily Sermonettes for Home Worship* (1939). Both had 365 different contributors! All of the contributors were listed inside of each book, with very little duplication between the two.

On a page inside *God's Purpose* was an acknowledgement of thanks to all the contributors, along with this: "It is our sincere regret that we could not include all of the sermonettes so graciously sent." Wow! There were more than 365 submitted for that one publication! I had been working on this book for more than two years and had received about 70 from other contributors.

I had a good laugh when I realized that my little idea of having a devotional compiled of stories written by different women wasn't so original after all. But the real reason for my joy was because I knew that God was there with me unpacking that box. He wasn't rubbing in the fact that someone else was able to pull off receiving all the stories they needed. No, I felt my God sweetly encouraging me, showing me it could be done.

I had allowed those feelings of discouragement into my heart—again. Because of current circumstances, I had not devoted as much time to writing as I wanted and this book was progressing very slowly. Plus, I hadn't received a story from another "contributor" in weeks. But my dear Father led me to this box of hidden treasures on that day for a reason. He wanted to protect me from being discouraged and losing my enthusiasm for a project that He ordained.

He planted the seed in my heart for this book. He will not ask me to do something without equipping me with all I need. I know that. I can't see the last story yet, but I have faith that one day I will. This book isn't going to have 366 different writers, but each story will be inspired by the greatest author of all time—the Author of our faith.

Today is 11/1. Let's try committing Hebrews 11:1 to memory in our hearts. The words are right here on this page for you to see. But more importantly, let's try keeping our eyes fixed on the unseen—our place with God in heaven.

November 2

"Heaven and earth will pass away, but my words will never pass away." —**Matthew 24:35**

The new slow-cooker recipe for vegetable soup sounded amazingly easy, healthy and delicious. With my five-item grocery list in hand, along with my reusable grocery bag, I went inside the store. Planning to stop only in the produce department to buy veggies for the soup, I anticipated a quick trip.

I must confess I have a deep infatuation with grocery stores. I basically grew up in one. My dad owned a small chain when I was born in Corpus Christi, Texas. Even though he filed for bankruptcy and lost the stores when he and mom divorced in 1961, he remained in the business in some form or fashion until his death in 2003.

After college in 1974, I spent the next 29 years working for him in various capacities in his Houston-based supermarket chain. I was captivated by the business. Grocery stores were in my blood and, to this day, I love to roam a store, eye new products and scrutinize the shelf displays.

On this particular day, I was strolling the aisles like I had nothing else in the world to do. I had just left Bible study and my heart was full of joy, so perhaps that was why I was enjoying my shopping experience more than usual. I walked the aisles and was especially enthralled by all the new items. For some reason, my eyes automatically search out what's new on the shelf. However, this day I felt overwhelmed—almost out of touch—with all the new ones I noticed.

After I stocked up on all the veggies for the soup, I remembered needing sugar. Just plain, white, real sugar. On the baking aisle, I walked by the section with all the boxed muffin, brownie and cake mixes. I used to buy those items when my boys were home, but now my husband and I don't need to eat such things. When did all these sugar-free and gluten-free boxed mixes show up? Plus, all the labels had changed on all the familiar ones. So many enticing new choices on the shelves. Had it been that long since I purchased a store-bought mix?

Then I remembered using the last of the milk for my morning coffee, so off to the dairy section. Back in the 1950s, the milkman delivered to our home. Then when the watery skim milk was introduced, and Mom started buying it at the store, I was saddened to lose contact with the friendly milkman. Now, the selections are mind-boggling. There's not only no-fat, 2% and regular, there's no-fat, 2% and regular *organic* milk, available with added DHA Omega-3 for added brain health—plain or chocolate. (I jumped all over that added brain-health milk when it was first introduced.) Plus, there's lactose-free, soy, almond, coconut, almond, hemp, oak and rice milk. What happened to the premise that milk came from cows?

An hour after entering the store, I was in the checkout lane. So much for my quick trip through the produce department. Apologizing to the sacker for having only one canvas bag—after all, I just came in for five items—I told him plastic would be fine for the rest. Twenty-five years ago, who would have thought there would be such an issue with paper, plastic or reusable bags?

As I looked at the display on the cash register and the total quickly adding up, I thought about how simple grocery shopping used to be. Also how much cheaper! There weren't as many choices on the shelf screaming for us to buy them. The stores weren't as large, jam-packed with lawn and garden equipment, books, dinnerware and kitchen appliances. No, just groceries. My, how times have changed.

As I walked out to my car, I mused over all the changes in the grocery industry during my lifetime. When I opened my door, I glanced over to the passenger side and noticed my Bible on the seat. Thankfully, we can all hold tight to God's Word—it will endure for eternity and never change.

November 3

We know that we have come to know him if we obey his commands. The man who says, "I know him," but does not do what he commands is a liar, and the truth is not in him. But if anyone obeys his words, God's love is truly made complete in him. This is how we know we are in him: Whoever claims to live in him must walk as Jesus did.
—1 John 2: 3-6

There is a big joke at my house on Lake Travis in Austin about the "rules" I have posted. When you have a place on the water with water toys, there tends to be a lot of company. With so many "guests," it gives me a sense of orderliness to have some rules posted in strategic places.

For example, we have a septic system, so not just everything can be flushed down the toilet. I have placed some polite reminders in each bathroom of what *not* to flush. Also, if you spend the night, you are requested to change your own sheets before you leave. I have specific written instructions on what to do with the dirty sheets and where to find the clean ones. And whatever you do, don't lie on top of the bedspreads or comforters! People cover themselves with sun screen or suntan oil, stay out in the sun all day, then come in the house and flop on the bed. That really gets me upset! How hard is it to pull back the bedspread?

When I was seeking contributors for this book, I sent out an email with some basic information and general guidelines to follow, such as how long the stories should be and when I needed them returned. My dear, sweet friend Linda emailed me several months later, asking me to resend that email with my "rules." It just struck me as being kind of funny that I was now being accused of having "rules" for my book too.

I asked if there was a problem with that. Linda's response: "Rules are good. Obviously, God thought so, too. I think you are in good company." She put a whole new perspective on that little word. Yes, God does indeed have rules for us to follow. He wants our obedience to His commands. I know how upset I get when my rules at the lake house aren't followed. Is it so difficult to follow a few simple requests? How must God feel when the whole world breaks His?

November 4

I press on toward the goal to win the prize for which God has called me heavenward in Christ Jesus.—**Philippians 3:14**

I enjoy cooking for large groups. I'm not a great cook; I just have no qualms with big crowds. So when I was asked to provide taco soup for 50 people, I didn't anticipate any problems.

If you have ever made taco soup, you will probably agree that it actually tastes better the next day. I prepared the soup, planning to re-heat it the following morning before taking it to the luncheon. A pot of soup for 50 is sizeable, and I knew that it would take a while to thoroughly warm up slowly, to prevent scorching.

I stirred the pot often during the morning, but finally realized that being on the safe side at simmer wasn't doing the trick because the soup was still cold after two hours. OK, time to turn up the heat.

Being a tad forgetful, I set the timer and felt comfortable to just leave it on the stove. Big mistake! When I walked back into the kitchen at the sound of the buzzer, the soup was boiling!

I dragged the spoon across the bottom of the pot and, sure enough, I came up with a big glob of black, charred pinto beans. I quickly sampled the soup and it was fine; not even a hint of that distinct, burnt taste. The soup had been rescued in the knick of time.

Don't stir the pot, don't make waves and *avoid intentional agitation* have always been words I have tried to live by. However, if I had paid closer attention and stirred the pot more frequently, my soup never would have reached the boiling point and there would have been no charred beans.

Sometimes I feel like that taco soup and I am at the boiling point. Life is crazy-busy, and self-destruction is close at hand. If left unattended, I, too, will get trapped at the bottom, stuck in my stuff. But along comes the Master Chef. At the perfect time, He adds just the right ingredients to this life of mine, allows it all to simmer slowly, stirring it often with His love, grace and mercy so that I will become all He meant for me to be.

But what about the glob I scrapped off the bottom of the pot? When I dragged the spoon, the burnt beans ended up floating around in the soup, just like the shame from past sins can resurface, trying to overshadow the grace of God's forgiveness in my life.

The ladies who ate that soup never knew about my little mishap. Now, don't get grossed out here, but I ladled the soup from the pot, one dip at a time. If there were any black clumps, I spooned them out and washed them down the drain. With each spoonful, I thought how God has lovingly cleaned up the gunk in my life too. All my sins are thrown away like I threw out the charred beans. The soup looked just fine and all traces of the near catastrophe were gone. But more important than looking good, it tasted just as wonderful as it was supposed to.

"Stirring the pot" never sounded so full of promise. My Creator loves me so much that He won't allow me to get trapped at the bottom permanently. No matter what ingredients He has planned to include in my life recipe, I will end up exactly as He intended. For whatever amount of time God allows me to cook, I know the King is in the kitchen with me "stirring constantly." The Master will never set the timer and simply walk away from His creation. He will discard my sins and mistakes and, in the end, His recipe will win the prize as I am called heavenward to be with Christ Jesus.

November 5

For the kingdom of God is not a matter of eating or drinking, but of righteousness, peace and joy in the Holy Spirit, because anyone who serves Christ in this way is pleasing to God and approved by men.—**Romans 14:17-18**

I am not Supermom. I don't cut out the cute projects I find in parenting magazines. I don't make the interesting food snacks that look like animals, nor do I use things around the house to make inventive crafts. But I was desperate. So I grabbed the kids, loaded them into the car and drove to Target. I bought the poster board, the ruler, the magic markers, the stickers and a handful of treats. I came home, spread the materials out and did it. I made two Happy Heart Charts. They looked just like the ones I had envisioned when reading an article from *Growing Kids God's Way.*

Why was I so desperate? Because I couldn't stand the whining, pouting and stomping of feet that followed every request I made to my then 4-year old twins. While Cooper and Lucy usually ultimately obeyed, there was significant drama that ensured I knew they were not happy about my request.

That afternoon, I sat them down in front of the charts. "I'm proud that you all are learning to obey, but now that you are 4, it is time to do something more," I explained. "When I ask you to do something, I want you to obey right away, all the way, and with a happy heart. When you do this, you get a sticker on the chart. When you get ten stickers, you'll get to pick a treat."

We walked through numerous examples. We role-played having happy hearts and obeying quickly, and then we pretended to have not-so-happy hearts and to procrastinate. I felt like they actually understood! And ever so slowly, over the next few weeks, I saw a transformation. It took lots of praise and positive reinforcement (and a little negative reinforcement too), but the results were worth it. Oh, the joy it brought when I asked for something and heard a cheerful "Yes, Mommy," followed by immediate obedience!

But I didn't get to bask in the joy of having obedient children long before the Holy Spirit whispered to me, "And what about you?" When God impresses something on my heart, do I make excuses? Do I groan inwardly as I agree to help someone in need? Or do I cheerfully exclaim, "Yes, Father"? Am I joyful for the opportunities that God provides or do I think, *Why me?*

I had to think. For me, it was a mixed bag. There are times I am genuinely happy to obey. But there are also times when I obey out of duty. Then there are times when I make excuses, grumble and procrastinate.

Fortunately, I don't think God keeps a Heavenly Happy Heart Chart. But I do believe it pleases Him when we serve with righteousness, peace and joy. So the next time I get that little prompting, I will think of the joy that I bring my Father when I not only obey, but do so right away, all the way and with a happy heart.

Julie Zavodny
Austin, TX

November 6

Jesus Christ is the same yesterday and today and forever. — **Hebrews 13:8**

With the instability of the economy, it became common to see businesses close or change hands. Since my husband and I often ate out, I was more aware of the high number of restaurants that became a statistic. Just when we got used to a menu and the folks who worked there, everything could change the next time we went to eat.

Trying new restaurants was fun, but we also had our favorites. There was one where we didn't even have to look at the menu — we knew exactly what we would order before we walked in. We had a rude awakening when we saw the sign "under new management" as we walked through the doors.

My husband questioned the hostess and she assured us that everything was the same — same menu, wait staff, prices and good food. All right, we would give it a fair chance. Unfortunately, we weren't impressed. We had to ask for bread and the yummy garlic-herb butter was no longer as tasty. The new cook prepared my husband's favorite dish using a new recipe that wasn't even close to the previous one, and my salad was missing the olives that I craved. Perhaps if we hadn't had expectations, we wouldn't have been disappointed. (I understand these are totally trivial disappointments in light of other major changes many have faced because of this unstable economy.)

A few days later, I was driving from my home in Austin to Katy. There is a church on the outskirts of a small town I pass through that always has catchy little messages on the marquee out front. As I drove by, I read, "Under the same management for 2000 years."

After our restaurant experience, I had to chuckle at the sign. But then I thought about those clever words and felt so reassured. While I can expect things of this world to change and leave me disappointed, I know my Lord and Savior is the same yesterday and today — and forever (Hebrews 13:8).

November 7

We have confidence before God and receive from him anything we ask, because we obey his commands and do what pleases him. — **1 John 3:21-22**

Raising kids is just not the easiest thing to do — especially if our quest is to do it "right"! So, as a Christian, I knew that in order to accomplish this difficult task, all three of my children needed to be surrounded daily with the Holy Spirit directing them in the decisions they would make. For that to happen in a school district going through the woes and, many times, the horrors of integration in its early stages, I knew that my prayers for them were essential.

As a Christian mother, I studied many Christian books on childrearing; I knew all the Scriptures that built trust in a God who would hear and answer our prayers for our children. I also knew Scripture that told me how to get my prayers answered. (1 John 3:21-22 is one good example.) But I also knew that just having the knowledge of how God works was not enough — my responsibility was to activate God's work in my children's life through prayer.

At this time in our lives, not only did we have three children of our own, but we also had my niece and a nephew living with us who had come from a dysfunctional family. Having them come into our home during their teenage years was difficult in itself because they did not know the unwritten rules within our family and had lived seemingly without boundaries. Thus, much prayer was needed to understand how to parent them in such a way that they felt comfortable while learning to live within an established family.

Now, where was I to find the time to pray as I should? Being a busy school administrator myself with a university football coach as a husband who worked long hours each day, I began to pray: "God help me to find the time to do this right, time to pray protection for these five children at school, and to pray for myself in order that I might show my love and patience and kindness to each of these children."

That "extra" hour came often at 3:11 a.m. God would awaken me just wide-eyed (and I am such a good sleeper) at this particular time. With that exact time showing on my bedside clock, I knew it was God speaking to me, answering my plea for more time—giving me that hour of time to visit with Him.

I would gladly jump out of bed, put on my robe, get a glass of orange juice and go outside in our lovely backyard.

So many times there would be a full moon, and sitting there looking up to the heavens through the lovely drooping arms of a Weeping Willow, I would sense God's presence. He would direct my prayers for the coming day at school, where I was one of the high school counselors. Not only would God bring the names and needs of my own children, niece and nephew to me, but also the needs of the multitudes of children who would come through my door at school seeking help with a debilitating problem in their own lives.

I often wonder about the outcome in the lives of children with whom I spent time and know that one day many of those outcomes will be revealed to me because I prayed for so many of them. The most beautiful blessing is that all three of my own children and the niece and nephew all love the Lord Jesus and are rearing children to do the same.

Praise God for getting me up on those mornings to be with Him and also for giving me the ability to go right back to bed and sleep soundly until the alarm clock went off to start a new day.

Jo
Austin, TX

November 8

"But the Counselor, the Holy Spirit, whom the Father will send in my name, will teach you all things and will remind you of everything I have said to you."—**John 14:26**

Both of my sons inherited a few of my not-so-good personality traits. While Zach seems to be outgrowing most of them, my younger son is still battling one in particular—time management. I am too.

Trevor called the other night and, to my delight, was in a talkative mood. He is a self-employed photographer, and making the best use of his time has been a challenge, so that was the main topic of our conversation. I suggested that he try getting up earlier in the mornings, since he has a tendency to sleep in.

If a mother is going to give advice, she should probably make sure she lives by her words. I sometimes linger in bed a bit longer than I should, but justify my actions by the fact that I am a retired Empty Nester. However, since starting this book, my days are full. I sure would get much more accomplished if I would just get up earlier.

God must have decided I needed to practice what I was preaching to my son. The very next morning after Trevor and I had our conversation, the sensation of a tap on my shoulder woke me up. I was in a deep sleep, but shot up out of bed, quite startled. You see, my husband was out of town and no one else could have been in the house.

Immediately I looked over to his side of the bed. The pillow and blanket were still neat and smooth. Sure enough, he hadn't slipped in during the middle of the night. But I honestly felt "someone" tap me on my shoulder!

I lay back down and that's when I heard that quiet voice. *What did you tell your son last night? Get up, Brenda.* I looked at the clock and it was only 6:15. Really? Get up this early? I could still feel that finger tapping me on the shoulder. You'd better believe I got up.

When God goes out of His way to reveal Himself to me, I am in total awe. I can't explain "who" tapped me on the shoulder as I slept. An angel? Perhaps it was just a very vivid dream. However, when I heard that small voice, I knew it was the whisper of the Holy Spirit.

Jesus promised the Holy Spirit would come to us, and I know He is here within me. He is constantly reminding me of God's Word, trying to help me along my spiritual journey. This particular morning He had a lesson to teach me in time management.

A little tap on the shoulder, a soft knock on the door of my heart, a gentle nudge of encouragement, a helping hand from a friend—He won't force His way, but He's there, if I choose to let Him in.

"Here I am! I stand at the door and knock. If anyone hears my voice and opens the door, I will come in and eat with him and he with me" (Revelation 3:20).

November 9

"See, I have written your name on the palms of my hands." —**Isaiah 49:16 (NLT)**

Finally, someone remembered my name! I had been going to the same gym for more than a year and not one of the people behind the front desk had ever greeted me by my first name—until now. When that nice, retired gentleman who works the desk on Fridays said, "Hello, Brenda," before I signed in, I was elated. Simply being recognized made me feel so special.

My editor, Rick Weber, includes the words of Isaiah 49:16 on the signature of his emails. I have seen that verse hundreds of times through all of our online communications. However, after that day when Ken called me by my name, I began to ponder the words.

If I was filled with joy when someone I barely knew called me by my name, what will it be like when I see Jesus face to face? The King of Kings holds out His arms to embrace me and welcome me home. I look down at the scars on His hands and see *my* name written on the palms of *His* hands. Oh, my!

My name has never been in bright lights or one that is recognized by millions of people, like an actress or sports hero or rock star. I have received some recognition plaques with my name engraved on them that I displayed in my office back in my working days. But etched on the hands of God?

Isaiah 49:16 tells me that God *has written* my name on the palms of His hands. My name is already there—He already knows it. I don't have to wait to hear Him whisper *Brenda*. I have the choice to listen to the whispers of the Holy Spirit every day on this side of heaven.

There shouldn't be anything that brings more joy than knowing the Creator of the universe knows my name, so why do I long to be recognized by others? Scripture tells me "it is better to take refuge in the LORD than to trust in man" (Psalm 118:8). There is not one single living person who will ever know me like my Father knows me. Why isn't that enough?

Certainly we all want to be appreciated and recognized during our life, but there have been times I allowed that desire to overshadow the fact that I have already been blessed with all the recognition I will ever need. The clamor of this busy world can drown out His words, and I end up going down my own path, instead of following His voice.

I pray God will give discernment to both me, and you, so that when we venture out into the busyness of life today, we listen for the voice of our Shepherd as He calls out each of us by name. May He give us the ears to hear and the obedience to follow. "The watchman opens the gate for him, and the sheep listen to his voice. He calls his own sheep by name and leads them out" (John 10:3).

November 10

*"Peace I leave with you; my peace I give you. I do not give to you as the world gives. Do not let your hearts be troubled and do not be afraid." —***John 14:27**

My friend Debbie posted on Facebook that her oldest son, Brad, would be leaving very soon for Afghanistan and asked her friends to lift him up in prayer. This was what he had trained for. He was ready to go.

Not having any family connections to the military, I have no idea if a mother is ever ready to send her child to war. I had spoken to Debbie several months prior to the scheduled deployment and I knew she was anxious then. How must she be feeling now, knowing his departure was imminent?

The day of his departure, Debbie sent an email to her prayer warriors and said, "I am quietly freaking out." One of her immediate concerns was the activity going on in the volatile border region between Afghanistan and Pakistan, where Brad and his brigade were going. Only a few days before, the Taliban had launched an attack against the military base in that city. Taliban suicide fighters disguised as Afghan soldiers attacked the same military base only months before. In Debbie's words, "It is not a good place to be right now."

Debbie and I met in 2005. Our youngest sons were among the incoming freshman football players at the University of Texas. Over the years, we developed a special friendship. One incident that happened between us will stay etched in my heart forever.

At the annual spring UT Orange and White scrimmage in 2007, I was the anxious one, the one "quietly freaking out." My son was fighting for a starting position and I was nervous. Debbie could read my face and knew I needed to calm down. She discreetly gave me a bracelet with John 14:27 inscribed on it. I clutched that bracelet the whole game. How sweet that she knew I needed to hear from God at that moment. I certainly had no control over how well Trevor was going to perform that day. Worrying wasn't going to help one bit! Yes, I desperately needed some peace—the peace that could only come from God.

The bracelet Debbie gave me came with a little card, asking the recipient to give it away when she saw someone else who was "quietly freaking out" and needed God's peace. I even went online and purchased more of them because I knew I would encounter more than one person who just might need an extra dose of peace. Sure enough, all those extra bracelets, and the original one Debbie gave me, have been given away.

Back in those days, our lives revolved around UT football. But this was not a game. I look back and feel quite sheepish that I was overly anxious as my son was fighting for a spot on the depth chart; Debbie's son would soon be fighting a real battle. A serious life-and-death situation. Debbie's oldest son was going to war. He was ready, willing and able to risk his life for you and for me. I am humbled beyond words.

The day I received Debbie's email, I knew the peace she needed could only come from God. The bracelet she gave me was long gone, but I could still pray John 14:27 for Debbie. Isn't it sweet that the same words of encouragement she gave me were the ones that I could give back to her? How important to put the command from Hebrews 10:25 into action: *"Let us encourage one another."* You just never know when your own words may come back around.

November 11

*Praise be to the God and Father of our Lord Jesus Christ, the Father of compassion and the God of all comfort, who comforts us in all our troubles, so that we can comfort those in any trouble with the comfort we ourselves have received from God. —***2 Corinthians 1:3-5**4

Yesterday, you read a story about my friend Debbie's son being deployed to Afghanistan. After I wrote it, I received a call from another friend whose son was already there. After I spoke to her, I felt a "part two" being written to that story.

During our five years of being football moms at the University of Texas, I had the privilege of getting to know Debbie's other kids. During those years, her son Brad was stationed at Fort Bliss in El Paso and was able to attend several of the football games to watch his younger brother. The last game Brad attended was in November 2009. It was Senior Night, and family members were allowed to go down on the field as our senior players were honored.

Dressed in his Army uniform, Brad looked handsome and distinguished. During the playing of the National Anthem, the crowd started clapping, and I looked at the huge Jumbotron screen. The cameras were focused on Brad—standing so proud, saluting the American flag, an incredible, larger-than-life sight. The expression on his face was one I will never forget!

The list of friends with children or spouses in active military duty continues to grow—people who are in harm's way, risking their lives for us. I am so thankful these women have reached out, asked for prayers and shared their hearts. They have also provided informative websites that provide such things as video tours of military bases or blog posts from other parents.

How else are the rest of us, who don't have family members in the military, supposed to have any understanding of what they go through? The more a military parent communicates, the more we will know how to offer encouragement. The more we take it upon ourselves to learn about the sacrifices, the better equipped we are to reach out to them. Once I got started looking at some of the websites these moms provided, I have found numerous resources that help me be better informed.

My friend's son was in the same volatile region that Brad was being deployed to, and she was elated that he would be coming home the following month, but her son–in–law would be deployed in the following months.

After our phone conversation, I felt God at work. Even if I don't have a family member deployed right now, I have sisters in Christ who do. All of us have dear, sweet friends who need our support, along with the thousands whose names we will never know.

Many of you faithfully cry out to God for the safety, peace and protection of our soldiers and their families. Or perhaps you are like me and tend to forget to pray for them on a daily basis. Every day, there are families waiting for the safe return of their loved ones who are risking their lives for us. God is nudging me to be more consistent in my prayers for our soldiers, plus He is providing me with numerous resources to equip me to be a greater source of comfort to family members. I felt God urging me to write this story, asking readers to do the same.

Today is Veteran's Day—the day set aside to honor and thank all who served in the military, in both wartime and peacetime, to acknowledge appreciation for their contributions to our national security. Please join me in praying for our veterans and those still enlisted.

November 12

Therefore, as God's chosen people, holy and dearly loved, clothe yourselves with compassion, kindness, humility, gentleness and patience. Bear with each other and forgive whatever grievances you may have against one another. Forgive as the Lord forgave you. And over all these virtues put on love, which binds them all together in perfect unity. —**Colossians 3: 12-14**

My husband, Jim, and I were both raised in Christian homes. We are fortunate to be surrounded with generations of believers in Christ. I wanted to lay that foundation so that you understand that disunity and separation can happen in any family.

A few years back, my family experienced a heartbreaking separation where close family members no longer wanted to be in relationship. Hurtful words were spoken, feelings became wounded, and it seemed impossible for loved ones to be in the same room together or even talk on the phone with each other. I would have never believed that this could happen to our family.

Jim had determined that this should not be. We began praying, he started reading up on how to facilitate reconciliation, making phone calls and sending out emails. Jim set a date for the reconciliation meeting and he kept in weekly communication with the other men involved. With the date quickly approaching, we began visiting the couples involved because fear had begun to set in and people were choosing not to participate. I became fearful that no one would show up and I felt protective of my husband's feelings. On several occasions I told him that this might not work because we had no control over the people showing up and participating.

He would always respond that his God is bigger and God would see that reconciliation would happen. He was placing his faith in God, not man. You see, God is all about unity, relationship and reconciliation. Why else would He send His only Son to die on the cross for us? He paved the way for reconciliation to Himself through Christ. In Colossians, He actually tells His chosen people that we are holy and dearly loved, how to dress every morning and to bear with each other and forgive whatever grievances we may have against one another. Forgive as the Lord forgave you. And over all these virtues put on love, which binds them all together in perfect unity.

There you have it: Perfect unity involves knowing that we are loved and holy, clothing ourselves with compassion, kindness, humility, gentleness and patience. We have to forgive and finally but not least, love. God is bigger, for everyone that dared to show up and bear each other's grievance, reconciliation happened. It was not easy. There were many tears and anxious moments but God brought this family back together. Holidays and birthdays are once again celebrations. Praise be to God!

Cathy Hale
Katy, TX

November 13

Be kind and compassionate to one another, forgiving each other, just as in Christ God forgave you.— **Ephesians 4:32**

True forgiveness: what freedom it brings. Three years into our marriage, my husband came to me, saying he wasn't happy and wanted a separation. I was devastated and hurt. My world was destroyed. He left our home and filed for a divorce. With much prayer from family and friends, he came back. All was forgiven.

Even many years later, there were times I would still get upset over the whole issue with the separation. One day God showed me, with a little help from a friend, that I had not totally forgiven my husband. You see, I forgave him and loved him, but I still felt like he owed me something for the things that I went through. For example, I felt he created my poor self-esteem, and I wanted to be treated like a queen and to always be loved. When I finally realized my husband owed me nothing—and he really doesn't—I had that total forgiveness with the healing of my emotions. I was free to love my husband like I needed, and get this: He was free to love me.

You see, I was holding my husband's sin against him. This is not the forgiveness God has for us. God does not hold our past sins against us. We are all undeserving. God sent His Son to die on the cross for our sins—past, present and future. By His mighty mercy and grace we are forgiven. "For it is by grace you have been saved, through faith—and this not from yourselves, it is the gift of God" (Ephesians 2:8).

So I thank You, God, for the gift of Your Son, Jesus Christ, and my precious husband and blessed marriage of over 30 years.

This is quite a blessing from God. He is faithful when we are willing to keep His Word. My three sons are married now, and we are now Empty Nesters. My husband and I are totally enjoying each other and our time together to the point where even if the boys aren't around for the holidays, we will still have a great season. We are free in many ways by God's grace.

Jayne Couch
Katy, TX

November 14

Be joyful always; pray continually; give thanks in all circumstances, for this is God's will for you in Christ Jesus.
—**1 Thessalonians 5:16-17**

Many years ago, when my sons were ages 6 and 4, I experienced a spiritual renewal of my love for Jesus, all through the power of the Holy Spirit.

Our family was not attending a church at the time, or pursuing God in any way. The Spirit soon led me to start praying with my boys at bedtime. I also started reading a devotional to them at the breakfast table. We used two books, *Little Visits with God* and *I Meet God in the Strangest Places*. The time spent at the table with my sons became a wonderful bonding time for us, with God being at the center of our reading and conversations. My husband and I started attending a church near our home, and we had our sons baptized. We were all on our spiritual journey together as a family!

One morning, during my quiet time with Him, I felt led to pray that my sons "would be ministers of Jesus' love"—words I would not have chosen on my own. I knew deep down that these words had come from the Holy Spirit.

Since praying that prayer, I have watched my sons grow up into godly men with a deep faith and filled with the Spirit of the Living God. We went through the high school years with the usual teen "stuff" and with them both being part of the church youth group, Young Life, sports and, of course, girls! Then they were off to college, a challenging time for us all, with them both being away from home for the first time. My oldest son is now 38 and is in full-time ministry. My second son is an engineer and is in leadership at his church. They are both married to godly women, and have blessed my husband and me with five grandchildren.

What an amazing God we have! I know that prayer I whispered many years ago was heard and answered in His Way and in His Timing. God's leading in the prayer gave Him two kingdom workers who are spreading the Word of God's redeeming love for all of His creation.

I hope that you will "pray continually" for your children. He is a God who loves us beyond our understanding and always hears His children when they pray!

By the way, I think now is the time to get the books off the shelf and read them to my grandchildren!

Irene Peeler
Spicewood, TX

November 15

Cast your burden on the LORD, and he will sustain you; he will never permit the righteous to be moved.
—**Psalm 55:22 (ESV)**

My husband and I were about to purchases a new house. We had spent months searching online, weeks with a realtor viewing first-hand what looked promising on the computer, and finally found the perfect place. The night before the closing, my realtor called to tell us there was a unique problem with the seller (who lived out of the country) and we wouldn't be able to close the following morning. It would have to be postponed for several weeks while the Power of Attorney documents were corrected.

How did this oversight happen? We had everything planned already. The movers, the utilities, the time off—now what? Immediately we felt God was saying this wait was a good thing. Perhaps this wasn't the perfect house. Or this was a teachable moment in patience. When my realtor gave us a few options, we didn't like any of them and told her we needed some time to talk to God and pray.

Did we ever pray that night! We asked for wisdom to know what to do. We asked God to help us make the right decision. We read Scripture about waiting and patience. Afterwards I felt at peace, knowing we had turned the situation over to God and He would give us guidance. Well, it didn't exactly happen as I expected.

The next morning, I just knew I would wake up with a peaceful feeling of how to proceed, but I didn't. If we didn't close and move in that day as planned, there were conflicts too numerous to mention here. Waiting several weeks to close didn't seem like a viable option, so was God telling us to stop and walk away? At 8:30, my realtor called, and I didn't even want to answer. What would I say? I didn't have to speak a word. In the middle of the night, she sat up in bed as a light bulb went off.

I had prayed that God and I would come up with a path to follow. Oh, He so faithfully answered my prayer, but through someone else. Besides giving Cindi the insight on how to resolve this unusual legal issue (one that I later discovered had never occurred in her lengthy professional career or that of the seller's agent), He also gave me an opportunity to talk to my realtor about Him.

Cindi and I had spent a lot of time together looking at houses. We talked about our kids, cooking, our husbands and our favorite restaurants, but we didn't actually talk about God.

But there we sat at the title company. We had almost walked away from a sale, but it turned out to be the perfect chance for two women to share their faith. I told her how I had prayed for wisdom, prayed for an answer, prayed for patience to wait if that was God's will. I sensed that Cindi was quite moved by the fact she had woken in the middle of the night with a clear solution, and she knew it was God who gave her the wisdom.

All we had to do was lease the house for a few weeks—that was easy. And, by the way, acceptable to both parties. God had intentionally used this little bump in the road to demonstrate that He knows a thing or two about real estate and is involved with every aspect of my life and Cindi's too.

Now, here we were at the end of our business relationship and God was there with us at the table. He had been with us during the night finding the perfect resolution, in His own special way. I thought He would certainly give me the clear answer since I had so faithfully given Him the problem. (When will I learn that it's not about me?) However, He used Cindi as the messenger of His simple solution. We never know how important every person we encounter is to fulfilling God's purpose and plan for our life.

I just love how time after time, He proves just how powerful and in control He is! My Father only asks that I faithfully surrender all to Him. It really is just that easy.

November 16

But I trust in you, O Lord; I say, "You are my God." My times are in your hands.—**Psalm 31:14-15**

My family doctor referred me to a hematologist because of some unusual results from my recent blood work. She was 99% sure it was nothing serious, but wanted a second opinion. She did warn me that I would see some very sick people in the waiting room because this doctor was also an oncologist and his office was located at the South Austin Cancer Center.

When I walked into the waiting room, I almost felt guilty. Yes, these people did look sick. There were some very thin, bald-headed people. Old and young, men and women, black, brown and white. I did actually feel like I was the oddball in the room because I was the healthy one. Here, the normal was cancer.

Sitting in the waiting room, I assumed I was the healthy one, but what if this specialist found something different than my family doctor? What if I fell into that 1% "unsure" category? The "what if" questions were screaming at me, and I was suddenly overwhelmed with fear as I heard the nurse call my name.

As I got up out of the chair, my cell phone rang. Glancing at the caller, it was my younger son. He sends text messages during the day, but an actual phone call only occurs about once a week, and I had spoken to him a few days earlier. This must be important. The nurse who called my name suddenly motioned for me to wait in the hall because the room wasn't quite ready, so I decided to take his call while I just stood there.

Trevor was helping me with a photograph for a blog post I had written for my church. It was about God's perfect timing and Trevor had taken some photos of a clock next to a Bible. He was calling to tell he had emailed the pictures and wanted my thoughts. Trevor knows I spend most of my time at the computer, but at that moment, I didn't have time to look at the email on my phone.

At that precise moment in time, his call was such a blessing. First of all, I have written several stories about my wayward sons, so just to have one of them involved in anything related to God is a hallelujah! Second, the call was a reminder that all events of my life occur in God's perfect time. Exactly what I had written the blog post about! Did God orchestrate Trevor's call at that specific second to reassure me that nothing happens that He isn't fully aware of? I believe so. My time *is* in His hands.

God knew I was walking into a situation where I feared the unknown. I needed Him right at that precise second! So what does my God do? He sent me a phone call to reassure me He knew exactly where I was and He was there, too. If that room had been ready, I couldn't have taken that call. Now, that's some perfect timing!

November 17

All bitterness, anger and wrath, insult and slander must be removed from you, along with all wickedness. And be kind and compassionate to one another, forgiving one another, just as God also forgave you in Christ.
—**Ephesians 4:31-32 (HCSB)**

Yesterday, I wrote about going to a hematologist for a second opinion (for something completely minor). It was a story about God's perfect timing, and so is this one. I can also use the expression "a God-incidence" because what happened was no coincidence.

As I was leaving the South Austin Cancer Center, I glanced into the waiting room and noticed a familiar face. The person I saw wasn't actually one of my favorites. As a matter of fact, I harbored a great deal of resentment towards him. I just couldn't seem to shake the bitterness that I felt.

My feelings were completely unjustified and in total disobedience to the Scripture at the top of this page, so the who and what isn't important. What is noteworthy is the lesson God had planned for me that day. He wasn't pleased with my feelings—I had been forgiven, so shouldn't I forgive others as well? Besides, there is never justification for failure to obey God.

We chatted for a few minutes, but I mentioned that if he was in the waiting room of South Austin Cancer Center, there must be a problem. He got the most serious look on his face, and I immediately saw a man I had never seen before. This wasn't the same man I had conversations with in the past, when I had to try to maintain my composure. This wasn't the man I had pegged as being arrogant, aloof and uncaring.

He confessed his wife was one month away from her five-year anniversary of being cancer-free—and she had just found out her cancer was back. I saw a man who was completely heartbroken and could barely speak at all.

Right then, his wife walked up and the look he had for her was so tender, so sweet—so unlike any I had ever seen on his face before. I was humbled into total remorse for my ugly thoughts of him. Here was a loving husband, totally overwhelmed with sadness, fear and uncertainty. Suddenly, I actually felt empathy for this person who only minutes before I had deep, hidden feelings of resentment in my heart.

I was so thankful God planned that meeting, to close the door on animosity. I had been praying for God to help me overcome the bitterness I felt surrounding that season of life. I knew my feelings were sinful. I am commanded to forgive, just as I have been forgiven. God, in His faithfulness, did provide that help. Most importantly, He changed my heart and showed me how wrong I had been in my previous assessment of this person.

Bitterness was removed from me and replaced with compassion. Prayers for his wife have become a constant, and even for this man. This seemingly chance meeting in a waiting room was just another example of the God-incidences planned for our lives. My Heavenly Father continues to amaze me with how He orchestrates the events of my daily life, answers my prayers and changes my heart. And He is doing the same for you.

November 18

"The thief comes only to steal and kill and destroy; I have come that they may have life, and have it to the full."
—**John 10:10**

By age 28, I had given many areas of my life over to the Lord, but I was more self-reliant than I realized. Then came November 18, 2008—the day my world was shattered. That morning, I found my sweet mother. After many years of struggling with depression, she had taken her own life and gone to be with Jesus. That evening, my husband and I arrived home to find that our house had been broken into. The words of John 10:10 rang in my head: "Steal. . . kill. . . destroy."

Gone was that self-reliance, as I could barely take care of myself and our infant daughter. It was the beginning of my "refining season." The next several months were filled with great pain as I stumbled through the acute stages of grief. Almost exactly one year after my mom died, I lost the baby I was carrying, followed by another miscarriage a few months later. *Really, God? Really? This is your plan for a hope and a future?* My understanding of who the Lord is and how He operates was completely rocked.

I read an interview of a silversmith in Kristen's Milligan's book, *Consider it Pure Joy,* that helped me better understand what happens in the refining process. I learned that when a silversmith refines silver, he holds it in the hottest part of the flame to cause the impurities to rise to the surface so they can be scraped away. He must keep his eyes on the silver the entire time; if he leaves it in there a moment too long, it will burn up. When the silversmith was asked how he knows when the silver is ready, he answered, "That's easy—when I can see my image in it." That is exactly what the Lord does with us (Psalm 66:10). I am choosing to see my own personal hell as the Lord's refining fire. While I would never choose any of the events of those years, I am eternally grateful for the changes that they brought in my life. I am more desperate for the Lord because of the flames.

This refining season has taught me that Jesus' promise of life to the full includes depth as well as height. Yes, the enemy killed, stole and destroyed life as I knew it. I am not the person I once was, but what has risen from the ashes is a woman refined by God's holy fire who, by the grace of God, more clearly reflects the face of her Maker. To God be the glory.

Sweet friend, if you are going through a "refining season," hold on tightly to the Word of God. From everything I have experienced, the Lord really is who He claims to be. Our God is so faithful!

Katherine
Austin, TX

November 19

He who goes out weeping, carrying seed to sow, will return with songs of joy, carrying sheaves with him.—**Psalm 126:6**

The months following my mother's death, that I wrote about yesterday, were long and dark. Everything felt black and I could see no light at the end of the tunnel. I faced a crisis of belief. If I chose to trust my feelings, I was pretty sure I was going to lose my mind. According to 2 Timothy 1:7, God had given me a sound mind. The two didn't reconcile. I decided to take God at His Word; it was better than the alternative.

Upon making this decision, one of the passages I memorized was 1 Peter 1:3-9. According to these verses, I had a living hope through Christ's death and resurrection, an inheritance that could never perish, spoil or fade. I was shielded by God's power, and because of these things, I greatly rejoice.

How do you rejoice when your circumstance would lead you to believe that you are being exposed and pummeled by the Enemy? The passage goes on to say that for a little while, I had to suffer grief in all kinds of trials. These trials have come to prove the genuineness of my faith when Christ is revealed, and that because of this I am filled with an "inexpressible and glorious joy." Joy? Really? *This* is what joy looked like? Could this really be *my* God, the God of *love*? I was devastated.

Our neighborhood at that time had a two-mile loop that I could run mindlessly while working on Scripture memory. I would run that loop over and over, Scripture cards balanced on the jogging stroller, bawling my eyes out, trying to reconcile the fact that while my heart was a shattered mess, according to Scripture, I was filled with an "inexpressible and glorious joy."

No part of me felt joyful. In fact, for months I was convinced that I would never laugh or smile again; I was too broken. What God said in His Word was so contrary to what I was feeling.

During those months, I learned what it meant to sow in tears—to humbly choose to believe the Word of God beyond the blinding darkness of difficult circumstances and to be raw before the Lord, weeping over the heartache of it all. Christ was so merciful to cover the gaps in my understanding and bring forth an abundant harvest that could only come out of being down in the dirt with Him. He proved Himself and His word true. This harvest was one of the gifts of my suffering.

Katherine
Austin, TX

November 20

But by the grace of God I am what I am, and his grace to me was not without effect. No, I worked harder than all of them—yet not I, but the grace of God that was with me.—**1 Corinthians 15:10**

HE has broken me and I am reminded daily how weak I am. I don't understand this process. The only thing I am sure of is that HE truly exists and HE loves HIS creation.

I realize, from the outside and to the world, I would be considered a bit of a failure, but as I walk through this journey with GOD, HE teaches me HIS ways are so much more peaceful, kind, and true.

It is me who is the cheater in this relationship. God stays and waits. HE is so patient with my slow progress. Why have I fallen so deeply in love with HIM? Yet, I still cheat? I want to be faithful, but my self-destruction is more comfortable for me. I can't believe HE is such a gentleman.

I wish HE would just heal me quickly, but then I realize there would be no journey to share with others who might be questioning HIM in their own hearts.

I want to be the perfect bride, but when I look in the mirror, I am not perfect, but messy, needing only HIS strength, mercy and grace daily. Oh, how HE loves HIS creation!

Traci E. Irwin
Austin, TX

November 21

She had a sister called Mary, who sat at the Lord's feet listening to what he said. But Martha was distracted by all the preparations that had to be made.—**Luke 10:39-40**

Mom and I were in Omaha, Nebraska, to visit her friend Charles again. Instead of the normal six months between visits, it had been only four this time. Mom was concerned about his health—which was deteriorating more rapidly than expected—and was anxious to see him.

When she asked if I would take her back so quickly, I hesitated. November—seriously? That's Thanksgiving and Christmas is right around the corner. I just can't leave. Not right now!

Those are the words I wanted to say, but I couldn't tell her no. The trips meant so much to both mom and Charles. There's no possible way she could make the trip without some assistance. Of course, I would take her.

So, off we went. We would get back home three days before Thanksgiving, before the air-travel frenzy started. With the family gathering at my sister's, the only preparation I had was to cook a few sides and a dessert, so the timing worked fine.

As much as I love and miss my dog, not having to take Holly for her daily walks sure does save time. There are no trips to the grocery store or meals to cook, no clothes to wash or house to clean in Omaha. Even though I cherish my time with my girlfriends and mentees, all meetings had been rescheduled. Attending my Pilates class at home is a priority, but I have never even looked for another workout facility that offers Pilates in Omaha. (I do take the stairs as often as possible instead of the elevator though to get a little bit of exercise.)

On these trips my only responsibility is to be a chauffeur for my mom and Charles. All I do is drive back and forth from the hotel to the retirement home and to area restaurants. The hidden gem of these trips has been the time I get to myself.

As I was driving back to the hotel from dropping mom off to visit Charles one morning, I was amazed at the incredible peace that consumed me. I didn't have to drive on the freeway, so there was no traffic to contend with, only quiet, picturesque neighborhoods. When I returned to the hotel, there was nothing on my agenda until late afternoon, when I would pick them up for dinner. I had all day to myself—the opportunity to write with no interruptions.

That's when it hit me—back home I don't have uninterrupted days. There is always something to get me side-tracked. How often do I go off and just spend time alone with God? Sure I have my quiet time in the morning, reading my daily devotions and Scriptures. But there is always an obligation for busyness lurking on the horizon. By golly, Omaha is the perfect place to escape!

Thinking back on all our previous trips, I have had some productive writing time. Finally, after numerous trips to visit Charles, I figured it out. It's quality time because there are no distractions in Omaha.

These trips with Mom have been a selfish inconvenience, and I have done more than grumble about them. However, each time God has had a lesson for me to learn. Every time we have come, I leave with a new God story—or two. That certainly makes the trip worthwhile.

Back to the busyness and distractions that keep me sidetracked from time with God—I can't plan on trips to Omaha just to keep my focus on Him. Now that I have experienced that peace that surpasses all understanding because of no distractions, I want more of it! What do I need to do about uncluttering my life at home?

Right now I don't have the answer to that question. I have some pretty good ideas though, but I need to do some serious praying about this. How about your life? Is it full of clutter and distractions too? I will ask God to reveal to us both His solution to this dilemma.

November 22

Consider it pure joy, my brothers, whenever you face trials of many kinds because you know that the testing of your faith develops perseverance. Perseverance must finish its work so that you may be mature and complete, not lacking anything.—**James 1:2-4**

I suppose I have always had a bit of pride when it came to my health. As a child, I was "healthy," with only the usual bouts of measles, mumps and chickenpox. Oh, I had a few colds and the flu, but no broken bones or allergies. As an adult, when I visited a doctor for my yearly checkup, he would invariably say, "Well, you are the healthiest person I've seen all day!"

So when I heard the diagnosis of uterine cancer that would require a complete hysterectomy, I was shocked. After the surgery, I was reassured that it had removed all the disease and the chance of recurrence was very rare. I should be just fine and no further treatment was required. Of course, I put the episode out of my mind and went on with my life with gratitude to the Lord for healing me.

Unfortunately, two years later, I noticed a pain in my abdomen and went to an emergency room. There was a tumor, as well as, nodules on both lungs and a suspicious spot on my spine. Although rare, the cancer had spread. "How could this be happening to me?" I asked God.

I went into a real tailspin of fear, dread and anger as I plodded through tests, scans and procedures, and finally 10 rounds of chemotherapy. However, during those days and months, the Lord provided everything I needed to get through the ordeal. Family and friends were attentive and caring, and I felt the Lord's closeness, love and peace more profoundly than ever before. Once again, I was told the cancer was gone, and I rejoiced.

I am convinced that the Lord's ways are not our ways, and He has a perfect plan for the lives of His children. That assurance helped me cope with the news a year later that my daughter Amy had extensive thyroid cancer, but not without asking the Lord, "How could this be happening to Amy?" She was a healthy, young mother of three children, fit and active! Nevertheless, we could see that my illness helped prepare us both, and I could encourage her through her trial. I was well, too, so I was available to go to her during her surgery to help out with her children. God's timing is perfect!

Fast-forward another year, after many clear CT scans, my cancer again returned. I must admit, I was panicked thinking of losing my hair again and going through more debilitating chemo. This time, I sought a second opinion in another city just to be thorough. That ordeal proved to be the most upsetting, frustrating, and confusing event I can remember. After many, many tears, I pleaded with God for clarity and wisdom to decide on the course of treatment. I was in distress, needing help. It came so clearly from Him, saying to me, "Keep it simple! Stay in Austin for radiation only, trust Me and continue to draw near to Me."

Around the same time, to make matters more stressful and complicated, Amy's doctors found her cancer had spread to her lungs. Could it be that the trials we were experiencing were all part of God's design to test us both and refine us, in the fire, you might say? We encouraged one another with what we had learned about God's character—that His plan is perfect, always for our good, no matter how it appears, and that He loves us and never intends harm toward us.

Having both completed recent treatments, our hope is to keep cancer at bay for a while. Whatever the future brings, we know we can trust a sovereign God with it. He is good all the time and He is in control. As a lifelong "control freak," relinquishing that control has been a challenge, but so freeing! The Lord continues to be my steady and reliable Guide and Companion through all of life's ups and downs. He has given me confidence to face whatever may come, and I praise Him for His always-sufficient provision.

"In this you greatly rejoice, even though now for a little while, if necessary, you have been distressed by various trials, so that the proof of your faith, being more precious than gold which is perishable, even though tested by fire, may be found to result in praise and glory and honor at the revelations of Jesus Christ" (1 Peter 1:6-7 NASB).

Ann Temple
Austin, TX

November 23

Lift your eyes and look to the heavens: Who created all these? He who brings out the starry host one by one, and calls them each by name.—**Isaiah 40:26**

Since 1979, we have gathered for Thanksgiving at the family ranch in Weimar, Texas. Sometimes our feast was the day after, but it was still a cherished celebration, no matter if it was a day late. However, Thanksgiving of 2011 brought about some changes.

My son Zach went to Louisiana with his wife. Lauren's grandfather had passed the previous month and it was important for them to be with her Grandma Jeri. (Plus an added bonus of being close to Baton Rouge meant they could attend the LSU-Arkansas football game.) My other son was invited to his then steady girlfriend's home in Houston and was torn between where he should go.

Trevor is very sentimental and doesn't like change, so I knew the thought of not going to the ranch was difficult for him, but being with his girlfriend was important too. When her mom invited my husband and me to come as well, I eagerly accepted. That way, I would at least be able to spend time with one of my sons.

Desiring the best of both worlds, I tried to figure out a way to still see my sisters and mom at the ranch, either before or after Thanksgiving, so we planned dinner the night before. The next morning, Austin and I could drive on to Houston. It would seem weird leaving Thanksgiving morning, just when all the hustle and bustle in the kitchen was getting started in preparation for the traditional feast. However, spending time with my sisters, their husbands and my mom on Wednesday night would be special.

After dinner that Wednesday night and before going to bed, I took my dog for a walk. The night air was crisp and the sky was brilliant. Being so far away from any city lights out in the country, the heavens appeared closer, with an abundance of stars. On our walk I saw a raccoon, possum, armadillo and rabbit. I could hear the cows mooing in the distance, and the fallen leaves crunched as I walked on top of them. Why did I feel so close to God that night?

As I looked into the sky, I thought about the words from Isaiah 40:26 I read earlier that morning from a devotion in *Daily Guideposts 2010*. I couldn't help but sing Chris Tomlin's "Indescribable." Yes, *He placed the stars in the sky and He knows them by name!*

I honestly can't remember a Thanksgiving when I have ever been more thankful than I was at that moment. I had just had a fun dinner—it wasn't the traditional turkey and dressing, but beef from one of the ranch cows. Still, my stomach and heart were full, unlike millions of others in this world. My boys and my niece and nephews, along with their spouses and kiddos weren't there, but my mom sure was happy dining with her three daughters and our husbands. Afterwards, I had the privilege of being one on one with the Creator of the universe. Just me—and the animals and stars—and God!

Thanksgiving 2011 was the first deviation from the norm since 1979, and it was delightful. I knew He wanted me to embrace our time together as the most profound memory. How sweet to be reminded that it's not the date on the calendar or traditions or the rituals that make it special. The attitude of love in my heart for my Father, family, friends and fellow man makes every day worthy of thanksgiving!

My editor, Rick Weber, had just moved from Texas to Florida, and had no family there. He spent Thanksgiving Day delivering meals to shut-ins. A friend in my Pilates class who wouldn't have her grown children home decided to invite others over who were in the same boat. My "mentee" from church had to work the whole week, so her parents spent the day feeding the homeless in Houston and had their family time over the weekend. New experiences for all.

As our children continue to grow the family through marriage and babies, as we move and loved ones pass on, all of our previous traditions will change. When adjustments to holiday traditions must be made (not if, but when), be prepared to listen as God calls us to something new.

November 24

Sing and make music in your heart to the Lord, always giving thanks to God the Father for everything, in the name of our Lord Jesus Christ.—**Ephesians 5:19-20**

Yesterday, I shared a story about being tolerant of inevitable changes to holiday traditions. I pridefully felt very convicted by my own words! However, after our Thanksgiving of 2012, I was humbly reminded of an incident that wasn't so warmly accepted at our annual family feast.

My husband and I were already middle-aged when we married and found that trying to mesh two worlds of traditions presented some challenges, but nothing too difficult. However, at one of the first Thanksgivings while dating,

Austin not only ruffled my feathers, but also those of my two sisters when he tried to introduce something new to our very established menu.

Dad used to be the chef for our gatherings at the family ranch. He wasn't very good at close relationships and interacting with the family, but he was a master in the kitchen. After he became ill (and later passed), my sisters and I took over. Before long, we had a scrumptious set-in-stone menu.

When anyone else offered to bring something, we gave them a simple task, such as a dessert or condiment, but nothing that interfered or competed with any of our dishes. When Austin said he was going to bring some dressing that first year, I tried to discourage him. My sister Rhonda prepared that side dish and my family loved hers. We didn't need a new recipe introduced.

Austin's wasn't just any dressing—it was oyster dressing! Ugh! I knew that no one in my family would eat it, but if it was so important, he would be "allowed" to bring a small pan. Rhonda still prepared her recipe and we reluctantly accepted his addition to our perfect menu.

We obviously had a different idea of what constituted "small," and he cooked a large 9x11 pan of it. I was right. No one else in the family ate a bite. Oysters at Thanksgiving? I don't think so. Not in my family. When it was time to go home, he insisted on leaving the leftovers with my sister Nancy, and she was anything but thrilled to have that yucky stuff in her already jam-packed refrigerator.

The following year, I was asked to gently persuade Austin not to bring his oyster dressing. My sister doesn't let anything go to waste, but she said the dogs wouldn't even eat it. He abided by my request and never fixed it again—until 2012. It had been part of his family's traditional meal before meeting me, and my sisters and I had shamed him into never bringing it again. Austin decided that even though no else liked it, there was no reason he should continue to go without.

When we walked into Nancy's kitchen, I told her what Austin had prepared. She thought that fiasco was a one-time thing, never to be dealt with again. Nope. He did it again. But to our amazement, others actually ate it! My oldest son, who now loves oysters, thought it was wonderful. I actually tried some myself. And when it came time to pack up the leftovers, my mother, of all people, asked to take some home.

For several years, we had lovingly joked about that dressing, and Austin had been a great sport. But this year when it reappeared on the table, we were all more receptive. Considering all the changes that have transpired through deaths, divorces, births, marriages and distance, a little pan of oyster dressing was quite easy to accept. It was time for me to heed the words from yesterday's story—when adjustments to holiday traditions must take place, be open-minded to the "new" that will come.

Even taste buds change over time and now oyster dressing was considered an acceptable addition to the Thanksgiving menu. Looking back, I can certainly acknowledge that change can be a good thing, starting with the dramatic transformation in my own life.

I am overflowing with joy for that blessing from God and have so much praise to offer up to Jesus for His redemptive power. Though the holiday feast may be subject to change over the years, I want to make sure words of thanksgiving and praise are always a staple on my daily prayer menu.

November 25

Be still before the Lord and wait patiently for him.—**Psalm 37:7**

It was a sunny day in Austin, and I was on summer break from teaching. My husband, Andy, and I sat eagerly in the ultrasound room at my 20-week prenatal appointment. We were both pretty excited about the new baby and the new experiences that were to come.

A few days earlier, we had returned from a trip that I had spent the last year secretly planning for my husband's 30th birthday. Feeling rested and energized by our recent vacation, we were so happy, and I was finally ready to start planning for the baby.

284

Andy smiled and squeezed my knee as the ultrasound technician came in to begin our exam. She pointed out arms, legs, tiny hands and facial features on the overhead screen and printed out pictures for us to take home. She spent some time looking at the baby's organs and heart, and soon the doctor came in to take a look as well. They seemed to spend quite awhile looking at the baby's heart, during which time their facial expressions became more serious and polite chatting quickly turned to an uncomfortable silence.

The doctor suggested we move to a different room to get a clearer view of the baby's heart and to make a video recording of what they were seeing. Finally, he explained that he was sure there was something terribly wrong with the way the heart had developed, and that we would need to follow up with a pediatric cardiologist. We were then escorted to see the genetic counselor who suggested I have an amniocentesis procedure done to check our child's chromosomes for abnormalities that may be linked to congenital heart defects.

The news that our baby would be born with a broken heart was devastating. Only a year earlier, I'd had a miscarriage, and this time around, we thought for sure that nothing could possibly go wrong. As we sat there, we were given some possible scenarios of the exact defect, although we would not know for sure until the baby was born. As long as I was still pregnant, my body would supply all the oxygen that the baby would need in order to grow and develop. However, after birth the baby would have a hard time supplying oxygen on his own. If not surgically corrected, the baby could possibly die of congestive heart failure within a few months of birth.

I spent the next few days in a panic. I emailed everyone I knew to pray for us. I emailed our church pastor, radio stations, churches I used to attend in other towns, friends, relatives, even speaker/author Beth Moore. When I wasn't praying, I researched *Truncus Arteriosus*, the name of the baby's potential and most likely defect. I learned the anatomy of the human heart and the surgery to repair the defect, and I read stories of other parents who had sat where I was now sitting.

While all this information was very helpful and reassuring, I couldn't escape the black hole of fear, helplessness and panic I felt as the due date came closer. I knew people were praying for me, but I still didn't feel better. I just didn't think prayers were enough to help me get through this. I was waiting for a divine revelation of some sort. I wanted the doctor to call and tell me there was a mistake, and that the baby was fine. I was reading my Bible and praying, and I wasn't allowing myself to stop and breathe, because I knew somehow I could do something to fix all this myself. I thought that if I prayed enough, that the baby would be miraculously cured, and I would be spared from the pain and fear of sending my first child to the operating room.

Have you ever searched frantically for your keys only to find them in your purse, where you left them? Or have you looked everywhere for the pencil you just had in your hand only to find it tucked behind your ear? In my frantic state, I was searching for loopholes and answers, and I kept hearing the word "wait" whispered quietly in the back of my mind. *Surely that isn't God talking to me*, I thought, and I continued in my frantic state. The next day, I received a reply from one of the pastors at our church advising me to heed the words of Psalm 37:7: "Be still before the Lord and wait patiently for him."

WAIT! I laughed when I read it. I knew that's what I needed to do all along, but I was too selfish and arrogant to trust that God could handle this on His own.

A few days later, I talked to the genetic counselor on the phone. I held my breath as she told me the results of the amniocentesis. Thankfully, the results concluded that the heart defect was completely isolated. The baby's chromosomes were normal, and there would be no syndrome connected with the heart problems. This was great news, but there was still a heart defect, and the baby would still require open-heart surgery.

The doctors advised us to just go on and plan for the baby like we would have done all along. Andy and I felt robbed. Why did we even have to know about the defect if there was nothing we could do? It wasn't fair. My husband and I are the type of people who like to fix things as soon as they are broken. If there is something that needs fixing around our house, and even our friends' and neighbors' houses, Andy does it. He won't pay someone to do something that he knows he has the tools to do himself. But this time there was nothing for us to fix. We could only wait.

I knew my options were either to wait in a panic and have a miserable pregnancy, or I could wait upon the Lord and hope and pray for peace. I decided this was the best time ever to completely depend on God for strength and peace. Andy and I prayed together, and not only did we receive peace, but also great joy! We were not expecting to be happy throughout this process. Instead of allowing this devastating diagnosis to destroy our spirits and our marriage, we turned it into an opportunity to fully trust in God to carry us through every day. It was liberating! In the most fearful and helpless place in my life, I was able to bring glory to God just by admitting there was nothing I could do on my own in all this.

After our son, Cody, was born, he was quickly taken away to the neonatal intensive care unit. He looked great and impressed all of his doctors and nurses by his color and weight. Nine days later, he was strong enough for his open-heart surgery. There were no complications, and he recovered steadily. I can't say that that month in the hospital wasn't hard, but God truly carried us through.

I didn't realize it then, but looking back, I believe that God used Cody's heart to show me just how defective my own heart was. Today, Cody is the happiest and sweetest little boy. His heart defect has not slowed him down one bit, and he seems to be developmentally ahead of other kids his age. He will continue to need maintenance on his heart and the arteries around it, and I welcome each procedure as a chance to examine my own heart.

Meghan Patterson
Austin, TX

November 26

The steadfast love of the LORD *never ceases; his mercies never come to an end; they are new every morning; great is your faithfulness.*—**Lamentations 3:22-23 (ESV)**

The daily verse for today was also the daily reading in one of the online devotions I received. How thoughtful that God would send me these words. They were exactly what I needed to hear.

Throughout this book, I have written about the rejuvenation I receive from God. There are stories of how God has awakened my soul, softened my heart and changed my attitude. But then I revert back to my old ways. What's the deal with me?

Many stories reflect my ongoing struggle to surrender all to God, love Him more, be more thankful for what I have, guard my heart and mouth, get more organized and stop procrastinating. When am I ever going to grow up and be a mature Christian?

There are days I feel so close to God. Days I am on fire for Him. Days I am more obedient, kind and loving. I feel that I see God in everything I do and everywhere I go. I know He is with me and that I am abiding in Him. I am thankful for my blessings and acknowledge His magnificence. Why can't every day be like that?

There are just days I get down on myself and feel I don't measure up to the other women I hang out with. I know better than to compare myself to others. I just love what The Message says in Romans 12:6: ". . . let's just go ahead and be what we were made to be, without enviously or pridefully comparing ourselves with each other, or trying to be something we aren't." But sometimes, I just can't help but do the comparison thing.

However, there are days, like this very one, when God goes out of His way to quiet my soul, sit me down and love on me. On this morning He spoke, I listened and heard His message of love. He gave me not one, but two verses, reminding me that every day is a brand new day—a new beginning. I read "Let me hear of your unfailing love each morning" (Psalm 143:8 NLT) in a posting on Facebook. His unfailing love is there each morning! How do I miss it?

I might not get it right today, but tomorrow He will be there with a whole new batch of love and mercy so I can try again. That's what the Christian walk is all about—a series of new beginnings. We will all reach new mountaintops, when we are on top of the world and sing of His praises all day. But then how easily we stumble when we take our eyes off Him. We must be careful not to tarry there too long and become complacent. No, each morning we must look up to God for a new beginning, as He picks us up and brushes off the dirt.

My Father is taking me on this journey up and down peaks and valleys for a reason, and there will always be a "next step" to maturity, as well as a slip and fall backwards. This side of heaven there will not be perfection in my walk, but God *is* perfect and great is His faithfulness.

November 27

I am sending you to them to open their eyes and turn them from darkness to light, and from the power of Satan to God, so that they may receive forgiveness of sins and a place among those who are sanctified by faith in me.—**Acts 26:18**

Thanksgiving weekend is noted for family and food—and college football. It seems that there is always some crucial game on the line that could determine who will or won't go to a bowl game or to the national championship game.

I am not a huge football fanatic, but I do keep track of the University of Texas and LSU because my two sons graduated from those fine universities. UT and Texas A&M played their final regular-season game against each other on Thanksgiving night 2011 (A&M left the Big 12, going to the Southeastern Conference), with the Longhorns winning in the final seconds. LSU beat Arkansas on Friday, securing a place in the national championship game.

After watching those two games, I was a bit bored with football. However, something I saw in the Boise State and Wyoming game on Saturday of that Thanksgiving weekend got my attention—it was probably the "cutest" play I have ever seen. Now, my husband cringed when I used the word "cute" to describe something about football, but it literally brought tears to my eyes just thinking about it. Yes, it was cute, it was darling, it was such a God thing!

With the score tied and only one second left in the first half, quarterback Kellen Moore of Boise State threw a 46-yard Hail Mary pass to the goal line. However, a Wyoming defender tipped the ball. Now, I don't know who the intended receiver was, but sprawled out, flat on his back, in the end zone just beyond the goal line was Boise State's Matt Miller.

Miller said that he had his eyes open because he was trying not to get stepped on. He looked up and there was the ball, literally falling into his arms. He just put his arms up in the air and grabbed the ball for a touchdown. Talk about being in the right place at the right time! I bet his mom was just screaming with excitement for her son!

This particular play in the end zone was so perfectly orchestrated, with a player flat on his back with outstretched arms. No one would ever have dreamed up such a "cute" touchdown, but with God in the end zone, anything is possible. No matter who is playing, no matter which one is supposed to be the better team, God is the One in control of the outcome.

What if Matt Miller's eyes had been closed? Would he still have caught the ball? We will never know that answer, but having his eyes wide open certainly aided in the catch. How about for you and me? What happens when our eyes are sealed shut due to layers of scales on them, preventing us from seeing all that God has promised and prepared for our life? Might we miss out on the big play?

What if Saul hadn't been on that road to Damascus and met Jesus? What if Ananias hadn't done what God told him to do? Would the scales ever have fallen off of Saul's eyes? Pretty silly to worry about the what-ifs of that story. God had a plan for Saul to become Paul and nothing could stop His purpose.

Is a good life the luck of being in the right place at the right time? Or does being in God's light and doing what is right result in a life being good? Thankfully, God's Word provides the answer to that question.

November 28

Gideon replied, "If now I have found favor in your eyes, give me a sign that it is really you talking to me.—**Judges 6:17**

"Look, it's 6:17 a.m. There must be an important Bible verse corresponding to those numbers," my husband said to me, with just a hint of sarcasm in his voice. Let me clarify, Austin wasn't being sarcastic about the verse in the Bible—he was just letting me know that we were 13 minutes early to the hospital.

My surgery was at 8:00, and we had been asked to arrive at 6:30. As usual, I was overly anxious about arriving on time. Austin's schedule is so hectic. He is always rushing to arrive in just the nick of time, and he handles that stress very well. On the other hand, I get in a tizzy if I'm not early. We have had this little time discrepancy our entire marriage. You would think I would be used to it by now.

There have been a few stories written about the associations I make with the time on a digital clock and Scripture. A time display can spur me on to search for or think of a corresponding verse in one of the books of the Bible. (Example: If I see 3:16 on a clock, I think of John 3:16.)

We left the house later than planned and then Austin made a wrong turn. It was foggy and dark, and I was irritated. Since I was going in for a very minor surgical procedure that required general anesthesia, I hadn't had anything to eat or drink since midnight. I can do without the food, but I don't do so well without my morning coffee. Yes, I was grumpy and admittedly a bit anxious about the procedure.

My husband has always tried to make me laugh and not be so testy. This time thing has given him all kinds of ammunition to make jokes. I know he just wants me to relax a bit, so why do I let his comments get under my skin? Then we arrived at the hospital—with 13 minutes to spare. He was right again.

Yes, I worried over nothing. Plus, after arriving, we had to wait an additional 15 minutes. And, believe me, he took every opportunity to joke about being early. (I really do love how he is such a good natured, fun-loving husband!)

When we pulled in the parking lot and Austin noted the time, I was curious if there was a 6:17 verse with special significance to the situation. However, as we walked into the hospital, my mind went back to worrying about surgery and anesthesia.

Routine procedures can go wrong, but after signing all the paperwork, calmness enveloped me, and I wasn't the least bit anxious anymore. Surgery went well, and I woke up, thankful for God's gift.

The next morning, my husband drove me back to the doctor for a quick follow-up. I was reading my online devotions on my iPhone and came to a weekly entry from Max Lucado. And what was one of the Scriptures he referenced? Hebrews 6:17. "Because God wanted to make the unchanging nature of his purpose very clear to the heirs of what was promised, he confirmed it with an oath." Lucado paraphrased that verse as God's promise of being the same yesterday, today and tomorrow.

Out of curiosity, I began scrolling through other books on my Olive Tree Bible App, and when I read Judges 6:17, I had to smile. "Gideon replied, 'If now I have found favor in your eyes, give me a sign that it is really you talking to me.'"

The peace I felt the previous day before going into surgery was all the assurance I needed from my Heavenly Father that He was there with me. I wasn't actually looking for a sign from God, but I just love how He always just shows up and lets me know He's around. God *was* and *is* and *will be* there to lead the way and shower me with His loving presence. He remains the same, yesterday, today and tomorrow.

Two powerful verses from one glance towards the clock at 6:17 a.m.—that's the bonus for arriving early.

November 29

Behold, I am doing a new thing.—**Isaiah 43:19 (AMP)**

A question I've been asking myself over the last two years is, "What's next, Lord?" My kids are getting older (middle school) and college is not too far away. I have often thought about returning to the classroom. It's comfortable, familiar and I loved it for the 10 years I did it.

However, something keeps stopping me. Fear? After all, public schools and kids have changed. Lack of confidence? It's been so long. Would I remember anything? Two kids and years later, I'm not sure I have any brain cells left!

I don't believe any of these is the reason.

God said, "Behold, I am doing a new thing." I am not the same person I was 13 years ago. So often, I limit God. I cuddle up into my nice cocoon instead of branching out and allowing Him to reveal something new and different to me, challenging me to press on, continuing the walk, and maturing.

As I was reading the Bible the other day, I was continually reminded that age does not limit God's call! Man does! After two years of praying, waiting, seeking and moving forward, I have a clearer picture of what the next step is in this journey with Him. After all, that's all He asks—to trust Him, walk in faith and move forward. Are you asking God, "What's next in this journey?" Or are you covering yourself in what's comfortable?

Chris Barr Freeman
Austin, TX

November 30

Let us not become weary in doing good, for at the proper time we will reap a harvest if we do not give up.—**Galatians 6:9**

The ladies in my Tuesday morning Bible study are such a source of encouragement. They know my joys and concerns. Sounding like a broken record, repeatedly asking the mighty prayer warriors to lift up my wayward children, they never tire of my requests.

Weeks before Christmas, Debbie sent me a link to a book she had purchased for her own adult children, thinking I too might be interested for my sons. It was Rick Warren's new expanded edition of his highly acclaimed *The Purpose Driven Life*.

After meeting a friend at Starbucks in my local Barnes & Noble, I browsed around and quickly found it piled high on a table. Before picking up copies to give my boys, on that very same table I caught a glimpse of a very unusual picture on the cover of another best-selling author's book.

Are you familiar with Nick Vujicic? Along with being an author, he is an incredible motivational speaker. There are many exceptional speakers in this world, but none like Nick. When listening and watching his presentations, it is extremely difficult to dwell upon your own problems as he addresses overcoming adversity and trials. It is almost impossible not to be inspired by this man's ability to enjoy an abundant, joy-filled life.

You see, Nick was born without arms or legs. But God gave him all he needs to live—a brain to think clearly and a torso to hold his loving heart. The picture on the cover of Vujicic's *Unstoppable* shows him riding a surfboard—an unusual image that prompted me to immediately snatch it up. I had viewed some of his talks on YouTube and knew of his ability to captivate an audience. Now I was anxious to read how God would use him through words on a page.

Excitedly, I read the back cover. *Hmm, this sounds like something my boys might find inspiring.* Both Zach and Trevor had different issues in their life at that moment, but how could they not focus less on their own circumstances after reading this young man's journey, with God by his side?

Folks were sitting all over the place in big comfy chairs reading, so I decided to do the same and "randomly" opened the book to pages 56 and 57. I couldn't believe the timeliness of what I read. Those two pages were devoted to romantic relationships gone wrong and the hope found through God to survive the heartbreak.

It was so timely because my unmarried son was experiencing a devastating "break" in a relationship with his girlfriend of several years. However, my main concern was the break he had taken from Jesus.

Please understand that I was also distraught about the possibility of losing "her." However, I wondered how Trevor would endure the heartache, without depending on the loving arms of Jesus to hold him up? It was more important for my son to have Jesus in his life than anyone or anything else. Nick provided insight to likely purposes God has for relationship woes. The words on those two pages were exactly what Trevor needed to hear—words spoken by someone other than his mom. And I "randomly" opened the book to those two pages?

I didn't wait for Christmas to give him the book. Also, during this "break" we had some of the best God conversations in many years. Would this be the time Trevor asked Jesus back into his life? If not, God certainly helped me plant a harvest of seeds. Oh, the good that can come out of the trials in life!

There are many instances when this mom is at a loss on how to communicate the love of Jesus to her adult children (who have taken a "break" from Him) as they struggle through their difficulties—whether it's a broken relationship, unemployment, poor decisions, financial crisis or loneliness. But with the perfect Parent in the picture, I know where to go for help. God the Father will lead the way.

There's no doubt in my mind Who led me to *Unstoppable* and specifically to pages 56 and 57. There is nothing random about His perfect plan.

December 1

And let us consider how to stir up one another to love and good works, not neglecting to meet together, as is the habit of some, but encouraging one another, and all the more as you see the Day drawing near.—**Hebrews 10:24-25 (ESV)**

According to Wikipedia, the free encyclopedia found through a search on Google, "the liturgical year, also known as the church year, consists of the cycle of liturgical seasons in Christian churches which determines when feast days, including celebrations of saints, are to be observed, and which portions of Scripture are to be read. The dates of the festivals vary somewhat between the different churches, though the sequence and logic is largely the same."

Protestant churches observe far fewer festivals than Catholic and Orthodox, in particular with regard to feasts of the Virgin Mary and the other Saints. Non-denominational Bible churches, like the one I attend in Austin, don't actually observe a church calendar year. However, growing up in the United Methodist Church, I did become accustomed to some of the traditions, in particular the observance of Advent, the four Sundays preceding Christmas Day.

I grew up understanding that Advent was a time of expectant waiting and anticipation of the birth of Christ. Also, for most churches, the church calendar year begins with the first Sunday of Advent. However, I wasn't aware that some of the early churches observed the last Sunday before Advent (and the last Sunday of the church year) as a special day as well.

Stir-Up Sunday, as that last Sunday of the church year was called, is an informal term that was coined in the early Anglican church from the opening words of the Collect for the Day in the Book of Common Prayer: *Stir up, we beseech thee, O Lord, the wills of thy faithful people; that they, plenteously bringing forth the fruit of good works, may be plenteously rewarded; through Jesus Christ our Lord. Amen.*

Since most recipes for Christmas pudding called for the mixture to stand for several weeks before cooking, the congregation would go to church, hear the words "stir up" and be reminded that it was time to start stirring up the puddings and other seasonal recipes for Christmas.

The prayer is clearly referencing more than the action of using a spoon to mix up ingredients in a bowl. The prayer asks for God to stir up the wills of the people, so that we can bring forth the fruit of good works that He has planned for us to do. A prayer for God to stir us into action, so that each of us can be used to accomplish His purpose.

Every morning I start off my day with a cup of coffee, adding two spoons of real sugar and milk. I absolutely savor the taste of that first cup! What a blessing to be able to walk into the warmth (or coolness) and security of my own kitchen and pour a cup of coffee, and I do thank God every single morning for that privilege. However, if I forget to stir, the sweetness just sits at the bottom and that first sip is extremely bitter. Immediately, my happy thoughts of thanksgiving are interrupted, as I reach for the spoon.

Today, think of what you and God need to work on together to get that sweet taste of joy and love into your day. He will stir you into all kinds of situations and with all kinds of people to use you for His purpose. Don't just sit at the bottom of the cup, interrupting His plans for your life. Allow the Creator to stir you up into His unique and special creation, all for His glory.

December 2

"You will seek me and find me when you seek me with all your heart. I will be found by you, declares the LORD, and will bring you back from captivity." —**Jeremiah 29:12-14**

My husband and I went to the 2010 Make A Difference Tour in Austin featuring recording artists Michael W. Smith, Third Day, TobyMac, and Jason Gray, along with renowned author, speaker and minister Max Lucado. It was certainly a lively, loud, inspirational evening. Even though it was several years ago, memories of that concert remain etched in my heart.

I first saw Michael W. Smith sometime around 1994 at his solo performance at a church in Houston. I took my sons, Zach and Trevor, because, at the time, Michael W. Smith was one of Zach's favorite artists. TobyMac used to be part of the Christian rock band dc Talk, which was another of his favorites as well. I must admit, when I had Zach and Trevor at that small concert way back then, I was feeling quite sure about myself as a parent.

There I was, with my two boys, listening to a Christian recording artist. Certainly that meant that they would always love Christian music and they would be good Christian boys. Right?

Seated in the row in front of us at the Make A Difference Tour was a group of eight boys, probably about 10 years old, the same age as Zach in 1994. Now this concert was much livelier than what we saw way back then. TobyMac is known for his rapper-style Christian music and Michael W. Smith and Third Day had a full band on stage. The venue wasn't a church and it was extremely loud—it was a REAL concert. But I still couldn't stop looking at those young boys in front of us and think back.

As Zach got older, Contemporary Christian music was no longer his favorite. When he was in college, he began to question his own faith. I know Zach believes in God, but struggles with having a relationship with Jesus. As I was examining how Zach's life has changed since 1994, God led me to look at my own.

I attended church weekly and taught Sunday school all through the boys' elementary and junior high years, and read my daily devotionals, of course. I called myself a Christian, but looking back, I know I didn't have a relationship with Jesus Christ. I wasn't earnestly seeking Him and, to be honest, wasn't even aware I needed to. God had some plans for my life though and in 1997, I quit work (totally a God thing) and started attending a women's Bible study for the first time. From that point on, everything started to change. Slowly, ever so slowly, I began a relationship with that man Jesus, seeking Him with all my heart. I am certainly a work in progress, and I can't even imagine how in the world I ever got through one day without *knowing* Him and the hope of His promises.

Did you notice I kind of skipped some parts of my life? Oh, my college years, when church and God were the last things on my mind, how He carried and protected me! Through all my years of being lost, He kept me in His sight. He let me flounder around, like the Israelites in the desert, but He always knew exactly where I was. He brought me out of that scorched desert and into His holy presence, where I have found joy beyond belief.

I understand exactly what's going on. Zach is in the same place I was. If God could save a wretch like me, I trust with my heart that He can do the same for my sweet son.

Yes, much has changed since I took my boys to see Michael W. Smith in 1994. I have an incredible relationship with Jesus Christ, my Lord and Savior. Through the trials and the joys, He has carried me like one of His precious sheep, from the desert to His Promised Land. My journey has been in His perfect timing—Zach's will be also.

December 3

The LORD does not look at the things man looks at. Man looks at the outward appearance, but the LORD looks at the heart. —**1 Samuel 16:7**

It seems like Christmas decorations go up earlier and earlier every year. The pressure is on to get the tree up and the manger scene out in the yard. One year we ran into a little problem though: Almost all the Christmas decorations were in storage.

We started our house remodel back in the spring of 2012, and the builder promised it would be completed in time for Christmas. My husband and I moved to the small garage apartment and only the bare necessities came with us. The decorations went to the storage unit, along with all the other "stuff."

We were naïve enough to think it would be done on schedule and didn't think to put the decorations in at the very last, making them easily accessible. At the end of November, we were looking at four to five more months until completion—not exactly in time for Christmas. Even if I could have found the boxes, there was no room for the big tree in the tiny apartment. However, there was a bright point: A few of the outdoor decorations were in a separate storage building behind our garage.

The weekend after Thanksgiving, my sweet husband got it done. From the street, we looked festive and ready. However, come up the driveway a bit and it was another story. It was a construction disaster zone with no visible sign of Christmas anywhere.

Driving home one night, I heard Bing Crosby's "It's Beginning to Look a Lot Like Christmas" on the radio, and indeed my neighborhood looked festive. I saw the lights of decorated trees sparkling through the windows and imagined the stockings hung by the chimney with care, with garland adorning the staircase and mantle. I visualized a nativity scene on a shelf and most certainly some glittery centerpieces on the table, along with the Christmas dishes. But not at my house.

For a few minutes, I actually felt sorry for myself. How could I get into the Christmas spirit without my decorations? Oh, the Holy Spirit didn't waste anytime before He had a little talk with me. How silly was that notion of mine that I needed a tree, some garland and stockings to celebrate the birth of Christ?

The outside of my house may have looked like one ready for Christmas with the lighted nativity scene and wreaths on the gate, but what would someone say about not seeing anything Christmassy inside my home? Would the lights on a decorated tree be an indicator of Jesus' love shining in my home? God knows my heart and what's inside. Does He see a heart overflowing with the light of His Son's love?

Please know that I absolutely love Christmas decorations and preparations. I think part of the magic of the season is the beautiful lights, candles, stockings, glittery centerpieces and decorated trees, along with festive gatherings of friends and family, carols and special Christmas Eve church services. But what is the reason behind all of those efforts? Are we trying to bring glory to our glitter and glitz or to God? When our love for Jesus is the reason for all we do, *every day*, then we know that our hearts are in good condition. Most importantly, God knows!

"Woe to you, teachers of the law and Pharisees, you hypocrites! You are like whitewashed tombs, which look beautiful on the outside but on the inside are full of the bones of the dead and everything unclean. In the same way, on the outside you appear to people as righteous but on the inside you are full of hypocrisy and wickedness" (Matthew 23:27-28). In Matthew 23, Jesus spoke loud and clear about hypocrisy. Woe to us indeed, if we are more concerned with outside appearances than the inside of our hearts. Are our visible decorations truthfully signs of our adoration for the King? Oh, looks can be so deceiving!

Honestly, I missed going through all my boxes of ornaments and the memories each one held, but I know that no-frills Christmas didn't just happen by accident. Having all those decorations out of reach was such a special gift of time and reflection. If you are in the middle of putting up your tree right now, I am sure you can identify with the amount of time I saved that year.

God gave me the opportunity to simply focus on the message behind that unassuming nativity scene in the front of my house—it's all about baby Jesus in the manger.

December 4

"Everyone to whom much was given, of him much will be required, and from him to whom they entrusted much, they will demand the more."—**Luke 12:48**

Stepping Out is an annual event sponsored by the Women's Ministry of my church. It is an evening of food and fellowship where we work together to benefit local and international ministries with hands-on service projects. Most of the projects are Christmas-related, so it was a fun way to kick off the season.

Since I am a retired Empty Nester, with a husband who spends much time working out of town, I volunteered to arrive early to help set up and stay late for cleanup duty. After all, I had more of the luxurious gift of time than many of the other women, especially the young moms. In previous years, I noticed how those young mothers thoroughly enjoyed lingering around at the close of the evening. The kids were being taken care of at home or church with a sitter, and this was an evening for them to step out and enjoy some adult fellowship while serving others.

Stepping Out was certainly an opportunity to bring glory to God by doing projects that would benefit His children. However, on this particular night, I just didn't want to go. How's that for a really bad attitude? I was in the middle of writing a devotion. The thought of getting dressed and venturing out in the chilly damp night, interrupting my thoughts, had no appeal at all.

My writing is important too. There would be plenty of other women at Stepping Out to do that bit of God's work, and surely one less body wouldn't be a problem. While I tried to convince myself it would be all right to stay home, the Holy Spirit let me know otherwise.

What a transformation, that after all these years I can recognize His voice. I might not always listen, but I hear it. This time I surrendered to God instead of to my selfish self. Yes, I got dressed, went to Stepping Out and had an absolutely delightful evening visiting and serving. God even opened the door to two additional project needs where my time and resources would be put to good use. Though I undoubtedly deserved it, I never heard the Holy Spirit say, "I told you so."

The next morning, when I sat down to gather my thoughts, ponder the events of the previous night and have some quiet time with God, I heard something else from the Holy Spirit: The words from the daily verse rang clearly in my head. The previous Sunday, Pastor Brad spoke of the importance of serving in his sermon, based on Luke 12:35-49, and now I was being reminded of his message.

Brad was wrapping up a sermon series that focused on ways to serve others. In the sermon notes he wrote, "If we knew when Jesus was going to return, would it make a difference in how you live? I think the Bible does not tell us the day or hour so that we live each moment with an alert expectation of our Lord returning." In Luke 12:36 (ESV) we read, "Stay dressed for action," and Brad added, *"Serving people* stay dressed for action!"

Ouch! Who didn't want to go to all the trouble to get dressed—put on makeup and fix her hair—to go serve others? Who was more concerned about her own conveniences than making life a little more convenient for others? Who was the one, despite all her abundant blessings, thought she earned an excuse from blessing others? Yes, I was that person who felt it was OK to sit in front of my computer, doing what I wanted instead of making a simple effort to reach out.

Besides being able to recognize the small voice of the Holy Spirit, I have also learned to decipher the loud screams from the Evil One. Satan attempts to take every act of disobedience to God and turn it into shame and guilt, which causes us to focus on the sin and turn away from God. The result is a feeling of condemnation; a feeling of hopeless despair that we have messed up—again.

Conviction is the constructive emotion that comes from the Holy Spirit. Being aware we sinned against our Father, and did something that wasn't pleasing in His sight, we draw closer to Him. We allow God to speak truth into our hearts, which leads to repentance and change, resulting in the promise of hope, not hopeless despair.

As I recalled the truths from Brad's message on serving, I was most definitely convicted and sought forgiveness for my poor attitude. I had messed up again, but I wouldn't remain separated from the love of my Father—not this time.

December 5

Glory to God in the highest, and on earth peace to men on whom his favor rests.—**Luke 2:14**

The holiday season is upon us, bringing family gatherings, cooking, shopping and hosting parties. But often, in all the frenzy and frivolity, we end up so tired and grumpy that we feel like the Grinch. Here are a few things you can do to keep the **PEACE** in your soul while being the gracious mother/wife/friend/hostess/volunteer that you are.

Practice saying "no." This is one of the hardest things for women to do. It is our nature to be all things to all people, to be "superwoman," while neglecting ourselves. But saying "yes" to too many things actually costs you energy. Make a "Do Not Do" list along with your "To-Do" list, and be committed to it, sticking to your priorities. View your "no" as giving someone else the opportunity to say "yes!"

Eliminate the stressors. *Simplify* your life, don't over-schedule and be flexible. Send that family letter after the holidays, when others have more time to read it anyway. Eat on paper plates, purchase your sides, or your entire meal for that matter. In a few weeks, your family and friends won't remember that you scrubbed the floor or spent 12 hours in the kitchen. They *will* remember your attitude.

Allow some time for yourself. This is the most important thing you can do to keep yourself going during the busyness of the season. Schedule some personal time in every day, even if it is just 15 minutes. Take a walk, exercise, pamper yourself with a pedicure or massage, read a book, or just sit outside in the quiet. Do something that rejuvenates you mentally and physically to avoid exhaustion. You won't enjoy the season if your energy is drained.

Celebrate the traditions that are most meaningful and bring your family joy; set aside those that exhaust you. Try asking each family member what one tradition they view as sacred and focus on those. If a lavishly decorated home is not important to them, then lighten up! If they don't want to bake and decorate dozens of cookies for the neighbors, then spend that time doing something that everyone wants to do. Celebrate those special things that bring you closer, and toss the things that are just "ho-hum."

Express your emotions. If you feel like crying, then let it out! If you have experienced the death of a loved one during the year and are grieving, know that it is OK to be sad. If you are lonely, then seek out ways to be involved in the community. It is not healthy to hold your emotions in for the sake of appearances, and it will only drain you in the end.

Most of all, express your gratitude! Every day, thank God for at least one thing that you are blessed with. We all have things that make us smile, things that we take for granted. Be grateful for a roof over your head, running water, transportation—things that many others live without. Give thanks for friends and family who love you unconditionally, and tell them how much they mean to you.

This may sound odd, but *thank yourself:* for all you do for others to inspire them and lift them up, for the mother, wife or good friend you are, and for the unique woman God created you to be. Remember who you are: a beautiful gift to others every day of the year!

Susan Tolles
Austin, TX

December 6

"These things I have spoken unto you, that my joy might remain in you, and that your joy might be full."
—John 15:11 (KJV)

I don't care how early the rest of the world wants to start getting ready for Christmas; I am just not an early-bird person. I love the hustle and bustle. I want to shop when the malls are full of people, the carols are playing and the Christmas rush is on. However, one particular Christmas the hustle and bustle got to me.

My two sons must have been 2 and 4. I worked part-time, and it was a Friday, my day off. I drove a full-sized van that was only a few months old; my previous vehicle was a Suburban. It was a cold, rainy day in the urban sprawl of Houston. Friday traffic, coupled with inclement weather, was a challenge. I wasn't feeling great, but shopping had to be done, with the two guys in tow. We were grumpy, and all I wanted was to get home and all three of us take a nap.

Finally, I was home, going up the driveway and straight into the garage. Relief was in sight! Whoops, just one problem. What was I thinking? The van didn't fit in the garage like the Suburban! I knew that. It was a taller vehicle and the luggage rack would hit the top of the garage doorframe, so I always parked it on the driveway.

When I heard the crunch, my heart just sank. I backed it out to survey the damage. Yep, the luggage rack now had new shape to it and the bottom of the garage door was bent, plus there was a piece of wood hanging down from the frame. Not much I could do at that point but take the boys inside for that much-needed nap.

I laugh when I think about driving that van right into the garage. Where was my mind? Unfortunately, I was focused on all the negatives of the day. I just simply forgot that my van never had, and never would, fit in my garage. I failed to take in the joys of the season and the precious time I was spending with my children.

That day still serves as a reminder to not allow the hustle and bustle consume me with have-to's and got-to's so that I overlook God's presence all around me. I am so thankful that early on He taught me to cherish the spirit of Christmas, along with the memorable shopping outings with my children. Oh, how they loved the magical atmosphere of the malls!

Fast forward to a trip to the mall one December day with my youngest, who was then 24 years old. He commented on how much fun he had during our shopping excursions during the Christmas season when he was a little boy and shared some of his special memories, many I had long forgotten. My eyes just welled up with tears. You see I had just started to write this story about the van that very morning! What a special God-incidence.

Thank You, dear Heavenly Father, for a van that wouldn't fit in the garage, and for the joy that fills my life from being in Your holy presence—during the Christmas shopping season and every day. Amen!

December 7

This is the confidence we have in approaching God; that if we ask anything according to his will, he hears us. And if we know he hears us—whatever we ask—we know that we have what we asked of him.—**1 John 5:14-15**

Don't ever underestimate the power of our Lord. When He sets out to show how powerful He is, He just might take your breath away. That's what He did for me one December day.

There are stories in this book about my two sons and their lack of faith. I have also written several about the highs and lows of this book. God let me know, without a shadow of doubt, that He heard my prayers regarding those specific circumstances.

Don't get me wrong; I don't doubt that God hears my prayers. I know that He will answer according to His will and certainly not mine. It was just one of those days that He chose to make a profound statement.

Every year, I give my sons a daily devotional for Christmas. I have been doing that since they were in elementary school. Even when I knew their faith was dwindling in college and they had stopped reading them, I still gave a new one—just in case that was to be the year they re-opened their hearts to God. I wasn't going to allow their lack of faith to stop me from sharing mine.

On this day, one of my sons told me how much he had been enjoying his new devotional. Yes, he had actually been reading it! First time in over five years, but a small step in the right direction. What a hallelujah moment!

Later that day, I received a call from a special young lady from church. God placed us in each other's life for a specific reason, and we sensed that. She was one of the first to whom I disclosed my thoughts about this book, and she was supportive and encouraged me to pursue my dream. I had sent her several emails, seeking feedback. I didn't hear anything from her. I felt awkward making additional attempts to contact her—I didn't want to appear pushy. Not knowing the best approach, I asked God for His intervention. He told me to be patient and wait. I listened. She called. What an incredible gift to hear her voice.

Stories from other women for this book had been coming in so slowly. I had prayed to trust God more in all aspects of this project because I couldn't do it myself. On this day of answered prayers I received two devotions. Now, that is something to praise God for!

I discovered a while back that I didn't really know how to pray. I spent my time bombarding God with my selfish desires, trying to convince God to do things my way. Right before Christmas one year, we had completed a sermon series on 1 John. I love what Pastor Brad said: "We treat God like a piñata. Prayer is the stick. We whack Him and He's supposed to give us the goods." I have been guilty of that many times, wondering why my pleas were going unanswered.

God's promise to us is that He hears and He answers *when* we ask according to His will. Plain and simple. He is the One in control and He will answer when and how, according to His perfect plan. But He does expect us to obey His command and trust Him to provide. To be blessed with so many answers in one day just took my breath away. I know it was a banner day and not every one will be like that, but the reassurance that He gave me made it one to put in my memory bank—for those times when I doubt, wondering where He is.

Are you praying God's will or demanding the goods? Jehovah-Jireh, The Lord Who Provides, already knows what you need. Trust Him.

December 8

But God demonstrated his own love for us in this: While we were still sinners, Christ died for us.—**Romans 5:8**

Our family's life for several years has been consumed by circumstances and events driven by the treatment and care of our youngest daughter following one life-changing moment. Suddenly, one December, she was beset with severe and stubborn epilepsy. After countless emergency-room trips, hospital stays, treatments and surgeries, her seizures are still numerous and daily.

This Christmastime, I was pondering the incredible gift that God gave to us all in the birth of the precious baby Jesus, knowing that Christ's birth is the very gift of hope which has sustained us through these years. I noticed that while the Bible is rich with Scripture that recounts the experiences of Christ's life, suffering and sacrifice for us, it is seemingly silent on the Father's experience during Jesus' time on earth.

Watching my child suffer and being utterly helpless to intervene has ignited in me a great awareness of what God may have endured in order to give us this immeasurable gift of hope and redemption. He knew exactly what Jesus would endure. He knew the undeserved pain and suffering. Yet He restrained His very able hand and allowed it all.

It has been excruciating, at times almost unbearably so, to watch our precious girl suffer and yet be able to do nothing. It would be so much worse to withhold help, for the good and mercy of a "wicked and perverse" genera-tion—for us and for me.

As I come face-to-face with the character of God once more, I cannot bend low enough to express my awe and humility before a love so great as this.

In this season, as we celebrate the glorious hope of redemption that entered our world in the form of the Babe, may we remember as well, to acknowledge and to celebrate how wide and long and deep and high is the love that compelled that merciful gift.

Terri Carriker
Austin, TX

December 9

How great is the love the Father has lavished on us, that we should be called children of God! And that is what we are! —**1 John 3:1**

Today, I received an early Christmas present. It wasn't a material gift. Oh, no, it was something much more meaningful. It was a gift from my son's heart and from God, and it will go down in my memory bank as one of those significant moments.

When my boys were little, one of our favorite outings of the Christmas season was a trip to the upscale Galleria in Houston. Since we lived in the suburb of Katy, the Galleria wasn't the mall we normally shopped, so it was a special trip to go there any time, but Christmas was a real treat. The decorations were spectacular, the carols joyful and the magic of Christmas was everywhere. The real highlight, though, of our excursion was ice-skating. It didn't matter that the outside temperature in Houston might be in the 80s, because it felt like Christmas, with a frigid skating rink and a brightly lit tree right in the middle.

Both of my sons have graduated from college, live in Houston and enjoy all the big-city attractions on a regular basis, including the Galleria. My youngest son was there on this particular day to pick up his computer at the Apple Store, and he sent me a text message.

This wasn't just a plain text message. It included a picture—a picture of the ice-skating rink and that huge Christmas tree. Along with the picture Trevor wrote, "I am just eating and watching people skate and it brought back so many wonderful memories." I just gazed at that picture, reminiscing—and shedding a few tears of pure joy and thanksgiving. How precious that my grown son would share that thought with me! What a meaningful gift!

I was having a difficult morning, and God was doing everything He could to let me know how much He loved me. My devotions were so uplifting and full of encouragement, speaking to my tired and troubled heart. The songs I heard on the radio as I drove to the doggie park were my favorites. I could feel my Heavenly Father reaching out, lavishing His love on me.

Then my own son reached out to me, too. I have no doubt God had His hand in that. Trevor hadn't planned on being at the Galleria. His computer crashed the previous day and he took it to be repaired, being told it would take several days. He got the call that it was already fixed, after only one day, and went by at noon to pick it up. Just so he could send me a picture and a sweet message to perk me up? Yes, I think that's exactly why!

God *lavished* His love on me and my son blessed me also. It's significant because I was reminded, again, of just how important I am to my Father, that He would orchestrate such a lovely gift for me, just when I needed some extra encouragement. My sweet friend, He is ready to lavish His love on you too! Be ready to accept it!

December 10

Every good and perfect gift is from above, coming down from the Father of the heavenly lights, who does not change like shifting shadows.—**James 1:17**

For the Christmas of 1960, a Barbie doll was at the top of my Christmas wish list. The dolls had recently come on the market and I wanted one. Mom and Dad gave me one, and my grandmother made a box of outfits for her. I had the best-dressed doll, and what fun I had playing with her!

A few years later, my Christmas wish took on a different style. I just had to have a pair of purple suede, fringe, go-go boots. My grandmother tried to talk me into choosing blue boots, but I wouldn't budge. She gave me the purple boots. Come to find out, I had nothing to wear with the boots. I kept those boots for about 12 years, never really wearing them, and feeling very guilty about asking to have them when I finally gave them away.

In my senior year in high school, the only thing on my Christmas wish list was to get to go on the Young Life ski trip to Colorado over Christmas break. My mother didn't want me to go because she had a feeling that I was going to break a leg while skiing. By November, she relented and gave me the trip. After three days of skiing, my legs were OK and I fell in love with a great sport. Unfortunately, I did break my left leg playing powder-puff football on the fourth and final day of the trip. This was a bum thing to happen during my senior year but the accident and the talks I had heard during the ski trip did lead me to examine my spiritual life. I realized that I had never accepted Christ as my Savior and that I had many questions about the Christian faith. My journey to salvation began on that ski trip.

By the time I was a senior in college, my Christmas wish involved a relationship. I had been dating my future husband Randy for over two years. That Christmas I had been invited to travel with his family to celebrate their Christmas. I was deeply wishing for a marriage proposal and an engagement ring. I didn't get my wish that Christmas. He gave me a beautiful robe and slippers that I needed very much. I was very grateful for my gifts but I was hugely disappointed. My wish did happen five months later.

My husband and I shared a Christmas wish in 1977. We were expecting our first child, due on Christmas Eve, and our wish (and prayer) was for a healthy baby. God answered our prayers and gave us a healthy girl two weeks early on December 10. What joy and blessings we received with our early Christmas gift. God also blessed us with two sons over the next few years but they were not born in December.

Many of the gifts I received for Christmas over the years were fun and frivolous, like the Barbie doll and the purple boots. I no longer have them, but I have memories of them. The ski trip and broken leg led me to make a decision to accept Christ as my Savior. This gift had eternal promises for me. The robe and slippers were useful for years and they taught me to wait upon the Lord's timing in my life. In God's timing, I received the gift of marriage (for over 40 years and counting) to a wonderful man. Our three children have blessed our lives beyond measure. It seemed that overnight that they were grown and we were at their weddings, giving away our precious gifts to their mates. We then had a new son and two new daughters. Now we have four grandchildren and another on the way, adding incredible joy to our lives. Children are the gifts that keep on giving.

Of all the gifts I have received, there is no comparison to the amazing gift that God gave to me and to the world by sending His son at the first Christmas. Jesus was sent to us to die on the cross for our sins. This is the free gift of salvation. All we need to do is accept it. Yes, every perfect gift comes from Him. God knows exactly what we need and gives to us accordingly. All others are temporal, but the gift of salvation is eternal. I praise the Lord and give Him thanks for His goodness to me.

Rhonda Bonham Goss
Austin, TX

December 11

Because your love is better than life, my lips will glorify you. I will praise you as long as I live, and in your name I will lift up my hands.—**Psalm 63:3-4**

I read somewhere that a fetus can hear sounds at 17 weeks. That is a reassuring thought as I look back on the day that I first told my baby girl, "I love you."

Trinity Hope Woods was born on December 11, 2009, and she is loved. She was a hope of her mom and dad's. A prayer answered. She was a heart's desire of her mother's for 10 years.

Unfortunately, that prayer didn't get answered as I had hoped. Ten years prior, I gave birth to a beautiful baby boy, Noah. He was an unexpected gift to my husband and me. We had been married only a few months before we found out I was pregnant. So we wanted to wait a little bit before trying for a sibling.

The waiting lasted a decade. I was waiting on God to answer my prayers for a sibling for Noah and He finally answered in 2009. In the spring, I found out I was pregnant, but almost as quickly as I found out, I was told the devastating news that we lost the baby.

I was heartbroken. I had hoped for another child, but started accepting that we were only going to have one child, when I realized I was pregnant. And then, the baby was taken away.

I was angry and numb, confused and depressed. I questioned my faith during the months that followed. I wanted to run away and hide from God—like that was possible! I had no words to form a prayer. I didn't know what to say. My faith was turned upside down. What did I believe? Was it real? Who is this God that I believed in? Why would He allow this to happen to me? Is this God's punishment for my sins?

As I searched for answers with my Bible open wide, I knew I had to start with the heart of my faith. I believed that God is—that He exists. I was reminded in that moment of Psalm 139:7: "Where can I go from your Spirit? Where can I flee from your presence?" And I believed. I believed He was there. I knew God was calling me; reminding me that He was right there in my pain. I cried out, "I thought I knew You." And I heard Him say to me clearly, "You don't know Me. Come and know Me."

So that is where my faith journey began. I felt God leading me to read Psalms so that I may know Him a little more like David. I felt that rather than asking for things in prayer, I needed to simply praise and thank Him for who He is. Slowly, my spirit was strengthened and my joy and peace was found in Christ alone. I was standing on the Rock again. My faith was renewed. Little did I know how God was preparing me for a greater loss.

Only a few months later, I received news that I was pregnant again. I passed through my first trimester with lingering nausea—a good sign I was told and reminiscent of my first pregnancy with Noah. Strawberry cake and chicken burrito supreme from Taco Bell were my little baby's favorites.

Around the 16th week, I started feeling tinges of pain. I was told at a later ultrasound appointment that the fibroids I had were growing and it would be good to continue monitoring them regularly. In that same appointment, it was confirmed—my baby was a girl. My husband and I hoped for a girl. I remember being relieved as the ultrasound tech told me that she was developing well. Verse 14 from Psalm 139 came to mind: "I praise you because I am fearfully and wonderfully made." I was grateful and filled with peace.

Not long after this good news, I found myself in labor, being told that I had to give birth to my little baby girl and that she wouldn't survive because it was too early in the pregnancy. The fibroids caused me to go into labor. This was the hardest day of my life. We prayed. I felt God's peace cover me. Scriptures I read over many years came flooding back to me as God carried me through this dark and stormy evening.

Trinity Hope entered the world wrapped in her mother's arms, showered with words of love and through tears of deep sorrow. I watched her chest rise and fall with each breath. I wanted time to stand still, but I could only keep her with me for seven minutes. She died holding my pinky and knowing she was loved, even if she didn't understand the words I was speaking. Her short life has impacted me in ways I am still figuring out. She left a legacy.

The days, months and years after her passing have been filled with many emotions. But, through it all, it was the Lord that got me through then and He still does. I poured into Scripture and praised His name. I clung to Him for my daily bread and strength for each day. I don't know why things happened as they did, but I know Who is in control and Who loves me through it all. He is faithful. He gives me His Strength, His Peace, His Joy. And in the midst of enduring the loss of my child, I learned what was meant in Psalm 73:26: "My flesh and my heart may fail, but God is the strength of my heart and my portion forever."

He is my testimony, in whom I give glory, and the praise of my lips forever.

In Loving Memory of Trinity Hope Woods
December 11, 2009

Sheji Woods
Wimberley, TX

December 12

Weeping may remain for a night, but rejoicing comes in the morning. — **Psalm 30:5**

I just love reminiscing as I put the ornaments on the tree—I have quite a collection that brings back all kinds of memories. Listening to carols is also part of the decorating routine, and I thoroughly enjoy my Christmas playlist on my iPod.

For some strange reason, one song played twice in a row: "It's the Most Wonderful Time of the Year" by Andy Williams. I honestly don't remember that song even being on my iPod. (I have "O Holy Night" on five times, all by different recording artists, but it's my favorite, so five times is OK.) I couldn't get the words of that song out my head, though. Christmas really isn't such a wonderful time of the year for so many people.

I thought about the lonely, older folks who no longer have their spouses, like my own mother, who lives in a retirement community, with many other widows and widowers. What about the people who have loved ones in the hospital with a terminal illness or on foreign soil in the military? But today, I was thinking of two women in particular who would probably testify that Christmas isn't the most wonderful time of their year.

Yesterday my friend Sheji, shared her story. On December 11, 2009, she was 17 weeks pregnant and delivered her daughter, Trinity, who lived for only seven minutes. Sheji and her husband have an older son and have been trying all these years for another baby. She had a previous miscarriage and was so hopeful that God had finally answered their prayers with Trinity. I know my sweet friend struggled to get through the day yesterday. No, this Christmas season will not go down as the happiest one of all for her.

Today, my friend Vickie celebrates her son Nick's birthday. However, it will be another birthday without him since his untimely death on September 16, 2006. He was 27 when he went home to be with Jesus. I know that today Vickie is thanking God for her son's remarkable life and honoring his memory, but shedding tears because she is a mom who misses her son. As the song tells us, loved ones are supposed to be near at Christmas, but her Nick is in heaven. Oh, my heart was breaking for my dear friends.

I was having a joyous time reliving my own memories of Christmases past as each ornament was lovingly placed on the tree, while Sheji and Vickie were filled with thoughts of a dead child. If we could just stay focused on God's truths—that He will never leave us or forsake us (Deuteronomy 31:5), that we are to consider it pure joy when we suffer trials (James 1:2)—then we should be able to endure anything He puts in our path. Right? Would Sheji and Vickie agree with that statement? Absolutely!

While we rejoice over the birth of our Savior Jesus Christ at Christmas time and the special joys of the season, there are those who must cope with very real feelings of loss, who must endure the pain of not having loved ones present. I pray for my sweet friends and for all who never want to hear Andy Williams sing that song again. We all know that trials will come, that bad things will happen, but we also have God's promises. How does anybody get by without the words of assurance that our Heavenly Father has left for us?

I know that Sheji and Vickie have unwavering faith in their sovereign Lord. This isn't the most wonderful time of the year for them, but I know they both love God, no matter what. These two women have been my inspiration. They have a powerful testimony, professing their love and devotion to their Heavenly Father despite the sadness and loss in their hearts.

Oh, dear Father, please comfort these women You have put in my life who will glorify You, no matter what the circumstances—women with faith so strong they know that although they may be crying right now, joy will come in the morning.

December 13

"So do not fear, for I am with you; do not be dismayed, for I am your God. I will strengthen you and help you; I will uphold you with my righteous right hand." —**Isaiah 41:10**

When I was a young girl, my mother would occasionally take my younger brother and me to the drive-in movies. Back then, there were no multiplex, IMAX 3D theaters. But the drive-ins had a picnic area with a cool children's playground located directly underneath the large movie screen. Families would arrive well before dark and let the kids play before the movie began. We'd already be in our pajamas. When I think back on that now, it's funny. Surely the bath we took before leaving home was all for naught after playing in the dirt and on the swings and slides.

Just before the movie would begin, the parents in their cars would either flash their lights or honk their horns, signaling for the children to go to the bathroom and get back to the car. The pillows would all be fluffed in the back seat. The mosquito coils would be lit and sitting on the dashboards. The crackling speaker (there was only one per vehicle) would be securely placed on the partially rolled down window of the driver's seat. The snacks from home would come out, ready for the show to begin.

I remember one particular night when a double feature was playing. The first feature was a kid's film that I really wanted to see. I took my place behind the driver. I lay down and looked out my window up into the early evening sky. Then I saw it and froze with fear—the face of Jesus. I can still see it today. When I collected myself, I sat up to see the reaction of everyone else. I fully expected everyone in the park to be screaming and running around wildly like something out of a horror film. But no one else seemed to notice what I could so clearly see. I got out of the car to get a better look. My mother told me to get back in before all of the mosquitoes came in. I looked up from my window for a long time. The face did not fade as a cloud would by softly changing form. I started to cry uncontrollably. My mother thought I was afraid of the movie and suggested we go home. I buried my face into the pillow and never spoke of what I had seen for more than 20 years.

Through the years, I often pondered the meaning and the reason why I had seen something that no one else did. We attended church on Easter and Christmas, and I suppose a few times in between. I always *knew* that Jesus lived and protected children. My parents divorced when I was in the first grade. *Fear not, for I am with you. . . .* My mother worked hard, often holding two jobs and taking a class here and there at the college. My brother and I were alone a lot. *Do not fear, for I am with you. . . .* We had to move a lot. I attended nine different schools before graduating from high school. For about 18 months, my brother and I lived in a different state with a dad we barely knew along with his new family. I truly feared my stepmother. I didn't realize it at the time, but she suffered from mental illness. I had to remain strong for my brother who needed me. That conviction prevented me from committing suicide at the age of 14. *I will strengthen you and help you.*

There have been two times in my adult life when the face of Jesus brought me a calmness and peace that even today I have difficulty explaining. At the age of 19, I was raped. I *knew* I would live through the ordeal because He was with me protecting me. *I will uphold you with my righteous right hand. . . .* He certainly did! The second time was when I was being taken to the delivery room for an emergency C-section on December 13. I was only 25 weeks

301

pregnant with triplets! I was hemorrhaging so badly that my doctor told me the next day that all four of us should have died. *Fear not, for I am with you. . . .* I was actually almost giddy with the peace I felt as the medical team was scurrying into position. I *knew* that everything would be OK.

I have learned in my 50-plus years that life is not easy, and it's not supposed to be. We are all here for a purpose and a reason. I find my daily peace in Him, knowing that I am not alone. I have never been alone, nor will I EVER be alone. *Do not be dismayed, for I am your God. . . .* Dismayed? No. Amazed? YES!

JSN
Sanford, FL

December 14

"She did what she could." —**Mark 14:8**

I recently attended a women's ministry conference at Dallas Theological Seminary. The guest speaker was Elisa Morgan, former CEO of MOPS (Mothers of Preschoolers), and the title of her talk was the title of a book she had written: *She Did What She Could.*

She took that title from a story in Mark 14:1-9. Mary has just anointed Jesus with expensive perfume, and those watching begin criticizing her. Jesus steps in on her behalf and says, "Leave her alone. . . . She did what she could."

In a world that places such a high value on having things "perfect," on doing more and more and more until we're exhausted, isn't that the most freeing thing? To hear Jesus-—the only perfect man—say in a woman's defense, "She did what she could."

Think about that this Christmas season. When you are decorating every inch of your home and still thinking about what else you could add. When you are fighting traffic and lines to buy one more present, and you really should be home cooking dinner. When you are saying "yes" to every invitation that comes along even though what you really want to do is decline.

"She did what she could."

What would that look like for you to say at the end of each day, "I did what I could"? There's still an action verb there: *did.* This isn't an excuse to be lazy. It's a reason to be wise.

Will you ask God each morning to give you wisdom to know what must be done, what needs to be done, and what can be left undone during this Christmas season?

Marilyn Ingram
Austin, TX

December 15

You will find a baby wrapped in clothes and lying in a manager. —**Luke 2:12**

I love nativities and enjoy collecting them from all over the world. Perhaps it's because I delight in seeing Jesus through different people's eyes. Or maybe it's because I have been enamored with nativities since I was a teenager and visited the Holy Land 40 years ago with my parents.

I was awestruck when our tour guide took us into an underground cave in Bethlehem on the grounds of the church of the Nativity. It was representative of the kind of manger/cave in which Jesus was born, as "tradition" has it. It did have an opening in the ground large enough for cows and donkeys, but people had to duck down low to enter in.

But this just couldn't be right! The pictures I had always seen depicted baby Jesus in a wooden stable, not in a rock cave. However, the Holy Land doesn't have much wood worthy of building the kind of stables we have in Texas. Caves around Bethlehem are probably where the animals, and most likely shepherds, stayed to keep warm on cold winter nights. Yes, it gets cold in Bethlehem, and evens snows due to the elevation, so it isn't surprising Joseph and Mary sought shelter in a cave that December night so long ago.

I had been looking but had yet to find a nativity in a cave—until now. Last year, my thoughtful husband purchased a soapstone nativity on a mission trip to Nicaragua. I opened the package last Christmas and set it aside, knowing I would open it again this year and help it find a new home on the shelf somewhere. I was running out of places to display the nativities I already had, but surely I could find one more nook or cranny.

This past fall we moved into our new home, and I have been struggling with where to put our Christmas decorations and many nativity sets. For 21 years I have known where every nativity had its place. The handmade ceramic set from Colorado my parents gave us for our first Christmas after we were married. The carved ebony figures from Africa. The Eskimo nativity from Alaska. The little handmade clay pot nativity figures from our children's Advent workshop days. Even the new "Little People" nativity bought last year for our grandson to play with, *"So we don't touch Gran's others ones, right, Brayden?"*

Unpacking some more Christmas boxes from the garage, I found the soapstone nativity from Central America. So unusual, so beautifully hand-carved, so perfect. Was it? Yes, it was. I had forgotten. Finally I had my nativity cave. And then it happened. I looked twice, but there was no mistake. Someone had packed two Jesus figures in the bag.

I have an extra Jesus. My first thought was how disappointed someone would be when she got home with no Jesus, and I have two! (So, if you went on the trip and are missing baby Jesus, call me.)

Then I thought, *Could this be a God message directed to me?* In all the hustle and bustle of the Christmas schedule of seemingly unending activities, I needed more Jesus. More Jesus in every part of my day. How about you? Need some extra Jesus? You don't have to look far. He's right here.

Lynn Harper
Kingwood, TX

December 16

After Jesus was born in Bethlehem in Judea, during the time of King Herod, Magi from the east came to Jerusalem.
—**Matthew 2:1**

Finding the perfect Christmas gift for Elizabeth, my Pilates instructor, should have been easy. After all, she had casually mentioned one day in class that she needed something in particular. All I had to do was go to the little specialty athletic-wear shop at that upscale mall and I would find it.

One problem: That upscale mall wasn't one that I often frequented. As a matter of fact, I had only been there once—several years before. Not being familiar with the layout, I Googled the location and actually felt well prepared.

Have I ever mentioned that I don't read maps well? Upon arrival, I was totally turned around. The parking garage that I thought was directly behind the store was completely on the opposite end of the mall, which just so happened to be one of those open-air, pedestrian-friendly concepts. I could either move my car and park closer to the store or just walk.

It was an unseasonably warm day for mid-December, even by Austin standards. Besides being almost hot, it was extremely windy. I should have driven, but that idea made me feel really lazy. I honestly think the trek was at least a mile to that little store, and by the time I arrived, I was a wind-blown, sweaty mess!

This shopping excursion was so unlike me. While I thoroughly enjoy the hustle and bustle of Christmas shopping and have great fun searching for the perfect gift for the special people in my life, I prefer "my" mall where I am familiar with all the stores and where to park—and am not exposed to the elements.

A muggy, gusty two-mile round trip hike to purchase one small gift might have been silly, but Elizabeth was worth it. Unless she reads this story, she will never know about the minor inconvenience. Had she not been special to me, I never would have driven to that out-of-the-way mall. The trip and the walk were all part of my gift because I love her so much.

The remainder of the day, as I continued shopping (at "my" mall), I pondered the situation. Why was I stuck on the thought of going to such extremes for one simple gift?

A few days later, the Holy Spirit led me to Matthew 2 and the story of the Magi. Growing up, I had associated the Three Wise Men as being present at the birth of Jesus because all the nativity scenes included three kings. The one in my own home did too, along with the pictures in the pretty Christmas storybooks.

To reiterate the Scripture, a recent Christmas Eve sermon was based upon Matthew 2. Exactly how far the men traveled isn't known for sure, but most scholars agree that it was a great distance that took many months, on camelback. There is so much that remains a mystery about the Magi, but from what is revealed in Scripture, we know they traveled from somewhere in the east and "when they saw the star they were overjoyed. On coming to the house, they saw the child with his mother Mary, and they bowed down and worshiped him. Then they opened their treasures and presented him with gifts" (Matthew 2:10-11). They weren't at the manger, but a house, and the Jesus they saw wasn't described as a baby, but a child.

Then it hit me. I made such a big deal about walking a few sweaty miles for a gift that I believed was well worth the trouble, but the Holy Spirit wanted me to think about those men. Along with their special treasures of gold, incense and myrrh, the sacrifice of their long journey was part of their gift of love to the promised Messiah.

My mind raced with questions. I might have sacrificed some extra time and energy for Elizabeth's gift, but how much am I willing to give up for Jesus, the Messiah, my Savior? Is it only what's convenient and within my comfort zone? Would I follow the light of a star as long and far as the Magi to give Jesus my gift of love, worship and obedience? Am I willing to surrender all—even just for a day?

My prayer is that this Christmas season and in the coming new year, with God's help, I will travel greater distances for Christ and obediently venture into unfamiliar territory for God's glory. May I be *overjoyed* to go wherever Jesus calls.

December 17

Listen to my prayer, O God, do not ignore my plea; hear me and answer me.—**Psalm 55:1**

My favorite box of Christmas ornaments is full of handmade treasures my two sons made when they were young. Most were made in Sunday school, and a few from their public elementary. I might have had something to do with a few of these ornaments, though.

I was their Sunday school teacher back in those days and made sure they created priceless heirlooms because I wanted them for my tree. After all these years, I wonder how many of those glittery stars are still hung with care, along with those constructed out of Popsicle sticks, on the trees of others from my classes?

Their works of art are lovingly displayed on the tree every year, but I rotate them. They are fragile and I don't want them to get worn out. One year, I discovered a smaller box of hand-made treasures that I presume were put on the tree one year, and then boxed separately so I wouldn't put them back on the following year.

What caught my attention wasn't actually a handmade decoration, but a store-bought Christmas card. I had asked each child in the class to write "What Christmas Means to Me." The back of the card was dated 1994, when my oldest was a fourth-grader. Zach wrote:

Christmas means joy and love and the birth of Christ. Being able to spend time with my family, Christmas songs, and giving to one another. That's what Christmas means to me.

I cherish those days of innocence. Both boys had a relationship with Jesus, and their faith progressed with their ages. But both of them became increasingly non-Christ-focused in high school and totally out of focus while in college. Unfortunately, I can identify with their path because I also went my own direction during my high school and college days, and know all too well what it's like to live in the pit of darkness.

In my heart, I believe that just as we can do nothing to earn our salvation, we can't do anything to lose it either. For many years, I was a disobedient child of God and far removed from walking in His light. He was still the Light of the World though—unmoved and unchanged—and waited on my return.

While nothing can separate us from the love of God, the quality of our relationship depends on the amount of time we choose to spend with Him in obedience. I can stand firm in that statement because I am living proof. Almost 30 years ago, I made the decision to follow Christ, and each step of the journey brings me closer and closer to my Lord Jesus. The more time I spend in His presence, the stronger our relationship grows, and that relationship is priceless to me.

That precious card was placed on one of the branches of the Christmas tree—a special reminder that my Zach was and always will be a child of God. He is an incredible young man, with a determined work ethic. I am proud of his determination and commitment, but sad that he is missing out on the joy of a relationship with Jesus.

At this stage of my journey, my time spent with Jesus does take precedence. The Lord hears my prayers and answers, according to His will, in His perfect timing. While he might not want to spend time with God, Zach is defenseless against my time spent in prayer, that one day, sooner than later, their relationship will flourish once again. *Listen to my prayer, O God, do not ignore my plea; hear me and answer me. Amen!*

December 18

So they hurried off and found Mary and Joseph, and the baby, who was lying in the manger. When they had seen him, they spread the word concerning what had been told them about the child, and all who heard it was amazed at what the shepherds said to them. But Mary treasured up all these things and pondered them in her heart.—**Luke 2:16-19**

The word "ponder" has suddenly become a new buzzword for me. I see it everywhere. There is even a woman in my Tuesday morning Bible study whose last name is Ponder, and she has touched my heart in a very special way.

The Encarta World Dictionary defines ponder as "to think about something carefully over a period of time." Some of the synonyms: consider, contemplate, wonder about and muse. I think the reason I like this word so much is that it implies thinking, without worry. It's like stress-free contemplation. I just love how sweet and gentle "ponder" sounds.

As I began to "ponder" my schedule for Christmas, I soon realized that my mind was straying from "pondering" and heading towards worrying. The "hurry-ups" and the "got-to's" were entering into the picture. Somehow, the birth of Jesus was put on the back burner, and my focus was on shopping, planning the Christmas Day meal, and wrapping presents. All at the last minute.

The scripture above implies that even at the time of the birth of Christ, folks were scurrying around. *They* (the shepherds) *hurried off and found Mary and Joseph.* But what was going on with Mary?

Now, one might expect a new mother to be anxious. I know after the birth of my first son, Zach, I was overwhelmed with the newness of it all. I thought all those books on parenting would prepare me. Yeah, right! As soon as I held my son in my arms, I realized that nothing had prepared me for that moment. (And as time went on, I really discovered that those books left out way too much.)

Can you imagine how hectic it must have been for Mary? At least I could enjoy the first night with my baby in a relatively quiet hospital room, in a clean bed. My only interruption was the nurse coming in to check my vitals, while my son lay beside me in a clean bassinet. (Oh, I can't omit his little interruptions all during the night.) There were no animals to contend with, no mooing or yucky odors, prickly hay or cold air. Yet Mary wasn't anxious and she wasn't the least bit concerned about the hustle and bustle around her. She *treasured up all the things and pondered them in her heart.* Those sweet words just take my breath away.

I thought giving birth to my son was noteworthy and one of the most spiritual, life-changing events of my life, but Mary had just given birth to the Son of God! Angels announced His birth. The greatest event in history had just

305

occurred. Yet she wasn't overwhelmed. She wasn't going to let anything interfere with the special moment. She took it all in, cherished all the events, and *pondered them in her heart.*

All the hurrying stopped with those words, *but Mary.* She took the time to gaze upon her child. The precious King sleeping in the manger. Didn't I stop and marvel at the wonder of creation when I gazed upon my newborn son? I may be getting older and forgetful, but I still remember that day like it was yesterday, those memories stored in my heart. Mary had much more to ponder than the average new mother. *But Mary* had no sense of worry, no sense of anxiety.

Stop, right now. Ponder the Scripture above. If Mary, mother of the Son of God, can stop and treasure the moment, so can we. Treasure everything that God puts into your day, every day of the year. Ponder. Think carefully about what the birth of His Son means in your life. Without His birth, there would have been no death on the cross or resurrection. We would have no hope or future. Our promise of eternal life in John 3:16 was fulfilled with the birth of precious Jesus.

"For God so loved the world that he gave his one and only Son, that whoever believes in him shall not perish but have eternal life."

December 19

I lift my eyes to you, to you whose throne is in heaven.—**Psalm 123:1**

One year at Christmas I did something very unusual—I purchased a Christmas gift very early in December. It's not like me to do something like that. I am more of a last-minute shopper, but I just happened to be in Barnes & Noble and spotted the perfect manly devotional to get for my husband. Also on the shelf was the 35th annual edition of *Daily Guideposts 2011* that I just couldn't resist buying for myself.

I also picked up Beth Moore's *Jesus: 90 Days with the One and Only.* Beth Moore is absolutely one of my favorite speakers/authors. (If you aren't from Texas, you might not even know who she is. Please go online and find her. Get to know her. Listen to her. I promise you, your life will be changed!)

After I brought the books home, I lost track of them. I put them somewhere, but they were nowhere to be found.

One morning, I stooped down to pick up the delightful mess my precious golden retriever had made on the floor of my office. Holly just loves to dig out the papers from the trash can and shred them. I know it's not the cleanest trick in the book, but she has never torn up anything that's not from the trash, so I consider it a good tradeoff. Most retrievers are known for chewing shoes or furniture—mine just shreds paper.

As I stood up, I looked up. Lo and behold, right on top of my tall bookcase were the books. I just smiled! Isn't that just so typical of me? I get so caught up in my own little world, in my fleshy stuff, that I don't take time to look up—past the circumstances of my messy life—to the One who has all the answers, the One who wants my time and attention.

Once again, a song came to mind, "Praise You in the Storm," by Casting Crowns, that takes some of the exact words from Psalm 121:1-2: "I lift my eyes to the hills. Where does my help come from?"

Take some time right now to lift your eyes up to your Maker of heaven and earth and give Him praise for this day and all of His provisions. By the way, I started my Beth Moore book today. Oh, my goodness! What a wonderful gift.

December 20

On a good day, enjoy yourself; on a bad day, examine your conscience. God arranges both kinds of days so that we won't take anything for granted.—**Ecclesiastes 7:14 (MSG)**

My day was planned. I would meet a group of women to do some volunteer work in Austin and then have lunch with them. Afterwards, I would go Christmas shopping at the mall. My outing would end at the grocery store so I could get all that I needed to start preparing for a dinner I was helping with the following night.

Living on Lake Travis, I feel the need to take advantage of my trips "into town." After all, it is a 45-minute drive. I try to do as much shopping as possible with the businesses close to my home, but there are times when I just need the big-city shopping experience.

When I reached into my purse to pay for lunch, I couldn't find the small holder for my driver's license and credit cards. I didn't panic because I instantly remembered where it was. I had purchased a gift on line the day before and needed my credit card number. I knew it was right next to my computer—at home.

I did have some cash in my purse to pay for lunch. But wait! What about my plans for the day? I couldn't very well go to the mall without my credit card. I couldn't even write a check without my license or go to the bank without my ATM card.

Christmas shopping could wait, but not the grocery store. I wasn't happy about wasting all that time driving home, then returning to the store—that same supermarket I would pass when I went back to the house. Would the money in my purse be enough to pay for groceries so I wouldn't need to go get my credit card?

I could at least buy the ingredients necessary to get a head start on the dinner I was helping with the following night. If I didn't do some of the baking and preparation before hand, the next day would be way too hectic. For the first time in I don't know how many years, I was going to pay cash for my groceries and I would have to pay close attention that I didn't buy more than what I had money to pay for.

I don't mean to sound frivolous, but swiping that plastic sure does make shopping easy. I literally charge everything to accumulate those all-important points. Thankfully there is enough money in my bank account to pay the bills that roll in every month.

I do realize that for many, these are extremely difficult economic times and having money in the bank to cover monthly expenditures is indeed a blessing. My circumstances for the day could by no means give me a taste of what it must feel like to actually be experiencing critical financial difficulties. However, I know that when daily plans get completely overturned, God is out to teach me a lesson.

My grocery list was long. I had much to purchase for that dinner. The cash in my purse wasn't enough to cover the whole list so I could only buy the absolute necessities.

I couldn't afford the luxury of putting everything I wanted in my shopping cart. There could be no impulse buying, and I had to resist my temptation to try any enticing new items. Doesn't sound like much of a sacrifice or anything too traumatic, but I became so mindful of just how easy and stress-free my shopping experience typically is.

At the checkout counter, I anxiously watched the computer screen. I would have to stop the checker if I got too close to my budgeted amount, but with a sigh of relief, the total was six dollars less than the cash in my purse. However, as I walked out to my car the feeling of relief turned into an overwhelming sadness.

What about all the people just in this city of Austin who never get to put everything they need into a shopping cart or who don't even have a kitchen to cook or store the food? Folks wondering where the money will come from to pay the rent and all the other bills? Parents unable to buy even one item on their child's Christmas wish list?

Thank You, God, for this very small lesson in humility and thanksgiving. And thank You for the privilege of going to the grocery store and the means to pay. Amen!

December 21

"He will reply, 'Truly I tell you, whatever you did not do for one of the least of these, you did not do for me.'"
—**Matthew 25:46**

Deck the halls with boughs of holly, Fa la la la la, la la la la. Tis the season to be jolly, Fa la la la la, la la la la.
Is it really the season to be jolly?

For many of us, it certainly is. However, the Capital Area Food Bank of Texas put a different spin to the classic Christmas carol on a billboard in Austin. Written across the face of the sign were the words, *'Tis the season to be jolly*, but "be jolly" was crossed out with a single black line and "feed the hungry" was written above it.

Very clever. Hopefully thousands of other motorists let their eyes stray from the freeway (just long enough) to read that sign and were convicted to reach out to the less fortunate. For those not prone to generosity, Christmas is the time to pull at those with callous heartstrings. However, for those who know God and His Word, we have a year-round calling, don't we?

Today, I am including the whole text from Matthew 25:31-46, subtitled "The Final Judgment," in my ESV, just as a reminder of what Jesus said:

"When the Son of Man comes in his glory, and all the angels with him, then he will sit on his glorious throne. Before him will be gathered all the nations, and he will separate people one from another as a shepherd separates the sheep from the goats. And he will place the sheep on his right, but the goats on the left.

"Then the King will say to those on his right, 'Come, you who are blessed by my Father, inherit the kingdom prepared for you from the foundation of the world. For I was hungry and you gave me food, I was thirsty and you gave me drink, I was a stranger and you welcomed me, I was naked and you clothed me, I was sick and you visited me, I was in prison and you came to me.'

"Then the righteous will answer him, saying, 'Lord, when did we see you hungry and feed you, or thirsty and give you drink? And when did we see you a stranger and welcome you, or naked and clothe you? And when did we see you sick or in prison and visit you?'

"And the King will answer them, 'Truly, I say to you, as you did it to one of the least of these my brothers, you did it to me.'

"Then he will say to those on his left, 'Depart from me, you cursed, into the eternal fire prepared for the devil and his angels. For I was hungry and you gave me no food, I was thirsty and you gave me no drink, I was a stranger and you did not welcome me, naked and you did not clothe me, sick and in prison and you did not visit me.'

"Then they also will answer, saying, 'Lord, when did we see you hungry or thirsty or a stranger or naked or sick or in prison, and did not minister to you?'

"Then he will answer them, saying, 'Truly, I say to you, as you did not do it to one of the least of these, you did not do it to me.' And these will go away into eternal punishment, but the righteous into eternal life."

This Christmas, and every season, may we experience the joy of reaching out to the least of our Shepherd's children.

December 22

The virgin will be with child and will give birth to a son, and they will call him Emmanuel — which means, "God with us." — **Matthew 1:23**

My husband told me all he wanted for Christmas was a devotion. My life is pretty much consumed with that right now so I am sure he thought he was doing me a favor. I could kill two birds with one stone; give him a present, plus get one day closer to filling my book. I have been thinking for weeks what I should write, and here I am, down to the wire, as usual.

Austin and I are in the "empty nest" season of our lives. Have you ever wondered who came up with the term "empty nest"? I Googled the term and chuckled at all of the websites. However, I wasn't able to determine who coined the phrase, other than it became a popular expression in the 1970s.

We have only been married since July 31, 2005. We started off our married life as Empty Nesters, with my youngest son leaving home for the University of Texas in June of that year. However, our life has been anything but empty.

Just a few days ago, we were driving, listening to our favorite Christian radio station when we heard *God Bless the Broken Road*. We agreed that could be our theme song. Yes, we both went through divorces, in total disobedience to God's commands. But somewhere along the broken roads of our lives, God brought us together.

It is very interesting how close in proximity we have actually been to each other since the early 1970s, when I moved to Houston after graduating from college. At one point, I was working in the office at my dad's grocery store, where Austin shopped. Later, we lived in the same apartment complex. We both ended up in Katy, Texas, in early 1980, living only a few miles from each other. We never met until Divorce Recovery class in 1999 at the church where I had been a member for many years and where Austin had recently started attending.

God has done some mighty work in our lives since our divorces and in our marriage. Besides bringing Austin and I together in a marital relationship, God brought us into a closer relationship with Him. He led us to another church, which was exactly what we needed, to open our eyes to how much we didn't know. Both of us "thought" we were Christians, but God knew we were ready to strengthen our relationship and took us down the road to spiritual renewal. He was with us as we walked the broken roads of our lives, and He so lovingly guided us as He gave us the opportunity to repent and change our direction in life.

I am so thankful for this loving, patient, hard-working man God led me to. We have such a blessed existence, but without the righteous, guiding hand of our Heavenly Father, we would just be walking along another broken road. God filled the empty places of our hearts with His love, grace and mercy. He gave us another chance to live an abundant life, free of the guilt and shame associated with our divorce and all of the sin in our lives, just like He gave the sinful world another chance over 2000 years ago with the birth of Jesus.

Living in God's light is something we have the opportunity to do each day of the year, not just December 25, as we make the choice to live in obedience to His commands. Jesus lived and died for our salvation, and that free gift is ours for the taking. Every day with my husband is Christmas, not just because of our wonderful life together, but because we share our home with our Father, in the good and the bad, for better or for worse. Our nest is far from empty— because of this Christ child we welcome at Christmas and all 365 days of the year. Hallelujah for Emmanuel, *God with us*.

December 23

Jesus Christ is the same yesterday, today and forever.—**Hebrews 13:8**

I was talking with some friends the other day about our favorite Christmas traditions. Honestly, traditions aren't a big deal in my family; however, one thing that remained a constant with my two boys was what we did on Christmas morning.

The boys were instructed to stay in bed on Christmas morning until I went upstairs to get them (and they actually listened). While gifts from Mom and Dad were wrapped, toys from Santa weren't and we wanted to capture their precious reactions on camera when they came down the stairs. As the boys got older, this "tradition" remained. They wouldn't come downstairs until they got the OK. One Christmas after their dad and I divorced, they spent Christmas Eve with him. They came back home on Christmas morning, only to immediately dash upstairs, jump in bed and wait for me to call them back down. This ritual continued all through high school and college and even post-college! Of course, by then, I actually had to go upstairs and wake them up!

Our little tradition came to an end in 2009. My older son married his high school sweetheart and her family had their own traditions. They have a wonderful Christmas Eve celebration with family and friends. What is really a blessing is that our family has been included for several years!

Now that they are married, Zach and Lauren spend Christmas Eve at her parents' house and come over to our house later on Christmas Day. I thought I would be devastated with the end of our Christmas morning ritual, but to my amazement, I wasn't even sad.

God had prepared my heart over the past few years for my boys to leave the nest, and I am so thankful He allowed me to embrace this particular change with joy. With God's help, I was able to focus on all that I had, not the little tradition that had ended. There is nothing wrong with tradition, but we can't get so caught up with the routine that we are lost with the change. As long as Christ remains the constant in my Christmas, I have all I need for a joyous celebration—a promise of life eternal, through Christ Jesus.

Zach called me a few days ago and asked if he and Lauren could come back to our house Christmas Eve, after the party at her parents' and spend the night—so this year we could do Christmas morning like we used to. What a surprise and what fun it will be! However, I understand that how we used to do Christmas morning is no longer a family tradition and for this mom, that's OK. Life brings changes, but thankfully Jesus Christ is the same yesterday, today and forever. Yes, Christ is the constant, not only in Christmas, but every day of my life.

December 24

Where is the one who has been born king of the Jews. We saw his star in the east and have come to worship him. —**Matthew 2:2**

My golden retriever was born on December 24. When I was thinking of a name for her, something Christmas-oriented seemed appropriate, such as Holly, Joy or Noel. When the breeder "requested" that each puppy from the litter (of 13) be registered with the AKC as a Christmas song, I decided on *Holly, Jolly Christmas* since Holly had been on my mind. Besides, the breeder had put a different color of ribbon around the neck of each puppy for identification purposes and she just happened to have a dark green one.

That song isn't one of my favorite Christmas songs. *Mary Did You Know* and *O Holy Night* fall into that category. Mary just didn't sound right for a dog and I sure didn't think this puppy would start out very holy, so Holly it was!

As I was driving, listening to all the Christmas music on the radio, *Holly, Jolly Christmas* came on. As Burl Ives' voice filled my car, I listened with renewed interest. She certainly is a jolly dog, with such a fun, sweet disposition, so the song fits her well. However, I felt bad that she wasn't named after a song that at least mentioned the birth of Jesus. After all, I could have named her *O Holy Night*, for the official record, but called her Holly. As I sang along, I was even more convicted that I had made a terrible mistake in my choice of a completely secular song for my special Christmas Eve dog.

The next song that played was *O Come All Ye Faithful*. I heard the Holy Spirit ask me a question. "How are you doing in the faithful department?" What do my character and actions say about me and my faith in the Lord Almighty? A name doesn't define us. Our character and actions do. I smiled at God for giving me such a sweet message.

I also listened to *O Come All Ye Faithful* with renewed interest. I am being called to come and adore Christ, the newborn King. Am I giving my King all of the glory that is due Him? Does He feel my love and adoration? I am sure a secular song name for my Christmas Eve dog is OK with God, just as long as I am faithful in my love and obedience to Him.

Oh, that I would keep the words of this classic carol in my heart, not just during the Christmas season, but everyday of the year! May we all start each day seeking to adore and bring glory to Christ. Come; let's sing out to Him. Yes, come all ye faithful, let us worship Christ our newborn King right now! You know the words. Sing out to Him. It's just you and your audience of One.

December 25

A savior has been born to you; he is Christ the Lord. —**Luke 2:11**

At Chris Tomlin's *Glory in the Highest* concert, pastor and speaker Louie Giglio introduced the audience to what he dubbed "The Twelve Words of Christmas." *A savior has been born to you; he is Christ the Lord.*

There's certainly nothing new about those words. According to the Bible, the Book of Luke was written about 60 A.D. The greatest story ever told, the birth of Jesus Christ, began with those 12 words spoken by the angel of the Lord over 2000 years ago.

In an article published in the *Houston Chronicle* after the concert in 2009, Giglio said, "I don't think the 'Twelve Days of Christmas' song has changed anyone, but these 12 words change everything!"

I couldn't agree with him more. I was mesmerized by his sermon and left the concert feeling like I had heard the Christmas story for the very first time in my life, even though I have heard it for as long as I can remember. However, Giglio shared some facts that were new to me in his sermon, specifically information about Reginald Fessenden. He was an inventor who performed experiments in radio. Fessenden is responsible for the world's first Trans-Oceanic radio communication—on Christmas Eve 1906.

In this historic transmission, he played a phonograph recording from Handel's Messiah and then he himself played "O Holy Night" on the violin. He ended by reading the Christmas story from Luke 2:9-14. I thought that was incredible!

Several years later I wanted to hear Giglio's sermon again, so I purchased the DVD. The anticipation I felt as I sat down to watch it surprised me. I had heard it before. I knew what he was going to say. But I also knew just how powerful and moving his words were. I think I cried all the way through it. That's just how good it is!

There's no way that I can do justice to the eloquence of Giglio's sermon in an attempt to summarize his message, so I'm not even going to try. I am going to suggest that you make every effort to listen to it for yourself. But for now, I just wanted to share "The Twelve Words of Christmas." Our Savior came to be with us that night over 2000 years ago. After 400 years of not hearing from God, the silence was broken with the cries of the baby. There is no more waiting. He is with us—right now. *"A savior has been born to you; he is Christ the Lord."*

December 26

Because Joseph her husband was a righteous man and did not want to expose her to public disgrace, he had in mind to divorce her quietly. But after he had considered this, an angel of the Lord appeared to him in a dream and said, "Joseph, son of David, do not be afraid to take Mary home as your wife, because what is conceived in her is from the Holy Spirit." —**Matthew 1:19-20**

As women, we have all had thoughts about the miracle of the virgin birth, and the responsibility that was placed on Mary. But what about Joseph? We don't hear too much about him. As a matter of fact, after Jesus turned 12, Joseph is never mentioned again in the Bible.

At a Sunday LifeGroup meeting, Jeff, our small-group leader at the time, posed some questions concerning Joseph. For the first time, I pondered what it must have been like to be Jesus' father on earth.

According to the Book of Deuteronomy, Chapter 22, the punishment for "marriage violations" was severe, even punishable by death. The angel of the Lord appeared before both Mary and Joseph, explaining the situation, but would everyone else believe that story? If your son or daughter came to you confessing an out-of-wedlock pregnancy, orchestrated by God, what would your first reaction be?

Not only was Mary faced with being humiliated, but Joseph was as well. However, he agreed to the angel's instructions. His obedience and actions revealed four admirable qualities, as the NIV Bible explained in footnotes for Matthew 1:19-25: righteousness in verse 19, and also, in that same passage, sensitivity by not wanting to expose her to public disgrace; his responsiveness to God is proven is verse 24 when "he did what the angel of the Lord had commanded" and took Mary home as his wife; and in Mathew 1:25, we read that "he had no union with her until she gave birth to a son," revealing his admirable self-discipline.

My NIV Bible footnotes also explained that Joseph thought there were only two options. He could divorce her quietly or let her be stoned to death. But God had a different plan and a third option—to take her home to his parents as his wife. Thankfully, he had the wisdom to discern the will of God. Isn't it interesting how often we try to orchestrate the plans of our life, only to have God show us another way? I could write volumes in answer to that question!

Joseph was indeed a man of great character. We shouldn't be surprised that God handpicked individuals with high moral standards to raise His Son on earth. Even when it came to choosing human parents for the King of Kings, moral character was more important than prestige in the community, wealth or fame. Living a righteous life and being obedient to God appeared to be deciding factors in this situation.

Thinking about both of these parents, Mary and Joseph, I had to ask myself if I would have been in the running to be the chosen mom for Jesus?

"Greetings, you who are highly favored! The Lord is with you" (Luke 1:28). Would an angel ever have appeared to me with those words?

Would I have responded with Mary's same words of obedience? "I am the Lord's servant" (Luke 1:38). Or would I have allowed the fear of ridicule and humiliation to take precedence over serving my Father?

Dear Father, You know the answer to those questions. I pray Psalm 139:23 right now: *Search me, O God, and know my heart; test me and know my anxious thoughts. See if there is any offensive way in me, and lead me in the way everlasting. Amen!*

December 27

"Martha, Martha," the Lord answered, "you are worried and upset about many things, but only one thing is needed. Mary has chosen what is better, and it will not be taken from her." —**Luke 10:41-42**

There were no more shiny, wrapped packages under the tree. The last dish was washed, the kitchen clean and tidy again. It was just my husband and I in the house, along with our golden, Holly, and all was quiet. Christmas Day had come to an end.

The previous few days seemed like a blur. I don't know how my grandmother used to prepare the whole meal, have all the family over and make it look so easy. I spent half a day just making trips to the grocery store, battling the traffic and long lines. Thankfully my husband is the real cook in the family so there were two of us in the kitchen, but it still got a bit frantic.

It was lovely to spend Christmas Eve at church and at the home of my daughter-in-law's parents—something we had done for the past eight or so years. What a blessing that our families could share such a special evening together. We got home way too late though, and morning came quickly.

I thought of the childhood poem, "The Night Before Christmas," as I lay in bed that Christmas Eve, but there were no visions of sugarplums dancing in my head. No, I was worried about timing issues for the next day. Most everyone coming was on a tight schedule and if anyone was late, that would create a problem for the next house they were to visit.

When it comes to holidays, the consequences of divorce and re-marriage and blended families are very clear—especially when the kids are older and married, adding even more families into the schedule. All involved have made a heartfelt effort to make sure the day goes as smooth as possible, and that is a huge hallelujah. (And all of the families live in the same town or at least in the same state. I can't even imagine how crazy it would be if some lived out of Texas.)

I also wrote my Christmas letters to my two sons (in my head) that night. Don't ask me why I wait until the very last hour to do that, but the words just don't come to me any earlier. So after only a few hours of sleep, I was up and at 'em way before the sun on Christmas morning at my computer.

It was dark again outside, the day was over and it was early to bed. As my husband and I said our prayers, I was overcome with sadness and remorse. It was Christmas Day, and I had missed it! It had been a day of do, do, do and hurry, hurry, hurry. When had I stopped to actually reflect on the day? Even as my mother said grace before the meal, my mind was racing, hoping the buzzer for the rolls in the oven wouldn't go off during her prayer.

How could I even come before God in prayer after missing His Son's birth? I felt so distant from my Father and so unworthy. I thought of Martha, who had been distracted by all the preparations that had to be made for Jesus and the disciples, as Mary sat at the feet of Jesus, listening to Him teach. I could just hear Jesus saying, *"Brenda, Mary has chosen what is better."*

Two days after Christmas I was playing catch-up on reading my daily devotions. Yep, I had let that slide too. When I picked up *Jesus Calling*, I randomly went to December 26—or so I thought. No, Jesus called me to that exact day for a reason, even though it was the 27th.

Sarah Young wrote, "When you are discouraged with your behavior, you tend to feel unworthy of My Love." *Oh, yes! That is exactly how I feel, God.* She went on to write that His Love is unconditional. He simply wants me to come to Him, so He can hold me in His arms.

I missed celebrating the birth of Jesus on December 25—the One and Only perfect gift. However, I found an unopened present on December 27—God's unfailing love and forgiveness. It is available to me every day; sometimes I just fail to see it. All I have to do is stop long enough to look, and there is my Heavenly Father, with His arms wide open, waiting—for me!

December 28

You will be with child and give birth to a son, and you are to give him the name Jesus. He will be great and will be called the Son of the Most High. The Lord God will give him the throne of his father David, and he will reign over the house of Jacob forever; his kingdom will never end.—**Luke 1:31-33**

No matter how long my Christmas decorations are up, I linger in the effort to put them away in boxes, cabinets and storage containers after the holidays have passed. It doesn't matter if the decorations went up the day after Thanksgiving or December 24—I have trouble getting out the boxes to pack them up after the holidays are gone.

My excuse for years was that my birthday fell so close to Christmas and New Year's that I didn't want to be taking precious family time putting everything away instead of enjoying the full extent of the holidays. The truth is, I just love Christmas, and it is so difficult to "put it away." Anyway, I really adore the sparkle and twinkle of the lights and the memories recalled with each special ornament or unique nativity. Christmas lights give such a spectacular glimmer and glow to any home, and the decorations can add such extraordinary expressions of God's love to any decor.

One year, my children joked that I was going to have a Valentine's Tree. I did consider the challenge, but finally relented and put the decorations away before February 14. I was going for the record, and Valentine's Day would have been a personal best. Actually, I do know someone who keeps *all* her Christmas decorations out all year long, including several fully decorated trees, but I think that is pushing the limit a bit.

Someone mentioned to me that we shouldn't have to "put Christmas away." I was listening intently to her rationale and planned to use it as ammunition for my family's protests and admonitions, since Christmas was still out at our house on February 1 one year. My friend explained she carefully chooses certain decorations to display in her home that remind her of Christmas after the holiday has come and gone.

What's wrong with this scenario? Can't we keep just a few reflections of Christmas strategically placed to keep the joy, love and sparkle of Christmas in our homes and hearts year round? Sounds like a fabulous plan to me. So, as I pack my treasures away until next Christmas, except for a few well-placed chosen ones, I will be giving great thought to how I can keep Christmas every day in my heart and in my home. What about you? How will you "keep Christmas"?

Heavenly Father, may we keep the memories of Christmas and the celebration of the birth of Your Son in our hearts and homes each day of the year and never "put Christmas away." Amen!

Lynn Harper
Kingwood, TX

December 29

The fruit of the Spirit is love, joy, peace, patience, kindness, goodness, faithfulness, gentleness and self-control.
—**Galatians 5:22**

To celebrate my husband's parents' 60th wedding anniversary, a book of letters and special photos was compiled by all of the family members. This was my letter to them:

I remember the first time I met the two of you, in 1975. Scott and I were out on a date and he asked me if I wanted to meet his parents. I remembered thinking that I would love to meet his parents, although nervously. Scott drove us to your home and opened up the door to the den, and there you were sitting, watching television and eating popcorn. The picture right there relaxed me. Mom said, "We get to meet someone new!" I don't remember much else of the conversation, but I do remember leaving with a smile in my heart and on my face.

I have stored many treasured moments in my heart from that first day on. Another remembrance I cherish is the first Christmas Scott and I were together. He was attending Michigan Tech and I was attending Michigan State. The distance and time apart were agonizing. Back in the day, the only way to make long-distance calls was to use your home phone. Scott called me often, charging the calls to your home phone, as he did not have access to charging calls to his school address.

On Christmas Eve at your house, he told me that he had to write a check out to Dad for $80 for the phone calls he made to me. I was devastated that we had racked up such a large bill. Of course, we needed to take responsibility. Later that evening, the family was gathered in the living room, opening presents. Dad handed Scott and I a small box. Inside was the phone bill, with PAID IN FULL written across Scott's check. Dad had added the note, "We love you two, but please write!" I wept at your generosity and outpouring of love. And we did heed your advice and wrote.

Your arms have been around us since that very first day. You traveled to see us and visited us in every home we lived in during our journey. You came to celebrate new life, birthdays, graduations, weddings, holidays and the passing of life. And you made these trips seem so easy, even if they weren't always. This will forever be etched on my heart. And you taught me about the love of Jesus.

I watched as you became grandparents to Nicholas and Molly. You were their beloved Grams and Gramps from day one. Even though there was much distance between our homes, your grandchildren felt your presence every day, as if you were right next-door. You played games with them that enhanced their imaginations. Memories were made that they loved to relive. You called often and sent them each letters, sharing the events of the day. Molly has kept your letters all these years. The letters are a treasure in a box and in her heart.

You talked to them about Jesus, teaching them to pray by example. During one of your visits, Nicholas and you were playing and out of the blue he said to you, "Grandma, you have God antennas; you hear from God." He was only four years old. You touched his heart and planted a seed. They knew the unconditional love of Jesus with your love and devotion.

I watched and listened all those years. I did not realize then what I know now. You were teaching me just as you were teaching Nicholas and Molly. I learned so much about grand parenting by being on the outside looking in. Watching my children light up at the mere mention of your names was seeing the light of Jesus shine so brightly. I remember thinking that this was the kind of grandparent I wanted to be. You truly showed how the Spirit produces love, joy, peace, patience, kindness, goodness and faithfulness. What an amazing blessing!

God bless you, both, as you celebrate and remember 60 years of marriage. May the loving embrace of God be around you.

Vickie Sayles
Katy, TX

December 30

*"I no longer call you servants, because a servant does not know his master's business. Instead I have called you friends, for everything I have learned from my Father I have made known to you." —***John 15:15**

I know the year is coming to an end when there aren't many pages left in my daily devotionals. I read several online, but my favorites are the old-fashioned kind—the ones written on the pages of a book.

There are verses underlined and sticky notes placed on the corners. I have read, and re-read, several over the years, but somehow the message sounds fresh and relevant for the current day. With each new morning, God has something different to show me, even though His Word never changes.

This year is coming to an end and a new one will start January 1. What exactly does that signify? Most of us use the calendar year for income-tax purposes. Earnings are based on monies paid from January 1 through December 31. Property and school tax valuations are connected to those same dates too. They also determine our age and the number of years we have left to pay off the mortgage and car note.

There are New Year's Eve celebrations throughout the world on December 31 as people get ready to bring in the New Year, closing out the old by singing "Auld Lang Syne." Do we even know what those words mean? According to Merriam-Webster's Dictionary, auld lang syne is a noun defined as "the good old times."

I have simply been amazed at where God has taken me in writing stories for this book. The thought of the year ending led me to think of that song, which took me on a Google search to find the definition. I ended up at an article written in the *Ottawa Citizen* posted exactly nine hours previous to my search, titled "The Mysterious Roots of Auld Lang Syne." Seems that the Morgan Library & Museum in Manhattan had just opened an entire exhibit in tribute to the history of that song.

Scottish poet Robert Burns is attributed with composing the ballad in 1788, but he himself claimed he "took it down from an old man's singing" that had never been put into print. Many history buffs and fans of the famous poet have pondered whether he actually just copied the mysterious man's song or whether Burns himself is the actual author.

In 1799, after Burns had died, words and music were put together to come up with the final song as we know it today. It would be another 200 years for it to become a global phenomenon, popularized by American big band leader Guy Lombardo. However, no one really knows how such a ballad with hard-to-pronounce words became one of the most widely recognized songs on this planet, after "Happy Birthday."

In case you don't know the modern version, here is the first verse:

Should old acquaintance be forgot, and never brought to mind?
Should old acquaintance be forgot, and old lang syne?

CHORUS:
For auld lang syne, my dear,
For auld lang syne,
We'll take a cup of kindness yet,
For auld lang syne.

The song may simply be interpreted as a call to remember the good times of long-standing friendships. I do hope that you have some friends that come to your mind. Memories of people who have touched your heart, changed your life and been at your side through difficult and joyful times.

Hopefully the first person who comes to mind is your sweet friend, Jesus. In John 15:15, Jesus calls *us* His friend. I find that to be a powerful thought to hold in my heart as I think back on the times He and I have spent together. Oh, how He has touched my life and made this a year to remember. I can't wait to see what He has planned for the next one.

December 31

And now, O Lord, for what do I wait? My hope is in you. — **Psalm 39:7**

What a glorious last day of the year! It was dreary, foggy, chilly, rainy, and I was absolutely ecstatic about the gloomy New Year's Eve forecast.

There had been some rain during the fall, but Lake Travis was still 50 feet low and the drought conditions in the Texas Hill Country remained classified as severe. However, the lessons God taught me during the years of the ongoing dry spell were priceless. He did indeed show me how to dance and be joyful, even in a drought — a physical drought due to a lack of rain and a spiritual one caused by my lack of dependence on Him.

The weather forecast predicted heavy thunderstorms during that last day of the year. The heavy rain never materialized, but the constant drizzle throughout the morning and afternoon was such a welcome reprieve. However, by early evening the clouds parted to make way for a true-to-Texas burnt-orange sunset. The western horizon was graced with soft hues of orange and pink as the fiery ball slipped away, bringing an end to the last day of the year.

Sure, I would have been happier with a deluge, but my heart was full of thanksgiving for the moisture God gave. All day long, I was reminded of His promises and faithfulness. *My hope is in you.* What a special way to end the year — being showered with God's gift of love.

My husband prepared a yummy dinner for just the two of us that night. He is the most fabulous cook and such a hopeless romantic. He goes to great lengths to make me happy and to serve me. However, when it comes to dog duty, that task is usually mine. After ringing in the New Year (with the thousands on TV in Times Square), I took Holly out to potty.

There was a firework frenzy going on and after Holly did her business, she high-tailed it back to the house. For some reason though, I lingered in the yard. The wind picked up and then it happened — it started to pour!

My first reaction was laughter. God is just so funny sometimes in how He reveals Himself. It's like He just wants to make sure we don't miss Him. There I was in the middle of the yard, no umbrella, and I was drenched. Kind of hard to miss that God sign. But then I started to cry because I was completely awed by how God works, giving me glimpses of His power and glory — and unending love.

When I was standing out in the rain, some of the lyrics to "My Hope is in You" (recorded by Aaron Shust) were stuck in my head: *My hope is in you Lord all the day long. I won't be shaken by drought or storm.* Through something so simple as a rain shower, God demonstrated, once again, that He alone is the great Provider of life-sustaining water — both for the rivers and lakes, plants and trees — and my soul.

Even though the physical drought hadn't ended, my spiritual thirst was being quenched by Jesus' promise to provide me with living water, as He did to the Samaritan women at the well. As He pursued her, He keeps on coming after me with signs of His presence and provision. "Everyone who drinks this water will be thirsty again, but whoever drinks the water I give him will never thirst. Indeed, the water I give him will become in him a spring of water welling up to eternal life" (John 4:13-14).

My online dictionary defined hope as "a feeling of expectation and desire for a certain thing to happen." Through His Word we have hope for what is to come — eternal life. Before that time comes, the promises in His God-breathed Scriptures provide all we need to face any circumstances — joy or trial.

Years will come and go, but God's Word never changes. Tomorrow will be a new year on the calendar. Do you have expectations or desires? Are you anxious or at peace about what's ahead? It might be a sweet, welcomed rain shower or we could face a drought or a storm, but there's no need to be shaken. We can go forward with great hope, knowing we won't be alone. Father God, our hope is in You!

CPSIA information can be obtained at www.ICGtesting.com
Printed in the USA
LVOW09s2133281113

362884LV00001B/1/P